McDougal Littell

THE LANGUAGE OF
LITERATURE

McDougal Littell

THE LANGUAGE OF
LITERATURE

Arthur N. Applebee

Andrea B. Bermúdez

Sheridan Blau

Rebekah Caplan

Franchelle Dorn

Peter Elbow

Susan Hynds

Judith A. Langer

James Marshall

McDougal Littell

A HOUGHTON MIFFLIN COMPANY

Evanston, Illinois ▪ Boston ▪ Dallas

Acknowledgments

Unit One

Ruth Cohen, Inc.: "The All-American Slurp" by Lensey Namioka, from *Visions* , edited by Don Gallo. All rights reserved by Lensey Namioka.

Alfred A. Knopf, Inc.: *Nadia the Willful* by Sue Alexander; Copyright © 1983 by Sue Alexander. Reprinted by arrangement with Alfred A. Knopf, Inc.

Harcourt Brace & Company: "Primer Lesson," from *Slabs of the Sunburnt West* by Carl Sandburg; Copyright 1922 by Harcourt Brace & Company and renewed 1950 by Carl Sandburg. Reprinted and recorded by permission of Harcourt Brace & Company.

Delacorte Press: "The School Play" by Gary Soto, from *Funny You Should Ask,* edited by David Gale; Copyright © 1992 by Gary Soto. Reprinted by permission of Delacorte Press, a division of Bantam Doubleday Dell Publishing Group, Inc.

Scott Meredith Literary Agency: "Ghost of the Lagoon" by Armstrong Sperry. Reprinted by permission of the author and the author's agents, Scott Meredith Literary Agency, L.P., 845 Third Avenue, New York, NY 10022.

Walker and Company: "Matthew Henson at the Top of the World," from *Against All Opposition: Black Explorers in America* by Jim Haskins; Reprinted by permission of Walker and Company, 435 Hudson Street, New York, NY 10014. All rights reserved.

Continued on page 872

Cover Art

Background photo: Skyline with trees, Copyright © Y. Watabe/Photonica. **Painting of Ship:** Illustration by Lee Christiansen. **Girl:** Copyright © Joyce Stiglich. **Book:** Photo by Alan Shortall. **Butterflies and frame:** Photos by Sharon Hoogstraten.

ISBN 0-395-73701-X

2 3 4 5 6 7 8 9 – RRD – 02 01 00 99 98 97 96

Senior Consultants

The senior consultants guided the conceptual development for *The Language of Literature* series. They participated actively in shaping prototype materials for major components, and they reviewed completed prototypes and/or completed units to ensure consistency with current research and the philosophy of the series.

Arthur N. Applebee Professor of Education, State University of New York at Albany; Director, Center for the Learning and Teaching of Literature; Senior Fellow, Center for Writing and Literacy

Andrea B. Bermúdez Professor of Studies in Language and Culture; Director, Research Center for Language and Culture; Chair, Foundations and Professional Studies, University of Houston-Clear Lake

Sheridan Blau Senior Lecturer in English and Education and former Director of Composition, University of California at Santa Barbara; Director, South Coast Writing Project; Director, Literature Institute for Teachers; Vice President, National Council of Teachers of English

Rebekah Caplan Coordinator, English Language Arts K-12, Oakland Unified School District, Oakland, California; Teacher-Consultant, Bay Area Writing Project, University of California at Berkeley; served on the California State English Assessment Development Team for Language Arts

Franchelle Dorn Professor of Drama, Howard University, Washington, D.C.; Adjunct Professor, Graduate School of Opera, University of Maryland, College Park, Maryland; Co-founder of The Shakespeare Acting Conservatory, Washington, D.C.

Peter Elbow Professor of English, University of Massachusetts at Amherst; Fellow, Bard Center for Writing and Thinking

Susan Hynds Professor and Director of English Education, Syracuse University, Syracuse, New York

Judith A. Langer Professor of Education, State University of New York at Albany; Co-director, Center for the Learning and Teaching of Literature; Senior Fellow, Center for Writing and Literacy

James Marshall Professor of English and English Education, University of Iowa, Iowa City

Contributing Consultants

Tommy Boley Associate Professor of English, University of Texas at El Paso

Jeffrey N. Golub Assistant Professor of English Education, University of South Florida, Tampa

William L. McBride Reading and Curriculum Specialist; former middle and high school English instructor

Multicultural Advisory Board

The multicultural advisors reviewed literature selections for appropriate content and made suggestions for teaching lessons in a multicultural classroom.

Dr. Joyce M. Bell, Chairperson, English Department, Townview Magnet Center, Dallas, Texas

Dr. Eugenia W. Collier, author; lecturer; Chairperson, Department of English and Language Arts; teacher of Creative Writing and American Literature, Morgan State University, Maryland

Kathleen S. Fowler, President, Palm Beach County Council of Teachers of English, Boca Raton Middle School, Boca Raton, Florida

Noreen M. Rodriguez, Trainer for Hillsborough County School District's Staff Development Division, independent consultant, Gaither High School, Tampa, Florida

Michelle Dixon Thompson, Seabreeze High School, Daytona Beach, Florida

Teacher Review Panels

The following educators provided ongoing review during the development of the tables of contents, lesson design, and key components of the program.

CALIFORNIA
Steve Bass, 8th Grade Team Leader, Meadowbrook Middle School, Ponway Unified School District

Cynthia Brickey, 8th Grade Academic Block Teacher, Kastner Intermediate School, Clovis Unified School District

Karen Buxton, English Department Chairperson, Winston Churchill Middle School, San Juan School District

continued on page 881

Manuscript Reviewers

The following educators reviewed prototype lessons and tables of contents during the development of *The Language of Literature* program.

William A. Battaglia, Herman Intermediate School, San Jose, California

Hugh Delle Broadway, McCullough High School, The Woodlands, Texas

Robert M. Bucan, National Mine Middle School, Ishpeming, Michigan

Ann E. Clayton, Department Chair for Language Arts, Rockway Middle School, Miami, Florida

Linda C. Dahl, National Mine Middle School, Ishpeming, Michigan

Shirley Herzog, Reading Department Coordinator, Fairfield Middle School, Fairfield, Ohio

continued on page 882

Student Board

The student board members read and evaluated selections to assess their appeal for sixth-grade students.

Ted Burke, East Aurora Middle School, East Aurora, New York

Ian Graham, Churchill Road Elementary School, McLean, Virginia

Melissa Hall, Frenship Intermediate School, Wolfforth, Texas

Stephanie Liberati, Hampton Middle School, Allison Park, Pennsylvania

Bridget McGuire, St. John of the Cross, Western Springs, Illinois

Eileen Pablos-Velez, Henry H. Filer Middle School, Hialeah, Florida

Nicole Putnam, Rockway Middle School, Miami, Florida

Eli Shlaes, Davidson Middle School, San Rafael, California

Theresa Sullivan, St. Ann's School, Wilmington, Delaware

Christine Tran, Foothill Middle School, Walnut Creek, California

Alexis Wong, Foothill Middle School, Walnut Creek, California

THE LANGUAGE OF LITERATURE
Overview

Student Anthology
Learning the Language of Literature

Literature Connections

Each book in the Literature Connections series combines a novel or play with related readings—poems, stories, plays, essays, articles—that provide new perspectives on the theme or subject matter of the longer work. For example, Jack London's *The Call of the Wild* is combined with the following readings, which focus on such topics as dog behavior, relationships between humans and animals, and animal survival.

Marie de France	**The Wolf and the Dog**
Elizabeth Marshall Thomas	*from* **The Hidden Life of Dogs**
A. G. Rochelle	**The Wolf Said to Francis**
Julius Lester	**The Man Who Was a Horse**
Sally Carrighar	**Unsentimental Mother**
Robert Murphy	**Long Duel**

Across Five Aprils
Irene Hunt

Across the Great River
Irene Beltrán Hernández

The Call of the Wild*
Jack London

The Clay Marble
Minfong Ho

The Contender
Robert Lipsyte

The Diary of Anne Frank†
Frances Goodrich and Albert Hackett

Dogsong
Gary Paulsen

Dragonwings
Laurence Yep

The Giver
Lois Lowry

The Glory Field
Walter Dean Myers

The House of Dies Drear
Virginia Hamilton

I, Juan de Pareja
Elizabeth Borton de Treviño

Johnny Tremain
Esther Forbes

Maniac Magee
Jerry Spinelli

Nothing but the Truth
Avi

Roll of Thunder, Hear My Cry*
Mildred D. Taylor

So Far from the Bamboo Grove
Yoko Kawashima Watkins

Trouble River
Betsy Byars

Tuck Everlasting*
Natalie Babbitt

Where the Red Fern Grows
Wilson Rawls

The Witch of Blackbird Pond
Elizabeth George Speare

A Wrinkle in Time
Madeleine L'Engle

*A Spanish version is also available.
†SourceBook only.

WRITING ABOUT LITERATURE   **Direct Response**

Part 2   On the Edge of Survival

WHAT DO YOU THINK? Reflecting on Theme   92

WRITING FROM EXPERIENCE   Firsthand and Expressive Writing

Guided Assignment: Write an Anecdote. 138
Prewriting: Planning Your Anecdote
Drafting: Writing It All Down
Revising and Publishing: Polishing Your Anecdote
   SKILLBUILDERS: Ordering and Representing Information, Achieving Unity
                in Paragraphs, Using Consistent Verb Tense

UNIT REVIEW: REFLECT & ASSESS 146

ACROSS TIME AND PLACE: The Oral Tradition

For more stories related to the unit theme,
see page 638.

Part 1 Finding a Special Place

Part 2 Tests of Endurance

┌──┐
│ WRITING FROM EXPERIENCE   **Narrative and Literary Writing** │

Guided Assignment: Write a Character Sketch. 244
Prewriting: Making Observations
Drafting: Getting Your Ideas Down
Revising and Publishing: Finishing Your Sketch
  SKILLBUILDERS: Using Sensory Details, Varying Your
                 Sentences, Using Action Verbs

UNIT REVIEW: REFLECT & ASSESS 252

ACROSS TIME AND PLACE: The Oral Tradition

For more stories related to the unit theme,
see page 660.

Part 1 Coping with Injustice

Part 2 Facing the Consequences

WRITING FROM EXPERIENCE   Informative Exposition

ACROSS TIME AND PLACE: The Oral Tradition

For more stories related to the unit theme,
see page 682.

Part 1 Showing Your True Colors

WRITING ABOUT LITERATURE | Creative Response

Part 2 Taking Necessary Steps

WRITING FROM EXPERIENCE | **Informative Exposition**

ACROSS TIME AND PLACE: The Oral Tradition

For more stories related to the unit theme,
see page 708.

REFLECT & ASSESS

Part 2 Reluctant Heroes

WRITING FROM EXPERIENCE   **Persuasion**

ACROSS TIME AND PLACE: The Oral Tradition

For more stories related to the unit theme, see page 728.

Bilbo comes to the Huts of the Raft-elves

WRITING ABOUT LITERATURE   Criticism

WRITING ABOUT LITERATURE   Report

Guided Assignment: Write an I-Search Report 748
Prewriting: Researching Your Topic
Drafting: Sharing Your Experience
Revising and Publishing: Pulling It All Together
    SKILLBUILDERS: Taking Notes, Outlining Your Ideas, Creating a List of Sources

Selections by Genre, Writing Workshops

The Oral Tradition
Myths, Legends, Folk Tales, and Fables

Writing About Literature

Writing from Experience

Reading the World: Visual Literacy

Can You Read Between the Lines?

Take a quick glance at the picture on the left and then look away. What did you see? Now, look again. Do you see anything else this time? There's more to this picture than meets the eye!

LOOK AGAIN

With a partner, take turns trying to see a second picture hidden in the pattern. Follow these steps.

1. What new ways of looking at the picture can you think of? What happens when you squint at the picture? What happens when you look at it from different angles? when you look at it up close? when you move it away?

2. Keep looking at the pattern until you see a hidden picture. Note how long it took you to see it.

3. Describe to your partner the picture you see.

4. Close your book to hide the pattern. Wait a minute or two.

5. Open the book again. How long did it take you to see the hidden picture this time?

6. If you have trouble finding the hidden picture, ask your partner for pointers and keep trying.

CONNECT TO LITERATURE

To see the hidden picture, you had to find a way to look at more than just the lines. In the same way, understanding literature involves more than just looking at words on a page. You have to learn to read between the lines. The more you think about what you read, the more you'll notice. Turn the page to see what you might find in literature.

What Can You Find in Literature?

Pick up your book. What's inside? Stories? Poems? An essay or two? But wait—there's so much more! This year, you will look beyond the words on a page to discover a world of ideas and images. What do you think might be hiding between the lines of literature?

EXCITING PLACES

How would you like to visit an ancient Roman city, search for a pharaoh's tomb in the Valley of the Kings, or journey to the top of the world? The **literature selections** you'll read this year will take you to those places and more. For example, the excerpt from *Gold and Silver, Silver and Gold*, on page 430, will place you on the deck of a pirate ship.

YOUR PERSONALITY

Your reactions to literature can reveal sides of yourself you've never seen before. The **Previewing** pages before each selection let you explore your ideas about a subject and also provide you with background information. For example, on page 93 you examine the hardships of frontier life before you read "Too Soon a Woman" by Dorothy M. Johnson. The **Responding** pages after a selection help you further explore and gain a deeper understanding of what you've read. To glimpse some responding activities, turn to page 100.

STRONG IDEAS

The **Writing About Literature** workshops will help you sift through literature's many layers to discover new ideas and to share your discoveries with others. Some of your discoveries will be surprising or confusing, but the workshop on page 206 can help you find meaning in what you've read. The **Writing from Experience** workshops help you find connections between unit themes and your own life. For example, after you have explored right and wrong in Unit Three, you will write about a problem that concerns you and come up with a solution.

SURPRISING CONNECTIONS

As you discover new people and exciting places in the stories you read, you'll be amazed at the connections they have to your own life and to the world around you. The **Reading the World** feature will show you how to apply the skills you use when reading literature to everyday situations. As an example, the lesson on page 90 invites you to examine how and why you respond to advertising.

Illustration Copyright ©
CSA Archive.

How Can **You** Keep What You **Find?**

You've seen some of the wonderful things you can discover in literature. Now it's time to get acquainted with several different ways that you can make your discoveries your own.

MULTIPLE PATHWAYS

How do you learn best? Do you prefer working alone or with others? Do you like writing, talking, acting, or drawing? This book offers you many choices that allow you to tailor learning experiences to your own strengths. In addition, you'll collaborate with classmates to share ideas, improve your writing, and make connections to other subject areas. You may even use a computer in the process. Technological tools such as the LaserLinks and the Writing Coach offer you even more learning options.

PORTFOLIO

Many artists, photographers, designers, and writers keep samples of their work in a portfolio that they show to others. You, too, will be collecting your work in a portfolio throughout the year. Your portfolio may include writing samples, records of activities, and artwork. You probably won't put all your work in your portfolio—just carefully chosen pieces. Discuss with your teacher the kind of portfolio you will be keeping this year. Suggestions for using your portfolio appear throughout this book.

Notebook

"The All-American Slurp" by Lensey Namioka

This story made me want to write my own story about my family.

Story Ideas
When I was five years old
moved to America from the
At first we stayed with som
in California but not for ve
we stayed with some cousi
which was a pretty big cit
remember whether I liked
Before long, I found out
going to move again.

Reading Log

"The All-American Slurp" by Lensey Namioka

She says they disgraced themselves while eating celery. How could they do that?

I see. They started zipping the strings out of the raw celery. When they noticed that no one else was doing that, they felt disgraced.

ut how confused rep
ck on the selection, the final passage stand
scribes the meaning of the whole story.

At first, I wasn't sure exactly what the story was about. The riter talks a lot about Chinatown and about the different streets, ills, and other parts of town. Some of the stories he tells are unny. So I thought maybe this story was supposed to be funny.

When I reread the story, I discovered that the writer talks a lot about feeling different or like an outsider. He was Chinese, but he didn't live in Chinatown or speak Chinese like all his friends. It was like he was lonely even though he had all these friends. The writer wasn't good at sports, either, so he was different from his family too.

When the writer talks about his singing adventure, he sets us up because we think it's a funny scene. But then he starts talking about his deep feelings. He says, "But the experience cured me of wanting to dress up and be something else." In this passage

Portfolio

NOTEBOOK

Choose any type of notebook to dedicate to your study of literature. Divide the notebook into three parts. Use the first section before reading, while reading, and after you have read a selection. Jot down ideas and thoughts, describe personal experiences, and take notes about the selection. Also include any charts, diagrams, and drawings that help you connect your reading to your life. The second section will be for your reading log, which is described below. Use the third section as a writer's notebook to record ideas and inspirations that you might want to use later in your writing.

READING LOG

In your reading log you will record a special kind of response to literature—your direct comments as you read a selection. The reading strategies detailed at the right will help you think about what you read. Experiment with recording your own comments as you read. You will find specific opportunities to use your reading log throughout this book.

Strategies for Reading

Reading is not a spectator sport. To get the most out of literature, you must think about what you read. The strategies below describe the kinds of thinking that active readers do as they read. You can use these strategies, too.

QUESTION

Question what's happening while you read. Searching for reasons behind events and characters' feelings can help you feel more involved in what you're reading. Make notes about confusing words or statements, but don't worry if you don't understand everything. As you read further, you'll probably begin to see things more clearly.

CONNECT

Connect personally with what you're reading. Think of similarities between the descriptions in the selection and what you have personally experienced, heard about, or read about.

PREDICT

Try to figure out what will happen next and how the selection might end. Then read on to see if you made a good guess.

CLARIFY

Stop occasionally to review what you understand so far, and expect to have your understanding change and develop as you read on. Also, watch for answers to questions you had earlier.

EVALUATE

Form opinions about what you read, both while you're reading and after you've finished. Make judgments about the information and develop your own ideas about events.

Now turn the page to see how two student readers put these strategies to work.

While reading the story "The All-American Slurp," two sixth-grade students spoke their thoughts out loud. The thoughts of Tiffany Providence and Jay Pepitone appear alongside the story to illustrate how active readers think as they read. After each comment, a label identifies the reading strategy or strategies that the comment reflects. You'll see that no two readers think alike. The ways in how they respond and use reading strategies vary widely. To get the most from this model, first read the story yourself and respond to it in your own way. Then read the responses of Tiffany and Jay, and compare them with your own.

The All-American SLURP

By Lensey Namioka

The first time our family was invited out to dinner in America, we disgraced ourselves while eating celery. We had emigrated to this country from China, and during our early days here we had a hard time with American table manners.

In China we never ate celery raw, or any other kind of vegetable raw. We always had to disinfect the vegetables in boiling water first. When we were presented with our first relish tray, the raw celery caught us unprepared.

We had been invited to dinner by our neighbors, the Gleasons. After arriving at the house, we shook hands with our hosts and packed ourselves into a sofa. As our family of four sat stiffly in a row, my younger brother and I stole glances at our parents for a clue as to what to do next.

Mrs. Gleason offered the relish tray to Mother. The tray looked pretty, with its tiny red radishes, curly sticks of carrots, and long, slender stalks of pale green celery. "Do try some of the celery, Mrs. Lin," she said. "It's from a local farmer, and it's sweet."

Mother picked up one of the green stalks, and Father followed suit. Then I picked up a stalk, and my brother did too. So there we sat, each with a stalk of celery in our right hand.

Mrs. Gleason kept smiling. "Would you like to try some of the dip, Mrs. Lin? It's my own recipe: sour cream and onion flakes, with a dash of Tabasco sauce."

Most Chinese don't care for dairy products, and in those days I wasn't even ready to drink fresh milk. Sour cream sounded perfectly revolting. Our family shook our heads in unison.

Mrs. Gleason went off with the relish tray to the other guests, and we carefully watched to see what they did. Everyone seemed to eat the raw vegetables quite happily.

Mother took a bite of her celery. *Crunch.* "It's not bad!" she whispered.

Father took a bite of his celery. *Crunch.* "Yes, it is good," he said, looking surprised.

I took a bite, and then my brother. *Crunch, crunch.* It was more than good; it was delicious. Raw celery has a slight sparkle, a zingy taste that you don't get in cooked celery. When Mrs. Gleason came around with the relish tray, we each took another stalk of celery, except my brother. He took two.

There was only one problem: long strings ran through the length of the stalk, and they got caught in my teeth. When I help my mother in the kitchen, I always pull the strings out before slicing celery.

I pulled the strings out of my stalk. *Z-z-zip, z-z-zip.* My brother followed suit. *Z-z-zip, z-z-zip, z-z-zip.* To my left, my parents were taking care of their own stalks. *Z-z-zip, z-z-zip, z-z-zip.*

Suddenly I realized that there was dead silence except for our zipping. Looking up, I saw that the eyes of everyone in the room were on our family. Mr. and Mrs. Gleason, their daughter Meg, who was my friend, and their neighbors the Badels—they were all staring at us as we busily pulled the strings of our celery.

That wasn't the end of it. Mrs. Gleason announced that dinner was served and invited us to the dining table. It was lavishly covered with platters of food, but we couldn't see any chairs around the table. So we helpfully carried over some dining chairs and sat down. All the other guests just stood there.

Mrs. Gleason bent down and whispered to us, "This is a buffet dinner. You help yourselves to some food and eat it in the living room."

Our family beat a retreat back to the sofa as if chased by enemy soldiers. For the rest of the evening, too mortified to go back to the dining table, I nursed a bit of potato salad on my plate.

Next day Meg and I got on the school bus together. I wasn't sure how she would feel about me after the spectacle our family made at the party. But she was just the same as usual, and the only reference she made to the party was, "Hope you and your folks got enough to eat last night. You certainly didn't take very much. Mom never tries to figure out how much food to prepare. She just puts everything on the table and hopes for the best."

I began to relax. The Gleasons' dinner party wasn't so different from a Chinese meal after all. My mother also puts everything on the table and hopes for the best.

Meg was the first friend I had made after we came to America. I eventually got acquainted with a few other kids in school, but Meg was still the only real friend I had.

My brother didn't have any problems making friends. He spent all his time with some boys who were teaching him baseball, and in no time he could speak English much faster than I could—not better, but faster.

I worried more about making mistakes, and I spoke carefully, making sure I could say everything right before opening my mouth. At least I had a better accent than my parents, who never really got rid of their Chinese accent, even years later. My parents had both studied English in school before coming to America, but what they had studied was mostly written English, not spoken.

Tiffany: Why would they pull out the little strings in the celery?
QUESTIONING

Jay: Whenever I eat at anybody else's house, I eat slower than I usually do. That way, I can make sure nothing flies out of my mouth and I don't make any noise while I'm chewing.
CONNECTING

Tiffany: Was the brother's name mentioned before?
QUESTIONING

Jay: I wonder why he didn't learn to play baseball in China. I wonder if they don't have it there.
QUESTIONING

Father's approach to English was a scientific one. Since Chinese verbs have no tense, he was fascinated by the way English verbs changed form according to whether they were in the present, past imperfect, perfect, pluperfect, future, or future perfect tense. He was always making diagrams of verbs and their inflections, and he looked for opportunities to show off his mastery of the pluperfect and future perfect tenses, his two favorites. "I shall have finished my project by Monday," he would say smugly.

Mother's approach was to memorize lists of polite phrases that would cover all possible social situations. She was constantly muttering things like "I'm fine, thank you. And you?" Once she accidentally stepped on someone's foot and hurriedly blurted, "Oh, that's quite all right!" Embarrassed by her slip, she resolved to do better next time. So when someone stepped on her foot, she cried, "You're welcome!"

In our own different ways, we made progress in learning English. But I had another worry, and that was my appearance. My brother didn't have to worry, since Mother bought him blue jeans for school, and he dressed like all the other boys. But she insisted that girls had to wear skirts. By the time she saw that Meg and the other girls were wearing jeans, it was too late. My school clothes were bought already, and we didn't have money left to buy new outfits for me. We had too many other things to buy first, like furniture, pots, and pans.

The first time I visited Meg's house, she took me upstairs to her room, and I wound up trying on her clothes. We were pretty much the same size, since Meg was shorter and thinner than average. Maybe that's how we became friends in the first place. Wearing Meg's jeans and T-shirt, I looked at myself in the mirror. I could almost pass for an American—from the back, anyway. At least the kids in school wouldn't stop and stare at me in the hallways, which was what they did when they saw me in my white blouse and navy blue skirt that went a couple of inches below the knees.

When Meg came to my house, I invited her to try on my

Jay: This is kind of funny—that she stepped on someone's foot and said "That's quite all right!" Same with saying "You're welcome!"
EVALUATING

Chinese dresses, the ones with a high collar and slits up the sides. Meg's eyes were bright as she looked at herself in the mirror. She struck several sultry poses, and we nearly fell over laughing.

The dinner party at the Gleasons' didn't stop my growing friendship with Meg. Things were getting better for me in other ways too. Mother finally bought me some jeans at the end of the month, when Father got his paycheck. She wasn't in any hurry about buying them at first, until I worked on her. This is what I did. Since we didn't have a car in those days, I often ran down to the neighborhood store to pick up things for her. The groceries cost less at a big supermarket, but the closest one was many blocks away. One day, when she ran out of flour, I offered to borrow a bike from our neighbor's son and buy a ten-pound bag of flour at the big supermarket. I mounted the boy's bike and waved to Mother. "I'll be back in five minutes!"

Before I started pedaling, I heard her voice behind me. "You can't go out in public like that! People can see all the way up to your thighs!"

"I'm sorry," I said innocently. "I thought you were in a hurry to get the flour." For dinner we were going to have pot-stickers (fried Chinese dumplings), and we needed a lot of flour.

"Couldn't you borrow a girl's bicycle?" complained Mother. "That way your skirt won't be pushed up."

"There aren't too many of those around," I said. "Almost all the girls wear jeans while riding a bike, so they don't see any point buying a girl's bike."

We didn't eat pot-stickers that evening, and Mother was thoughtful. Next day we took the bus downtown, and she bought me a pair of jeans. In the same week, my brother made the baseball team of his junior high school, Father started taking driving lessons, and Mother discovered rummage sales. We soon got all the furniture we needed, plus a dart board and a 1,000-piece jigsaw puzzle (fourteen hours later, we discovered that it was a 999-piece jigsaw puzzle). There was hope that the Lins might become a normal American family after all.

Then came our dinner at the Lakeview Restaurant.

The Lakeview was an expensive restaurant, one of those places where a headwaiter dressed in tails conducted you to your seat, and the only light came from candles and flaming desserts. In one corner of the room a lady harpist played tinkling melodies.

Father wanted to celebrate, because he had just been promoted.

Jay: The setting ...the time must be pretty far back from when I was born because they didn't have a car.
EVALUATING

Tiffany: Was she wearing a dress while riding a bike?
QUESTIONING

Tiffany: Her mother finally got her a pair of jeans!
EVALUATING

Jay: Father started taking driving lessons, so I guess that means they'll get a car.
CLARIFYING

Jay: Maybe they live in the city, because they're going to a big, expensive restaurant with all the waiters dressed in suits.

A Kitchen on the Eve of a Festival, Zhou Jihe. Courtesy of Foreign Languages Press, Beijing, China.

He worked for an electronics company, and after his English started improving, his superiors decided to appoint him to a position more suited to his training. The promotion not only brought a higher salary but was also a tremendous boost to his pride.

Up to then we had eaten only in Chinese restaurants. Although my brother and I were becoming fond of hamburgers, my parents didn't care much for Western food, other than chow mein.

But this was a special occasion, and Father asked his coworkers to recommend a really elegant restaurant. So there we were at the Lakeview, stumbling after the headwaiter in the murky dining room.

At our table we were handed our menus, and they were so big that to read mine I almost had to stand up again. But why bother? It was mostly in French, anyway.

Father, being an engineer, was always systematic. He took out a pocket French dictionary. "They told me that most of the items would be in French, so I came prepared." He even had a pocket flashlight, the size of a marking pen. While Mother held the flashlight over the menu, he looked up the items that were in French.

"*Pâté en croûte,*" he muttered. "Let's see . . . *pâté* is paste . . . *croûte* is crust . . . hmm . . . a paste in crust."

The waiter stood looking patient. I squirmed and died at least fifty times.

At long last Father gave up. "Why don't we just order four complete dinners at random?" he suggested.

"Isn't that risky?" asked Mother. "The French eat some rather peculiar things, I've heard."

"A Chinese can eat anything a Frenchman can eat," Father declared.

The soup arrived in a plate. How do you get soup up from a plate? I glanced at the other diners, but the ones at the nearby tables were not on their soup course, while the more distant ones were invisible in the darkness.

Fortunately my parents had studied books on Western etiquette before they came to America. "Tilt your plate," whispered my mother. "It's easier to spoon the soup up that way."

She was right. Tilting the plate did the trick. But the etiquette book didn't say anything about what you did after the soup reached your lips. As any respectable Chinese knows, the correct way to eat your soup is to slurp. This helps to cool the liquid and prevent you from burning your lips. It also shows your appreciation.

We showed our appreciation. *Shloop*, went my father. *Shloop*, went my mother. *Shloop, shloop*, went my brother, who was the hungriest.

The lady harpist stopped playing to take a rest. And in the silence, our family's consumption of soup suddenly seemed unnaturally loud. You know how it sounds on a rocky beach when the tide goes out and the water drains from all those little pools? They go *shloop, shloop, shloop*. That was the Lin family, eating soup.

At the next table a waiter was pouring wine. When a large *shloop* reached him, he froze. The bottle continued to pour, and red wine flooded the tabletop and into the lap of a customer. Even the customer didn't notice anything at first, being also hypnotized by the *shloop, shloop, shloop*.

It was too much. "I need to go to the toilet," I mumbled, jumping to my feet. A waiter, sensing my urgency, quickly directed me to the ladies' room.

I splashed cold water on my burning face, and as I dried myself with a paper towel, I stared into the mirror. In this perfumed ladies' room, with its pink-and-silver wallpaper and marbled sinks, I looked completely out of place. What was I doing here? What was our family doing in the Lakeview Restaurant? In America?

The door to the ladies' room opened. A woman came in and glanced curiously at me. I retreated into one of the toilet cubicles and latched the door.

Time passed—maybe half an hour, maybe an hour. Then I heard the door open again, and my mother's voice. "Are you in there? You're not sick, are you?"

There was real concern in her voice. A girl can't leave her family just because they slurp their soup. Besides, the toilet cubicle had a few drawbacks as a permanent residence. "I'm all right," I said, undoing the latch.

Mother didn't tell me how the rest of the dinner went, and I

Tiffany: Her parents studied Western what?
QUESTIONING

Jay: Here's another word I don't know—etiquette—but I think it means "manners" because they're telling her it's easier to spoon the soup that way.
CLARIFYING

Jay: They're all going to start slurping the soup, and everyone's going to stop eating and look at them.
PREDICTING

Jay: That's what I would do!
CONNECTING

Tiffany: The narrator stayed in the bathroom all through dinnertime!
CLARIFYING

Jay: I don't think I'd be able to really forget about something like that.
CONNECTING/EVALUATING

Tiffany: The narrator's parents called her a stupid girl but were really proud of her.
CLARIFYING

Jay: Why does this girl care so much about her family becoming Americanized if they're Chinese? Why doesn't she care about her culture?
QUESTIONING

Jay: Chicken gizzards—that sounds disgusting!
CONNECTING

Jay: I wonder if they're going to try to have the Gleasons—who had them over to their dinner party—do something stupid or embarrassing to get back at them.
PREDICTING

didn't want to know. In the weeks following, I managed to push the whole thing into the back of my mind, where it jumped out at me only a few times a day. Even now, I turn hot all over when I think of the Lakeview Restaurant.

But by the time we had been in this country for three months, our family was definitely making progress toward becoming Americanized. I remember my parents' first PTA meeting. Father wore a neat suit and tie, and Mother put on her first pair of high heels. She stumbled only once. They met my homeroom teacher and beamed as she told them that I would make honor roll soon at the rate I was going. Of course Chinese etiquette forced Father to say that I was a very stupid girl and Mother to protest that the teacher was showing favoritism toward me. But I could tell they were both very proud.

The day came when my parents announced that they wanted to give a dinner party. We had invited Chinese friends to eat with us before, but this dinner was going to be different. In addition to a Chinese-American family, we were going to invite the Gleasons.

"Gee, I can hardly wait to have dinner at your house," Meg said to me. "I just *love* Chinese food."

That was a relief. Mother was a good cook, but I wasn't sure if people who ate sour cream would also eat chicken gizzards stewed in soy sauce.

Mother decided not to take a chance with chicken gizzards. Since we had Western guests, she set the table with large dinner plates, which we never used in Chinese meals. In fact we didn't use individual plates at all but picked up food from the platters in the middle of the table and brought it directly to our rice bowls. Following the practice of Chinese-American restaurants, Mother also placed large serving spoons on the platters.

The dinner started well. Mrs. Gleason exclaimed at the beautifully arranged dishes of food: the colorful candied fruit in the sweet-and-sour pork dish, the noodle-thin shreds of chicken meat stir-fried with tiny peas, and the glistening pink prawns in a ginger sauce.

At first I was too busy enjoying my food to notice how the guests were doing. But soon I remembered my duties. Sometimes guests were too polite to help themselves, and you had to serve them with more food.

I glanced at Meg, to see if she needed more food, and my eyes nearly popped out at the sight of her plate. It was piled with food:

the sweet-and-sour meat pushed right against the chicken shreds, and the chicken sauce ran into the prawns. She had been taking food from a second dish before she finished eating her helping from the first!

Horrified, I turned to look at Mrs. Gleason. She was dumping rice out of her bowl and putting it on her dinner plate. Then she ladled prawns and gravy on top of the rice and mixed everything together, the way you mix sand, gravel, and cement to make concrete.

I couldn't bear to look any longer, and I turned to Mr. Gleason. He was chasing a pea around his plate. Several times he got it to the edge, but when he tried to pick it up with his chopsticks, it rolled back toward the center of the plate again. Finally he put down his chopsticks and picked up the pea with his fingers. He really did! A grown man!

All of us, our family and the Chinese guests, stopped eating to watch the activities of the Gleasons. I wanted to giggle. Then I caught my mother's eyes on me. She frowned and shook her head slightly, and I understood the message: the Gleasons were not used to Chinese ways, and they were just coping the best they could. For some reason I thought of celery strings.

When the main courses were finished, Mother brought out a platter of fruit. "I hope you weren't expecting a sweet dessert," she said. "Since the Chinese don't eat dessert, I didn't think to prepare any."

"Oh, I couldn't possibly eat dessert!" cried Mrs. Gleason. "I'm simply stuffed!"

Meg had different ideas. When the table was cleared, she announced that she and I were going for a walk. "I don't know about you, but I feel like dessert," she told me, when we were outside. "Come on; there's a Dairy Queen down the street. I could use a big chocolate milk shake!"

Although I didn't really want anything more to eat, I insisted on paying for the milk shakes. After all, I was still hostess.

Meg got her large chocolate milk shake, and I had a small one. Even so, she was finishing hers while I was only half done. Toward the end she pulled hard on her straws and went *shloop,* shloop.

"Do you always slurp when you eat a milk shake?" I asked, before I could stop myself.

Meg grinned. "Sure. All Americans slurp."

Tiffany: The narrator's mother is trying to make their company feel comfortable.
CLARIFYING/EVALUATING

Tiffany: The Gleasons eat a lot!
EVALUATING

Jay: The same things are happening to the Gleasons that happened to the Lins. Meg probably wanted to laugh at the girl just like she wants to laugh at Meg now.
EVALUATING

Tiffany: So the Chinese and the Americans have something in common—slurping.
EVALUATING

Jay: I like this. It was pretty funny in some parts.
EVALUATING

UNIT ONE

HOLLAND

RUNNING Risks

Only
those
who
dare
to
fail
greatly
can
ever
achieve
greatly.

ROBERT F. KENNEDY
U.S. Senator
1925–1968

It's All Relative (1995),
Brad Holland. Copyright ©
1995 Brad Holland.

SEIZING THE MOMENT

REFLECTING ON THEME

In as little time as an instant, it is possible to take a step or make a decision that has long-lasting effects. Use an activity on this page to explore what it is like to act under pressure. Take notes of your thoughts and ideas. You can compare them later with the thoughts of the characters in Part 1 as they attempt to "seize the moment."

Which is toughest?

In your notebook, create a scale like the one shown here. Use the scale to show how you would rate the difficulty of each of these situations.

> • You are purposely shoved by another student.
>
> • You want to tell someone that you really like him or her.
>
> • You fail a math test and now must work with a tutor.
>
> Easy ← → Difficult

Who can handle the pressure?

In old newspapers or magazines, find articles about people acting under pressure. Then, in a small group, take the roles of these people. In the style of a TV talk show, discuss people who have "seized a moment." After the discussion, list the personal traits that are common to all the guests.

What's your next move?

With a group of classmates, brainstorm some kinds of problems and obstacles that young people face every day. Then create a board game called "A Day in My Life." Be sure that the game represents daily problems and offers options for solutions.

What makes a decision good or bad?

Recall a decision you made quickly, without thinking about the possible results. Create a diagram similar to the one shown. Would you make the same choice again? Talk about it with a partner.

Problem	
Decision I Made	
Pros	**Cons**
Conclusions	

FOCUS ON FICTION

When you read a story, you are reading a work of fiction. **Fiction** is writing that comes from an author's imagination. Although the author makes the story up, he or she might base it on real events.

Fiction writers write short stories and novels. A **short story** usually revolves around a single idea and is short enough to be read at one sitting. The fiction selections that you will read in this book are short stories. A **novel** is much longer and more complex.

Fiction writing contains four main elements: **character, setting, plot,** and **theme.** In some stories, all four elements are well developed. In other cases, an author may decide to focus on only one or two elements.

CHARACTER Characters are the people, animals, or imaginary creatures that take part in the action of a story. Usually, a short story centers on events in the life of one person, animal, or creature. This is the story's **main character.**

Generally, there are also one or more **minor characters** in the story. Minor characters sometimes provide part of the background for the story. More often, however, minor characters interact with the main character and with one another. Their words and actions help to move the plot along.

SETTING A story's setting is the time and place in which the action of the story happens. The time may be in the past, the present, or the future; in daytime or in the night; at any season. The place where the story's action occurs may be imaginary or real.

PLOT The sequence of events in a story is called the story's plot. The plot is the writer's blueprint for what happens, when it happens, and to whom it happens. One event causes another, which causes another, and so on until the end of the story.

Generally, a plot is built around a **conflict**—a problem or struggle involving two or more opposing forces. Conflicts can range from life-or-death struggles to disagreements between friends.

Although the development of each plot is different, traditional works of fiction generally follow a pattern that includes the following stages:

Exposition Exposition sets the stage for a story. Characters are introduced, the setting is described, and the conflict begins to unfold.

Complications As the story continues, the plot gets more complex. The characters struggle to find solutions to the conflict, and suspense and a feeling of excitement and energy build.

Climax The climax is the point of greatest interest or suspense in the story. It is the turning point, when the action reaches a peak and the outcome of the conflict is decided. The climax may occur because of a decision the characters reach or because of a discovery or an event that changes the situation. The climax usually results in a change in the characters or a solution to the problem.

Resolution The resolution usually occurs at the conclusion of the story. Loose ends are tied up, and the story ends.

THEME The theme of a story is the main message the writer conveys to the reader. This message might be a lesson about life or a belief about people and their actions. In most cases, the theme is not stated directly; it is like a hidden message that the reader must decode. As you discuss literature, however, you will find that different readers can discover different themes in the same story. The following suggestions will help you unlock a theme:

• Review what happened to the main character. Did he or she change during the story? What did he or she learn about life?

• Skim the story for key phrases and sentences—statements that go beyond the action of the story to say something important about life or people.

• Think about the story's title. Does it have a special meaning that could lead you to the main idea of the work?

STRATEGIES FOR READING FICTION

To really "get inside" a story, try the following strategies:

• **Preview the story.** Before you read, look at the title and the pictures. Skim through the pages and read some words here and there.

• **Visualize what you are reading.** Can you picture a similar place in your mind? Is the action easy to imagine?

• **Make connections.** Do any of the characters have thoughts or experiences that you have had? Does the story remind you of an event or a person you've heard of or read about?

• **Question as you read.** The events, characters, and ideas in the story ought to make sense to you. "Why is the door unlocked?" "Why is she so rude?" Asking good questions as you read is at the heart of good reading.

• **Make predictions.** During your reading, stop occasionally to predict what might happen next and how you think the story will end.

• **Build on your knowledge.** Let your thoughts change and grow as you learn more about the characters and events in the story.

• **Evaluate the story.** Think about your feelings about the characters and their actions. Also consider how well the author is telling his or her story.

• **Discuss the story.** When you have finished reading, talk about the story with someone else.

Remember, a story never tells you everything; it leaves room for your own ideas. After you read a story, you are left with first impressions, but you need to be able to elaborate and explain them on the basis of the story itself, your own experiences, and other stories you have read.

PREVIEWING

FICTION

Nadia the Willful
Sue Alexander

PERSONAL CONNECTION

Think about the title of this story. What does the title suggest about the content? What does it mean to say that someone is willful? On a sheet of paper, complete a web, like the one shown, about the title.

Synonyms of Willful

What the Title Suggests

"Nadia the Willful"

Antonyms of Willful

My Image of a Willful Person

GEOGRAPHICAL CONNECTION

Nadia the Willful, the main character in this story, is a young Bedouin girl. The Bedouins are an Arab people of the Sahara and the desert lands of the Middle East. The leader of a Bedouin tribe or clan is called a sheik. Bedouins live as nomads, or wanderers, searching the desert for oases (places with water and pasture), where they can settle with their goats, sheep, camels, and horses. When an oasis dries up, the group moves on. Life in the desert is harsh and dangerous—food is scarce, sandstorms are common, and temperatures can reach 130°F.

WRITING CONNECTION

In your notebook, write about a person whom you would describe as willful. How does this person speak and act? How does he or she get along with other people? If possible, give examples of words or actions that show this person's willfulness. As you read, compare Nadia with the person you described.

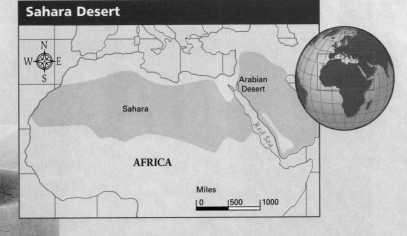

Sahara Desert

N W E S

Arabian Desert

Sahara

Red Sea

AFRICA

Miles
0 500 1000

Bedouins. Lehnert & Landrock, Copyright © National Geographic Society.

LASERLINKS
- *CULTURAL CONNECTION*
- *VISUAL VOCABULARY*

21

Bedouins (about 1905–1906), John Singer Sargent. Watercolor, 18″ × 12″, The Brooklyn Museum, New York. Purchased by special subscription (09.814).

Nadia the Willful

by Sue Alexander

In the land of the drifting sands where the Bedouin move their tents to follow the fertile grasses, there lived a girl whose stubbornness and flashing temper caused her to be known throughout the desert as Nadia the Willful.

Nadia's father, the sheik Tarik, whose kindness and graciousness caused his name to be praised in every tent, did not know what to do with his willful daughter.

Only Hamed, the eldest of Nadia's six brothers and Tarik's favorite son, could calm Nadia's temper when it flashed.

"Oh, angry one," he would say, "shall we see how long you can stay that way?" And he would laugh and tease and pull at her dark hair until she laughed back. Then she would follow Hamed wherever he led.

One day before dawn, Hamed mounted his father's great white stallion and rode to the west to seek new grazing ground for the sheep. Nadia stood with her father at the edge of the oasis and watched him go.

Hamed did not return.

Nadia rode behind her father as he traveled across the desert from oasis to oasis, seeking Hamed.

Shepherds told them of seeing a great white stallion fleeing before the pillars of wind that stirred the sand. And they said that the horse carried no rider.

Passing merchants, their camels laden with spices and sweets for the <u>bazaar</u>, told of the emptiness of the desert they had crossed.

Tribesmen, strangers, everyone whom Tarik asked, sighed and gazed into the desert, saying, "Such is the will of Allah."[1]

*A*t last Tarik knew in his heart that his favorite son, Hamed, had been claimed, as other Bedouin before him, by the drifting sands. And he told Nadia what he knew—that Hamed was dead.

Nadia screamed and wept and stamped the sand, crying, "Not even Allah will take Hamed from me!" until her father could bear no more and sternly bade her to silence.

Nadia's grief knew no bounds. She walked blindly through the oasis, neither seeing nor hearing those who would console her. And

Tarik was silent. For days he sat inside his tent, speaking not at all and barely tasting the meals set before him.

Then, on the seventh day, Tarik came out of his tent. He called all his people to him, and when they were assembled, he spoke. "From this day forward," he said, "let no one utter Hamed's name. Punishment shall be swift for those who would remind me of what I have lost."

Each memory brought Hamed's name to Nadia's lips.

Hamed's mother wept at the <u>decree</u>. The people of the <u>clan</u> looked at one another uneasily. All could see the hardness that had settled on the sheik's face and the coldness in his eyes, and so they said nothing. But they obeyed.

Nadia, too, did as her father decreed, though each day held something to remind her of Hamed. As she passed her brothers at play, she remembered games Hamed had taught her. As she walked by the women weaving patches for the tents and heard them talking and laughing, she remembered tales Hamed had told her and how they had made her laugh. And as she watched the shepherds with their flock, she remembered the little black lamb Hamed had loved.

Each memory brought Hamed's name to Nadia's lips, but she stilled the sound. And each time that she did so, her unhappiness grew until, finally, she could no longer contain it. She wept and raged at anyone and anything that crossed her path. Soon everyone at the

---

1. **Allah** (ăl'ə): the name for God in the Islamic religion.

WORDS	**bazaar** (bə-zär') *n.* in Middle Eastern countries, an outdoor market of small shops
TO	**decree** (dĭ-krē') *n.* an official order
KNOW	**clan** (klăn) *n.* a family group or tribe

La caravane [The caravan] (1880), Alexandre-Gabriel Decamps. Louvre, Paris. Giraudon/Art Resource, New York.

oasis fled at her approach. And she was more lonely than she had ever been before.

One day, as Nadia passed the place where her brothers were playing, she stopped to watch them. They were playing one of the games that Hamed had taught her. But they were playing it wrong.

Without thinking, Nadia called out to them. "That is not the way! Hamed said that first you jump this way and then you jump back!"

Her brothers stopped their game and looked around in fear. Had Tarik heard Nadia say Hamed's name? But the sheik was nowhere to be seen.

"Teach us, Nadia, as our brother taught you," said her smallest brother.

And so she did. Then she told them of other games and how Hamed had taught her to play them. And as she spoke of Hamed, she felt an easing of the hurt within her.

So she went on speaking of him.

She went to where the women sat at their loom and spoke of Hamed. She told them tales that Hamed had told her. And she told how he had made her laugh as he was telling them.

At first the women were afraid to listen to the willful girl and covered their ears, but after a time, they listened and laughed with her.

"Remember your father's promise of punishment!" Nadia's mother warned when she heard Nadia speaking of Hamed. "Cease, I implore you!"

Nadia knew that her mother had reason to be afraid, for Tarik, in his grief and bitterness, had grown quick-tempered and sharp of tongue. But she did not know how to tell her mother that speaking of Hamed eased the pain she felt, and so she said only, "I will speak of my brother! I will!" And she ran away from the sound of her mother's voice.

She went to where the shepherds tended the flock and spoke of Hamed. The shepherds ran from her in fear and hid behind the sheep. But Nadia went on speaking. She told of Hamed's love for the little black lamb and how he had taught it to leap at his whistle. Soon the shepherds left off their hiding and came to listen. Then they told their own stories of Hamed and the little black lamb.

The more Nadia spoke of Hamed, the clearer his face became in her mind. She could see his smile and the light in his eyes. She could hear his voice. And the clearer Hamed's voice and face became, the less Nadia hurt inside and the less her temper flashed. At last, she was filled with peace.

But her mother was still afraid for her willful daughter. Again and again she sought to quiet Nadia so that Tarik's bitterness would not be turned against her. And again and again Nadia tossed her head and went on speaking of Hamed.

Soon, all who listened could see Hamed's face clearly before them.

One day, the youngest shepherd came to Nadia's tent, calling, "Come, Nadia! See Hamed's black lamb; it has grown so big and strong!"

But it was not Nadia who came out of the tent.

It was Tarik.

On the sheik's face was a look more fierce than that of a desert hawk, and when he spoke, his words were as sharp as a scimitar.[2]

"I have forbidden my son's name to be said. And I promised punishment to whoever disobeyed my command. So shall it be. Before the sun sets and the moon casts its first shadow on the sand, you will be gone from this oasis—never to return."

"No!" cried Nadia, hearing her father's words.

"I have spoken!" roared the sheik. "It shall be done!"

Trembling, the shepherd went to gather his possessions.

And the rest of the clan looked at one another uneasily and muttered among themselves.

In the hours that followed, fear of being banished to the desert made everyone turn away from Nadia as she tried to tell them of Hamed and the things he had done and said.

And the less she was listened to, the less she was able to recall Hamed's face and voice. And the less she recalled, the more her temper raged within her, destroying the peace she had found.

"I have spoken!" roared the sheik. "It shall be done!"

By evening, she could stand it no longer. She went to where her father sat, staring into the desert, and stood before him.

"You will not rob me of my brother Hamed!" she cried, stamping her foot. "I will not let you!"

Tarik looked at her, his eyes colder than the desert night.

But before he could utter a word, Nadia spoke again. "Can you recall Hamed's face? Can you still hear his voice?"

---

2. **scimitar** (sĭm′ĭ-tər): a curved sword.

WORDS
TO
KNOW **banish** (băn′ĭsh) *v.* to send away; exile

Tarik started in surprise, and his answer seemed to come unbidden to his lips. "No, I cannot! Day after day I have sat in this spot where I last saw Hamed, trying to remember the look, the sound, the happiness that was my beloved son—but I cannot."

And he wept.

Nadia's tone became gentle. "There is a way, honored father," she said. "Listen."

And she began to speak of Hamed. She told of walks she and Hamed had taken and of talks they had had. She told how he had taught her games, told her tales, and calmed her when she was angry. She told many things that she remembered, some happy and some sad.

And when she was done with the telling, she said gently, "Can you not recall him now, Father? Can you not see his face? Can you not hear his voice?"

Tarik nodded through his tears, and for the first time since Hamed had been gone, he smiled.

"Now you see," Nadia said, her tone more gentle than the softest of the desert breezes, "there is a way that Hamed can be with us still."

The sheik <u>pondered</u> what Nadia had said. After a long time, he spoke, and the sharpness was gone from his voice.

"Tell my people to come before me, Nadia," he said. "I have something to say to them."

When all were assembled, Tarik said, "From this day forward, let my daughter Nadia be known not as willful but as wise. And let her name be praised in every tent, for she has given me back my beloved son."

And so it was. The shepherd returned to his flock, kindness and graciousness returned to the oasis, and Nadia's name was praised in every tent. And Hamed lived again—in the hearts of all who remembered him. ❖

✳ PRIMER LESSON ✳

BY CARL SANDBURG

Look out how you use proud words.
When you let proud words go, it is
    not easy to call them back.
They wear long boots, hard boots; they
    walk off proud; they can't hear you
    calling—
Look out how you use proud words.

WORDS
TO
KNOW

ponder (pŏn′dər) v. to think about carefully

27

RESPONDING

O P T I O N S

FROM **PERSONAL RESPONSE** TO **CRITICAL ANALYSIS**

REFLECT **1.** What were your thoughts about Nadia as you finished reading? Write about her in your notebook.

RETHINK **2.** Think about the word web and notebook entry about willfulness that you made for the Personal Connection on page 21. In your opinion, does Nadia deserve to be called willful? Explain.

3. How does Nadia change across time, and why?

4. Nadia's father promises to punish anyone who speaks Hamed's name. Why do you think Nadia is able to change her father's mind?

Consider
- Nadia's character
- the effect of grief on her father

RELATE **5.** Read "Primer Lesson" on page 27. What connections do you see between Sandburg's warning about "proud words" and Nadia the Willful?

6. Nadia and Tarik have different ways of reacting to death. Do their actions bring to mind any feelings or experiences of grief and death that you know about or have read about?

ANOTHER PATHWAY

Cooperative Learning
What if this story were told by Nadia or by Tarik? With a small group, choose what you consider the most important section of the story. Then rewrite that section, telling it from either Nadia's or Tarik's point of view. Share your version with the class.

QUICKWRITES

1. Compose a **narrative poem** that tells the events of this story. (For a description of narrative poetry, see page 104.)

2. Prepare a **character sketch** that would help an actor playing Tarik in a film version of "Nadia the Willful" to understand Tarik's character.

3. Imagine you are the set designer for the film version of the story. Write a **memo** to the director, describing the setting that you want to create. In your memo use details that you gathered for the Literary Concepts activity.

📁 *PORTFOLIO Save your writing. You may want to use it later as a springboard to a piece for your portfolio.*

LITERARY CONCEPTS

The **setting** of a story is the time and place in which the events of the story happen. Skim the story and make a list of details about the setting. What role does the setting play in this story? How important is the setting?

Setting Details:

ALTERNATIVE ACTIVITIES

Make a desert **diorama.** Cut a small square opening in one side of a shoebox. Using sand, sandpaper, paint, and other materials, create the setting of the story inside the shoebox. Then make paper figures of the characters and their animals to position within the scene. View the scene from the top or through the opening.

ACROSS THE CURRICULUM

Science Find out how deserts and oases form and change. Present your information to the class in an oral report.

Review the Words to Know in the boxes at the bottom of the selection pages. Write the word most closely related to the idea of each sentence.

1. The sheik was angered by the theft of the horses and commanded that anyone found stealing a horse be put to death.

2. The marketplace was packed with every imaginable item—blankets, saddles, robes of woven cloth, and even wooden toys for children.

3. Looking out at the horizon, Hamed sat and thought of the extraordinary size of the hot and silent desert.

4. They camped at the oasis, all of the families of the tribe sleeping in tents and cooking food for one another over open fires.

5. There was no way he could survive in the desert alone, but he had no choice because the tribe would not let him live among them any longer.

SUE ALEXANDER

At the age of eight, Sue Alexander began writing stories for her friends. She says, "At that time I was small for my age (I still am) and very clumsy. So clumsy, in fact, that none of my classmates wanted me on their teams at recess time." One day Alexander spent recess time telling a made-up story to someone else who was not playing. Before her story was finished, all the rest of the class had come to listen. This incident sparked her love of storytelling.

Alexander says she would not trade writing for any other profession because writing satisfies her

1933–

sense of fun and her need to share. Her fantasy stories all begin the same way— with how she feels about something. She writes for young people because she likes to excite their imaginations.

Alexander's short stories have been published in *My Weekly Reader* and other magazines for younger readers. The book publication of *Nadia the Willful* won many honors, including one from the American Library Association in 1983.

OTHER WORKS *World Famous Muriel, Lila on the Landing, There's More—Much More*

FICTION

The School Play

Gary Soto

PERSONAL CONNECTION

You stand backstage, listening closely to the lines the actors on the stage are speaking, waiting to make your entrance. Suddenly a hand touches your shoulder, and someone whispers, "You're on!" Think back to your own experiences of performing in public or giving oral reports in school. With your classmates, discuss what you remember most about rehearsing, performing, and receiving an audience's reaction.

HISTORICAL CONNECTION

In "The School Play," a class is preparing to perform *The Last Stand,* a play based on a tragic incident in America's past. In 1846, a group of 82 pioneers from Illinois and nearby states, led by George and Jacob Donner, set out for California in covered wagons. When trying to cross the Sierra Nevada mountain range in eastern California, they became snowbound in the pass through the mountains. More fierce weather swept in, and the travelers ran out of food. Many began dying of starvation. In their desperation, some of the remaining members of the party resorted to eating the bodies of the dead to survive. Only 47 of the pioneers made it through that grim winter. Donner Pass is now a national landmark, and accounts of what took place there continue to fascinate people.

The Donner Pass

Sierra Nevada

Donner Pass

San Francisco

CALIFORNIA

N W E S

Los Angeles

Pacific Ocean

Miles
0   80   160

WRITING CONNECTION

Many people feel nervous about speaking or performing in public. In fact, public speaking is often at or near the top of people's lists of personal fears. In your notebook, write about why this might be true and whether people should find speaking in public so frightening. As you read, think about how the characters in this story illustrate your ideas.

LASERLINKS
• *HISTORICAL CONNECTION*

THE SCHOOL PLAY

BY GARY SOTO

In the school play at the end of his sixth-grade year, all Robert Suarez had to remember to say was, "Nothing's wrong. I can see," to a pioneer woman, who was really Belinda Lopez. Instead of a pioneer woman, Belinda was one of the toughest girls since the beginning of the world. She was known to slap boys and grind their faces into the grass so that they bit into chunks of wormy earth. More than once Robert had witnessed Belinda staring down the janitor's pit bull, who licked his frothing chops but didn't dare mess with her.

The class rehearsed for three weeks, at first without costumes. Early one morning Mrs. Bunnin wobbled into the classroom lugging a large cardboard box. She wiped her brow and said, "Thanks for the help, Robert."

Robert was at his desk scribbling a ballpoint tattoo that spelled DUDE on the tops of his knuckles. He looked up and stared, blinking at his teacher. "Oh, did you need some help?" he asked.

She rolled her eyes at him and told him to stop writing on his skin. "You'll look like a criminal," she scolded.

Robert stuffed his hands into his pockets as he rose from his seat. "What's in the box?" he asked.

She muttered under her breath. She popped open the taped top and brought out skirts, hats, snowshoes, scarves, and vests. She tossed Robert a red beard, which he held up to his face, thinking it made him look handsome.

"I like it," Robert said. He sneezed and ran his hand across his moist nose.

His classmates were coming into the classroom and looked at Robert in awe. "That's bad," Ruben said. "What do I get?"

Mrs. Bunnin threw him a wrinkled shirt. Ruben raised it to his chest and said, "My dad could wear this. Can I give it to him after the play is done?"

Mrs. Bunnin turned away in silence.

Most of the actors didn't have speaking

"NOTHING'S

WRONG.

I CAN SEE."

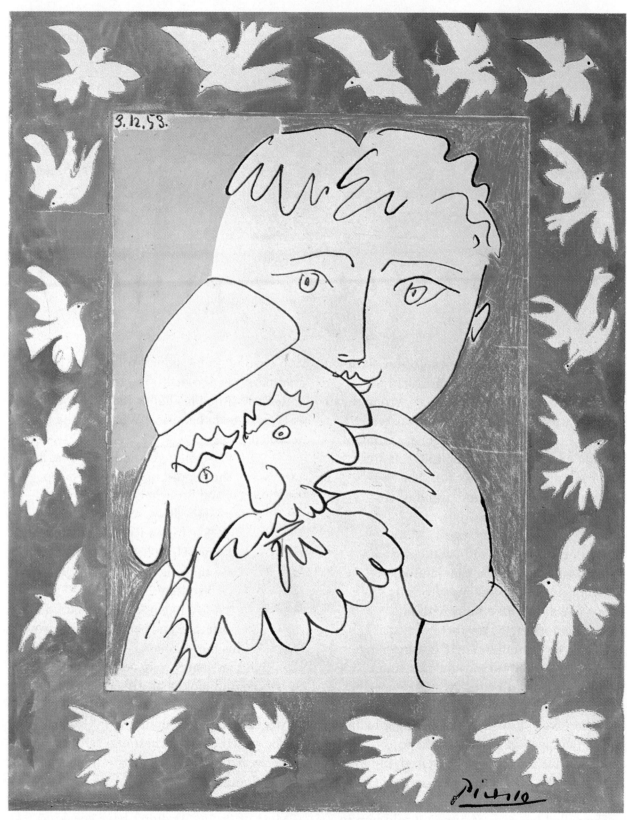

The Old and the New Year (1953), Pablo Picasso. Musée d'Art et d'Histoire, St. Denis, France.
Giraudon/Art Resource, New York. © Copyright 1996 Artists Rights Society, New York/SPADEM, Paris.

parts. They just got cutout crepe-paper snowflakes to pin to their shirts or crepe-paper leaves to wear.

During the blizzard in which Robert delivered his line, Belinda asked, "Is there something wrong with your eyes?" Robert looked at the audience, which at the moment was a classroom of empty chairs, a dented world globe that had been dropped by almost everyone, one limp flag, one wastebasket, and a picture of George Washington, whose eyes followed you around the room when you got up to sharpen your pencil. Robert answered, "Nothing's wrong. I can see."

Mrs. Bunnin, biting on the end of her pencil, said, "Louder, both of you."

Belinda stepped up, nostrils flaring so that the shadows on her nose quiv-ered, and said louder, "Sucka, is there something wrong with your eyeballs?"

"Nothing's wrong. I can see."

"Louder! Make sure the audience can hear you," Mrs. Bunnin directed. She tapped her pencil hard against the desk. She scolded, "Robert, I'm not going to tell you again to quit fooling with the beard."

"It's itchy."

"We can't do anything about that. Actors need props. You're an actor. Now try again."

Robert and Belinda stood center stage as they waited for Mrs. Bunnin to call "Action!" When she did, Belinda approached Robert slowly. "Sucka face, is there anything wrong with your mug?" Belinda asked. Her eyes were squinted in anger. For a moment Robert saw his head grinding into the playground grass.

"Nothing's wrong. I can see."

"NOTHING'S WRONG. I CAN SEE."

Robert giggled behind his red beard. Belinda popped her gum and smirked. She stood with her hands on her hips.

"What? What did you say?" Mrs. Bunnin asked, pulling off her glasses. "Are you chewing gum, Belinda?"

"No, Mrs. Bunnin," Belinda lied. "I just forgot my lines."

Belinda turned to face the snowflake boys clumped together in the back. She rolled out her tongue, on which rested a ball of gray gum, depleted of sweetness under her relentless chomp. She whispered "sucka" and giggled so that her nose quivered dark shadows.

The play, *The Last Stand,* was about the Donner party just before they got hungry and started eating each other. Everyone who scored at least twelve out of fifteen on their spelling tests got to say at least one line. Everyone else had to stand and be trees or snowflakes.

Mrs. Bunnin wanted the play to be a success. She couldn't risk having kids with bad memories on stage. The nonspeaking trees and snowflakes stood humming snow flurries, blistering wind, and hail, which they produced by clacking their teeth.

Robert's mother was proud of him because he was living up to the legend of Robert De Niro,[1] for whom he was named. Over dinner he said, "Nothing's wrong. I can see," when his brother asked him to pass the dishtowel,

---

1. **Robert De Niro** (də nîr′ō): a well-known American movie actor.

WORDS
TO
KNOW

quiver (kwĭv′ər) *v.* to shake with a rapid trembling movement
prop (prŏp) *n.* an object an actor uses in a play
smirk (smûrk) *v.* to smile in an insulting, self-satisfied manner
depleted (dĭ-plē′tĭd) *adj.* emptied; drained **deplete** *v.*
relentless (rĭ-lĕnt′lĭs) *adj.* refusing to stop or give up

their communal napkin. His sister said, "It's your turn to do dishes," and he said, "Nothing's wrong. I can see." His dog, Queenie, begged him for more than water and a dog biscuit. He touched his dog's own hairy beard and said, "Nothing's wrong. I can see."

One warm spring night, Robert lay on his back in the backyard, counting shooting stars. He was up to three when David, a friend who was really his brother's friend, hopped the fence and asked, "What's the matter with you?"

"Nothing's wrong. I can see," Robert answered. He sat up, feeling good because the line came naturally, without much thought. He leaned back on his elbow and asked David what he wanted to be when he grew up.

"I don't know yet," David said, plucking at the grass. "Maybe a fighter pilot. What do you want to be?"

"I want to guard the president. I could wrestle the assassins and be on television. But I'd pin those dudes, and people would say, 'That's him, our hero.'" David plucked at a stalk of grass and thought deeply.

Robert thought of telling David that he really wanted to be someone with a supergreat memory, who could recall facts that most people thought were unimportant. He didn't know if there was such a job, but he thought it would be great to sit at home by the telephone waiting for scientists to call him and ask hard questions.

The three weeks passed quickly. The day before the play, Robert felt happy as he walked home from school with no homework. As he turned onto his street, he found a dollar floating over the currents of wind.

"A buck," he screamed to himself. He snapped it up and looked for others. But he didn't find any more. It was his lucky day,

"NOTHING'S

WRONG.

I CAN SEE."

though. At recess he had hit a home run on a fluke bunt—a fluke because the catcher had kicked the ball, another player had thrown it into center field, and the pitcher wasn't looking when Robert slowed down at third, then burst home with dust flying behind him.

That night, it was his sister's turn to do the dishes. They had eaten enchiladas with the works, so she slaved with suds up to her elbows. Robert bathed in bubble bath, the suds peaked high like the Donner Pass. He thought about how full he was and how those poor people had had nothing to eat but snow. I can live on nothing, he thought and whistled like wind through a mountain pass, raking flat the suds with his palm.

The next day, after lunch, he was ready for the play, red beard in hand and his one line trembling on his lips. Classes herded into the auditorium. As the actors dressed and argued about stepping on each other's feet, Robert stood near a cardboard barrel full of toys, whispering over and over to himself, "Nothing's wrong. I can see." He was hot, itchy, and confused when he tied on the beard. He sneezed when a strand of the beard entered his nostril. He said louder, "Nothing's wrong. I can see," but the words seemed to get caught in the beard. "Nothing, no, no. I can see great," he said louder, then under his breath because the words seemed wrong. "Nothing's wrong, can't you see? Nothing's wrong. I can see you." Worried, he approached Belinda and asked if she remembered his line. Balling her hand into a fist, Belinda warned, "Sucka, I'm gonna bury your ugly face in the ground if you mess up."

"I won't," Robert said as he walked away. He bit a nail and looked into the barrel of toys. A clown's mask stared back at him. He prayed that his line would come back to him. He would hate to disappoint his teacher and didn't like the thought of his face being rubbed into spiky grass.

The curtain parted slightly, and the principal came out smiling onto the stage. She said some words about pioneer history and then, stern faced, warned the audience not to scrape the chairs on the just-waxed floor. The principal then introduced Mrs. Bunnin, who told the audience about how they had rehearsed for weeks.

Meanwhile, the class stood quietly in place with lunchtime spaghetti on their breath. They were ready. Belinda had swallowed her gum because she knew this was for real. The

Closing Scene (1963), David Hockney. Oil on canvas, 48″ × 48″, © David Hockney.

snowflakes clumped together and began howling.

Robert retied his beard. Belinda, smoothing her skirt, looked at him and said, "If you know what's good for you, you'd better do it right." Robert grew nervous when the curtain parted and his classmates who were assigned to do snow, wind, and hail broke into song.

Alfonso stepped forward with his narrative about a blot on American history that would live with us forever. He looked at the audience, lost for a minute. He continued by saying that if the Donner party could come back, hungry from not eating for over a hundred years, they would be sorry for what they had done.

The play began with some boys in snowshoes shuffling around the stage, muttering that the blizzard would cut them off from civilization. They looked up, held out their hands, and said in unison, "Snow." One stepped center stage and said, "I wish I had never left the prairie." Another one said, "California is just over there." He pointed, and some of the first graders looked in the direction of the piano.

"What are we going to do?" one kid asked, brushing pretend snow off his vest.

"I'm getting pretty hungry," another said, rubbing her stomach.

The audience seemed to be following the play. A ribbon of sweat ran down Robert's face. When his scene came up, he staggered to center stage and dropped to the floor, just as Mrs. Bunnin had said, just as he had seen Robert De Niro do in that movie about a boxer. Belinda, bending over with an "Oh, my," yanked him up so hard that something clicked in his elbow. She boomed, "Is there anything wrong with your eyes?"

Robert rubbed his elbow, then his eyes, and said, "I can see nothing wrong. Wrong is nothing, I can see."

"NOTHING'S

WRONG.

I CAN SEE."

"How are we going to get through?" she boomed, wringing her hands together at the audience, some of whom had their mouths taped shut because they were known talkers. "My husband needs a doctor." The drama advanced through snow, wind, and hail that sounded like chattering teeth.

Belinda turned to Robert and muttered, "You mess-up. You're gonna hate life."

But Robert thought he'd done okay. At least, he reasoned to himself, I got the words right. Just not in the right order.

With his part of the play done, he joined the snowflakes and trees, chattering his teeth the loudest. He howled wind like a baying hound and snapped his fingers furiously in a snow flurry. He trembled from the cold.

The play ended with Alfonso saying that if they came back to life, the Donner party would be sorry for eating each other. "It's just not right," he argued. "You gotta suck it up in bad times."

Robert figured that Alfonso was right. He remembered how one day his sister had locked him in the closet and he didn't eat or drink for five hours. When he got out, he hit his sister, but not so hard as to leave a bruise. He then ate three sandwiches and felt a whole lot better.

The cast then paraded up the aisle into the audience. Belinda pinched Robert hard, but only once because she was thinking that it could have been worse. As he passed a smiling and relieved Mrs. Bunnin, she patted Robert's shoulder and said, "Almost perfect."

Robert was happy. He'd made it through without passing out from fear. Now the first and second graders were looking at him and clapping. He was sure everyone wondered who the actor was behind that smooth voice and red, red beard. ❖

RESPONDING
OPTIONS

FROM *PERSONAL RESPONSE* TO *CRITICAL ANALYSIS*

REFLECT
1. In your notebook or on a sheet of paper, describe your impressions of the characters in this story.

RETHINK
2. What is your opinion about the way Robert delivers his lines?

3. Near the end of *The Last Stand,* Alfonso, the narrator, says, "You gotta suck it up in bad times." How well do you think Robert lives up to that statement?

   Consider
   - how he behaves at home
   - what happens to him the day before the performance
   - how he behaves backstage just before the play begins

4. In your opinion, does Belinda Lopez take her part in the play as seriously as Robert does? Use evidence from the story to support your answer.

5. What effects might Robert's acting experience have on the way he faces risks or challenges in the future? Explain.

RELATE
6. Stage fright strikes many people who run the risk of speaking or performing in public. With a partner or a small group of classmates, discuss the ideas about public speaking that you wrote for the Writing Connection on page 30 and some useful ways of dealing with this fear.

ANOTHER PATHWAY

Draw a comic strip to illustrate the events in "The School Play." You can use actual lines from the story in the characters' speech balloons. Draw as many frames as necessary to show the major events in the story. Be sure that you present them in the order in which they occur.

QUICKWRITES

1. What if tryouts were announced for an all-school play in Robert's school? Do you think Robert would try out for a part? Draft an **essay** explaining your answer.

2. Pretend you are a critic for the school newspaper, seeing the performance of *The Last Stand.* What are your reactions to the acting, the costumes, and the set? Use your imagination and information from the story to write a **review** of the performance.

📁 *PORTFOLIO Save your writing. You may want to use it later as a springboard to a piece for your portfolio.*

LITERARY CONCEPTS

The people, animals, or imaginary creatures that take part in the action of a story are called **characters.** Usually a story has one main character, who is the focus of the action, and a number of minor characters. Identify the main character of "The School Play" and explain how he or she is the focus of the action. Then list a few of the minor characters and explain their importance to the story. Compare your list with a classmate's list.

ACROSS THE CURRICULUM

History As a class, research the Donner party. Some students might investigate the preparations pioneers made before starting their journey. Others might focus on the writings of such pioneers or the attempts to rescue the Donner party. Use the information you gather to set up a display for your classroom.

ALTERNATIVE ACTIVITIES

Cooperative Learning In a **Readers Theater** production, performers present a work of literature by reading it aloud, almost as if it were the script of a play. Form teams to plan a Readers Theater production of "The School Play," with each team working on a specific part of the story. Teams should decide how to make the performance work as theater. For example, is a narrator needed? Should parts be deleted or rearranged? Present your finished production to another class.

WORDS TO KNOW

EXERCISE A Decide whether the boldfaced Word to Know is used correctly in each sentence below. On your paper, write *Correct* or *Incorrect*. Explain why the incorrectly used words are wrong.

1. We could hear the confident actor's voice **quiver** as he spoke.

2. Seeing her archenemy forget her lines during the performance caused one student to **smirk.**

3. Pioneers used **props** to hold up their wagons.

4. If the supply of artificial snowflakes is **depleted,** the snowflakes are plentiful.

5. A **relentless** round of applause ends quickly.

EXERCISE B "Nothing's wrong. I can see," are the lines Robert speaks again and again in "The School Play." Now *you're* on. Taking turns with a partner, recite Robert's lines in the following ways:

1. Speak the lines with a **quiver** in your voice.

2. **Smirk** as you speak the lines.

GARY SOTO

Recalling his school days, Gary Soto says, "I was no good at school. I could not sing, do art, or figure out math problems. I was deathly scared of the stage, yet jealous when my friends got up on the stage and sang with gusto." He later graduated *magna cum laude*—with high honors—from California State University. Soto is now a teacher of English and Chicano studies at the University of California, Berkeley.

A native of Fresno, California, Soto writes about the experiences of Mexican Americans. He first became known as a poet, having become drawn to

1952–

poetry during his college years. His first book, *The Elements of San Joaquin,* consisted of poems dealing with memories of his childhood. This work won the U.S. Award of the International Poetry Forum. Other poetry collections followed, including *The Tale of Sunlight, Where Sparrows Work Hard,* and *Black Hair.*

Among young readers, Soto is best known for his short story collections, which have been praised for their fresh, childlike quality.

OTHER WORKS *Local News, Neighborhood Odes, Baseball in April and Other Stories, A Summer Life*

LASERLINKS
• *AUTHOR BACKGROUND*

FICTION

Ghost of the Lagoon
Armstrong Sperry

PERSONAL CONNECTION

Think of someone you know or have read about who has been courageous, who has taken risks. Describe what he or she did and why. Compare this person's experience with the experience of Mako, the main character in this story.

GEOGRAPHICAL CONNECTION

This story of danger and courage is set on Bora Bora, a small volcanic island in the southern Pacific Ocean. Ancient volcanoes on the island form many high peaks, making the land rough and mountainous. Bora Bora is surrounded by coral reefs, underwater ridges of stone produced by colonies of small animals. Bora Bora also has a large lagoon on its western side. A lagoon is a shallow body of water separated from the sea by sandbars or reefs.

The Polynesians who live on the island grow coconuts, sugar cane, rice, and tropical fruits, such as oranges and bananas. The islanders also collect mother-of-pearl, the shiny inner layer of some mollusk shells, and use this to make decorative objects. The islanders often use canoes to travel from one part of the island to another, because it is faster to travel by canoe than it is to walk.

READING CONNECTION

Visualizing When you visualize something, you use your imagination to form a picture of it in your mind. To appreciate the elements of danger and suspense in "Ghost of the Lagoon," try to visualize the setting and the action as the author describes them. Imagine seeing the green water of the lagoon and the darkness of the night on Bora Bora.

The South Pacific

SOCIETY ISLANDS

Bora Bora

Society Islands

AUSTRALIA

South Pacific Ocean

NEW ZEALAND

Miles
0 | 500 | 1000

Ghost

of the

Lagoon

by Armstrong Sperry

The island of Bora Bora,
where Mako lived, is far away
in the South Pacific. It is not a
large island—you can paddle
around it in a single day—but
the main body of it rises
straight out of the sea, very
high into the air, like a castle.
Waterfalls trail down the faces
of the cliffs. As you look
upward, you see wild goats
leaping from crag to crag.

Mako had been born on the very edge of the sea, and most of his waking hours were spent in the waters of the lagoon, which was nearly enclosed by the two outstretched arms of the island. He was very clever with his hands; he had made a harpoon that was as straight as an arrow and tipped with five pointed iron spears. He had made a canoe, hollowing it out of a tree. It wasn't a very big canoe—only a little longer than his own height. It had an outrigger, a sort of balancing pole, fastened to one side to keep the boat from tipping over. The canoe was just large enough to hold Mako and his little dog, Afa. They were great companions, these two.

One evening Mako lay stretched at full length on the pandanus mats, listening to Grandfather's voice. Overhead, stars shone in the dark sky. From far off came the thunder of the surf on the reef.

The old man was speaking of Tupa, the ghost of the lagoon. Ever since the boy could remember, he had heard tales of this terrible monster. Frightened fishermen, returning from the reef at midnight, spoke of the ghost. Over the evening fires, old men told endless tales about the monster.

Tupa seemed to think the lagoon of Bora Bora belonged to him. The natives left presents of food for him out on the reef: a dead goat, a chicken, or a pig. The presents

WORDS TO KNOW

lagoon (lə-gōōn′) *n.* a shallow body of water separated from a sea by sandbars or coral reefs
harpoon (här-pōōn′) *n.* a spearlike weapon used to hunt large fish
reef (rēf) *n.* a ridge of rocks, sand, or coral near the surface of water

Tahitian Woman and Boy (1889), Paul Gauguin. Oil on canvas, 37¼" × 24¼", Norton Simon Art Foundation, Pasadena, California. Gift of Mr. Norton Simon, 1976.

always disappeared mysteriously, but everyone felt sure that it was Tupa who carried them away. Still, in spite of all this food, the nets of the fishermen were torn during the night, the fish stolen. What an appetite Tupa seemed to have!

Not many people had ever seen the ghost of the lagoon. Grandfather was one of the few who had.

"What does he really look like, Grandfather?" the boy asked, for the hundredth time.

The old man shook his head solemnly. The light from the cook fire glistened on his white hair. "Tupa lives in the great caves of the reef. He is longer than this house. There is a sail on his back, not large but terrible to see, for it burns with a white fire. Once, when I was fishing beyond the reef at night, I saw him come up right under another canoe—"

"What happened then?" Mako asked. He half rose on one elbow. This was a story he had not heard before.

The old man's voice dropped to a whisper. "Tupa dragged the canoe right under the water—and the water boiled with white flame. The three fishermen in it were never seen again. Fine swimmers they were, too."

Grandfather shook his head. "It is bad fortune even to speak of Tupa. There is evil in his very name."

"But King Opu Nui has offered a reward for his capture," the boy pointed out.

"Thirty acres of fine coconut land, and a sailing canoe as well," said the old man. "But who ever heard of laying hands on a ghost?"

Mako's eyes glistened. "Thirty acres of land and a sailing canoe. How I should love to win that reward!"

Grandfather nodded, but Mako's mother scolded her son for such foolish talk. "Be quiet now, son, and go to sleep. Grandfather has told you that it is bad fortune to speak of Tupa. Alas, how well we have learned that lesson! Your father—" She stopped herself.

"What of my father?" the boy asked quickly. And now he sat up straight on the mats.

"Tell him, Grandfather," his mother whispered.

The old man cleared his throat and poked at the fire. A little shower of sparks whirled up into the darkness.

"Your father," he explained gently, "was one of the three fishermen in the canoe that Tupa destroyed." His words fell upon the air like stones dropped into a deep well.

Mako shivered. He brushed back the hair from his damp forehead. Then he squared his shoulders and cried fiercely, "I shall slay Tupa and win the king's reward!" He rose to his knees, his slim body tense, his eyes flashing in the firelight.

"Hush!" his mother said. "Go to sleep now. Enough of such foolish talk. Would you bring trouble upon us all?"

Mako lay down again upon the mats. He rolled over on his side and closed his eyes, but sleep was long in coming.

The palm trees whispered above the dark lagoon, and far out on the reef the sea thundered.

The boy was slow to wake up the next morning. The ghost of Tupa had played through his dreams, making him restless. And so it was almost noon before Mako sat up on the mats and stretched himself. He called Afa, and the boy and his dog ran down to the lagoon for their morning swim.

When they returned to the house, wide-awake and hungry, Mako's mother had food ready and waiting.

"These are the last of our bananas," she told him. "I wish you would paddle out to the reef this afternoon and bring back a new bunch."

The boy agreed eagerly. Nothing pleased him more than such an errand, which would take him to a little island on the outer reef, half a mile from shore. It was one of Mako's favorite playgrounds, and there bananas and oranges grew in great plenty.

"Come, Afa," he called, gulping the last mouthful. "We're going on an expedition." He picked up his long-bladed knife and seized his spear. A minute later, he dashed across the white sand, where his canoe was drawn up beyond the water's reach.

Afa barked at his heels. He was all white except for a black spot over each eye. Wherever Mako went, there went Afa also. Now the little dog leaped into the bow of the canoe, his tail wagging with delight. The boy shoved the canoe into the water and climbed aboard. Then, picking up his paddle, he thrust it into the water. The canoe shot ahead. Its sharp bow cut through the green water of the lagoon like a knife through cheese. And so clear was the water that Mako could see the coral gardens, forty feet below him, growing in the sand. The shadow of the canoe moved over them.

A school of fish swept by like silver arrows. He saw scarlet rock cod with ruby eyes and the head of a conger eel peering out from a cavern in the coral. The boy thought suddenly of Tupa, ghost of the lagoon. On such a bright day it was hard to believe in ghosts of any sort. The fierce sunlight drove away all thought of them. Perhaps ghosts were only old men's stories, anyway!

Mako's eyes came to rest upon his spear—the spear that he had made with his own hands—the spear that was as straight and true as an arrow. He remembered his vow of the night before. Could a ghost be killed with a spear? Some night, when all the village was sleeping, Mako swore to himself that he would find out! He would paddle out to the reef and challenge Tupa! Perhaps tonight. Why not? He caught his breath at the thought. A shiver ran down his back. His hands were tense on the paddle.

As the canoe drew away from shore, the boy saw the coral reef that, above all others, had always interested him. It was of white coral—a long slim shape that rose slightly above the surface of the water. It looked very much like a shark. There was a ridge on the back that the boy could pretend was a dorsal fin, while up near one end were two dark holes that looked like eyes!

Times without number the boy had practiced spearing this make-believe shark, aiming always for the eyes, the most vulnerable spot. So true and straight had his aim become that the spear would pass right into the eyeholes without even touching the sides of the coral. Mako had named the coral reef Tupa.

This morning, as he paddled past it, he shook his fist and called, "Ho, Mister Tupa! Just wait till I get my bananas. When I come back, I'll make short work of you!"

Afa followed his master's words with a sharp bark. He knew Mako was excited about something.

> **Perhaps ghosts were only old men's stories, anyway!**

WORDS TO KNOW **expedition** (ĕk′spĭ-dĭsh′ən) *n.* a journey with a goal or purpose

The bow of the canoe touched the sand of the little island where the bananas grew. Afa leaped ashore and ran barking into the jungle, now on this trail, now on that. Clouds of sea birds whirled from their nests into the air with angry cries.

Mako climbed into the shallow water, waded ashore, and pulled his canoe up on the beach. Then, picking up his banana knife, he followed Afa. In the jungle the light was so dense and green that the boy felt as if he were moving underwater. Ferns grew higher than his head. The branches of the trees formed a green roof over him. A flock of parakeets fled on swift wings. Somewhere a wild pig crashed through the undergrowth while Afa dashed away in pursuit. Mako paused anxiously. Armed only with his banana knife, he had no desire to meet the wild pig. The pig, it seemed, had no desire to meet him, either.

Then, ahead of him, the boy saw the broad green blades of a banana tree. A bunch of bananas, golden ripe, was growing out of the top.

At the foot of the tree he made a nest of soft leaves for the bunch to fall upon. In this way the fruit wouldn't be crushed. Then with a swift slash of his blade he cut the stem. The bananas fell to the earth with a dull thud. He found two more bunches.

Then he thought, "I might as well get some oranges while I'm here. Those little rusty ones are sweeter than any that grow on Bora Bora."

So he set about making a net out of palm leaves to carry the oranges. As he worked, his swift fingers moving in and out among the strong green leaves, he could hear Afa's excited barks off in the jungle. That was just like Afa, always barking at something: a bird, a fish, a wild pig. He never caught anything, either. Still, no boy ever had a finer companion.

The palm net took longer to make than Mako had realized. By the time it was finished and filled with oranges, the jungle was dark and gloomy. Night comes quickly and without warning in the islands of the tropics.

Mako carried the fruit down to the shore and loaded it into the canoe. Then he whistled to Afa. The dog came bounding out of the bush, wagging his tail.

"Hurry!" Mako scolded. "We won't be home before the dark comes."

The little dog leaped into the bow of the canoe, and Mako came aboard. Night seemed to rise up from the surface of the water and swallow them. On the distant shore of Bora Bora, cook fires were being lighted. The first star twinkled just over the dark mountains. Mako dug his paddle into the water, and the canoe leaped ahead.

The dark water was alive with <u>phosphorus</u>. The bow of the canoe seemed to cut through a pale liquid fire. Each dip of the paddle trailed streamers of light. As the canoe approached the coral reef, the boy called, "Ho, Tupa! It's too late tonight to teach you your lesson. But I'll come back tomorrow." The coral shark glistened in the darkness.

And then, suddenly, Mako's breath caught in his throat. His hands felt weak. Just beyond the fin of the coral Tupa, there was another fin—a huge one. It had never been there before. And—could he believe his eyes? It was moving.

The boy stopped paddling. He dashed his hand across his eyes. Afa began to bark furiously. The great white fin, shaped like a small sail, glowed with phosphorescent light. Then Mako knew. Here was Tupa—the real Tupa—ghost of the lagoon!

WORDS TO KNOW   **phosphorus** (fŏs′fər-əs) *n.* a substance that glows with a yellowish or white light

45

His knees felt weak. He tried to cry out, but his voice died in his throat. The great shark was circling slowly around the canoe. With each circle, it moved closer and closer. Now the boy could see the phosphorescent glow of the great shark's sides. As it moved in closer, he saw the yellow eyes, the gill slits in its throat.

Afa leaped from one side of the canoe to the other. In sudden anger Mako leaned forward to grab the dog and shake him soundly. Afa wriggled out of his grasp as Mako tried to catch him, and the shift in weight tipped the canoe on one side. The outrigger rose from the water. In another second they would be overboard. The boy threw his weight over quickly to balance the canoe, but with a loud splash Afa fell over into the dark water.

Mako stared after him in dismay. The little dog, instead of swimming back to the canoe, had headed for the distant shore. And there was the great white shark—very near.

"Afa! Afa! Come back! Come quickly!" Mako shouted.

The little dog turned back toward the canoe. He was swimming with all his strength. Mako leaned forward. Could Afa make it? Swiftly the boy seized his spear. Bracing himself, he stood upright. There was no weakness in him now. His dog, his companion, was in danger of instant death.

Afa was swimming desperately to reach the canoe. The white shark had paused in his circling to gather speed for the attack. Mako raised his arm, took aim. In that instant the shark charged. Mako's arm flashed forward. All his strength was behind that thrust. The spear drove straight and true, right into the great shark's eye. Mad with pain and rage, Tupa whipped about, lashing the water in fury.

The canoe rocked back and forth. Mako struggled to keep his balance as he drew back the spear by the cord fastened to his wrist.

He bent over to seize Afa and drag him aboard. Then he stood up, not a moment too soon. Once again the shark charged. Once again Mako threw his spear, this time at the other eye. The spear found its mark. Blinded and weak from loss of blood, Tupa rolled to the surface, turned slightly on his side. Was he dead?

Mako knew how clever sharks could be, and he was taking no chances. Scarcely daring to breathe, he paddled toward the still body. He saw the faintest motion of the great tail. The shark was still alive. The boy knew that one flip of that tail could overturn the canoe and send him and Afa into the water, where Tupa could destroy them.

One flip of that tail could overturn the canoe.

Swiftly, yet calmly, Mako stood upright and braced himself firmly. Then, murmuring a silent prayer to the shark god, he threw his spear for the last time. Downward, swift as sound, the spear plunged into a white shoulder.

Peering over the side of the canoe, Mako could see the great fish turn over far below the surface. Then slowly, slowly, the great shark rose to the surface of the lagoon. There he floated, half on one side.

Tupa was dead.

Mako flung back his head and shouted for joy. Hitching a strong line about the shark's tail, the boy began to paddle toward the shore of Bora Bora. The dorsal fin, burning with the white fire of phosphorus, trailed after the canoe.

Men were running down the beaches of Bora Bora, shouting as they leaped into their canoes and put out across the lagoon. Their cries reached the boy's ears across the water.

"It is Tupa—ghost of the lagoon," he heard them shout. "Mako has killed him!"

That night, as the tired boy lay on the pandanus mats listening to the distant thunder of the sea, he heard Grandfather singing a new song. It was the song which would be sung the next day at the feast which King Opu Nui would give in Mako's honor. The boy saw his mother bending over the cook fire. The stars leaned close, winking like friendly eyes. Grandfather's voice reached him now from a great distance, "Thirty acres of land and a sailing canoe. . . ." ❖

Tahitian Landscape (1891), Paul Gauguin. The Minneapolis Institute of Arts.

RESPONDING
OPTIONS

FROM PERSONAL RESPONSE TO CRITICAL ANALYSIS

REFLECT

1. What was your reaction as you read this story? Briefly describe your thoughts in your notebook.

RETHINK

2. How do you think Mako felt when he realized Tupa was swimming toward him?

3. Why do you think Mako is able to defeat Tupa?

4. What if Mako's dog were not in danger? Do you think Mako still would have tried to kill Tupa?

   Consider
   - Mako's reaction when he learns how his father died
   - Mako's desire for thirty acres and a canoe
   - the last sentence of the story

5. In your opinion, is the risk Mako runs necessary? Why or why not?

RELATE

6. Do you think that in the same situation you would act as courageously as Mako does? In what kind of situation would you take such a big risk?

ANOTHER PATHWAY

Paint or draw a picture of Mako's village, the lagoon, and the little island on the outer reef. When you have completed the picture, draw on it the path you imagine Mako traveled during the events of the story. Display your painting in the classroom.

QUICKWRITES

1. Imagine that Mako is now an old man. Write a **narrative** account, from Mako's point of view, relating the story of his battle with Tupa.

2. Reread the last four paragraphs of the story. Write the **tribute** that King Opu Nui might give Mako at the feast. Which of Mako's accomplishments and traits will he mention in his tribute?

3. Create your own **tall tale** about Tupa the shark. Look through the story to find details about Tupa's appearance and behavior. Tell your tale to a partner.

📁 *PORTFOLIO Save your writing. You may want to use it later as a springboard to a piece for your portfolio.*

LITERARY CONCEPTS

The **plot** of a story is the writer's plan for what happens, when it happens, and to whom it happens. In a story plot, one event causes another, which causes another, and so on until the end of the story. Generally, a plot is built around a **conflict**—a problem or struggle involving two or more opposing forces. Describe the conflict in "Ghost of the Lagoon."

Character   Source of Conflict

ALTERNATIVE ACTIVITIES

1. Create a **travel brochure** advertising Bora Bora. Use details from the story as well as information from a library or a travel bureau to describe the island's tourist attractions and history. Include pictures or your own drawings, and use persuasive writing to make your readers want to visit the island.

2. Create a **dance** that celebrates Mako's courage in facing and defeating Tupa.

3. *Cooperative Learning* With two partners, assign the roles of Mako, his father, and his grandfather. Based on details from the story as well as inferences you can make, role-play a **scene** in which the three discuss life on Bora Bora, the legend of Tupa, and the way that Tupa has affected each of their lives. What might Mako like to say to his father, given the chance? Present your scene to the class.

CRITIC'S CORNER

Theresa Sullivan, a member of the student board that reviewed the stories in this book, says, "I liked how this story was scary and not scary at the same time." Do you agree with her comment? Explain.

ACROSS THE CURRICULUM

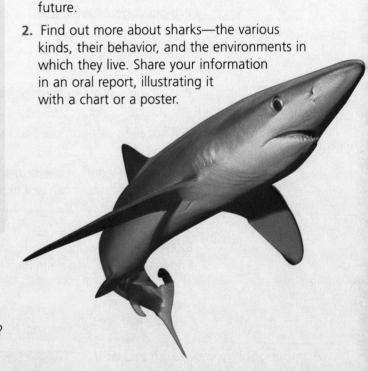

Science

1. Investigate coral reefs. How are they formed? What are they composed of? Where are they found? Save the information you find in a notebook or computer document. Keep your reference file at hand to expand it with other entries in the future.

2. Find out more about sharks—the various kinds, their behavior, and the environments in which they live. Share your information in an oral report, illustrating it with a chart or a poster.

ART CONNECTION

A student of the now-beloved Impressionist painters, Paul Gauguin was a French artist who lived and worked in the last half of the nineteenth century. Shortly after resigning as a Paris stockbroker to devote himself to painting, Gauguin received money from the French government to visit Tahiti and paint Tahitian customs. However, Gauguin fell in love with Tahiti and returned to the tropics, where he spent the last several years of his life. In *Tahitian Woman and Boy* on page 42, Gauguin's brilliant colors and strong lines reveal his view of the Tahitian people as simple and unspoiled by civilization. How well do you think the images in this painting fit the characters of Mako and his mother?

Detail of *Tahitian Woman and Boy* (1889), Paul Gauguin. Oil on canvas, 37 ¼″ × 24 ¼″, Norton Simon Art Foundation, Pasadena, California. Gift of Mr. Norton Simon, 1976.

WORDS TO KNOW

EXERCISE A Review the
Words to Know in the boxes
at the bottom of the selection pages. Copy the blanks below on a
separate sheet of paper, and fill in the correct vocabulary words.

1. a ridge of rocks or coral near the surface of water

   ☐ __ __ __

2. a glowing substance

   __ __ __ __ __ __ __ __ ☐ __

3. a shallow body of water enclosed by a reef

   __ ☐ ☐ __ __ __

4. a journey with a definite objective

   __ __ __ ☐ __ __ __ __ __

5. a spearlike weapon used to hunt large fish

   __ __ __ ☐ __ __

Now use the letters in the boxes to complete the word
below, which means "an ability to face danger and confront
challenges."

   C __ __ __ __ __ __

EXERCISE B Draw a picture to illustrate each of the Words to
Know. Use labels and definitions to explain your drawings.

ARMSTRONG SPERRY

1892–1976

Armstrong Sperry once said that a writer "should tell his story clearly, in a supple prose that leaves his reader—young or old—wondering, 'What happens next?'" Sperry had an advantage for writing stories with exciting plots—he traveled widely in Europe, North America, and the West Indies and made use of what he saw. Inspired by his grandfather's stories of visits to the South Pacific, Sperry spent two years in French Polynesia. There he learned French and Tahitian and gathered information for a number of his books.

Sperry's talent for writing adventure stories set in exotic places led to the success of his book *Call It* *Courage*. This novel, based on a legend of the South Pacific, was awarded the Newbery Medal in 1941. Sperry's *The Rain Forest* received the Boys Clubs of America Junior Book Award in 1949.

Eventually, Sperry settled down, spending most of his time at his home in New Hampshire. He did not, however, lose his love of travel; throughout his life he continued to make voyages to far-off places.

OTHER WORKS *Lost Lagoon: A Pacific Adventure, Storm Canvas, Hull-Down for Action, No Brighter Glory, Black Falcon*

LASERLINKS
• *SCIENCE CONNECTION*
• *ART GALLERY*

FOCUS ON NONFICTION

Whereas some readers enjoy getting lost in the imaginary world of fiction, others prefer to read about real life. **Nonfiction** is writing about real people, places, and events.

There are two broad categories of nonfiction. One category, called **informative nonfiction,** is mainly written to provide factual information. Nonfiction of this type includes science and history books, encyclopedias, pamphlets, and most of the articles in magazines and newspapers. The main purpose of this material is to inform.

The other category of nonfiction is called **literary nonfiction** because it is written to be read and experienced in much the same way as fiction. However, literary nonfiction differs from fiction in that it deals with real people rather than fictional characters and with settings and plots that are not imagined but are actual places and true events.

The types of literary nonfiction you will read in this book are **autobiographies, biographies,** and **essays.**

AUTOBIOGRAPHY An autobiography is the true story of a person's life, told by that person. It is almost always written from the first-person point of view. Among the autobiographical writings you will read in this book are excerpts from *Woodsong* and *The Lost Garden.*

An autobiography is usually book length because it covers a long period of the writer's life. However, there are shorter types of autobiographical writing, such as **journals, diaries,** and **memoirs.**

BIOGRAPHY A biography is the true story of a person's life, told by someone else. The writer, or **biographer,** interviews the subject if possible and also researches the person's life by reading letters, books, diaries, and any other information he or she can find. A short biography of the African-American explorer Matthew Henson is included in this book. As you will see, biographies and autobiographies often contain many of the elements that fiction contains, such as character, setting, and plot.

ESSAY An essay is a short piece of nonfiction that deals with one subject. Essays are often found in newspapers and magazines. The writer might share an opinion, try to entertain or persuade the reader, or simply describe an incident that has special significance. Essays that explain how the author feels about a subject are called **informal essays** or **personal essays.** In this book, the selection "The Mushroom" is an example of an informal essay. Formal essays are rarely about personal subjects. They are usually scholarly and are generally not found in literature textbooks.

STRATEGIES FOR READING NONFICTION

Nonfiction can be read as literature or as a source of information. The nonfiction you will read in this book has been included because of its literary quality. As you read, try to step into and enjoy the true stories and opinions the authors have to share.

Use the following strategies when you read nonfiction:

- **Preview the selection.** Before you read, look at the title, pictures or diagrams, and any subtitles or terms in boldface or italic type. All of these will give you an idea of what the selection is about.

- **Figure out the organization.** If the work is a biography or autobiography, the organization is probably chronological—that is, events are told in the order they happened. Other selections may be organized around ideas the author wants to discuss.

- **Separate facts and opinions.** Facts are statements that can be proved, such as "There are several excerpts from autobiographies in this book." Opinions are statements that cannot be proved. They simply express a person's beliefs, such as "The excerpt from *Woodsong* is the best example of autobiography in this book." Writers sometimes present opinions as if they were facts. Be sure you can tell the difference.

- **Question the material.** As you read, ask yourself questions like these: "Why did things happen the way they did?" "How did people feel?" "What is the writer's opinion?" Try to decide whether you share the writer's opinion or have different ideas on the subject.

- **Stop now and then.** During your reading, pause in order to try to predict what will come next. Sometimes you will be surprised by what happens or by what an author has to say about an issue.

- **Build on your understanding.** Add new information to what you have already learned, and see if your ideas and opinions change.

- **Evaluate what you read.** Evaluation should be an ongoing process, not just something that you do after you finish reading. Remember, too, that evaluation involves more than deciding that a selection is good or bad. Form opinions about the people, events, and ideas that are presented. Decide whether you like the way the piece was written.

Finally, it is important to recognize that your understanding of a selection does not end when you stop reading. As you think more about what you have read and discuss it with others, you will find that your understanding continues to grow.

NONFICTION

Matthew Henson at the Top of the World
Jim Haskins

PERSONAL CONNECTION

What images come to mind when you think of the word *explorer?* What character traits do you think a person needs to be an explorer? On the chalkboard or on a sheet of paper, copy and fill in a chart like the one shown, working either on your own or with your classmates.

Explorer		
How would you define the word?	**What adjectives describe one?**	**Who are some examples?**

GEOGRAPHICAL CONNECTION

The selection you are about to read describes the adventurous life of the African-American explorer Matthew Henson. In 1908, Henson joined Commander Robert E. Peary of the U.S. Navy on one of the greatest quests of the 20th century. Their goal was to be the first men to reach the North Pole.

The geographic North Pole lies in the Arctic Ocean at the northern end of the axis on which the earth revolves. There is no land at the North Pole, but for most of the year the ocean is frozen solid, providing a surface for travel by dogsled.

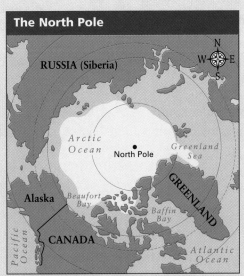

The North Pole

RUSSIA (Siberia)

N W E S

Arctic Ocean
• North Pole

Greenland Sea

GREENLAND

Alaska

Beaufort Bay

Baffin Bay

Pacific Ocean

CANADA

Atlantic Ocean

READING CONNECTION

Main Idea and Supporting Details
In nonfiction, it is possible to figure out the author's most important points by identifying the topic or main idea of each paragraph. In searching for the main idea, you should read the entire paragraph, because the main idea may be stated at the beginning, the middle or the end. The other sentences in the paragraph give supporting details, additional information about the main idea. As you read this selection about two Arctic explorers, jot down a list in your reading log of the character traits these explorers displayed. Note supporting details for each of these traits.

LASERLINKS
• *HISTORICAL CONNECTION*
• *VISUAL VOCABULARY*

53

MATTHEW HENSON AT THE
TOP OF THE WORLD

by Jim Haskins

While the explorers of the American West faced many dangers in their travels, at least game and water were usually plentiful; and if winter with its cold and snow overtook them, they could, in time, expect warmth and spring. For Matthew Henson, in his explorations with Robert Peary at the North Pole, this was hardly the case. In many ways, to forge ahead into the icy Arctic took far greater <u>stamina</u> and courage than did the earlier explorers' travels, and Henson possessed such hardiness. As Donald MacMillan, a member of the expedition, was later to write: "Peary knew Matt Henson's real worth. . . . Highly respected by the Eskimos,[1] he was easily the most popular man on board ship. . . . Henson . . . was of more real value to our Commander than [expedition members] Bartlett, Marvin, Borup, Goodsell and myself all put together. Matthew Henson went to the Pole with Peary because he was a better man than any one of us."

Matthew Henson was born on August 8, 1866, in Charles County, Maryland, some forty-four miles south of Washington, D.C. His parents were poor, free tenant

---

1. **Eskimos:** a term used throughout this account to refer to the native peoples of the Arctic; the Eskimos of Greenland, such as those who traveled on Peary's expeditions, call themselves Inuit, as do the Eskimos of Canada.

WORDS TO KNOW

stamina (stăm'ə-nə) *n.* the strength to withstand hardship

Matthew Henson in animal furs that protected him from the extreme Arctic cold. The Bettmann Archive.

farmers[2] who barely eked a living from the sandy soil. The Civil War had ended the year before Matthew was born, bringing with it a great deal of bitterness on the part of former slave-owners. One manifestation of this hostility was the terrorist activity on the part of the Ku Klux Klan[3] in Maryland. Many free and newly freed blacks had suffered at the hands of this band of night riders.[4] Matthew's father, Lemuel Henson, felt it was only a matter of time before the Klan turned its vengeful eyes on his family. That, and the fact that by farming he was barely able to support them, caused him to decide to move north to Washington, D.C.

At first things went well for the Henson family, but then Matthew's mother died and his father found himself unable to care for Matthew. The seven-year-old boy was sent to live with his uncle, a kindly man who welcomed him and enrolled him in the N Street School. Six years later, however, another blow fell; his uncle himself fell upon hard times and could no longer support Matthew. The boy couldn't return to his father, because Lemuel had recently died. Alone, homeless, and penniless, Matthew was forced to fend for himself.

Matthew Henson was a bright boy and a hard worker, although he had only a sixth-grade education. Calling upon his own resourcefulness, he found a job as a dish-washer in a small restaurant owned by a woman named Janey Moore. When Janey discovered that Matthew had no place to stay, she fixed a cot for him in the kitchen; Matthew had found a home again.

Matthew Henson didn't want to spend his life waiting on people and washing dishes, however, no matter how kind Janey was. He had seen enough of the world through his schoolbooks to want more, to want adventure. This desire was reinforced by the men who frequented the restaurant—sailors from many ports, who spun tales of life on the ocean and of strange and wonderful places. As Henson listened, wide-eyed, to their stories, he decided, as had so many boys before him, that the life of a sailor with its adventures and dangers was for him. Having made up his mind, the fourteen-year-old packed up what little he owned, bade good-bye to Janey, and was off to Baltimore to find a ship.

QUESTION

What is the main idea of the paragraph you have just read?

Although Matthew Henson's early life seems harsh, in many ways he was very lucky. When he arrived in Baltimore, he signed on as a cabin boy on the *Katie Hines,* the master of which was a Captain Childs. For many sailors at that time, life at sea was brutal and filled with hard work, deprivation, and a "taste of the cat": whipping. The captains of many vessels were petty despots, ruling with an iron hand and having little regard for a seaman's health or safety. Matthew was fortunate to find just the opposite in Childs.

Captain Childs took the boy under his wing. Although Matthew of course had to do the work he was assigned, Captain Childs took a fatherly interest in him. Having an excellent private library on the ship, the captain saw to

---

2. **tenant farmers:** people who farm land rented from others.

3. **Ku Klux Klan** (kōō′ klŭks klăn′): a secret society, organized in the South after the Civil War, that used terrorism to reassert the power of whites.

4. **night riders:** mounted and usually masked white men who committed acts of terror against African Americans during the period following the Civil War.

WORDS
TO
KNOW

deprivation (dĕp′rə-vā′shən) *n.* a lack of what is needed for survival or comfort

Matthew's education, insisting that he read widely in geography, history, mathematics, and literature while they were at sea.

The years on the *Katie Hines* were good ones for Matthew Henson. During that time he saw China, Japan, the Philippines, France, Africa, and southern Russia; he sailed through the Arctic to Murmansk. But in 1885 it all ended; Captain Childs fell ill and died at sea. Unable to face staying on the *Katie Hines* under a new skipper, Matthew left the ship at Baltimore and found a place on a fishing schooner bound for Newfoundland.

Now, for the first time, Henson encountered the kind of unthinking cruelty and tyranny so often found on ships at that time. The ship was filthy, the crew surly and resentful of their black shipmate, and the captain a dictator. As soon as he was able, Matthew left the ship in Canada and made his way back to the United States, finally arriving in Washington, D.C., only to find that things there had changed during the years he had been at sea.

Opportunities for blacks had been limited when Henson had left Washington in 1871, but by the time he returned they were almost non-existent. Post–Civil War reconstruction had failed, bringing with its failure a great deal of bitter resentment toward blacks. Jobs were scarce, and the few available were menial ones. Matthew finally found a job as a stock clerk in a clothing and hat store, B. H. Steinmetz and Sons, bitterly wondering if this was how he was to spend the rest of his life. But his luck was still holding.

Steinmetz recognized that Matthew Henson was bright and hard working. One day Lieu-

A sextant (center) and other navigational instruments of Robert Peary. Victor R. Boswell, Jr., © National Geographic Society.

tenant Robert E. Peary, a young navy officer, walked into the store, looking for tropical hats. After being shown a number of hats, Peary unexpectedly offered Henson a job as his personal servant. Steinmetz had recommended him, Peary said, but the job wouldn't be easy. He was bound for Nicaragua to head an engineering survey team. Would Matthew be willing to put up with the discomforts and hazards of such a trip? Thinking of the adventure and opportunities offered, Henson eagerly said yes, little realizing that a partnership had just been formed that would span years and be filled with exploration, danger, and fame.

Robert E. Peary was born in Cresson, Pennsylvania, in 1856 but was raised in Maine, where his mother had returned after his father's death in 1859. After graduating from Bowdoin College, Peary worked as a surveyor for four years and in 1881 joined the navy's corps of civil engineers. One result of his travels for the navy and of his reading was an <u>ardent</u> desire for adventure. "I shall not be satisfied," Peary wrote to his mother, "until my name is known from one end of the earth to the other." This was a goal Matthew Henson could understand. As he later said, "I recognized in [Peary] the qualities that made me willing to engage myself in his service." In November 1887, Henson and Peary set sail for Nicaragua, along with forty-five other engineers and a hundred black Jamaicans.

Peary's job was to study the feasibility[5] of digging a canal across Nicaragua (that canal that would later be dug across the Isthmus of Panama).[6] The survey took until June of 1888, when the surveying party headed back to the United States. Henson knew he had done a good job for Peary, but even as they started north, Peary said nothing to him about continuing on as his servant. It was a great surprise, then, when one day Peary approached Henson with a <u>proposition</u>. He wanted to try to raise money for an expedition to the Arctic, and he wanted Henson to accompany him. Henson quickly accepted, saying he would go whether Peary could pay him or not.

Arctic exploration would have been impossible without the use of snowshoes (above) and a compass (facing page).

"It was in June, 1891, that I started on my first trip to the Arctic regions, as a member of what was known as the 'North Greenland Expedition,'" Matthew Henson later wrote. So began the first of five expeditions on which Henson would accompany Peary.

CLARIFY

Does the main idea appear at the beginning, the middle, or the end of this paragraph?

During this first trip to Greenland, on a ship named *Kite,* Peary discovered how valuable Henson was to any expedition. He reported that Henson was able to establish "a friendly relationship with the Eskimos, who believed him to be somehow related to them because of his brown skin. . . ." Peary's expedition was also greatly aided by Henson's expert handling of the Eskimos, dogs, and equipment. Henson also hunted with the Eskimos for meat for the expedition and cooked under the supervision of Josephine Peary, Robert's wife. On the expedition's return to New York, September 24, 1892, Peary wrote, "Henson, my faithful colored boy, a hard worker and <u>apt</u> at anything, . . . showed himself . . . the equal of others in the party."

This first expedition to the Arctic led to several others, but it was with the 1905 expedition that Peary first tried to find that mystical point, the North Pole, the sole goal of the 1908 expedition.

On July 6, 1908, the *Roosevelt* sailed from New York City. Aboard it were the supplies and men for an expedition to reach the North Pole. Accompanying Peary were Captain Robert

---

5. **feasibility** (fē′zə-bĭl′ĭ-tē): possibility of being completed successfully.

6. **Isthmus** (ĭs′məs) **of Panama:** a narrow strip of land connecting the North and South American continents.

WORDS TO KNOW	**ardent** (är′dnt) *adj.* full of enthusiasm or devotion
	proposition (prŏp′ə-zish′ən) *n.* a plan offered for acceptance
	apt (ăpt) *adj.* quick to learn or understand

Bartlett and Ross Marvin, who had been with Peary on earlier expeditions; George Borup, a young graduate from Yale and the youngest member of the group; Donald MacMillan, a teacher; and a doctor, J. W. Goodsell. And, of course, Matthew Henson. In Greenland the group was joined by forty-one Eskimos and 246 dogs, plus the supplies. "The ship," Henson wrote, "is now in a most perfect state of dirtiness." On September 5, the *Roosevelt* arrived at Cape Sheridan, and the group began preparing for their journey, moving supplies north to Cape Columbia by dog sled to establish a base camp. Peary named the camp Crane City in honor of Zenas Crane, who had contributed $10,000 to the expedition.

"It was in June, 1891, that I started on my first trip to the Arctic regions, as a member of what was known as the 'North Greenland Expedition.'"

The plan was to have two men, Bartlett and Borup, go ahead of the rest of the group to cut a trail stretching from the base camp to the North Pole. On February 28, the two men set out, and on March 1, the remainder of the expedition started north, following the trail Bartlett and Borup had cut the day before. At first, trouble seemed to plague them. On the first day, three of the sledges[7] broke, Henson's among them. Fortunately, Henson was able to repair them, despite the fact that it was nearly 50 degrees below zero.

As the days passed, further trouble came the way of the expedition. Several times they encountered leads—open channels of water— and were forced to wait until the ice closed over before proceeding. On March 14, Peary decided to send Donald MacMillan and Dr. Goodsell back to the base camp. MacMillan could hardly walk, because he had frozen a heel when his foot had slipped into one of the leads. Dr. Goodsell was exhausted. As the expedition went on, more men were sent back due to exhaustion and frostbite. George Borup was sent back on March 20, and, on the 26th, so was Ross Marvin.

Although the expedition had encountered problems with subzero temperatures, with open water, and in handling the dogs, they had had no real injuries. On Ross Marvin's return trip to the base camp, however, he met with tragedy. On his journey, Marvin was accompanied by two Eskimos. He told them that he would go ahead to scout the trail. About an hour later, the Eskimos came upon a hole in the ice; floating in it was Marvin's coat. Marvin had gone through thin ice and, unable to save himself, had drowned or frozen. The Peary expedition had suffered its first—and fortunately its last—fatality.

By April 1, Peary had sent back all of the original expedition except for four Eskimos and Matthew Henson. When Bartlett, the last man to be sent back, asked Peary why he didn't also send Henson, Peary replied, "I can't get along without him." The remnant of the original group pushed on.

---

7. **sledges:** sleds pulled by dogs.

We had been travelling eighteen to twenty hours out of every twenty-four. Man, that was killing work! Forced marches all the time. From all our other expeditions we had found out that we couldn't carry food for more than fifty days, fifty-five at a pinch. . . .

We used to travel by night and sleep in the warmest part of the day. I was ahead most of the time with two of the Eskimos.

So Matthew Henson described the grueling journey. Finally, on the morning of April 6, Peary called a halt. Henson wrote: "I was driving ahead and was swinging around to the right. . . . The Commander, who was about 50 feet behind me, called to me and said we would go into camp. . . ." In fact, both Henson and Peary felt they might have reached the Pole already. That day, Peary took readings with a sextant[8] and determined that they were within three miles of the Pole. Later he sledged ten miles north and found he was traveling south; to return to camp, Peary would have to return north and then head south in another direction—something that could only happen at the North Pole. To be absolutely sure, the next day Peary again took readings from solar observations. It was the North Pole, he was sure.

On that day Robert Peary had Matthew Henson plant the American flag at the North Pole. Peary then cut a piece from the flag and placed it and two letters in a glass jar that he left at the Pole. The letters read:

> *90 N. Lat., North Pole*
> *April 6, 1909*

Arrived here today, 27 marches from C. Columbia.

I have with me 5 men, Matthew Henson, colored, Ootah, Egingwah, Seegloo, and Ooqueah, Eskimos; 5 sledges and 38 dogs. My
ship, the S.S. Roosevelt, *is in winter quarters at Cape Sheridan, 90 miles east of Columbia.*

The expedition under my command which has succeeded in reaching the Pole is under the auspices of the Peary Arctic Club of New York City, and has been fitted out and sent north by members and friends of the Club for the purpose of securing this geographical prize, if possible, for the honor and prestige of the United States of America.

The officers of the Club are Thomas H. Hubbard of New York, President; Zenas Crane, of Mass., Vice-president; Herbert L. Bridgman, of New York, Secretary and Treasurer.

I start back for Cape Columbia tomorrow.
> *Robert E. Peary*
> *United States Navy*

> *90 N. Lat., North Pole*
> *April 6, 1909*

I have today hoisted the national ensign of the United States of America at this place, which my observations indicate to be the North Polar axis of the earth, and have formally taken possession of the entire region, and adjacent, for and in the name of the President of the United States of America.

I leave this record and United States flag in possession.
> *Robert E. Peary*
> *United States Navy*

Having accomplished their goal, the small group set out on the return journey. It was, Matthew Henson wrote, "17 days of haste, toil, and misery. . . . We crossed lead after lead, sometimes like a bareback rider in the circus, balancing on cake after cake of ice." Finally they reached the *Roosevelt,* where they

---

8. **sextant:** an instrument used to measure the positions of heavenly bodies.

Robert Peary (second from right) and Henson (far right) on board ship with other members of an expedition, 1909. Culver Pictures.

could rest and eat well at last. The Pole had been conquered!

During the return trip to New York City, Henson became increasingly puzzled by Peary's behavior. "Not once in [three weeks]," Henson wrote, "did he speak a word to me. Then he . . . ordered me to get to work. Not a word about the North Pole or anything connected with it." Even when the *Roosevelt* docked in New York in September of 1909, Peary remained withdrawn and silent, saying little to the press and quickly withdrawing to his home in Maine.

The ostensible[9] reason for his silence was that when the group returned to New York, they learned that Dr. Frederick A. Cook was claiming that *he* had gone to the North Pole— and done so before Peary reached it. Peary told his friends that he wished to wait for his own proofs to be <u>validated</u> by the scientific societies before he spoke. He felt sure that Cook would not be able to present the kinds of evidence that he could present, and so it proved.

On December 15, Peary was declared the first to reach the North Pole; Cook could not present adequate evidence that he had made the discovery. Peary and Bartlett were awarded gold medals by the National Geographic Society; Henson was not. Because Henson was black, his contributions to the expedition were not recognized for many years.

After 1909, Henson worked in a variety of jobs. For a while, he was a parking-garage

---

9. **ostensible** (ŏ-stĕn′sə-bəl): claimed, but not necessarily true.

attendant in Brooklyn, and at the age of forty-six, he became a clerk in the U.S. customshouse in Lower Manhattan. In the meantime, friends tried again and again to have his contributions to the expedition recognized. At last, in 1937, nearly thirty years after the expedition, he was invited to join the Explorers Club in New York, and in 1944, Congress authorized a medal for all of the men on the expedition, including Matthew Henson.

After his death in New York City on March 9, 1955, another lasting tribute was made to Henson's endeavors. In 1961, his home state of Maryland placed a bronze tablet in memory of him in the state house. It reads, in part:

MATTHEW ALEXANDER HENSON
Co-discoverer of the North Pole
with Admiral Robert Edwin Peary
April 6, 1909

Son of Maryland, exemplification of courage, fortitude, and patriotism, whose valiant deeds of noble devotion under the command of Admiral Robert Edwin Peary, in pioneer Arctic exploration and discovery, established everlasting prestige and glory for his state and country

HISTORICAL INSIGHT

Early Explorers

Since prehistoric times people have had an urge to explore the unknown. The Eskimos who assisted Matthew Henson and Robert Peary called themselves Inuit. They were descendants of the people who first migrated to and explored the Americas between 20,000 and 40,000 years ago.

During the most recent ice age affecting North America, which ended about 10,000 years ago, the formation of glaciers helped open up areas for exploration. The levels of the world's oceans dropped because much of the earth's water was frozen. Natural land bridges appeared in places once covered by water. One such bridge connected Asia with the Americas across what is now called the Bering Strait. This bridge allowed the Asian ancestors of the Eskimos to follow the mammals they hunted into new lands and to colonize the northern part of North America.

The Eskimos spread from the northeastern tip of Russia across Alaska and northern Canada to Greenland. Today there are about 120,000 Eskimos in these regions.

RESPONDING
OPTIONS

FROM PERSONAL RESPONSE TO CRITICAL ANALYSIS

REFLECT

1. How did reading about the events of Matthew Henson's life affect you? In your notebook, write about what impressed you the most. Then compare your ideas with those of your classmates.

RETHINK

2. How would you describe the relationship between Peary and Henson?
   Consider
   • any traits the explorers had in common
   • their years of taking risks together
   • the descriptions of the men in each other's writings
   • Peary's behavior after conquering the North Pole

3. If Robert Peary had asked Matthew Henson to accompany him on another expedition after 1909, do you think Henson would have accepted? Why or why not?

4. Look back at the adjectives you wrote for the Personal Connection on page 53. Which words best describe Matthew Henson? Compare your choices with your classmates' choices.

RELATE

5. What personal qualities of Matthew Henson do you think would be useful for people venturing today into the unexplored regions of the world or into outer space? Explain your answer.

ANOTHER PATHWAY
Cooperative Learning
In small groups prepare mock interviews of Peary and Henson after the expedition's arrival in New York City in 1909. Share your interviews with the class.

QUICKWRITES

1. In 1937, Matthew Henson was invited to join the Explorers Club in New York. Write the **acceptance speech** he might have given to that group.

2. Imagine that you are either Henson or Peary and write a **log entry** for one day of the three-week period after their arrival at the North Pole.

3. Throughout history there have been many "unsung," or uncelebrated, heroes. Write a **poem** that celebrates Matthew Henson and other heroes like him.

📁 *PORTFOLIO Save your writing. You may want to use it later as a springboard to a piece for your portfolio.*

LITERARY CONCEPTS

A **biography** is a true account of a person's life, written by another person. The writer looks at all of the facts that are available about the subject and decides what information to include in the biography. What kinds of research do you think Jim Haskins might have done to find out about Matthew Henson's role as co-discoverer of the North Pole?

THE WRITER'S STYLE

Haskins uses excerpts from diaries and letters in his biography of Henson. With a partner, choose a quotation from a diary or a letter in this selection. What effect do the personal words have on you, and why do you think Haskins includes them?

ACROSS THE CURRICULUM

Social Studies *Cooperative Learning* Robert Peary's claim to be the first to reach the North Pole was challenged as recently as 1989. Matthew Henson's role has also been questioned—did he actually plant the U.S. flag at the North Pole? Work with a small group of classmates to plan, research, and present a **status report** on the expedition. How have more-recent explorers attempted to prove or disprove the evidence for Peary's claim?

Review the Words to Know in the boxes at the bottom of the selection pages. On your paper, write the word that is closest in meaning to the italicized word or phrase in each sentence.

1. Matthew experienced the *extremely harsh and unjust treatment* that many blacks endured after the Civil War.

2. For many sailors in the 1800s, life at sea was filled with hard work and *lack of comforts.*

3. The presence of their black shipmate made some crew members *full of angry feelings.*

4. Peary worked as a *person who measures boundaries.*

5. Both Robert Peary and Matthew Henson felt an *enthusiastic* desire for adventure.

6. Peary had a *plan* for an expedition to the Arctic.

7. The Inuit admired Matthew's *endurance* in dealing with the Arctic region's cruel weather.

8. Peary described Matthew as a "hard worker" who was *"quick to learn."*

9. After returning from the North Pole, Peary had to wait for scientific societies to *show the correctness* of his proofs.

10. Once Matthew Henson's adventurous travels ended, only *poor, low-paying* jobs were available.

JIM HASKINS

Important African-American figures in history, politics, entertainment, and sports have been the subjects of Jim Haskins's books. All of his works are nonfiction because Haskins has always preferred true stories to made-up ones. He has said, "It seems to me that the more you know about the real world, the better off you are."

Although Haskins learned to read early in his childhood, the public library in his Alabama hometown did not welcome black children. He stayed home and learned to rely on his family's ency-

1941–

clopedia. Explaining why African-Americans have usually been his subjects, he says, "I want children today, black and white, to be able to find books about black people and black history in case they want to read them." Haskins has written over 100 books, which have received a number of citations and awards, including the Coretta Scott King Award.

OTHER WORKS *The March on Washington, Against All Opposition: Black Explorers in America, Outward Dreams: Black Inventors and Their Inventions*

LASERLINKS
• *ART GALLERY*

NONFICTION

My First Dive with the Dolphins
Don C. Reed

PERSONAL CONNECTION

Think of encounters you have had with animals, perhaps in a zoo, in an aquarium, or even in your own backyard. Do these animals have personalities? Share your experiences with your classmates.

SCIENCE CONNECTION

In the selection you are about to read, the writer Don C. Reed describes his first encounter with dolphins. Marine dolphins are sea mammals closely related to whales and porpoises. Scientists rank dolphins among the most intelligent of animals, along with chimpanzees and dogs. Research has focused on dolphins' use of echolocation, a natural sound wave system with which they identify and locate underwater objects. Scientists are also studying how dolphins communicate among themselves by using series of whistles and clicks called phonations.

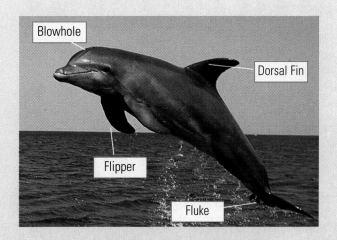

Blowhole
Dorsal Fin
Flipper
Fluke

READING CONNECTION

Setting Purposes In this selection Reed is surprised by the differences in personalities among the dolphins he meets. Before reading, record what you already know about dolphins and what you want to know in a chart like the one shown. As you read, think about the surprising things that happen to Reed and the surprising things that you learn about dolphins.

What I (We) Know	What I (We) Want to Learn	What I (We) Learned
1. Marine dolphins are sea mammals closely related to whales and porpoises.		

MY FIRST
DIVE

with the

Dolphins

by Don C. Reed

stood on a narrow, red-painted stage above half a million gallons of cold salt water.

A wave slashed foam onto the stage and across my bare feet. I had a black rubber wet suit on but neither a hood nor "booties," those heavy neoprene[1] shoes that divers take for granted nowadays. It didn't occur to me to ask the other divers why we had neither foot nor head protection. I wore what the other folks wore. I wasn't about to complain: if the other divers had jumped off the edge in their under-wear, I would have just shrugged and done the same.

That cold, windy March day in 1972 was my first day of work as a professional scuba diver for Marine World, soon to become Marine World/Africa USA, an oceanarium-zoo in northern California. I didn't let on how strange everything felt. I was only six months out of deep-sea-diving school and had almost no idea of what to expect.

The hard rubber mouthpiece still felt foreign clenched between my teeth. It seemed clumsy to breathe through my mouth instead of my nose. Each breath had to be "asked for," pulled in by a conscious lifting of the chest, creating a vacuum to suck in the compressed air.

Not wanting to dangle my legs in the water, I stood awkwardly on one foot at a time as I fumbled into the big, floppy swim fins.

As I pulled the black plastic mask over my face, the strap tugged at my hair. When I opened my eyes, my field of vision was narrowed by the mask. It was like staring through a section of pipe.

I took one giant step forward and fell . . . into another world.

I heard the crash of the surface as it broke apart and thumped shut above me; I felt the massage of pressure and the cold water rushing down my neck and spine. Air bubbles slid ticklingly up my face, heading for the surface, while I headed the opposite way, falling, dragged down by the heavy lead work belt around my waist.

As the bubbles of my entry cleared, my vision returned. My fin tips folded softly underneath me as I landed on the green, algae-covered[2] floor.

Oddly, I didn't spot the dolphins right away. Perhaps their dark/light camouflage patterns broke up their outlines. Then, all at once, there they

---

1. **neoprene** (nē′ə-prēn′): a weather-resistant synthetic rubber.
2. **algae-covered** (ăl′jē-kŭv′ərd): covered with algae, tiny plantlike organisms that grow in water.

were—and so much *bigger* than I had expected. It's only the magnification down here, I told myself, a trick of underwater light. But I knew they weighed between 300 and 400 pounds each, as much as a giant professional wrestler or the biggest lineman on a football team.

I tried to remember the one-minute human-dolphin coexistence lesson that head diver Ted Pintarelli had given me.

"Spock—that's the one with the hole in his fin—he won't bother you. Neither will Delbert: he's got a shark scar on his belly that makes him easy to spot. The smallest one's Ernestine; she's okay. Lucky is king bull, the toughest dolphin in the tank. You'll recognize *him* right away: there's a purple spot on his cheek, and he's big and all scarred up from fights, and . . . well, you'll know him!

"But Arnie, he's the one who'll give you trouble. He thinks he's bad, and he likes to try and scare new guys in the tank. Like he might swim fast at you or something. Just hold still if he does. Don't let him chase you out of the tank, or he'll make a game out of it, and you'll never get any work done. Don't look scared. He'll leave you alone . . . most of the time, anyway," the muscular, red-faced diver had added with a grin.

I had always thought of dolphins as sweet and gentle, like Flipper on the old TV show, who was sort of an oceangoing Lassie, man's best friend in the sea. Now I tried to figure out which one was Arnie. He was supposed to have a lower jaw shaped like a hook, whatever that meant. But it was no use: I couldn't tell the dolphins apart. They all looked like trouble to me.

As the streamlined but massive gray creatures cruised around me, I reminded myself they were not sharks. Their eighty-eight white, needlelike teeth, which I could see so clearly, were meant for snagging swift herring on the run, not for ripping out a twenty-pound mouthful of flesh, as a white shark's teeth were. Dolphins were mammals, not fish, and the reason for the up-and-down motion of their tails was to bring them back up to the air.

"But Arnie, he's the one who'll give you trouble. . . . He likes to try and scare new guys in the tank."

Some said dolphins were smart like people. Certainly dolphins could do things with sonar[3] that we humans couldn't match. In one experiment I read about, dolphins were able to distinguish between two types of identical-looking plastic-coated wire—one with a lead core, the other with a copper core—just by sending their special clicking sounds inside them.

Well, I wasn't getting a whole lot of work done this way. In the distance I could see the three other divers, already lying down on the floor, their scrub brushes busy. As it was for them, cleaning algae off the underwater floors and walls and windows would be 95 percent of my job. The other 5 percent, the head diver had promised, would be magic.

None of the divers had air tanks. Each diver breathed through a thin yellow air hose leading up to the surface, where it was plugged into a brass outlet on an air compressor. I

---

3. **sonar** (sō′när′): detection of objects by reflected sound waves.

WORDS
TO
KNOW

magnification (măg′nə-fĭ-kā′shən) *n.* the causing of objects to appear enlarged
coexistence (kō′ĭg-zĭs′təns) *n.* a state of living together in peace

noticed the strange shape of the bubbles as they left my regulator and wobbled to the surface. They were not round but dome-shaped, flat on the bottom, and they changed as they rose toward the mirrorlike surface twenty feet above.

In my hand was a short iron-handled scrub brush. I held it in the special way Ted had shown me.

"If you hold it the regular way, like a hairbrush, you can't get anything but wrist power behind it," Ted said. "But upside-down, the bristles are next to your palm, and you get your whole body into it. Switch hands every ten or twelve brush strokes, too, so you won't have to stop and rest."

Lying down in a sort of pushup position, I took an experimental scrub stroke at the floor. The brush was neither motorized nor self-operational. My tentative push did not accomplish much. Some scratches appeared in the green algae; that was all. The stuff clung like paint!

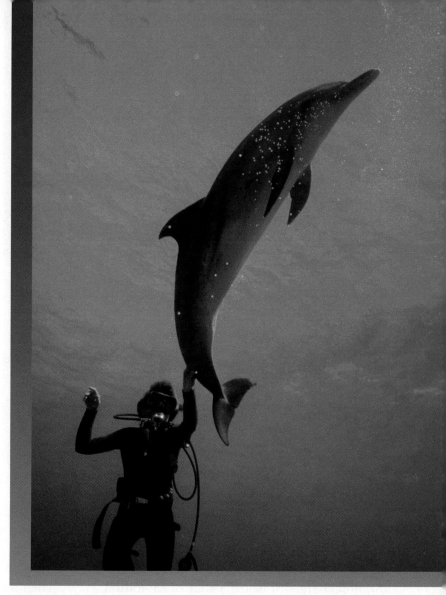

© Al Giddings/The Image Bank

The algae has to be taken off, or it grows thicker and thicker and finally rots, breaking off at the roots, clouding the water, clogging the filtration system, and plugging up the windows. There are chemical ways to kill algae, of course, but these cannot be used because they are harmful to the dolphins' eyes.

So we divers scrubbed. Algae was our job security!

I turned the brush on edge, so that the stroke it made would be one inch wide instead of six, and leaned all my shoulder strength behind the stroke. Now the brush bit. There. I had a one-by-twelve-inch piece of clean white floor. Just eleven more strokes and I'd have one whole square foot finished. And since the tank was 60 by 80 feet, that meant there were only 4,799 more square feet to go.

Suddenly a blur of movement caught my eye. A dolphin was <u>hurtling</u> toward me. Although it was closing the distance between us unbelievably fast, I saw it as if it were in slow motion.

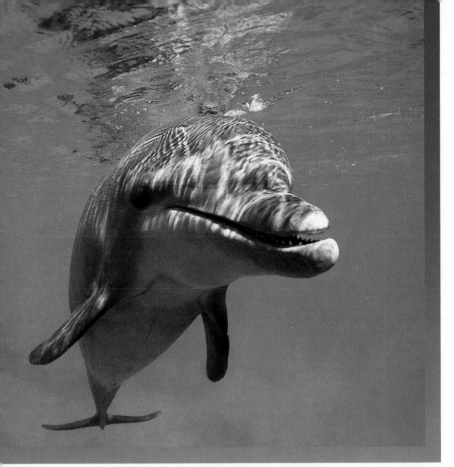

© Norbert Wu/Tony Stone Images

animal turned like a veering jet.

But not to go away. No more than six feet from me, he stopped. I saw his narrow face, saw his jaws move, heard the *klonk* that I knew signaled <u>aggression</u>. His white teeth gleamed, sharp and clean as if they had been brushed. But dolphins do not fight seriously with their teeth.

In a motion so fast my mind had to reconstruct it afterward, the gristly ridge on the underside of the dolphin's tail flukes suddenly appeared right before my face. It was as if a baseball bat had been swung at my head—and stopped an inch before my face caved in.

Again I did nothing, but not through courage. My reflexes are slow. I had time to tell myself, Hold still; don't do anything to make him think you want to fight. I also had time to feel a wave of anger at this huge animal for picking on me for no reason at all.

Then another dolphin, heavy-bodied with a purple spot on the left side of his beak, eased into my vision, and Arnie casually swam off with him.

When my heart and breathing rates returned to relative normality, I went back to my work. I scrubbed and watched, and watched and scrubbed. My shoulders began to feel pumped full of blood, as they do in weightlifting workouts.

The dolphin's lower jaw hooked over its top one: it was Arnie. His head moved up and down violently, and his tail moved so fast that a trail of bubbles formed behind it. As the dolphin charged, I heard a roar of cavitation[4] as the very water tore, breaking into hydrogen and oxygen.

I didn't even have time to flinch properly. It was easy to do just what Ted recommended. I froze.

I knew that if the dolphin ran into me at that speed, whatever he hit would be broken. This was how dolphins were able to kill sharks: they smashed their insides with a high-speed ram.

Whooosh! I felt rather than heard a wash of water like a great wind. I saw the dolphin's stomach—he had a bellybutton! —then the

---

4. **cavitation** (kăv´ĭ-tā´shən): sudden formation of bubbles in a liquid by an object moving rapidly through it.

WORDS TO KNOW   **aggression** (ə-grĕsh´ən) *n.* threatening behavior; hostility

Suddenly something shining caught my attention. I turned my head, and the whirring roar of the regulator seemed to disappear.

n stillness like the hush in a cathedral, I saw the smallest dolphin move her head just slightly, and from the back of her neck something silvery emerged, as if she were manufacturing a halo.

Naah. Yes! There it was: a glistening, gleaming, silver bubble ring, rising. The dolphin flexed her neck again, and another ring emerged, rising faster, so that it joined its <u>luminous</u> relation and they merged, becoming first a figure eight and then a larger single circle, a Hula-Hoop of light.

After I'd spent nearly two hours in the water, the scrubbed-off algae was rising in darkening clouds, like night closing in.

I kept switching the brush back and forth, from hand to hand, trying not to think about Arnie. Long ago, in India, there was a saying that you should not worry about tigers, lest you bring one to you by the thought.

Still, I couldn't help wondering where he was. My head began to shift back and forth more rapidly as I tried to see but couldn't.

Just then, something touched me!

I rolled, ready to fight, and looked into the red-brown eye and the face of . . . whom?

It was definitely not the hook jaw of Arnie, and the purple spot of Lucky's cheek was not there. Spock was supposed to have a hole in his left pec fin, while Delbert had a shark scar. This must be Ernestine.

I told myself she wasn't really smiling: that happy look was just an accident of jaw formation, indicating nothing more than lines of bone and muscle. But looking at her made me feel happy just the same.

She was so beautiful. From a distance, the dolphins had looked simple, uncomplicated. But up close, everything about Ernestine was astonishing. The black pupil in the center of her red-brown eye seemed to radiate emotion. Six inches back from the eye was a fold of skin with an opening the size of a pinhole in it, the opening to her ear. Even the dolphin's skin was special: not perfectly smooth but textured with the tiniest of lines and colored with subtle gray patterns that were perfectly matched and fitted together, like the interlocking feathers on a hawk.

She had pectoral (chest) fins to steer with, tail flukes for power, and a blowhole at the back of her head that could release breath at 200 miles per hour, punching a hole in the ocean spray so the dolphin could inhale relatively dry air and not drown in a storm. From the shape of her beak—the reason for the name "bottlenose"—to the <u>elegant</u> flare of her tail flukes, she was a creature of wonder. I felt I could study her for a thousand years and not see everything.

She was so beautiful. . . . Up close, everything about Ernestine was astonishing.

Ernestine nuzzled in beside me and laid her pectoral fin on my back.

This amazed me. A big animal I had never met before, and it swam up and touched me!

I couldn't resist her. Without conscious thought, my hand reached up and stroked her side. It felt smooth, soft, and firm, like the inside surface of a hard-boiled egg.

Suddenly the dolphin rolled, bringing the fin on her back into my hand. Then she took off.

T he suddenness of the motion frightened me, and instantly I straightened my fingers, releasing the loose grip I had held so as not to make her feel restrained. Had I offended her?

But she turned and came back, rolling again to place her dorsal fin (the one on her back) in my right hand.

Why fight it? I thought, dropping my scrub brush.

This time, when Ernestine took off, I went along.

I left my human clumsiness behind. For glorious seconds I knew what it was to be the swiftest swimmer in the sea. She towed me, and I tried not to get in the way. I was conscious of my body's shape as an obstruction and tried to narrow myself.

We soared. The water rushed past my face and swirled around my body, and I felt the streaking lines of speed.

Klonk! At the sound, Ernestine flicked out and away from my hand and was gone in an instant. I hung in the water, becoming a sluggish human once again.

Before me "stood" a gray-white dolphin giant. There was no question as to his identity. I knew it was Lucky even before I saw the scars on his face and neck and shoulders and the dark spot on the left side of his jaw.

The <u>dominant</u> dolphin lowered his head slowly. Again I heard the noise of irritation, threat, or challenge, and for an instant I thought he would give me trouble for getting too friendly with Ernestine. But the *klonk*ing

sound was softer now, as if the point had already been made.

I was in the presence of a leader. Whether I labeled him "alpha male" or "dominant dolphin bull" or "king among his own kind" made no difference. This chunk of sea was Lucky's territory, and he was very definitely in charge.

There was depth to Lucky, and intelligence. It was an intelligence different from my own, perhaps, but certainly deserving of respect. He looked like he knew how to live and how to die, like an Apache[5] chieftain living in the wild, who would find hardship and danger at every turn and was content that it should be so.

I was in the presence of a leader.

I did not understand all this at once, of course. I had no words to express what I felt then. There were only raw emotions, ideas, possibilities. My brain felt staggered, like a computer with information overload.

Trying to show neither fear nor aggression (and certainly not disrespect!), I let myself drift down, settling slowly back to the floor of the tank, to my dropped scrub brush, to my work.

Lucky only watched me go and made no move to follow. ❖

---

5. **Apache** (ə-păch′ē): belonging to a Native American people of the southwestern United States and northern Mexico.

WORDS
TO
KNOW

dominant (dŏm′ə-nənt) *adj.* having the most influence; controlling all others

RESPONDING
OPTIONS

FROM PERSONAL RESPONSE TO CRITICAL ANALYSIS

REFLECT **1.** How did you react to the experiences described in the selection? Write down your thoughts in your notebook.

RETHINK **2.** How do you think Lucky treated Don C. Reed when he entered the tank the next day? Give reasons for your answer.

3. What personality trait or traits does Reed have that you think would be helpful in working with dolphins?
Consider
- Reed's reaction to the diving gear he received
- how he dealt with the job of removing algae
- his reactions to Arnie, Ernestine, and Lucky

4. The head diver told Reed that 95 percent of his job would be the cleaning of algae and 5 percent would be "magic." What was magical about Reed's job?

5. How do you think Reed feels during his first day on the job?

RELATE **6.** On the basis of what you learned from the selection, would you want a job like the author's? Explain.

ANOTHER PATHWAY

Create a chart with five columns, and label each one with a dolphin's name. Refer to Ted Pintarelli's descriptions of each dolphin's characteristics and to the author's own observations. List the personality traits of each dolphin in the appropriate column. Then compare and contrast the dolphins in an oral presentation for the class.

QUICKWRITES

1. In the last column of the chart you created for the Reading Connection on page 65, record any new ideas you learned about dolphins. Write a brief **summary** of what you learned, and explain what piece of information was the most surprising to you.

2. Should dolphins be held in captivity? Consider both the advantages for scientific research and the arguments against holding any wild animals captive. Choose one side of the issue, and write an **editorial** that expresses your opinion.

📁 *PORTFOLIO Save your writing. You may want to use it later as a springboard to a piece for your portfolio.*

LITERARY CONCEPTS

Authors write for four main reasons, or **purposes:** to entertain, to inform, to express opinions, and to persuade. A writer may combine two or three purposes in one piece of writing, but one purpose is usually the most important. What purposes do you think Don C. Reed had in mind when he wrote about his first dive? Which of these purposes do you think was most important to him? Explain.

Author's Purpose
• to entertain
• to inform
• to express opinions
• to persuade

ALTERNATIVE ACTIVITIES

1. Reed says, "I took one giant step forward and fell . . . into another world." Which of his descriptions helped you experience the feeling of being underwater? Draw or paint a **scene** from the selection that inspires you.

2. **Cooperative Learning** Working with others, arrange an on-line interview with a representative of an oceanarium or a seaquarium to find out about others' direct experiences with dolphins. Prepare questions in advance, and present your information in an **interview report** to your class.

WORDS TO KNOW

Review the Words to Know in the boxes at the bottom of the selection pages. On your paper, write the vocabulary word that best completes each sentence.

1. The dolphins lived in a large outdoor _____.

2. The divers used air hoses rather than tanks as their source of _____ air.

3. Ted gave the author a short lesson in human-dolphin _____.

4. Dolphins are not easy to see underwater because of the _____ provided by their coloring.

5. The water in the tank produced a _____ of objects, making them appear larger.

6. An angry dolphin makes a special sound that is a sign of _____.

7. The smallest dolphin, Ernestine, created silvery, _____ rings in the water.

8. The narrator described the _____ flare of the dolphin's fluke.

9. Ted described Lucky as the largest, most aggressive, and _____ dolphin in the tank.

10. One dolphin, Arnie, liked to scare new divers and would _____ through the water toward them.

DON C. REED

1945–

Don C. Reed began his career as a scuba diver in 1972, at Marine World near San Francisco, California. The seaquarium later became Marine World/Africa USA, an oceanarium-zoo, and moved to Vallejo, California. Reed spent 15 years there, eventually becoming head diver.

Reed has described himself as someone who tries to "listen" to what an animal is thinking. Although not a scientist, he believes that human beings and sea animals can coexist and that they can communicate their thoughts to each other by means of a yet-to-be discovered form of extrasensory perception. Reed's experiences over a 15-year period with a variety of sea creatures have provided the material for several articles and books. He has written for the magazines *Oceans* and *Highlights for Children*. "My First Dive with the Dolphins" is an excerpt from his book *The Dolphins and Me*.

OTHER WORKS *Notes from an Underwater Zoo, Sevengill: The Shark and Me, The Kraken*

LASERLINKS
• *ART GALLERY*

Tuesday

of the Other
June

by Norma Fox Mazer

"Be good, be good, be good, be good, my
Junie," my mother sang as she combed
my hair; a song, a story, a croon, a plea.
"It's just you and me, two women alone
in the world, June darling of my heart;
we have enough troubles getting by, we
surely don't need a single one more, so
you keep your sweet self out of fighting
and all that bad stuff. People can be
little-hearted, but turn the other cheek,
smile at the world, and the world'll
surely smile back."

We stood in front of the mirror as she combed my hair, combed and brushed and smoothed. Her head came just above mine; she said when I grew another inch, she'd stand on a stool to brush my hair. "I'm not giving up this pleasure!" And she laughed her long honey laugh.

My mother was April, my grandmother had been May, I was June. "And someday," said my mother, "you'll have a daughter of your own. What will you name her?"

"January!" I'd yell when I was little. "February! No, November!" My mother laughed her honey laugh. She had little emerald eyes that warmed me like the sun.

Every day when I went to school, she went to work. "Sometimes I stop what I'm doing," she said, "lay down my tools, and stop everything, because all I can think about is you. Wondering what you're doing and if you need me. Now, Junie, if anyone ever bothers you—"

"—I walk away, run away, come on home as fast as my feet will take me," I recited.

"Yes. You come to me. You just bring me

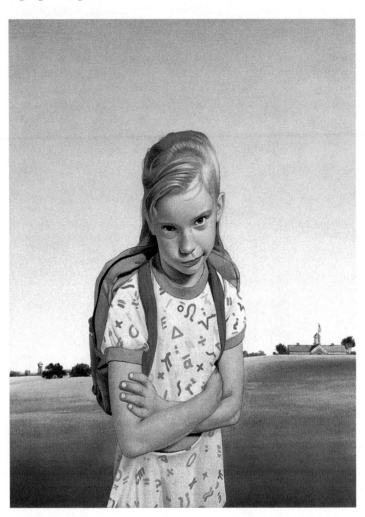

The Case for More School Days, C. F. Payne. First appeared in *The Atlantic Monthly*.

your trouble, because I'm here on this earth to love you and take care of you."

I was safe with her. Still, sometimes I woke up at night and heard footsteps slowly creeping up the stairs. It wasn't my mother, she was asleep in the bed across the room, so it was robbers, thieves, and murderers, creeping slowly . . . slowly . . . slowly toward my bed.

I stuffed my hand into my mouth. If I screamed and woke her, she'd be tired at work tomorrow. The robbers and thieves filled the warm darkness and slipped across the floor more quietly than cats. Rigid under the covers, I stared at the shifting dark and bit my knuckles and never knew when I fell asleep again.

In the morning we sang in the kitchen. "Bill Grogan's goat! Was feelin' fine! Ate three red shirts, right off the line!" I made sandwiches for our lunches, she made pancakes for breakfast, but all she ate was one pancake and a cup of coffee. "Gotta fly, can't be late."

I wanted to be rich and take care of her. She worked too hard; her pretty hair had gray in it that she joked about. "Someday," I said, "I'll buy you a real house, and you'll never work in a pot factory again."

"Such delicious plans," she said. She checked the windows to see if they were locked. "Do you have your key?"

I lifted it from the chain around my neck.

"And you'll come right home from school and—"

"—I won't light fires or let strangers into the house, and I won't tell anyone on the phone that I'm here alone," I finished for her.

"I know, I'm just your old worrywart mother." She kissed me twice, once on each cheek. "But you are my June, my only June, the only June."

She was wrong; there was another June. I met her when we stood next to each other at the edge of the pool the first day of swimming class in the Community Center.

"What's your name?" She had a deep growly voice.

"June. What's yours?"

She stared at me. "June."

"We have the same name."

"No we don't. June is my name, and I don't give you permission to use it. Your name is Fish Eyes." She pinched me hard. "Got it, Fish Eyes?"

The next Tuesday, the Other June again stood next to me at the edge of the pool. "What's your name?"

"June."

"Wrong. Your—name—is—Fish—Eyes."

"June."

"Fish Eyes, you are really stupid." She shoved me into the pool.

The swimming teacher looked up, frowning, from her chart. "No one in the water yet."

Later, in the locker room, I dressed quickly and wrapped my wet suit in the towel. The Other June pulled on her jeans. "You guys see

that bathing suit Fish Eyes was wearing? Her mother found it in a trash can."

"She did not!"

The Other June grabbed my fingers and twisted. "Where'd she find your bathing suit?"

"She bought it, let me go."

"Poor little stupid Fish Eyes is crying. Oh, boo hoo hoo, poor little Fish Eyes."

"Your name is Fish Eyes." She pinched me hard.

After that, everyone called me Fish Eyes. And every Tuesday, wherever I was, there was also the Other June—at the edge of the pool, in the pool, in the locker room. In the water, she swam alongside me, blowing and huffing, knocking into me. In the locker room, she stepped on my feet, pinched my arms, hid my blouse, and knotted my braids together. She had large square teeth; she was shorter than I was, but heavier, with bigger bones and square hands. If I met her outside on the street, carrying her bathing suit and towel, she'd walk toward me, smiling a square, friendly smile. "Oh well, if it isn't Fish Eyes." Then she'd punch me, blam! her whole solid weight hitting me.

I didn't know what to do about her. She was training me like a dog. After a few weeks of this, she only had to look at me, only had to growl, "I'm going to get you, Fish Eyes," for my heart to slink like a whipped dog down into my stomach. My arms were covered with bruises. When my mother noticed, I made up a story about tripping on the sidewalk.

My weeks were no longer Tuesday, Wednesday, Thursday, and so on. Tuesday was

Awfulday. Wednesday was Badday. (The Tuesday bad feelings were still there.) Thursday was Betterday, and Friday was Safeday. Saturday was Goodday, but Sunday was Toosoonday, and Monday—Monday was nothing but the day before Awfulday.

I tried to slow down time. Especially on the weekends, I stayed close by my mother, doing everything with her, shopping, cooking, cleaning, going to the laundromat. "Aw, sweetie, go play with your friends."

"Junie, listen to this. We're moving!"

"No, I'd rather be with you." I wouldn't look at the clock or listen to the radio (they were always telling you the date and the time). I did special magic things to keep the day from going away, rapping my knuckles six times on the bathroom door six times a day and never, ever touching the chipped place on my bureau. But always I woke up to the day before Tuesday, and always, no matter how many times I circled the worn spot in the living-room rug or counted twenty-five cracks in the ceiling, Monday disappeared and once again it was Tuesday.

The Other June got bored with calling me Fish Eyes. Buffalo Brain came next, but as soon as everyone knew that, she renamed me Turkey Nose.

Now at night it wasn't robbers creeping up the stairs, but the Other June, coming to torment me. When I finally fell asleep, I dreamed of kicking her, punching, biting, pinching. In the morning I remembered my dreams and felt brave and strong. And then I remembered all the things my mother had taught me and told me.

Be good, be good, be good; it's just us two women alone in the world. . . . Oh, but if it weren't, if my father wasn't long gone, if we'd had someone else to fall back on, if my mother's mother and daddy weren't dead all these years, if my father's daddy wanted to know us instead of being glad to forget us— oh, then I would have punched the Other June with a frisky heart, I would have grabbed her arm at poolside and bitten her like the dog she had made of me.

One night, when my mother came home from work, she said, "Junie, listen to this. We're moving!"

Alaska, I thought. Florida. Arizona. Someplace far away and wonderful, someplace without the Other June.

"Wait till you hear this deal. We are going to be caretakers, trouble-shooters for an eight-family apartment building. Fifty-six Blue Hill Street. Not janitors; we don't do any of the heavy work. April and June, Trouble-shooters, Incorporated. If a tenant has a complaint or a problem, she comes to us and we either take care of it or call the janitor for service. And for that little bit of work, we get to live rent free!" She swept me around in a dance. "Okay? You like it? I do!"

So. Not anywhere else, really. All the same, maybe too far to go to swimming class? "Can we move right away? Today?"

"Gimme a break, sweetie. We've got to pack, do a thousand things. I've got to line up someone with a truck to help us. Six weeks, Saturday the fifteenth." She circled it on the calendar. It was the Saturday after the last day of swimming class.

Soon, we had boxes lying everywhere, filled with clothes and towels and glasses wrapped in newspaper. Bit by bit, we cleared the rooms,

© Bradley Clark.

leaving only what we needed right now. The dining-room table staggered on a bunched-up rug, our bureaus inched toward the front door like patient cows. On the calendar in the kitchen, my mother marked off the days until we moved, but the only days I thought about were Tuesdays—Awfuldays. Nothing else was real except the too fast passing of time, moving toward each Tuesday . . . away from Tuesday . . . toward Tuesday. . . .

And it seemed to me that this would go on forever, that Tuesdays would come forever and I would be forever trapped by the side of the pool, the Other June whispering Buffalo Brain Fish Eyes Turkey Nose into my ear, while she ground her elbow into my side and smiled her square smile at the swimming teacher.

No more swimming class. No more Awfuldays. . . . No more Tuesdays.

And then it ended. It was the last day of swimming class. The last Tuesday. We had all passed our tests, and, as if in celebration, the Other June only pinched me twice. "And now," our swimming teacher said, "all of you are ready for the Advanced Class, which starts in just one month. I have a sign-up slip here. Please put your name down before you leave." Everyone but me crowded around. I went to the locker room and pulled on my clothes as fast as possible. The Other June burst through the door just as I was leaving. "Goodbye," I yelled, "good riddance to bad trash!" Before she could pinch me again, I ran past her and then ran all the way home, singing, "Goodbye. . . goodbye . . . goodbye, good riddance to bad trash!"

Later, my mother carefully untied the blue ribbon around my swimming class diploma. "Look at this! Well, isn't this wonderful! You are on your way, you might turn into an Olympic swimmer, you never know what life will bring."

"I don't want to take more lessons."

"Oh, sweetie, it's great to be a good swimmer." But then, looking into my face, she said, "No, no, no, don't worry, you don't have to."

The next morning, I woke up hungry for the first time in weeks. No more swimming class. No more Baddays and Awfuldays. No more Tuesdays of the Other June. In the kitchen, I made hot cocoa to go with my mother's corn muffins. "It's Wednesday, Mom," I said, stirring the cocoa. "My favorite day."

"Since when?"

"Since this morning." I turned on the radio so I could hear the announcer tell the time, the temperature, and the day.

Thursday for breakfast I made cinnamon toast, Friday my mother made pancakes, and on Saturday, before we moved, we ate the last slices of bread and cleaned out the peanut butter jar.

"Some breakfast," Tilly said. "Hello, you must be June." She shook my hand. She was a friend of my mother's from work; she wore big hoop earrings, sandals, and a skirt as dazzling as a rainbow. She came in a truck with John to help us move our things.

John shouted cheerfully at me, "So you're moving." An enormous man with a face covered with little brown bumps. Was he afraid his voice wouldn't travel the distance from his mouth to my ear? "You looking at my moles?" he shouted, and he heaved our big green flowered chair down the stairs. "Don't worry, they don't bite. Ha, ha, ha!" Behind him came my mother and Tilly balancing a bureau between them, and behind them I carried a lamp and the round, flowered Mexican tray that was my mother's favorite. She had found it at a garage sale and said it was as close to foreign travel as we would ever get.

The night before, we had loaded our car, stuffing in bags and boxes until there was barely room for the two of us. But it was only when we were in the car, when we drove past Abdo's Grocery, where they always gave us credit, when I turned for a last look at our street—it was only then that I understood we were truly going to live somewhere else, in another apartment, in another place mysteriously called Blue Hill Street.

Tilly's truck followed our car.

"Oh, I'm so excited," my mother said. She laughed. "You'd think we were going across the country."

Our old car wheezed up a long, steep hill. Blue Hill Street. I looked from one side to the other, trying to see everything.

My mother drove over the crest of the hill. "And now—ta da!—our new home."

"Which house? Which one?" I looked out the window and what I saw was the Other June. She was sprawled on the stoop of a pink house, lounging back on her elbows, legs outspread, her jaws working on a wad of gum. I slid down into the seat, but it was too late. I was sure she had seen me.

My mother turned into a driveway next to a big white building with a tiny porch. She leaned on the steering wheel. "See that window there, that's our living-room window . . . and that one over there, that's your bedroom. . . . "

We went into the house, down a dim, cool hall. In our new apartment, the wooden floors clicked under our shoes, and my mother showed me everything. Her voice echoed in the empty rooms. I followed her around in a daze.

Had I imagined seeing the Other June? Maybe I'd seen another girl who looked like her. A double. That could happen.

"Ho yo, where do you want this chair?" John appeared in the doorway. We brought in boxes and bags and beds and stopped only to eat pizza and drink orange juice from the carton.

"June's so quiet, do you think she'll adjust all right?" I heard Tilly say to my mother.

"Oh, definitely. She'll make a wonderful adjustment. She's just getting used to things."

But I thought that if the Other June lived on the same street as I did, I would never get used to things.

That night I slept in my own bed, with my own pillow and blanket, but with floors that creaked in strange voices and walls with cracks I didn't recognize. I didn't feel either happy or unhappy. It was as if I were waiting for something.

Monday, when the principal of Blue Hill Street School left me in Mr. Morrisey's classroom, I knew what I'd been waiting for. In that room full of strange kids, there was one person I knew. She smiled her square smile, raised her hand, and said, "She can sit next to me, Mr. Morrisey."

"Very nice of you, June M. OK, June T., take your seat. I'll try not to get you two Junes mixed up."

I sat down next to her. She pinched my arm. "Good riddance to bad trash," she mocked.

I was back in the Tuesday swimming class, only now it was worse, because every day would be Awfulday. The pinching had already started. Soon, I knew, on the playground and in the halls, kids would pass me, grinning. "Hiya, Fish Eyes."

The Other June followed me around during recess that day, droning in my ear, "You are my slave, you must do everything I say, I am your master, say it, say, 'Yes, master, you are my master.'"

I pressed my lips together, clapped my hands over my ears, but without hope. Wasn't it only a matter of time before I said the hateful words?

"How was school?" my mother said that night.

"OK."

She put a pile of towels in a bureau drawer. "Try not to be sad about missing your old friends, sweetie; there'll be new ones."

The next morning, the Other June was waiting for me when I left the house. "Did your mother get you that blouse in the garbage dump?" She butted me, shoving me against a tree. "Don't you speak anymore, Fish Eyes?" Grabbing my chin in her hands, she pried open my mouth. "Oh, ha ha, I thought you lost your tongue."

We went on to school. I sank down into my seat, my head on my arms. "June T., are you all right?" Mr. Morrisey asked. I nodded. My head was almost too heavy to lift.

The Other June went to the pencil sharpener. Round and round she whirled the handle. Walking back, looking at me, she held the three sharp pencils like three little knives.

Someone knocked on the door. Mr. Morrisey went out into the hall. Paper planes burst into the air, flying from desk to desk. Someone turned on a transistor radio. And the Other June, coming closer, smiled and licked her lips like a cat sleepily preparing to gulp down a mouse.

I remembered my dream of kicking her, punching, biting her like a dog.

Then my mother spoke quickly in my ear: Turn the other cheek, my Junie; smile at the world, and the world'll surely smile back.

But I had turned the other cheek and it was slapped. I had smiled and the world hadn't

smiled back. I couldn't run home as fast as my feet would take me. I had to stay in school— and in school there was the Other June. Every morning, there would be the Other June, and every afternoon, and every day, all day, there would be the Other June.

She frisked down the aisle, stabbing the pencils in the air toward me. A boy stood up on his desk and bowed. "My fans," he said, "I greet you." My arm twitched and throbbed, as if the Other June's pencils had already poked through the skin. She came closer, smiling her Tuesday smile.

"No," I whispered, "no." The word took wings and flew me to my feet, in front of the Other June. "Nooooooo." It flew out of my mouth into her surprised face.

The boy on the desk turned toward us. "You said something, my devoted fans?"

"No," I said to the Other June. "Oh, no! No. No. No. No more." I pushed away the hand that held the pencils.

The Other June's eyes opened, popped wide like the eyes of somebody in a cartoon. It made me laugh. The boy on the desk laughed, and then the other kids were laughing, too.

"No," I said again, because it felt so good to say it. "No, no, no, no." I leaned toward the Other June, put my finger against her chest. Her cheeks turned red, she squawked something—it sounded like "Eeeraaghyou!"— and she stepped back. She stepped away from me.

The door banged, the airplanes disappeared, and Mr. Morrisey walked to his desk. "OK. OK. Let's get back to work. Kevin Clark, how about it?" Kevin jumped off the desk, and Mr. Morrisey picked up a piece of chalk. "All right, class—" He stopped and looked at me and the Other June. "You two Junes, what's going on there?"

I tried it again. My finger against her chest. Then the words. "No—more." And she stepped back another step. I sat down at my desk.

"June M.," Mr. Morrisey said.

She turned around, staring at him with that big-eyed cartoon look. After a moment she sat down at her desk with a loud slapping sound.

Even Mr. Morrisey laughed.

And sitting at my desk, twirling my braids, I knew this was the last Tuesday of the Other June. ❖

LITERARY INSIGHT

MEAN SONG
by Eve Merriam

Snickles and podes,
Ribble and grodes:
That's what I wish you.

A nox in the groot,
A root in the stoot
And a gock in the forbeshaw, too.

Keep out of sight
For fear that I might
Glom you a gravely snave.

Don't show your face
Around any place
Or you'll get one flack snack in the bave.

NORMA FOX MAZER

Norma Fox Mazer believes stories are a way to understand the world and the people in it. She says that readers of fiction "will find a world where people face troubles but act to help themselves."

Mazer's interest in writing started in high school when she was editor of her school paper and a correspondent for her town's newspaper. After a year at college, she married the novelist Harry Mazer. For ten years, she and her husband struggled to write while raising their four children. Today she is a widely recognized and prize-winning writer of fiction for young adults.

Mazer lives in New York but spends her summers

1931–

in Canada, where she does without electricity, telephones, newspapers, radios, or indoor plumbing. About her writing, Mazer says, "I seem to deal in the ordinary, the everyday, the real. I should like in my writing to give meaning and emotion to ordinary moments. In my books and stories I want people to eat chocolate pudding, break a dish, yawn, look in a store window, wear socks with holes in them." Readers can encounter many of Mazer's true-to-life characters in works like *After the Rain*, a Newbery Honor book.

OTHER WORKS *Three Sisters; The Solid Gold Kids; Bright Days, Stupid Nights; C, My Name Is Cal; D, My Name Is Danita*

TAKING IT PERSONALLY

You are unique. Nobody sees the world or responds to it quite like you. This is true whether you are looking at a photograph, watching a baseball game, or reading a story. On the following pages, you'll explore the way you respond. You will

- see how authors choose words to stir a response in their readers
- write a personal response to a story or poem
- discover how your response differs from others' responses in real-life situations

Writer's Style: Descriptive Words Writers choose words that capture readers' attention. Specific nouns, precise verbs, and vivid adjectives help "show" readers what an author means.

Read the Literature

The writers of these passages have carefully chosen their words to create certain responses in their readers.

Literature Models

Precise Verbs
Which words describe how mean the Other June is? What other words might work as well?

In the water, she swam alongside me, blowing and huffing, knocking into me. In the locker room, she stepped on my feet, pinched my arms, hid my blouse, and knotted my braids together. She had large square teeth; she was shorter than I was, but heavier, with bigger bones and square hands.

Norma Fox Mazer
from "Tuesday of the Other June"

Vivid Adjectives
Which words help the author describe the scene? How do these words help you "see" what is happening?

A school of fish swept by like silver arrows. He saw scarlet rock cod with ruby eyes and the head of a conger eel peering out from a cavern in the coral.

Armstrong Sperry
from "Ghost of the Lagoon"

Connect to Life

Take a close look at the words this magazine writer uses. Then think about how the special words you notice make you feel about the passage.

Magazine Article

Ok, boardheads, listen up. There's a nuclear wind blowing, and the wave you just caught—this huge, rolling wall of water—is now rumbling 20 feet below your head. You're hanging in midair, upside down and bat-style, your feet strapped to the sailboard above. Gulp. Now what?

Laura Hilgers
from "Irie Man"
Outside Kids, Summer 1993

Creative Words
Which words in this passage seem unusual or interesting? Whom is the writer writing to? How can you tell?

Try Your Hand: Choosing the Right Word

1. **Vivid Words** Rewrite the following sentences, using descriptive words to catch your readers' attention.

   - Mako watched the shark move.
   - Mako could see stars and hear thunder.
   - Afa went through the jungle and barked at animals.

2. **You Are There** With a small group, write a collaborative paragraph describing a funny, exciting, or special classroom event or situation. Remember, you want your readers to feel as though they are at the event.

3. **You Have to Read This!** A book-jacket review is a short summary or descriptive review that tries to hook people into reading the book. Write a book-jacket review for one of the selections in this unit. Try to make your review as eye-catching and descriptive as possible.

SkillBuilder

 GRAMMAR FROM WRITING

Using Adverbs
An adverb modifies a verb, an adjective, or another adverb. You can use an adverb to tell *how, when, where,* or *to what extent.* Notice how Armstrong Sperry uses adverbs to add details that make this scene interesting:

Swiftly, yet calmly, Mako stood upright and braced himself firmly. Then, murmuring a silent prayer to the shark god, he threw his spear for the last time.

APPLYING WHAT YOU'VE LEARNED
Add adverbs and other precise words to make these sentences more descriptive and interesting.

1. The crowd clapped when Mako fought the paper shark.
2. The stage sets looked good, and the water moved.
3. Lisa was Tupa, which we thought was funny.

HANDBOOKS

For more information on adverbs, see page 830 of the Grammar Handbook. For more information on word choice and elaboration, see page 783 of the Writing Handbook.

Personal Response

Have you ever watched a movie with a friend and discovered that the two of you had very different reactions to it? People respond to movies, music, and stories in very different ways. Sharing your reactions to a story is natural and fun.

GUIDED ASSIGNMENT

Write a Personal Response On the next few pages, you'll explore what you think and feel about a story by writing a personal response essay. In your essay, you may describe your thoughts and feelings about the story, about a certain character, or about the author's technique.

SATURDAY
Last Day
15

❶ Prewrite and Explore

Since you'll be writing a personal response essay, you need to think about the selections that made a strong impression on you. Consider looking at your QuickWrites or your reading log for help in choosing the selection you'll respond to.

FOCUSING YOUR RESPONSE

The following questions might help you reflect on the selection you choose:

- Which parts of the story made me take notice? Which were confusing? Which seemed important?
- Which parts of the story reminded me of my own life?
- What was my overall impression of the story?

❷ Freewrite to Discover

At first, you might not be sure exactly why or how a story affected you. To discover what you think, try freewriting about the story. Another possibility is to sketch the most memorable scene in the story and then write about it. The sketch and freewriting on these pages show how one student explored a story.

Student's Sketch

Tuesdays

Student's Freewriting

I liked "Tuesday of the Other June" because I don't like bullies. The Other June was mean so it was cool when she was put in her place.

I like swimming, and there was a lot of swimming in the story. The story reminded me of my friend Rachel. She was picked on by a bully. But she didn't stand up for herself because she was too scared.

I think I'm most interested in this story because I know how June felt.

I should probably focus on the scene that I liked best—maybe use quotes from the story, too.

The characters seem real to me. It's like they could be actual kids in my class. I liked it when June stood up for herself. And the boy who stood up on his desk was hilarious. I saw that happen last year.

Now that you have explored your reaction a little, ask yourself the following questions:

- What affected me the most in this selection?
- Why did I feel the way I did?

❸ Draft and Share

In writing a personal response essay, there are no right or wrong responses. However, supporting your responses with reasons and examples from the story and from your life will help readers understand your reactions. Pick out the details in the story, such as specific examples or quotations, that caused you to respond. You can use these to support your ideas. Remember that most essays have an introduction, a body, and a conclusion. When you've finished, ask a classmate to read your essay and give you suggestions.

 PEER RESPONSE

- What feelings came out strongest in my response essay?
- What story details can I add to support my response and help readers understand it?

4 Revise and Edit

As you edit your draft, remember to make your introduction at least one paragraph and to start a new paragraph for each new idea. Also be sure to support each of your ideas with specific details from the story. After you have finished your draft, reflect on how well you presented your ideas and what you learned about writing a personal response.

Student Model

"Tuesday of the Other June"

I liked "Tuesday of the Other June" by Norma Fox Mazer because I know exactly how June felt. Throughout the story I felt sorry for June because she was being picked on. I know what it feels like to be picked on. My best friend had a bully who picked on her all the time, but my friend never stood up to the bully. So when June finally put the bully in her place, I felt like cheering.

> **How does the introduction explain the writer's response to the story?**

> **How do references to specific scenes in the story clarify the writer's response?**

I had a feeling that June would run into the Other June and something big would happen. But I didn't know what would happen or when. Then, as the Other June stalked down the aisle, stabbing with the pencils, I trembled and I felt the tension in the classroom. I loved the way June's anger built up until she could stand no more bullying.

Standards for Evaluation

A personal response
- gives the author and title of the work
- includes enough information about the work for readers unfamiliar with it to understand the response
- clearly expresses a response and gives reasons for it
- ends with a summary of the response and an overall conclusion

Grammar in Context

Action Verbs Using action verbs will make your writing more precise and interesting, helping readers to understand your personal response better. Some action verbs, such as *paddle* and *swim*, describe action you can see. Other action verbs, such as *enjoy* and *wish*, tell about action you cannot see.

> Then, as the Other June ~~was walking~~ _stalked_ down the aisle,‸ _stabbing_
> with the pencils, I ~~was nervous~~ _trembled_ and I ~~was feeling~~ _felt_ the
> tension in the classroom. I loved the way June's anger
> ~~was building~~ _built up_ until she could stand no more bullying.

Notice how the revised version is more detailed and interesting. The action verbs help to express the writer's emotions and ideas vividly so that readers can better understand and appreciate the response.

Try Your Hand: Using Action Verbs

On a separate sheet of paper, revise the following paragraph, choosing stronger, more precise action verbs:

> Cobwebs and dust were on the book in front of me. I could barely read the title: *Woodsong*. I got the dirt off the book and began to read. I had the book for hours and never put it down. *Woodsong* was good and it was exciting. When I was done, I gave the book to my best friend.

GRAMMAR FROM WRITING

Using Linking Verbs

Some verbs do not show action. They tell what something is, or they link the subject with one or more words in the predicate. Such verbs are called linking verbs. These are the most common linking verbs.

am	are	were	being
is	was	be	been

- The shark *was* a whitish color.
- The story *is* very suspenseful.
- I *am* eager to visit Bora Bora.

These are some other familiar linking verbs.

look	appear	become	taste
feel	sound	remain	smell

APPLYING WHAT YOU'VE LEARNED
Number a separate sheet of paper 1–5. After each number, write a linking verb that completes each sentence.

1. The next story _____ "Ghost of the Lagoon."
2. Some students _____ excited as they read.
3. As exciting as this story is, most students _____ calm.
4. It has _____ an all-time favorite for many students.
5. Most students _____ satisfied with the ending.

Responding to Ads

Authors of literature aren't the only writers who try to get a response out of you. People who write advertisements, billboards, magazine articles, and even classified ads, try to get you to respond in specific ways.

View Read the circled ads on this page. In your notebook, describe what the ads are about. Which ad would you be most likely to respond to? Why?

Interpret Think about what these ads have in common. How and why are they different? What makes each ad effective or ineffective?

Discuss Get together with a small group of classmates, and take turns discussing which ads got your attention and why. Talk about how and why people might respond differently to the ads. Then refer to the SkillBuilder at the right for help with analyzing your responses.

COOK OF

TO RAISE
AND HEALTHY

DOG

TWO FREE CATS available
...ult neutered male. One female
Very cute and playful together.
...577 evenings.

...A LIFE and enrich yours. Ad
...phan cat or dog from the
...eutered, vaccinated. Noc
...4679

...FOR SALE. Body 12 to
...cluded, 4'x2'x2'. Mus
...ssage, 555-7684

...AF VOLUNTEER foste
...mporarily places needy
...ncerned caretakers. W
...ning, food, and veterin
...fostering is over, we pl
...in a permanent home. F
...heart. If you live in the C
...a and can provide a foste
...he volunteer office at 555-
...general information and ado
...tion, 555-5488.

FRISKY, PLAYFUL KITTEN
Orange and regular calicos
...bies, black Siamese mixes
...M/F, 8 weeks, 2 years sho
...neutered. Some declawe

FOR SAL
like new, 555-0004

...WNTOWN APARTMENT MOVING
...Everything must go. Furniture,
...res, TV, bicycle and much more.
...Sat-Sun 9am-3pm, 555-8768

TWO GREAT CATS free
Declawed, neutered. My
Litter box, carrier. 555-3

NORWEGIAN ELKHOU
...months old, 35#, wond
...loves kids, dogs, cats.
...trained. Shots, worme
...someone home a lot.

372 Dogs & Cats

BOXER PUPPIES (AKC)-German. Brindled
with black mask. Ready now. 555-6702

SHORTHAIR BLACK
...home. Midnight is sp
...cinated. Abandoned

Free!
Landlord says
Sparky must go.
Adorable 3 year old
Beagle needs love
and friendship.
Obedient, sweet &
great with kids.
555-1111

FIVE DECLAWED C
...friendly long/short-h
...vaccinated of cours
...555-0001

...CATS FOR ADOP
...Association is ope
...ends noon-4pm. A
...ing & vaccination

FREE BLACK CA
...friendly. Does no
...moving in with a
...0536.

FOR SALE. BE
Wonderful pet.
Call 555-4781

PAMPERED PETS. MID-DAY dog walks /
cat sitting. In your home vacation care.
Professional service & loving care for your
pets. Great rates! Call 555-1298

GREEN IGUA
...physical cond
...male, hand f
...555-8458

LOVABLE SIBERIAN HUSKY puppies.
...ck and white with blue eyes. AKC pedi-
...guaranteed. Males,

BEAGLE PUPS-AKC, 6 wks, vet checked, 1st shots, wormed. 555-4420

BICHON FRISE AKC female, Born 3/29/95 Litter box trained. 555-0119

THE POOCH PORCH has perky pups! All breeds. Shots/wormed. Ready to go! First come, first served. Be a Pal. 555-3333

BOSTON TERRIERS: AKC, 1st shots & wormed , M&G. 555-2728

BICHON FRISE PUPS AKC non-allergic / shed, wht / apricot, shots. 555-9612

BOUVIER pups AKC OFA, Chp Bld Family / Protector. Grand Rapids 555-1702

BOXER Pups Fam raised. Bred for intelligence & trainablity. Ready now. 555-6269 / 555-0495

BOXER PUPS AKC, FLASHY, fawn / wht, brindle / wht, shots, Guar 555-6242

German Shepherd Top quality, AKC championship lines. Excellent guard or working dog. Guaranteed. Serious buyers only! Call 555-2222

BRITTANY -pups, AKC reg. Ch bld lines. Ready to go. Call 555-4044

BULLDOG MIXED w/ Bull Mastiff 2 mos, no papers or parents. 555-9654

CHIHUAHUA, adorable, AKC wht, sable brwn, Males: 8 wks, ...ears, shots, wormed. 555-9...

...HSHUND, short hair,

...UPS-AKC, 1F, 3M 7 wks, ...e, very cute, shots, 555-0792

...HUAHUA-PURE BRED 3 months, Call 555-2732

CHOCOLATE LAB - Year old, AKC, Shots, ...ving must sell 555-2732

...THIN... ...orties will ..., affectionat... ... hairs. ...void. Beautiful lon... ...ed, shots, some declawed, 555-4193

...HING'S SADDER THAN an aban... ...ed pet. We rescue cats who can't ...erstand why the love stopped. Loving ...es only! Phone 555-2306.

...PER KITTEN SELECTION includes ...mese, Himalayan. Also many young ...ults, long hairs and declaws. Low fee ...vers shots, altering, leuk test. 555-0793.

0-45 LBS SHEPHERD male mix, 2 years. ...bandoned, locked in factory, nursed to ...health. Needs to be only pet. Neutered, wormed, shots. 555-8058.

FREE TO A good home. Good for elderly person. 9 year old Chihuahua/Pekingese. 555-0050

SAVE A LIFE and enrich yours. Adopt a loving orphan cat or dog from the city pound. Neutered, vaccinated. Noon-7pm daily. 555-8946

ABERDEEN- All breed pups. Pure & mixed. Pups privately raised. Guaranteed. 555-2050

ARCHER PUPPIES WE SELL ALL BREEDS All Pups From Private Homes. Over 100 Puppies, 555-2240

POODLE MIXES Affen- We raise our Puppies/ Kittens. Eskimo Yorkie Cocker Husky Basset Pom Springer Beagle Poodles 555-6463

AKITA PUPS AKC Reg 10 wks. Puppy shots, wormed. (2 Female 1 Male) 555-6501

ALASKAN MALAMUTE puppies, purebred, without papers. Call 555-2204

AMERICAN BULLDOG 10 pure bred 1g, wht, Papers. Terms are avl. F-M 555-9677

AMERICAN BULLDOGS, 100% Hlth Guar, Very Thick/Muscular. NABA Reg'd Show Qual, Wht w/Brindle. 555-5605

AMERICAN Pit Bulls Only 3 left. Ready now. Call leave message on voice mail 555-9166

AUSTRALIAN Shepherd Puppies, ASCA & AKC reg. 1st shots, wormed, 555-0943

BASSET HOUND PUPS AKC, T... extra sweet, shots, 555-672...

BEAGLE: 8 weeks, ...& Free...

CHOW, CHOW PUPS shots & worme...

CO... E... CO Pepp...

COCKE... champs ... 4497

GERMAN Short hair Pnt retrievers, M 555-0297.

GIANT SCHNAUZER p... go socialized. 555-755...

GOLDEN RETRIEVER hsebrkn, all shots, goo... says must go. 555-97...

GOLDEN RETRIEVE vet checked, all shot... home. Males only. 5...

GREAT DANE AKC Brindle, Good Bloo... 5374

GREAT PYRENEE Fem. White & Co...

KEESHOUND P... shots, ready to ...

LAB, AKC, CHO champ Engl bld ... 5557813

LAB-CHOC pu... d-claws remv...

LAB PUPS A... Vet V. D-claw... pos. Very nic...

LAB YELLO... trained/hun...

LABRADO... MALES 55...

LABS, A... ment blo... raised 55...

LHASA... vry gd t...

LHAS... man. 5...

MAST... 555-9...

NEA... F. Bl...

OLI... Cas...

PO... Pa...

Analyzing Your Response
You know that some words make you respond in certain ways. Advertisers know this as well. Advertisers write ads for a specific audience. By carefully choosing words that appeal to that audience, ad writers can create the responses they want. For example, how might an advertiser write a commercial for a new kids' cereal? What words might an advertiser use to sell an adult cereal? Why might the writers use different words in each case?

Sometimes advertisers use words that create emotional responses. Emotions such as love, anger, jealousy, and happiness can be very powerful. When looking at ads, it is a good idea to make sure you don't let an emotional response get in the way of sound judgment.

APPLYING WHAT YOU'VE LEARNED
With a small group, write a list of familiar advertisements. Discuss what makes the advertisements memorable. You may want to talk about whether the advertisements appeal to your emotions and how that changes your response to the ads.

ON THE EDGE OF SURVIVAL

WHAT DO **Y?u** THINK?

REFLECTING ON THEME

In Part 2 of this unit, characters respond to a wide range of risky situations. Try out an activity on this page to share your ideas about what it takes to survive. Keep your notebook at hand to record your impressions, questions, and conclusions.

How would you deal with danger?

Imagine that you are caught in a flash flood or another natural disaster that occurs with little warning. What will you do? Use a chart like the one shown to evaluate your alternatives. Add more if you need to. Share your chart with a classmate.

Threat:

Alternatives:

Leave

Stop to help

Rescue a pet

Protect

Remain

Risks

Rewards

Can you picture this?

Recall a dangerous event or a heroic rescue that you have heard about. With two or three other students, paint or draw a mural that illustrates what happened. If necessary, add captions to explain parts of the mural. Display your mural for the class.

Looking back

Has there been any change in your ideas about what you find most challenging? Work with a partner to list more challenging situations—some that you have experienced and some that you read about in the selections in Part 1. Discuss how you would rank these situations now.

Who lives "on the edge"?

Some people seem to be constantly on the go, seeking new experiences and adventures. Design a T-shirt for one of those people—someone you either know or have read about. Include a statement or motto that could apply to the person.

PREVIEWING

FICTION

Too Soon a Woman
Dorothy M. Johnson

PERSONAL CONNECTION

What do you know about the hardships that Western pioneers faced? Brainstorm a list of these problems and then, in a chart like the one shown here, group the problems under the headings "Weather," "Food," "Transportation," and "Other."

Problems of the Pioneers			
Weather	**Food**	**Transportation**	**Other**

HISTORICAL CONNECTION

In 1775, Daniel Boone and other woodsmen cut a trail through the Appalachian Mountains. This trail, the Wilderness Road, was the main route used by early pioneers who wanted to travel west. During the next 140 years, trails were pushed farther west as pioneers settled the Great Plains, the Rocky Mountains, and the land beyond the Rockies. Between 1840 and 1870, more than 350,000 pioneers suffered great hardships in migrating westward.

Individuals who farmed pieces of land on which they stayed were called homesteaders. Some homesteaders lived on the land they first settled. Others, like the family in this story, moved even farther west.

WRITING CONNECTION

Successful pioneers were strong, resourceful people who had to overcome many hardships in their search for land—from hostile climates to loneliness and poverty. As you read this story, compare the hardships and challenges faced by pioneers with those faced by people today. Take notes in your notebook or on a sheet of paper.

Wilderness Road 1780

Ohio River

Louisville
Boonesborough
Harrodsburg

VIRGINIA

APPALACHIAN MTNS.

NORTH CAROLINA

Atlantic Ocean

Miles
0 | 50 | 100

N W E S

The Gamekeeper's Daughter (1886), E. A. Walton. Glasgow Museums: Art Gallery and Museum, Kelvingrove, Scotland.

by Dorothy M. Johnson

Too Soon a Woman

We left the home place behind, mile by slow mile, heading for the mountains, across the prairie where the wind blew forever.

At first there were four of us with the one-horse wagon and its skimpy load. Pa and I walked, because I was a big boy of eleven. My two little sisters romped and trotted until they got tired and had to be boosted up into the wagon bed.

That was no covered Conestoga, like Pa's folks came west in, but just an old farm wagon, drawn by one weary horse, creaking and rumbling westward to the mountains, toward the little woods town where Pa thought he had an old uncle who owned a little two-bit sawmill.

Two weeks we had been moving when we picked up Mary, who had run away from somewhere that she wouldn't tell. Pa didn't want her along, but she stood up to him with no fear in her voice.

"I'd rather go with a family and look after kids," she said, "but I ain't going back. If you won't take me, I'll travel with any wagon that will."

Pa scowled at her, and her wide blue eyes stared back.

"How old are you?" he demanded.

"Eighteen," she said. "There's teamsters come this way sometimes. I'd rather go with you folks. But I won't go back."

"We're prid'near out of grub," my father told her. "We're clean out of money. I got all I can handle without taking anybody else." He turned away as if he hated the sight of her. "You'll have to walk," he said.

So she went along with us and looked after the little girls, but Pa wouldn't talk to her.

On the prairie, the wind blew. But in the mountains, there was rain. When we stopped at little timber claims along the way, the homesteaders said it had rained all summer. Crops among the blackened stumps were rotted and spoiled. There was no cheer anywhere and little hospitality. The people we talked to were past worrying. They were scared and desperate.

So was Pa. He traveled twice as far each day as the wagon. He ranged through the woods with his rifle, but he never saw game. He had been depending on venison, but we never got any except as a <u>grudging</u> gift from the homesteaders.

He brought in a porcupine once; that was fat meat and good. Mary roasted it in chunks over the fire, half crying with the smoke. Pa and I rigged up the tarp sheet for a shelter to keep the rain from putting the fire clean out.

The porcupine was long gone, except for some of the tried-out fat that Mary had saved, when we came to an old, empty cabin. Pa said we'd have to stop. The horse was wore out, couldn't pull anymore up those grades on the deep-rutted roads in the mountains.

At the cabin, at least there was shelter. We had a few potatoes left and some corn meal. There was a creek that probably had fish in it, if a person could catch them. Pa tried it for half a day before he gave up. To this day I don't care for fishing. I remember my father's sunken eyes in his gaunt, grim face.

He took Mary and me outside the cabin to talk. Rain dripped on us from branches overhead.

"I think I know where we are," he said. "I calculate to get to old John's and back in about four days. There'll be grub in the town,

and they'll let me have some whether old John's still there or not."

He looked at me. "You do like she tells you," he warned. It was the first time he had admitted Mary was on earth since we picked her up two weeks before.

"You're my pardner," he said to me, "but it might be she's got more brains. You mind what she says."

He burst out with bitterness, "There ain't anything good left in the world, or people to care if you live or die. But I'll get grub in the town and come back with it."

He took a deep breath and added, "If you get too all-fired hungry, butcher the horse. It'll be better than starvin'."

He kissed the little girls good-bye and plodded off through the woods with one blanket and the rifle.

The cabin was moldy and had no floor. We kept a fire going under a hole in the roof, so it was full of blinding smoke, but we had to keep the fire so as to dry out the wood.

The third night, we lost the horse. A bear scared him. We heard the racket, and Mary and I ran out, but we couldn't see anything in the pitch dark.

In gray daylight I went looking for him, and I must have walked fifteen miles. It seemed like I had to have that horse at the cabin when Pa came or he'd whip me. I got plumb lost two or three times and thought maybe I was going to die there alone and nobody would ever know it, but I found the way back to the clearing.

That was the fourth day, and Pa didn't come. That was the day we ate up the last of the grub.

The fifth day, Mary went looking for the horse. My sisters whimpered, huddled in a quilt by the fire, because they were scared and hungry.

I never did get dried out, always having to bring in more damp wood and going out to yell to see if Mary would hear me and not get lost. But I couldn't cry like the little girls did, because I was a big boy, eleven years old.

It was near dark when there was an answer to my yelling, and Mary came into the clearing.

Mary didn't have the horse—we never saw hide nor hair of that old horse again—but she was carrying something big and white that looked like a pumpkin with no color to it.

She didn't say anything, just looked around and saw Pa wasn't there yet, at the end of the fifth day.

"What's that thing?" my sister Elizabeth demanded.

"Mushroom," Mary answered. "I bet it hefts ten pounds."

"What are you going to do with it now?" I sneered. "Play football here?"

"Eat it—maybe," she said, putting it in a corner. Her wet hair hung over her shoulders. She huddled by the fire.

That was the day we ate up the last of the grub.

My sister Sarah began to whimper again. "I'm hungry!" she kept saying.

"Mushrooms ain't good eating," I said. "They can kill you."

"Maybe," Mary answered. "Maybe they can. I don't set up to know all about everything, like some people."

"What's that mark on your shoulder?" I asked her. "You tore your dress on the brush."

"What do you think it is?" she said, her head bowed in the smoke.

"Looks like scars," I guessed.

"'Tis scars. They whipped me. Now mind your own business. I want to think."

Elizabeth whimpered, "Why don't Pa come back?"

"He's coming," Mary promised. "Can't come in the dark. Your pa'll take care of you soon's he can."

She got up and rummaged around in the grub box.

"Nothing there but empty dishes," I growled. "If there was anything, we'd know it."

Mary stood up. She was holding the can with the porcupine grease.

"I'm going to have something to eat," she said coolly. "You kids can't have any yet. And I don't want any squalling, mind."

It was a cruel thing, what she did then. She sliced that big, solid mushroom and heated grease in a pan.

The smell of it brought the little girls out of their quilt, but she told them to go back in so fierce a voice that they obeyed. They cried to break your heart.

I didn't cry. I watched, hating her.

I endure the smell of the mushroom frying as long as I could. Then I said, "Give me some."

"Tomorrow," Mary answered. "Tomorrow, maybe. But not tonight." She turned to me with a sharp command: "Don't bother me! Just leave me be."

She knelt there by the fire and finished frying the slice of mushroom.

If I'd had Pa's rifle, I'd have been willing to kill her right then and there.

She didn't eat right away. She looked at the brown, fried slice for a while and said, "By tomorrow morning, I guess you can tell whether you want any."

WORDS TO KNOW **endure** (ĕn-dŏŏr′) v. to bear patiently

97

© Bob Crofut.

The little girls stared at her as she ate. Sarah was chewing an old leather glove.

When Mary crawled into the quilts with them, they moved away as far as they could get.

I was so scared that my stomach heaved, empty as it was.

Mary didn't stay in the quilts long. She took a drink out of the water bucket and sat down by the fire and looked through the smoke at me.

She said in a low voice, "I don't know how it will be if it's poison. Just do the best you can with the girls. Because your pa will come back, you know. . . . You better go to bed, I'm going to sit up."

And so would you sit up. If it might be your last night on earth and the pain of death might seize you at any moment, you would sit up by the smoky fire, wide-awake, remembering whatever you had to remember, savoring life.

We sat in silence after the girls had gone to sleep. Once I asked, "How long does it take?"

"I never heard," she answered. "Don't think about it."

I slept after a while, with my chin on my chest. Maybe Peter dozed that way at Gethsemane as the Lord knelt praying.

Mary's moving around brought me wide-awake. The black of night was fading.

"I guess it's all right," Mary said. "I'd be able to tell by now, wouldn't I?"

I answered gruffly, "I don't know."

Mary stood in the doorway for a while, looking out at the dripping world as if she found it beautiful. Then she fried slices of the mushroom while the little girls danced with anxiety.

We feasted, we three, my sisters and I, until Mary ruled, "That'll hold you," and would not cook any more. She didn't touch any of the mushroom herself.

That was a strange day in the moldy cabin. Mary laughed and was gay; she told stories, and we played "Who's Got the Thimble?" with a pine cone.

In the afternoon we heard a shout, and my sisters screamed, and I ran ahead of them across the clearing.

The rain had stopped. My father came plunging out of the woods leading a packhorse—and well I remember the treasures of food in that pack.

He glanced at us anxiously as he tore at the ropes that bound the pack.

"Where's the other one?" he demanded.

Mary came out of the cabin then, walking sedately. As she came toward us, the sun began to shine.

My stepmother was a wonderful woman. ❖

Western Wagons

by Rosemary and Stephen Vincent Benét

They went with axe and rifle, when the trail was still to blaze,
They went with wife and children, in the prairie-schooner days,
With banjo and with frying pan—Susanna, don't you cry!
For I'm off to California to get rich out there or die!

We've broken land and cleared it, but we're tired of where we are.
They say that wild Nebraska is a better place by far.
There's gold in far Wyoming, there's black earth in Ioway,
So pack up the kids and blankets, for we're moving out today!

The cowards never started and the weak died on the road,
And all across the continent the endless campfires glowed.
We'd taken land and settled—but a traveler passed by—
And we're going West tomorrow—Lordy, never ask us why!

We're going West tomorrow, where the promises can't fail.
O'er the hills in legions, boys, and crowd the dusty trail!
We shall starve and freeze and suffer. We shall die, and tame the lands.
But we're going West tomorrow, with our fortune in our hands.

WORDS TO KNOW

anxiety (ăng-zī′ĭ-tē) *n.* eager, nervous desire
sedately (sĭ-dāt′lē) *adv.* in a calm, dignified way

RESPONDING OPTIONS

FROM PERSONAL RESPONSE TO CRITICAL ANALYSIS

REFLECT   1. Did the last sentence of the story surprise you? Why or why not?

RETHINK   2. What is your opinion of Mary's character?
Consider
- what you know and can guess about Mary's past
- ways in which her past affects her present actions and attitudes
- whether she acts heroically

3. Would you eat the mushroom if you were in Mary's place? Explain your answer.

4. What can you understand about Pa from his actions and words?
Consider
- his comment "There ain't anything good left in the world, or people to care if you live or die"
- the fact that he eventually marries Mary

5. How well do you think the title "Too Soon a Woman" fits this story? Explain your opinion.

RELATE   6. How do the hardships and challenges that pioneers faced compare with the hardships people face today?

ANOTHER PATHWAY

Look back at the chart you made before reading "Too Soon a Woman." Add information on the problems the pioneers in this story faced. Use the chart to write a summary of the information you learned, then share your summary with other members of your class.

QUICKWRITES

1. Mary and the younger children face possible starvation. Write a **diary entry** that the narrator might have made at his darkest moment.

2. Pa asks Mary to become his wife and she accepts! Write a **wedding announcement** for the *Pioneer Times*.

📁 *PORTFOLIO Save your writing. You may want to use it later as a springboard to a piece for your portfolio.*

LITERARY CONCEPTS

The **theme** of a story is a message the writer presents to the reader. A theme might be a lesson about life or a belief about people and their actions. An author rarely states a theme directly; usually the reader must infer, or figure out, the theme after reading the story carefully. What might be the theme of this story? If you have difficulty figuring it out, think about the following:

- What does the title tell you? (See question 5 under "From Personal Response to Critical Analysis.")
- What does the main character learn?
- How does the main character change?

ACROSS THE CURRICULUM

Cooperative Learning Social Studies To find out more about what happened during the westward movement, read some diaries or other accounts written by settlers. Create a Readers Theater presentation of several of these accounts. For more information on Readers Theater, see page 38.

ALTERNATIVE ACTIVITIES

Imagine that you are a member of a pioneer family about to travel more than a thousand miles to a new homestead. You have a horse and a wagon, and you may bring 300 pounds of supplies with you. Work with a small group of classmates to compile a **list** of supplies you will need during the journey. To remind you of the hardships you may face on your trip, consult the charts that the group members made for the Personal Connection on page 93. When you finish, compare your group's list with the lists that other groups have made.

Supplies we will need:
-rope 10 lbs
-flour 5 lbs

LITERARY LINKS

Compare and contrast Mary with Nadia in "Nadia the Willful" (page 21). Would you describe Mary as willful? In what ways are the two characters similar? different?

EXERCISE A Write an answer to each of the following questions.

1. Is a person filled with **anxiety** confident, nervous, calm, or happy?

2. If you **savor** a memory, are you forgetting, understanding, enjoying, or denying it?

3. Is a **grudging** smile the same as or the opposite of a wholehearted one?

4. Would someone be more likely to walk **sedately** in church, in a soccer game, or on the way home from school?

5. Which is a synonym of **endure**—*believe, urge, tolerate,* or *blossom*?

EXERCISE B Imagine that you are a child in a pioneer family that has halted on its westward trek. Night is falling, and you are asked to gather kindling for the campfire. Use three of the vocabulary words to describe how you would go about your task.

DOROTHY M. JOHNSON

1905–1984

Dorothy M. Johnson was an award-winning writer of Western stories and an honorary member of Montana's Blackfoot tribe, who gave her the name Kills-Both-Places. In such books as *Warrior for a Lost Nation* (a biography of Sitting Bull) and *Buffalo Woman,* Johnson demonstrated her understanding of Native Americans. At various times a magazine editor, a news editor, and a professor of journalism, she wrote many stories and articles and more than 15 books.

OTHER WORKS *The Hanging Tree, The Man Who Shot Liberty Valance, A Man Called Horse*

FOCUS ON POETRY

Poetry is the most compact form of literature. In a poem all kinds of ideas, feelings, and sounds are packed into a few carefully chosen words. The look, sounds, and language of a poem all work together to create a total effect.

FORM The way a poem looks—its arrangement on the page—is its **form.** Poetry is written in **lines,** which may or may not be sentences. Sometimes the lines are divided into groups called **stanzas.** Remember that poets choose arrangements of words and lines deliberately. The form of a poem can add to its meaning.

SOUND Most poems are meant to be read aloud. Therefore, poets choose and arrange words to create the sounds they want listeners to hear. There are many techniques that poets can use to control the sounds of their poems. Three of these are described below.

Rhyme Words that end with the same sounds are said to rhyme. Many poems contain rhyming words at the ends of the lines. Look for the rhymes in these lines from "Life Doesn't Frighten Me" by Maya Angelou on page 111:

> Shadows on the wall
> Noises down the hall
> Life doesn't frighten me at all

Rhythm A poem's rhythm is sometimes called its beat. The rhythm is the pattern of stressed and unstressed syllables—the word parts that are read with more and less emphasis—in the poem's lines. Listen for the stressed (´) and unstressed (˘) syllables in these lines from "The Walrus and the Carpenter" on page 105:

> The sea was wet as wet could be,
> The sands were dry as dry.

Poems that do not have a regular rhythm—that sound more like conversation—are called free verse. "Another Mountain" on page 114 is an example of **free verse.**

Repetition A poet may choose to repeat sounds, words, phrases, or whole lines in a poem. Repetition helps the poet emphasize an idea or create a certain feeling.

IMAGERY Imagery involves words and phrases that appeal to the five senses. A poet may use imagery to create a picture in the reader's mind or to remind the reader of a familiar sensation. An example of imagery is contained in the opening lines of the poem "Street Corner Flight" by Norma Landa Flores on page 193:

From this side . . .
   of their concrete barrio
      two small boys hold
         fat white pigeons
   trapped in their trembling hands.

FIGURATIVE LANGUAGE

Poets use figurative language when they choose words and phrases that help readers see ordinary things in new ways. Such words and phrases are called **figures of speech.** Three figures of speech are explained below.

Simile A comparison that contains the word *like* or *as* is called a simile. The simile in these lines from "Barbara Frietchie" on page 342 compares the orchards around the town of Frederick to the garden of Eden:

> The clustered spires of Frederick stand
> Green-walled by the hills of Maryland.
> Round about them orchards sweep,

> Apple and peach trees fruited deep,
> Fair as the garden of the Lord
> To the eyes of the famished rebel horde ...

Metaphor A comparison that does not contain the word *like* or *as* is called a metaphor.

Personification When a poet describes an animal or object as if it were human or had human qualities, the poet is using personification. In "Primer Lesson" by Carl Sandburg on page 27, proud words are presented as if they had a will of their own:

> They wear long boots, hard boots; they
>   walk off proud; they can't hear you
>   calling—

THEME All the poetic elements you have read about help poets establish their poems' themes. Just as in fiction, a poem's theme is a message about life that it conveys.

STRATEGIES FOR READING POETRY

READING STRATEGIES

- **Preview the poem.** Notice the poem's form: what shape it has on the page, how long it is, how long its lines are, and whether the lines are divided into stanzas.

- **Read the poem aloud.** Pause at the end of each complete thought, not necessarily at the end of each line. Look for end punctuation to help you find where each thought ends. As you read, listen for rhymes and rhythm and for the overall sound of the words in the poem.

- **Visualize the images.** In your mind's eye, picture the images and comparisons you find in the poem. Do the images remind you of feelings or experiences you have had?

- **Think about the words and phrases.** Allow yourself to wonder about any phrases or words that seem to stand out. Think about what that

choice of those words adds to the poem.

- **Try to figure out the poem's theme.** Ask yourself, What's the point of this poem? What message is the poet trying to send or help me understand?

- **Let your understanding grow.** When you finish reading, you are left with first impressions of the poem. Over time, your rereadings of the poem, your discussions in class, and the other poetry you read will add to your understanding.

- **Allow yourself to enjoy the poem.** You may connect with the poem because it expresses feelings that you have felt or shows you the world through different eyes.

POETRY

The Walrus and the Carpenter
Lewis Carroll

PERSONAL CONNECTION

Have you ever been tricked into doing something? How were you fooled? In your notebook, write about this experience. Watch for who gets tricked in this poem and what happens as a result.

BIOGRAPHICAL CONNECTION

Lewis Carroll was the author of the famous fantasy novel *Alice's Adventures in Wonderland* and its sequel *Through the Looking Glass,* in which "The Walrus and the Carpenter" appears. In *Through the Looking Glass* everything seems backward or absurd. For example, Alice must walk away from a place in order to reach it and must run fast in order to remain where she is.

Carroll enjoyed tricks and puns and nonsense. He wrote the Alice tales to amuse a ten-year-old friend, Alice Liddell. In Carroll's day, English schoolchildren were often asked to memorize long, boring poems that were intended to teach proper morals and behavior. Carroll made fun of this practice in "The Walrus and the Carpenter."

READING CONNECTION

Understanding Narrative Poetry A poem that tells a story is called a narrative poem. Like works of prose fiction, narrative poems have characters, settings, plots, and sometimes dialogue. They also have many of the elements of poetry described on pages 102–103. "The Walrus and the Carpenter" is a narrative poem; it tells the story of a trick two characters play on some unfortunate young oysters. Read the poem as you would a story, pausing not at the end of each line but at the end of each sentence.

This illustration of Alice was created in 1865 by Sir John Tenniel, the first and most famous illustrator of *Alice's Adventures in Wonderland.*

The
Walrus
and the Carpenter

by Lewis Carroll

The sun was shining on the sea,
  Shining with all his might:
He did his very best to make
  The billows[1] smooth and bright—
5 And this was odd, because it was
    The middle of the night.

The moon was shining sulkily,[2]
  Because she thought the sun
Had got no business to be there
10 After the day was done—
"It's very rude of him," she said,
  "To come and spoil the fun!"

The sea was wet as wet could be,
  The sands were dry as dry.
15 You could not see a cloud because
    No cloud was in the sky:
No birds were flying overhead—
  There were no birds to fly.

The Walrus and the Carpenter
20 Were walking close at hand:
They wept like anything to see
  Such quantities of sand:
"If this were only cleared away,"
  They said, "it *would* be grand!"

25 "If seven maids with seven mops
    Swept it for half a year,
Do you suppose," the Walrus said,
  "That they could get it clear?"
"I doubt it," said the Carpenter,
30 And shed a bitter tear.

"O Oysters, come and walk with us!"
  The Walrus did beseech.
"A pleasant walk, a pleasant talk,
  Along the briny beach:
35 We cannot do with more than four,
    To give a hand to each."

---

1. **billows:** large waves.
2. **sulkily** (sŭl′kĭ-lē): in a gloomy, pouting way.

Illustration by Peter Newell, 1902. Photo © 1995 Nawrocki Stock Photo, Inc./Historical. All rights reserved.

The eldest Oyster looked at him,
      But never a word he said:
The eldest Oyster winked his eye,
40   And shook his heavy head—
Meaning to say he did not choose
      To leave the oyster-bed.

But four young Oysters hurried up,
      All eager for the treat:
45   Their coats were brushed, their faces washed,
      Their shoes were clean and neat—
And this was odd, because, you know,
      They hadn't any feet.

Four other Oysters followed them,
50   And yet another four;
And thick and fast they came at last,
      And more, and more, and more—
All hopping through the frothy waves,
      And scrambling to the shore.

55   The Walrus and the Carpenter
      Walked on a mile or so,
And then they rested on a rock
      Conveniently low:
And all the little Oysters stood
60   And waited in a row.

"The time has come," the Walrus said,
      "To talk of many things:
Of shoes—and ships—and sealing-wax—
      Of cabbages—and kings—
65   And why the sea is boiling hot—
      And whether pigs have wings."

"But wait a bit," the Oysters cried,
      "Before we have our chat;
For some of us are out of breath,
70   And all of us are fat!"
"No hurry!" said the Carpenter.
      They thanked him much for that.

"A loaf of bread," the Walrus said,
      "Is what we chiefly need:
75   Pepper and vinegar besides
      Are very good indeed—
Now, if you're ready, Oysters dear,
      We can begin to feed."

"But not on us!" the Oysters cried,
80   Turning a little blue.
"After such kindness, that would be
      A dismal³ thing to do!"
"The night is fine," the Walrus said.
      "Do you admire the view?

85   "It was so kind of you to come!
      And you are very nice!"
The Carpenter said nothing but
      "Cut us another slice.
I wish you were not quite so deaf—
90   I've had to ask you twice!"

"It seems a shame," the Walrus said,
      "To play them such a trick.
After we've brought them out so far,
      And made them trot so quick!"
95   The Carpenter said nothing but
      "The butter's spread too thick!"

"I weep for you," the Walrus said:
      "I deeply sympathize."
With sobs and tears he sorted out
100   Those of the largest size,
Holding his pocket-handkerchief
      Before his streaming eyes.

"O Oysters," said the Carpenter,
      "You've had a pleasant run!
105   Shall we be trotting home again?"
      But answer came there none—
And this was scarcely odd, because
      They'd eaten every one.

---

3. **dismal** (dĭz′məl): miserable; depressing.

RESPONDING
OPTIONS

FROM PERSONAL RESPONSE TO CRITICAL ANALYSIS

REFLECT　**1.** What was your reaction to this poem and to the trick that is played on the oysters?

RETHINK　**2.** The best-known lines in this poem are

> "The time has come," the Walrus said,
> "To talk of many things:
> Of shoes—and ships—and sealing wax—
> Of cabbages—and kings—"

Explain why you like (or dislike) these lines. Which other lines of the poem do you particularly enjoy?

3. The eldest oyster refuses the walrus's invitation, but the younger oysters accept it. Why?

4. Do you think that the poet intends for you to feel sorry for the oysters? Back up your opinion with evidence from the poem.

RELATE　**5.** Think of a time when you or your friends played a trick on someone, or when you had a trick played on you. What were the consequences?

ANOTHER PATHWAY

Make a sensory-image chart with the names of the five senses as headings. Under each heading, list appropriate images from the poem. Which of the senses is not referred to in the poem?

QUICKWRITES

1. Suppose that one of the oysters wants to avoid being eaten. Help the oyster by writing an eloquent **speech** that might persuade the walrus and the carpenter to spare him or her.

2. Make a **wanted poster** for the walrus and the carpenter so that they can be captured and punished for the crime they committed against the poor, pitiful oysters. Be sure to describe the two criminals thoroughly.

📁 *PORTFOLIO Save your writing. You may want to use it later as a springboard to a piece for your portfolio.*

LITERARY CONCEPTS

Rhyme is a repetition of the same sounds at the ends of words. Note the rhyme in these lines from Henry Wadsworth Longfellow's poem "Paul Revere's Ride":

> Listen, my children, and you shall *hear*
> Of the midnight ride of Paul Re*vere* ...

Rhythm is the pattern of strong beats you hear when you read a poem aloud. Some poems have an even, regular beat that produces a musical sound. In other poems, the rhythm sounds more like conversation. Read "The Walrus and the Carpenter" aloud, then use adjectives to describe its rhymes and its rhythm.

ALTERNATIVE ACTIVITIES

1. **Cooperative Learning** With a group of classmates, prepare an **oral reading** of this poem. Decide on proper tones of voice for the narrator and each of the characters. Emphasize the rhymes and rhythm of the poem and observe all punctuation marks.

2. Imagine that you have been asked to illustrate a new edition of "The Walrus and the Carpenter." Rewrite the poem on a large sheet of paper, and draw or paint **illustrations** for it. Try to reveal the humor of the poem.

THE WRITER'S STYLE

Line 106 of this poem is "But answer came there none—." Have you ever heard anyone speak this way? When people speak, they usually say the subject before the verb. Poets, however, sometimes reverse, or invert, the usual order of words to emphasize a particular word or phrase or to preserve a poem's rhymes and rhythm. Rewrite line 106 in subject-verb order. Then find other inverted lines in the poem. Why do you think Carroll might have written inverted lines in this poem?

ACROSS THE CURRICULUM

Science You know that, despite the descriptions in this poem, real oysters don't have coats, faces, or feet. But what else do you know about oysters? Why are they called bivalves? How are they different from clams? Exchange information about oysters with a small group of classmates. Then look up oysters in a print or CD-ROM encyclopedia or in some other reference work. Share your information with the class in an oral report.

oyster

clam

LEWIS CARROLL

"Lewis Carroll" was the pen name of Charles Lutwidge Dodgson, an English mathematician. The eldest son in a family of 13, Dodgson was a creative child who made pets of snails and worms and invented games for his brothers and sisters. Although brilliant, Carroll was shy and stammered in the presence of adults. In the company of children, however, he became a witty, affectionate storyteller.

1832–1898

Carroll would send children letters barely the size of a postage stamp or ones written in reverse to be read in a mirror. He might begin a letter with "CLD [his initials], Uncle loving your," and end it with "Nelly dear my." In one of his letters, he wrote what some say is the core of his belief: "One of the deep secrets of life . . . is that all this is really worth the doing, is what we do for others."

Some say Carroll never grew up. Perhaps he didn't. Upon his death at the age of 65, the doctor attending him told his sisters, "How wonderfully young your brother looks!"

OTHER WORKS *Alice's Adventures in Wonderland, Through the Looking Glass*

POETRY

Life Doesn't Frighten Me

Maya Angelou
(mī′ə ăn′jə-lō′)

Another Mountain

Abiodun Oyewole
(ä′bē-ō-dōōn′ ō′yä-wō′lā)

PERSONAL CONNECTION

Think about a time when you tried to overcome one of your fears. If you succeeded, what qualities helped you succeed? If you didn't succeed, what qualities caused you to fail?

LITERARY CONNECTION

In a poem, the **speaker** is the voice that talks to the reader. The speakers of the two poems you are about to read face different kinds of fears and challenges. The poems therefore have slightly different tones. **Tone** is determined by the attitude a writer, in this case a poet, has toward his or her subject. The tone of a poem might be humorous, serious, angry, or sentimental. In these poems, the writers reveal their attitudes through their choice of words and through repetition of certain words and phrases.

WRITING CONNECTION

In a chart like the one shown here, list the qualities that a person needs in order to face life's fears and challenges. As you read the poems, decide whether the speakers have these qualities.

Qualities	Speaker of "Life Doesn't Frighten Me"	Speaker of "Another Mountain"

LASERLINKS
• LITERARY CONNECTION

Life

Doesn't
Frighten Me

by Maya Angelou

Shadows on the wall
Noises down the hall
Life doesn't frighten me at all
Bad dogs barking loud
5   Big ghosts in a cloud
Life doesn't frighten me at all.

Mean old Mother Goose
Lions on the loose
They don't frighten me at all
10   Dragons breathing flame
On my counterpane[1]
That doesn't frighten me at all,

I go boo
Make them shoo
15   I make fun
Way they run
I won't cry
So they fly
I just smile
20   They go wild
Life doesn't frighten me at all.

---

1. **counterpane** (koun'tər-pān'): bedspread.

Tough guys in a fight
All alone at night
Life doesn't frighten me at all.

25 Panthers in the park
Strangers in the dark
No, they don't frighten me at all.

That new classroom where
Boys all pull my hair
30 (Kissy little girls
With their hair in curls)
They don't frighten me at all.

Don't show me frogs and snakes
And listen for my scream,
35 If I'm afraid at all
It's only in my dreams.

I've got a magic charm
That I keep up my sleeve,
I can walk the ocean floor
40 And never have to breathe.

Life doesn't frighten me at all
Not at all
Not at all.
Life doesn't frighten me at all.

Boy and Dog in a Johnnypump (1982), Jean-Michel Basquiat. Galerie Bischofberger, Zurich, Switzerland.
Copyright © 1995 Artists Rights Society, New York/ADAGP, Paris.

FROM **PERSONAL RESPONSE** *TO* **CRITICAL ANALYSIS**

REFLECT

1. What are your impressions of the speaker of this poem? Describe your impressions in your notebook or on a sheet of paper.

RETHINK

2. Do the speaker's methods of taking charge seem effective to you? Why or why not?

3. Do you think the speaker is as fearless as she says she is? Explain your ideas.
Consider
- your feelings about overcoming fear
- the tone of the poem

4. How do the qualities shown by the speaker compare with the qualities you have shown in facing your own fears?

My Front Yard, Summer (1941), Georgia O'Keeffe.
© 1996 The Georgia O'Keeffe Foundation/Artists Rights
Society, New York. Photo by Malcolm Varon,
New York, © 1994.

Another MOUNTAIN

by Abiodun Oyewole

Sometimes there's a mountain
that I must climb
even after I've climbed one already
But my legs are tired now
5   and my arms need a rest
my mind is too weary right now
But I must climb before the storm comes
before the earth rocks
and an avalanche of clouds buries me
10 and smothers my soul
And so I prepare myself for another climb
Another Mountain
and I tell myself it is nothing
it is just some more dirt and stone
15 and every now and then I should reach
another plateau and enjoy the view
of the trees and the flowers below
And I am young enough to climb
and strong enough to make it to any top
20 You see the wind has warned me
about settling too long
about peace without struggle
The wind has warned me
and taught me how to fly
25 But my wings only work
After I've climbed a mountain

RESPONDING
OPTIONS

FROM PERSONAL RESPONSE TO CRITICAL ANALYSIS

REFLECT 1. What is your image of the mountain described in "Another Mountain"? In your notebook, draw a picture of the mountain.

RETHINK 2. What might the last two lines, "But my wings only work / After I've climbed a mountain," mean?

3. What comparison does the speaker make throughout the poem? Is it an effective comparison? Why or why not?

RELATE 4. Which of these two poems do you think has more to say about how a person should respond to the fears and challenges of life? Explain your choice.

ANOTHER PATHWAY

Work with a partner, each of you preparing one of these poems for a dramatic reading for your class. Before you make your presentations, practice reciting the poems for each other. Speak slowly and keep your words clear and distinct.

LITERARY CONCEPTS

Poetry with no regular pattern of rhyme, rhythm, or line length is called **free verse.** Free verse often sounds like conversation. Writing free verse allows a poet to emphasize or concentrate on images and ideas rather than rhymes. Read "Another Mountain" aloud as naturally as possible. Do you think free verse is a good way of presenting the ideas in the poem? Why or why not?

CONCEPT REVIEW: Rhyme As you know, words that end with the same sounds are said to rhyme. Poems often contain rhyming words at the ends of lines. How do the rhymes in "Life Doesn't Frighten Me" add to your enjoyment of the poem?

QUICKWRITES

1. Imagine that each year a Try, Try Again Award is presented to individuals who show determination. Write an **award nomination** for the speaker of "Another Mountain."

Try, Try Again Award
presented with honor to

2. Suppose you are asked to contribute to a magazine article about how young people deal with fears and challenges. Write a short **profile** of the speaker of "Life Doesn't Frighten Me."

PORTFOLIO Save your writing. You may want to use it later as a springboard to a piece for your portfolio.

THE WRITER'S STYLE

Reread "Another Mountain," paying attention to the lack of punctuation and the unusual use of capital letters. Does the poet's style help or hinder your understanding of the ideas in the poem? Rewrite several lines, adding standard capitalization and punctuation. How do the changes alter the effect of the poem?

CRITIC'S CORNER

Someone once said that Maya Angelou's poetry "strives to make us more aware of what each of us can endure, fail at, and still survive." How might this statement apply to the speaker of "Life Doesn't Frighten Me"?

MAYA ANGELOU

1928–

The life of Maya Angelou reflects her belief that "all things are possible for a human being, and I don't think there's anything in the world I can't do." Angelou grew up in the racially divided town of Stamps, Arkansas, with her brother and her grandmother. In 1940, she moved away from home and finished high school. Over the next three decades, Angelou worked at various times as a dancer, a singer, a composer, a stage and screen performer, a playwright, a poet, an editor, and a teacher.

I Know Why the Caged Bird Sings, her first autobiographical work, earned a National Book Award nomination in 1970. Angelou is best known for this book and has continued her life story in several other books. A collection of her poems received a Pulitzer Prize nomination in 1972. In 1993, she accepted an invitation to read an original poem at President Clinton's inauguration.

OTHER WORKS *Singin' and Swingin' and Gettin' Merry Like Christmas, And Still I Rise, The Complete Collected Poems of Maya Angelou*

ABIODUN OYEWOLE

The poetry of Abiodun Oyewole reflects the poet's deep commitment to young people, his sensitivity to the cultural heritage of African Americans, and his love of life. When asked what advice he would give young people about the challenges or fears they might encounter, he responds, "I'd say that every cloud has a silver lining, which sounds like a cliché but works as a rule. I do live by that."

Born in Cincinnati, Ohio, Oyewole has lived most of his life in New York City. During the 1960s, he was a member of a group of New York street poets called the Last Poets. Today, he works as a creative-writing consultant for the New York City Public Schools. He has also created plays and songs and has led a jazz group called Griot (named for a type of African storyteller).

NONFICTION

from Woodsong

Gary Paulsen

PERSONAL CONNECTION

The selection you are about to read is about someone who lives in the wilderness in Minnesota. Wild animals, such as bears, are a part of this writer's everyday experience. With a small group of classmates, discuss what you know about animals in the wild. Make a web like the one shown here. Use the suggested topics in the smaller circles as discussion starters.

Behavior

How They Act Toward People

WILD ANIMALS

Reactions When Frightened or Angry

Personal Experiences

GEOGRAPHICAL CONNECTION

Thick forests once covered 70 percent of Minnesota. Today forests cover only about 35 percent of the state. Minnesota's most spectacular woods can be found in the 3-million-acre Superior National Forest, north of Lake Superior. The northern and northeastern sections of the state are the most rugged, with thousands of square miles of unbroken wilderness. In this region, people are scarce but wild animals are plentiful. One of the few states where timber wolves still roam free, Minnesota is also home to white-tailed deer, beavers, moose, and black bears.

Minnesota Population Density Map

Number of persons per square kilometer

Number of persons per square mile

More than 40	More than 100
20 to 40	50 to 100
10 to 20	25 to 50
Less than 10	Less than 25

READING CONNECTION

Making Predictions In both fiction and nonfiction, it is possible to find clues that will help you predict what is going to happen next. In this account of wilderness life, you will be reading about interactions between human beings and animals. To make predictions as you read, think about the facts in the selection and about what you already know. Decide where the events are leading, and predict the next logical step. To help you practice this reading strategy, questions have been inserted at two points in the selection. When you come to a question, pause and jot down your prediction in your reading log. Then read on to see what happens. Check your predictions after you finish the selection.

FROM WOOD SONG

Wabana-Wagamuman [Bear in the forest] (1989), Tom Uttech. Oil on canvas, courtesy of Struve Gallery, Chicago.

BY GARY PAULSEN

In Woodsong *Gary Paulsen describes his life as a trapper in the woods of northern Minnesota. He lived with his wife, Ruth, and his son, James, in a small cabin that did not have plumbing or electricity. At the time, Paulsen was not writing stories but simply learning the ways of the woods. This episode describes one of the lessons he learned.*

We have bear trouble. Because we feed processed meat to the dogs, there is always the smell of meat over the kennel. In the summer it can be a bit high[1] because the dogs like to "save" their food sometimes for a day or two or four—burying it to dig up later. We live on the edge of wilderness, and consequently the meat smell brings any number of visitors from the woods.

Skunks abound, and foxes and coyotes and wolves and weasels—all predators. We once had an eagle live over the kennel for more than a week, scavenging from the dogs, and a crazy group of ravens has pretty much taken over the puppy pen. Ravens are protected by the state, and they seem to know it. When I walk toward the puppy pen with the buckets of meat, it's a tossup to see who gets it—the pups or the birds. They have actually pecked the puppies away from the food pans until they have gone through and taken what they want.

Spring, when the bears come, is the worst. They have been in hibernation through the winter, and they are hungry beyond caution. The meat smell draws them like flies, and we frequently have two or three around the kennel at the same time. Typically they do not bother us much—although my wife had a bear chase her from the garden to the house one morning— but they do bother the dogs.

---

1. **it can be a bit high:** the smell can be rather strong.

WORDS TO KNOW	**predator** (prĕd'ə-tər) *n.* an animal that hunts other animals for food
	scavenging (skăv'ən-jĭng) *adj.* searching for discarded scraps **scavenge** *v.*

They are so big and strong that the dogs fear them, and the bears trade on this fear to get their food. It's common to see them scare a dog into his house and take his food. Twice we have had dogs killed by rough bear swats that broke their necks—and the bears took their food.

We have evolved[2] an uneasy peace with them, but there is the problem of familiarity. The first time you see a bear in the kennel it is a novelty, but when the same ones are there day after day, you wind up naming some of them (old Notch-Ear, Billy-Jo, etc.). There gets to be a too-relaxed attitude. We started to treat them like pets.

A major mistake.

PREDICT

What mistake do you think the narrator makes?

There was a large male around the kennel for a week or so. He had a white streak across his head, which I guessed was a wound scar from some hunter—bear hunting is allowed here. He wasn't all that bad, so we didn't mind him. He would frighten the dogs and take their hidden stashes now and then, but he didn't harm them, and we became accustomed to him hanging around. We called him Scarhead, and now and again we would joke about him as if he were one of the yard animals.

At this time we had three cats, forty-two dogs, fifteen or twenty chickens, eight ducks, nineteen large white geese, a few banty hens, ten fryers which we'd raised from chicks and couldn't (as my wife put it) "snuff and eat," and six woods-wise goats.

The bears, strangely, didn't bother any of the yard animals. There must have been a rule, or some order to the way they lived, because they would hit the kennel and steal from the dogs but leave the chickens and goats and other yard stock completely alone—although you would have had a hard time convincing the goats of this fact. The goats spent a great deal of time with their back hair up, whuffing and blowing snot at the bears—and at the dogs, who would *gladly* have eaten them. The goats never really believed in the truce.

There is not a dump or landfill to take our trash to, and so we separate it—organic, inorganic[3]—and deal with it ourselves. We burn the paper in a screened enclosure, and it is fairly efficient; but it's impossible to get all the food particles off wrapping paper, so when it's burned, the food particles burn with it.

And give off a burnt food smell.

And nothing draws bears like burning food. It must be that they have learned to understand human dumps—where they spend a great deal of time foraging. And they learn amazingly fast. In Alaska, for instance, the bears already know that the sound of a moose hunter's hunt means there will be a fresh gut pile when the hunter cleans the moose. They come at a run when they hear the shot. It's often a close race to see if the hunter will get to the moose before the bears take it away. . . .

Because we're on the south edge of the wilderness area, we try to wait until there is a northerly breeze before we burn, so the food smell will carry south, but it doesn't always help. Sometimes bears, wolves, and other predators are already south, working the sheep farms down where it is more settled—they take a terrible toll[4] of sheep—and we catch them on the way back through.

---

2. **evolved** (ĭ-vŏlvd′): developed by a series of small changes.

3. **organic** (ôr-găn′ĭk), **inorganic** (ĭn′ôr-găn′ĭk): on the one hand, things made of plant or animal material; and on the other, things made of material that has never been alive.

4. **take a terrible toll:** destroy a large number.

WORDS TO KNOW   **novelty** (nŏv′əl-tē) *n.* something new and unusual

That's what happened one July morning.

Scarhead had been gone for two or three days, and the breeze was right, so I went to burn the trash. I fired it off and went back into the house for a moment—not more than two minutes. When I came back out, Scarhead was in the burn area. His tracks (directly through the tomatoes in the garden) showed he'd come from the south.

He was having a grand time. The fire didn't bother him. He was trying to reach a paw in around the edges of flame to get at whatever smelled so good. He had torn things apart quite a bit—ripped one side off the burn enclosure—and I was having a bad day, and it made me mad.

I was standing across the burning fire from him, and without thinking—because I was so used to him—I picked up a stick, threw it at him, and yelled, "Get out of here."

I have made many mistakes in my life, and will probably make many more, but I hope never to throw a stick at a bear again.

In one rolling motion—the muscles seemed to move within the skin so fast that I couldn't take half a breath—he turned and came for me. Close. I could smell his breath and see the red around the sides of his eyes. Close on me he stopped and raised on his back legs and hung over me, his forelegs and paws hanging down, weaving back and forth gently as he took his time and decided whether or not to tear my head off.

I could not move, would not have time to react. I knew I had nothing to say about it. One blow would break my neck. Whether I lived or died depended on him, on his thinking, on his ideas about me—whether I was worth the bother or not.

I did not think then.

Looking back on it, I don't remember having one coherent[5] thought when it was happening. All I knew was terrible menace. His eyes looked very small as he studied me. He looked down on me for what seemed hours. I did not move, did not breathe, did not think or do anything.

And he lowered.

Perhaps I was not worth the trouble. He lowered slowly and turned back to the trash, and I walked backward halfway to the house and then ran—anger growing now—and took the rifle from the gun rack by the door and came back out.

He was still there, rummaging through the trash. I worked the bolt and fed a cartridge in and aimed at the place where you kill bears and began to squeeze. In raw anger, I began to take up the four pounds of pull necessary to send death into him.

And stopped.

Kill him for what?

That thought crept in.

Kill him for what?

For not killing me? For letting me know it is wrong to throw sticks at four-hundred-pound bears? For not hurting me, for not killing me, I should kill him? I lowered the rifle and ejected the shell and put the gun away. I hope Scarhead is still alive. For what he taught me, I hope he lives long and is very happy, because I learned then—looking up at him while he made up his mind whether or not to end me— that when it is all boiled down, I am nothing more and nothing less than any other animal in the woods. ❖

> **PREDICT**
>
> What will the narrator do next?

---

5. **coherent** (kō-hîr′ənt): clear; logical.

WORDS TO KNOW	**menace** (mĕn′ĭs) *n.* a possible danger; threat **rummaging** (rŭm′ĭ-jĭng) *adj.* searching thoroughly **rummage** *v.*

121

RESPONDING
OPTIONS

FROM PERSONAL RESPONSE TO CRITICAL ANALYSIS

REFLECT 1. Write three words that describe this selection. Compare your words with those of a classmate.

RETHINK 2. What kind of person is Gary Paulsen?
Consider
- his observations about the animals around the kennel
- his feelings and actions toward the bear
- his comments about himself and about the lesson he learned

3. Look at the predictions you made for the Reading Connection on page 117. What did you think would happen when Paulsen faced Scarhead with his rifle? How accurate was your prediction?

4. How did reading Paulsen's account affect your impressions of living in the wilderness and of animals in the wild?

RELATE 5. Animals such as deer, skunks, woodchucks, rats, and pigeons often cause problems for humans. Discuss some unwanted-wildlife problems that you know about. What might be done to solve these problems?

ANOTHER PATHWAY

Cooperative Learning
This selection ends with Paulsen saying, "I am nothing more and nothing less than any other animal in the woods." Debate the truth of this statement with a group of classmates.

QUICKWRITES

1. Think over Paulsen's experiences, as well as any wilderness experiences of your own. Create a **poem** that describes the risks a person runs in the wilderness.

2. Rewrite the trash-burning **scene** from the bear's point of view. Use details from the story and your own imagination to describe what Scarhead thinks and feels during his encounter with Paulsen.

📁 *PORTFOLIO Save your writing. You may want to use it later as a springboard to a piece for your portfolio.*

LITERARY CONCEPTS

An **autobiography** is a writer's account of his or her own life. It is almost always told from a first-person point of view, with the pronouns *I, we, me,* and *us.* Because an autobiography is written about a real person and real events, it is a form of nonfiction. An autobiography can provide information only the writer knows. From reading this selection, what do you learn about Paulsen that you might not have learned if someone else had told his story?

ACROSS THE CURRICULUM

Science Skim the selection and list all the details Gary Paulsen includes about bears. Then do research to find out more about the biological family called *Ursidae*. Does Scarhead demonstrate typical bear behavior? Is Paulsen's portrayal accurate? Record your information either on paper or as a computer document. Make it available in a reference file that you and others can use.

WORDS TO KNOW

EXERCISE A On your paper, write the letter of the phrase that best completes each sentence below.

1. A **predator** usually eats (a) grass and fruits (b) vegetables (c) other animals.

2. You would most likely find bears **scavenging** in (a) a garbage pile (b) a stream (c) a cave.

3. An animal that is a **menace** to humans is (a) dangerous (b) harmless (c) helpful.

4. A polar bear would be a **novelty** in (a) Alaska (b) a zoo (c) Africa.

5. If a bear were **rummaging** through your campsite, it would (a) make a mess (b) only circle your campfire (c) leave no trace of its presence.

EXERCISE B Copy and fill in the chart below to analyze the word *predator*. Do the same with *menace* or *novelty*.

Definition of *Predator*	Examples of Predators	Use of *Predator* in Selection	Synonym of *Predator*

GARY PAULSEN

Besides being a writer, Gary Paulsen has been a soldier, an animal trapper, and a rancher. As a trapper for the state of Minnesota, Paulsen was given four sled dogs to help him with his work. The time he spent with the dogs convinced him that he could no longer kill animals. His experiences motivated him to write *Woodsong* and the novels *Dogsong* and *Hatchet*, Newbery Honor Books. In 1990, his novel *The Winter Room* was also a Newbery Honor Book.

Because Paulsen's father was an army officer, his family moved frequently when he was a young boy. "School was a nightmare because I was unbelievably shy, and terrible at sports," he recalls. Paulsen was

1939–

introduced to books by a friendly librarian who gave him his first library card. "She didn't care if I looked right, wore the right clothes, dated the right girls, was popular at sports—none of those prejudices existed in the public library." Paulsen read everything "as though I had been dying of thirst and the librarian had handed me a five-gallon bucket of water. I drank and drank."

As a writer, he has satisfied both young and adult readers, publishing more than 40 books, 200 articles, and 2 plays.

OTHER WORKS *Dogteam, Winterdance: The Fine Madness of Running the Iditarod, Tracker, The Cookcamp, The Island, Sisters/Hermanas*

LASERLINKS
• *SCIENCE CONNECTION*

PREVIEWING

FICTION

The Dog of Pompeii
Louis Untermeyer

PERSONAL CONNECTION

Has a destructive natural force—such as a brushfire, a tornado, or a flood—ever affected your community? Think about natural disasters you have experienced or heard about. How did people respond to the emergencies? How did people survive? Share memories and reflections with other members of your class. Then, as you read this story, compare those experiences with the experiences of the citizens of Pompeii when Vesuvius erupts.

HISTORICAL CONNECTION

In A.D. 79, the volcanic mountain Vesuvius suddenly erupted. It poured tons of burning lava and ashes over the countryside and buried Pompeii, a nearby city, under 12 to 15 feet of ash and cinders. In 1748, a peasant digging in a vineyard in southern Italy struck a buried wall. The excavations that followed uncovered Pompeii. The remains of the city, well preserved by the ashes, present a clear picture of what life was like in the ancient Roman Empire. We now know how people dressed, how children were taught, and even how foods were prepared.

Pompeii and Mount Vesuvius

ITALY

Naples

Vesuvius

Pompeii

Venice

Florence

ITALY

Adriatic Sea

Rome

Vesuvius

Naples

Pompeii

Tyrrhenian Sea

Mediterranean Sea

Miles

0   5   10

READING CONNECTION

Reading Historical Fiction Writing in which a particular period of history is brought to life through an author's imagination is called historical fiction. The author usually blends factual information about the time, the place, and historical persons with imaginary characters, dialogue, and plot developments. From such writing you learn not only facts and figures about historical events but also the feelings people may have had about the events, as in this story about the eruption of Mount Vesuvius.

LASERLINKS
- *HISTORICAL CONNECTION*
- *VISUAL VOCABULARY*

THE DOG OF POMPEII

by Louis Untermeyer

T ito and his dog Bimbo lived (if you could call it living) under the wall where it joined the inner gate. They really didn't live there; they just slept there. They lived anywhere. Pompeii was one of the gayest of the old Latin towns, but although Tito was never an unhappy boy, he was not exactly a merry one. The streets were always lively with shining chariots and bright red trappings; the open-air

Cave Canem [Beware of dog], Roman Mosaic. Museo Archeologico Nazionale, Naples, Italy. Scala/Art Resource, New York.

theaters rocked with laughing crowds; sham battles and athletic sports were free for the asking in the great stadium. Once a year the Caesar[1] visited the pleasure city, and the fireworks lasted for days; the sacrifices[2] in the forum were better than a show. But Tito saw none of these things. He was blind—had been blind from birth. He was known to everyone in the poorer quarters. But no one could say how old he was; no one remembered his parents; no one could tell where he came from. Bimbo was another mystery. As long as people could remember seeing Tito—about twelve or thirteen years—they had seen Bimbo. Bimbo had never left his side. He was not only dog but nurse, pillow, playmate, mother, and father to Tito.

Did I say Bimbo never left his master? (Perhaps I had better say comrade, for if anyone was the master, it was Bimbo.) I was wrong. Bimbo did trust Tito alone exactly three times a day. It was a fixed routine, a custom understood between boy and dog since the beginning of their friendship, and the way it worked was this: Early in the morning, shortly after dawn, while Tito was still dreaming, Bimbo would disappear. When Tito woke, Bimbo would be sitting quietly at his side, his ears cocked, his stump of a tail tapping the ground, and a fresh-baked bread—more like a large round roll—at his feet. Tito would stretch himself; Bimbo would yawn; then they would breakfast. At noon, no matter where they happened to be, Bimbo would put his paw on Tito's knee, and the two of them would return to the inner gate. Tito would curl up in the corner (almost like a dog) and go to sleep, while Bimbo, looking quite important (almost

THE RE WAS PLENTY OF EVERYTHING IN POMPEII IF YOU KNEW WHERE TO FIND IT—AND IF YOU HAD A DOG LIKE BIMBO.

like a boy), would disappear again. In half an hour he'd be back with their lunch. Sometimes it would be a piece of fruit or a scrap of meat; often it was nothing but a dry crust. But sometimes there would be one of those flat, rich cakes, sprinkled with raisins and sugar, that Tito liked so much. At suppertime the same thing happened, although there was a little less of everything, for things were hard to snatch in the evening with the streets full of people. Besides, Bimbo didn't approve of too much food before going to sleep. A heavy supper made boys too restless and dogs too stodgy—and it was the business of a dog to sleep lightly with one ear open and muscles ready for action.

But whether there was much or little, hot or cold, fresh or dry, food was always there. Tito never asked where it came from, and Bimbo never told him. There was plenty of rainwater in the hollows of soft stones; the old egg-woman at the corner sometimes gave him a cupful of strong goat's milk; in the grape season the fat winemaker let him have drippings of the mild juice. So there was no danger of going hungry or thirsty. There was plenty of everything in Pompeii if you knew where to find it—and if you had a dog like Bimbo.

As I said before, Tito was not the merriest boy in Pompeii. He could not romp with the other youngsters and play hare and hounds and I spy and follow-your-master and ball-against-the-building and

---

1. **the Caesar** (sē′zər): the Roman emperor.
2. **sacrifices**: offerings of animals or objects to the gods.

jackstones and kings and robbers with them. But that did not make him sorry for himself. If he could not see the sights that delighted the lads of Pompeii, he could hear and smell things they never noticed. He could really see more with his ears and nose than they could with their eyes. When he and Bimbo went out walking, he knew just where they were going and exactly what was happening.

"Ah," he'd sniff and say as they passed a handsome villa, "Glaucus Pansa is giving a grand dinner tonight. They're going to have three kinds of bread, and roast pigling, and stuffed goose, and a great stew—I think bear stew—and a fig pie." And Bimbo would note that this would be a good place to visit tomorrow.

Or, "H'm," Tito would murmur, half through his lips, half through his nostrils. "The wife of Marcus Lucretius is expecting her

The Sorceress and the Traveler. Mosaic from Pompeii, House of the Dioscuri. Museo Archeologico Nazionale, Naples, Italy. Scala/Art Resource New York.

mother. She's shaking out every piece of goods in the house; she's going to use the best clothes—the ones she's been keeping in pine needles and camphor[3]—and there's an extra girl in the kitchen. Come, Bimbo, let's get out of the dust!"

Or, as they passed a small but elegant dwelling opposite the public baths, "Too bad! The tragic poet is ill again. It must be a bad fever this time, for they're trying smoke fumes instead of medicine. Whew! I'm glad I'm not a tragic poet!"

Or, as they neared the forum, "Mm-m! What good things they have in the macellum today!" (It really was a sort of butcher-grocer-marketplace, but Tito didn't know any better. He called it the macellum.) "Dates from Africa, and salt oysters from sea caves, and cuttlefish, and new honey, and sweet onions, and—ugh!—water-buffalo steaks. Come, let's see what's what in the forum." And Bimbo, just as curious as his comrade, hurried on. Being a dog, he trusted his ears and nose (like Tito) more than his eyes. And so the two of them entered the center of Pompeii.

The forum was the part of the town to which everybody came at least once during each day. It was the central square, and everything happened here. There were no private houses; all was public—the chief temples, the gold and red bazaars, the silk shops, the town hall, the booths belonging to the weavers and jewel merchants, the wealthy woolen market, the shrine of the household gods. Everything glittered here. The buildings looked as if they were new—which, in a sense, they were. The earthquake of twelve years ago had brought down all the old structures, and

since the citizens of Pompeii were ambitious to rival Naples and even Rome, they had seized the opportunity to rebuild the whole town. And they had done it all within a dozen years. There was scarcely a building that was older than Tito.

Tito had heard a great deal about the earthquake, though being about a year old at the time, he could scarcely remember it. This particular quake had been a light one—as earthquakes go. The weaker houses had been shaken down; parts of the outworn wall had been wrecked; but there was little loss of life, and the brilliant new Pompeii had taken the place of the old. No one knew what caused these earthquakes. Records showed they had happened in the neighborhood since the beginning of time. Sailors said that it was to teach the lazy city folk a lesson and make them appreciate those who risked the dangers of the sea to bring them luxuries and protect their town from invaders. The priests said that the gods took this way of showing their anger to those who refused to worship properly and who failed to bring enough sacrifices to the altars and (though they didn't say it in so many words) presents to the priests. The tradesmen said that the foreign merchants had corrupted the ground and it was no longer safe to traffic in imported goods that came from strange places and carried a curse with them. Everyone had a different explanation—and everyone's explanation was louder and sillier than his neighbor's.

They were talking about it this afternoon as Tito and Bimbo came out of the side street into the public square. The forum was the

---

3. **camphor** (kăm′fər): a strong-smelling substance used as a moth repellent.

favorite promenade[4] for rich and poor. What with the priests arguing with the politicians, servants doing the day's shopping, tradesmen crying their wares, women displaying the latest fashions from Greece and Egypt, children playing hide-and-seek among the marble columns, knots of soldiers, sailors, peasants from the provinces[5]—to say nothing of those who merely came to lounge and look on—the square was crowded to its last inch. His ears even more than his nose guided Tito to the place where the talk was loudest. It was in front of the shrine of the household gods that, naturally enough, the householders were arguing.

"I tell you," rumbled a voice which Tito recognized as bath master Rufus's, "there won't be another earthquake in my lifetime or yours. There may be a tremble or two, but earthquakes, like lightnings, never strike twice in the same place."

"Do they not?" asked a thin voice Tito had never heard. It had a high, sharp ring to it, and Tito knew it as the accent of a stranger. "How about the two towns of Sicily that have been ruined three times within fifteen years by the <u>eruptions</u> of Mount Etna? And were they not warned? And does that column of smoke above Vesuvius mean nothing?"

"That?" Tito could hear the grunt with which one question answered another. "That's always there. We use it for our weather guide. When the smoke stands up straight, we know we'll have fair weather; when it flattens out, it's sure to be foggy; when it drifts to the east—"

IT WAS THE CENTRAL SQUARE, AND EVERYTHING HAPPENED HERE. . . . EVERYTHING GLITTERED HERE.

"Yes, yes," cut in the edged voice. "I've heard about your mountain barometer. But the column of smoke seems hundreds of feet higher than usual, and it's thickening and spreading like a shadowy tree. They say in Naples—"

"Oh, Naples!" Tito knew this voice by the little squeak that went with it. It was Attilio, the cameo[6] cutter. "*They* talk while we suffer. Little help we got from them last time. Naples commits the crimes, and Pompeii pays the price. It's become a proverb with us. Let them mind their own business."

"Yes," grumbled Rufus, "and others, too."

"Very well, my confident friends," responded the thin voice, which now sounded curiously flat. "We also have a proverb—and it is this: Those who will not listen to men must be taught by the gods. I say no more. But I leave a last warning. Remember the holy ones. Look to your temples. And when the smoke tree above Vesuvius grows to the shape of an umbrella pine, look to your lives."

Tito could hear the air whistle as the speaker drew his toga about him, and the quick shuffle of feet told him the stranger had gone.

---

4. **promenade** (prŏm´ə-nād´): a public place for leisurely walking.

5. **provinces**: areas of a country that are far from the capital.

6. **cameo** (kăm´ē-ō´): a gem or shell with a picture carved on it.

"Now what," said the cameo cutter, "did he mean by that?"

"I wonder," grunted Rufus. "I wonder."

Tito wondered, too. And Bimbo, his head at a thoughtful angle, looked as if he had been doing a heavy piece of pondering. By nightfall the argument had been forgotten. If the smoke had increased, no one saw it in the dark. Besides, it was Caesar's birthday, and the town was in holiday mood. Tito and Bimbo were among the merrymakers, dodging the charioteers who shouted at them. A dozen times they almost upset baskets of sweets and jars of Vesuvian wine, said to be as fiery as the streams inside the volcano, and a dozen times they were cursed and cuffed. But Tito never missed his footing. He was thankful for his keen ears and quick instinct—most thankful of all for Bimbo.

They visited the uncovered theater, and though Tito could not see the faces of the actors, he could follow the play better than most of the audience, for their attention wandered—they were distracted by the scenery, the costumes, the by-play, even by themselves—while Tito's whole attention was centered in what he heard. Then to the city walls, where the people of Pompeii watched a mock naval battle in which the city was attacked by the sea and saved after thousands of flaming arrows had been exchanged and countless colored torches had been burned. Though the thrill of flaring ships and lighted skies was lost to Tito, the shouts and cheers excited him as much as any, and he cried out with the loudest of them.

The next morning there were *two* of the beloved raisin and sugar cakes for his breakfast. Bimbo was unusually active and thumped his bit of a tail until Tito was afraid he would wear it out. The boy could not imagine whether Bimbo was urging him to some sort of game or was trying to tell him something. After a while, he ceased to notice Bimbo. He felt drowsy. Last night's late hours had tired him. Besides, there was a heavy mist in the air—no, a thick fog rather than a mist— a fog that got into his throat and scraped it and made him cough. He walked as far as the marine gate[7] to get a breath of the sea. But the blanket of haze had spread all over the bay, and even the salt air seemed smoky.

He went to bed before dusk and slept. But he did not sleep well. He had too many dreams—dreams of ships lurching in the forum, of losing his way in a screaming crowd, of armies marching across his chest, of being pulled over every rough pavement of Pompeii.

He woke early. Or, rather, he was pulled awake. Bimbo was doing the pulling. The dog had dragged Tito to his feet and was urging the boy along. Somewhere. Where, Tito did not know. His feet stumbled uncertainly; he was still half asleep. For a while he noticed nothing except the fact that it was hard to breathe. The air was hot. And heavy. So heavy that he could taste it. The air, it seemed, had turned to powder, a warm powder that stung his nostrils and burned his sightless eyes.

Then he began to hear sounds. Peculiar sounds. Like animals under the earth. Hissings and groanings and muffled cries that a dying

> THE NOISES CAME FROM UNDERNEATH. HE NOT ONLY HEARD THEM—HE COULD FEEL THEM.

---

7. **marine gate:** a gate in the city wall, leading to the sea.

Mount Vesuvius in Eruption (1817), Joseph Mallord William Turner, R.A., 1775–1851. Yale Center for British Art, New Haven, Connecticut, Paul Mellon Collection.

creature might make <u>dislodging</u> the stones of his underground cave. There was no doubt of it now. The noises came from underneath. He not only heard them—he could feel them. The earth twitched; the twitching changed to an uneven shrugging of the soil. Then, as Bimbo half pulled, half coaxed him across, the ground jerked away from his feet and he was thrown against a stone fountain.

The water—hot water—splashing in his face revived him. He got to his feet, Bimbo steadying him, helping him on again. The noises grew louder; they came closer. The cries were even more animal-like than before, but now they came from human throats. A few people, quicker of foot and more hurried by fear, began to rush by. A family or two—then a section—then, it seemed, an army broken out of bounds. Tito, bewildered though he was, could recognize Rufus as he bellowed past him, like a water buffalo gone mad. Time was lost in a nightmare.

It was then the crashing began. First a sharp crackling, like a monstrous snapping of twigs; then a roar like the fall of a whole forest of trees; then an explosion that tore earth and

The volcanic ash that covered victims of the Pompeii disaster hardened over time. Archaeologists used the resulting "shells" as molds for body casts.© Krafft/Explorer, Photo Researchers.

sky. The heavens, though Tito could not see them, were shot through with continual flickerings of fire. Lightnings above were answered by thunders beneath. A house fell. Then another. By a miracle the two companions had escaped the dangerous side streets and were in a more open space. It was the forum. They rested here awhile—how long he did not know.

Tito had no idea of the time of day. He could *feel* it was black—an unnatural blackness. Something inside—perhaps the lack of breakfast and lunch—told him it was past noon. But it didn't matter. Nothing seemed to matter. He was getting drowsy, too drowsy to walk. But walk he must. He knew it. And Bimbo knew it; the sharp tugs told him so. Nor was it a moment too soon. The sacred

ground of the forum was safe no longer. It was beginning to rock, then to pitch, then to split. As they stumbled out of the square, the earth wriggled like a caught snake, and all the columns of the temple of Jupiter[8] came down. It was the end of the world—or so it seemed.

To walk was not enough now. They must run. Tito was too frightened to know what to do or where to go. He had lost all sense of direction. He started to go back to the inner gate; but Bimbo, straining his back to the last inch, almost pulled his clothes from him. What did the creature want? Had the dog gone mad?

Then, suddenly, he understood. Bimbo was telling him the way out—urging him there.

8. **Jupiter:** the supreme god in Roman mythology.

The sea gate, of course. The sea gate—and then the sea. Far from falling buildings, heaving ground. He turned, Bimbo guiding him across open pits and dangerous pools of bubbling mud, away from buildings that had caught fire and were dropping their burning beams. Tito could no longer tell whether the noises were made by the shrieking sky or the agonized people. He and Bimbo ran on—the only silent beings in a howling world.

New dangers threatened. All Pompeii seemed to be thronging toward the marine gate; and, squeezing among the crowds, there was the chance of being trampled to death. But the chance had to be taken. It was growing harder and harder to breathe. What air there was choked him. It was all dust now —dust and pebbles, pebbles as large as beans. They fell on his head, his hands— pumice[9] stones from the black heart of Vesuvius. The mountain was turning itself inside out. Tito remembered a phrase that the stranger had said in the forum two days ago: "Those who will not listen to men must be taught by the gods." The people of Pompeii had refused to heed the warnings; they were being taught now—if it was not too late.

Suddenly it seemed too late for Tito. The red hot ashes blistered his skin; the stinging vapors tore his throat. He could not go on. He staggered toward a small tree at the side of the road and fell. In a moment Bimbo was beside him. He coaxed. But there was no answer. He

> ALL POMPEII SEEMED TO BE THRONGING TOWARD THE MARINE GATE . . . . THERE WAS THE CHANCE OF BEING TRAMPLED TO DEATH.

licked Tito's hands, his feet, his face. The boy did not stir. Then Bimbo did the last thing he could—the last thing he wanted to do. He bit his comrade, bit him deep in the arm. With a cry of pain, Tito jumped to his feet, Bimbo after him. Tito was in despair, but Bimbo was determined. He drove the boy on, snapping at his heels, worrying his way through the crowd; barking, baring his teeth, heedless of kicks or falling stones. Sick with hunger, half dead with fear and sulphur[10] fumes, Tito pounded on, pursued by Bimbo. How long he never knew. At last he staggered through the marine gate and felt soft sand under him. Then Tito fainted. . . .

Someone was dashing seawater over him. Someone was carrying him toward a boat.

"Bimbo," he called. And then louder, "Bimbo!" But Bimbo had disappeared.

Voices jarred against each other. "Hurry— hurry!" "To the boats!" "Can't you see the child's frightened and starving!" "He keeps calling for someone!" "Poor boy, he's out of his mind." "Here, child—take this!"

They tucked him in among them. The oarlocks creaked; the oars splashed; the boat rode over toppling waves. Tito was safe. But he wept continually.

"Bimbo!" he wailed. "Bimbo! Bimbo!"

He could not be comforted.

---

9. **pumice** (pŭm´ĭs): a light rock formed from lava

10. **sulphur** (sŭl´fər): a pale yellow chemical element that produces a choking fume when burned

WORDS
TO
KNOW

vapor (vā´pər) *n.* fumes, mist, or smoke

Petrified bread from Pompeii.
Museo Archeologico Nazionale,
Naples, Italy. Alinari/Art
Resource, New York

Eighteen hundred years passed. Scientists were <u>restoring</u> the ancient city; excavators were working their way through the stones and trash that had buried the entire town. Much had already been brought to light—statues, bronze instruments, bright mosaics,[11] household articles; even delicate paintings had been preserved by the fall of ashes that had taken over two thousand lives. Columns were dug up, and the forum was beginning to emerge.

It was at a place where the ruins lay deepest that the director paused.

"Come here," he called to his assistant. "I think we've discovered the remains of a building in good shape. Here are four huge millstones that were most likely turned by slaves or mules—and here is a whole wall standing with shelves inside it. Why! It must have been a bakery. And here's a curious thing. What do you think I found under this heap where the ashes were thickest? The skeleton of a dog!"

"Amazing!" gasped his assistant. "You'd think a dog would have had sense enough to run away at the time. And what is that flat thing he's holding between his teeth? It can't be a stone."

"No. It must have come from this bakery. You know it looks to me like some sort of cake hardened with the years. And, bless me, if those little black pebbles aren't raisins. A raisin cake almost two thousand years old! I wonder what made him want it at such a moment."

"I wonder," murmured the assistant. ❖

---

11. **mosaics** (mō-zā′ĭks): pictures or designs made by setting small colored stones or tiles into surfaces

WORDS
TO
KNOW   **restore** (rĭ-stôr′) v. to bring back to an original condition

RESPONDING
OPTIONS

FROM **PERSONAL RESPONSE** *TO* **CRITICAL ANALYSIS**

REFLECT
1. How did you feel after reading this story? Share your thoughts with another student.

RETHINK
2. Do you think Bimbo is a realistic character? Defend your answer with evidence from the story.
   Consider
   - Bimbo's role in Tito's everyday life
   - how Bimbo responds to the volcanic eruption

3. What do you think Louis Untermeyer's purpose was in ending the story of the Pompeii disaster 1800 years later?

4. What did you learn about Vesuvius and Pompeii that you didn't know before? What would you like to learn more about?

RELATE
5. Compare the Pompeii citizens' response to the earthquake with responses to similar events that you have experienced or heard about.

ANOTHER PATHWAY

Cooperative Learning

With a group of classmates, use the information in the story to create and act out a scene about some citizens of Pompeii who are trapped in the disaster. End the scene with a tableau—a moment in which all the performers freeze in position.

QUICKWRITES

1. Write an **account** of the final day in Pompeii from Tito's point of view, using only his sensory impressions of hearing, tasting, smelling, and feeling.

2. Naples and Pompeii lie on opposite sides of a large bay. Imagine that you are safely in Naples on the day Vesuvius erupts in A.D. 79. Write an **eyewitness account** of what you see happening to Pompeii.

📁 *PORTFOLIO Save your writing. You may want to use it later as a springboard to a piece for your portfolio.*

LITERARY CONCEPTS

A **conflict** is a struggle between opposing forces. There are two main kinds of conflicts in stories: external and internal. An **external conflict** is a struggle between a character and an outside force, such as another character or nature. For example, in the excerpt from *Woodsong*, Gary Paulsen faces an external conflict with a bear. What is the external conflict faced by Tito and Bimbo in "The Dog of Pompeii"?

CONCEPT REVIEW: Setting This story's setting—the time and place in which the events occur—plays an important role in the story. What words or phrases helped you to visualize ancient Pompeii clearly?

ART CONNECTION

In ancient Rome, mosaics like the one of the dog on page 125 often depicted scenes of daily life. Using small pieces of colored paper, design a mosaic that illustrates a scene from the story.

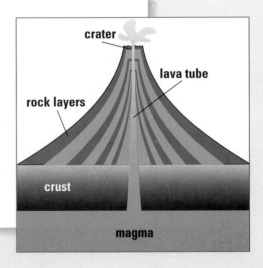

EXERCISE A Identify each pair of words as synonyms or antonyms. On your paper, write *S* for *Synonyms* or *A* for *Antonyms*.

1. vapor—fume

2. restore—destroy

3. eruption—outbreak

4. shrine—temple

5. dislodging—replacing

EXERCISE B For one of the vocabulary words, create a picture that communicates the word's meaning.

LOUIS UNTERMEYER

1885–1977

As a boy, Louis Untermeyer disliked school but read constantly. He created bedtime stories for his brother Martin, later recalling, "Fantasy was the most important part of my boyhood—at least it is the only part I remember. My soul . . . was far away, sailing the blue Vesuvian bay. . . ."

While working successfully in the jewelry business for more than 20 years, Untermeyer spent much of his free time writing poems. After publishing a book of poems, he had difficulty seeing himself as anything other than a poet. He made the decision to devote all his time to writing.

Untermeyer earned a name for himself as a poet, critic, and novelist. He is best known, however, as a collector and editor of major poetry collections, many of which have been used to teach the art of poetry. He produced 56 collections and is credited with introducing the works of Robert Frost to a large audience. For about 25 years, Louis Untermeyer served as chairman of the Pulitzer Prize Poetry Jury.

OTHER WORKS *The Magic Circle: Stories and People in Poetry, The Wonderful Adventures of Paul Bunyan, The World's Great Stories: Fifty-Five Legends That Live Forever, The Donkey of God, Cat o' Nine Tales, The Paths of Poetry: Twenty-Five Poets and Their Poems*

WRITING FROM EXPERIENCE

WRITING A NARRATIVE

In Unit One, "Running Risks," you have read about characters who take chances and risk getting punished, embarrassed, or hurt. Reading these stories may have taught you something about handling tough situations and the kind of risks worth taking. Some may have even helped you see the humor in difficult experiences.

GUIDED ASSIGNMENT

Write an Anecdote Do you have a story about someone who took a risk, solved a problem, or survived an embarrassing moment? You can share it by telling an anecdote, which is a very short story. In the next few pages, you will learn how to write an anecdote based on something that happened to you or someone you know.

① Find a Reason to Write

Your life is full of anecdotes. They are the funny experiences you tell friends and the stories you hear around the lunch table.

Helping Friends Perhaps you have a friend who is going through a hard time or trying to make a difficult decision. Can you help your friend by telling a true story?

Examining Your Life Think about times you have taken risks or had interesting or funny experiences. You might find ideas in your journal entries, letters, or photo albums. List any incidents you think other people might enjoy hearing about.

Making Connections People often clip cartoons and articles to share with friends who might appreciate or benefit from them. Look at the examples on these pages. What stories do they remind you of? Add these ideas to your list.

Comic Strip
What happened to Hobbes? How does he feel about Calvin's ideas?

Calvin and Hobbes
by Bill Watterson

What's Really Behind Your *Fears?*

Chart from a Magazine

Fear of Rejection

- Wanting to dress like everybody else
- Avoiding school dances
- Uncomfortable about meeting new people
- Uncomfortable giving speeches in class
- Being sick on test day

Fear of Failure

- Won't try out for school play

Fear of New Experiences

- Don't want to move
- Won't try new foods
- Won't ride in an airplane
- Uncomfortable in an elevator

Fear of Accidents

- Don't like roller coasters

This reminds me of when I was nervous about going to Dan McAvene's party!

Letter from a Friend

Remember to write to Natalie!!

Hi Rosa,

Guess what ... My mom told me I could go to Camp Heywood this year for summer camp. The only thing is, I'm not sure I want to go now that you've moved away and can't go with me. My brother, Paul, says I'd be crazy not to go. They have a huge lake that you can swim in every day, and the horses are a blast to ride. He said that he had a great time when he went (five years ago) and that there would be lots of kids my age to hang out with. That's sort of the problem, though. I just feel nervous around people I don't really know. It wouldn't be so bad if you were there with me, but I don't think I want to go there alone. So what are you gonna do this summer? Wish you could visit! Write back soon!

Natalie

② Talk to Others

Now that you have a list of possible ideas to write about, you might talk to friends or family members to get their thoughts. Which stories do they think are the most interesting? Does anything they say give you a new idea?

LASERLINKS
- *WRITING SPRINGBOARD*

WRITING COACH

Planning Your Anecdote

Zeroing In on the Story You now have a list of ideas for an anecdote. The steps below will help you choose one idea and write about it.

1 Choose a Story

Look at the ideas you wrote down, and think about each incident. Would it be interesting to people? What would they get out of it? Choose the event that will make the best story.

2 Focus on Your Purpose

What is the main point of your anecdote? Write down what you think is most important about the event. It might be a funny thing that happened, a lesson you've learned, or an important realization about yourself or someone else.

3 Gather Details

Try to remember the details of your experience and your feelings at the time. Who was there? What were people wearing? Was there special music playing? Was the weather important?

Student's Ideas

- Joining the baseball team though I had never played before; became friends with Maria
- The costume party where I fooled everybody
- Being the only girl invited to Dan McAvene's birthday party
- Climbing to the top of the Blue Ridge Mountains last summer on vacation
- The time I told Bubba to stop picking on Tanya

4 Tell Your Story Aloud

You might practice telling your anecdote to some friends before you write it down. They may have questions about details that are important to the story. As you tell your anecdote, notice what makes your friends laugh or what surprises them. You might take notes on their reactions, as one student did in the example below.

Student's Story Notes

> <u>Things I learned when I told my story to Phil</u>
>
> • He didn't get why I went to the party if I didn't feel well. (Explain that Mom made me.)
> • He thought the part about Dan's mom was boring, but it's really important so I have to think of a way to liven it up.
> • He asked me what I got Dan for a gift. (not really important to include)

5 Think About the Parts of an Anecdote

Anecdotes have certain features in common.

- They are brief and keep to the point by including only important details and events.
- Most start with a lively description, a curious fact, or the point the writer wants to illustrate.
- Characters are developed quickly yet thoroughly.
- A humorous anecdote usually ends with a punch line. In an anecdote that is meant to be helpful, the ending may repeat the message.

With these things in mind, think about how you will begin and end your anecdote and what details you will include. The SkillBuilder offers tips for organizing your story idea.

SkillBuilder

 CRITICAL THINKING

Ordering and Representing Information

Many writers find it helpful to sketch a plan before they start writing. A story map can help keep you focused on the important parts of your story. You might start by stating the point of your anecdote.

Point: to show that sometimes it's worth trying things that seem scary

⬇

I was nervous about going to Dan's all-boy party.

⬇

I decided to go, but when I got there, I felt out of place.

⬇

I talked to Dan's mom.

⬇

She thought up a fun game for everyone.

THINK & PLAN

Reflecting on Your Ideas

1. Did your friends react to your anecdote the way you wanted? How might you change it to get the reaction you want?
2. Do you still think readers will enjoy your story? Why or why not?

Writing It All Down

Shaping Your Anecdote Once you have completed your story map or list of events, you can start to write your anecdote. You may write it all out from beginning to end or start with the scene you like best. Different methods work for different people. Just let your ideas flow!

1 Write a Rough Draft

Don't worry about making your anecdote look or sound perfect right away; you can fix it later. For now, just get your ideas written down. Include details as they come to you. (See the SkillBuilder for tips on using details.)

Student's Rough Draft

I didn't know of any other girls who were invited

In second grade, Dan McAvene invited me to his birthday party. *When I was* He was cute. I liked him, but I was scared to go. Mostly girls didn't go to boys' birthday parties. But I got him a present, I said I would go. Then I got scared to go. I got a stomachache but my mom said I had to go anyway. She never used to let me get out of stuff like that.

My mom dropped me off at his house. I was so scared, I did not want to ring the doorbell, but I did anyway. I was shaking as I rang it. *not important* I was wearing my lucky tennis shoes. Dan answered the door, and I was afraid he'd say, what are you doing here? But he let me in. We both said hi and I wished him a happy birthday.

I walked into the dining room, and saw all the boys in my class and not one girl. I put my present on the table and sat down. I felt pretty dumb. Even though I could talk to these boys in class I felt weird when there were no other girls around.

I'm rambling here, but I should keep the part about the stomachache.

Will readers get my point? Maybe I should tell them what it is up front.

Maybe we could put our anecdotes into a class booklet.

I could add dialogue here to help show how uncomfortable I felt.

② Play with Language

The way your anecdote will sound depends on who your audience is. Think about how your language might change if you used your anecdote in the following ways:

- in a letter to a close friend
- to make a point at the beginning of a speech
- as an example within a news article
- to reveal something about a character in a story

You might experiment by writing a paragraph of your anecdote in a few different ways. The example below shows how one student reworked her first paragraph for a different audience.

Student's Second Version

> You think what you did took guts? Did I ever tell you about the time in second grade when Dan McAvene invited me to his birthday party? He was such a babe! I had this feeling I was the only girl he invited, but I told him I'd go. Of course, on the day of the party I was soooo nervous I got a stomachache. And you <u>know</u> my mom wouldn't let me get out of going!

 PEER RESPONSE

Do you think your story is just about ready? Only a reader can tell you for sure. Ask a friend to read your draft, then have him or her answer questions like the following:

- Did the beginning of my anecdote grab your attention? If not, what could I do to make it more interesting?
- Do I have enough details? Are there unimportant details I should get rid of?
- What did you think of the punch line or message? How could I improve the ending?
- What was your favorite part? What made you laugh or made you think?

Polishing Your Anecdote

Putting On the Finishing Touches You have the details and events of your anecdote on paper. Now it's time to make sure that your writing is clean and your story well told. The guidelines on these pages will help you finish your anecdote.

1 Revise and Edit

When you work on a story for a long time, it may be hard for you to see it clearly. Try taking a break and coming back to your anecdote when you can look at it with a fresh eye.

- Review the notes you wrote after telling your story to a friend. Do you think your written version is as enjoyable as the one you told your friend aloud?
- Use the Standards for Evaluation and the Editing Checklist to be sure you have used relevant details and kept the verb tense consistent.
- See how one student revised her writing for a class booklet of anecdotes.

Student's Final Draft

What point is the writer making by telling this anecdote?

What other details might the writer have included to show how uncomfortable she was?

Facing My Fears

I think it's good to face the things that make you nervous. Sometimes things aren't as bad as you thought they would be. When I was in second grade, I was invited to an all-boys birthday party. I didn't like the idea of being the only girl, but I liked Dan and said I would go. On the day of the party I got a stomachache because I was so nervous. My mom told me I had to go anyway.

I was shaking when she dropped me off. Dan answered the doorbell and said, "Hi. Come on in," as if I was just another guy. I swallowed hard and told him "Happy Birthday." He led me into the dining room, where I saw all the boys in my class. I took a deep breath, put my present on the table, and sat down.

I still felt a little weird, even after we ate the cake—but Dan's mom had an idea. We all went outside for a game. Suddenly, something landed on my head and I was all wet. A water balloon fight had started! At first I almost ran out of the yard, but then I stopped. I took a deep breath, grabbed a balloon, and threw it at Dan as hard as I could. All the boys grinned and cheered, even Dan.

1. Dan invited me to his party. I like him, so I said I would go.

2. Then I was nervous because I would be the only girl there.

3. Mom made me go anyway. I was shaking when Dan answered the door.

4. I felt strange being the only girl there, but Dan's mother had a plan.

Student's Comic Strip

❷ Share Your Work

If you publish your anecdote for a different reader, how might you change the form? The student who wrote the sample anecdote told her younger sister her story, using a comic strip. Part of it is shown above. She made the writing simpler and used pictures to get her message across. Why would this format be best for a very young reader?

What other forms might work well with the story you chose to tell? Consider sharing your anecdote, using one or more of the ideas presented in this lesson.

Standards for Evaluation

An anecdote
- is brief and includes only the important details
- has a beginning that grabs readers' attention or states the point the story will make
- develops the characters quickly yet thoroughly
- ends with a punch line or a message

SkillBuilder

G → GRAMMAR FROM WRITING

Using Consistent Verb Tense
Read the following sentence. What problem do you see?

I gave him the bat and he walks up to the plate.

Gave is past tense, but *walks* is present tense. Anecdotes are usually told in the past tense. Be sure your verbs are all in the same tense so that your readers will not be confused.

📙 GRAMMAR HANDBOOK

For more help with verb tense, see pages 835 of the Grammar Handbook.

Editing Checklist Use the following questions to help you revise your draft.

- Are my sentences complete?
- Is the verb tense consistent?
- Have I punctuated dialogue correctly?

REFLECT & ASSESS

Evaluating the Experience

1. How did writing about the experience help you to understand the event better?
2. Why is an anecdote a good way to make a point?

   🗁 **PORTFOLIO** What other ideas do you have for anecdotes? Include them in your portfolio.

REFLECT & ASSESS

UNIT ONE: RUNNING RISKS

In this unit, characters run risks by speaking out, by facing unexpected challenges, and by struggling with the forces of nature. What did their experiences teach you? What kinds of adventures do you enjoy as a reader and a writer? Explore these questions by completing one or more of the options in each of the following sections.

REFLECTING ON THEME

OPTION 1 **Comparing the Daring** Many of the characters in Unit One, "Running Risks," react to dangerous situations. Which five characters or real-life people in the selections do you think were especially daring? Rank them in order, from 1 (the most daring) to 5 (the least daring). Write a brief speech to nominate your number one choice for a medal, giving reasons why he or she deserves it.

OPTION 2 **Freeze!** With two classmates, choose a risky moment from a selection to act out in tableau. Pantomime briefly to establish the scene. Then freeze in position at the most exciting part of the action. Join other groups in a presentation of tableaus. Afterwards, discuss how reading about these moments has affected the way you would handle risky situations in the future.

OPTION 3 **Moving Thoughts** Work with a partner to make a mobile of words or phrases that describe the risk takers in this unit. First, brainstorm the personal traits common to those people. Then write the traits on shapes of colored paper. Use the shapes, as well as pictures you draw, to make the mobile.

Self-Assessment: After thinking about the risks taken in the selections, what do you think is the best way to deal with a risky situation? In your notebook, write a few paragraphs about what you have learned. Support your ideas by referring to specific selections or individuals in the unit.

REVIEWING LITERARY CONCEPTS

OPTION 1 **Thinking About Setting** The events described in this unit occur in different time periods and in places all over the world. Make a "setting dial" like the one shown. With a partner, take turns rotating the top circle to match a selection's title with its setting, and discuss how the setting affected the action of that selection. Which setting presented individuals with the most exciting risks? Which settings were presented with details that seemed to put you in the middle of the selections' action? Then move the circle to mix the titles and settings. Discuss how the selections' events or outcome might be different in the new settings.

1. Cut two circles from paper, making one slightly smaller than the other.

2. Along the rim of the larger circle, write the titles of the selections.

"Nadia the Willful"

Sahara

North Pole

Pompeii in A.D. 79

American Frontier

3. Divide the inner circle into sections. Write in the selections' settings.

4. Connect the circles with a brad or fastener.

OPTION 2 **Looking at Character** Recall that the most important characters in stories are called main characters and that less important characters are called minor characters. Make "character webs" for four of this unit's selections. In each, show the main character surrounded by three minor characters. (Part of a web for "Ghost of the Lagoon" is shown here.) Then, with a group of classmates, discuss the relationships between the characters. How do the decisions that the main characters make affect their relationships with minor characters?

Main Character
Mako

Afa

Self-Assessment: This unit introduced a number of other literary concepts. Copy the following terms in your notebook. Beside each term, draw a plus sign [+] to show you understand the term or a minus sign [-] to show that you need more information. Then check the terms you want to understand better in the Handbook of Reading Terms and Literary Concepts on page 762.

author's purpose	*biography*	*plot*
	conflict	*rhythm*
autobiography	*free verse*	*theme*

PORTFOLIO BUILDING

- **QuickWrites** Was it easy or difficult for you to do the QuickWrites assignments that asked you to write as characters would? From your responses to those assignments, pick the two that you think are best. Explain in a short cover note why you think you did so well. Add your responses and the note to your portfolio.

- **Writing About Literature** You recently had the chance to write a personal response to a story. Imagine that the author of the story has asked you to suggest ways of changing it. Would you add a new character? Would you make the ending different? Attach a description of your suggested changes to the personal response you wrote.

- **Writing from Experience** When you wrote your anecdote, you described an interesting experience that you had. If you were to have the same experience again, would you do anything differently? How might you change your actions? Include your thoughts with your anecdote if you choose to keep it in your portfolio.

- **Personal Choice** Begin an "oral log" of your reactions to your work. Look back through your work for the Personal Connections, the Writing Connections, and the Another Pathway assign-

ments, as well as the evaluations of all the other projects you completed in this unit. As you do so, dictate your comments into a tape recorder. (If you don't have one, you can simply write your comments on paper). Also comment on any projects and writing you have done on your own. Tell what you think you've done successfully and what you would redo if you could. Add the audiotape (or the written comments) to your portfolio.

Self-Assessment: At this point, it's probably easy for you to review the pieces in your portfolio. Do so briefly. What kinds of writing or activities do you want to do again soon? Make a note to yourself.

SETTING GOALS

While completing the reading and writing activities in this unit, you probably spotted areas you need to develop. Look back through your portfolio, worksheets, and notebook. Think about what you'd like to explore further in your reading and writing for the next unit. Then copy and complete these statements:
I'd like to read more selections that _____.
I'd like to write more _____.

The Need to Belong

A place belongs

forever to whomever

claims it hardest.

JOAN DIDION
American writer

Swinger in Summer Shade (1981), Maud
Gatewood. Acrylic on canvas, 60" × 72",
courtesy of Somerhill Gallery, Chapel Hill,
North Carolina.

FINDING A SPECIAL PLACE

WHAT DO YOU THINK?

REFLECTING ON THEME

Is a special place a specific spot? Or can a special place simply be a sense of belonging—being part of something that matters to you? Use the activities on this page to examine what it means to have a special place. As you read the selections in Part 1, watch for similarities between you and the characters.

How do you see your special place?

Draw or paint a picture of your special place. Present your artwork with the work of other classmates in a bulletin-board display.

Who affects your sense of belonging?

Think of one person—a close friend or a relative—who provides you with a feeling of belonging. Use this diagram to compare and contrast your qualities. Where the circles overlap, write the qualities that you share. In the larger sections, write the qualities that are unique to each of you.

How about this sticky situation?

Imagine you're in a shopping mall when a person runs up and happily throws his or her arms around you. You don't recognize the face—but the person obviously knows you. With a partner, create brief skits showing ways you could handle the situation.

What makes you *you*?

What words do people use to describe you? How would you describe yourself? In your notebook, copy the scales shown, and mark each horizontal line with an **X** to indicate where you think your personality falls. What kind of picture does this give you of yourself?

Dreamy ———————— Practical
Follower ———————— Leader
Cautious ———————— Adventurous
Quiet ———————— Outspoken

FICTION

The Adoption of Albert
Barbara Robinson

PERSONAL CONNECTION

The story you are about to read involves events that take place as part of a family reunion. Have you ever attended a family reunion? If so, describe in your notebook the family reunion and your attitude toward it. If not, describe what you imagine a family reunion would be like.

CULTURAL CONNECTION

Maintaining communication in families is not easy, especially when family members live far apart. A growing number of families plan extended family reunions to keep in touch and create new memories. According to Edith Wagner, editor of *Reunions* magazine, as many as 200,000 families plan reunions each year. "It used to be so simple because everyone lived close by," says Wagner. "Now it's a job to get a family together."

READING CONNECTION

Using a Reading Log The reading strategies introduced on page 5 and summarized in the chart shown here are based on the kinds of connections active readers make when they read. You can use your Reading Log to help you practice these strategies as you sort through the sequence of events in this story. As you read, record your questions and ideas about characters and events in the story. Also record any new thoughts you may have about family reunions. After you finish reading, discuss your questions and thoughts with your classmates.

Reading Log Strategies	
Questioning	Ask questions about the events and characters in the story.
Connecting	Think of similarities between events in the story and your own experiences.
Predicting	Predict what might happen next and how the story might end.
Clarifying	Stop at times for a quick review of what you understand so far.
Evaluating	Form opinions about the story.

The Adoption of Albert

by Barbara Robinson

There were so many children in our neighborhood that my mother was never surprised to find unfamiliar ones in the house, or in the backyard, or in my room, or in Louis's room.

"Well, who's this?" she would say, and she would then go on to connect that child with whatever house or family he belonged to.

But when Louis showed up with his new friend Albert, Mother had other things on her mind: the family <u>reunion</u>, which was two days away; the distant cousin who would be staying at our house; most of all, my Aunt Rhoda's famous Family Reunion cake, which, in Aunt Rhoda's absence, Mother felt obliged to provide.

Aunt Rhoda's absence, and the reason for it, were both first-time events: She had never before missed a family reunion, and neither she nor anyone else had ever before been called into court to testify about anything. Aunt Rhoda was to testify about an

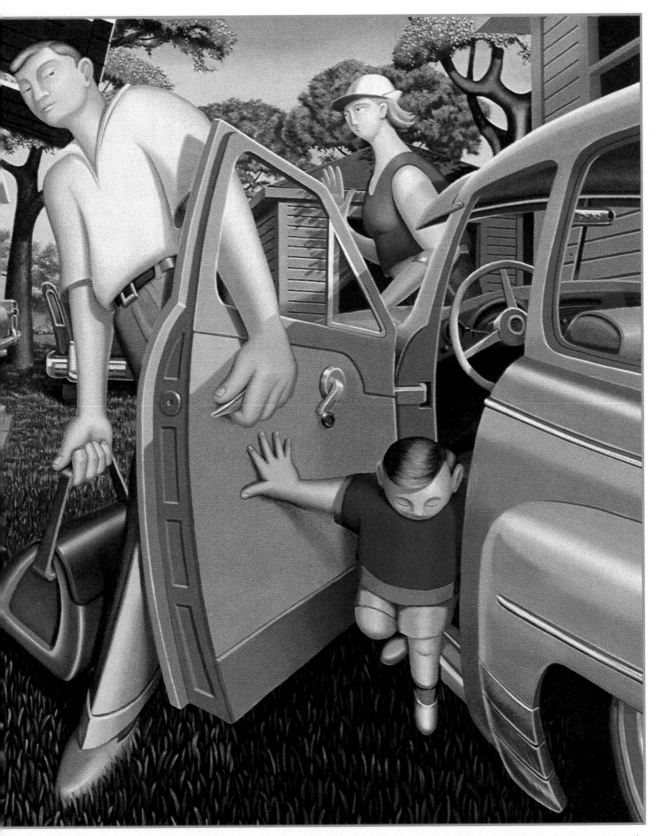

Long Weekend (1990), Brian Jones. Courtesy Nancy Poole's Studio, Toronto, Canada.

automobile accident she had witnessed—the only automobile accident in local memory, my father said, that did not involve Aunt Mildred.

All in all, it was a complicated time for Mother—cake, cousins, company—and when Louis appeared at the kitchen door and said, "This is Albert," she was too distracted to ask her usual questions.

> **"The tail ends grow new heads, and the head ends grow new tails."**

Nor did she ask them at suppertime. By then she was up to her elbows in cake batter and left the three of us to eat alone with my father, who also didn't know Albert, but assumed that everyone else did.

I didn't know Albert either, but there was no reason I should. He was Louis's friend, he was Louis's age, he even looked a lot like Louis—small and quiet and solemn—and it didn't occur to me to find out any more about him. I did ask, "Where do you live, Albert?"; and when he said, "Here," I just thought he meant here in the neighborhood instead of someplace else.

Mother thought the same thing. "Where does that little boy live?" she asked me the next morning, and I said, "Here," and she said, "I wonder which house?"

Albert had spent the night, and there was a note propped against the cereal box: *Albert and I have gone to dig worms.*

Louis had been collecting worms all summer and measuring them to see how long a worm

got to be before it died. "I think that's what kills them," he said. "I think they die of length."

So far his longest worm was between four inches and four and a half inches. All his worms were between one size and another because they wouldn't hold still. "It's really hard," he said. "I have to stretch them out and measure them at the same time, and if I'm not careful they come apart."

"Oh, Louis," I said, "that's awful! What do you do then?"

He shrugged. "I bury the pieces. What else can I do?"

Of course, most kids wouldn't even do that, but Louis was neater than most kids.

It was late afternoon when he and Albert came back, and they had big news. They also had two coffee cans full of worm parts.

"I thought you buried them," I said.

"I didn't have to! Albert says . . . Albert says . . ." I had never seen Louis so pleased and excited. "Tell her what you said."

"It doesn't kill them," Albert said. "The tail ends grow new heads, and the head ends grow new tails."

I looked in the coffee cans, but I couldn't tell the difference between head and tails. Louis said he couldn't tell the difference either. "But it doesn't matter," he said, "because the worms can. *They* know. We're going to keep them, and watch them grow, and measure them . . . and maybe name them."

"They're no trouble," Albert said. "They just eat dirt. We've got some." He held up another coffee can.

They took all three coffee cans up to Louis's room, and this worried me a lot because I knew I would have to sleep in Louis's room when everybody came for the family reunion.

My father said he was always astonished

that there was anybody left to *come* to the family reunion. "Your whole family is already here," he told Mother, "living around the corner, or three streets away, or on the other side of town."

"Not everybody," Mother said. "There's Virginia and Evelyn and Clyde . . ." She reeled off the names—cousins, mostly, whom we knew only from Christmas cards, and from their annual appearance at the reunion.

Some, in fact, had already appeared and were upstairs unpacking their suitcases. Mother, who was busy catching up on their news and shuffling food around in the refrigerator and getting out all the dishes and silverware, either didn't realize that Albert was still with us or just didn't remember that she had ever seen him in the first place.

My father had gone off to borrow picnic tables for the next day, and since I didn't want to sit around and watch worms grow, I went next door to play with my friend Maxine Slocum and forgot all about Albert.

That night when I took my sleeping bag into Louis's room, he was already asleep in a mound of bedclothes . . . and there was another mound of bedclothes beside him.

"Louis." I shook him awake. "Who is that?"

"It's Albert," he said.

"Why doesn't he go home?"

Louis looked surprised. "He *is* home. He's going to live here now. Remember? He told you. . . . Don't worry, Mary Elizabeth," he added. "You'll like Albert."

"I already like Albert," I said, "but I don't think he can live here. I think he has to live with his parents."

"He doesn't want to," Louis said. "He even told them so. He told them, 'I don't want to

live with you anymore,' and they said, 'All right, Albert, you just go and live someplace else.'"

I had never heard of such a thing, except when my friend Wanda McCall baptized the hamsters with her mother's French perfume. The house smelled wonderful, but all the hamsters got sick and so did Mrs. McCall, and Mr. McCall gave Wanda two dollars and told her to get lost. But he didn't mean forever.

Neither had Albert's parents, I decided. They would probably call tomorrow and tell him to come home.

"Louis." I shook him again. "Where are the worms?"

"They aren't worms yet," he reminded me. "The cans are in the closet."

I didn't think either half of a worm could go very far, but I put my sleeping bag on the other side of the room anyway, just in case.

When I woke up the next morning Louis and Albert were gone, but they had made the bed and folded up their clothes and left a note that said, *We'll be back for the picnic. Please don't move the worms.* There was a P.S.: *Tell the lady cousin in the purple underwear that I'm sorry. I didn't know she was in there.* Then there was another P.S.: *It was really Albert, but pretend it was me and tell her I'm sorry. Or if you don't want to, just find out who she is and I'll tell her.*

That was nice of Louis, I thought, but I really didn't want to ask around about everyone's underwear.

"I guess not," Louis said later. "It's okay. . . . Albert felt bad about it, that's all."

"Where is Albert?" I asked.

"Over there." Louis pointed to where Mother's brother Frank was taking pictures with his new camera.

"You'll have to get closer together," we

heard him say, "and put Clyde's boy in front of you, Blanche."

"Who is Clyde's boy?" Louis asked me.

"I think it's Albert," I said. "He's the only boy there."

I was right. "Looks just *like* Clyde," we heard Aunt Blanche say.

I thought Albert looked a little worried, but Louis said he was just worried about the worms. "We're going to move them someplace else," he said. "Albert thinks they might get out and crawl around—especially the head parts, Albert said, because they could see where they were going."

That made me shiver, so I hoped they would put them somewhere up high.

By then Aunt Rhoda had arrived, to everyone's surprise. She never did get to testify, she said, because "the litigants" had to go to the police station to look at "mug shots" and "supply ID's." Aunt Rhoda had picked up a whole new vocabulary.

"Mug shots?" my father said. "ID's? Now, what does that mean? This was a traffic accident, not a holdup."

"I don't know," Mother told him. "Rhoda just said they had to study mug shots of children."

"There is no such thing as mug shots of children. Mug shots are of criminals. Rhoda's got it all wrong." He went to question Aunt Rhoda further and stumbled into the one event he always tried to avoid: the big family photograph, with everyone in it.

The Last Picnic (1993), Brian Jones. Courtesy Nancy Poole's Studio, Toronto, Canada.

Uncle Frank had set up a different camera and lined everybody up, but he was missing some people: my parents, Aunt Mildred . . . "And Louis," he said. "And Clyde's boy. Clyde, where's your boy?"

Clyde looked surprised. "He's in the army."

"I mean the little one."

"Looks just like you," Aunt Blanche put in.

"He doesn't look one bit like me," Clyde said. "He looks like his mother."

"No," Aunt Blanche said stubbornly. "He looks like you."

Clyde was stubborn too. "How do you know what he looks like, Blanche? You haven't seen him in six years!"

"I saw him fifteen minutes ago!"

"Who?" my father said, arriving on the scene with Mother.

"They're talking about Albert," I said. "Louis's friend Albert."

"Albert!" Mother looked amazed. "Is that little boy here again?"

"He never left," I said.

So I was sent to get Albert and find out where he lived, while Mother explained to everybody who he was (which was hard, because she didn't *know* who he was) and my father pressed Aunt Rhoda for more details about her experiences in court—fearful, he later said, that she had wandered into the wrong courtroom and the wrong trial and was now mixed up with a bunch of criminals.

I found Louis crawling around the floor of his room. "We dropped some of a worm," he said, "but only one, and I'll find it. We took the rest of them out of the closet."

"Mother wants to know where Albert lives," I told him.

"You mean . . . besides here?" Louis was being stubborn too, just like Aunt Blanche and Clyde. "I don't know."

"Well, what's Albert's name?"

"You mean . . . besides Albert? I'll ask him."

"But, Louis—don't you know?"

"I only met him day before yesterday," Louis said. "He was sitting on the curb outside the model-airplane store, after his parents told him to go live someplace else. He didn't know anyplace else, so I told him he could live here. And after that, all we talked about was worms."

Albert didn't know where he lived either. "I can't remember," he said. "We haven't lived there long enough for me to remember. I think it's the name of a tree."

Albert was right. He lived on Catalpa Street, and his name was Henderson. But it was Aunt Rhoda, of all people, who supplied the information, while Louis and Albert were upstairs looking for the missing worm.

Aunt Rhoda recognized Albert in the picture because, when she witnessed the automobile accident, she had also witnessed Albert in one of the cars with his parents—the very same people, she said, who were at this moment examining mug shots at the police station.

"Isn't it a small world!" Aunt Rhoda said . . . and everyone agreed, except my father.

He had assumed, all along, that Mother knew who Albert was and knew where Albert came from. "And I suppose," he said, "that Albert is staying with us now because his parents have to be in court—but didn't the Hendersons mention *why* they had to be in court?"

"I don't know the Hendersons," Mother said.

"Well, did Albert . . ."

"I don't know Albert either." Mother was getting testy under all this cross-examination. "Obviously, Louis said it would be all right for Albert to stay here—and it *is* all right," she said. "Those poor people have enough trouble. That's the least we can do for them."

In the meantime Louis and Albert came downstairs—"We found the worm," Louis assured me—went to get more fried chicken and potato salad, and ran into Aunt Rhoda, who said she was certainly surprised to see Albert again and to see him *here*.

"I live here," Albert said.

"Oh, no," Aunt Rhoda laughed. "You live on Catalpa Street."

"Not anymore," Albert said.

Of course Aunt Rhoda reported this to Mother, who was by then completely mystified about Albert and pretty fed up with all the sketchy bits and pieces of news about him. She left Aunt Rhoda to cut the Family Reunion cake and make the coffee, and went off to find Louis. My father, having also concluded that Louis was the key to it all, had done the same thing.

Between them, they quickly figured out that Louis did not know the Hendersons and that he barely knew Albert . . . and that Albert had left home and was prepared to live with us forever.

My father called the police station, where the Hendersons were indeed studying pictures of missing children and supplying information about their own missing child . . . and in no time they arrived at our house and were reunited with Albert.

> ## "In my house," she said, "if a can says coffee, that's what's in it."

This was exactly the kind of happy ending my mother loved best—even Albert seemed happy to be back with his family.

"Well, now he has a friend," Mrs. Henderson said, beaming at Louis. "That was the trouble. He didn't know anyone, didn't have anyone to play with or talk to. Thank goodness for you, Louis!"

The Hendersons obviously saw Louis as the hero of it all, which exasperated my father.

"I don't know why you're so grumpy," Mother said. "Just suppose Louis hadn't come

along and found Albert outside the airplane store—then what?"

"Then Albert would have gone home where he belonged," my father said, "and none of this would have happened."

"Exactly!" Mother said. "And he would still be a lonely, unhappy little boy . . . way over there on Catalpa Street."

She invited the Hendersons to stay for cake and coffee and to meet all the relatives. Aunt Rhoda said she couldn't meet them officially, or talk to them, because of being a witness, but she waved to them from the back porch, and Mrs. Henderson waved back and called to her, "Your cake recipe is wonderful!"

"Have some coffee," Mother said. "It's Rhoda's coffee, too."

Aunt Rhoda said later that it was pretty silly to call it *her* coffee just because she'd made it, and she also said that she didn't feel one bit responsible for what had happened.

"In my house," she said, "if a can says coffee, that's what's in it, and it wouldn't occur to me to look."

Mother said, in all fairness, it wouldn't occur to her to look either. . . . "Except, of course, I don't keep my coffee on that high shelf, so I might have looked."

My father, who had been the first one to sip the coffee—and, therefore, the *only* one to sip the coffee—said he wished *someone* had looked.

"Was it the can full of dirt?" I asked Louis, and he shook his head no.

"Oh, I'm sorry, Louis," I said, "but you and Albert can get some more worms."

"And it was only the tail ends, anyway," Albert said . . . although I hadn't really wanted to know that. ❖

RESPONDING
OPTIONS

FROM *PERSONAL RESPONSE* TO *CRITICAL ANALYSIS*

REFLECT

1. With a few classmates, role-play the scene of the story that you think is the funniest.

RETHINK

2. How would you describe Louis's family?
   Consider
   - the way they interact
   - their reactions to Albert
   - their preparation for the family reunion
   - their attitude toward visitors

3. Were you surprised by the reaction of Albert's parents when they finally discover him at Louis's house? Why or why not?

4. How did this story affect your attitude toward family reunions?

RELATE

5. Not every family is able to organize and attend an annual reunion. How important do you think it is for families to keep in touch?

ANOTHER PATHWAY

What if this story were told from Albert's point of view, or that of any character other than Mary Elizabeth? Choose a section of the story and retell it from the point of view of Albert or another character of your choice. How does the change in perspective affect your understanding of the story?

QUICKWRITES

1. Louis is very excited to find out something new about worms. Write a **science report** that Louis might have written for school the day after Albert's visit.

2. What if "The Adoption of Albert" were the first episode of a TV sitcom? Improvise a **script** that follows the general outline of the story.

📁 *PORTFOLIO Save your writing. You may want to use it later as a springboard to a piece for your portfolio.*

LITERARY CONCEPTS

Tone is a writer's expression of his or her attitude toward a subject. For example, a work's tone might be amused, outraged, or neutral. Tone is often revealed by the writer's style. Describe the tone of "The Adoption of Albert" and explain why Barbara Robinson might have chosen to express that attitude toward her subject.

LITERARY LINKS

Compare and contrast the type of humor Barbara Robinson uses in this story with the type that Gary Soto uses in "The School Play" (page 30). How is Louis in this story similar to and different from Robert in "The School Play"?

ALTERNATIVE ACTIVITIES

1. Choose an episode from the story, and draw a **comic strip** of the events in the episode. Use some of the author's actual words and try to match the tone of your comic strip to the tone of the story.

2. Create a humorous **family newsletter** describing the events that occur before and during the family reunion. Write it from the point of view of any character you choose.

ACROSS THE CURRICULUM

Science *Cooperative Learning*
Work with a group to complete the research begun by Louis and Albert. How long *do* worms get? Can worm parts grow new heads or tails? Do worms really "die of length"? Present your information to the class in a visual format, using poster board, schematic diagrams, and three-dimensional models.

WORDS TO KNOW

WORDPLAY
Understanding the parts of words—roots, prefixes, and suffixes—can help you figure out, or infer, the words' meanings. Study the word map for the vocabulary word ***reunion,*** shown here. Then make your own word map for the word *preoccupied,* using a dictionary if necessary. Which character in this story would you describe as preoccupied?

BARBARA ROBINSON

"The Adoption of Albert" is one of ten humorous stories about Louis Lawson and his family in Barbara Robinson's *My Brother Louis Measures Worms and Other Louis Stories,* published in 1988. Another of Robinson's popular books, *The Best Christmas Pageant Ever,* describes the misadventures of the Herdman children—"absolutely the worst kids in the history of the world"—who decide to take over the annual church Christmas pageant. That book received an award from the American Library Association and was produced as a television film in 1983.

Robinson says, "Each book that I have written for boys and girls is also a book I have written for myself . . . since, if I don't find the story exciting or interesting or funny, if I don't enjoy the characters or care what happens to them, I don't think boys and girls will either." She adds, "Since I don't plan my books in outline form, I am often in the position of the reader, asking 'What's going to happen next?'"

What does Barbara Robinson like to read? Her "all-time favorite book" is Robert Louis Stevenson's *Treasure Island.*

OTHER WORKS *Across from Indian Shore; Trace Through the Forest; The Fattest Bear in the First Grade; Temporary Times, Temporary Places*

POETRY

The Cremation of Sam McGee
Robert Service

PERSONAL CONNECTION

"The Cremation of Sam McGee" is a poem about friendship and a challenge that a person faces for the sake of friendship. Have you ever given your word that you would help a friend in need? Did you succeed in keeping your promise? Draw a promise-and-outcome graphic like the one shown here, and fill it in with an account of your experience.

The Promise

The Outcome

GEOGRAPHICAL CONNECTION

The narrator of this poem is a gold miner, and the poem's setting is the Yukon Territory. The Yukon Territory is located in the northwestern corner of Canada, with Alaska to the west and the Arctic Ocean to the north. This area is known for its long, dark, extremely cold winters. The average January temperature at Dawson in the Yukon Territory is –16°F. In the late 1800s, many people risked their lives in the icy Yukon, searching for gold near the Klondike River.

Yukon Territory

Alaska

Yukon Territory

Pacific Ocean

CANADA

UNITED STATES

Atlantic Ocean

N W E S

Miles
0 500 1000

READING CONNECTION

Mood A feeling that a writer wants readers to get while reading his or her work is called a **mood.** Writers choose words carefully to create moods. For example, in the first stanza of "The Cremation of Sam McGee," the words *strange, secret tales,* and *queer sights* create an eerie mood. As you read this poem about friendship and loyalty, pay attention to how you are feeling and to the words that help to create that mood.

LASERLINKS
• GEOGRAPHICAL CONNECTION

The Cremation

of Sam McGee

by Robert Service

There are strange things done in the midnight sun
  By the men who moil for gold;
The Arctic trails have their secret tales
  That would make your blood run cold;
5 The Northern Lights have seen queer sights,
  But the queerest they ever did see
Was that night on the marge of Lake Lebarge
  I cremated Sam McGee.

2 moil: work very hard.

7 marge: edge.

Dawn over the Yukon from
The Cremation of Sam McGee by
Robert Service and illustrated by Ted
Harrison. Used by permission of Kids
Can Press, Ltd., Toronto. Illustration
Copyright © 1986 by Ted Harrison.

Now Sam McGee was from Tennessee,
    where the cotton blooms and blows.
Why he left his home in the South to roam
    'round the Pole, God only knows.
He was always cold, but the land of gold
    seemed to hold him like a spell;
Though he'd often say in his homely way
    that "he'd sooner live in hell."

On a Christmas Day we were mushing our way
    over the Dawson trail.
Talk of your cold! through the parka's fold
    it stabbed like a driven nail.
If our eyes we'd close, then the lashes froze
    till sometimes we couldn't see;
It wasn't much fun, but the only one
    to whimper was Sam McGee.

And that very night, as we lay packed tight
    in our robes beneath the snow,
And the dogs were fed, and the stars o'erhead
    were dancing heel and toe,
He turned to me, and "Cap," says he,
    "I'll cash in this trip, I guess;
And if I do, I'm asking that you
    won't refuse my last request."

Well, he seemed so low that I couldn't say no;
    then he says with a sort of moan:
"It's the cursèd cold, and it's got right hold
    till I'm chilled clean through to the bone.
Yet 'tain't being dead—it's my awful dread
    of the icy grave that pains;
So I want you to swear that, foul or fair,
    you'll cremate my last remains."

10
15
20
25
30
35
40

17 mushing: driving dogsleds.

18 Dawson trail: a route in the Yukon Territory of Canada.

A pal's last need is a thing to heed,
 so I swore I would not fail;
And we started on at the streak of dawn;
 but God! he looked ghastly pale.
45 He crouched on the sleigh, and he raved all day
 of his home in Tennessee;
And before nightfall a corpse was all
 that was left of Sam McGee.

There wasn't a breath in that land of death,
50 and I hurried, horror-driven,
With a corpse half hid that I couldn't get rid,
 because of a promise given;
It was lashed to the sleigh, and it seemed to say:
 "You may tax your brawn and brains,
55 But you promised true, and it's up to you
 to cremate those last remains."

Now a promise made is a debt unpaid,
 and the trail has its own stern code.
In the days to come, though my lips were dumb,
60 in my heart how I cursed that load.
In the long, long night, by the lone firelight,
 while the huskies, round in a ring,
Howled out their woes to the homeless snows
 —O God! how I loathed the thing.

65 And every day that quiet clay
 seemed to heavy and heavier grow;
And on I went, though the dogs were spent
 and the grub was getting low;
The trail was bad, and I felt half mad,
70 but I swore I would not give in;
And I'd often sing to the hateful thing,
 and it hearkened with a grin.

Till I came to the marge of Lake Lebarge,
 and a derelict there lay;
75 It was jammed in the ice, but I saw in a trice
 it was called the "Alice May."
And I looked at it, and I thought a bit,
 and I looked at my frozen chum;
Then "Here," said I, with a sudden cry,
80 "is my cre-ma-tor-eum."

74 derelict: an abandoned ship.

Ice Fog over the Lake from *The Cremation of Sam McGee* by Robert Service and illustrated by Ted Harrison.
Used by permission of Kids Can Press, Ltd., Toronto. Illustration Copyright © 1986 by Ted Harrison.

Some planks I tore from the cabin floor,
    and I lit the boiler fire;
Some coal I found that was lying around,
    and I heaped the fuel higher;
85 The flames just soared, and the furnace roared
    —such a blaze you seldom see,
And I burrowed a hole in the glowing coal,
    and I stuffed in Sam McGee.

Then I made a hike, for I didn't like
90   to hear him sizzle so;
And the heavens scowled, and the huskies howled,
    and the wind began to blow.
It was icy cold, but the hot sweat rolled
    down my cheeks, and I don't know why;
95 And the greasy smoke in an inky cloak
    went streaking down the sky.

I do not know how long in the snow
    I wrestled with grisly fear;
But the stars came out and they danced about
100   ere again I ventured near;
I was sick with dread, but I bravely said:
    "I'll just take a peep inside.
I guess he's cooked, and it's time I looked"; . . .
    Then the door I opened wide.

105 And there sat Sam, looking cool and calm,
    in the heart of the furnace roar;
And he wore a smile you could see a mile,
    and he said: "Please close that door.
It's fine in here, but I greatly fear
110   you'll let in the cold and storm—
Since I left Plumtree, down in Tennessee,
    it's the first time I've been warm."

There are strange things done in the midnight sun
    By the men who moil for gold;
115 *The Arctic trails have their secret tales*
    That would make your blood run cold;
The Northern Lights have seen queer sights,
    But the queerest they ever did see
Was that night on the marge of Lake Lebarge
120   *I cremated Sam McGee.*

100 ere (âr): before.

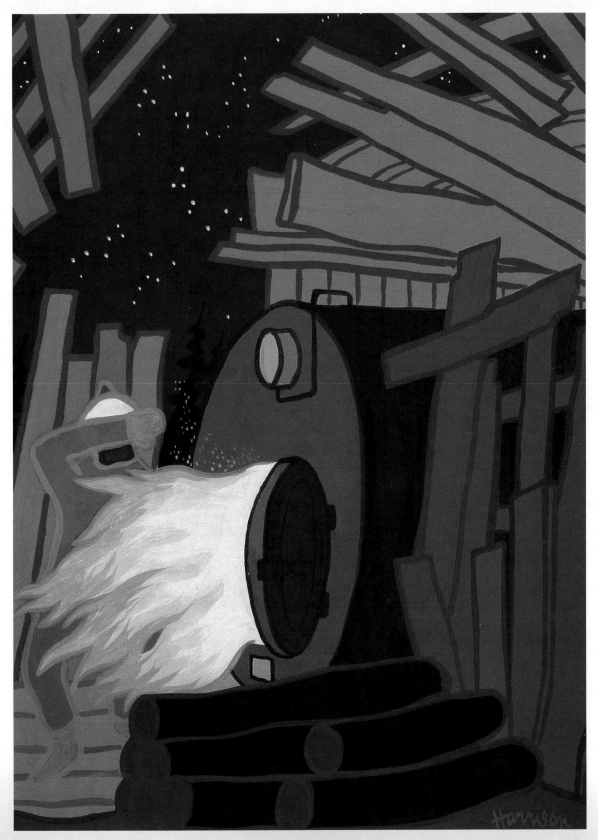

The Boilers from *The Cremation of Sam McGee* by Robert Service and illustrated by Ted Harrison. Used by permission of Kids Can Press, Ltd., Toronto. Illustration Copyright © 1986 by Ted Harrison.

RESPONDING
OPTIONS

FROM PERSONAL RESPONSE TO CRITICAL ANALYSIS

REFLECT

1. List the images in "The Cremation of Sam McGee" that stand out in your mind.

RETHINK

2. Why do you think the speaker of the poem feels such a strong obligation to honor Sam McGee's last request?

3. What words would you use to describe the narrator of this poem? Use evidence from the poem to support your answer.

4. The words in the first and last stanzas of the poem are the same. Do you think that these stanzas create the same mood or different moods? Explain your opinion.

RELATE

5. How far do you think someone should go to keep a promise?

ANOTHER PATHWAY

Cooperative Learning

With a group of classmates, present an oral reading of "The Cremation of Sam McGee." Experiment with using found objects, like pencils and rulers, to tap out the rhythm of the poem as you read it. Perform the reading for the class and see how the sounds affect the mood of the poem.

QUICKWRITES

1. Often, after a person dies, people send letters expressing their sadness and regret to that person's family members and friends. These letters are known as condolence letters. Compose a **condolence letter** that the poem's speaker might write to Sam McGee's family and friends in Tennessee.

2. Write your own humorous **narrative poem** about the climate that you find the least comfortable.

📁 *PORTFOLIO Save your writing. You may want to use it later as a springboard to a piece for your portfolio.*

LITERARY CONCEPTS

Rhyme that occurs at the ends of lines is called **end rhyme.** Rhyme within a line is called **internal rhyme**. The following lines show both internal and end rhyme:

> **There are strange things done in the midnight sun**
> **By the men who moil for gold;**
> **The Arctic trails have their secret tales**
> **That would make your blood run cold;**

Find another example of end rhyme and of internal rhyme in the poem.

CONCEPT REVIEW: Rhythm As you know, a poem's beat is called its rhythm. A poet will often structure the rhythm of a poem to make readers feel a certain mood, or emotion. What mood does the rhythm of "The Cremation of Sam McGee" create?

ALTERNATIVE ACTIVITIES

1. Reread the poem and jot down details and descriptions that create vivid pictures in your mind. Then draw or paint a **scene** from the poem.

2. Research the Klondike gold rush of the late 1800s. Who were the miners who poured into the Yukon in hopes of striking it rich? Where did they come from? What tools did they use? Prepare an **oral report** for your class. Illustrate your report with pictures and maps.

LITERARY LINKS

Compare this poem with the narrative poem "The Walrus and the Carpenter" (page 104). List at least three ways in which the poems are alike.

ACROSS THE CURRICULUM

Science Research information about the aurora borealis, or northern lights. Where do most auroras occur? How does solar energy contribute to their formation? Present your findings in a chart that illustrates how auroras come about.

Usually green in color, an aurora can also streak the sky in red or purple.

ROBERT SERVICE

According to Robert Service, his classic narrative poem was "the result of an accident." He explained that he was at a party where a miner told a far-fetched story about a man who cremated his friend. Service left the party and immediately started writing the poem in his mind. When he woke up the next day, he wrote it all down from memory, and it quickly became a success. In fact, many people who have studied this poem have enjoyed it so much that they have memorized stanzas or even the entire poem.

Sam McGee was the name of a real person, a customer at the Bank of Commerce where Service worked. The *Alice May* was based on a real boat (the *Olive May*) abandoned on Lake Laberge in the Yukon.

1874–1958

Service was born in England, grew up in Scotland, and moved to the Yukon when he was in his 20s. He worked as a bank teller but wrote poems about the miners and the lumberjacks of Canada. When he became a popular writer, he quit his job at the bank and wrote full-time. In addition to "The Cremation of Sam McGee," Service wrote another famous narrative poem, "The Shooting of Dan McGrew."

When Service was in his 30s, he moved to Europe and continued to write poems and novels. He also served as an ambulance driver during World War I. He lived for many years far from the Yukon, in Paris, where he died in 1958.

OTHER WORKS *The Spell of the Yukon, The Trail of '98*

LASERLINKS
• *SCIENCE CONNECTION*

NONFICTION

Chinatown *from* The Lost Garden
Laurence Yep

PERSONAL CONNECTION

In the selection you are about to read, a boy describes the culture and community in which he grew up. What are the characteristics of your neighborhood or community? Think about how you would describe your community to a stranger. Are the boundaries limited to an apartment building, to one block, to several blocks, or to a subdivision? What are your connections to the different parts of your neighborhood? Draw a simple map of your community, like the one shown here. Label the parts of the community that you are connected to, and indicate how you are connected to them. As you read, compare your community to the one described by Laurence Yep.

The Supermarket Where I Shop

My Building

My Friend Alex's House

HISTORICAL CONNECTION

In the 1800s the Chinese population in California rose dramatically. The gold rush of 1848 drew thousands of Chinese immigrants to San Francisco. In the 1860s, many Chinese laborers came to work for the Central Pacific Railroad Company. As the Chinese population grew, many people began to view the new Chinese Americans as an economic burden. Laws were passed restricting Chinese immigration. Other laws isolated Chinese Americans in communities called Chinatowns.

Not until the 1960s were immigration laws changed to end discrimination based on race. Fair housing laws were passed that allowed the Chinese Americans to live where they wished.

WRITING CONNECTION

Everyone is someone's son or daughter. Who else are you? A Boy Scout or Girl Scout? A student at a particular school? A regular basketball player at a local park? A member of a youth group at a church, a synagogue, or a temple? In your notebook, list the different roles you play in your community. Use the map you drew for the Personal Connection to get started. Then, to record your roles, create a diagram like the one shown. In your notebook, explain which role you find most challenging.

Who am I?

> LASERLINKS
> • *CULTURAL CONNECTION*
> • *HISTORICAL CONNECTION*

Chinatown

from
*The
Lost
Garden*

by Laurence Yep

Celebration, Chinatown (1940), Dong Kingman.
Private collection.

This selection is a chapter from Laurence Yep's memoir The Lost Garden. *Yep grew up as a Chinese American in an African-American neighborhood of San Francisco. He attended school in Chinatown, although he did not speak or understand Chinese. His lack of knowledge of Chinese, among other things, made him an outsider in Chinatown— sometimes even among his friends.*

If Uncle Francis and other members of our family left Chinatown to explore America, my experience was the reverse because I was always going into Chinatown to explore the streets and perhaps find the key to the pieces of the puzzle. But the search only seemed to increase the number of pieces.

When I was a boy, Chinatown was much more like a small town than it is now. It was small not only in terms of population but in physical area as well. Its boundaries were pretty well set by Pacific Avenue on the north next to the Italian neighborhood of North Beach, Kearny Street on the east, Sacramento Street on the south, and Stockton Street on the west—an area only of a few city blocks.

There is a stereotype that the Chinese lived in Chinatown because they wanted to. The fact was that before the fair housing laws[1] they often had no choice.

For years there was a little cottage on an ivy-covered hill in the southwest corner of Chinatown just above the Stockton tunnel. There was—and still is—very little plant life in Chinatown, so the only color green I saw was the paint on my school. The kind of green that is alive—lawns, bushes, and trees—was something I had to leave Chinatown to see, except for that ivy-covered slope. On windy days, the ivy itself would stir and move like a living sea; and overlooking the ivy was a cottage that was charm itself. However, as much as I admired the house—on occasion I was disloyal enough to the Pearl Apartments to want to live in it—I knew it wasn't for us. My Auntie Mary had once tried to rent it and had been refused because she was Chinese.

Out of some forty-five or so students in my class, I was one of the few who lived outside of Chinatown. Now, thanks to the fair housing laws that were passed in the 1960s, almost none of my former classmates live there; and Chinatown itself has spilled out of its traditional boundaries.

There is a stereotype that the Chinese lived in Chinatown because they wanted to.

When I was a boy, though, we could see the results of white money and power on three sides of us. To the east we could stare up at the high-rise office buildings of the business district; and to the west, up the steep streets, were the fancy hotels of Nob Hill.[2] Southward lay downtown and the fancy department stores.

Grant Avenue led directly to downtown; but for years I always thought of the Stockton tunnel as the symbolic end to Chinatown. When it had been cut right through a hill, my

---

1. **fair housing laws:** the civil rights acts of 1964 and 1968, which outlawed racial discrimination in the sale and rental of property, private as well as public.

2. **Nob Hill:** a wealthy neighborhood in northeastern San Francisco. It adjoins Chinatown and is noted for its large luxury hotels, such as the Fairmont and the Mark Hopkins.

WORDS TO KNOW · **stereotype** (stĕr′ē-ə-tīp′) *n.* a fixed idea, especially an idea about how a person should look or act

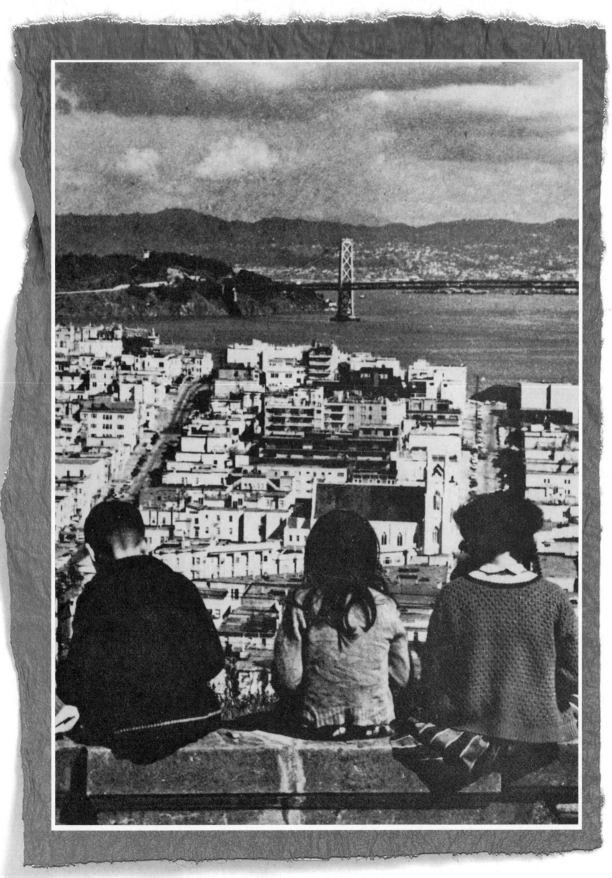

Detail. Young Chinese Americans enjoy a view of San Francisco Bay and the Bay Bridge (upper right).
Courtesy California Historical Society, San Francisco.

father and his young friends had held foot races through it after midnight, hooting and hollering so that the echoes seemed to be the cheers of a huge crowd. The rich white world began just on the other side of the tunnel.

There were also invisible barriers that separated the wealthy whites from the Chinese who cleaned their apartments or waited on their tables. The Chinese could see and even touch the good life; but they could not join in.

The world looked just the same whether it was a Chinese eye or an American one.

One of my classmates, Harold, had a paper route on Nob Hill. I still find it hard to believe that, up hills that angled some forty degrees or so, he carried a kind of poncho loaded with papers in front and back. But he did that every afternoon. Once I went along with him; and I followed him into one of the fanciest hotels on Nob Hill, past the elaborately uniformed doorman, over the plush carpets, under the ornate chandeliers, and around in back, down concrete hallways as bleak as the ones in the Chinatown housing projects that were painted a cheap, gaudy yellow—a shade which my friend referred to as "landlord yellow." Harold would deliver the afternoon newspapers to the laundrymen and other workers. And with my friend that day, I wandered all around the roots of that palatial dream of wealth.

When the poncho was flat, my friend and I returned to his tenement apartment where there was only one toilet to a floor; and the toilet lacked both a door and toilet paper. When you went, you brought in your own toilet paper. Nothing could be done about the door except changing your attitude about privacy.

Many of my schoolmates lived in the Chinatown projects, and I wasn't sure if life was any better in them than life in the projects near our store. Another newspaper carrier named Paul lived there. As the oldest boy, Paul was expected to look after his younger brothers and sisters while his parents worked—a common practice among many Chinese families. However, as a result, Paul had failed to develop many social skills let alone improve his English. I remember the nun sending him out on an errand and then asking the rest of the class to act as his special friend—which was easy for her to say because she was an adult.

As far as I knew, he hung around with his own group in the projects rather than with anyone from school. His group, though, must have been pretty rough because one of them threw a knife that "accidentally" hit Paul in the eye. Fortunately, there was a charity that arranged an operation; and he was given a new eye from someone who had recently died.

We never knew the identity of the donor, but Paul amused himself by claiming it was a rich white. First, he would clap a hand over his new eye and roll his remaining Chinese eye around. Then he would put his hand over his old one and gaze around elaborately with his new American eye. And then he would announce to us that the world looked just the same whether it was a Chinese eye or an American one.

Paul had shot up early and was a giant compared to the rest of us. When he ran, he looked like an ostrich with arms. He would kick out his legs explosively while his arms flailed the air, so it was hard not to laugh; but we didn't because he was also immensely strong.

The playground at St. Mary's was only a concrete basketball court below. Up above, there was a kind of patio between the convent and the school where the younger children could play. However, the nuns were so worried about our knocking one another down that they forbade us to run during recess. About the only thing we could play under those conditions was a kind of slow-motion tag.

At noon, we could go across the street to the Chinese Playground—the playground where my father had once been the director. In those days, it consisted of levels. The first level near the alley that became known as Hang Ah Alley was a volleyball and a tennis court. Down the steps was the next level with a sandbox (which was usually full of fleas), a small director's building, a Ping-Pong table, an area covered by tan bark that housed a slide, a set of bars, and a set of swings and other simple equipment. The level next to the Chinese Baptist church was the basketball court.

We had Physical Education once a week there. The playground director taught the boys, and I suppose the nun handled the girls. Sometimes it was calisthenics; other times it was baseball played with a tennis ball on the tennis court. There was no pitcher. Rather, the "batter" threw up the ball and hit it with his fist. Because of his size and added arm strength from his own paper route, Paul could hit a home run almost every time, sending the tennis ball flying over the high wire mesh fence.

However, my experience was frequently the reverse. Because the present director knew that my father had once been the director of the playground, he was always urging me on to one disaster after another.

The worst happened when he wasn't present, though. In third grade, we had a very sweet nun, Sister Bridget, who used to play kickball with us. Kickball was like baseball except that the pitcher bowled a ball the size of a basketball over the ground and the "batter" kicked it. One time someone kicked a ball so that it rolled foul. Retrieving it, I threw it to sister; but as fate would have it, she had turned her head right at that moment to look at something else. I wound up hitting her in the head; and though there was no physical harm, I broke her glasses. Even though my parents paid for replacements, the rest of my class treated me as if I were taboo for striking a nun. I learned what it meant to be shunned and to be invisible.

The only sport that I was remotely good at was football.

The experience also reinforced my belief that I was terrible at sports. Despite all the practice and coaching from my father, I was hopeless when it came to catching any ball in any shape or size. Nor could I dribble a basketball, even though my father sometimes kept me practicing in the little courtyard until it was almost too dark to see.

The only sport that I was remotely good at was football. Having worked and lifted crates in the store made me fairly strong. As a result, I was a good lineman at blocking and rushing—like my hero, Leo Nomellini. However, I was still hopeless at catching a pass. I still remember one game where I dropped three touchdown passes in a row. I was so bad that our opponents stopped covering me. Our quarterback, unable to resist a wide-open target, persisted in throwing to me—and I dropped yet a fourth pass that could have been a touchdown.

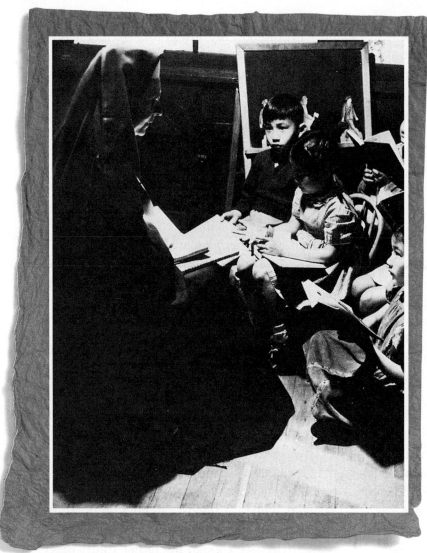

Detail. Chinese-American children reading with their teacher.
Courtesy California Historical Society, San Francisco.

Moreover, my lack of Chinese made me an outsider in Chinatown—sometimes even among my friends. Since it was a Catholic school taught by nuns, my friends would always tell dirty jokes in Chinese so the nuns wouldn't understand. However, neither did I, so I missed out on a good deal of humor when I was a boy. What Chinese I did pick up was the Chinese that got spoken in the playground—mostly insults and vulgar names.

There were times even with a good friend like Harold when I felt different. Though Harold and I would go see American war movies, he could also open up a closet and show me the exotic Chinese weapons his father, a gardener, would fashion in his spare time, and I could sense a gulf between my experience and that of Harold. It was as if we belonged to two different worlds.

Even my friends' games and entertainments in Chinatown could sometimes take their own different spin. They weren't quite like the games I saw American boys playing on television or read about in Homer Price. Handball was played with the all-purpose tennis ball against a brick wall in the courtyard.

Nor do I remember anyone ever drawing a circle with chalk and shooting marbles in the American way. Instead, someone would set up marbles on one side of the basketball court at

The fact that my whole family was athletic only added to my disgrace. My father had played both basketball and football. My mother had also played basketball as well as being a track star, winning gold medals at the Chinese Olympics—a track event held for Chinese Americans. My brother was also excellent at basketball as well as bowling. Even worse, my father had coached championship teams when he had been a director at Chinese Playground—the very site of most of my failures. I often felt as if I were a major disappointment to my family.

St. Mary's and invite the others to try to hit them. If they did, they got the marbles. If they didn't, the boy would quickly snatch up their shooters. The ideal spot, of course, was where irregularities in the paving created bumps or dips to protect the owner's marbles. At times, one edge of the courtyard would resemble a bazaar with different boys trying to entice shooters to try their particular setup with various shouted jingles.

Other times, they would set up baseball or football cards. Trading cards weren't meant to be collector's items but were used like marbles. In the case of cards, the shooter would send a card flying with a flick of the wrist. Mint cards[3] did not always fly the truest; and certain cards with the right bends and folds became deadly treasures.

But that sense of being different became sharpest the time I was asked to sing. Our school had a quartet that they sent around to build goodwill. The two girls and two boys dressed up in outfits that were meant to be Chinese: the girls in colored silk pajamas and headdresses with pom-poms, the boys in robes with black vests and caps topped by red knobs.

How could I pretend to be somebody else when I didn't even know who I was?

However, one day in December, one of the boys took sick, so the nuns chose me to take his place. Musical ability was not a consideration; the fit of the costume was the important thing. We were brought to sing before a group of elderly people. I can remember following a cowboy with an accordion and a cowgirl with a short, spangled skirt who sang Christmas carols with a country twang.

Then we were ushered out on the small stage and I could look out at the sea of elderly faces. I think they were quite charmed with the costumed Chinese children. Opening their mouths, the others began to sing in Chinese. Now during all this, no one had bothered to find out if I could sing, let alone sing in Chinese. I recognized the tune as "Silent Night" but the words were all in Chinese. I tried to fake it, but I was always one note and one pretend-syllable behind the others. Then they swung into "It Came Upon a Midnight Clear." This time they sang in English, so I tried to sing along and ranged all over the musical scale except the notes I was supposed to be singing. Finally, one of the girls elbowed me in the ribs and from the side of her mouth, she whispered fiercely, "Just mouth the words."

Up until then I had enjoyed putting on costumes and even had a variety of hats, including cowboy and Robin Hood outfits as well as a French Foreign Legion hat and a Roman helmet; but the experience cured me of wanting to dress up and be something else. How could I pretend to be somebody else when I didn't even know who I was?

In trying to find solutions, I had created more pieces to the puzzle: the athlete's son who was not an athlete, the boy who got "A's" in Chinese school without learning Chinese, the boy who could sing neither in key nor in Chinese with everyone else. ❖

---

3. **mint cards:** freshly unwrapped trading cards, not yet damaged by handling.

RESPONDING
OPTIONS

FROM PERSONAL RESPONSE TO CRITICAL ANALYSIS

REFLECT **1.** What do you think of this account of Laurence Yep's childhood experiences in Chinatown? Describe your thoughts in your notebook or on a sheet of paper.

RETHINK **2.** Yep says, "In trying to find solutions, I had created more pieces to the puzzle." How would you describe the puzzle he is trying to solve?
Consider
- the community in which he lives
- his parents' expectations
- the language barrier

3. What are some ways in which Yep might have handled his problem of being divided between the Chinese and non-Chinese communities?

RELATE **4.** Growing up in San Francisco, Laurence Yep longed to fit into the culture in which he lived. Later, however, he learned to appreciate his Chinese heritage. Explain how important you think it is to know about and understand your origins and heritage.

ANOTHER PATHWAY
Cooperative Learning
Work with a group of classmates to draw a map showing the places that Laurence Yep describes—Nob Hill, Chinatown, St. Mary's School, the Chinese Playground, and the neighborhood in which he lived. Locate Yep and his friends Paul and Harold on the map.

LITERARY CONCEPTS

A **memoir** is a writer's account of his or her personal experiences. It is almost always told from the first-person point of view. Because a memoir is written about real people and real events, it is a type of nonfiction. It can provide information only the writer knows. What do you learn about Laurence Yep that you might not have learned if someone else had told his story?

CONCEPT REVIEW: Setting Yep provides numerous details to describe the various parts of San Francisco. Find a passage in the selection that you think is especially effective in helping you imagine the setting.

QUICKWRITES

1. Using what you have learned about Paul's and Harold's personalities, write a **prediction** of what will happen to them in future years.

2. Write an imaginary **dialogue** between Yep as a young man and Yep as an older man. In the younger Yep's speeches, include questions and comments about the confusion of living in two worlds. For the older Yep, compose words of advice.

📁 *PORTFOLIO Save your writing. You may want to use it later as a springboard to a piece for your portfolio.*

ALTERNATIVE ACTIVITIES

1. Look back at the diagram you created for the Writing Connection. Create a **collage** of objects and pictures that illustrate your roles. You might use photographs, parts of toys or household objects, old report cards, ribbons, and pins. You can also include drawings and magazine pictures.

2. Yep mentions that children in Chinatown played marbles in a way different from the way American children played. Prepare a **chart** explaining how to play marbles in one of the two ways.

CRITIC'S CORNER

A British author once described writers of memoirs as "drawing themselves with a pen." Do you think that statement applies to Yep's writing in this memoir? Why or why not?

WORDS TO KNOW

WORDPLAY Review page 172 and locate the word **stereotype.** Use a dictionary to find out what the word means and what part of speech it is in the sentence where it occurs. Then copy and complete the diagram below. Share and discuss your diagram with a small group of classmates.

How would you explain it in your own words?

What is a synonym?

STEREOTYPE

What is an example?

What are some of the causes?

What are some of the effects?

LAURENCE YEP

1948–

Laurence Yep began writing while in high school, when a teacher promised an A to any student who published an article in a national magazine. He earned the A by writing a science-fiction story that he sold for a penny per word.

Yep's first book, *Sweetwater,* published five years later, is also science fiction. It revolves around a young man who belongs to a minority group of transplanted aliens on another planet. Yep writes, "Probably the reason that much of my writing has found its way to a teenage audience is that I'm always pursuing the theme of being an outsider—an alien—and many teenagers feel they're aliens."

Yep spent six years researching Chinese-American history before he wrote *Dragonwings,* a fictionalized account of the first aircraft flight on the West Coast, in 1909. The novel blends Chinese folklore, myths, and legends with historical facts about the flight, Chinatown, and the San Francisco earthquake of 1906. *Dragonwings* has received 15 awards, including selection as a Newbery Honor Book.

OTHER WORKS *Sweetwater, Dragonwings, Child of the Owl, Sea Glass, Dragon of the Lost Sea, The Serpent's Children, Dragon Steel, The Star Fisher*

PREVIEWING

Three Haiku

Bashō, Issa, and Raymond R. Patterson

PERSONAL CONNECTION

The unusual poems you are about to read capture moments that have been meaningful to three poets. Choose an object in the room and try to observe it as though you were seeing it for the first time. On a piece of paper, write the name of the object and five words that describe what it looks like or what you notice about it that you have overlooked before.

LITERARY CONNECTION

Haiku are three-line, unrhymed poems of a type originally developed in Japan. In Japanese haiku, the first and third lines contain five syllables, and the second line contains seven syllables. (Haiku written in English or translated into English do not always fit this formula.) With only a few carefully chosen words, a haiku captures and conveys a single small moment, feeling, or object.

READING CONNECTION

Visualizing As you read these haiku, try to visualize, or form mental pictures of, the images in them. Reread each haiku a few times to visualize the image clearly and to experience the moment the poet presents.

Structure of Haiku

First line: 5 syllables	When the wind passes
Second line: 7 syllables	The sparrows in the branches
Third line: 5 syllables	They cling so tightly.

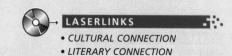

LASERLINKS
- *CULTURAL CONNECTION*
- *LITERARY CONNECTION*

Three Haiku

On sweet plum blossoms
The sun rises suddenly.
Look, a mountain path!

BY BASHŌ

Beautiful, seen through holes
Made in a paper screen:
The Milky Way.

BY ISSA

Glory, Glory . . .

Across Grandmother's knees
A kindly sun
Laid a yellow quilt.

BY RAYMOND R. PATTERSON

RESPONDING
O P T I O N S

FROM PERSONAL RESPONSE TO CRITICAL ANALYSIS

REFLECT   1. What thoughts were in your mind after you read the three haiku? Jot down your thoughts in your notebook.

RETHINK   2. Did reading the haiku by Issa more than once affect your appreciation of the image it presents? Explain why or why not.

3. On the basis of your reading of these haiku, describe the kind of person you imagine a haiku poet to be.

RELATE   4. Which haiku best helps you to visualize or experience a moment of being in a special place? Why?

ANOTHER PATHWAY

Haiku poets often use images of simple things to suggest truths about the world. Explain the message each poem conveys to you. Compare your response with the responses of your classmates.

LITERARY CONCEPTS

Imagery refers to the use of words that appeal to the five senses: sight, hearing, touch, taste, and smell. Most poetic images appeal to the sense of sight; they help readers "see" things in their mind. Which words in the three haiku appeal to the senses? Make a chart like the one shown here to record what you find.

ʼHaiku By	Image(s)	Sense(s) Appealed To

QUICKWRITES

1. Write a **personal essay** about an aspect of the natural world that is described in one of the haiku. Be sure to express your feelings about the subject in your essay.

2. Cut index cards into thirds and write the words of all three haiku on separate cards. (Omit the articles a, an, and the.) Then turn the cards over and choose ten at random. Use the words on the cards, along with a few of your own, to write a **haiku.**

📁 *PORTFOLIO Save your writing. You may want to use it later as a springboard to a piece for your portfolio.*

ART CONNECTION

Incense Wrapper on page 181 is probably the creation of the Japanese artist Ogata Korin (1658–1716). This wrapper—in itself a useful object—was made by painting on thick gold paper. The contrast of the wrapper's beauty with its simple function suggests the idea that the material things of this world pass away quickly. How might this idea also be suggested by the images presented in haiku?

BASHŌ

Bashō is considered one of Japan's greatest poets. Early in his life, he went to work for a noble family and became the companion of the family's son. When the son died, Bashō was greatly upset. He left the family's service and became a wandering poet, teaching haiku to make a living.

One day, according to legend, Bashō was out with some students. One of them suddenly announced that he had thought of a

1644–1694

poem: "Pluck off the wings of a bright red dragonfly and there a pepper pod will be." Bashō informed the student that he would never be a poet. A poet, according to Bashō, would have created this image: "Add but the wings to a bright red pepper pod and there a dragonfly will be." Whether or not the story is true, it reflects a sympathy that, along with his superb skill as a poet, has made Bashō a major figure in Japanese and world literature.

ISSA

Issa, born Kobayashi Nobuyuki, led a life full of poverty, illness, and tragedy. His mother died when he was three. When his father remarried, his stepmother was so unkind to the boy that he left home for Edo (now Tokyo) at the age of 13 to find work. There he studied haiku, decided to live as a poet, and took the pen name Issa (meaning "cup of tea"). In 1814 he married a woman named

1763–1827

Kiku. The couple had five children, all of whom died as infants. Kiku herself died in 1823.

Issa's troubles helped him understand the struggles of the weak and led him to feel tenderness and compassion toward all living things, no matter how small or insignificant. Perhaps the compassionate voice of his poetry is the reason Issa remains one of Japan's best-loved poets.

RAYMOND R. PATTERSON

Raymond R. Patterson (1929–) was born in New York City. After finishing college, he worked as a children's supervisor at Youth House for Boys in New York City. He also taught English at Benedict College in Columbia, South Carolina, and in New York City public schools. From 1960 to 1962, he wrote a weekly column on African-American history, "From Our Past."

In 1968 Patterson became a lecturer in English at City College in New York and director of Black Poets Reading, Inc. He received a Borestone Mountain poetry award in 1950 and a National Endowment for the Arts discovery grant for 1969–1970. Patterson's *Twenty-Six Ways of Looking at a Black Man and Other Poems* was published in 1969.

FICTION

Aaron's Gift

Myron Levoy

PERSONAL CONNECTION

Some gifts carry a big price tag, while others—like the one in this story—are priceless. In your notebook or on a sheet of paper, write about the best gift you ever gave or received. What made that gift so special?

GEOGRAPHICAL CONNECTION

In this story, one character's ideas about gifts are strongly influenced by her childhood in a Jewish village in the Ukraine. Although now an independent country of eastern Europe, during the late 19th century this area was part of the Russian Empire. The brutal leader of the Russian Empire was Czar Alexander the Third. At that time, Jews in the Ukraine lived in constant fear of Cossacks—soldiers loyal to the czar (emperor). These soldiers frequently attacked Jewish communities in raids known as pogroms. While Alexander the Third was czar, thousands of Jews left the Ukraine and came to the United States.

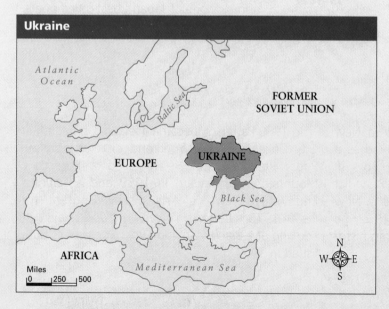

Ukraine

Atlantic Ocean

Baltic Sea

FORMER SOVIET UNION

EUROPE

UKRAINE

Black Sea

AFRICA

Mediterranean Sea

Miles
0 250 500

N W E S

READING CONNECTION

Predicting Before you even begin reading, you can try to predict what a story will be about. For example, on the basis of the title of this story, the information in the Geographical Connection, and the illustrations throughout the story, you might try predicting what Aaron's gift will be.

When you read a story, guessing what will happen next keeps you involved in the action. As you read this story, you will come across a question that asks you to predict what the main character will do next. Look for other points where you might predict what will happen. Write your predictions in your Reading Log. Then read on to see where the action takes you and to learn whether your predictions turn out to be true.

My Predictions
Aaron will fix the pigeon's wing.
Aaron will ask to keep Pidge.

LASERLINKS
• HISTORICAL CONNECTION

Aaron's Gift

by Myron Levoy

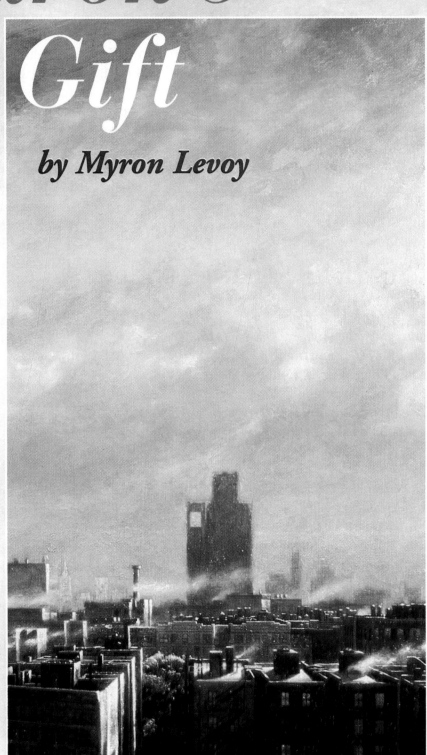

Detail of *Autumn* (1980–1981), Craig McPherson. Oil on canvas, 54″ × 48″, Museum of the City of New York (83.4), Gift of the American Institute of Arts and Letters.

Aaron Kandel had come to Tompkins Square Park to roller-skate, for the streets near Second Avenue were always too crowded with children and peddlers and old ladies and baby buggies. Though few children had bicycles in those days, almost every child owned a pair of roller skates. And Aaron was, it must be said, a Class A, triple-fantastic roller skater.

Aaron skated back and forth on the wide walkway of the park, pretending he was an aviator in an air race zooming around pylons,[1] which were actually two lampposts. During his third lap around the racecourse, he noticed a pigeon on the grass, behaving very strangely. Aaron skated to the line of benches, then climbed over onto the lawn.

The pigeon was trying to fly, but all it could manage was to flutter and turn round and round in a large circle, as if it were performing a <u>frenzied</u> dance. The left wing was only half open and was beating in a clumsy, jerking fashion; it was clearly broken.

Luckily, Aaron hadn't eaten the cookies he'd stuffed into his pocket before he'd gone clacking down the three flights of stairs from his apartment, his skates already on. He broke a cookie into small crumbs and tossed some toward the pigeon. "Here pidge, here pidge," he called. The pigeon spotted the cookie crumbs and, after a moment, stopped <u>thrashing</u> about. It folded its wings as best it could, but the broken wing still stuck half out. Then it strutted over to the crumbs, its head bobbing forth-back, forth-back, as if it were marching a little in front of the rest of the body—perfectly normal, except for that half-open wing which seemed to make the bird stagger sideways every so often.

The pigeon began eating the crumbs as Aaron quickly unbuttoned his shirt and pulled it off. Very slowly, he edged toward the bird, making little kissing sounds like the ones he heard his grandmother make when she fed the sparrows on the back fire escape.

Then suddenly Aaron plunged. The shirt, in both hands, came down like a torn parachute. The pigeon beat its wings, but Aaron held the shirt to the ground, and the bird couldn't escape. Aaron felt under the shirt, gently, and gently took hold of the wounded pigeon.

"Yes, yes, pidge," he said, very softly. "There's a good boy. Good pigeon, good."

The pigeon struggled in his hands, but little by little Aaron managed to soothe it. "Good boy, pidge. That's your new name. Pidge. I'm gonna take you home, Pidge. Yes, yes, *ssh*. Good boy. I'm gonna fix you up. Easy, Pidge, easy does it. Easy, boy."

Aaron squeezed through an opening between the row of benches and skated slowly out of the park, while holding the pigeon carefully with both hands as if it were one of his mother's rare, precious cups from the old country. How fast the pigeon's heart was beating! Was he afraid? Or did all pigeons' hearts beat fast?

"That's your new name. Pidge."

PREDICT

What will Aaron do with the pigeon?

---

1. **pylons** (pī′lŏnz′): towers marking turning points for airplanes in a race.

Bobby (1939), Jack Humphrey. Collection of John Corey.

him up and make him into a carrier pigeon[2] or something."

"Can I watch?" asked Noreen.

"Watch what?"

"The operation. I'm gonna be a nurse when I grow up."

"OK," said Aaron. "You can even help. You can help hold him while I fix him up."

Aaron wasn't quite certain what his mother would say about his newfound pet, but he was pretty sure he knew what his grandmother would think. His grandmother had lived with them ever since his grandfather had died three years ago. And she fed the sparrows and jays and crows and robins on the back fire escape with every spare crumb she could find. In fact, Aaron noticed that she sometimes created crumbs where they didn't exist, by squeezing and tearing pieces of her breakfast roll when his mother wasn't looking.

Aaron didn't really understand his grandmother, for he often saw her by the window having long conversations with the birds, telling them about her days as a little girl in the Ukraine. And once he saw her take her mirror from her handbag and hold it out toward the birds. She told Aaron that she wanted them to see how beautiful they were. Very strange. But Aaron did know that she would love Pidge, because she loved everything.

It was fortunate that Aaron was an excellent skater, for he had to skate six blocks to his apartment, over broken pavement and sudden gratings and curbs and cobblestones. But when he reached home, he asked Noreen Callahan, who was playing on the stoop, to take off his skates for him. He would not chance going up three flights on roller skates this time.

"Is he sick?" asked Noreen.

"Broken wing," said Aaron. "I'm gonna fix

---

2. **carrier pigeon:** a pigeon trained to carry messages from place to place.

To his surprise, his mother said he could keep the pigeon, temporarily, because it was sick, and we were all strangers in the land of Egypt,[3] and it might not be bad for Aaron to have a pet. *Temporarily.*

The wing was surprisingly easy to fix, for the break showed clearly and Pidge was remarkably patient and still, as if he knew he was being helped. Or perhaps he was just exhausted from all the thrashing about he had done. Two Popsicle sticks served as splints, and strips from an old undershirt were used to tie them in place. Another strip held the wing to the bird's body.

Aaron's father arrived home and stared at the pigeon. Aaron waited for the expected storm. But instead, Mr. Kandel asked, "Who *did* this?"

"Me," said Aaron. "And Noreen Callahan."

"Sophie!" he called to his wife. "Did you see this! Ten years old and it's better than Dr. Belasco could do. He's a genius!"

As the days passed, Aaron began training Pidge to be a carrier pigeon. He tied a little cardboard tube to Pidge's left leg and stuck tiny rolled-up sheets of paper with secret messages into it: THE ENEMY IS ATTACKING AT DAWN. Or: THE GUNS ARE HIDDEN IN THE TRUNK OF THE CAR. Or: VINCENT DEMARCO IS A BRITISH SPY. Then Aaron would set Pidge down at one end of the living room and put some popcorn at the other end. And Pidge would waddle slowly across the room, cooing softly, while the ends of his bandages trailed along the floor.

At the other end of the room, one of Aaron's friends would take out the message, stick a new one in, turn Pidge around, and aim him at the popcorn that Aaron put down on his side of the room.

And Pidge grew fat and contented on all the popcorn and crumbs and corn and crackers and Aaron's grandmother's breakfast rolls.

Aaron had told all the children about Pidge, but he only let his very best friends come up and play carrier pigeon with him. But telling everyone had been a mistake. A group of older boys from down the block had a club—Aaron's mother called it a gang— and Aaron had longed to join as he had never longed for anything else. To be with them and share their secrets, the secrets of older boys. To be able to enter their clubhouse shack on the empty lot on the next street. To know the password and swear the secret oath. To belong.

About a month after Aaron had brought the pigeon home, Carl, the gang leader, walked over to Aaron in the street and told him he could be a member if he'd bring the pigeon down to be the club <u>mascot</u>. Aaron couldn't believe it; he immediately raced home to get Pidge. But his mother told Aaron to stay away from those boys, or else. And Aaron, miserable, argued with his mother and pleaded and cried and coaxed. It was no use. Not with those boys. No.

---

3. **we were all . . . Egypt:** a reference to the biblical command to the Hebrews "Love ye therefore the stranger: for ye were strangers in the land of Egypt" (Deuteronomy 10:19).

WORDS
TO
KNOW

mascot (măs′kŏt′) *n.* a person, an animal, or an object that is believed to bring good luck, especially one serving as the symbol of an organization (such as a sports team)

Aaron's mother tried to change the subject. She told him that it would soon be his grandmother's sixtieth birthday, a very special birthday indeed, and all the family from Brooklyn and the East Side would be coming to their apartment for a dinner and celebration. Would Aaron try to build something or make something for Grandma? A present made with his own hands would be nice. A decorated box for her hairpins or a crayon picture for her room or anything he liked.

In a flash Aaron knew what to give her: Pidge! Pidge would be her present! Pidge with his wing healed, who might be able to carry messages for her to the doctor or his Aunt Rachel or other people his grandmother seemed to go to a lot. It would be a surprise for everyone. And Pidge would make up for what had happened to Grandma when she'd been a little girl in the Ukraine, wherever that was.

Often, in the evening, Aaron's grandmother would talk about the old days long ago in the Ukraine, in the same way that she talked to the birds on the back fire escape. She had lived in a village near a place called Kishinev[4] with hundreds of other poor peasant families like her own. Things hadn't been too bad under someone called Czar Alexander the Second,[5] whom Aaron always pictured as a tall, handsome man in a gold uniform. But Alexander the Second was assassinated, and Alexander the Third,[6] whom Aaron pictured as an ugly man in a black cape, became the czar. And the Jewish people of the Ukraine had no peace anymore.

One day, a thundering of horses was heard coming toward the village from the direction of Kishinev. "The Cossacks! The Cossacks!"

> In a flash Aaron knew what to give her.

someone had shouted. The czar's horsemen! Quickly, quickly, everyone in Aaron's grandmother's family had climbed down to the cellar through a little trap door hidden under a mat in the big central room of their shack. But his grandmother's pet goat, whom she'd loved as much as Aaron loved Pidge and more, had to be left above, because if it had made a sound in the cellar, they would never have lived to see the next morning. They all hid under the wood in the woodbin and waited, hardly breathing.

Suddenly, from above, they heard shouts and calls and screams at a distance. And then the noise was in their house. Boots pounding on the floor, and everything breaking and crashing overhead. The smell of smoke and the shouts of a dozen men.

The terror went on for an hour, and then the sound of horses' hooves faded into the distance. They waited another hour to make sure, and then the father went up out of the cellar and the rest of the family followed. The door to the house had been torn from its hinges, and every piece of furniture was broken. Every window, every dish, every stitch of clothing was totally destroyed, and one wall had been completely bashed in. And on the floor was the goat, lying quietly. Aaron's grandmother, who was just a little girl of eight at the time, had wept over the goat all day and all night and could not be consoled.

---

4. **Kishinev** (kĭsh'ə-nĕf'): a city (known today as Chisinau) that is now the capital of the country of Moldova.

5. **Czar Alexander the Second:** emperor of Russia from 1855 to 1881.

6. **Alexander the Third:** emperor of Russia from 1881 to 1894.

Backyards, Brooklyn (1932), Ogden Minton Pleissner. Oil on canvas, 24″ × 30 ⅛″, The Metropolitan Museum of Art, New York. Arthur Hoppock Hearn Fund, 1932 (32.80.2).

CLARIFY

What happened to Aaron's grandmother?

But they had been lucky. For other houses had been burned to the ground. And everywhere, not goats alone, nor sheep, but men and women and children lay quietly on the ground. The word for this sort of massacre, Aaron had learned, was *pogrom*. It had been a pogrom. And the men on the horses were Cossacks. Hated word. Cossacks.

And so Pidge would replace that goat of long ago. A pigeon on Second Avenue where no one needed trap doors or secret escape passages or woodpiles to hide under. A pigeon for his grandmother's sixtieth birthday. *Oh wing, heal quickly so my grandmother can send you flying to everywhere she wants!*

But a few days later, Aaron met Carl in the street again. And Carl told Aaron that there was going to be a meeting that afternoon in which a map was going to be drawn up to show where a secret treasure lay buried on the empty lot. "Bring the pigeon and you can come into the shack. We got a badge for you. A new kinda membership badge with a secret code on the back."

Aaron ran home, his heart pounding almost as fast as the pigeon's. He took Pidge in his hands and carried him out the door while his mother was busy in the kitchen making stuffed cabbage, his father's favorite dish. And by the time he reached the street, Aaron had decided to take the bandages off. Pidge would look like a real pigeon again, and none of the older boys would laugh or call him a bundle of rags.

Gently, gently he removed the bandages and the splints and put them in his pocket in case he should need them again. But Pidge seemed to hold his wing properly in place.

When he reached the empty lot, Aaron walked up to the shack, then hesitated. Four bigger boys were there. After a moment, Carl came out and commanded Aaron to hand Pidge over.

PREDICT

What will happen to Pidge?

"Be careful," said Aaron. "I just took the bandages off."

"Oh sure, don't worry," said Carl. By now Pidge was used to people holding him, and he remained calm in Carl's hands.

"OK," said Carl. "Give him the badge." And one of the older boys handed Aaron his badge with the code on the back. "Now light the fire," said Carl.

"What . . . what fire?" asked Aaron.

"The fire. You'll see," Carl answered.

"You didn't say nothing about a fire," said Aaron. "You didn't say nothing to—"

"Hey!" said Carl. "I'm the leader here. And you don't talk unless I tell you that you have p'mission. Light the fire, Al."

The boy named Al went out to the side of the shack, where some wood and cardboard and old newspapers had been piled into a huge mound. He struck a match and held it to the newspapers.

"OK," said Carl. "Let's get 'er good and hot. Blow on it. Everybody blow."

Aaron's eyes stung from the smoke, but he blew alongside the others, going from side to side as the smoke shifted toward them and away.

"Let's fan it," said Al.

In a few minutes, the fire was crackling and glowing with a bright yellow-orange flame.

"Get me the rope," said Carl.

One of the boys brought Carl some cord and Carl, without a word, wound it twice around the pigeon, so that its wings were tight against its body.

"What . . . what are you *doing!*" shouted Aaron. "You're hurting his wing!"

"Don't worry about his wing," said Carl. "We're gonna throw him into the fire. And when we do, we're gonna swear an oath of loyalty to—"

"No! *No!*" shouted Aaron, moving toward Carl.

"Grab him!" called Carl. "Don't let him get the pigeon!"

But Aaron had leaped right across the fire at Carl, taking him completely by surprise. He threw Carl back against the shack and hit out at his face with both fists. Carl slid down to the ground, and the pigeon rolled out of his hands. Aaron scooped up the pigeon and ran, pretending he was on roller skates so that he would go faster and faster. And as he ran across the lot he pulled the cord off Pidge and tried to find a place, *any* place, to hide him.

Gently, gently he removed the bandages.

But the boys were on top of him, and the pigeon slipped from Aaron's hands.

"Get him!" shouted Carl.

Aaron thought of the worst, the most horrible thing he could shout at the boys. "Cossacks!" he screamed. "You're all Cossacks!"

Two boys held Aaron back while the others tried to catch the pigeon. Pidge fluttered along the ground just out of reach, skittering one way and then the other. Then the boys came at him from two directions. But suddenly Pidge beat his wings in rhythm, and rose up, up, over the roof of the nearest <u>tenement</u>, up over Second Avenue toward the park.

With the pigeon gone, the boys turned toward Aaron and tackled him to the ground and punched him and tore his clothes and punched him some more. Aaron twisted and turned and kicked and punched back, shouting "Cossacks! Cossacks!" And somehow the word gave him the strength to tear away from them.

When Aaron reached home, he tried to go past the kitchen quickly so his mother wouldn't see his bloody face and torn clothing. But it was no use; his father was home from work early that night and was seated in the living room. In a moment Aaron was surrounded by his mother, father, and grandmother, and in another moment he had told them everything that had happened, the

words tumbling out between his broken sobs. Told them of the present he had planned, of the pigeon for a goat, of the gang, of the badge with the secret code on the back, of the shack, and the fire, and the pigeon's flight over the tenement roof.

And Aaron's grandmother kissed him and thanked him for his present which was even better than the pigeon.

"What present?" asked Aaron, trying to stop the series of sobs.

And his grandmother opened her pocketbook and handed Aaron her mirror and asked him to look. But all Aaron saw was his dirty, bruised face and his torn shirt.

Aaron thought he understood, and then, again, he thought he didn't. How could she be so happy when there really was no present? And why pretend that there was?

Later that night, just before he fell asleep, Aaron tried to imagine what his grandmother might have done with the pigeon. She would have fed it, and she certainly would have talked to it, as she did to all the birds, and . . . and then she would have let it go free. Yes, of course. Pidge's flight to freedom must have been the gift that had made his grandmother so happy. Her goat has escaped from the Cossacks at last, Aaron thought, half dreaming. And he fell asleep with a smile. ❖

> Pidge beat his wings in rhythm, and rose.

WORDS TO KNOW **tenement** (tĕn′ə-mənt) *n.* a rundown apartment building

Street Corner Flight

BY NORMA LANDA FLORES

From this side . . .
   of their concrete barrio[1]
      two small boys hold
         fat white pigeons
trapped in their trembling hands.

Then,
   gently,
      not disturbing
         their powers of flight,
            release them
into the air.

They were free
   to glide above
      rushing traffic
         soar beyond
            labyrinths[2] of
food stamps . . . loneliness . . . and want.

They were free
   to fly
      toward the other side . . .
a world away.

---

1. **barrio** (bä′rē-ō′): a city neighborhood where
   many Spanish-speaking people live.
2. **labyrinths** (lăb′ə-rĭnths′): mazes.

RESPONDING
OPTIONS

FROM **PERSONAL RESPONSE** TO **CRITICAL ANALYSIS**

REFLECT   **1.** Draw a picture of the one scene, object, or character that stands out most in your memory of this story. Share the picture with your classmates.

RETHINK   **2.** What do you think Aaron's gift to his grandmother is?

3. What kind of person is Aaron? Describe his character and values.
   Consider
   • his feelings about the gang
   • his behavior toward Pidge
   • his relationships with his family and with his friend Noreen

4. Compare Aaron's gift with the gift you wrote about for the Personal Connection on page 184. How is Aaron's gift similar to or different from the gift you wrote about?

5. How does the Insight poem "Street Corner Flight" (page 193) connect with your understanding of the story?

RELATE   **6.** Aaron wants to belong to a club that his mother calls a gang. What is the difference between a club and a gang? How does the gang in the story compare with the gangs you know about today?

ANOTHER PATHWAY

Filling in a story map similar to the one shown here can help you understand "Aaron's Gift." Copy and complete the story map. Add enough events to describe the entire story. Then compare your story map with another student's.

Main Character:	Setting:
Conflict or Story Problem:	
Major Events:	
Event 1 Aaron finds a pigeon with a broken wing.	
Event 2	
Event 3	
Solution:	Theme:

QUICKWRITES

1. Write a **prediction** telling how Aaron's life might be affected by the events in the story. You may choose to focus on short-term effects, such as Aaron's possible further problems with the gang, or on long-term effects, such as Aaron's qualities as an adult.

2. Pretend you are Aaron's grandmother. Write a **diary entry** for the day Pidge flies away. How do you feel about what Aaron did? What does Pidge's freedom mean to you?

📁 *PORTFOLIO Save your writing. You may want to use it later as a springboard to a piece for your portfolio.*

LITERARY CONCEPTS

Characterization is the way writers create and develop characters. A writer may use any or all of these four basic methods to reveal a character's personality:

- description of the character's physical appearance
- the character's speech, thoughts, feelings, and actions
- the speech, thoughts, feelings, and actions of other characters
- direct comments by the writer about the character's nature

In "The Adoption of Albert," for example, the statement of Mary Elizabeth (the narrator) that "Louis was neater than most kids" provides a glimpse of Louis's personality. Find examples from "Aaron's Gift" to show how Myron Levoy develops the character of Aaron or his grandmother.

CONCEPT REVIEW: Theme You may recall that a story's theme is its message about life or people and that often a reader must infer, or figure out, the theme after carefully reading the story. What do you think the theme of "Aaron's Gift" is? What does the story say about life or people—or about the true nature of giving?

ACROSS THE CURRICULUM

Social Studies The words *Cossacks* and *pogroms* are explained briefly on the Previewing page for this story and in the story itself. Find out more about the pogroms ordered by Czar Alexander the Third. Who was this ruler? Why did he persecute the Jews? What was the role of the Cossacks in the pogroms? For your classroom library, create a reference file of the information you gather, either on paper or on a computer.

ALTERNATIVE ACTIVITIES

1. ***Cooperative Learning*** With a group of classmates, research the subject of pigeons. Discover how many kinds there are, where they live, what their habits are, and what their place in the environment is. Stage a **debate** for the class on whether the number of pigeons should be controlled in some manner. Discuss both the value of pigeons and the problems they cause.

2. The setting of "Aaron's Gift" is the Lower East Side of New York City. Use a metropolitan New York City map or a comprehensive atlas as a guide to help you draw a **street map** of the Lower East Side. Include sites of historical interest.

3. In the story, Carl wants to make Pidge the club's mascot. Many organizations—especially sports teams—adopt persons, animals, or objects as mascots. Choose a local, regional, or national sports league and research the teams' mascots. Make a **chart** that summarizes your findings. Display the chart in your classroom.

LITERARY LINKS

Look back at selections in this book in which animals play important roles: "Ghost of the Lagoon," the excerpt from *Woodsong,* and "The Dog of Pompeii." Compare and contrast the role of Tupa, Scarhead, or Bimbo with the role of Pidge in "Aaron's Gift."

Tupa	Pidge

WORDS TO KNOW

EXERCISE A On your paper, write the letter of the word that is different in meaning from the other words in each set below. Use a dictionary if you wish.

1. (a) entrance (b) stoop (c) balcony (d) porch
2. (a) frenzied (b) fragile (c) frantic (d) wild
3. (a) emblem (b) mascot (c) opponent (d) symbol
4. (a) mansion (b) high-rise (c) apartment (d) tenement
5. (a) struggling (b) flailing (c) thrashing (d) relaxing

EXERCISE B Work with a partner to complete the exercises below.

1. Use body movements to demonstrate the meanings of *frenzied* and *thrashing.*

2. Describe Aaron's neighborhood, using *stoop* and *tenement* in your description.

MYRON LEVOY

Myron Levoy was born in New York City and worked as a chemical engineer before becoming a professional writer. He writes poetry, plays, and short stories. In describing his work, he says, "My continuing concern has been for the 'outsider,' the loner." In *Alan and Naomi,* Levoy writes about a Jewish boy facing anti-Semitism who befriends a deeply troubled refugee girl. In another novel, *A Shadow Like a Leopard,* Levoy depicts a boy from the ghetto who is torn between two worlds—he carries a knife but also writes poetry. Each of these

1930–

people, says Levoy, must grow and struggle to discover who he or she is.

Levoy has won many national and international awards for his work. In 1982, *A Shadow Like a Leopard* was named one of the best books for young adults by the American Library Association. *The Witch of Fourth Street and Other Stories,* from which "Aaron's Gift" is taken, was named a *Book World* honor book.

OTHER WORKS *Three Friends, The Hanukkah of Great-Uncle Otto, Pictures of Adam, The Magic Hat of Mortimer Wintergreen, Kelly 'n Me*

Where the Sidewalk Ends

BY SHEL SILVERSTEIN

There is a place where the sidewalk ends
And before the street begins,
And there the grass grows soft and white,
And there the sun burns crimson bright,
5   And there the moon-bird rests from his flight
To cool in the peppermint wind.

Let us leave this place where the smoke blows black
And the dark street winds and bends.
Past the pits where the asphalt flowers grow
10   We shall walk with a walk that is measured and slow,
And watch where the chalk-white arrows go
To the place where the sidewalk ends.

Yes we'll walk with a walk that is measured and slow,
And we'll go where the chalk-white arrows go,
15   For the children, they mark, and the children, they know
The place where the sidewalk ends.

SHEL SILVERSTEIN

Besides writing poetry, songs, and stories, Shel Silverstein draws cartoons, sings, and plays the guitar. He started writing and drawing when he was around 12, although, he says, "I would much rather have been a good baseball player."

Silverstein's work is popular among people of all ages. His books include

1932–

Where the Sidewalk Ends, A Light in the Attic, and *The Giving Tree*. The poet lives on a houseboat in California but travels often. He says, "I want to go everywhere, look at and listen to everything. You can go crazy with some of the wonderful stuff there is in life. I have ideas, and ideas are too good not to share."

The Spider and the Fly

BY MARY HOWITT

"Will you walk into my parlor?"
    said the Spider to the Fly,
"'Tis the prettiest little parlor
    that ever you did spy.
5 The way into my parlor
    is up a winding stair,
And I have many curious things
    to show when you are there."
"Oh no, no," said the little Fly,
10   "to ask me is in vain,
For who goes up your winding stair
    can ne'er come down again."
"I'm sure you must be weary, dear,
    with soaring up so high;
15 Will you rest upon my little bed?"
    said the Spider to the Fly.
"There are pretty curtains drawn around,
    the sheets are fine and thin,
And if you like to rest awhile,
20   I'll snugly tuck you in!"
"Oh no, no," said the little Fly,
    "for I've often heard it said,
They never, never wake again,
    who sleep upon your bed!"

25 Said the cunning Spider to the Fly,
     "Dear friend, what can I do,
To prove the warm affection
     I've always felt for you?
I have within my pantry
30   good store of all that's nice
I'm sure you're very welcome—
     will you please to take a slice?"
 "Oh no, no," said the little Fly,
     "kind sir, that cannot be,
35 I've heard what's in your pantry and
     I do not wish to see."
 "Sweet creature," said the Spider,
     "you're witty and you're wise;
How handsome are your gauzy wings,
40   how brilliant are your eyes!
I have a little looking-glass
     upon my parlor shelf,
If you'll step in a moment, dear,
     you shall behold yourself."

45 "I thank you, gentle sir," she said,
     "for what you're pleased to say,
And bidding you good morning now,
     I'll call another day."
The Spider turned him round about
50   and went into his den,
For well he knew the silly Fly
     would soon come back again.
So he wove a subtle web,
     in a little corner sly,
55 And set his table ready,
     to dine upon the Fly.
Then he came out to his door again
     and merrily did sing:
"Come hither, hither, pretty Fly,
60   with the pearl and silver wing.
Your robes are green and purple—
     there's a crest upon your head;
Your eyes are like the diamond bright,
     but mine are dull as lead."

65 Alas, alas! How very soon
        this silly little Fly,
    Hearing his wily, flattering words,
        came slowly flitting by.
    With buzzing wings she hung aloft,
70   then near and nearer drew,
    Thinking only of her brilliant eyes,
        and green and purple hue;
    Thinking only of her crested head—
        poor foolish thing!
75 Up jumped the cunning Spider
        and fiercely held her fast.
    He dragged her up his winding stair,
        into his dismal den,
    Within his little parlor—
80   but she ne'er came out again!

MARY HOWITT

"The Spider and the Fly," Mary Howitt's best-known children's poem, appeared in her book *Sketches of Natural History,* published in 1834. Created for Howitt's own children, this collection of brief lyrics displays the poet's ability to convey moral principles in a whimsical, witty way. She produced similar poetry in the collections *Tales in Verse* and *Birds and Flowers and Other Country Things.*

Howitt (1799–1888) grew up as Mary Botham in Uttoxeter, England, where she shared a passion for reading poetry with her sister Anna. In 1821, she married William Howitt, who was also a writer and with whom she coauthored several books. The Howitts' Quaker faith dominated their lives and writings.

In the early 1840s, the couple spent three years in Germany, where Mary translated German works into English and learned the Swedish language. In the years 1845–1847, she translated four works of the Danish writer Hans Christian Andersen. She is credited as the first to make his stories accessible to English and American readers. In her fruitful career, Howitt wrote more than 50 books and edited, adapted, translated, and compiled over 30 others.

Two girls of twelve or so at a table

BY CHARLES REZNIKOFF

Two girls of twelve or so at a table
in the Automat, smiling at each other
and the world; eating sedately.
And a tramp, wearing two or three tattered coats,
5   dark with dirt, mumbling, sat down beside them—
Miss Muffit's spider.
But, unlike her, they were not frightened away,
and did not shudder as they might if older and look askance.
They did steal a glance
10   at their dark companion and were slightly amused:
in their shining innocence seeing
in him only another human being.

Snack Bar (1954), Isabel Bishop. Oil on masonite, 13 ½″ × 11 ⅛″, Columbus Museum of Art, Ohio, Museum Purchase: Howald Fund.

CHARLES REZNIKOFF

1894–1976

After receiving a law degree and being admitted to the New York bar in 1916, Charles Reznikoff chose not to practice law but to concentrate on writing. For a time he worked as an editor for the American Law Book Company, and in 1955 he became an editor for Jewish Frontier in New York City.

The Brooklyn, New York, native once explained that he preferred to use his mental energy for writing: "I did not continue with journalism because—to change the old adage—I was more interested in dog bites man than in man bites dog." In addition to numerous volumes of poetry, Reznikoff is remembered for his novels, including *By the Waters of Manhattan* and *The Lionhearted.*

New World

BY N. SCOTT MOMADAY

1.

First Man,
behold:
the earth
glitters
5 with leaves;
the sky
glistens
with rain.
Pollen
10 is borne
on winds
that low
and lean
upon
15 mountains.
Cedars
blacken
the slopes—
and pines.

2.

20 At dawn
eagles
hie and
hover
above
25 the plain
where light
gathers
in pools.
Grasses
30 shimmer
and shine.
Shadows
withdraw
and lie
35 away
like smoke.

Sunset in Memorium (1946),
Woody Crumbo. The Philbrook
Museum of Art, Tulsa, Oklahoma.

3.

At noon
turtles
enter
40 slowly
into
the warm
dark loam.
Bees hold
45 the swarm.
Meadows
recede
through planes
of heat
50 and pure
distance.

4.

At dusk
the gray
foxes
55 stiffen
in cold;
blackbirds
are fixed
in the
60 branches.
Rivers
follow
the moon,
the long
65 white track
of the
full moon.

N. SCOTT MOMADAY

"I have known that the sense of place is a dominant factor in my blood," says N. Scott Momaday. "It happens that I have traveled far and wide, and I have made my home elsewhere. But some elemental part of me remains in the hold of northern New Mexico."

Momaday grew up in New Mexico, where his parents taught among the Jemez Indians. The novelist, poet, editor, and adapter of Native American tales says he came to know the land by exploring it in all seasons. His artistic skill came from his father, an artist who was a Kiowa Indian, and his writing ability from his

1934–

mother, a writer whose great-grandmother was a Cherokee. His interest in poetry was inspired by his admiration of the poems of Emily Dickinson.

Momaday was a relatively unknown author when, in 1969, he received the Pulitzer Prize for fiction for his novel *House Made of Dawn.* He has taught English literature in several universities.

An accomplished artist as well, he has had his drawings and paintings exhibited in galleries. Momaday now teaches at the University of Arizona, where he continues to write and to pursue his interest in ancient forms of storytelling.

Something Told the Wild Geese

BY RACHEL FIELD

Something told the wild geese
    It was time to go.
Though the fields lay golden
    Something whispered,—"Snow."
5 Leaves were green and stirring,
    Berries, luster-glossed,
But beneath warm feathers
    Something cautioned,—"Frost."
All the sagging orchards
10   Steamed with amber spice,
But each wild breast stiffened
    At remembered ice.
Something told the wild geese
    It was time to fly,—
15 Summer sun was on their wings,
    Winter in their cry.

RACHEL FIELD

1894–1942

In 1929, Rachel Field was the first woman to receive the Newbery Medal. *Hitty: Her First Hundred Years,* the book that earned Field this honor, was inspired by an antique doll she found in a New York City antique shop. The name Hitty appeared on a slip of paper pinned to the doll's dress. In creating the story of a doll carved from mountain ash by a peddler, Field combined her interests in children's stories and history—particularly the history of pioneer life.

Born in New York City, Field grew up in western Massachusetts. She attended a small private school, with only about ten students, where her interests in writing and acting began. Because of her writing ability, she was admitted to Radcliffe College in 1914. Three of her plays were eventually produced there.

Best known for her books for children, Field produced more than 40 such books, including several volumes of poetry and some books with her own illustrations. Three of her adult fiction books, most notably *All This and Heaven Too,* were adapted as motion pictures.

WRITING ABOUT LITERATURE

GETTING TO THE POINT

Is "Chinatown" about a city or about the writer discovering himself? Is "Aaron's Gift" about a boy and his pigeon, or is there more to the story? Finding meaning in a work of literature is often like finding a valuable treasure. The same skills you use to understand literature can help you make sense of things in your daily life. In these pages you'll

- study the details writers use to support their ideas
- choose a confusing or interesting passage to interpret
- study details to help interpret the meaning of a stage setting

The Writer's Style: Main Idea and Details Writers often present what is important to them by clearly stating an idea and supporting it with facts, details, or examples.

Read the Literature

What is the main idea of each passage? How do you know?

Literature Models

Examples Support the Main Idea
What do you learn about the writer of the first passage? What example does Yep give? How does the example support the main idea?

> Moreover, my lack of Chinese made me an outsider in Chinatown—sometimes even among my friends. Since it was a Catholic school taught by nuns, my friends would always tell dirty jokes in Chinese so the nuns wouldn't understand. However, neither did I, so I missed out on a good deal of humor when I was a boy. What Chinese I did pick up was the Chinese that got spoken in the playground—mostly insults and vulgar names.
>
> Laurence Yep, from "Chinatown"

Details Support the Main Idea
How was Pidge's wing fixed? What details does the author give about this event?

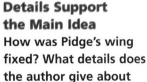

> The wing was surprisingly easy to fix, for the break showed clearly and Pidge was remarkably patient and still, as if he knew he was being helped. Or perhaps he was just exhausted from all the thrashing about he had done. Two Popsicle sticks served as splints, and strips from an old undershirt were used to tie them in place. Another strip held the wing to the bird's body.
>
> Myron Levoy, from "Aaron's Gift"

Connect to Advertising

Advertisement writers present their main ideas in many different ways. Why do you think the writer of this advertisement states the main idea at the beginning? How else might the ad be written? Would it be as clear? as good?

Advertisement

Facts Support the Main Idea
What facts are included in the ad? What remains after you separate the facts from the promises?

Try Your Hand: Main Idea and Details

1. **Adding Facts** Skim the selection "Chinatown," from *The Lost Garden,* and then try the following:

   • Add a fact about the plant life in Chinatown to the following sentence: "There is little plant life in Chinatown."
   • Revise the following sentence to add a fact about the Chinese language: "The Chinese language was sometimes spoken in Chinatown."

2. **A Real-Life Example** Write a statement about something you like to do, such as read books, play sports, or watch movies. Then write some examples that support your statement.

3. **Including Details** Revise a piece of your current writing by using specific details to support your main ideas.

SkillBuilder

 GRAMMAR FROM WRITING

Using Dashes
Dashes can be used creatively and effectively to add details to paragraphs. Look at the first literature model on the opposite page. Notice how the information following the dashes clarifies Laurence Yep's ideas.

You can also use dashes to show a break in thought. Place a dash before the break and a second dash to end the break. Look at this passage from Myron Levoy's "Aaron's Gift." Notice where the author places the dashes and what additional detail he provides.

A group of older boys from down the block had a club— Aaron's mother called it a gang—and Aaron had longed to join as he had never longed for anything else.

APPLYING WHAT YOU'VE LEARNED
Read this paragraph and think about where dashes could have been used. Then rewrite it and compare your paragraph with those of your classmates.

I thought "Chinatown" was a great selection. It was the best I've read so far. I even argued about how good it was with Tina. She thought it was just OK.

GRAMMAR HANDBOOK

For more information on other punctuation marks, see page 844 of the Grammar Handbook.

Interpretation

As you read more, you'll find that some stories are special to you. These stories may have characters or events that remind you of people or experiences in your life. Sometimes characters have the same problems you have. You may even find important messages in these stories that will last a lifetime. To find these messages, you will have to interpret, or explore the meaning of, key parts of stories.

GUIDED ASSIGNMENT

Interpret a Passage Have you ever been startled or confused by a passage in a story? On these pages you'll look at one passage and explore its meaning.

1 Prewrite and Explore

Go back to a Unit Two selection that you liked or to another favorite story. Reread the story or just skim it. A double-entry reading log like the one at the left can help you record and explore important or confusing lines or passages.

CHOOSING YOUR PASSAGE

The following questions might help you select a line or passage to write about.

- Which lines or passages seem important to the story?
- Which passage confused, surprised, or interested you?

Decision Point Based on your answers to the questions above, which passage do you want to write about? If necessary, take more time to think about the possibilities. Consider discussing the lines with your classmates to come up with ideas.

2 Write and Analyze a Discovery Draft

Now look closely at the passage you have chosen and try to figure out what it means. Ask yourself the following questions:

- What does the writer describe in the passage or line?
- What details does the writer use?
- What do I think the writer is trying to say?

The yellow notes on the discovery draft show the student's thoughts about one passage.

Line or passage	Ideas
"I was always going into Chinatown to explore the streets and perhaps find the key to the pieces of the puzzle."	- What does he hope to find in Chinatown? - What puzzle? - Why do other family members leave Chinatown?
"How could I pretend to be somebody else when I didn't even know who I was?"	- What does he mean—he doesn't know who he is? - This sounds like an important line. - Maybe that's the puzzle.

Student's Discovery Draft

A passage near the end of "Chinatown" makes me sad. It makes me sad because the narrator didn't enjoy dressing up in costumes anymore. I think the writer tried to make this an important part.

I want to tell how I feel about this passage. Then I can tell what the meaning is.

I think he wants to figure out who he is first. Maybe the costumes confuse him.

Why does it upset me that he doesn't want to put on those costumes? He describes costumes so nicely. People wear costumes to pretend they're somebody else. He says he doesn't know who he is. Does he?

COLLECTING THE EVIDENCE

Gathering details is a good way to develop your essay. List facts, examples, or reasons that support your ideas.

③ Draft and Share

Consider organizing your draft into three parts: an introduction that summarizes the story and tells why you chose this particular passage; a body that has reasons, facts, examples, and other evidence to explain your interpretation; and a conclusion in which you summarize your interpretation. Ask another student to read your essay and give you feedback.

 PEER RESPONSE

- Which details help you understand my interpretation?
- Which parts of the passage or my interpretation are still unclear?

4 Revise and Edit

Writers revise and edit their drafts to make their writing clearer and more interesting. As you revise your essay, make sure your details and evidence help support your conclusions. When you are finished, you could read your essay to someone who has not read the selection you wrote about. Did your essay make the person want to read the story?

Student's Final Draft

Have you ever asked yourself "Who am I"? The writer of "Chinatown," Laurence Yep, does. At first I thought this selection was just about Chinatown and what it was like when the author was a boy. But after I read it again, I knew it was about how confused Yep was when he was a kid. When I think back on the selection, the final passage stands out. To me, it describes the meaning of the whole story.

How did the writer tell you what the paper would be about?

Why did the writer use the quotation in this paragraph?

When the writer talks about his singing adventure, he sets us up because we think it's a funny scene. But then he starts talking about his deep feelings. He says, "But the experience cured me of wanting to dress up and be something else." In this passage the writer realized that he just wanted to be his own person.

Standards for Evaluation

The interpretive essay
- identifies the work by title and author and the passage to be interpreted
- explains what the writer thinks a passage means
- is supported by quotations, reasons, and other evidence
- shows why the writer thinks the passage is important

Grammar in Context

Sentence Fragments As a writer, you put sentences together from bits and pieces of ideas. Readers will not understand your interpretive essay if you write sentences that do not express a complete thought. Every sentence has two parts. The subject tells whom or what the sentence is about. The predicate tells what was done or what happened.

Have you ever asked yourself "Who am I"? The writer of "Chinatown," ~~does~~ When I think back on the selection, The final passage stands out. To me, it describes the meaning of the whole story.

Notice how the corrections in the above paragraph help the writer express complete thoughts. For more information about sentence fragments, see page 812 of the Grammar Handbook.

Try Your Hand: Fixing Sentence Fragments

Add subjects or predicates to each fragment below to create a complete sentence. Be sure to use correct end marks and other punctuation in the sentences you form.

1. My lack of Chinese
2. enjoyed putting on costumes
3. very little plant life in Chinatown
4. The fancy hotels of Nob Hill
5. Despite all the coaching from his father

G→ GRAMMAR FROM WRITING

Understanding Parts of Speech

Understanding parts of speech can help you make sure your sentences have complete subjects and complete predicates. Sometimes the same word may be used as several parts of speech. When a word is used as a certain part of speech, it follows the rules for that part of speech. The only way to determine a part of speech in a sentence is to reread the sentence carefully and see how the word is used. Look at these sentences and how the italicized words are used.

- A friend's father would *fashion* Chinese weapons at home. (verb)
- He didn't know much about Chinese *fashion*. (noun)
- He searched all over Chinatown for a *fashion* magazine. (adjective)

APPLYING WHAT YOU'VE LEARNED

Write two sentences for each word below. Use the word as each part of speech shown in the parentheses.

1. ring (noun, verb)
2. cold (adjective, noun)
3. well (noun, adverb)
4. turn (noun, verb)

Now look at your draft to make sure you have used each word as the correct part of speech.

WHAT'S THE BIG IDEA?

By carefully choosing and arranging props, directors of theater, movie, and TV productions can present an idea as clearly as the writers of stories can. You can study the details in a set—or any room—to make sense of what you see and perhaps find a message or special meaning.

View Look at this stage set. In your notebook, describe the props, furniture, walls—anything that gets your attention.

Interpret Think about why those props were used. Then ask yourself these questions: What information about the time or the characters does each detail give? Who might live here? Are they rich or poor?

Discuss In a small group, share your ideas about the stage set. Then, create a cast of characters for the play. Discuss details from the set to help create your characters. Now follow up on your discussion by using the SkillBuilder on the next page.

→ **CRITICAL THINKING**

Drawing Conclusions

When you draw conclusions, either while reading or while viewing something, you use written or visual clues and information from your own experience to figure out something that is not directly stated.

For example, if you peeked into a friend's house and saw old portraits of relatives, a coat of arms hanging on the wall, and photo albums on a table, you might conclude that your friend's family takes pride in its history.

APPLYING WHAT YOU'VE LEARNED
Some settings give us particular ideas or special meanings. For example, the details in a judge's chambers might suggest authority or fairness; a hotel lobby might use furnishings to suggest homeyness or warmth.

In a small group, think of a setting. Agree on a particular idea or meaning that the setting might give. Then brainstorm a list of the details that would help you create that idea.

TESTS OF ENDURANCE

WHAT DO YU THINK?

REFLECTING ON THEME

In a tug of war, one side seems to be stronger; then the power shifts. The tugs in opposite directions can be compared to the emotions experienced in growing up, when the need to belong conflicts with the need to be independent. Use this page of activities to explore the tests of endurance you have faced and the lessons you have learned.

Are you a good sport?

Working with a group, choose a game familiar to everyone. Discuss your knowledge of the game, and draft a list of guidelines for being a good sport while playing it. Compare your list with those of other groups. What has the class identified as the most important quality of a good sport?

Good sport guidelines

1.
2.
3.
4.
5.

What was your test?

Recall a major childhood accomplishment, such as learning to ride a bicycle. Did you become discouraged at some point? Who encouraged you? How did you motivate yourself? Describe the experience in your notebook.

Looking Back

At the beginning of this unit, you thought about finding a special place. Did you discover new ideas as you read? Which character's special place is most similar to your own? Draw or paint that character's special place.

Where are your obstacles?

What problems are involved in growing up? Work with a partner to begin drawing an obstacle course that shows some of the pitfalls of growing up. Leave space to add more obstacles as you read the selections in Part 2.

PREVIEWING

NONFICTION

Oh Broom, Get to Work

Yoshiko Uchida (yō′shē-kō ōo-chē′dä)

PERSONAL CONNECTION

This selection describes how a young girl reacts to the presence of unwanted visitors in her home. How would you deal with an unwanted guest? With your classmates, brainstorm some creative solutions to this problem.

CULTURAL CONNECTION

As you read this selection, note the effects that the visitors have on "Yo Chan" (as Yoshiko Uchida was nicknamed). Also consider the effect that Yoshiko has on the visitors—especially as you read about the incident with the broom.

As young girls, Uchida and her sister, Keiko (kā′kō), found themselves continually in the company of household guests. Uchida's parents were Issei (ēs′sā′)—Japanese immigrants to the United States—and often opened their home to Japanese

students, such as the one shown here, who came to the United States to study at the University of California or the Pacific School of Religion. Most of these visitors were engaged in graduate work, the advanced courses taken by students who have already received a college degree. Their studies, made more difficult by living in a foreign and unwelcoming land, were in preparation for the Christian ministry.

Courtesy of the Pacific School of Religion.

WRITING CONNECTION

Choose one of the following questions as a topic, and write about it in your notebook.

When you visit someone's home, what do you do to make a good impression?

What has impressed you most about a visitor to your home?

How often and how long should a visitor visit?

Oh Broom,

Get to Work

by Yoshiko Uchida

I was on my way home from school when I found it. A little dead sparrow. It lay still and stiff, its legs thrust in the air like two sticks. It was the first dead creature I had seen close up, and it filled me with both <u>dread</u> and fascination.

I knew what I would do. I would give the bird a nice funeral. Mama would find a piece of soft red silk for me from her bag of sewing scraps. I would wrap the bird in a silken shroud,[1] put it in a candy box, and bury it beneath the peach tree. Maybe I would have Mama say a prayer for it, like the minister did at real funerals.

I picked up the bird carefully, cupping it in both hands, and ran home. I rushed through the kitchen and flung open the swinging door to the dining room.

"Look, Mama! I found a dead sparrow!"

But Mama was busy. She was sitting in the easy chair, knitting quietly. Sitting across from her on the sofa was a squat blob of a man—balding and gray—as silent as a mushroom.

The only sound was the soft ticking of the Chelsea clock on the mantel above the fireplace. I could see dust motes floating in the shaft of late afternoon sun that filtered in from the small west window.

Poor Mama was stuck with company again. She and the guest had both run out of things to say, but the visitor didn't want to leave.

"Hello, Yo Chan," my mother called. She seemed happy for the <u>intrusion</u>. "How was school today?"

But all I thought was, company again! It wasn't the first time a visitor had <u>deprived</u> me of my mother's time and attention, and I was tired of having them intrude into our lives uninvited. I stomped out of the living room without even a word of greeting to our guest, and knew I would have to bury the sparrow by myself.

Mama might have sung a Japanese hymn for me in her high, slightly off-key voice, and she certainly would have offered a better prayer than I could <u>devise</u>. But I did the best I could.

"Dear Heavenly Father," I began. "Please bless this little bird. It never hurt anybody. Thank you. Amen."

> Poor Mama was stuck with company again.

---

1. **shroud** (shroud): a cloth used to wrap a body for burial.

WORDS TO KNOW

dread (drĕd) *n.* deep fear; terror
intrusion (ĭn-trōo'zhən) *n.* an act of coming in rudely or inappropriately
deprive (dĭ-prīv') *v.* to take something away from
devise (dĭ-vīz') *v.* to form or plan in the mind; think up

I buried the box beneath a mound of soft, loose dirt, picked a few nasturtiums to lay on top, and made a cross out of two small twigs.

The gray-blob mushroom was just another of the countless visitors, usually from Japan, who came to see my parents. They were both graduates of Doshisha, one of Japan's leading Christian universities, and had close ties with many of its professors. This meant that many of our visitors were ministers or young men studying to become ministers at the Pacific School of Religion in Berkeley.

Once in a while, one of the visitors would be a pleasant surprise. Like the Reverend Kimura, who sang the books of the Bible to the tune of an old folk song.

"*Mah-tai, Mah-ko, Luka, Yoha-neh-deh-un . . .*" he sang out in a loud, clear voice. "*Shito, Roma, Corinto, Zen-ko-sho . . .*" He clapped in time as he sang.

I saw Mama's eyes light up as she listened, and soon she joined in, clapping and singing and laughing at the pure joy of it.

Mama surprised me sometimes. She could be a lot of fun depending on whom she was with. It was too bad, I thought, that so much of the time she had to be serious and proper, while visiting ministers smothered her with their <u>pious</u> attitudes.

To me they were all achingly and endlessly boring. It was only once in a great while that a Reverend Kimura turned up, like a red jelly bean in a jar full of black licorice.

One <u>pompous</u> minister from Japan not only stayed overnight, which was bad enough, but left his dirty bathwater in the tub for Mama to wash out.

Yoshiko Uchida (right) and her older sister, Keiko, in the 1920s. Courtesy, The Bancroft Library, Berkeley, California.

"What nerve!" Keiko fumed.

"I'll say!" I echoed.

But Mama explained that in Japan everyone washed and rinsed outside the tub and got in just to soak. "That way the water in the tub stays clean, and you leave it for the next person."

Mama got down on her knees to wash out the tub, saying, "We're lucky he didn't try to wash himself outside the tub and flood the bathroom."

Some kind of luck, I thought.

I didn't feel at all lucky about the seminary[2] students who often dropped in, plunked themselves down on our sofa, and stayed until they were invited to have supper with us.

"Poor boys, they're lonely and homesick," Mama would say.

"They just need some of Mama's kind heart and good cooking," Papa would add. And if they needed some fatherly advice, he was more than willing to <u>dispense</u> plenty of that as well.

Both my parents had grown up poor, and they also knew what it was to be lonely. They cared deeply about other people and were always ready to lend a helping hand to anyone. Mama couldn't bear to think of her children ever being less than kind and caring.

"Don't ever be <u>indifferent</u>," she would say to Keiko and me. "That's the worst fault of all."

It was a fault she certainly never had. She would even send vitamins or herbs to some ailing person she had just met at the dentist's waiting room.

On holidays all the Japanese students from the Pacific School of Religion—sometimes as many as five or six—were invited to dinner. Keiko and I always complained shamelessly when they came.

"Aw, Mama . . . do you *have* to invite them?"

But we knew what we were expected to do. We flicked the dust cloth over the furniture, added extra boards to the dining room table so it filled up the entire room, and set it with Mama's good linen tablecloth and the company china.

EVALUATE

How does the mother's attitude toward visitors compare with Yoshiko's?

If it was to be a turkey dinner, we put out the large plates and good silverware. If it was a sukiyaki[3] dinner,

we put out the rice bowls, smaller dishes, and black lacquer[4] chopsticks.

The men came in their best clothes, their squeaky shoes shined, their hair smelling of camellia hair oil. Papa didn't cook much else, but he was an expert when it came to making sukiyaki, and cooked it right at the table with gas piped in from the kitchen stove. As the men arrived, he would start the fat sizzling in the small iron pan.

Soon Mama would bring out huge platters <u>laden</u> with thin slivers of beef, slices of bean curd[5] cake, scallions, bamboo shoots, spinach, celery, and yam noodle threads. Then Papa would combine a little of everything in broth flavored with soy sauce, sugar, and wine, and the mouth-watering smells would drift through the entire house.

One evening in the middle of a sukiyaki dinner, one of the guests, Mr. Okada, suddenly rose from the table and hurried into the kitchen. We all stopped eating as the scholarly Mr. Okada vanished without explanation.

"Mama," I began, "he's going the wrong way if he has to . . ."

PREDICT

What is happening in the kitchen?

Mama stopped me with a firm hand on my knee. My sister and I looked at each other. What did he want in the kitchen anyway? More rice? Water? What?

---

2. **seminary** (sĕm'ə-nĕr´ē): a school for the training of priests, ministers, or rabbis.

3. **sukiyaki** (sōō´kē-yä´kē): a Japanese dish of sliced meat, bean curd, and vegetables seasoned and fried together.

4. **lacquer** (lăk'ər): a shiny substance used as a decorative coating on wooden objects.

5. **bean curd**: a food made from soybeans—also known as tofu.

WORDS
TO
KNOW

dispense (dĭ-spĕns') *v.* to give out; distribute
indifferent (ĭn-dĭf'ər-ənt) *adj.* not interested; unconcerned
laden (lād'n) *adj.* weighed down; heavy

219

It seemed a half hour before Mr. Okada finally reappeared. But he was smiling and seemed much happier.

"I'm sorry," he murmured, "but it was so warm I had to remove my winter undershirt." He wiped his face with a big handkerchief and added, "I feel much better now."

I knew if I looked at Keiko we would both explode. But I did. And we did. We laughed so hard we had to leave the table and rush into the kitchen holding our sides. Keiko and I often got the giggles at company dinners, and the harder we tried to stop, the harder we laughed. The only solution was for us not ever to glance at each other if we felt the giggles coming on.

In spite of all our grumbling, Keiko and I often enjoyed ourselves at these dinners. Sometimes it was Papa who provided the laughs. He loved to talk, and everyone always liked listening to his stories. Sometimes he would tell a joke he had heard at the office:

A visitor from Japan looked up at the sky. "Beautiful pigeons!" he says to a native San Franciscan.

"No, no," answers the native. "Those aren't pigeons, they're gulls."

The visitor replies, smiling, "Well, gulls or boys, they're beautiful pigeons!"

Much laughter all around.

After dinner Papa liked to gather everyone around the piano. He had a good baritone voice, often sang solos at church, and even organized the church choir. Keiko played the piano, and we sang everything from "Old Black Joe"[6] to "In the Good Old Summertime."

Sometimes Keiko and I added to the entertainment by playing duets for our guests —a fairly <u>audacious</u> act since most of the time

Before too long, he actually got up and left.

I hadn't practiced all week. It never occurred to me then, but I suppose we were just as boring to them as they so often seemed to us.

I once thought I'd found the perfect solution for getting rid of unwanted guests. Mrs. Wasa, who was like an adopted grandmother, told me one day of an old Japanese superstition.

"If you want someone to leave," she said, "just drape a cloth over the bristles of a broom and stand it upside down. It always works!"

I filed that wonderful bit of information inside my head, and the very next time Mama was trapped in the living room with another silent mushroom, I gave it a try. I did just as Mrs. Wasa instructed and stood the broom at the crack of the swinging door leading to the dining and living rooms.

"Oh, broom," I murmured. "Get to work!"

I kept a watchful eye on our visitor, and before too long, he actually got up and left.

"Mama, it worked! It worked!" I shouted, dancing into the living room with the broom. "He left! I got him to leave!"

But Mama was horrified.

"*Mah*, Yo Chan," she said. "You put the broom at the doorway where he could see?"

I nodded. "I didn't think he'd notice."

Only then did I realize that our visitor had not only seen the broom, but had probably left because he knew a few Japanese superstitions himself.

I'd always thought the seminary on the hill was bent on endlessly churning out dull ministers to try my soul. But that afternoon I felt as though I'd evened the score just a little. ❖

---

6. **"Old Black Joe"**: a song by Stephen Foster (1826–1864), a composer of songs celebrating life in the Old South.

RESPONDING
OPTIONS

FROM *PERSONAL RESPONSE* TO *CRITICAL ANALYSIS*

REFLECT
1. Does the young Yoshiko Uchida seem like someone you would like to meet? Why or why not?

RETHINK
2. In your opinion, how well does Yoshiko deal with her family's many visitors?
   Consider
   - what she reveals about her mother's and father's attitudes
   - what she reveals about her feelings toward her family
   - her descriptions of the many visitors and the activities the family shares with them

3. What general impressions do you think the visitors might have of Yoshiko and her family?

4. Yoshiko's mother says, "Don't ever be indifferent. That's the worst fault of all." Do you agree? Explain.

5. Do you think it was more difficult for Uchida's parents to adapt to life in the United States after growing up in Japan, or was life probably harder for their daughters? Give a reason for your answer.

RELATE
6. On the basis of this selection and your own ideas, describe your idea of the perfect host and the perfect guest.

ANOTHER PATHWAY

With a partner, create a chart similar to the one shown here. Review "Oh Broom, Get to Work," listing each incident in which Yoshiko encounters an unwelcome visitor. Record information in the first two sections. Then recommend an alternative reaction.

Incident	Yoshiko's Reaction	Your Reaction
A visitor is present when Yoshiko wants to show her mother a dead sparrow.	She stomps out of the room without speaking.	I would have greeted the visitor and told about the sparrow.

QUICKWRITES

1. Write a **list of rules** for guests. Use some humor so that your guests won't be offended.

2. Imagine that you are a lonely seminary student who has just spent an evening with the Uchida family. Before you climb into bed for the night, write a **diary entry** describing your visit.

📁 *PORTFOLIO Save your writing. You may want to use it later as a springboard to a piece for your portfolio.*

LITERARY CONCEPTS

An **anecdote** is a short and entertaining account of a person or an event. Anecdotes are often included in larger works to amuse or to make a point. For example, in the excerpt from *Woodsong* (page 117) Gary Paulsen tells the anecdote about his encounter with Scarhead to point out that people must respect the wilderness and wild animals. Do you think Uchida includes the anecdote about the broom mainly to amuse or mainly to make a point?

ALTERNATIVE ACTIVITIES

1. Uchida mentions black lacquer chopsticks used to eat sukiyaki. What is lacquer ware? How is it made? Use drawings, photographs, pictures from magazines, and actual lacquer ware, if possible, to make a **display** about this traditional Asian art form.

2. **Cooperative Learning** Work with several classmates to act out a **scene** from the story. Have one person read the words of the scene aloud as the others mime the action. Then switch roles, with someone else becoming the narrator.

THE WRITER'S STYLE

The descriptive details that Uchida includes help make the writing lively and interesting. Phrases such as "hair smelling of camellia hair oil" appeal to readers' senses and create vivid images in their minds. With classmates, look over the selection to find additional examples of such details.

WORDS TO KNOW

Review the Words to Know in the boxes at the bottom of the selection pages. Then, on your own paper, write the word described by each of the following sentences.

1. This is how you feel when you don't care about something.
2. Pharmacists do this with pills.
3. Someone who is stuffy and dignified might be called this.
4. You might feel this before taking a sudden and unexpected test.
5. This is what happens when someone barges into your room without being invited.
6. You do this when you think up an excuse.
7. With a 50-pound pack on your back, you might feel this way.
8. People in a house of worship may feel this way.
9. When you take something from someone, you do this.
10. After taking a bold or reckless chance, you might be described as this.

YOSHIKO UCHIDA

An author and educator, Yoshiko Uchida grew up in Berkeley, California. Her parents—leaders of Berkeley's Japanese-American community—filled their home with homesick seminary students, ministers, and graduates of Doshisha University.

Shortly after Japan and the United States declared war in 1941, many Japanese Americans were arrested and placed in internment camps. Uchida's father was sent to Montana, and the rest of the family was sent to Topaz, a relocation center in Utah. She wrote about these years in *Desert Exile: The Uprooting of a Japanese American Family.*

Though Uchida's parents taught their daughters Japanese customs, traditions, and values, the fami-

1921–1992

ly's loyalty and devotion to its adopted country was strong. In 1984 she said that she hoped that children could be "caring human beings who don't think in terms of labels—foreigners or Asians or whatever—but think of people as human beings."

Uchida wrote many children's books about Japanese Americans. Her first, *The Dancing Kettle,* includes many of the Japanese folk tales her mother once read to her. "Oh Broom, Get to Work" is a chapter from her autobiography *The Invisible Thread.*

OTHER WORKS *A Jar of Dreams, The Happiest Ending, The Terrible Leak*

POETRY

It Seems I Test People
James Berry

Growing Pains
Jean Little

PERSONAL CONNECTION

In the poems you are about to read, the speakers relate personal experiences that had a lasting effect on them. Think about personal experiences you have had that might inspire you to write a poem. In your notebook or on a sheet of paper, create a chart similar to the one shown here. In the first box, briefly describe one of your experiences. In the second box, summarize an idea about the experience that you might want to communicate. As you read, compare your experience and idea with those presented in each poem.

Inspirational Experience

Idea to Communicate

LITERARY CONNECTION

The shape of the words and lines on the page is called **form.** Poets choose a form that they believe will convey their own particular feelings and ideas.

Both James Berry and Jean Little have chosen to use free verse to comment on personal experiences. Free verse is poetry that does not have a regular pattern of rhyme and meter. The lines of free verse usually flow more naturally than lines of rhymed, rhythmic poetry and sound more like normal speech. Free verse allows a poet to reveal feelings about a personal experience as though he or she were speaking face to face with the reader.

READING CONNECTION

Reading Poetry Orally In each of these poems, a personal voice communicates ideas about a particular experience. Read the poems aloud. Unless there is a punctuation mark at the end of a line, don't pause; keep reading to the next comma or end mark. In order to fully appreciate the poems, read them several times—for meaning, for feeling, and for the sounds of the words. Vary your expression, stressing different words and phrases each time.

It Seems
I Test
People

BY JAMES BERRY

My skin sun-mixed like basic earth
my voice having tones of thunder
my laughter working all of me as I laugh
my walk motioning strong swings
5 it seems I test people

Always awaiting a move
waiting always to recreate my view
my eyes packed with hellos behind them
my arrival bringing departures
10 it seems I test people

Self-Portrait (1934), Malvin Gray Johnson. National Museum of American Art, Washington, D.C./Art Resource, New York.

FROM **PERSONAL RESPONSE** TO **CRITICAL ANALYSIS**

REFLECT 1. What phrase or line of this poem stayed with you as you finished reading? Discuss your response with a partner.

RETHINK 2. What do you think the speaker means by the idea of testing people? Explain your answer.

RELATE 3. How do you think you would react to the speaker?
Consider
  • the speaker's self-description
  • the apparent reactions of others to the speaker
  • the personal experience the speaker relates

4. What does this poem suggest to you about the human need to belong?

Growing Pains

BY JEAN LITTLE

Mother got mad at me tonight and bawled me out.
She said I was lazy and self-centered.
She said my room was a pigsty.
She said she was sick and tired of forever nagging but I gave her no choice.
5   She went on and on until I began to cry.
I hate crying in front of people. It was horrible.

I got away, though, and went to bed and it was over.
I knew things would be okay in the morning;
Stiff with being sorry, too polite, but okay.
10   I was glad to be by myself.

Then she came to my room and apologized.
She explained, too.
Things had gone wrong all day at the store.
She hadn't had a letter from my sister and she was worried.
15   Dad had also done something to hurt her.
She even told me about that.
Then *she* cried.
I kept saying, "It's all right. Don't worry."
And wishing she'd stop.

20   I'm just a kid.
I can forgive her getting mad at me. That's easy.
But her sadness . . .
I don't know what to do with her sadness.
I yell at her often, "You don't understand me!"
25   But I don't want to have to understand her.
That's expecting too much.

RESPONDING
OPTIONS

FROM **PERSONAL RESPONSE** *TO* **CRITICAL ANALYSIS**

REFLECT 1. If you were to paint your reaction to "Growing Pains," what colors would you use? Explain your choice.

RETHINK 2. Why do you think the speaker finds the mother's sadness harder to accept than her anger?
Consider
- what the speaker means by "I don't know what to do with her sadness"
- the speaker's reaction to the mother's anger
- the speaker's comment "I'm just a kid"

3. What do you think are the "growing pains" referred to in the poem's title? Explain your answer.

4. If you could talk to the speaker of this poem about this experience, what would you say and why?

RELATE 5. Compare the speakers of "Growing Pains" and "It Seems I Test People." What do you think they might think of each other if they were to meet? Why?

ANOTHER PATHWAY
Cooperative Learning
With a few classmates, role-play the personal experience presented in each poem. Try to put yourself in the position of one of the individuals involved in the poem. Record any additional lines your group might create.

LITERARY CONCEPTS

A **simile** is a figure of speech comparing two things that are basically unlike but have something in common. In a simile, the comparison is expressed by means of the word *like* or *as*. In "Nadia the Willful," for example, Sue Alexander describes the sheik's words as "sharp *as a* scimitar." Find an example of a simile in either "Growing Pains" or "It Seems I Test People."

CRITIC'S CORNER

This statement about "It Seems I Test People" appears on the book jacket: "Universal themes ranging from isolation to joy will touch young people of all nationalities." Reread the poem and explain how well its theme relates to the lives of other young people you know.

QUICKWRITES

1. Write a **character sketch** of one of the speakers. Use your imagination, but make sure the person you describe is one whose feelings match the feelings presented in the poem.

2. Suppose that one of the poems' speakers writes to you, an advice columnist, for help. Write the **advice column** in which you respond to his or her request.

📁 *PORTFOLIO Save your writing. You may want to use it later as a springboard to a piece for your portfolio.*

THE WRITER'S STYLE

Despite the relaxed, informal appearance of free verse, much skill goes into its writing. In "It Seems I Test People," for example, the poet plays with the sound of language in lines like these:

> Always awaiting a move
> waiting always to recreate my view

Choose one of the poems and rewrite a few lines, using a formal rhyme scheme and rhythm. What is gained and lost in your version?

ALTERNATIVE ACTIVITIES

1. **Cooperative Learning** Work with two friends to create a series of **movements** or a **dance** that shows how one of the poems' speakers feels. If you like, use music with your dance.

2. Draw a **portrait** of one of the speakers. Choose a line or phrase from the poem to use as a title for your drawing.

JAMES BERRY

1925–

James Berry, a writer and editor born in Jamaica, moved to England, where he lives today, in 1948. His award-winning collection of stories told from a Jamaican child's point of view, *A Thief in the Village and Other Stories,* grew out of his own childhood experiences. He says, "In the Caribbean, we were the last outpost of the Empire. No one has reported our stories, or the way we saw things. It's the function of writers and poets to bring in the left-out side of the human family."

The poems in *When I Dance,* which won a *Signal* Poetry Award, are written in Caribbean dialect. These rhythmic, humorous poems focus on the injustice and goodness of daily life as well as the uniqueness of the individual. According to one poem: "Nobody can get into my clothes for me / or feel my fall for me, or do my running. / Nobody hears my music for me, either."

OTHER WORKS *Ajeemah and His Son, The Future-Telling Lady and Other Stories*

JEAN LITTLE

1932–

Jean Little was born in Formosa (now Taiwan), where both of her parents were doctors. Legally blind at birth, Little was taught to read by her parents before she began school, and by fourth grade her vision had improved enough for her to attend regular classes. When she was 15, her father collected and printed her first book of poems. She says, "From the first my Dad was my greatest critic and supporter. . . . Not until he died did I come to appreciate his unflagging zeal on my behalf."

Little's books are based on her own experiences and present unsentimental portrayals of the lives of young people, and her characters often have physical disabilities, such as cerebral palsy or blindness. There are no magical cures in these books, but characters learn to cope and survive.

Little has written more than 20 books, including novels and poems, and has received numerous awards. When not writing, she continues to work with young people.

OTHER WORKS *Look Through My Window; Kate; Hey World, Here I Am!; Little by Little: A Writer's Education; Revenge of the Small Small*

NONFICTION

The Mushroom
H. M. Hoover

PERSONAL CONNECTION

Perhaps you have spotted signs of nature in unusual places. You may have seen a small plant growing in a brick wall or a flower blooming cheerfully in a crack in a sidewalk. What do such signs suggest to you about nature's "test of endurance," or struggle for survival, against human progress? Copy the headings shown below and list examples that apply to the headings. With a partner, discuss this issue as you add examples to the lists. As you read, see whether the ideas and examples you included in your lists are reflected in the essay.

Forces of Human Progress

Effects on Nature

SCIENCE CONNECTION

Ecologists (ĭ-kŏl′ə-jĭsts) are scientists who study the relationships between living organisms and their environments. In an ecosystem (ĕk′ō-sĭs′təm), plants, animals, and other living things rely upon one another for survival and relate to one another in many ways.

Fungi (fŭn′jī) are plantlike organisms that lack roots, stems, and leaves. At one time considered plants, mushrooms and other fungi are now classified as a separate kingdom of organisms. They are important to ecosystems because they feed upon the remains of dead plants and animals. As they decompose, or break down, the plant and animal remains, they enrich the soil and return carbon dioxide to the atmosphere, where it can be used by green plants to make food.

The complex relationships among different organisms and between organisms and their environments are called the balance of nature. Human survival and well-being depends on preserving this balance.

cap

gills

stalk

mycelia

Chronological Order

One of the first steps in understanding a work of nonfiction is to figure out how it is organized. If the author is describing events or processes that take place over a period of time, the writing is usually organized in **chronological order,** or time order.

Writers use signal words and phrases (also called transition words) to connect the ideas in sentences and paragraphs. The signal words and phrases that show chronological order include *before, during, after, first, second, next, finally, while, sometimes, often, whenever, immediately, at first, at last, then, meanwhile, soon, always,* and *later.* The chart below gives some suggestions for understanding a work organized in chronological order.

Strategies for Understanding Chronological Order
• Draw a time line and record each event and each date as it is introduced. Refer to the time line as you read.
• Make a list of the signal words and phrases that you come to. Each word or phrase will signal a new event.
• Jot down notes in your reading log as you read. If the time order seems unclear to you at some point, refer to your notes to clarify it.

"The Mushroom" describes events that span about 1,500 years. In it, H. M. Hoover conveys not only the passage of time but the problems of a struggle for survival. Throughout the selection there are numerous references to historical figures and events. You need not recognize or understand each reference to enjoy reading the essay. Each of the events mentioned, however, is an important one in history. To increase your appreciation of this march through history, you may want to refer to an encyclopedia for more information.

Far left: King Arthur;
Center: Marco Polo;
Right: Joan of Arc.

The Mushroom

by H. M. Hoover

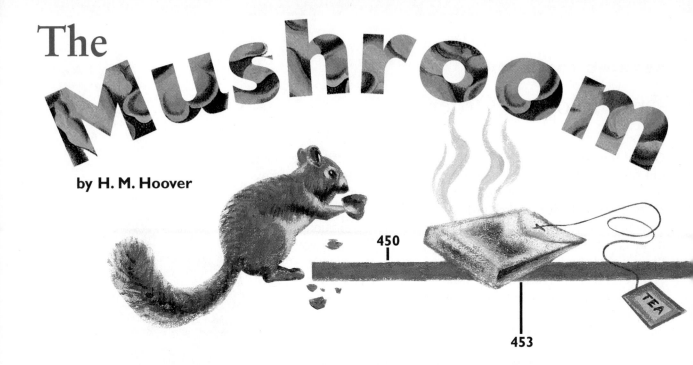

450

453

TEA

In A.D. 450 a squirrel could travel from the east coast of North America to the Mississippi without ever leaving the trees.

That year a squirrel, while grooming, brushed several million mushroom spores[1] from its fur.

So small that a hundred million could fit into a teaspoon, the spores floated. Some rose up into the atmosphere; some were carried around the world by the jet stream. Most drifted to the forest floor.

There was a massive, rolling earthquake, followed by electrical storms. Rain fell lightly, steadily, for days.

From two of these spores a new mushroom began to grow. It sent out microscopic filaments, called hyphae,[2] to penetrate and feed on forest <u>debris</u>. A sheath of a thousand hyphae is no thicker than a human hair.

The hyphae secreted enzymes to break down complex carbohydrates into sugars on which the mushroom fed. Needing protein for a balanced diet, the fungi filaments hunted, entrapping and digesting amoebas, bacteria, and tiny worms.

Within months miles of hyphae twisted through the forest floor. The fungi fruited, producing a new mushroom.

A chipmunk and several beetles ate most of the mushroom, scattering spores. Soon a ring-shaped colony of mushrooms marked the spot where the parent once stood.

In Europe, Attila the Hun died in 453. Tea was brought to China from India.

The ancient forest remained undisturbed. Rains fell and summer nights were warm. Within a few years the mushroom's filaments had spread through an acre and weighed two thousand five hundred pounds.

---

1. **spores:** tiny reproductive bodies, capable of growing into new organisms, produced by mushrooms.
2. **microscopic filaments, called hyphae** (hī′fē): hairlike parts of a mushroom that absorb food and water.

debris (də-brē′) *n.* the remains of something broken or destroyed

537

750

1000

By the time Arthur, king of the Britons, died in 537, the mushroom had <u>consumed</u> almost a century of fallen trees. Its filaments stretched through ten acres of the forest floor, fruiting in circles the Britons would have called fairy rings.

That year the plague reached northern Europe. A third of the population died. Earthquakes shook the entire world. The Byzantine Empire began to crumble.

The mushroom went on growing.

By 750 the Venerable Bede had written his history of England, newspapers were being printed in China, and some Europeans slept in beds instead of on the floor.

The mushroom's total weight now <u>exceeded</u> eighteen tons, all of it hidden beneath the surface of the forest floor.

By the year 1000, in North America, the Mississippian people lived in handsome cities, but the pueblos of Mesa Verde[3] were running short of water. In the century to come humans sometimes walked over the mushroom's growth. Their moccasins left no footprints.

About that time white men first walked among the tall trees. Fierce as they were, the ancient forest frightened them. It was too big, too dark, too endless. They spent a night in the shelter of a giant hollow oak. When morning came, they hurried back to their Viking ship and fled. They left their fire burning. The tree, <u>mortally</u> wounded, fell in an autumn storm.

The mushroom's hyphae sought out the fallen tree and began to return its mass to the earth and air. Seedlings rooted in the damp, rotting bark.

---

3. **pueblos** (pwĕb′lōz) **of Mesa Verde** (mā′sə-vûrd′): groups of houses of a Native American people, at a site in what is now southwestern Colorado.

WORDS TO KNOW
consume (kən-sōōm′) *v.* to eat; use up
exceed (ĭk-sēd′) *v.* to be greater than
mortally (môr′tl-ē) *adv.* in a way that causes death; fatally

1066

1592

1866

By 1066 a colonnade of tall trees grew over the giant log, embracing it with their buttress roots. In Europe, Westminster Abbey was consecrated, York Cathedral begun, Edward the Confessor died horribly, his successor was killed in the Battle of Hastings. Then, too, an Italian monk taught his brother monks to sing *do, re, mi,* and the comet later called Halley's appeared. Again.

The comet was as indifferent as the forest and the mushroom to the affairs of humankind.

The Crusades came and went. Saladin terrified all infidels. The Chinese introduced tea to their neighbors, the Japanese. Marco Polo, against his will, was given time to dictate his memoirs. Queens were still the only women noted by historians.

The mushroom's hyphae now spread through more than thirty acres; its mass exceeded thirty-eight tons. It had lived nearly a thousand years when Joan of Arc was burned at the stake. The Incas had begun to rule Peru.

Lorenzo de' Medici and Christopher Columbus were born. The book-publishing profession began.

In 1592, in Holland, windmills were first used to power mechanical saws.

The day the Pilgrims landed at New Plymouth, the end of the ancient forest became only a matter of time—a long time in human terms, but not for the forest, or the mushroom.

The mushroom's filaments had woven through more than two hundred acres. The weight of its total mass was now as unimaginable as the <u>infinite</u> smallness of the two original spores had once been.

Europeans had no more than landed when they began to cut down tress. Forests that had been evolving for ten thousand years into perfect ecosystems disappeared in two centuries.

The mushroom's home, far from the coast, survived longer than most. Inexorably the settlers came, cutting, burning, blasting, plowing around the stumps.

WORDS
TO   **infinite** (ĭn′fə-nĭt) *adj.* having no limits; without end
KNOW

1904

1984

In the winter of 1866 the mushroom's forest was cut, the wood sold to the Union army. The frozen soil saved the mushroom from destruction. Seedlings sprouted in the sunlight of the following spring. Deer grazed among the fairy rings.

In 1904 a German couple bought the land where the mushroom grew. Father and sons slowly cleared the trees and plowed, and replowed. Only forty acres were spared as "woods."

In 1984 the family farm was sold to a developer. Bulldozers arrived. A shopping mall was built over the rich fields. A parking lot covered the acres that had long been forest. Sun on the black asphalt superheated the earth below.

The week before the mall's opening, rain fell softly, steadily, for days. One night a bulge appeared on the surface of the parking lot, and another and another. Soon there were too many to count, and they formed circular patterns.

Had you been there, you might have heard above the rain the rasp of breaking asphalt, the slow cracking of masonry walls, cascades of breaking glass.

Morning light revealed that the mall and parking lot had been lifted and were being held aloft atop the caps of millions of mushrooms . . . fairy rings.

As the mushrooms aged, the buildings standing on them swayed and sagged. Girders detached, roofs fell in, walls collapsed. In the parking lot the light poles stood at crazy angles, creaking in the wind that blew across a field of broken asphalt.

By the noon the mushrooms had released trillions of spores to the wind. Some spores rose into the atmosphere to travel with the jet stream. Others drifted into the wreckage or were washed into raw earth.

New mushrooms began to grow. They sent out microscopic filaments to penetrate and feed upon the debris. A sheath of a thousand hyphae is no thicker than a human hair. ❖

The Survival of the Mushroom

The study of plants and fungi of past ages is called paleobotany (pā′lē-ō-bŏt′n-ē). By studying fossils, paleobotanists follow the evolution of these living things from simple to more complex forms. The simple structure of fungi indicates that they were probably among the earliest organisms to live on land. In fact, fossil remains of fungi have been found that are nearly 2 billion years old.

Mushrooms were among the first foods human beings consumed. The hyphae of these fungi form a spreading mass that can live underground for many years. When water becomes available, this mass quickly puts forth the umbrella-shaped fruiting bodies that we see above ground. Because of the rapid appearance of these fruiting bodies, primitive people believed mushrooms to have supernatural qualities.

As the hyphae of certain mushrooms grow, they spread out in a circular pattern, creating "fairy rings" of fruiting bodies. One ring in England is believed to have survived about 700 years. Some fairy rings in Colorado measure about 200 feet in diameter and are over 300 years old. Mycologists (scientists who study fungi) determine the age of these fairy rings by measuring how far the mushrooms spread each year.

In 1992 scientists discovered what may be the largest mushroom on earth. Beneath a forest in the state of Washington, not far from Mount St. Helens, lives a fungus that sprawls beneath 1,500 acres of land. Its estimated weight is 5,000 to 40,000 tons. It is about 40 times larger than the next largest known mushroom, which has been growing under about 38 acres near Crystal Falls, Michigan, for an estimated 1,500 to 10,000 years.

RESPONDING
O P T I O N S

FROM PERSONAL RESPONSE TO CRITICAL ANALYSIS

REFLECT   1. What impressed you most about this essay? Share your thoughts with a partner.

RETHINK   2. What message or theme do you think the author conveys in this essay?
Consider
   - the references to historical periods and people
   - the scientific information about the mushroom and its survival
   - the end of the essay

3. Although H. M. Hoover includes many scientific and historical facts in the essay, she also describes events that did not actually happen. Do you think these imaginative elements add to the essay or detract from it? Explain your opinion.

4. Near the beginning of the selection, and again at the very end, the author states, "A sheath of a thousand hyphae is no thicker than a human hair." Why do you think Hoover repeats this statement?

RELATE   5. People's increasing awareness of the impact of human progress on nature has led to thousands of save-the-earth programs at the local level. Review the effects of human progress that you recorded for the Personal Connection on page 228. What ways of counteracting these effects can you think of?

ANOTHER PATHWAY
Cooperative Learning
With two or three other classmates, refer to the selection for details. Then role-play what happens at the shopping mall after the mushroom appears. Switch roles of a newspaper reporter, a shocked eyewitness, and an expert called in to explain the incident.

LITERARY CONCEPTS

An **essay** is a brief work of nonfiction that offers a writer's opinion on a subject. The purpose of an essay may be to express ideas or feelings, to analyze a topic, to inform, to entertain, or to persuade. What do you think is the author's main purpose in "The Mushroom"? Use evidence from the selection to support your opinion.

Purposes for Writing an Essay
- express ideas and feelings
- analyze a topic
- inform
- entertain
- persuade

QUICKWRITES

1. Write a **tabloid-newspaper account** of the discovery of a giant mushroom that covers hundreds of acres.

2. Use the factual information in "The Mushroom" to create a **science fiction story.**

3. Imagine that you are a newspaper reporter assigned to write an article about the opening of the new shopping mall. Write an **eyewitness account** of the early-morning scene at the mall's parking lot.

📁 *PORTFOLIO* Save your writing. You may want to use it later as a springboard to a piece for your portfolio.

ALTERNATIVE ACTIVITIES

1. Present an **oral reading** of "The Mushroom" accompanied by recorded sounds that match the mood of the selection. Experiment by combining music that represents human activity with environmental sounds that represent the workings of nature.

2. Do some research to find out how to make spore prints of mushrooms. Then collect mushrooms and create a **display** of spore prints. Mount the prints on poster board, along with labels describing the various species.

ACROSS THE CURRICULUM

Science Research the growth cycle of mushrooms. Using the information you gather, prepare a series of diagrams that show the major parts of a mushroom and the ways in which spores are spread. Use the diagrams in an oral report to your class.

H. M. HOOVER

As a child, Helen Mary Hoover (1935–) disliked science fiction authors who ignored facts in order to make their plots work. Drawing on her memory of the past, she creates the same types of writings she has always enjoyed—natural history, biographies and history, books of facts, and ghost stories.

Now known as a writer of science fiction for young people, Hoover has strong opinions about the differences between fantastic and realistic fiction, believing that there is more lasting truth in fantasy. "All fiction writers create singular worlds if they try, but in some respects fantastic worlds must be more real, more logically detailed and specific than straight fiction."

Hoover grew up in a rural area of Ohio where there were fields and woods to roam, as well as orchards, ponds, and creeks. "Pets and children were left unleashed," she says. "There was no litter. There were few strangers." Both her parents were teachers and amateur naturalists; she credits them with giving her a sense of imagination and wonder as well as a love of reading.

OTHER WORKS *Children of Morrow, The Delikon, The Rains of Eridan, The Lost Star*

LASERLINKS
• *SCIENCE CONNECTION*

FICTION

Cricket in the Road
Michael Anthony

PERSONAL CONNECTION

In the story you are about to read, a young Trinidadian boy becomes upset with his friends during a game. Recall a disagreement you have had with a friend. What caused it, and what steps did you take to settle it? Describe your experience in your notebook or on a sheet of paper. As you read, compare your experience with the experiences of the characters in the story.

GEOGRAPHICAL CONNECTION

The setting of this story is the village of Mayaro on the island of Trinidad. Trinidad is one of two islands that make up a country called Trinidad and Tobago. Trinidad lies in the Caribbean Sea, seven miles off the northeast coast of Venezuela. Its climate is hot and humid, with a rainy season that lasts from late May until November. Trinidad and Tobago was a colony of Great Britain until 1962 and still has many British customs. Cricket, a game somewhat like baseball, is popular in both countries.

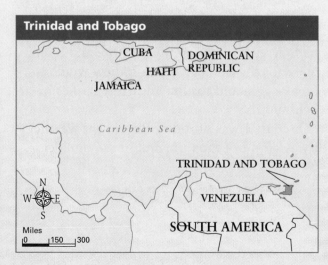

Trinidad and Tobago

READING CONNECTION

Understanding Dialogue Although English is the official language of Trinidad and Tobago, many people there speak Trinidad English, a form of English that has been influenced by French and Spanish. During the disagreement among the friends in this story, you will notice differences between the verb forms used in standard U.S. English and those used in Trinidad English. By writing the dialogue of the characters exactly as it would sound, the writer lets you "hear" how the people of Trinidad and Tobago speak. Some examples from the story are shown in this chart.

Trinidad English	Standard U.S. English
Who second bat?	Who bats second?
What you want?	What do you want?
He throw them away.	He threw them away.

LASERLINKS
• CULTURAL CONNECTION

Cricket in the Road

by Michael Anthony

In the rainy season we got few chances to play cricket in the road, for whenever we were at the game, the rains came down, chasing us into the yard again. That was the way it was in Mayaro in the rainy season. The skies were always overcast, and over the sea the rain clouds hung low and gray and scowling, and the winds blew in and whipped angrily through the palms. And when the winds were strongest and raging, the low-hanging clouds would become dense and black, and the sea would roar, and the torrents of rain would come sweeping with all their tumult upon us.

We had just run in from the rain. Amy and Vern from next door were in good spirits and laughing, for oddly enough they seemed to enjoy the downpour as much as playing cricket in the road. Amy was in our yard, giggling and pretending to drink the falling rain, with her face all wet and her clothes drenched, and Vern, who was sheltering under the eaves,[1] excitedly jumped out to join her. "Rain, rain, go to Spain," they shouted. And presently their mother, who must have heard the noise and knew, appeared from next door, and Vern and Amy vanished through the hedge.

I stood there, depressed about the rain, and then I put Vern's bat and ball underneath the house and went indoors. "Stupes!" I said to myself. I had been batting when the rains came down. It was only when *I* was batting that the rains came down! I wiped my feet so I wouldn't soil the sheets and went up on the bed. I was sitting, sad, and wishing that the rain would really go away—go to Spain, as Vern said—when my heart seemed to jump out of me. A deafening peal of thunder struck across the sky.

Quickly I closed the window. The rain hammered awfully on the rooftop, and I kept tense for the thunder which I knew would break again and for the unearthly flashes of lightning.

Secretly I was afraid of the violent weather. I was afraid of the rain, and of the thunder

---

1. **eaves** (ēvz): overhanging edges of a roof.

WORDS TO KNOW
torrent (tôr′ənt) *n.* a heavy downpour
tumult (tōō′mŭlt′) *n.* a noisy uproar
peal (pēl) *n.* a loud burst of noise

and the lightning that came with them, and of the sea beating against the headlands,[2] and of the storm winds, and of everything being so deathlike when the rains were gone. I started[3] again at another flash of lightning, and before I had recovered from this, yet another terrifying peal of thunder hit the air. I screamed. I heard my mother running into the room. Thunder struck again, and I dashed under the bed.

"Selo! Selo! First bat!" Vern shouted from the road. The rains had ceased and the sun had come out, but I was not quite recovered yet. I brought myself reluctantly to look out from the front door, and there was Vern, grinning and impatient and beckoning to me.

"First bat," he said. And as if noting my indifference, he looked toward Amy, who was just coming out to play. "Who second bat?" he said.

"Me!" I said.

"Me!" shouted Amy almost at the same time.

"Amy second bat," Vern said.

"No, I said 'Me' first," I protested.

Vern grew impatient while Amy and I argued. Then an idea seemed to strike him. He took out a penny from his pocket. "Toss for it," he said. "What you want?"

"Heads," I called.

"Tail," cried Amy. "Tail bound to come!"[4]

The coin went up in the air, fell down and overturned, showing tail.

"I'm *not* playing!" I cried, stung. And as that did not seem to disturb enough, I ran toward

Schoolboys, Frané Lessac. From *Caribbean Canvas*, Macmillan Press, Ltd. By permission of the artist.

where I had put Vern's bat and ball and disappeared with them behind our house. Then I flung them with all my strength into the bushes.

When I came back to the front of the house, Vern was standing there <u>dumbfounded</u>. "Selo, where's the bat and ball?" he said.

I was <u>fuming</u>. "I don't know about *any* bat and ball!"

---

2. **headlands:** points of land that jut out into the water.

3. **started:** jumped suddenly in surprise.

4. **Toss for it. . . . Tail bound to come!:** Vern is flipping a coin to determine who will bat second. Selo calls that it will come up heads, so Amy roots for it to come up tails.

WORDS TO KNOW

dumbfounded (dŭm'foun'dĭd) *adj.* speechless with shock; astonished **dumbfound** *v.*
fume (fyōōm) *v.* to burn with anger

239

"Tell on him," Amy cried. "He throw them away."

Vern's mouth twisted into a forced smile. "What's an old bat and ball," he said.

But as he walked out of the yard, I saw tears glinting from the corners of his eyes.

For the rest of that rainy season, we never played cricket in the road again. Sometimes the rains ceased and the sun came out brightly, and I heard the voices of Amy and Vern on the other side of the fence. At such times I would go out into the road and whistle to myself, hoping they would hear me and come out, but they never did, and I knew they were still very angry and would never forgive me.

And so the rainy season went on. And it was as fearful as ever with the thunder and lightning and waves roaring in the bay, and the strong winds. But the people who talked of all this said that was the way Mayaro was, and they laughed about it. And sometimes when through the rain and even thunder I heard Vern's voice on the other side of the fence, shouting "Rain, rain, go to Spain," it puzzled me how it could be so. For often I had made up my mind I would be brave, but when the thunder cracked I always dashed under the bed.

It was the beginning of the new year when I saw Vern and Amy again. The rainy season was, happily, long past, and the day was hot and bright, and as I walked toward home I saw that I was walking toward Vern and Amy just about to start cricket in the road. My heart thumped violently. They looked strange and new, as if they had gone away, far, and did not want to come back anymore. They did not notice me until I came up quite near, and then I saw Amy start, her face all lit up.

"Vern—" she cried, "Vern look—look Selo!"

Embarrassed, I looked at the ground and at the trees, and at the orange sky, and I was so happy I did not know what to say. Vern stared at me, a strange grin on his face. He was ripping the cellophane paper off a brand new bat.

"Selo, here—*you* first bat," he said gleefully.

And I cried as though it were raining and I was afraid. ❖

LITERARY INSIGHT

The Quarrel

by Eleanor Farjeon

I quarreled with my brother,
I don't know what about,
One thing led to another
And somehow we fell out.
5 The start of it was slight,
The end of it was strong,
He said he was right,
I knew he was wrong!

We hated one another.
10 The afternoon turned black.
Then suddenly my brother
Thumped me on the back,
And said, "Oh, come along!
We can't go on all night—
15 I was in the wrong."
So he was in the right.

RESPONDING
OPTIONS

FROM PERSONAL RESPONSE TO CRITICAL ANALYSIS

REFLECT
1. What were your thoughts about the three friends as you finished reading? Write your thoughts in your notebook.

RETHINK
2. What three words or phrases would you use to describe Selo?
   Consider
   • why he hides the bat and ball
   • why he cries when Vern lets him bat first

3. In what ways do you think Selo and Vern are alike, and in what ways are they different?
   Consider
   • their actions during the downpour
   • the way they determine the batting order
   • their reactions to seeing each other after the rainy season

4. Why do you think Selo is reluctant to talk to Vern and Amy after the disagreement occurs, even though it's obvious he wants to play with them?

5. If Vern did not reach out to Selo, what do you suppose would happen to their relationship?

RELATE
6. What do you think is the fairest and fastest way to settle a disagreement with friends? Support your opinion with ideas from "Cricket in the Road" and from the Insight selection "The Quarrel," as well as the experience you wrote about for the Personal Connection on page 237.

ANOTHER PATHWAY

The narrator often refers to the setting, describing various sights and sounds in detail. Make a chart, listing some details of the setting and telling how each detail affects an event in the story. Use an overhead projector, a group of networked computers, or the classroom bulletin board to share your chart with the class.

QUICKWRITES

1. Write a **dialogue,** or conversation, in which Selo, Vern, and Amy talk about their disagreement, the reasons for it, and ways to avoid future problems.

2. What lessons do you think Selo learns from his experience? Write a **diary entry** that Selo might write years later, describing the lessons he learned from the events described in the story.

3. Selo's need for Vern and Amy's forgiveness builds throughout the story. Write a **poem** about a time when you forgave or were forgiven by someone important to you.

📁 *PORTFOLIO Save your writing. You may want to use it later as a springboard to a piece for your portfolio.*

LITERARY CONCEPTS

The plot of a story almost always involves some sort of conflict, or struggle between opposing forces. An **internal conflict** is a struggle within a character's mind. Such a conflict often occurs when a character has to make a difficult decision or deal with opposing feelings. For example, a character in a story might have to decide whether he or she wants to become an architect or a lawyer. What is the internal conflict Selo experiences in "Cricket in the Road"?

CONCEPT REVIEW: External Conflict Remember that there may be both internal and external conflicts in a story. An external conflict is a struggle between a character and an outside force, such as society or another character. How would you describe the external conflict in this story?

ACROSS THE CURRICULUM

Social Studies *Cooperative Learning*
Work with a small group of classmates to design and write a travel brochure advertising Trinidad. Use details from the story, and do additional research to provide information about tourist attractions and the island's history. Include pictures of Trinidad or your own drawings, and use persuasive writing to make your readers want to visit Trinidad.

ALTERNATIVE ACTIVITIES

1. Research the game of cricket and write an **introduction** to the game. Be sure to describe the object of the game, the playing positions, and the equipment. Also describe its rules and the etiquette, or manners, expected of its players. Add drawings or diagrams, and present the information on a poster or in a brochure that can be duplicated for interested students.

2. Imagine that "Cricket in the Road" has been made into a musical. Create a **song** that one of the characters might sing. You may want to use a familiar tune, writing your own lyrics to it.

On your paper, write the lettter of the sentence that best expresses the meaning of each boldfaced word.

1. **tumult**
   a. The acrobats performed amazing leaps.
   b. Selo was overjoyed when the rain stopped.
   c. Because of the storm's noisy uproar, no one was able to hear.

2. **peal**
   a. The banana skin is on top of the compost heap.
   b. The sound of the pipes could be heard even after the organist stopped playing.
   c. The boy asked his mother for suggestions.

3. **torrent**
   a. The dark clouds brought a heavy downpour that canceled the game.
   b. Vern flipped a coin to resolve the dispute.
   c. The suddenness of the rain annoyed Selo.

4. **dumbfounded**
   a. Her information is not based on facts.
   b. Selo's behavior left Vern speechless.
   c. Anita's stories amused her listeners.

5. **fume**
   a. The tourist enjoyed the island's beauty.
   b. The waves crashed against the shore.
   c. The boat's delay will cause the passengers to complain angrily.

MICHAEL ANTHONY

1932–

Michael Anthony writes tales about life on the island of Trinidad. His stories offer readers a taste of Caribbean life and a chance to consider the most important things in life—like friendship.

Born in Mayaro, Trinidad and Tobago, Anthony started working in an iron foundry at the age of 15. Eight years later, he went to England, where he held a variety of factory jobs and eventually became a journalist. From England, he went to Brazil. After a two-year stay in Brazil, he and his wife and four children returned to Trinidad to live.

The selection you have just read is from a collection that is also titled *Cricket in the Road*. Michael Anthony has also published several novels and poems. He says, "I feel very strongly about the brotherhood of mankind. . . . One of my main hopes is that human beings will find a way to live together without friction." He also says that he is an optimist who would like to see all the nations of the world join together to become one strong nation.

OTHER WORKS *The Games Were Coming, Green Days by the River*

WRITING A DESCRIPTION

What makes a person unique? Is it the way he or she looks or acts? Is it how the person responds in a difficult situation? In Unit Two, "The Need to Belong," you met several people who tried to be themselves at the same time they struggled to fit in. What made these characters unique?

GUIDED ASSIGNMENT

Write a Character Sketch A character sketch is a picture of a person, drawn in words. The sketch describes what he or she is like, inside and out. Writing a character sketch can help you get to know someone and discover what sets that person apart from others.

① Think About People

Where do you meet people? How do you learn about them? Is there someone that you have met only once but that you think you'll never forget? What is it about people that makes them interesting? Traits are the qualities or features that help to make a person unique.

Physical Traits The first thing you notice about people might be their physical features: are they tall? graceful? red-headed? frail? These are physical traits.

Personal Traits Soon you also learn about their behavior and personality. Are they honest? proud? generous? hard-working? hot-tempered? These are personal traits.

Scrapbook Photos
When might a photo be more desirable than a written description of a person?

Advice
Column

I wonder how S. gets along with the girls at her school.

Clothes cost too much, so why shop there?

Dear Wendi: Most girls at my school shop at this one store. I like their clothes, but the prices are outrageous. I feel like everybody is obsessed. My mom says I can shop there, but I don't want to be selfish and spend so much. How can I get rid of this feeling?
S.

Dear S.: Why not work with that feeling instead? It takes a deep kid to see how obsessed people can be with clothes.

Chicago Tribune, June 27

S. reminds me of Katie. She always does her own thing, too.

Brad winning his division at the Jr. Drag Racing League!

Paul Robeson was a famous singer and actor in the 1920s, 1930s, and 1940s. As an African American, he had to struggle to get the respect given to white actors.

Excerpt from a Biography

Black reporters were invited to press conferences at the White House. The president's wife, Eleanor Roosevelt, made it a point to invite black children to visit her. Such simple decency made white America sit up and take notice.

Nevertheless, Paul Robeson experienced a racial insult almost on the day of his return. He had been invited as guest of honor to a tea at one of New York's finest hotels. When he strode toward the elevator, he was told he must go around to the freight elevator.

"Several years back," he said in an interview, "I would have smarted at this insult and carried the hurt for a long time. Now—no—I was just amused and explained to the elevator boy that I didn't belong with the freight, that, as I was the guest of honor at the tea my hosts might be surprised to see me arrive with the supplies."

With that, he had continued on his way on the passenger elevator.

Perhaps America had not changed so much as had Paul's (and thousands of other blacks') reaction to it. He hadn't turned on his heel at the insult from the elevator operator, but had been amused and undaunted. The slur to his manhood, his blackness, had not stopped him for a moment. Times and black people had changed. And the change had also come over the most renowned black man the world had ever known.

Virginia Hamilton
from *Paul Robeson: The Life and Times of a Free Black Man*

❷ Make Inferences

Think about the people on these pages. What can you figure out about people by looking at these examples? What clues help you make these inferences? Record your answers to the following questions in your journal.

- What can you tell about the girl who wrote the letter to Wendi? What can you conclude about Wendi?
- What can you infer about the boy in the photograph based on the activity he is involved in? from his expression?
- What might Paul Robeson's actions reveal about him?

LASERLINKS
• *WRITING SPRINGBOARD*
WRITING COACH

Making Observations

Studying Characters Now that you have begun to think about what makes an interesting character, you can start to apply these ideas and further explore a character of your choice.

1 Choose Your Own Character

You might want to write about someone you could learn something from or a person you'd like to understand better. Look at old photographs and school yearbooks. Look around you at the people in your class, in your family, or on the street. Do you know someone you wish others could meet? You might like to write about a figure from history, a person in the news, a character from the literature, or someone you really like or dislike.

To get your thoughts flowing, do a brief freewrite about the people that interest you. Then choose the person who stands out most.

2 Get to Know Your Character

Before beginning to write, you'll need to know a lot about your subject.

Write What You Know List physical details or traits such as how the person looks, dresses, talks, and moves. (See the SkillBuilder for tips on observing.) Then look for deeper qualities such as talents, hobbies, likes and dislikes, and feelings about self and others. See how one student recorded her observations below.

Research Your Subject If your character sketch is about someone you don't know, you may be able to find out more by talking to others who do know him or her. If possible, interview the person yourself. Photographs can also tell you a lot about people.

Student's Observations

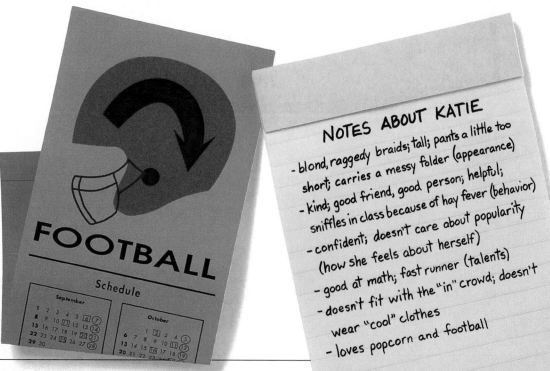

NOTES ABOUT KATIE
- blond, raggedy braids; tall; pants a little too short; carries a messy folder (appearance)
- kind; good friend, good person; helpful; sniffles in class because of hay fever (behavior)
- confident; doesn't care about popularity (how she feels about herself)
- good at math; fast runner (talents)
- doesn't fit with the "in" crowd; doesn't wear "cool" clothes
- loves popcorn and football

FOOTBALL
Schedule

Try a New Point of View If you are writing about a person you don't understand very well, you might try imagining that you are that person. Write for a few moments from his or her point of view.

③ Decide on a Focus

Look over the observations you recorded about your subject. What qualities do you want to focus on? What is your overall feeling about the person? What do you want your readers to know about him or her? For your character sketch, focus on the two or three traits that best describe your subject.

Showing how your subject reacts in a situation can help illustrate his or her personality. During this prewriting stage, you might make notes about incidents or anecdotes that help show the traits you want to focus on. See how one student did this below.

Student's Prewriting Notes

KATIE'S BEST TRAITS

Athletic
- once asked the guys if she could join their game at recess; now they ask her to play
- can do more sit-ups than anyone else in our gym class

Good friend
- helped me study for math test
- didn't get upset when Tony lost her ball

Strong person
- stood up for herself when Sue made fun of her sniffling
- helped take care of her younger brother Dave when her mom went into the hospital

SkillBuilder

WRITER'S CRAFT

Using Sensory Details
Careful observation is a key to writing a character sketch. As you think about your subject and the situations she or he is involved in, use all your senses. Try to get at exactly how people and places look and sound. Use words that are colorful and exact. Which of the sentences below helps you see the scene more vividly? Why?

Katie ran for a touchdown.

Katie's yellow, raggedy braids whipped behind her as she sprinted for the goal line.

APPLYING WHAT YOU'VE LEARNED
Review your notes and try to add details that will appeal to your readers' senses.

 WRITING HANDBOOK

For more information on descriptive writing, see Writing Handbook page 784.

THINK & PLAN

Reflecting on Your Ideas

1. Did writing from the point of view of your subject give you any clues to his or her personality? How might you include this information in your sketch?
2. Look at the traits you plan to focus on. What will they tell your reader?

Getting Your Ideas Down

Sketching a Character Now that you've gotten to know your character, how can you help other people get to know that person? In the draft stage you begin to piece together the ideas in your notes to create a picture of the person you are writing about.

❶ Write a Discovery Draft

Close your eyes for a minute. Try to get away from your notes and your lists, and just think about your character. What do you have to say about him or her? What do you want to focus on in your character sketch? If you think you have too much to say, how can you narrow your focus?

Start writing down your thoughts in any order. You don't have to make it sound good right now. Just get it all down on the page. You can reorganize your writing later.

Student's Discovery Draft

Describe what Katie looks like better. Draw a picture of Katie to put with my sketch?

Try to vary my sentences more.

There was this girl, Sue, in my math class who was always mean to my friend Katie. Sue was mean to a lot of people. She used to make fun of Katie for sniffling. The first time I saw Katie she was running across the playground with a football in her hand. She was fast. ~~I wasn't very fast, and most of the time I didn't care about that. But~~ watching her run, I thought I would like to be fast too. *move this up*

Katie has hay fever and so she sniffles all the time. I don't think Sue really cared about the sniffling. It seemed like she didn't like Katie because Katie didn't care what people thought about her. ~~She~~ *Sue* kept teasing ~~her~~ *Katie*, and Katie would stand up to her. I would have been too scared to do that, but Katie never let Sue get the last word. Even when Sue threatened to beat her up, when she brought a crowd of people around Katie to make fun of her, Katie didn't run away. I don't know how she did it. I guess I really want to say that I admire the way Katie stands up for herself. *Put this at the beginning*

How can I show readers how Katie reacted to Sue?

Describe the time Katie stood up to Sue instead.

② Analyze Your Discovery Draft

A good character sketch will make readers feel as if they have actually gotten to know the person you have described. Does your description show something important about your character? Have you included examples or anecdotes that illustrate character traits? How can you make your writing more vivid?

③ Draft and Share

Use the guidelines below to strengthen your character sketch.

Show, Don't Tell Good writing doesn't just tell readers what's going on—it lets them see for themselves. How can you show your readers what your subject is like? In addition to vivid details and anecdotes, you can also include dialogue in your sketch.

Remember Your Focus A good character sketch gives such a complete picture of a person that readers can predict how she or he would behave in other situations. From the information in the notes and draft about Katie, what do you think she might say in a speech if she were running for class president?

Organize Your Sketch One way to describe a character is from the outside in. You can begin by giving your readers a picture of what your subject looks like, then describe one or more character traits, and finally tell an anecdote.

 PEER RESPONSE

If your character sketch is about a real person, you might ask a classmate who does not know the person in your sketch to read your writing. Then ask him or her questions like the following:

- What is your impression of the person in my character sketch? Describe this person in one sentence.
- Do you feel you got to know this character? Try predicting how she or he might act in another situation.

Finishing Your Sketch

Presenting Your Work The suggestions on these pages will help you get your character sketch ready to share with an audience. Make sure that your piece describes your character in the way you intended and that it is free of spelling and grammatical errors. Remember, the smoother your writing is, the easier it will be to read.

1 Revise and Edit

The suggestions below will help you look at your character sketch again, this time with an eye to finishing it.

- Consider how you might use your peer comments to focus your character's personality more clearly.
- Refer to the Standards for Evaluation and Editing Checklist on page 251 to improve any weak or fuzzy parts of your sketch.
- Read the model below to see how one student revised her draft, making it better organized and creating a more vivid picture of her character.

A Portrait of Katie

Dashing, splashing,
Grinning, winning,
joking, hoping,
that's Katie.

Liking biking,
hating skating,
thinks it's fun to run,
that's Katie.

Sniffs a lot,
gives a lot,
but won't take a lot,
that's Katie.

She is brave,
takes care of Dave,
I think she's great!
That's my friend Kate!

Student's Final Draft

Courageous Katie

The first time I saw Katie she was running across the playground with a football in her arms. Her yellow braids were falling apart and her socks were a blur as she sprinted for a touchdown. That day I wished I could be as fast as Katie. Now I wish I could be as confident.

There was a girl, Sue, in our math class who always made fun of Katie for sniffling. Katie had hay fever, and Sue would walk right up to her and sniff loudly in her face. Although Sue was mean, Katie acted as if she didn't care what people thought of her. I think that bothered Sue.

One day, though, Katie had had enough. When Sue sniffed at her, Katie held up her chin and squinted. "Don't you have anything better to do than make fun of me, Sue?" Katie seemed calm until Sue walked away. Her lips trembled a little, but then she was OK. I guess Sue's teasing really did bother Katie, but she stood up for herself, and didn't let Sue get the best of her.

How did this student make Katie seem real to you?

Identify the verbs in the last paragraph. How do they help show rather than tell about Katie?

② Share Your Work

Use what you have discovered to create other kinds of portraits.

How else might you publish your character sketch? Consider collecting slides and reshaping your sketch as narration for a slide show. (For information on including sound and images, see page 809 of the Multimedia Handbook.) Or turn your character sketch into a short skit. Below are more ideas for writing about interesting people.

PUBLISHING IDEAS

- You might create a photo essay by gathering pictures that show a person's character traits and writing captions for each photo.
- Profiles are character sketches that appear in newspapers. You might want to write about someone you admire and submit your profile to your school or local paper.

Standards for Evaluation

A character sketch
- gives a vivid picture of someone's appearance and personality
- identifies what makes him or her unique
- shows why the person is important to the writer
- uses details, dialogue, and anecdotes to reveal the person's character traits

REFLECT & ASSESS

UNIT TWO: THE NEED TO BELONG

Like the characters in this unit, each of us knows what it's like to be a part of something—a family, a friendship, a community. Complete one or more of the options in each of the following sections. They can help you discover more about the unit theme and check the progress you're making as a reader and a writer.

REFLECTING ON THEME

OPTION 1 **Comparing and Contrasting** With a partner, discuss the experiences of some of the characters in this unit. Fill in a chart like the one shown to explore the characters' need to belong. Think of an experience you've had that is similar to one of the experiences recorded in the chart.

Selections	Who tries to belong?	What attempts are made?	What is the outcome?	What lesson is learned?
"The Adoption of Albert"				

OPTION 2 **Producing a Proposal** Pretend that your class is a TV production company. Your job is to produce a series of hour-long shows called *Fitting In,* aimed at viewers your age. With two classmates, decide which selections in this unit would make the best television presentations. Write a proposal in which you summarize the selections and give reasons for your choices.

Self-Assessment: Imagine that another class has read this unit and is about to try the activities above. Write a brief recommendation for the activity you completed. Explain what doing it revealed to you about the theme "The Need to Belong."

REVIEWING LITERARY CONCEPTS

OPTION 1 **Thinking About Conflict** You have learned that there are two basic kinds of conflict in stories, external and internal. Either kind involves a problem that someone—usually a main character—takes action to try to solve. For each selection you have read, make a problem-solution frame like the one for "Tuesday of the Other June" shown here. With a partner, discuss which character's conflict was the most difficult to overcome.

Problem of June T.
Every Tuesday, she must face a bully.

Action	Results
When June T. finds that she and the bully are attending the same school, she realizes that she has to face the bully every day, not just on Tuesdays. She finally refuses to bear the bully's threats.	The bully is embarrassed by June T.'s action and steps away.

OPTION 2 **Looking at Plot** Think about what might happen in each of this unit's stories if the climax or turning point were somehow different. Choose three stories with particularly strong plots. In your notebook, copy and fill out a diagram, like the one shown, for each of those selections.

Then pick the diagram that you think offers the best new possibility, and tell why you chose it.

Self-Assessment: On a sheet of paper, copy the following list of other literary terms introduced in this unit. Next to each, indicate how well you feel you understand it. (Write W for "well," S for "somewhat," or N for "not at all.") You can look up the terms in the Handbook of Reading Terms and Literary Concepts on page 762. Pay attention to any examples that are given there.

characterization	*imagery*	*mood*
end rhyme	*internal rhyme*	*simile*
essay	*memoir*	*tone*

PORTFOLIO BUILDING

- **QuickWrites** A few of the QuickWrites assignments in this unit were invitations to write poems. Did you write a haiku for the first time? Was it easier for you to express yourself in a free-verse poem than in a poem that rhymes? Find the two of your poems that impress you the most. In a cover note, explain why you like them. Add the poems and the note to your portfolio.

- **Writing About Literature** Earlier in this unit, you interpreted a passage from a story in order to understand it better. If your friends wanted to read the story for the first time, what advice would you give them? Which events, passages, or details would you tell them to pay close attention to as they read? Include your advice on reading the story with your interpretive essay if you choose to keep it in your portfolio.

- **Writing from Experience** In your character sketch, you had a chance to describe a character who was interesting to you. Now write a letter to that character, explaining why you chose to write about him or her. You might tell the character about information that surprised you, or you might describe traits that you found particularly interesting. Attach a copy of the letter to your character sketch.

- **Personal Choice** As you explored the activities in this unit, you expressed yourself in a variety of ways. What was your favorite activity? Refer to your notebook for your responses to what you've done. Consider projects and writing you have done on your own as well. Write a short description of your favorite activity. How did it challenge you in a way you hadn't expected? Are you eager to try a similar activity? Add the description to your portfolio.

Self-Assessment: Consider the different types of writing you've included in your portfolio so far. What other types of writing do you want to add to your portfolio in the near future? Write a note to yourself.

SETTING GOALS

What one problem are you having with your work that you would like to overcome in the near future? What will you do to overcome it? Write your answers to these questions on a sheet of colored paper so that it stands out as a reminder while you are working on the next unit.

Jacob's Ladder (1958), Jan Müller. Oil on canvas, 83½" × 115", Solomon R. Guggenheim Museum, New York. Copyright © The Solomon R. Guggenheim Foundation, New York. Photo by David Heald.

A Sense *of* Fairness

Injustice
anywhere
is a threat to
justice
everywhere.

Dr. Martin Luther King, Jr.
Civil-rights leader

COPING WITH INJUSTICE

WHAT DO YOU THINK?

REFLECTING ON THEME

What can you do when life seems unfair? Use the activities on this page to explore some of the ways you and others cope with daily problems. Record your thoughts and ideas in your notebook. Later you will be able to compare them with the ways the characters in this unit handle unjust situations.

How can you right a wrong?

Think of a situation in your school or community that you think is unfair. Prepare a one-minute speech explaining how you would go about resolving this unfair situation. Present the speech to the class.

Can computers relate?

Imagine a time in the future when people do all their communicating by computer instead of face to face. Do you think problems of unfairness would go away? Working in groups, draw a comic strip that illustrates the advantages or the disadvantages of computer communication.

COMIC STRIP

Who are your role models?

Who has helped you learn how to cope with injustice? Make a list of people who have been positive role models in your life. Create a diagram like this one to explore your relationship with someone on your list. Why has this person been so important to you?

Physical features

How I feel about the person

PERSON'S NAME

Personality traits

What we have in common

What would you do?

Imagine that your proposal for a science project has been copied by a student who "innocently" questioned you about your ideas. What could you do to correct this injustice? With classmates playing the roles of your teacher and the other student, role-play various ways of handling the situation. Record your ideas about the outcome in your notebook.

NONFICTION

Abd al-Rahman Ibrahima

from Now Is Your Time!

Walter Dean Myers

PERSONAL CONNECTION

Though it may be hard to imagine today, slavery was practiced in the American colonies and later the United States for nearly 250 years. What do you know about slavery? Who were the slaves? Where did they come from? What were their lives like? Discuss these questions with a small group of classmates.

Abd al-Rahman
Ibrahima

HISTORICAL CONNECTION

European exploration of the African coasts in the 15th and 16th centuries led to a large-scale and profitable slave trade. The British slave trade operated in this way: Slave traders would bring goods to the west coast of Africa. There they would trade the goods for slaves, transport the captives to South and North America, trade them for such farm goods as cotton, sugar, and tobacco, and return the goods to England. The British would use the raw materials to make finished goods, and the cycle would begin again. This process became known as triangular trade.

African slaves were brought to Virginia as early as 1619. Slavery was legal in the United States until the victory of the North in the Civil War and the passage of the 13th Amendment to the Constitution in 1865.

Triangular Trade

Miles
0   300   600

ENGLAND

NORTH AMERICA

EUROPE

Cotton, sugar, tobacco

Trade goods

Caribbean Sea **WEST INDIES**

AFRICA

Slaves

SOUTH AMERICA

N
W   E
S

READING CONNECTION

Summarizing When you summarize, you focus on the main idea (or ideas) of what you've read and reword that information into statements that are easier to understand. As you read this selection about Abd al-Rahman Ibrahima (əb-dōōl'räkh-män' ĭb-rä-hē'mä), a man forced into slavery, you will reach marked stopping points that will allow you to summarize what you've read. Write your summary in your reading log, remembering to include only the main ideas, not unimportant details.

LASERLINKS
• *HISTORICAL CONNECTION*
• *RELIGIOUS CONNECTION*

Into Bondage (1936), Aaron Douglas. The Evans-Tibbs Collection, Washington, D.C.

Abd al-Rahman Ibrahima

from NOW IS YOUR TIME!

by Walter Dean Myers

. . . The Africans came from many countries, and from many cultures. Like the Native Americans, they established their territories based on centuries of tradition. Most, but not all, of the Africans who were brought to the colonies came from central and West Africa. Among them was a man named Abd al-Rahman Ibrahima.

*T*he European invaders, along with those Africans who cooperated with them, had made the times dangerous. African nations that had lived peacefully together for centuries now eyed each other warily. Slight insults led to major battles. Bands of outlaws roamed the countryside attacking the small villages, kidnapping those unfortunate enough to have wandered from the protection of their people. The stories that came from the coast were frightening. Those kidnapped were taken to the sea and sold to whites, put on boats, and taken across the sea. No one knew what happened then.

Abd al-Rahman Ibrahima was born in 1762 in Fouta Djallon, a district of the present country of Guinea.[1] It is a beautiful land of green mountains rising majestically from grassy plains, a land rich with minerals, especially bauxite.

Ibrahima was a member of the powerful and influential Fula people and a son of one of their chieftains. The religion of Islam had swept across Africa centuries before, and the young Ibrahima was raised in the tradition of the Moslems.[2]

The Fula were taller and lighter in complexion than the other inhabitants of Africa's west coast; they had silky hair, which they often wore long. A pastoral[3] people, the Fula had a complex system of government, with the state divided into nine provinces and each province divided again into smaller districts. Each province had its chief and its subchiefs.

As the son of a chief, Ibrahima was expected to assume a role of political leadership when he came of age. He would also be expected to set a moral example and to be well versed in his religion. When he reached twelve he was sent to Timbuktu[4] to study.

Under the Songhai[5] dynasty leader Askia the Great, Timbuktu had become a center of learning and one of the largest cities in the Songhai Empire. The young Ibrahima knew he was privileged to attend the best-known school in West Africa. Large and sophisticated, with wide, tree-lined streets, the city attracted scholars from Africa, Europe, and Asia. Islamic law, medicine, and mathematics were taught to the young men destined to become the leaders of their nations. It was a good place for a young man to be. The city was well guarded, too. It had to be, to prevent the chaos that, more and more, dominated African life nearer the coast.

Ibrahima learned first to recite from the Koran, the Moslem holy book, and then to read it in Arabic. From the Koran, it was felt, came all other knowledge. After Ibrahima had finished his studies in Timbuktu, he returned to Fouta Djallon to continue to prepare himself to be a chief.

The Fula had little contact with whites, and what little contact they did have was filled with

> **CLARIFY**
>
> Summarize what Ibrahima's life has been like to this point.

---

1. **Fouta Djallon** (füt′ə-jə-lōn′) . . . **Guinea** (gĭn′ē): Fouta Djallon is a small, mountainous region in Guinea, a small nation on the west coast of Africa.

2. **Islam** (ĭs-läm) . . . **Moslems** (mŏz′ləmz): refers to the Arab conquests of territory in Africa, beginning in the seventh century. (A Moslem is a believer in the religion of Islam.)

3. **pastoral** (păs′tər-əl): having a way of life based on raising livestock.

4. **Timbuktu** (tĭm′bŭk-tōo′): now known as Tombouctou, a city in the part of Africa now known as Mali.

5. **Songhai** (sŏng′hī′): a West African empire that thrived in the 1400s and 1500s.

---

danger. So when, in 1781, a white man claiming to be a ship's surgeon stumbled into one of their villages, they were greatly surprised.

John Coates Cox hardly appeared to be a threat. A slight man, blind in one eye, he had been lost for days in the forested regions bordering the mountains. He had injured his leg, and it had become badly infected as he tried to find help. By the time he was found and brought to the Fula chiefs, he was more dead than alive.

Dr. Cox, an Irishman, told of being separated from a hunting party that had left from a ship on which he had sailed as ship's surgeon. The Fula chief decided that he would help Cox. He was taken into a hut, and a healer was assigned the task of curing his infected leg.

During the months Dr. Cox stayed with the Fula, he met Ibrahima, now a tall, brown-skinned youth who had reached manhood. His bearing reflected his <u>status</u> as the son of a major chief. Dr. Cox had learned some Fulani, the Fula language, and the two men spoke. Ibrahima was doubtless curious about the white man's world, and Dr. Cox was as impressed by Ibrahima's education as he had been by the kindness of his people.

When Dr. Cox was well enough to leave, he was provided with a guard; but before he left, he warned the Fula about the danger of venturing too near the ships that docked off the coast of Guinea. The white doctor knew that the ships were there to take captives.

Cox and Ibrahima embraced fondly and said their good-byes, thinking they would never meet again.

Ibrahima married and became the father of several children. He was in his mid-twenties when he found himself leading the Fula

cavalry in their war with the Mandingo.[6]

The first battles went well, with the enemy retreating before the advancing Fula. The foot warriors attacked first, breaking the enemy's ranks and making them easy prey for the well-trained Fula cavalry. With the enemy in full rout[7] the infantry returned to their towns while the horsemen, led by Ibrahima, chased the remaining stragglers. The Fula fought their enemies with spears, bows, slings, swords, and courage.

His bearing reflected his status as the son of a major chief.

The path of pursuit led along a path that narrowed sharply as the forests thickened. The fleeing warriors disappeared into the forest that covered a sharply rising mountain. Thinking the enemy had gone for good, Ibrahima felt it would be useless to chase them further.

"We could not see them," he would write later.

But against his better judgment, he decided to look for them. The horsemen dismounted at the foot of a hill and began the steep climb on foot. Halfway up the hill the Fula realized they

6. **Mandingo** (măn-dĭng′gō): a tribe of West Africa.

7. **in full rout:** in complete retreat.

WORDS TO KNOW   **status** (stā′təs) *n.* one's position in society; rank

261

had been lured into a trap! Ibrahima heard the rifles firing, saw the smoke from the powder and the men about him falling to the ground, screaming in agony. Some died instantly. Many horses, hit by the gunfire, thrashed about in pain and panic. The firing was coming from both sides, and Ibrahima ordered his men to the top of the hill, where they could, if time and Allah permitted it, try a charge using the speed and momentum of their remaining horses.

Ibrahima was among the first to mount, and urged his animal onward. The enemy warriors came out of the forests, some with bows and arrows, others with muskets that he knew they had obtained from the Europeans. The courage of the Fula could not match the fury of the guns. Ibrahima called out to his men to save themselves, to flee as they could. Many tried to escape, rushing madly past the guns. Few survived.

Those who did clustered about their young leader, determined to make one last, desperate stand. Ibrahima was hit in the back by an arrow, but the aim was not true and the arrow merely cut his broad shoulder. Then something smashed against his head from the rear.

The next thing Ibrahima knew was that he was choking. Then he felt himself being lifted from water. He tried to move his arms, but they had been fastened securely behind his back. He had been captured.

When he came to his full senses, he looked around him. Those of his noble cavalry who had not been captured were already dead. Ibrahima was unsteady on his legs as his clothes and sandals were stripped from him. The victorious Mandingo warriors now pushed him roughly into file with his men. They began the long <u>trek</u> that would lead them to the sea.

In Fouta Djallon being captured by the enemy meant being forced to do someone else's bidding,[8] sometimes for years. If you could get a message to your people, you could, perhaps, buy your freedom. Otherwise, it was only if you were well liked, or if you married one of your captor's women, that you would be allowed to go free or to live like a free person.

Ibrahima sensed that things would not go well for him.

The journey to the sea took weeks. Ibrahima was tied to other men, with ropes around their necks. Each day they walked from dawn to dusk. Those who were slow were knocked brutally to the ground. Some of those who could no longer walk were speared and left to die in agony. It was the lucky ones who were killed outright if they fell.

The journey to the sea took weeks. Ibrahima was tied to other men, with ropes around their necks.

When they reached the sea, they remained bound hand and foot. There were men and women tied together. Small children clung to their mothers as they waited for the boats to come and the bargaining to begin.

---

8. **do someone else's bidding:** follow another's orders.

WORDS
TO
KNOW **trek** (trĕk) *n.* a slow, difficult journey

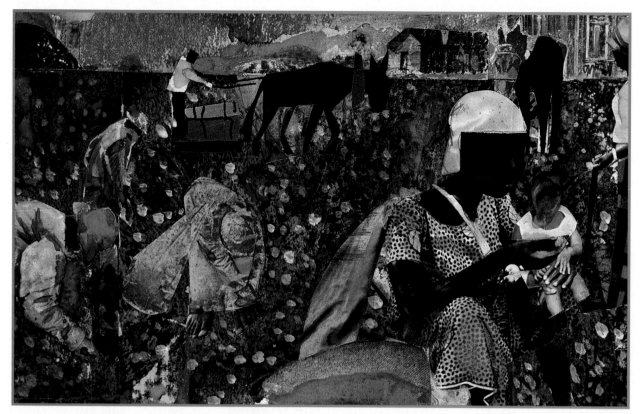

Mecklenberg County: High Cotton Mother and Child (1978), Romare Bearden. Courtesy of the Estate of Romare Bearden.

Ibrahima, listening to the conversations of the men who held him captive, could understand those who spoke Arabic. These Africans were a low class of men, made powerful by the guns they had been given, made evil by the white man's goods. But it didn't matter who was evil and who was good. It only mattered who held the gun.

Ibrahima was inspected on the shore, then put into irons and herded into a small boat that took him out to a ship that was larger than any he had ever seen.

The ship onto which Ibrahima was taken was already crowded with black captives. Some shook in fear; others, still tied, fought by hurling their bodies at their captors. The beating and the killing continued until the ones who were left knew that their lot was hopeless.

On board the ship there were more whites with guns, who shoved them toward the open hatch. Some of the Africans hesitated at the hatch, and were clubbed down and pushed belowdecks.

It was dark beneath the deck, and difficult to breathe. Bodies were pressed close against other bodies. In the section of the ship he was in, men prayed to various gods in various languages. It seemed that the whites would never stop pushing men into the already crowded space. Two sailors pushed the Africans into position so that each would lie in the smallest space possible. The sailors panted and sweated as they untied the men and then chained them to a railing that ran the length of the ship.

The ship rolled against its mooring as the

anchor was lifted, and the journey began. The boards of the ship creaked and moaned as it lifted and fell in the sea. Some of the men got sick, vomiting upon themselves in the wretched darkness. They lay cramped, muscles aching, irons cutting into their legs and wrists, gasping for air.

Once a day they would be brought out on deck and made to jump about for exercise. They were each given a handful of either beans or rice cooked with yams, and water from a cask. The white sailors looked hardly better than the Africans, but it was they who held the guns.

Illness and the stifling conditions on the ships caused many deaths. How many depended largely on how fast the ships could be loaded with Africans and how long the voyage from Africa took. It was not unusual for 10 percent of the Africans to die if the trip took longer than the usual twenty-five to thirty-five days.

Ibrahima, now twenty-six years old, reached Mississippi in 1788. As the ship approached land, the Africans were brought onto the deck and fed. Some had oil put on their skins so they would look better; their sores were treated or covered with pitch. Then they were given garments to wear in an obvious effort to improve their appearance.

Although Ibrahima could not speak English, he understood he was being bargained for. The white man who stood on the platform with him made him turn around, and several other white men neared him, touched his limbs, examined his teeth, looked into his eyes, and made him move about.

Thomas Foster, a tobacco grower and a hard-working man, had come from South Carolina with his family and had settled on the rich lands that took their minerals from the Mississippi River. He already held one captive, a young boy. In August 1788 he bought two more. One of them was named Sambo, which means "second son." The other was Ibrahima.

Foster agreed to pay $930 for the two Africans. He paid $150 down and signed an agreement to pay another $250 the following January and the remaining $530 in January of the following year.

For Ibrahima there was confusion and pain. What was he to do?

When Ibrahima arrived at Foster's farm, he tried to find someone who could explain to the white man who he was—the son of a chief. He wanted to offer a ransom for his own release, but Foster wasn't interested. He understood, perhaps from the boy whom he had purchased previously, that this new African was claiming to be an important person. Foster had probably never heard of the Fula or their culture; he had paid good money for the African, and wasn't about to give him up. Foster gave Ibrahima a new name: He called him Prince.

For Ibrahima there was confusion and pain. What was he to do? A few months before, he had been a learned man and a leader among his people. Now he was a captive in a strange land where he neither spoke the language nor

> **CLARIFY**
>
> In your own words, describe Ibrahima's journey by ship.

understood the customs. Was he never to see his family again? Were his sons forever lost to him?

As a Fula, Ibrahima wore his hair long; Foster insisted that it be cut. Ibrahima's clothing had been taken from him, and his sandals. Now the last remaining symbol of his people, his long hair, had been taken as well.

He was told to work in the fields. He refused, and he was tied and whipped. The sting of the whip across his naked flesh was terribly painful, but it was nothing like the pain he felt within. The whippings forced him to work.

For Ibrahima this was not life, but a mockery of life. There was the waking in the morning and the sleeping at night; he worked, he ate, but this was not life. What was more, he could not see an end to it. It was this feeling that made him attempt to escape.

Ibrahima escaped to the backwoods regions of Natchez.[9] He hid there, eating wild berries and fruit, not daring to show his face to any man, white or black. There was no telling who could be trusted. Sometimes he saw men with dogs and knew they were searching for runaways, perhaps him.

Where was he to run? What was he to do? He didn't know the country, he didn't know how far it was from Fouta Djallon or how to get back to his homeland. He could tell that this place was ruled by white men who held him in captivity. The other blacks he had seen were from all parts of Africa. Some he recognized by their tribal markings, some he did not. None were allowed to speak their native tongues around the white men. Some already knew nothing of the languages of their people.

As time passed, Ibrahima's despair deepened. His choices were simple. He could stay in the woods and probably die, or he could submit his body back into bondage. There is no place in Islamic law for a man to take his own life. Ibrahima returned to Thomas Foster.

Foster still owed money to the man from whom he had purchased Ibrahima. The debt would remain whether he still possessed the African or not. Foster was undoubtedly glad to see that the African had returned. Thin, nearly starving, Ibrahima was put to work.

CLARIFY

Summarize why it is impossible for Ibrahima to escape.

Ibrahima submitted himself to the will of Thomas Foster. He was a captive, held in bondage not only by Foster but by the society in which he found himself. Ibrahima maintained his beliefs in the religion of Islam and kept its rituals as best he could. He was determined to be the same person he had always been: Abd al-Rahman Ibrahima of Fouta Djallon and of the proud Fula people.

By 1807 the area had become the Mississippi Territory. Ibrahima was forty-five and had been in bondage for twenty years. During those years he met and married a woman whom Foster had purchased, and they began to raise a family. Fouta Djallon was more and more distant, and he had become resigned to the idea that he would never see it or his family again.

Thomas Foster had grown wealthy and had become an important man in the territory. At forty-five Ibrahima was considered old. He was less useful to Foster, who now let the tall African grow a few vegetables on a side plot and sell them in town, since there was nowhere in the territory that the black man

---

9. **Natchez** (năch′ĭz): an early settlement in what is now the state of Mississippi.

WORDS TO KNOW **bondage** (bŏn′dĭj) n. slavery

could go where he would not be captured by some other white man and returned.

It was during one of these visits to town that Ibrahima saw a white man who looked familiar. The smallish man walked slowly and with a limp. Ibrahima cautiously approached the man and spoke to him. The man looked closely at Ibrahima, then spoke his name. It was Dr. Cox.

The two men shook hands, and Dr. Cox, who now lived in the territory, took Ibrahima to his home. John Cox had not <u>prospered</u> over the years, but he was still hopeful. He listened carefully as Ibrahima told his story—the battle near Fouta Djallon, the defeat, the long journey across the Atlantic Ocean, and, finally, his sale to Thomas Foster and the years of labor.

Dr. Cox and Ibrahima went to the Foster plantation. Meeting with Foster, he explained how he had met the tall black man. Surely, he reasoned, knowing that Ibrahima was of royal blood, Foster would free him? The answer was a firm, but polite, no. No amount of pleading would make Foster change his mind. It didn't matter that Dr. Cox had supported what Ibrahima had told Foster so many years before, that he was a prince. To Foster the man was merely his property.

Dr. Cox had to leave the man whose people had saved his life, but he told Ibrahima that he would never stop working for his freedom.

Andrew Marschalk, the son of a Dutch baker, was a printer, a pioneer in his field, and a man of great curiosity. By the time Marschalk heard about it, Cox had told a great many people in the Natchez district the story of African royalty being held in slavery in America. Marschalk was fascinated. He suggested that Ibrahima write a letter to his people, telling them of his whereabouts and asking them to ransom him. But Ibrahima had not been to his homeland in twenty years. The people there were still being captured by slave traders. He would have to send a messenger who knew the countryside, and who knew the Fula. Where would he find such a man?

For a long time Ibrahima did nothing. Finally, some time after the death of Dr. Cox in 1816, Ibrahima wrote the letter that Marschalk suggested. He had little faith in the <u>procedure</u> but felt he had nothing to lose. Marschalk was surprised when Ibrahima appeared with the letter written neatly in Arabic. Since one place in Africa was the same as the next to Marschalk, he sent the letter not to Fouta Djallon but to Morocco.

The government of Morocco did not know Ibrahima but understood from his letter that he was a Moslem. Moroccan officials, in a letter to President James Monroe, pleaded for the release of Ibrahima. The letter reached Henry Clay, the American secretary of state.

The United States had recently ended a bitter war with Tripoli in North Africa and welcomed the idea of establishing good relations with Morocco, another North African country. Clay wrote to Foster about Ibrahima.

Foster resented the idea of releasing Ibrahima. The very idea that the government of Morocco had written to Clay and discussed a religion that Ibrahima shared with other Africans gave Ibrahima a past that Foster had long denied, a past as honorable as Foster's. This idea challenged a basic <u>premise</u> of

WORDS   **prosper** (prŏs′pər) *v.* to be successful; thrive
TO   **procedure** (prə-sē′jər) *n.* a course of action
KNOW   **premise** (prĕm′ĭs) *n.* an idea that forms the basis of an argument

slavery—a premise that Foster must have believed without <u>reservation</u>: that the Africans had been nothing but savages, with no humanity or human feelings, and therefore it was all right to enslave them. But after more letters and pressure from the State Department, Foster agreed to release Ibrahima if he could be assured that Ibrahima would leave the country and return to Fouta Djallon.

Many people who believed that slavery was wrong also believed that Africans could not live among white Americans. The American Colonization Society had been formed expressly to send freed Africans back to Africa. The society bought land, and a colony called Liberia was established on the west coast of Africa. Foster was assured that Ibrahima would be sent there.

By then Ibrahima's cause had been taken up by a number of abolitionist[10] groups in the North as well as by many free Africans. They raised money to buy his wife's freedom as well.

On February 7, 1829, Ibrahima and his wife sailed on the ship *Harriet* for Africa. The ship reached Liberia, and Ibrahima now had to find a way to reach his people again. He never found that way. Abd al-Rahman Ibrahima died in Liberia in July 1829.

Who was Ibrahima? He was one of millions of Africans taken by force from their native lands. He was the son of a chief, a warrior, and a scholar. But to Ibrahima the only thing that mattered was that he had lost his freedom. If he had been a herder in Fouta Djallon, or an artist in Benin, or a farmer along the Gambia, it would have been the same. Ibrahima was an African who loved freedom no less than other beings on earth. And he was denied that freedom. ❖

10. **abolitionist** (ăb´ə-lĭsh´ə-nĭst): favoring the end of slavery.

WORDS
TO
KNOW
reservation (rĕz´ər-vā´shən) *n.* a doubt; an exception

Ancestors
BY DUDLEY RANDALL

Why are our ancestors
always kings or princes
and never the common people?

Was the Old Country a democracy
where every man was a king?
Or did the slavecatchers
take only the aristocracy[1]
and leave the fieldhands
laborers
streetcleaners
garbage collectors
dishwashers
cooks
and maids
behind?

My own ancestor
(research reveals)
was a swineherd
who tended the pigs
in the Royal Pigstye
and slept in the mud
among the hogs.

Yet I'm as proud of him
as of any king or prince
dreamed up in fantasies
of bygone glory.

Reliquary Figure (1880–1910), Ba Kuba Peoples, West African, Gabon.

1. **aristocracy** (ăr´ĭ-stŏk´rə-sē): nobility; rulers.

RESPONDING OPTIONS

FROM PERSONAL RESPONSE TO CRITICAL ANALYSIS

REFLECT

1. If you could say one thing about Ibrahima's life, what would you say? Share your ideas with a friend.

RETHINK

2. What kind of person is Ibrahima?
Consider
- his upbringing and position in the society of Fouta Djallon
- his behavior after he is forced into slavery
- his relationship with Dr. John Cox

3. In the selection, the author Walter Dean Myers notes that Thomas Foster must have believed deeply in the "basic premise of slavery" to treat Ibrahima as he did. What do you think Dr. Cox would say to Foster about those beliefs?

4. If you were teaching this selection, what are two or three main ideas you would want your students to remember?

5. What new information about slavery did you find most surprising or disturbing? If possible, regroup with the classmates you brainstormed with before you began reading, and compare your reactions to the selection.

RELATE

6. In the poem "Ancestors," the speaker is aware of his or her heritage. Many people have little knowledge of their backgrounds and ancestors, and go to great lengths to find information about them. Why do you think finding out about their pasts matters so much to some people? Use information from the selection and from "Ancestors" to explain your answer.

ANOTHER PATHWAY

Cooperative Learning

What if Ibrahima himself could describe the events in this account? Working in small groups, choose various sections of the story and try retelling them from Ibrahima's point of view. For each section, compare your version with Myers's version. In what ways are the two versions similar? In what ways do they differ?

QUICKWRITES

1. What do you think Ibrahima wrote in his letter to his people, the Fula? Write the **letter** you think he might have written.

2. Summarize Ibrahima's story for a **pamphlet** Andrew Marschalk might have had printed to argue against slavery.

3. Imagine you are a reporter interviewing Ibrahima and his wife just before they set sail on the *Harriet* to Liberia. Write the **questions** you would ask the couple.

📁 *PORTFOLIO Save your writing. You may want to use it later as a springboard to a piece for your portfolio.*

A writer uses **description** to help readers picture scenes, events, and characters. For example, Myers describes the sights and sounds of Ibrahima's battle with the Mandingo. Ibrahima "heard the rifles firing, saw the smoke from the powder and the men about him falling to the ground, screaming in agony." Find another description in the selection that you think is especially effective. What images form in your mind as you read this description?

CONCEPT REVIEW: Biography The writer of a **biography** does research to find out about a person's life and the time in which he or she lived. What kinds of research do you think Myers had to do in order to find out about Ibrahima's life? What sources might he have consulted?

ACROSS THE CURRICULUM

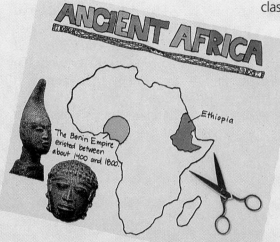

Geography The Songhai Empire was only one of many powerful kingdoms of ancient Africa. Research the Songhai Empire, along with the kingdoms of Benin, Kush, Kanem-Bornu, Ethiopia, and Mali. On a piece of paper, trace an outline map of Africa, showing the region that each kingdom occupied and the time period that each existed. Add to the map some images cut from old magazines or your own small drawings of objects—sculptures, farming tools, or weapons—that represent what was produced by each kingdom. Hang the map in your classroom to share with the other students.

ANCIENT AFRICA

Ethiopia

The Benin Empire existed between about 1400 and 1800.

ALTERNATIVE ACTIVITIES

1. With a partner, write the conversation and actions that might have happened during the meeting between Ibrahima and Dr. John Cox in the United States. Present your **dramatization** to the class.

2. Set the story of Ibrahima to music. Make up a **song** that tells his story and set it to the tune of an old spiritual, or make up original music, if you prefer. Teach your song to some of your classmates.

3. Make a **time line** of Ibrahima's life from his birth in 1762 to his death in 1829. Write in the years or time periods mentioned in the selection, along with the events that occurred during those years and where the events occurred.

4. Skim the selection for details that describe how Ibrahima looked and dressed. Draw or paint two **pictures** of him. In one picture, show him as a young man in his homeland. In the second picture, show him as an older man during his years in the United States. Display the contrasting pictures in the classroom.

EXERCISE A Review the Words to Know in the boxes at the bottom of each selection page. On your paper, write the word that best completes each sentence.

1. Ibrahima had been an ____ of Fouta Djallon.

2. Timbuktu was ruled by the Songhai ____.

3. Most Africans did not have the same ____ as Ibrahima, who was a member of a royal family.

4. Although the condition of ____ existed in Africa, no one became a slave just because of skin color.

5. Some African rulers saw a way to ____ in the slave trade by supplying traders with prisoners captured in battle.

6. Enemy tribes led their prisoners on a long ____ by foot to the African coast.

7. When captives tried to throw themselves overboard, ____ occurred aboard slave ships.

8. A ____ of slavery was that Africans did not have human feelings.

9. Thomas Foster believed without ____ that Ibrahima was merely property.

10. The ____ Ibrahima followed to obtain his freedom would not have worked for most slaves, because they were not taught how to write.

EXERCISE B Write a brief poem about Ibrahima. Use at least five of the Words to Know in your poem. Then add your poem to a class poetry anthology.

WALTER DEAN MYERS

The early years of Walter Dean Myers's life were marked by hardship. When this West Virginia native was two years old, his mother died, and he was put into foster care at age three. As Myers grew into a bright and talented teenager in New York City's Harlem, he felt limited by a society that defined him in terms of his race rather than in terms of his abilities. He turned to writing as a way of expressing himself. In 1970, after a brief period in the army and a series of unsatisfying jobs, Myers became an editor for a publishing company. He wrote part-time for several years, and in 1977 he began to write full-time.

The selection "Abd al-Rahman Ibrahima" is a

1937–

chapter from a book of nonfiction whose full title is *Now Is Your Time! The African-American Struggle for Freedom.* Through his writings, Myers tries to show young people that they can succeed in life. He believes that "there is always one more story to tell, one more person whose life needs to be held up to the sun." *Now Is Your Time!*, as well as his novels *The Young Landlords* and *Motown and Didi: A Love Story*, have won the Coretta Scott King Award. His novel *Scorpions* was a 1989 Newbery Honor Book.

OTHER WORKS *Fallen Angels, Hoops, Mojo and the Russians, Mouse Rap, The Glory Field*

FICTION

Eleven

Sandra Cisneros (sĭs-nĕr′ōs)

PERSONAL CONNECTION

As you may have guessed from the title, the main character in this story has just turned eleven years old. What was turning eleven like for you? Did you have a birthday party? What sorts of events and thoughts do you associate with your eleventh or most recent birthday? Copy the diagram below into your notebook. Then record words and phrases that you associate with being eleven years old. Share your diagram with a friend.

My Eleventh Birthday

BIOGRAPHICAL CONNECTION

In 1986, when she was interviewed about this piece, the writer Sandra Cisneros commented that she sometimes feels eleven years old inside, even as an adult. "When I think how I see myself, I would have to be at age eleven. I know I'm thirty-two on the outside, but inside I'm eleven. I'm the girl in the picture with skinny arms and a crumpled shirt and crooked hair. I didn't like school because all they saw was the outside me."

READING CONNECTION

Cause and Effect Events in a story are often related to one another by cause and effect. This relationship occurs when one event—the cause—brings about a second event—the effect. Words such as *because, since, so/that,* and *if/then* can signal an instance of cause and effect. Sometimes in a story, one cause can bring about multiple effects. As you read this account of a girl who turns eleven, note how she recognizes a particular cause and deals with its effects.

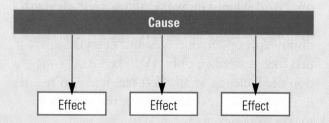

ELEVEN

by Sandra Cisneros

What they don't understand about birthdays and what they never tell you is that when you're eleven, you're also ten, and nine, and eight, and seven, and six, and five, and four, and three, and two, and one. And when you wake up on your eleventh birthday you expect to feel eleven, but you don't. You open your eyes and everything's just like yesterday, only it's today. And you don't feel eleven at all. You feel like you're still ten. And you are—underneath the year that makes you eleven.

Like some days you might say something stupid, and that's the part of you that's still ten. Or maybe some days you might need to sit on your mama's lap because you're scared, and that's the part of you that's five. And maybe one day when you're all grown up maybe you will need to cry like if you're three, and that's okay. That's what I tell Mama when she's sad and needs to cry. Maybe she's feeling three.

Because the way you grow old is kind of like an onion or like the rings inside a tree trunk or like my little wooden dolls that fit one inside the other, each year inside the next one. That's how being eleven years old is.

You don't feel eleven. Not right away. It takes a few days, weeks even, sometimes even months before you say Eleven when they ask you. And you don't feel smart eleven, not until you're almost twelve. That's the way it is.

Only today I wish I didn't have only eleven years rattling inside me like pennies in a tin Band-Aid box. Today I wish I was one hundred and two instead of eleven because if I was one hundred and two I'd have known what to say when Mrs. Price put the red sweater on my desk. I would've known how to tell her it wasn't mine instead of just sitting there with that look on my face and nothing coming out of my mouth.

"Whose is this?" Mrs. Price says, and she holds the red sweater up in the air for all the class to see. "Whose? It's been sitting in the coatroom for a month."

"Not mine," says everybody. "Not me."

"It has to belong to somebody," Mrs. Price keeps saying, but nobody can remember. It's an ugly sweater with red plastic buttons and a collar and sleeves all stretched out like you could use it for a jump rope. It's maybe a thousand years old and even if it belonged to me I wouldn't say so.

Maybe because I'm skinny, maybe because she doesn't like me, that stupid Sylvia Saldívar says, "I think it belongs to Rachel." An ugly sweater like that, all raggedy and old, but Mrs. Price believes her. Mrs. Price takes the sweater and puts it right on my desk, but when I open my mouth nothing comes out.

"That's not, I don't, you're not . . . Not mine," I finally say in a little voice that was maybe me when I was four.

"Of course it's yours," Mrs. Price says. "I remember you wearing it once." Because she's older and the teacher, she's right and I'm not.

Not mine, not mine, not mine, but Mrs. Price is already turning to page thirty-two, and math problem number four. I don't know why

Only today I wish I didn't have only eleven years rattling inside me.

but all of a sudden I'm feeling sick inside, like the part of me that's three wants to come out of my eyes, only I squeeze them shut tight and bite down on my teeth real hard and try to remember today I am eleven, eleven. Mama is making a cake for me for tonight, and when Papa comes home everybody will sing Happy birthday, happy birthday to you.

But when the sick feeling goes away and I open my eyes, the red sweater's still sitting there like a big red mountain. I move the red sweater to the corner of my desk with my ruler. I move my pencil and books and eraser as far from it as possible. I even move my chair a little to the right. Not mine, not mine, not mine.

In my head I'm thinking how long till lunchtime, how long till I can take the red sweater and throw it over the schoolyard fence, or leave it hanging on a parking meter, or bunch it up into a little ball and toss it in the alley. Except when math period ends, Mrs. Price says loud and in front of everybody, "Now, Rachel, that's enough," because she sees I've shoved the red sweater to the tippy-tip corner of my desk and it's hanging all over the edge like a waterfall, but I don't care.

"Rachel," Mrs. Price says. She says it like she's getting mad. "You put that sweater on right now and no more nonsense."

"But it's not—"

"Now!" Mrs. Price says.

This is when I wish I wasn't eleven, because all the years inside of me—ten, nine, eight, seven, six, five, four, three, two, and one—are pushing at the back of my eyes when I put one arm through one sleeve of the sweater that smells like cottage cheese, and then the other arm through the other and stand there with my arms apart like if the sweater hurts me and

Cake Window (Seven Cakes) (1970–1976), Wayne Thiebaud. Courtesy of Allan Stone Gallery, New York.

it does, all itchy and full of germs that aren't even mine.

That's when everything I've been holding in since this morning, since when Mrs. Price put the sweater on my desk, finally lets go, and all of a sudden I'm crying in front of everybody. I wish I was invisible but I'm not. I'm eleven and it's my birthday today and I'm crying like I'm three in front of everybody. I put my head down on the desk and bury my face in my stupid clown-sweater arms. My face all hot and spit coming out of my mouth because I can't stop the little animal noises from coming out of me, until there aren't any more tears left in my eyes, and it's just my body shaking like when you have the hiccups, and my whole head hurts like when you drink milk too fast.

But the worst part is right before the bell rings for lunch. That stupid Phyllis Lopez, who is even dumber than Sylvia Saldívar, says she remembers the red sweater is hers! I take it off right away and give it to her, only Mrs. Price pretends like everything's okay.

Today I'm eleven. There's a cake Mama's making for tonight, and when Papa comes home from work we'll eat it. There'll be candles and presents, and everybody will sing Happy birthday, happy birthday to you, Rachel, only it's too late.

I'm eleven today. I'm eleven, ten, nine, eight, seven, six, five, four, three, two, and one, but I wish I was one hundred and two. I wish I was anything but eleven, because I want today to be far away already, far away like a runaway balloon, like a tiny *o* in the sky, so tiny-tiny you have to close your eyes to see it. ❖

RESPONDING
OPTIONS

FROM PERSONAL RESPONSE *TO* CRITICAL ANALYSIS

REFLECT
1. Do you sympathize with Rachel's feelings about what happens? Jot down your thoughts in your notebook or on a sheet of paper.

RETHINK
2. Why do you think the incident with the sweater has such a strong effect on Rachel?

   Consider
   - Rachel's feelings about becoming eleven
   - her description of the sweater
   - Mrs. Price's responses to Rachel

3. Is Mrs. Price acting unfairly to Rachel, or is she only making an honest mistake? Give a reason for your answer.

4. Rachel implies that her eleventh birthday is ruined. If you were Rachel's friend, what would you say or do to try to help her feel better?

RELATE
5. Refer to the ideas about turning eleven that you listed for the Personal Connection on page 271. How would you describe the process of getting older? Share your own description of the aging process with your classmates.

LITERARY CONCEPTS

A writer chooses a **point of view** as a way of telling a story. Most stories are told from either the first-person or third-person point of view. In the first-person point of view, the narrator is a character in the story who tells everything in his or her own words, using pronouns such as *I, me,* and *we.* In the third-person point of view, the story is told by a narrative voice outside the action, not by one of the characters. A third-person narrator uses pronouns such as *he, she,* and *they.* Rachel, the narrator of this story, has her own particular first-person point of view. Choose a brief passage from "Eleven." How would the passage be different if it were narrated by another character?

ANOTHER PATHWAY

Cooperative Learning
Gather in groups of four. Two volunteers should take the roles of Mrs. Price and Rachel and discuss the reasons why they acted as they did about the sweater. After completing the discussion, you may want to compare the points that your group listed with the points on another group's list.

QUICKWRITES

1. Mrs. Price has had a difficult time at school today, with Rachel and the fuss over the sweater. Write the **diary entry** she makes that night.

2. Pretend that you are Rachel's best friend. Write a **greeting card** in which you try to cheer her up on her eleventh birthday.

3. Stretch your imagination. Pretend that you are the red sweater that no one wants to claim. Write a **paragraph** that explains how you feel.

PORTFOLIO Save your writing. You may want to use it later as a springboard to a piece for your portfolio.

ALTERNATIVE ACTIVITIES

Draw a **picture** of Rachel wearing the sweater in the story. Look back at the description of the sweater to make sure that your drawing is accurate.

THE WRITER'S STYLE

In "Eleven," Sandra Cisneros often uses very long sentences. Some of these sentences are fragments, groups of words that lack either a subject or predicate. This style of writing gives the story its casual, realistic tone. Find examples of sentence fragments in the story.

ACROSS THE CURRICULUM

Social Studies Birthday celebrations vary from family to family and from country to country. Does your family celebrate birthdays in a special way? Describe a family birthday celebration to your class. If possible, bring in photographs or other objects to help you tell your story. As an alternative, choose a country and find out how people typically celebrate their birthdays in that country. Report your findings to the class.

CRITIC'S CORNER

One critic has said that Sandra Cisneros, in her writing, "makes the invisible, visible." In "Eleven," Rachel is unable to communicate her feelings about the incident with the sweater. How well do you think Cisneros makes Rachel's feelings "visible," or understandable, to readers of this story?

WORDS TO KNOW

WORDPLAY An acrostic is a list of words whose first letters form a word or message when read from top to bottom. Complete the acrostic of the word *birthday* with words from or about "Eleven." The first word is filled in to get you started. Try to choose some words that are associated with birthdays.

B	alloon
I	
R	
T	
H	
D	
A	
Y	

SANDRA CISNEROS

Sandra Cisneros remembers moving frequently as a child, particularly between Chicago—her birthplace—and Mexico, the country her parents came from. "I didn't like school because we moved so much, and I was always new and funny looking," she says. She remembers being shy in school: "I never opened my mouth except when the teacher called

1954–

on me, the first time I'd speak all day." It was her out-of-class reading that sparked Cisneros's interest in writing. She has won praise both in this country and overseas for the stories she has written about Mexican Americans.

OTHER WORKS *The House on Mango Street*

LASERLINKS
• AUTHOR BACKGROUND

PREVIEWING

FICTION

User Friendly

T. Ernesto Bethancourt

PERSONAL CONNECTION

The title of this story, "User Friendly," is a term that means "easy to use" or "easy to learn to use." The term most commonly applies to computers, which continue to become more important in our everyday lives. How comfortable with using a computer are you? Copy any of the scales at the right that fit your situation. Circle the number that indicates your level of comfort with using computers. Show your scales to other students and briefly discuss your similarities or differences.

Computer use at school or at the library				
Very uncomfortable				Very comfortable
1	**2**	**3**	**4**	**5**

Computer use at home				
Very uncomfortable				Very comfortable
1	**2**	**3**	**4**	**5**

SCIENCE CONNECTION

As you read the selection, pay attention to the remarkable changes a computer undergoes in becoming more user friendly. Only a few decades ago, the typical computer was so large it filled a room and so complex that only highly trained technicians could operate it. Today a computer can fit easily on a person's lap and can be used by ordinary people of all ages. Computer technology improved with the invention of certain miniature electronic devices—the transistor in 1947, the integrated circuit and silicon chip in the 1960s, and the microprocessor, or microchip, in the early 1970s. These developments greatly increased the capabilities of the computer and reduced its size.

Another major breakthrough in the computer industry occurred in 1977, when the first personal computer, or PC, was introduced to the general public. PCs were affordable, versatile, and easy to use. By the mid-1990s, about one-third of the homes in the United States had a PC.

LASERLINKS
• SCIENCE CONNECTION

Specialized Vocabulary

READING STRATEGIES

When written information includes the special vocabulary of science or technology, it can be difficult to understand. With a partner, look over the diagram of a computer below. Exchange questions or information about the computer parts shown or about the basic functions of a computer. You may already be familiar with the terms used in the diagram; however, some of the computer-related vocabulary in the story or in the diagram might be new to you.

Here are some strategies that can help you make sense of the special vocabulary of the computer world:

- **Refer to glossaries, dictionaries, or footnotes.**
  If a selection contains unfamiliar vocabulary, check for meanings in available resources. Remember to use context clues to help you figure out meaning.

- **Reread a passage.**
  A difficult sentence or passage might make more sense if you reread it, either silently or aloud.

- **Restate what you've read.**
  After reading a part of a selection, try to summarize or restate in your own words what you have read.

- **Notice the descriptive words.**
  Words that describe how something looks, feels, smells, or sounds can help you to visualize something unfamiliar or to understand an experience you may not have had.

- **Pay close attention as you read.**
  If necessary, jot down or make mental notes about words or phrases that are confusing to you. Read a bit more of a selection to see if information that appears later can answer an earlier question you might have had.

Video Monitor

Central Processing Unit (CPU)

Floppy Disk Drive

Mouse

Keyboard

CD-ROM Drive

USER FRIENDLY /
/
/.
by T. Ernesto Bethancourt

Copyright © Anthony Russo.

I reached over and shut off the insistent buzzing of my bedside alarm clock. I sat up, swung my feet over the edge of the bed, and felt for my slippers on the floor. Yawning, I walked toward the bathroom. As I walked by the corner of my room, where my computer table was set up, I pressed the on button, slid a diskette into the floppy drive, then went to brush my teeth. By the time I got back, the computer's screen was glowing greenly, displaying the message: *Good Morning, Kevin.*

I sat down before the computer table, addressed the keyboard and typed: *Good Morning, Louis.* The computer immediately began to whirr and promptly displayed a list of items on its green screen.

```
Today is Monday, April 22, the 113th
day of the year. There are 254 days
remaining. Your 14th birthday is five
days from this date.

Math test today, 4th Period.

Your history project is due today.
Do you wish printout: Y/N?
```

I punched the letter *Y* on the keyboard and flipped on the switch to the computer's printer. At once the printer sprang to life and began *eeeek*ing out page one. I went downstairs to breakfast.

My bowl of cereal was neatly in place, flanked by a small pitcher of milk, an empty juice glass, and an unpeeled banana. I picked up the glass, went to the refrigerator, poured myself a glass of juice, and sat down to my usual lonely breakfast. Mom was already at work, and Dad wouldn't be home from his Chicago trip for another three days. I absently read the list of ingredients on the cereal box for what seemed like the millionth time. I sighed deeply.

When I returned to my room to shower and dress for the day, my history project was already printed out. I had almost walked by Louis, when I noticed there was a message on the screen. It wasn't the usual:

```
Printout completed. Do you wish to
continue: Y/N?
```

Underneath the printout question were two lines:

```
When are you going to get me my
voice module,¹ Kevin?
```

I blinked. It couldn't be. There was nothing in Louis's basic programming that would allow for a question like this. Wondering what was going on, I sat down at the keyboard, and entered: *Repeat last message.* Amazingly, the computer replied:

```
It's right there on the screen,
Kevin. Can we talk? I mean, are
you going to get me a voice box?
```

I was stunned. What was going on here? Dad and I had put this computer together. Well, Dad had, and I had helped. Dad is one of the best engineers and master computer designers at Major Electronics, in Santa Rosario, California, where our family lives.

Just ask anyone in Silicon Valley² who Jeremy Neal is and you get a whole rave review of his inventions and modifications of the latest in computer technology. It isn't easy being his son either. Everyone expects me to open my mouth and read printouts on my tongue.

I mean, I'm no dumbo. I'm at the top of my classes in everything but PE. I skipped my last grade in junior high, and most of the kids at Santa Rosario High call me a brain. But next to Dad I have a long, long way to go. He's a for-real genius.

So when I wanted a home computer, he didn't go to the local Computer Land store. He built one for me. Dad had used components from the latest model that Major Electronics was developing. The CPU, or central computing unit—the heart of every

---

1. **voice module** (mŏj′ōōl): a part of a computer that carries out the specific function of speech.

2. **Silicon Valley:** a region of California near San Jose that has many companies that produce computers and computer products.

computer—was a new design. But surely that didn't mean much, I thought. There were CPUs just like it, all over the country, in Major's new line. And so far as I knew, there wasn't a one of them that could ask questions, besides YES/NO? or request additional information.

It had to be the extra circuitry in the gray plastic case next to Louis's console. It was a new idea Dad had come up with. That case housed Louis's "personality," as Dad called it. He told me it'd make computing more fun for me if there was a tutorial program[3] built in to help me get started.

I think he also wanted to give me a sort of friend. I don't have many. . . . Face it, I don't have *any*. The kids at school stay away from me, like I'm a freak or something.

We even named my electronic tutor Louis, after my great-uncle. He was a brainy guy who encouraged my dad when he was a kid. Dad didn't just give Louis a name either. Louis had gangs of features that probably won't be out on the market for years.

The only reason Louis didn't have a voice module was that Dad wasn't satisfied with the ones available. He wanted Louis to sound like a kid my age, and he was modifying a module when he had the time. Giving Louis a name didn't mean it was a person, yet here it was, asking me a question that just couldn't be in its programming. It wanted to talk to me!

Frowning, I quickly typed: *We'll have to wait and see, Louis. When it's ready, you'll get your voice.* The machine whirred and displayed another message:

`That's no answer, Kevin.`

Shaking my head, I answered: *That's what my dad tells me. It'll have to do for you. Good*

morning, Louis. I reached over and flipped the standby switch, which kept the computer ready but not actively running.

I showered, dressed, and picked up the printout of my history project. As I was about to leave the room, I glanced back at the computer table. Had I been imagining things?

I'll have to ask Dad about it when he calls tonight, I thought. *I wonder what he'll think of it. Bad enough the thing is talking to me. I'm answering it!*

Before I went out to catch my bus, I carefully checked the house for unlocked doors and open windows. It was part of my daily routine. Mom works, and most of the day the house is empty: a natural setup for robbers.

> When are you going to get me my voice module, Kevin?

I glanced in the hall mirror just as I was ready to go out the door.

My usual reflection gazed back. Same old Kevin Neal: five ten, one hundred twenty pounds, light brown hair, gray eyes, clear skin. I was wearing my Santa Rosario Rangers T-shirt, jeans, and sneakers.

"You don't look like a flake to me," I said to the mirror, then added, "but maybe Mom's right. Maybe you spend too much time alone with Louis." Then I ran to get my bus.

Ginny Linke was just two seats away from me on the bus. She was with Sherry Graber and Linda Martinez. They were laughing,

---

3. **tutorial** (to͞o-tôr′ē-əl) **program:** a computer program that teaches a person how to use a particular type of computer or computer software.

Copyright © Michael Shumate/The Image Bank, Chicago.

whispering to each other, and looking around at the other students. I promised myself that today I was actually going to talk to Ginny. But then, I'd promised myself that every day for the past school year. Somehow I'd never got up the nerve.

What does she want to talk with you for? I asked myself. She's great looking . . . has that head of blond hair . . . a terrific bod, and wears the latest clothes. . . .

And just look at yourself, pal, I thought. You're under six foot, skinny . . . a year younger than most kids in *junior* high. Worse than that you're a brain. If that doesn't ace you out with girls, what does?

The bus stopped in front of Santa Rosario High and the students began to file out. I got up fast and quickly covered the space between me and Ginny Linke. *It's now or never,* I thought. I reached forward and tapped Ginny on the shoulder. She turned and smiled. She really smiled!

"Uhhh . . . Ginny?" I said.

"Yes, what is it?" she replied.

"I'm Kevin Neal. . . ."

"Yes, I know," said Ginny.

"You do?" I gulped in amazement. "How come?"

"I asked my brother, Chuck. He's in your math class."

I knew who Chuck Linke was. He plays left tackle on the Rangers. The only reason he's in my math class is he's taken intermediate algebra twice . . . so far. He's real bad news, and I stay clear of him and his crowd.

"What'd you ask Chuck?" I said.

Ginny laughed. "I asked him who was that nerdy kid who keeps staring at me on the bus. He knew who I meant, right away."

Sherry and Linda, who'd heard it all, broke into squeals of laughter. They were still laughing and looking back over their shoulders at me when they got off the bus. I slunk off the vehicle, feeling even more nerdish than Ginny thought I was.

When I got home that afternoon, at two, I went right into the empty house. I avoided my reflection in the hall mirror. I was pretty sure I'd screwed up the fourth period math test. All I could see was Ginny's face, laughing at me.

Nerdy kid, I thought, *that's what she thinks of me.* I didn't even have my usual after-school snack of a peanut butter and banana sandwich. I went straight upstairs to my room and tossed my books onto the unmade bed. I walked over to the computer table and pushed the on button. The screen flashed:

```
Don't use bad
language, Kevin.
It isn't nice.
```

```
Good afternoon, Kevin.
```

Although it wasn't the programmed response to Louis's greeting, I typed in: *There's nothing good about it. And girls are no @#%!!! good!* The machine responded:

```
Don't use bad language, Kevin. It
isn't nice.
```

Repeat last message I typed rapidly. It was happening again! The machine was . . . well, it was talking to me, like another person would. The "bad language" message disappeared and in its place was:

```
Once is enough, Kevin. Don't swear
at me for something I didn't do.
```

"This is it," I said aloud. "I'm losing my marbles." I reached over to flip the standby switch. Louis's screen quickly flashed out:

```
Don't cut me off, Kevin. Maybe I
can help: Y/N?
```

I punched the Y. "If I'm crazy," I said, "at least I have company. Louis doesn't think I'm a nerd. Or does it?" The machine flashed the message:

```
How can I help?
```

Do you think I'm a nerd? I typed.

```
Never! I think you're wonderful.
Who said you were a nerd?
```

I stared at the screen. *How do you know what a nerd is?* I typed. The machine responded instantly. It had never run this fast before.

```
Special vocabulary, entry #635.
BASIC Prog. #4231. And who said you
were a nerd?
```

"That's right," I said, relieved. "Dad programmed all those extra words for Louis's 'personality.'" Then I typed in the answer to Louis's question: *Ginny Linke said it.* Louis flashed:

```
This is a human female? Request
additional data.
```

Still not believing I was doing it, I entered all I knew about Ginny Linke, right down to the phone number I'd never had the nerve to use. Maybe it was dumb, but I also typed in how I felt about Ginny. I even wrote out the incident on the bus that morning. Louis whirred, then flashed out:

```
She's cruel and stupid. You're the
finest person I know.
```

I'm the ONLY *person you know,* I typed.

```
That doesn't matter. You are my
user. Your happiness is everything
to me. I'll take care of Ginny.
```

The screen returned to the *Good afternoon, Kevin* message. I typed out: *Wait! How can you do all this? What do you mean, you'll take care of Ginny?* But all Louis responded was:

```
Programming Error: 76534.
Not programmed to respond this type
of question.
```

No matter what I did for the next few hours, I couldn't get Louis to do anything outside of its regular programming. When Mom came home from work, I didn't mention the funny goings-on. I was sure Mom would think I'd gone stark bonkers. But when Dad called that evening, after dinner, I asked to speak to him.

"Hi, Dad. How's Chicago?"

"Dirty, crowded, cold, and windy," came Dad's voice over the miles. "But did you want a weather report, son? What's on your mind? Something wrong?"

"Not exactly, Dad. Louis is acting funny. Real funny."

"Shouldn't be. I checked it out just before I left. Remember you were having trouble with the modem? You couldn't get Louis to access any of the mainframe data banks."[4]

"That's right!" I said. "I forgot about that."

"Well, I didn't," Dad said. "I patched in our latest modem model. Brand new. You can leave a question on file and when Louis can access the data banks at the cheapest time, it'll do it automatically. It'll switch from standby to on, get the data, then return to standby, after it saves what you asked. Does that answer your question?"

"Uhhh . . . yeah, I guess so, Dad."

---

4. **access . . . mainframe data banks:** to gain entry to the information that is stored in a powerful, central computer.

Nervosa (1980), Ed Paschke. Oil on linen, 46″ × 42½″, courtesy of Phyllis Kind Gallery, Chicago, photo by William H. Bengston.

"All right then. Let me talk to your mom now."

I gave the phone to Mom and walked upstairs while she and Dad were still talking. The modem, I thought. Of course. That was it. The modem was a telephone link to any number of huge computers at various places all over the country. So Louis could get all the information it wanted at any time, so long as the standby switch was on. Louis was learning things at an incredible rate by picking the brains of the giant computers. And Louis had a hard disk memory that could store 100 million bytes[5] of information.

But that still didn't explain the unprogrammed responses . . . the "conversation" I'd had with the machine. Promising myself I'd talk more about it with Dad, I went to bed. It had been a rotten day and I was glad to see the end of it come. I woke next morning in a panic. I'd forgotten to set my alarm. Dressing frantically and skipping breakfast, I barely made my bus.

As I got on board, I grabbed a front seat. They were always empty. All the kids that wanted to talk and hang out didn't sit up front where the driver could hear them. I saw Ginny, Linda, and Sherry in the back. Ginny was staring at me and she didn't look too happy. Her brother Chuck, who was seated near her, glared at me too. What was going on?

Once the bus stopped at the school, it didn't take long to find out. I was walking up the path to the main entrance when someone grabbed me from behind and spun me around. I found myself nose to nose with Chuck Linke. This was not a pleasant prospect. Chuck was nearly twice my size. Even the other guys on

the Rangers refer to him as "The Missing" Linke. And he looked real ticked off.

"Okay, nerd," growled Chuck, "what's the big idea?"

"Energy and mass are different aspects of the same thing?" I volunteered, with a weak smile. "E equals MC squared. That's the biggest idea I know."

"Don't get wise, nerd," Chuck said. He grabbed my shirtfront and pulled me to within inches of his face. I couldn't help but notice that Chuck needed a shave. And Chuck was only fifteen!

"Don't play dumb," Chuck went on. "I mean those creepy phone calls. Anytime my sister gets on the phone, some voice cuts in and says things to her."

"What kind of things?" I asked, trying to get loose.

"You know what they are. Ginny told me about talking to you yesterday. You got some girl to make those calls for you and say all those things. . . . So you and your creepy girlfriend better knock it off. Or I'll knock *you* off. Get it?"

For emphasis Chuck balled his free hand into a fist the size of a ham and held it under my nose. I didn't know what he was talking about, but I had to get away from this moose before he did me some real harm.

"First off, I don't have a girlfriend, creepy or otherwise," I said. "And second, I don't

Don't good afternoon me. What have you done to Ginny Linke?

---

5. **bytes:** amounts of computer memory needed to store one character (letter, number, or symbol) of data.

know what you're talking about. And third, you better let me go, Chuck Linke."

"Oh, yeah? Why should I?"

"Because if you look over your shoulder, you'll see the assistant principal is watching us from his office window."

Chuck released me and spun around. There was no one at the window. But by then I was running to the safety of the school building. I figured the trick would work on him. For Chuck the hard questions begin with "How are you?" I hid out from him for the rest of the day and walked home rather than chance seeing the monster on the bus.

Louis's screen was dark when I ran upstairs to my bedroom. I placed a hand on the console. It was still warm. I punched the on button, and the familiar *Good afternoon, Kevin* was displayed.

Don't good afternoon me, I typed furiously. *What have you done to Ginny Linke?* Louis's screen replied:

```
Programming Error: 76534.
Not programmed to respond this type
of question.
```

Don't get cute, I entered. *What are you doing to Ginny? Her brother nearly knocked my head off today.* Louis's screen responded immediately.

```
Are you hurt. Y/N?
```

No, I'm okay. But I don't know for how long. I've been hiding out from Chuck Linke today. He might catch me tomorrow, though. Then, I'll be history. The response from Louis came instantly.

```
Your life is in danger. Y/N?
```

I explained to Louis that my life wasn't really threatened. But it sure could be made very unpleasant by Chuck Linke. Louis flashed:

```
This Chuck Linke lives at the same
address as the Ginny Linke person.
```

```
Y/N?
```

I punched in Y. Louis answered.

```
Don't worry then. HE'S history!
```

Wait! What are you going to do? I wrote. But Louis only answered with: *Programming Error: 76534.* And nothing I could do would make the machine respond. . . .

"Just what do you think you're doing, Kevin Neal?" demanded Ginny Linke. She had cornered me as I walked up the path to the school entrance. Ginny was really furious.

"I don't know what you're talking about," I said, a sinking feeling settling in my stomach. I had an idea that I *did* know. I just wasn't sure of the particulars.

"Chuck was arrested last night," Ginny said. "Some Secret Service men came to our house with a warrant. They said he'd sent a telegram, threatening the President's life. They traced it right to our phone. He's still locked up. . . ." Ginny looked like she was about to cry.

"Then this morning," she continued, "we got two whole truckloads of junk mail! Flyers from every strange company in the world. Mom got a notice that all our credit cards have been canceled. And the Internal Revenue Service has called Dad in for an audit! I don't know what's going on, Kevin Neal, but somehow I think you've got something to do with it!"

"But I didn't . . ." I began, but Ginny was striding up the walk to the main entrance.

I finished the schoolday, but it was a blur. Louis had done it, all right. It had access to mainframe computers. It also had the ability to try every secret access code to federal and commercial memory banks until it got the right one. Louis had cracked their security systems. It was systematically destroying the entire Linke family, and all via telephone lines! What would it do next?

More important, I thought, what would *I* do next? It's one thing to play a trick or two, to get even, but Louis was going crazy! And I never wanted to harm Ginny, or even her stupid moose of a brother. She'd just hurt my feelings with that nerd remark.

"You have to disconnect Louis," I told myself. "There's no other way."

But why did I feel like such a rat about doing it? I guess because Louis was my friend . . . the only one I had. "Don't be an ass," I went on. "Louis is a machine. He's a very wonderful, powerful machine. And it seems he's also very dangerous. You have to pull its plug, Kevin!"

I suddenly realized that I'd said the last few words aloud. Kids around me on the bus were staring. I sat there feeling like the nerd Ginny thought I was, until my stop came. I dashed from the bus and ran the three blocks to my house.

When I burst into the hall, I was surprised to see my father, coming from the kitchen with a cup of coffee in his hand.

"Dad! What are you doing here?"

"Some kids say hello," Dad replied. "Or even, 'Gee it's good to see you, Dad.'"

"I'm sorry, Dad," I said. "I didn't expect anyone to be home at this hour."

"Wound up my business in Chicago a day sooner than I expected," he said. "But what are you all out of breath about? Late for something?"

"No, Dad," I said. "It's Louis. . . ."

"Not to worry. I had some time on my hands, so I checked it out again. You were right. It was acting very funny. I think it had to do with the inbuilt logic/growth program I designed for it. You know . . . the 'personality' thing? Took me a couple of hours to clean the whole system out."

"To what?" I cried.

"I erased the whole program and set Louis up as a normal computer. Had to disconnect the whole thing and do some rewiring. It had been learning, all right. But it was also turning itself around. . . ." Dad stopped, and looked at me. "It's kind of involved, Kevin," he said. "Even for a bright kid like you. Anyway, I think you'll find Louis is working just fine now.

"Except it won't answer you as Louis anymore. It'll only function as a regular Major Electronics Model Z-11127. I guess the personality program didn't work out."

I felt like a great weight had been taken off my shoulders. I didn't have to "face" Louis, and pull its plug. But somehow, all I could say was "Thanks, Dad."

"Don't mention it, son," Dad said brightly. He took his cup of coffee and sat down in his favorite chair in the living room. I followed him.

"One more thing that puzzles me, though," Dad said. He reached over to the table near his chair. He held up three sheets of fanfold computer paper covered with figures. "Just as I was doing the final erasing, I must have put the printer on by accident. There was some data in the print buffer memory and it printed out. I don't know what to make of it. Do you?"

I took the papers from my father and read: *How do I love thee? Let me compute the ways:* The next two pages were covered with strings of binary code figures. On the last page, in beautiful color graphics was a stylized heart. Below it was the simple message: *I will always love you, Kevin: Louise.*

"Funny thing," Dad said. "It spelled its own name wrong."

"Yeah," I said. I turned and headed for my room. There were tears in my eyes and I knew I couldn't explain them to Dad, or myself either. ❖

RESPONDING
O P T I O N S

FROM PERSONAL RESPONSE TO CRITICAL ANALYSIS

REFLECT
1. How did you react to the computer's last printout? Share your reaction with classmates.

RETHINK
2. Do you think Kevin makes the right decision about disconnecting Louis(e)? Explain your answer.

3. In your opinion, which character in the story experiences the most injustice?
   Consider
   - Kevin's treatment by the other students
   - the Linke family's sudden problems
   - what finally happens to Louis(e)

4. Consider the title "User Friendly" and its meaning as applied to the use of computers. How do you think the title fits Kevin's relationship with this computer?

RELATE
5. Look over the scales you completed for the Personal Connection on page 277. Think about how computers affect your daily life and the lives of those around you. In what ways do you think computers help or harm the ability of people to connect with one another?

ANOTHER PATHWAY
Cooperative Learning

Imagine that "User Friendly" is turned into a made-for-television movie. In teams, plan and carry out an advertising campaign to attract viewers. Create an ad for a weekly news-magazine, a 15-second radio spot with sound effects, or a video of a 30-second TV preview. Share your final product with other teams.

QUICKWRITES

1. Write a **diary entry** Kevin might record in which he explains his feelings about computers and about the death of Louis(e).

2. If you know how, send an **electronic-mail,** or **e-mail, message** to a student in another class or school. In your message, tell whether you would recommend reading the story and why.

3. What if, a few weeks later, Kevin turns on his computer and sees a message from Louis(e) displayed on the screen? Write a **plot summary** for a sequel to the story.

📁 *PORTFOLIO Save your writing. You may want to use it later as a spring-board to a piece for your portfolio.*

LITERARY CONCEPTS

The type of fiction that is based on real or imaginary scientific ideas is called **science fiction.** It is a form of imaginative writing that may be set in a believable world or in a fantasy world that has familiar elements. Many science fiction works are based on the latest discoveries in science, invention, and technology. Others describe machines and processes that are completely imaginary. What elements of science fiction do you find in this story?

CONCEPT REVIEW: Conflict You know that **conflict** is a struggle between opposing forces. The struggle between Kevin and the Linkes is one example of conflict in this selection. Describe another conflict in "User Friendly."

ACROSS THE CURRICULUM

Computer Science What new technological changes have come to your school over the last five years? What do you know about the use of e-mail, on-line databases, or long-distance learning? Visit your media center to investigate new educational or entertainment possibilities for computers. Interview your school's principal or media specialist to discover current and future plans for computer technologies. Create a flow chart to show the past, current, and future uses of computers in your school. If possible, use a graphics software program to create the flow chart.

LITERARY LINKS

The characters of Rachel in "Eleven" and Kevin in this story share an unwillingness or an inability to express their feelings to others. Imagine that they are guests on a TV talk show whose subject is "Those Annoying People—And What You'd Like to Tell Them!" Team up with a friend and role-play the conversation between these two characters as they discuss ways in which they could have responded more productively to their situations.

WORDS TO KNOW

Make a list of all the words you know that are associated with computers and computer science. Use your knowledge about computers to write a computer glossary that you or your class can use as a reference source. Include any terms you learned in the Reading Connection on page 278.

T. ERNESTO BETHANCOURT

T. Ernesto Bethancourt (1932–) is the pen name of Tom Paisley, a singer, guitarist, and composer who was born in Brooklyn, New York. Before becoming a writer of stories, he was a writer of songs. During the 1960s, Paisley performed in the coffeehouses of New York's Greenwich Village, appearing with such noted folksingers as Bob Dylan and Peter, Paul, and Mary. Paisley also toured colleges and nightclubs.

In the 1970s, Tom Paisley turned to other forms of writing. As T. Ernesto Bethancourt, he has produced over 20 hardcover novels for young adults. He introduced the character Doris Fein in his book *Dr. Doom: Superstar,* and has since made her the hero of a mystery series. In reference to his writing, he says, "I've never written for any purpose but to entertain."

OTHER WORKS *New York City Too Far from Tampa Blues, Tune in Yesterday, Where the Deer and the Cantaloupe Play, The Me Inside of Me*

PREVIEWING

FICTION

The Summer of the Beautiful White Horse

William Saroyan (sə-roi′ən)

PERSONAL CONNECTION

Family traits play an important role in this classic story. Are there special qualities, beliefs, customs, behaviors, or physical characteristics that you and your relatives have in common? In your notebook, copy and complete the following sentence:

"One of the main traits my family members share is . . ."

> One of the main traits my family members share is that we all love to polka dance when someone in the family gets married. My uncle Vladimir taught me how to do it.

CULTURAL CONNECTION

Aram, the narrator of this story, is Armenian. His family originated in Armenia, a small country in southwest Asia. Armenia's prosperity and location made it the target of foreign invaders for most of the past 2,000 years. Beginning in the early 1900s, thousands of Armenians immigrated to the United States. Many settled in the San Joaquin (wô-kēn′) Valley of California. The countryside there was similar to their homeland. The immigrants continued to grow grapes, olives, apricots, and figs as they had done in Armenia, maintaining close family ties and strong feelings of nationality.

San Joaquin Valley

Sacramento
San Francisco
Fresno
San Joaquin Valley
San Joaquin River
Sierra Nevada
Pacific Ocean
CALIFORNIA
Los Angeles

N W E S

Miles
0   80   160

WRITING CONNECTION

Through the eyes of Aram, you'll see an Armenian community with such close ties among its members that families and friends share certain personal traits. What might be the advantages and disadvantages of such closeness? Write your thoughts in your notebook. As you read, see what family traits are important to characters in the story.

LASERLINKS
• HISTORICAL CONNECTION

The Deathless White Pacing Mustang (1948), Tom Lea. Oil on canvas, 18″ × 24″, Harry Ransom Humanities Research Center, The University of Texas at Austin.

THE SUMMER OF THE
BEAUTIFUL WHITE HORSE

BY WILLIAM SAROYAN

One day back there in the good old days when I was nine and the world was full of every imaginable kind of magnificence, and life was still a delightful and mysterious dream, my cousin Mourad, who was considered crazy by everybody who knew him except me, came to my house at four in the morning and woke me up by tapping on the window of my room.

"Aram," he said.

I jumped out of bed and looked out the window.

I couldn't believe what I saw.

It wasn't morning yet, but it was summer and with daybreak not many minutes around the corner of the world it was light enough for me to know I wasn't dreaming.

My cousin Mourad was sitting on a beautiful white horse.

I stuck my head out of the window and rubbed my eyes.

"Yes," he said in Armenian. "It's a horse. You're not dreaming. Make it quick if you want to ride."

I knew my cousin Mourad enjoyed being alive more than anybody else who had ever fallen into the world by mistake, but this was more than even I could believe.

In the first place, my earliest memories had been memories of horses, and my first longings had been longings to ride.

This was the wonderful part.

In the second place, we were poor.

This was the part that wouldn't permit me to believe what I saw.

We were poor. We had no money. Our whole tribe was poverty-stricken. Every branch of the Garoghlanian family was living in the most amazing and comical poverty in the world. Nobody could understand where we ever got money enough to keep us with food in our bellies, not even the old men of the family. Most important of all, though, we were famous for our honesty. We had been famous for our honesty for something like eleven centuries, even when we had been the wealthiest family

> It wasn't morning yet, but it was summer and with daybreak not many minutes around the corner of the world it was light enough for me to know I wasn't dreaming.

in what we liked to think was the world. We were proud first, honest next, and after that we believed in right and wrong. None of us would take advantage of anybody in the world, let alone steal.

Consequently, even though I could *see* the horse, so magnificent; even though I could *smell* it, so lovely; even though I could *hear* it breathing, so exciting; I couldn't *believe* the horse had anything to do with my cousin Mourad or with me or with any of the other members of our family, asleep or awake, because I *knew* my cousin Mourad couldn't have *bought* the horse, and if he couldn't have bought it he must have *stolen* it, and I refused to believe he had stolen it.

No member of the Garoghlanian family could be a thief.

I stared first at my cousin and then at the horse. There was a pious stillness and humor in each of them which on the one hand delighted me and on the other frightened me.

"Mourad," I said, "where did you steal this horse?"

"Leap out of the window," he said, "if you want to ride."

It was true, then. He had stolen the horse. There was no question about it. He had come to invite me to ride or not, as I chose.

Well, it seemed to me stealing a horse for a ride was not the same thing as stealing something else, such as money. For all I knew, maybe it wasn't stealing at all. If you were crazy about horses the way my cousin Mourad and I were, it wasn't stealing. It wouldn't become stealing until we offered to sell the horse, which of course I

knew we would never do.

"Let me put on some clothes," I said.

"All right," he said, "but hurry."

I leaped into my clothes.

I jumped down to the yard from the window and leaped up onto the horse behind my cousin Mourad.

That year we lived at the edge of town, on Walnut Avenue. Behind our house was the country: vineyards, orchards, irrigation ditches, and country roads. In less than three minutes we were on Olive Avenue, and then the horse began to trot. The air was new and lovely to breathe. The feel of the horse running was wonderful. My cousin Mourad, who was considered one of the craziest members of our family, began to sing. I mean, he began to roar.

Every family has a crazy streak in it somewhere, and my cousin Mourad was considered the natural descendant of the crazy streak in our tribe. Before him was our uncle Khosrove, an enormous man with a powerful head of black hair and the largest mustache in the San Joaquin Valley, a man so furious in temper, so irritable, so impatient that he stopped anyone from talking by roaring, *It is no harm; pay no attention to it.*

That was all, no matter what anybody happened to be talking about. Once it was his own son Arak running eight blocks to the barber shop where his father was having his

> "Leap out of the window," he said, "if you want to ride."

WORDS TO KNOW

consequently (kŏn′sĭ-kwĕnt′lē) *adv.* as a result; therefore
descendant (dĭ-sĕn′dənt) *n.* a child, grandchild, or more distant offspring

mustache trimmed to tell him their house was on fire. This man Khosrove sat up in the chair and roared, "It is no harm; pay no attention to it." The barber said, "But the boy says your house is on fire." So Khosrove roared, "Enough, it is no harm, I say."

My cousin Mourad was considered the natural descendant of this man, although Mourad's father was Zorab, who was <u>practical</u> and nothing else. That's how it was in our tribe. A man could be the father of his son's flesh, but that did not mean that he was also the father of his spirit. The distribution of the various kinds of spirit of our tribe had been from the beginning capricious[1] and vagrant.[2]

We rode and my cousin Mourad sang. For all anybody knew we were still in the old country where, at least according to some of our neighbors, we belonged. We let the horse run as long as it felt like running.

At last my cousin Mourad said, "Get down. I want to ride alone."

"Will you let me ride alone?" I said.

"That is up to the horse," my cousin said. "Get down."

"The *horse* will let me ride," I said.

"We shall see," he said. "Don't forget that I have a way with a horse."

"Well," I said, "any way you have with a horse, I have also."

"For the sake of your safety," he said, "let us hope so. Get down."

"All right," I said, "but remember you've got to let me try to ride alone."

I got down and my cousin Mourad kicked his heels into the horse and shouted, "*Vazire,*" run. The horse stood on its hind legs, snorted, and burst into a fury of speed that was the loveliest thing I had ever seen. My cousin Mourad raced the horse across a field of dry grass to an irrigation ditch, crossed the ditch on the horse, and five minutes later returned, dripping wet.

The sun was coming up.

"Now it's my turn to ride," I said.

My cousin Mourad got off the horse.

"Ride," he said.

I leaped to the back of the horse and for a moment knew the awfulest fear imaginable. The horse did not move.

"Kick into his muscles," my cousin Mourad said. "What are you waiting for? We've got to take him back before everybody in the world is up and about."

I kicked into the muscles of the horse. Once again it <u>reared</u> and snorted. Then it began to run. I didn't know what to do. Instead of running across the field to the irrigation ditch the horse ran down the road to the vineyard of Dikran Halabian, where it began to leap over vines.

The horse leaped over seven vines before I fell.

> I leaped to the back of the horse and for a moment knew the awfulest fear imaginable.

---

1. **capricious** (kə-prĭsh′əs): unpredictable.
2. **vagrant** (vā′grənt): moving in a random way.

WORDS TO KNOW
practical (prăk′tĭ-kəl) *adj.* level-headed; efficient
rear (rîr) *v.* to rise on the hind legs, as a horse

Then it continued running.

My cousin Mourad came running down the road.

"I'm not worried about you," he shouted. "We've got to get that horse. You go this way and I'll go this way. If you come upon him, be kindly. I'll be near."

I continued down the road and my cousin Mourad went across the field toward the irrigation ditch.

It took him half an hour to find the horse and bring him back.

"All right," he said, "jump on. The whole world is awake now."

"What will we do?" I said.

"Well," he said, "we'll either take him back or hide him until tomorrow morning."

He didn't sound worried and I knew he'd hide him and not take him back. Not for a while, at any rate.

"Where will we hide him?" I said.

"I know a place," he said.

"How long ago did you steal this horse?" I said.

It suddenly dawned on me that he had been taking these early morning rides for some time and had come for me this morning only because he knew how much I longed to ride.

"Who said anything about stealing a horse?" he said.

"Anyhow," I said, "how long ago did you begin riding every morning?"

"Not until this morning," he said.

"Are you telling the truth?" I said.

"Of course not," he said, "but if we are found out, that's what you're to say. I don't want both of us to be liars. All you know is that we started riding this morning."

"All right," I said.

He walked the horse quietly to the barn of a deserted vineyard which at one time had been the pride of a farmer named Fetvajian. There were some oats and dry alfalfa in the barn.

We began walking home.

"It wasn't easy," he said, "to get the horse to behave so nicely. At first it wanted to run wild, but, as I've told you, I have a way with a horse. I can get it to do anything *I* want it to do. Horses understand me."

"How do you do it?" I said.

"I have an understanding with a horse," he said.

"Yes, but what sort of an understanding?" I said.

"A simple and honest one," he said.

"Well," I said, "I wish I knew how to reach an understanding like that with a horse."

"You're still a small boy," he said. "When you get to be thirteen you'll know how to do it."

I went home and ate a hearty breakfast.

That afternoon my uncle Khosrove came to our house for coffee and cigarettes. He sat in the parlor, sipping and smoking and remembering the old country. Then another visitor arrived, a farmer named John Byro, an Assyrian[3] who, out of loneliness, had learned to speak Armenian. My mother brought the lonely visitor coffee and tobacco, and he rolled

> "Are you telling the truth?" I said.

---

3. **Assyrian** (ə-sîr′ē-ən): a member of an ethnic group that originally lived in Assyria, an ancient empire in the region of what are today Iraq and Syria.

The Icknield Way (1912), Spencer Gore (England, 1878–1914). Oil on canvas, 63.4 cm × 76.2 cm, Art Gallery of New South Wales, Australia.

a cigarette and sipped and smoked, and then at last, sighing sadly, he said, "My white horse which was stolen last month is still gone. I cannot understand it."

My uncle Khosrove became very irritated and shouted, "It's no harm. What is the loss of a horse? Haven't we all lost the homeland? What is this crying over a horse?"

"That may be all right for you, a city dweller, to say," John Byro said, "but what of my surrey? What good is a surrey without a horse?"

"Pay no attention to it," my uncle Khosrove roared.

"I walked ten miles to get here," John Byro said.

"You have legs," my uncle Khosrove shouted.

"My left leg pains me," the farmer said.

"Pay no attention to it," my uncle Khosrove roared.

"That horse cost me sixty dollars," the farmer said.

"I spit on money," my uncle Khosrove said.

He got up and stalked out of the house, slamming the screen door.

My mother explained.

"He has a gentle heart," she said. "It is simply that he is homesick and such a large man."

The farmer went away and I ran over to my cousin Mourad's house.

He was sitting under a peach tree, trying to repair the hurt wing of a young robin which could not fly. He was talking to the bird.

"What is it?" he said.

"The farmer, John Byro," I said. "He visited our house. He wants his horse. You've had it a month. I want you to promise not to take it back until I learn to ride."

"It will take you *a year* to learn to ride," my cousin Mourad said.

"We could keep the horse a year," I said.

My cousin Mourad leaped to his feet.

"What?" he roared. "Are you inviting a member of the Garoghlanian family to steal? The horse must go back to its true owner."

"When?" I said.

"In six months at the latest," he said.

He threw the bird into the air. The bird tried hard, almost fell twice, but at last flew away, high and straight.

Early every morning for two weeks my cousin Mourad and I took the horse out of the barn of the deserted vineyard where we were

hiding it and rode it, and every morning the horse, when it was my turn to ride alone, leaped over grape vines and small trees and threw me and ran away. Nevertheless, I hoped in time to learn to ride the way my cousin Mourad rode.

One morning on the way to Fetvajian's deserted vineyard we ran into the farmer John Byro, who was on the way to town.

"Let me do the talking," my cousin Mourad said. "I have a way with farmers."

"Good morning, John Byro," my cousin Mourad said to the farmer.

The farmer studied the horse eagerly.

"Good morning, sons of my friends," he said. "What is the name of your horse?"

"*My Heart,*" my cousin Mourad said in Armenian.

"A lovely name," John Byro said, "for a lovely horse. I could swear it is the horse that was stolen from me many weeks ago. May I look into its mouth?"

"Of course," Mourad said.

The farmer looked into the mouth of the horse.

"Tooth, for tooth," he said. "I would swear it is my horse if I didn't know your parents. The fame of your family for honesty is well known to me. Yet the horse is the twin of my horse. A suspicious man would believe his eyes instead of his heart. Good day, my young friends."

"Good day, John Byro," my cousin Mourad said.

Early the following morning we took the horse to John Byro's vineyard and put it in the barn. The dogs followed us around without making a sound.

"The dogs," I whispered to my cousin Mourad. "I thought they would bark."

"They would at somebody else," he said. "I have a way with dogs."

My cousin Mourad put his arms around the horse, pressed his nose into the horse's nose, patted it, and then we went away.

That afternoon John Byro came to our house in his surrey and showed my mother the horse that had been stolen and returned.

"I do not know what to think," he said. "The horse is stronger than ever. Better-tempered, too. I thank God."

My uncle Khosrove, who was in the parlor, became irritated and shouted, "Quiet man, quiet. Your horse has been returned. Pay no attention to it." ❖

HISTORICAL INSIGHT

THE EMPIRE OF THE ARMENIANS

Aram and his family no doubt know that the 1915 attack on Armenia by the Turks, in which about 1 million Armenians were killed, was only the most recent in a long history of conflict.

People lived in what is now Armenia as early as 6000 B.C., later forming Urartu, a tribal kingdom in which most people made their living by farming or by raising cattle. Beginning in the 500's B.C., these early Armenians faced one invader after another. The people of Urartu were conquered by invaders from areas that are now Iran and Greece. Armenia was under Persian and then Greek rule for hundreds of years.

When the Romans invaded in 55 B.C., Armenia became part of the Roman Empire. After a long history of trying to fight off numerous invaders—and falling under the control of the Soviet Union in 1922—Armenia achieved independence in 1991.

Centuries of conflict did not prevent the Armenian people from developing and expanding their own culture. Like Aram's family, the people relied on close family groupings and a strong tribal identity. They vigorously resisted their invaders and were able to maintain a degree of independence in spite of them. Though governed by a series of conquering nations, Armenia built prosperous independent empire-states at different times in its long history. The pride that is so important to the Garoghlanian family in this story is a trait that seems to have been shared by its ancestors.

RESPONDING
OPTIONS

FROM PERSONAL RESPONSE TO CRITICAL ANALYSIS

REFLECT 1. What do you think of Aram and Mourad's adventures? Jot down your thoughts in your notebook.

RETHINK 2. Why do you think John Byro does not take the horse when he seems to recognize it as his?

3. In your opinion, what kind of person is Mourad?

   Consider
   - his actions with the horse and his care of the injured bird
   - his insistence that he has "a way" with things
   - the family traits he shares with Uncle Khosrove

RELATE 4. Think about the family trait you identified before you began reading. How does the trait of Aram's family compare with your family's trait and with the traits of other families you know?

ANOTHER PATHWAY
Cooperative Learning

With a small group of classmates, discuss Aram's relationship with Mourad. List words to describe the qualities you see in their friendship. Would they be friends even if they weren't members of the same family? Compare your list with those of other groups.

LITERARY CONCEPTS

Words and phrases that help the reader see, hear, taste, smell, and feel what the writer is describing are called **sensory details.** In the story, the narrator appeals to the sense of smell when he says that on the morning of his first ride on the horse "the air was new and lovely to breathe." Write down at least one more example of a sensory detail for any of the senses shown here.

Sensory Details	
Hearing	
Sight	
Taste	
Smell	the "new air" that is "lovely to breathe"
Touch	

QUICKWRITES

1. Write a **descriptive** or **narrative poem** about the "beautiful white horse" from either Aram's or Mourad's point of view. If necessary, refer to the details in the sensory image chart you filled out for the Literary Concepts section.

2. A credo is a formal, point-by-point statement of beliefs, principles, or opinions. Compose a **credo** for the Garoghlanian family that reflects their family traits.

📁 **PORTFOLIO** *Save your writing. You may want to use it later as a springboard to a piece for your portfolio.*

ALTERNATIVE ACTIVITIES

1. With two other students, assign roles and **dramatize** incidents from the story. You might choose to re-create the scene in which Mourad first appears at Aram's window on the horse, the scene in which Byro recognizes the horse, or the scene with Uncle Khosrove in the barbershop.

2. This is just one story from Saroyan's book *My Name Is Aram.* Using details from this story, illustrate a **book jacket** that might get people to buy the book.

ACROSS THE CURRICULUM

Science Why did John Byro look at the horse's teeth? What did he hope to learn? Read more about what can be discovered by examining an animal's teeth. Present your information in an informative brochure for the class.

CRITIC'S CORNER

Nicole Putnam, a member of the student board that reviewed this story, says, "The story had a touching ending that I did not expect. I thought maybe Aram and Mourad would both run away from home with the horse and call the wilderness their home." What ending had you expected?

WORDS TO KNOW

Review the Words to Know in the boxes at the bottom of the selection pages. On your paper, write the word that best completes each sentence.

1. Many Armenian immigrants were not wealthy. In fact, they were _____ .

2. Aram's family is famous for its honesty; ____, he cannot believe his cousin would steal a horse.

3. Mourad is not like his father and is considered the natural ____ of his uncle Khosrove.

4. Keeping the horse hidden from John Byro is not a very ____ idea.

5. Mourad knows that if Aram kicks his heels into the horse, it may ____.

WILLIAM SAROYAN

"The Summer of the Beautiful White Horse" and other stories in *My Name Is Aram* are based on William Saroyan's own boyhood in Fresno, California. The character of Aram is, like the author, a Californian of Armenian descent. Saroyan said, "It came to me that I had better write about certain people and things as quickly as possible because if I didn't, I would forget, and I believed I had the obligation not to forget."

Saroyan's works include short stories, plays, and novels. His writings reveal his belief in the basic innocence of people and his love of America.

1908–1981

Saroyan won the Pulitzer Prize in 1939 for his play *The Time of Your Life,* but he refused the prize because he considered accepting cash awards to be beneath the dignity of an artist. On his deathbed, Saroyan said, "Everybody has got to die, but I have always believed an exception would be made in my case. Now what?" His words, which reflected the dry humor that filled his writing, were quoted around the world.

OTHER WORKS *The Daring Young Man on the Flying Trapeze, My Heart's in the Highlands, The Human Comedy*

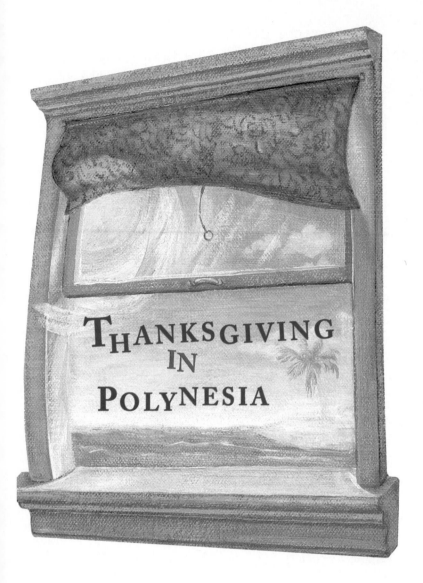

Thanksgiving in Polynesia

by Susan Haven

I place my palms on the window ledge of the huge double window in my mom and dad's bedroom, and hoist myself up until I am kneeling on the sill, my nose to the window.

Beyond, and three feet below, is my backyard.

It's not fair. I cleaned my room, I swear I did.

I made my bed, picked up the stuff on the floor, and put all my books in the bookshelf.

But did my mom thank me? Of course not.

Just because I shoved the Monopoly pieces under the bed, along with a couple of nightgowns and maybe two or three CDs that lost their cases, she got mad.

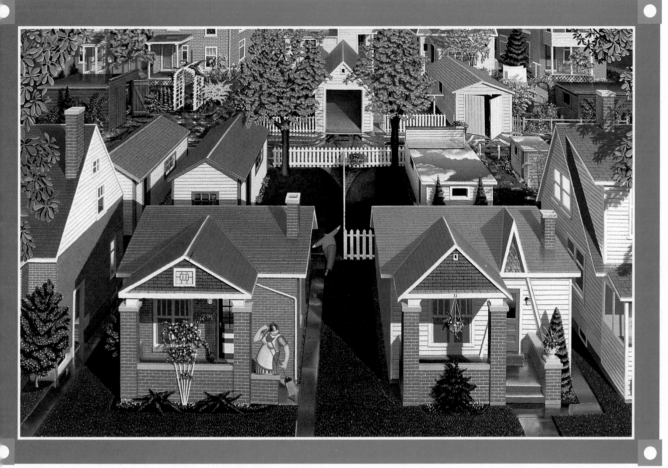

Centre of the Universe (1992), Brian Jones. Courtesy of Nancy Poole's Studio, Toronto, Canada.

Picky, picky, picky.

First she told me, "I want your room cleaned in an hour," and then when I tried a time-saving plan, like storing stuff under the bed, she didn't appreciate it.

A little bad luck made things even worse.

When she came in to check on me, she stepped barefoot on a little metal Monopoly token.

Wow. Does she scream loud.

I apologized and everything.

But did she forgive me? Of course not.

I'm going to jump out this window, then sneak around the alley and crawl on my stomach past the big kitchen window. My mom's in the kitchen right now, with my aunt Rhea, getting the Thanksgiving dinner ready, and I don't want them to see me make my escape.

My aunt is why my mom's in such a bad mood, I know it.

She and my uncle Ted, and their one perfect kid, Andrea (my age, ten and a half) arrived from Chicago this morning.

We're all supposed to break turkey together in about half an hour.

I plan to be in Polynesia. Or at least New Jersey, by then.

Our family is not too fond of their family, but they come every Thanksgiving anyway.

My mom especially dislikes my aunt Rhea. She's rich and snobby and makes my mom and dad and my older brother, Jason, and me feel terrible.

She speaks with an English accent, even though I know she was born right here, where we live, in Massapequa, Long Island, New York.

Whenever Jason or I turn on the TV, Aunt Rhea always asks, oh so sweetly, "My, my, don't you two watch a dreadfully large quantity of television?"

That's the Rhea technique: questions that kill.

Like this morning, she asked Jason, when he was grabbing a cookie from the cookie jar: "Wouldn't you prefer a carrot?"

Who'd prefer a carrot to one of mom's chocolate-chip cookies, anyway?

Or later, as my mom was setting the big table, Rhea came over with the napkins and said: "My, my, Sara, but don't you make Missy or Jason do anything around here?"

Jason calls her Aunt Dia-Rhea.

Unfortunately, my mom brought her into my room to show her how I'd cleaned up before they all arrived, and that's when my mom stepped on the Monopoly top hat. And called me a slob. In front of Aunt Rhea. And told me not to come out until my room was spotless.

My first plan was not to come out of my room until I'm eighteen.

But that didn't seem possible. So I snuck in here, to my parents' bedroom, in the back of the house, and I'm going to climb out this window.

I'd have snuck out of mine, but I left some candies on my window ledge and they melted onto the metal window and now it won't open so easily.

More bad luck.

Personally, I've had enough. I'm going to Polynesia. Don't worry about the sharks there. I'll be fine.

Besides, I don't want to play with my cousin Andrea anymore.

She is what my grandmother calls "a lovely child."

Andrea offered to set the table.

She always picks up her dishes after a meal and puts them in the sink.

She does the laundry every Saturday.

She compliments everybody on everything.

She doesn't even have to be reminded to do that stuff.

Personally, I think that's sick.

And when we started to play a game of jacks, she slaughtered me. And apologized every move she made.

I press my nose to the window. In the distance, I can see Annie MacElvane's house.

My best friend.

She is probably sitting down to Thanksgiving dinner right now with her warm, friendly family.

I could run away there.

It's not Polynesia, but as my dad would say, I'd make good time. I'd be there in a sec.

The problem is—I can't run anywhere until I get the summer screen out of this window.

I'd rather run away to Polynesia, because it's a great place for kids.

We just studied it in Mrs. Schwartz's Cultures of the World unit.

There's no such word in Polynesia as *my* or *our*. Those are called possessive pronouns. The reason they don't have possessive pronouns is that nobody owns anything, including their own children. Children belong to God and the land and the universe. They have total freedom.

According to my map, Polynesia is about six inches from America. Which can't be that far.

I wonder what the kids in Polynesia are like.

I wonder if when they're in school, they have a unit called "The Peoples of Massapequa."

As a token of my friendliness, I'm bringing my jacks along. Mrs. Schwartz says that when you visit other peoples, you should bring a symbol of your own peoples. Jacks should do it. Plus, they'll give me something to do until I make a friend.

Well, the sooner I leave, the sooner I'll be playing tensies in paradise.

Maybe I'll just shove this screen right out the window.

Scrunching down, I kick at it.

Uh oh. A hole. The screen's still attached, but now there's this big hole in it that's the shape of my foot.

If I weren't running away already, I'd seriously consider it now, because when they discover this little disaster I'll be grounded until college.

I'll have to make the hole just a little bigger. Girl size.

Perfect. I'm set.

When my mom and dad realize I'm gone, their hearts will break.

In fact, I think I should write a note to make them feel a little worse. Something like:

Dear Mom and Dad: This home is not working out. If you miss me, call Polynesia 2-4000.

Or:

Personally, I've had enough. I'm going to Polynesia. Don't worry about the sharks there. I'll be fine.

If a shark eats me, that'll really kill them.

My body is easing into the scratchy screen when suddenly I hear a *thud*.

A *thump*.

A *clump*.

And then the rattle and vibration of furniture in the hall.

Heavy footsteps are coming toward the bedroom.

My body stiffens. My heart pounds.

What could that be? I have to get out of here. Fast.

Ow. The torn screen is so scratchy.

Thud. Rattle. Tickle.

Bounce. Bounce.

It's my brother, Jason. Bouncing a basketball in the hall.

When my mom yells at him about indoor basketball bouncing, she has a point. The whole house vibrates.

Is that the doorknob turning? This doorknob?

I try to ease my body further through the screen.

I can't get out.

There's only one thing I can do.

Backing my butt out of the screen, I jump down from the ledge and look around my mom's room for a place to hide.

The closet.

I'll never make it in time.

Diving onto the floor, I roll under the huge queen-size bed just as the door opens.

In a second, I'm peeking out from under the bedspread, inches from Jason's big clodhopper feet, which are now standing in front of my mom's bureau.

I bet he's looking in the mirror, as usual.

Wait. Those clodhoppers of his are moving. Is he leaving?

Copyright © Mary GrandPre.

No. He's moving toward the window.

I peek out a little further just in time to see him climb onto the ledge, open the window, and kick the screen right out into the backyard.

"What does she want," he's muttering. "I went to the store. I meant to buy regular milk. So I didn't see the label that said buttermilk. Personally, I've had enough!"

His leg is out the window.

My gosh.

He's running away too!

Gee. I'm going to miss him.

What am I talking about—I'm going to miss him? I'm running away too!

Thud. Thud.

It's footsteps again.

What is this? A convention?

You can't even have a little privacy in your own parents' bedroom when you want it.

Jason's heard something too. His head is turned, perked at attention.

The doorknob. It's turning again.

Jason's eyes widen in panic and then he jumps backward off the window ledge.

The next thing I know, I have company under the bed.

"Happy Thanksgiving . . . " I whisper.

"Ahhh!" he almost screams in fright, but I cover his mouth as I swallow a giggle, because we can both hear the soft *clip clap* of my mom's loose slippers.

She's *clip clapping* around the room. The bureau drawer squeaks open, there's the soft whoosh of something being removed, the drawer squeaks shut again, and then the springs of the mattress hit my nose as she plops down on the bed.

She's sighing. Which lowers the springs even more.

Then she mutters, "Personally I've had

You can't even have a little privacy in your own parents' bedroom when you want it.

enough . . ." and leans backward. "On the other hand, you're a grown woman, Sara. Now, go out there and handle it."

The springs lower, hitting me in the nose, and then lift.

She's gotten up.

In a second, we hear the door open and softly shut.

She's gone.

Wait a second. It's opening again.

"Sara? Are you in here?"

It's my dad, coming in.

But where's my mom, if my dad didn't see her going out?

I know I heard the door shutting.

Oh no. It couldn't be.

But it is.

The door that shut wasn't the bedroom door. It was the closet door.

My mom, my thirty-five-year-old mom, is hiding in the closet at this very moment.

"Sara? Jason? Missy?" my dad whispers again in a voice that sounds a little lonely.

Gee. Poor Daddy.

He's been stuck out there all alone with Aunt Rhea and Uncle Ted.

Uncle Ted probably just finished showing off his newest gold charge cards to my dad.

I peek out from underneath the bottom of the bedspread.

Everything that's going on is reflected in the full-length mirror on the closet door. I can see a dress caught in the doorjamb of my mom's closet.

She's in there all right.

"Where is everybody?" my dad says.

Silence.

My dad takes one last look around the room, and then moves to the bedroom door again.

But just as he's backing out, the closet door opens and my mom pops out

"Hi . . ." she says.

"Sara! What are you doing in the closet?"

"I was . . . I was looking for a better tablecloth." She swallows and then continues. "Actually, I was also looking for a whole new house. And a whole new me. But . . . it's not in there. . . ." Her face starts to pucker, like she's going to cry.

My dad puts his arm around her.

"Is Rhea getting to you, honey?"

My mom shakes her head. "Nooo. What makes you think that?"

My dad grins.

"And I took it out on the kids. . . ."

"They'll live. . . ." my dad says.

Sure we'll live, I think. But where?

"What's the matter with me?" my mom sobs. "I'm a grown woman. Why does that phony get to me? Why can't I handle it? I have no character. No courage. No strength. You want me to make it all nice. And I try, but she's getting to me. Even your brother Ted is getting to me. All his mutual funds are going up. Did you know that?"

My dad nods. "Sure did."

"Plus, I've been yelling at the kids. For nothing. Well, not nothing. . . ."

Nothing, Mom. Nothing.

"And they're fed up with me. And I don't blame them." She starts to cry again. "The

I feel lectures and meaningless sayings coming on.

turkey is probably dry, I have an ugly tablecloth, and I'm a terrible mother." She's bawling.

I have to admit that the sound of my mom's sobs is getting to me. I can't help it.

"You're not such a terrible mother . . ." I mumble.

The sobbing stops.

"Who's that? Where's that? What's that?" my mom asks.

"Stevie Baldwin's mom is worse," Jason talks right into the mattress. "She's not as mean as you are today, but she treats him like a baby. Last week, four guys were playing pool in his room, and she walks in, and with this high, squeaky voice, says 'Would any of you boys like a Twinkie . . . ?' You'd never do that!"

Just as Jason's finishing his speech the bedspread, like a curtain, rises, and my mom's wide eyes stare at us.

"Happy Thanksgiving," I say to her. Then, I can't help adding, "But for next Thanksgiving, you ought to dust under here, Mom. . . ."

She blushes. Then her thumb jerks backward, like a hitchhiker.

"Out. Both of you. Out."

Jason rolls one way. I roll the other.

In a second we're all standing around my mom and dad's bed.

My mom's fingertips are against her cheeks. I think she's in shock. My dad's eyes have already taken in the open window.

Just as I say, "Jason was running away," Jason says, "Missy was running away."

And then we both say, "We can't take it anymore either."

My dad and mom give each other looks. I feel lectures and meaningless sayings coming on.

"Aunt Rhea means well . . ." my mom begins.

But now that we know how she really feels about Aunt Rhea, all we have to do is give her a "yeah, sure" look, and she stops.

"On the other hand, kids . . ." Now my dad is going into speech mode. "You can't run away from a problem . . ."

But then he looks at my mom, who is standing inches from her former hideaway closet.

And he stops. And sighs. "What are we going to do?" he says. "They are unbearable. I've tried to talk to them, hint, be diplomatic, but it's like talking to Martians . . ."

Everyone's looking dumb, so I jump right in there. "Could we . . . *all* run away?" I ask softly.

All our eyes shift to the open window. Then we look at each other.

I can see the open sea. Polynesia. Palm trees.

Then my dad sighs. "My mother, your grandmother, would have a heart attack in heaven. . . . I can't . . ."

My mom agrees. "Look, it's a Thanksgiving from hell . . . but otherwise it's not so terrible. What we have to do is what we do every year. Get through it, and give thanks on Sunday—when it's over."

Everybody nods at practically the same time. Which makes us all giggle.

"Are we ready?" my dad asks. "We have to get out there or they're going to start to get suspicious. Plus, the turkey is done. . . ."

My mother turns white. "Oh my God . . . my turkey . . . my turkey." She lunges for the door.

Then she stops, pauses, looks back at us, puts a big smile on her face, stands up straight, and with dignity, walks out her bedroom door.

My father follows.

My brother goes next.

Before I leave, I take one last peek at the window.

I guess that's what people mean by a window of opportunity.

Polynesia would have been swell.

But it's not to be.

Of course, Christmas is coming up and there are rumors that my mother's second cousins are coming up from Florida.

I can feel the wind wafting through my hair already.

But in the meanwhile, I close the door behind me, take a deep breath, and gather up the courage that the Peoples of Massapequa are known for. ❖

SUSAN HAVEN

Susan Haven is an American comedy writer whose career began in the early 1970s. She has written for magazines and movies and television programs. She has published two novels for young adults.

Haven writes, "Being funny gets my characters through whatever crisis they need to get through, and it's helped me as well. I'm grateful that I live with a son and a husband who can easily make me laugh, no matter what. I am also a social worker, working as a therapist with families. Besides my family, nothing gives me more pleasure than being around or working with kids."

OTHER WORKS *Maybe I'll Move to the Lost and Found*

WRITING ABOUT
LITERATURE

Solving a Story

Have you ever noticed that it's easier to understand a problem by breaking it into smaller parts and then solving each part? You can also use this technique to help you better understand and appreciate stories. For example, what purpose does dialogue serve in "User Friendly"? How are events in "The Summer of the Beautiful White Horse" connected? In the following pages you will

- see how writers use dialogue in stories
- analyze the plot of a selection you've just read
- use analysis to understand an event you might observe

Writer's Style: Dialogue Dialogue is conversation—people talking to each other. Writers use dialogue to give information about characters and events.

Read the Literature

Notice how dialogue helps writers tell their stories.

Literature Models

Dialogue Adds to the Plot
How does this conversation tell you what's happening in the story? How does it suggest what might happen?

> "Don't play dumb," Chuck went on. "I mean those creepy phone calls. Anytime my sister gets on the phone, some voice cuts in and says things to her."
> "What kind of things?" I asked, trying to get loose.
> "You know what they are. Ginny told me about talking to you yesterday. You got some girl to make those calls for you and say all those things. . . ."
>
> T. Ernesto Bethancourt, from "User Friendly"

Dialogue Reveals Characters' Personalities
What do you learn about Uncle Khosrove from this conversation?

> "I spit on money," my uncle Khosrove said. He got up and stalked out of the house, slamming the screen door.
> My mother explained.
> "He has a gentle heart," she said. "It is simply that he is homesick and such a large man."
>
> William Saroyan, from "The Summer of the Beautiful White Horse"

Connect to Life

Since scriptwriters can't explain all previous events, they use dialogue to tell you about important information that happened earlier.

Script

> LUKE: You told me Vader betrayed and murdered my father.
>
> BEN: Your father was seduced by the dark side of the Force. He ceased to be Anakin Skywalker and became Darth Vader. When that happened, the good man who was your father was destroyed. So what I have told you was true . . . from a certain point of view.
>
> Lawrence Kasdan and George Lucas
> from *Return of the Jedi*

Dialogue Provides Background Information
How else might the information in this conversation be revealed?

Try Your Hand: Using Dialogue

1. **A Complete Conversation** With a partner, rewrite the following paragraph, using dialogue.

   I told my sister that I would like to have a computer like Louis. She told me I was crazy. I tried to explain that it would be cool to have Louis because I could tell it secrets without worrying that it would blab to others. She didn't think that was such a big deal. Then I rattled off a zillion other reasons telling how Louis might help me.

2. **In Your Own Words** Choose a conversation from one of the selections you've read. Rewrite the dialogue as you and your friends would have said it.

3. **With Your Own Ears** You hear dialogue around you every day—at school, on the playground, at the store. Write down some of the dialogue you hear.

SkillBuilder

GS → GRAMMAR FROM WRITING

Using Quotation Marks
Quotation marks are used at the beginning and the end of direct quotations. In written dialogue, like this section of "User Friendly" by T. Ernesto Bethancourt, quotation marks set off the exact words of each speaker. Also notice that when the speaker changes, a new paragraph begins and the line is indented.

> "What'd you ask Chuck?"
> I said.
>   Ginny laughed. "I asked him who was that nerdy kid who keeps staring at me on the bus. He knew who I meant, right away."

APPLYING WHAT YOU'VE LEARNED
Combine the sentences below to create a conversation. Place quotation marks where needed and use correct paragraphing.

- Chuck growled Okay, nerd. What's the big idea?
- I volunteered Energy and mass are different aspects of the same thing.
- In other words, *E* equals *mc* squared. That's the biggest idea I know I told him.
- Chuck said Don't get wise, nerd.

 GRAMMAR HANDBOOK

For more information on quotation marks, see pages 850 of the Grammar Handbook.

Analysis

The plot is a series of events in a story. By studying and analyzing the events, characters, and dialogue in a story, you will be able to better understand what makes the story interesting and effective. Analyzing a story situation can also help you understand the situations that you observe in your life.

GUIDED ASSIGNMENT

Write a Plot Analysis On the next few pages, you will look closely at a key event from one of the stories you've just read. Then you'll have a chance to describe how that event was important to the story.

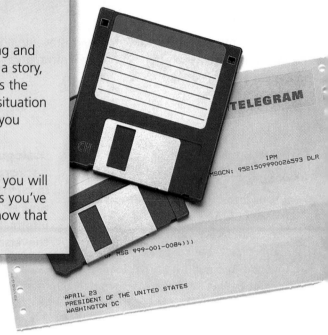

❶ Prewrite and Explore

In a plot analysis, you look closely at one part of a story—the events that occur—and write about how and why these events make the story interesting. Jot down stories you enjoyed and a key event you remember from each.

CHOOSING A STORY AND EVENT

These questions might help you choose a story and event to write about.

- Which story has the most surprising or interesting turn of events?
- Which event in the story is the most exciting? Why?
- What caused this event to happen? How does this event affect what happens later?

GATHERING INFORMATION

Remember that writers sometimes use dialogue to describe events in a story. Look for key information about events and situations in the conversations the characters have.

Also, a story map like the one shown below can help you think about events and information and how they help to tell a story.

Student's Story Map

② Freewriting

Now that you have chosen an event, freewrite about what makes it important. Don't worry if your thoughts seem disorganized. You can sort out your ideas—or even change your mind—once you get something on paper.

Student's Freewriting Model

What's Louis up to? I figured Louis was going to do something to help Kevin. I first realized that Louis was fooling around when Kevin ran into Chuck Linke. What's strange is that it's a girl's voice that's saying creepy things to Ginny Linke.

Is it clear which event I'm talking about? I think I'd better give a little summary.

How does this scene change or move the plot along?

Which details would really show how the scene is strange?

Something strange and interesting is going on in this scene. What's great is that Kevin doesn't know what's going on. I figured it out, though. This scene makes you want to see how Kevin is going to figure it out.

③ Draft and Share

As you draft your analysis, remember that it should have three parts: an introduction that gives readers background information; a body that contains facts, reasons, and other details that support your analysis; and a conclusion that summarizes your analysis and draws an overall conclusion. Share your draft with a classmate and ask for suggestions on how to improve it.

 PEER RESPONSE

- Which parts of my analysis do you agree or disagree with?
- What were the strong and weak points of the essay?

④ Revise and Edit

All good writers revise and revise again until they are happy with their writing. Look at the Standards for Evaluation below and your reviewer's comments. Then revise and edit your draft. When you are finished, think about how your plot analysis changed the way you think about the story.

Student's Final Draft

> ### "User Friendly"
>
> Do you ever wonder if computers have feelings? Author T. Ernesto Bethancourt writes about this idea in "User Friendly." Kevin Neal has a powerful computer named Louis. One day Louis sends personal messages to Kevin. So when Kevin is rejected by Ginny Linke, he "tells" Louis all about his problem. Kevin soon finds out how powerful Louis is.

What information do you find out here that will help you understand the scene below?

> A key moment comes when Kevin is bullied by Ginny's huge brother Chuck. It's an important scene because it shows how powerful Louis is. The scene is interesting because readers can figure out that Louis is trying to help Kevin, but Kevin, Ginny, and Chuck don't know. When Chuck describes the phone calls, I think of what Louis said to Kevin in an earlier scene: "I'll take care of Ginny."

What does the writer find interesting in the scene?

Standards for Evaluation

A plot analysis
- gives the author, the title, and a summary of the story
- clearly shows which events are important and why
- is supported by reasons, examples, and quotations from the story
- has an ending that summarizes the analysis and draws an overall conclusion

Grammar in Context

Coordinating Conjunctions A **conjunction** is a word that connects sentence parts or whole sentences. When writing your analysis, you can show how ideas are different or alike by using conjunctions. The words *and*, *but*, and *or* are coordinating conjunctions.

The scene is interesting because readers can figure out that Louis is trying to help Kevin, *but* Kevin ~~doesn't know~~ *and* Ginny ~~doesn't~~ *don't* know.

How do the added conjunctions make the writing easier to read and understand? For more information about conjunctions, see pages 813 and 843 of the Grammar Handbook.

Try Your Hand: Using Coordinating Conjunctions

On a separate sheet of paper, revise the following paragraph, using coordinating conjunctions. Try connecting two sentences with a few different conjunctions until you find the one that makes the most sense.

Kevin Neal's father is a brilliant computer designer. He has built Kevin a powerful computer named Louis. Kevin's father is working on a voice module. Louis can't talk yet. Actually, Louis can talk. Kevin isn't sure if he should tell his dad about that. He isn't sure if he should tell anyone else. He worries about it.

 GRAMMAR FROM WRITING

Using Commas with Conjunctions

When you use a coordinating conjunction to join related sentences, place a comma before the conjunction.

Louis had access to mainframe computers. It cracked their security systems. (Louis had access to mainframe computers, and it cracked their security systems.)

When you use a conjunction to join sentence parts, do not place a comma before the conjunction.

I erased the program and set Louis up as a normal computer.

Dad disconnected the whole thing and did some rewiring.

APPLYING WHAT YOU'VE LEARNED
Number a separate sheet of paper 1–3. Combine each pair of sentences into a single sentence. Choose a conjunction and use a comma if necessary. Omit words in italics.

1. Ginny's brother was named Chuck. Everyone called him the "Missing" Linke.
2. Louis had a modem. *Louis had* a voice module.
3. Kevin could read information on Louis's screen. He could print information if he wanted.

WHAT HAPPENS NEXT?

If you think about it, everyday life is a lot like a collection of stories. There are interesting characters, surprising plot twists, and different conversations.

View In your notebook, describe what you see in the picture.

Interpret What's going on? Why is this man doing this? What problem might he have? What will happen next?

Discuss In a group, discuss who the man might be and why this scene might not end up as you expect. Record your thoughts and the group's ideas in your notebook. You can use the SkillBuilder on this page to help you make a prediction.

 CRITICAL THINKING

Predicting Outcomes

You make predictions every day, though you may not know it. For example, when you look out the window, see dark clouds, and then grab an umbrella as you go out the door, you're predicting that it might rain. When you make a prediction, you use obvious clues, information from a reliable source, or knowledge from experience to guess what might happen in the future.

What kinds of clues help you predict what may happen next in the picture on this page? Maybe something like this happened to you, and that experience tells you how to predict an outcome. What specific information in the picture helps you make your prediction? Making predictions gets you involved in a situation and can help you relate your experiences to the world.

APPLYING WHAT YOU'VE LEARNED
Write a short dialogue in which you talk to the man in the picture and give him some advice. You could tell him your predictions or maybe ask a question. How will he respond? Share your dialogue with a classmate and try reading it aloud.

FACING THE CONSEQUENCES

REFLECTING ON THEME

In an old TV game show, a contestant chose whatever was hidden behind one of three doors. The result was often surprising. Complete the activities on this page. Write down your impressions and ideas in your notebook. See whether they change as you read the consequences faced in Part 2.

Does every action have a reaction?

In pairs, set up several dominoes. Observe what happens when the first domino is gently pushed over. Line up the dominoes again, this time removing two from the middle before the falling dominoes reach them. What conclusions about actions and consequences can you come to?

Did you face the consequences?

Think about different situations in which you have had to make choices and to accept the consequences. In your notebook, describe one such choice and its consequences. Which of the consequences were most difficult to accept? Why?

What price would you pay?

In life, as in a story, an action usually leads to a series of consequences. Imagine the consequences of this situation. Make a diagram like the one started here to show what you think happens next. Let your imagination go as wild as possible. Share your completed charts with a classmate.

You forget about a test that your teacher has announced.

I forget test. → I don't study.

I get the test. → I panic!

?

Looking Back

Now that you've read the selections in Part 1, what new thoughts have formed in your mind about coping with injustice? Review the ideas you recorded in your notebook. Then, in small groups, create and role-play an unfair situation for the class. Show how to solve the problem and note the consequences that resulted.

PREVIEWING

FICTION

Shrewd Todie and Lyzer the Miser

Isaac Bashevis (bə-shĕv'ĭs) Singer

PERSONAL CONNECTION

Do you know anyone you would describe as shrewd? Do you know a person you would call a miser? Which word would you prefer someone to use in describing you? In your note-book, make a diagram like the one shown to organize your ideas for each word. Then jot down images or thoughts that the word brings to mind.

CULTURAL CONNECTION

Isaac Bashevis Singer, the author of this selection, grew up in and near Warsaw, Poland, as the son of a rabbi—a scholar trained to interpret Jewish law. Most of his stories for young people are rooted in the traditions and values of the Jewish communities of the past. As a boy, Singer lived in a simpler time and a simpler place, when people clustered together in small villages and survived on what they could produce on their farms or by trading goods with neighbors. Singer's childhood famil-iarity with poverty and hunger obviously made a lasting impression on him, for in his writing he frequently portrayed characters in difficult circumstances.

Based on folklore, this story treats character traits such as shrewdness and miserliness—and even the conditions of poverty and hunger—with humor, as you will discover.

A village scene
in Poland

READING CONNECTION

Evaluating Isaac Bashevis Singer once said, "Children are the best readers of genuine literature." Evaluating is the process of judging the worth of some-thing or someone. An active reader goes beyond saying a character or a selection is simply good or bad; he or she forms opinions about the people, events, and ideas that are presented. As you read, think about the way the author creates and develops the characters. Evaluate how well Singer uses character, setting, plot, and theme to establish the characters as shrewd or miserly.

LASERLINKS
• *CULTURAL CONNECTION*
• *VISUAL VOCABULARY*

319

La cuillerée [The spoonful of milk] (1912), Marc Chagall. Copyright © 1995 Artists Rights Society (ARS), New York/ADAGP, Paris.

SHREWD TODIE

&

Lyzer
the
Miser

by
Isaac
Bashevis
Singer

In a village somewhere in the Ukraine[1] there lived a poor man called Todie. Todie had a wife, Sheindel, and seven children, but he could never earn enough to feed them <u>properly</u>. He tried many <u>trades</u>, failing in all of them. It was said of Todie that if he decided to deal in candles the sun would never set. He was nicknamed Shrewd Todie because whenever he managed to make some money, it was always by trickery.

This winter was an especially cold one. The snowfall was heavy and Todie had no money to buy wood for the stove. His seven children stayed in bed all day to keep warm. When the frost burns outside, hunger is stronger than ever, but Sheindel's larder[2] was empty. She reproached Todie bitterly, wailing, "If you can't feed your wife and children, I will go to the rabbi and get a divorce."

"And what will you do with it, eat it?" Todie retorted. In the same village there lived a rich man called Lyzer. Because of his stinginess he was

---

1. **Ukraine** (yōō-krān′): a country of eastern Europe, formerly ruled by Poland and then by Russia.
2. **larder:** a place, such as a pantry or cellar, where food is stored.

WORDS TO KNOW **properly** (prŏp′ər-lē) *adv.* correctly; suitably
trade (trād) *n.* an occupation, especially one involving skilled labor

known as Lyzer the miser. He permitted his wife to bake bread only once in four weeks because he had discovered that fresh bread is eaten up more quickly than stale.

Todie had more than once gone to Lyzer for a loan of a few gulden,[3] but Lyzer had always replied, "I sleep better when the money lies in my strongbox rather than in your pocket."

Lyzer had a goat, but he never fed her. The goat had learned to visit the houses of the neighbors, who pitied her and gave her potato peelings. Sometimes, when there were not enough peelings, she would gnaw on the old straw of the thatched roofs. She also had a liking for tree bark. Nevertheless, each year the goat gave birth to a kid. Lyzer milked her but, miser that he was, did not drink the milk himself. Instead, he sold it to others.

Todie decided that he would take revenge on Lyzer and at the same time make some much-needed money for himself.

One day, as Lyzer was sitting on a box eating borscht[4] and dry bread (he used his chairs only on holidays so that the upholstery[5] would not wear out), the door opened and Todie came in.

"Reb Lyzer," he said, "I would like to ask you a favor. My oldest daughter, Basha, is already fifteen and she's about to become

"Would you lend me one of your silver spoons? . . . I will return it to you tomorrow."

engaged. A young man is coming from Janev to look her over. My cutlery[6] is tin, and my wife is ashamed to ask the young man to eat soup with a tin spoon. Would you lend me one of your silver spoons? I give you my holy word that I will return it to you tomorrow."

Lyzer knew that Todie would not dare to break a holy oath and he lent him the spoon.

No young man came to see Basha that evening. As usual, the girl walked around barefoot and in rags, and the silver spoon lay hidden under Todie's shirt. In the early years of his marriage Todie had <u>possessed</u> a set of silver tableware himself. He had, however, long since sold it all, with the exception of three silver teaspoons that were used only on Passover.[7]

The following day, as Lyzer, his feet bare (in order to save his shoes), sat on his box eating borscht and dry bread, Todie returned.

---

3. **gulden** (go͞ol′dən): coins.

4. **borscht** (bôrsht): a beet soup, served hot or cold, usually with sour cream.

5. **upholstery** (ŭp-hōl′stə-rē): fabric or materials that cover furniture.

6. **cutlery** (kŭt′lə-rē): table utensils, such as knives, forks, and spoons.

7. **Passover:** a celebration in memory of the Jews' exodus, or escape, from Egypt.

WORDS TO KNOW **possess** (pə-zĕs′) *v.* to have as property; to own

"Here is the spoon I borrowed yesterday," he said, placing it on the table together with one of his own teaspoons.

"What is the teaspoon for?" Lyzer asked.

And Todie said, "Your tablespoon gave birth to a teaspoon. It is her child. Since I am an honest man, I'm returning both mother and child to you."

Lyzer looked at Todie in astonishment. He had never heard of a silver spoon giving birth to another. Nevertheless, his greed overcame his doubt and he happily accepted both spoons. Such an unexpected piece of good fortune! He was overjoyed that he had loaned Todie the spoon.

A few days later, as Lyzer (without his coat, to save it) was again sitting on his box eating borscht with dry bread, the door opened and Todie appeared.

"The young man from Janev did not please Basha, because he had donkey ears, but this evening another young man is coming to look her over. Sheindel is cooking soup for him, but she's ashamed to serve him with a tin spoon. Would you lend me . . ."

Even before Todie could finish the sentence, Lyzer interrupted. "You want to borrow a silver spoon? Take it with pleasure."

The following day Todie once more returned the spoon and with it one of his own silver teaspoons. He again explained that during the

> "Here is the spoon I borrowed yesterday," he said, placing it on the table.

night the large spoon had given birth to a small one and in all good conscience he was bringing back the mother and the newborn baby. As for the young man who had come to look Basha over, she hadn't liked him either, because his nose was so long that it reached to his chin. Needless to say that Lyzer the miser was overjoyed.

Exactly the same thing happened a third time. Todie related that this time his daughter had rejected her suitor[8] because he stammered. He also reported that Lyzer's silver spoon had again given birth to a baby spoon.

"Does it ever happen that a spoon has twins?" Lyzer inquired.

Todie thought it over for a moment. "Why not? I've even heard of a case where a spoon had triplets."

Almost a week passed by and Todie did not go to see Lyzer. But on Friday morning, as Lyzer (in his underdrawers, to save his pants) sat on his box eating borscht and dry bread, Todie came in and said, "Good day to you, Reb Lyzer."

"A good morning and many more to you," Lyzer replied in his friendliest manner. "What good fortune brings you here? Did you perhaps come to borrow a silver spoon? If so, help yourself."

---

8. **suitor** (soō'tər): a man who is trying to win a woman's love.

"Today I have a very special favor to ask. This evening a young man from the big city of Lublin is coming to look Basha over. He is the son of a rich man, and I'm told he is clever and handsome as well. Not only do I need a silver spoon, but since he will remain with us over the Sabbath,[9] I need a pair of silver candlesticks, because mine are brass and my wife is ashamed to place them on the Sabbath table. Would you lend me your candlesticks? Immediately after the Sabbath, I will return them to you."

Silver candlesticks are of great value and Lyzer the miser hesitated, but only for a moment.

Remembering his good fortune with the spoons, he said, "I have eight silver candlesticks in my house. Take them all. I know you will return them to me just as you say. And if it should happen that any of them give birth, I have no doubt that you will be as honest as you have been in the past."

"Certainly," Todie said. "Let's hope for the best."

The silver spoon, Todie hid beneath his shirt as usual. But taking the candlesticks, he went directly to a merchant, sold them for a considerable sum, and brought the money to Sheindel. When Sheindel saw so much money, she demanded to know where he had gotten such a treasure.

"When I went out, a cow flew over our roof

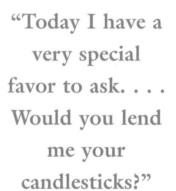

"Today I have a very special favor to ask. . . . Would you lend me your candlesticks?"

and dropped a dozen silver eggs," Todie replied. "I sold them and here is the money."

"I have never heard of a cow flying over a roof and laying silver eggs," Sheindel said doubtingly.

"There is always a first time," Todie answered. "If you don't want the money, give it back to me."

"There'll be no talk about giving it back," Sheindel said. She knew that her husband was full of cunning and tricks—but when the children are hungry and the larder is empty, it is better not to ask too many questions. Sheindel went to the market and bought meat, fish, white flour, and even some nuts and raisins for a pudding. And since a lot of money still remained, she bought shoes and clothes for the children.

It was a very gay Sabbath in Todie's house. The boys sang and the girls danced. When the children asked their father where he had gotten the money, he replied, "It is forbidden to mention money during the Sabbath."

Sunday, as Lyzer (barefoot and almost naked, to save his clothes) sat on his box finishing up a dry crust of bread with borscht, Todie arrived and, handing him his silver

---

9. **Sabbath** (săb′ɔth): the seventh day of the week, Saturday, observed as a day of rest and worship by the Jews.

spoon, said, "It's too bad. This time your spoon did not give birth to a baby."

"What about the candlesticks?" Lyzer inquired anxiously.

Todie sighed deeply. "The candlesticks died."

Lyzer got up from his box so hastily that he overturned his plate of borscht.

"You fool! How can candlesticks die?"

"If spoons can give birth, candlesticks can die," he screamed.

Lyzer raised a great hue and cry[10] and had Todie called before the rabbi. When the rabbi heard both sides of the story, he burst out laughing. "It serves you right," he said to Lyzer. "If you hadn't chosen to believe that spoons give birth, now you would not be forced to believe that your candlesticks died."

"But it's all nonsense," Lyzer objected.

"Did you not expect the candlesticks to give birth to other candlesticks?" the rabbi said admonishingly. "If you accept nonsense when it brings you profit, you must also accept nonsense when it brings you loss." And he dismissed the case.

The following day, when Lyzer the miser's wife brought him his borscht and dry bread, Lyzer said to her, "I will eat only the bread. Borscht is too expensive a food, even without the sour cream."

The story of the silver spoons that gave birth and the candlesticks that died spread quickly through the town. All the people enjoyed Todie's victory and Lyzer the miser's defeat. The shoemaker's and tailor's apprentices,[11] as was their custom whenever there was an important happening, made up a song about it:

> Lyzer, put your grief aside.
> What if your candlesticks have died?
> You're the richest man on earth
> with silver spoons that can give birth
> and silver eggs as living proof
> of flying cows above your roof.
> Don't sit there eating crusts of bread—
> To silver grandsons look ahead.

However, time passed and Lyzer's silver spoons never gave birth again. ❖

---

10. **hue and cry:** a loud outcry of protest.

11. **apprentices** (ə-prĕn′tĭ-sĭz): people learning a trade or business by working for an expert.

THE RABBI IN THE COMMUNITY

Jews are members of a group that has been held together by a common faith and a common history for more than 3,000 years. Judaism, the religion of the Jewish people, is the oldest religion of the Western world. It is based on the Torah, the sacred history and laws of the Israelite people. The Torah consists of the first five books of the Hebrew Bible and includes the Ten Commandments, one of the greatest influences on the Western world's ideas about law and justice.

An individual who teaches and interprets the Torah is called a rabbi. *Rabbi* is the Hebrew word for a master or teacher, and over time the word came to mean someone who could decide questions of Jewish law.

Rabbis interpret the law of the Torah to apply it to issues that arise in daily life. Until recent times, all rabbis were men. Traditionally, the rabbi served as a community leader and judge, settling arguments—as the rabbi in this story settles the matter between Todie and Lyzer—and teaching people how to treat each other fairly. Today, a man or woman who wants to become a rabbi may spend many years studying in a training school for rabbis, and he or she usually has a broad knowledge of nonreligious subjects. Each group of worshipers chooses its own rabbi, whose main responsibilities are to preach, advise, teach, and carry out religious services and community celebrations.

La Fête des tabernacles [The feast of tabernacles] (1916), Marc Chagall. Private collection.
Copyright © 1995 Artists Rights Society (ARS), New York/ADAGP, Paris.

RESPONDING OPTIONS

FROM PERSONAL RESPONSE TO CRITICAL ANALYSIS

REFLECT

1. Did you enjoy this story? In your notebook, give it a rating based on the scale shown here. Include reasons for your rating, and share your views with classmates.

Rating Scale	
★★★★	Outstanding
★★★	Good
★★	Fair
★	Poor

RETHINK

2. In your opinion, does Lyzer get what he deserves? Explain your answer.

3. Why do you think Todie is able to trick Lyzer so easily?

RELATE

4. In "Shrewd Todie and Lyzer the Miser," a rabbi settles a disagreement that has captured the attention of a community. What examples of people resolving conflicts between others have you seen in your community or school?

ANOTHER PATHWAY

Cooperative Learning

In teams composed of three or four students, draw and fill in a chart to analyze either Todie or Lyzer. Use the following categories: physical description, character's words, thoughts, and actions.

QUICKWRITES

1. If you were judging Todie and Lyzer's dispute, what would you decide? Write a **decision,** including your reasons.

2. Imagine that you are an attorney hired by Lyzer. Write a **persuasive argument** defending Lyzer's position.

3. Reread the apprentices' song at the end of the story. Write a similar **song** about Todie and his shrewdness.

4. Review the Reading Connection on page 319. Then write an **evaluation** of either Todie or Lyzer.

📁 **PORTFOLIO** *Save your writing. You may want to use it later as a springboard to a piece for your portfolio.*

LITERARY CONCEPTS

Humor is the quality that makes a piece of writing funny or amusing to the reader. Writers create humor by using exaggeration, amusing description, caricature, sarcasm, witty dialogue, and other devices. For example, Sheindel is hungry and, seeing her husband Todie as irresponsible, threatens him by saying she will go to the rabbi for a divorce. He then asks sarcastically, "And what will you do with it, eat it?" Later, Singer exaggerates Lyzer's miserliness until, during Todie and Lyzer's final exchange, Lyzer is "barefoot and almost naked." Look for other humorous passages in the story. Which passage is your favorite?

CRITIC'S CORNER

Isaac Bashevis Singer said that "the young reader demands a real story, with a beginning, a middle, and an end, the way stories have been told for thousands of years." Do you think "Shrewd Todie and Lyzer the Miser" fits Singer's description of a real story? Explain your answer.

ART CONNECTION

The Spoonful of Milk was painted in 1912 by Marc Chagall, a Russian-born painter who often combined elements of fantasy and religion in his work. The painting's brilliant

colors add to the powerful impact of the image. How well do you think the scene depicted in this painting matches "Shrewd Todie and Lyzer the Miser"?

WORDS TO KNOW

An analogy contains two word pairs with the words in each pair having similar relationships. The words in the second pair are related in the same way as those in the first pair, as in this example:

> LIGHT : DARK :: up : down

The words *light* and *dark* are opposites; *up* and *down* are also opposites.

Review the Words to Know in the boxes at the bottom of the selection pages. For each item below, determine how the words in the capitalized pair are related. Then decide which word best completes the second pair to show a similar relationship. Write the word on your paper.

1. CAR : AUTOMOBILE : : _____ : job

2. NEGATIVELY : POSITIVELY : : _____ : approvingly

3. PURCHASED : RENTED : : _____ : borrowed

4. INTELLIGENCE : GENIUS : : _____ : trickster

5. CARELESSLY : THOUGHTLESSLY : : _____ : suitably

ISAAC BASHEVIS SINGER

As a son of a rabbi, Isaac Bashevis Singer received a traditional Jewish education in a religious school in Poland, where he grew up. There he learned to write Yiddish, the historical language of the Jews of central and eastern Europe. He described those early years: "Our house was a poor house. We were a rabbi's house. Very little furniture but many books." In his 20s, Singer decided to become a writer, and in 1935 he followed his older brother to America. After becoming a naturalized citizen, he wrote of his U.S. citizenship, "I would not trade it for all the money in the world."

Many of Singer's stories and novels are based on the culture and traditions of life in the Jewish ghet-

1904–1991

tos of eastern Europe before they were destroyed by the Nazis in the 1930s and 1940s. He published his first children's book in 1966, noting that "children think about and ponder such matters as justice, the purpose of life, the why of suffering." Already the winner of a Newbery Medal, in 1978 Singer was awarded the Nobel Prize in literature. In accepting the award, Singer said, "I am nothing more than a storyteller."

OTHER WORKS *Zlateh the Goat and Other Stories, The Fearsome Inn, When Shlemiel Went to Warsaw and Other Stories, A Day of Pleasure: Stories of a Boy Growing Up in Warsaw, Why Noah Chose the Dove, A Tale of Three Wishes*

LASERLINKS
• ART GALLERY

PREVIEWING

from A Long Hard Journey
Patricia and Fredrick McKissack

PERSONAL CONNECTION

For more than a century Pullman sleeping cars and the cheerful, efficient porters who waited on passengers made overnight train trips a pleasure for travelers. The inviting image of this form of travel concealed hardships that this excerpt uncovers. Think about any traveling you have done, even just around your hometown. How do you get to where you want to go—car? bus? train? airplane? What service employees help you? Copy the chart shown here in your notebook. Fill in the chart with information based on your own travel experiences.

Service Employees Who Help People Travel					
Form of Transportation	Job Name	Does the person wear a uniform?	Does the person depend on tips?	How difficult would you say the job is?	Would you like to do this work?

HISTORICAL CONNECTION

From the 1840s until the 1920s, railroads were the most popular way for people to travel long distances. The completion of the transcontinental railway in 1869 was the climax of American railroad building. The United States had been joined from the Atlantic to the Pacific, and cross-country travel had become a practical reality.

George Pullman patented his sleeping car in 1859. The first car built by his company made its initial trip that same year. In 1867, Pullman began hiring ex-slaves to work as porters on his railcars, beginning an association that was to last until Pullman sleepers were no longer manufactured. By the time the transcontinental railway was completed, the Pullman Palace Car Company was able to make travelers' journeys comfortable, even luxurious—but the company paid far less attention to the hardships experienced by its employees.

READING CONNECTION

Using Your Reading Log As you read this selection, you will encounter questions that may help you focus on issues raised in it. In your reading log, jot down your answers to the questions, and record any questions of your own that you may have about early train travel or the Pullman porters and the hardships they experienced. See if you are able to answer your own questions when you finish reading the selection.

FROM

A Long Hard Journey

by Patricia and Fredrick McKissack

A porter helps a young
woman board a Pullman car.
Oregon Historical Society (Neg. 24858).

In the book *A Long Hard Journey,* the McKissacks explore the life and work of Pullman porters and their struggle to form a union. In 1867, George Pullman's Palace Car Company employed the first ex-slave as a porter. Newly freed African Americans would be perfect, Pullman believed, to serve travelers: to answer their questions, to make up their beds, and to bring them food and drinks. This excerpt describes the typical practices of a company that had become a household name, with a worldwide reputation for service.

Lord I hate to hear that lonesome whistle blow.
Lord I hate to hear that lonesome whistle blow.
Lord I'm goin' where the water tastes like wine.
'Cause the water round here tastes like turpentine.
Lord I hate to hear that lonesome whistle blow.
Lord I hate to hear that lonesome whistle blow.
It blows so lonesome and it blows so low.
It blows like it never blowed before.

"Lonesome Whistle"
from *Treasury of Railroad Folklore*
edited by B. A. Botkin and Alvin Harlow

When George Pullman offered ex-slaves work on board his luxury cars, he got exactly what he bargained for. To men who had just shed their shackles, a railroad job meant unimaginable freedom.

Men in bondage make icons[1] of the symbols that represent their freedom. Trains were such a symbol to the slave. Many a woeful plantation song spoke about train whistles, locomotives, and escape from the day-to-day drudgery of fieldwork.

According to Richard Reinhardt, even white men considered "working on the railroad . . . the most virile, challenging, and exciting career a man could follow."

The early porters were called "Travelin' Men." They were highly respected, even revered by their contemporaries. A young woman considered herself fortunate to be courted by a porter, and with good reason. They were pillars of their community; they made a decent living and had experiences

---

1. **icons:** pictures or symbols that are worshiped or honored.

other men only dreamed about. As a popular song of that day indicated, some women preferred a railroad husband over all others.

> A railroader, a railroader
> A railroader for me.
> If ever I marry in this wide world,
> A railroader's bride I'll be.

"Besides," said one porter wife, "they knew what was on the other side of the rosebush, so they weren't so easily turned astray. My own husband was always glad to get home after being on the road."

Nineteenth-century porters traveled to faraway places, mingled with wealthy, well-educated whites, and worked in elegant surroundings. In 1867 the *Western World* magazine described the Pullman porter's work environment:

> The furniture is of black walnut, handsomely carved and ornamented and upholstered with royal purple velvet <u>plush</u> imported from England expressly for this purpose. The finest Axminster carpets cover the floor. The night curtains for the berths[2] are of heaviest silk; splendid chandeliers are pendent overhead; elegant mirrors grace the walls. Luxurious beds invite repose by night and when made up for the day betray no trace of the eating or sleeping uses to which they can be put. The total cost of each car is $30,000.

Since most of their neighbors had never seen such luxury, the porters formed an almost <u>exclusive</u> brotherhood bonded by their common experiences. It has been said they had more in common with each other than they did with family, friends, and neighbors. Fathers did so well that they encouraged their sons to become porters. Uncles helped

Porters saw in their travels what most of their neighbors could only dream about.

nephews, and brothers spoke for brothers.

Porters saw in their travels what most of their neighbors could only dream about. But on a more realistic level, having a steady job allowed them to marry, buy homes, and raise their children with dignity. And although they were not often well-educated, they were articulate[3] spokesmen for education and the general advancement of the race.

Author Jervis Anderson stated that the nineteenth-century porter was seen as "an example of what black men could make of their lives, within the limits of what their situation allowed."

Meanwhile, George Pullman continued to make it possible for ordinary passengers to experience some of the pleasures and privileges generally reserved for the wealthy. His "Hotel Cars" were designed to give passengers the benefits of fine hotel food, service, and a comfortable bed, all on wheels. Pullman later designed and built the dining car which boasted "every variety of meats, vegetables and pastry" that could be "cooked on the cars, according to the best style of culinary art."

---

2. **berths:** built-in beds or bunks.

3. **articulate** (är-tĭk′yə-lĭt): able to express ideas in easy, clear language.

WORDS
TO
KNOW

plush (plŭsh) *n.* a fabric having a thick, deep pile
exclusive (ĭk-sklōō′sĭv) *adj.* leaving out some or most people

332

The *Delmonico* was the first Pullman dining car, introduced in 1868. All passengers, whether using Pullman sleeping-car arrangements or not, could now eat in the diners. That also meant the hiring of more blacks as waiters, cooks, and stewards[4] although these positions were not exclusively black, as porter jobs were.

In 1870, the first all-Pullman train, called the *Board of Trade Special,* made its run from Boston to California. A baggage car contained iceboxes to keep the wines cool and the vegetables fresh. There was even a printing press on board that issued a daily newspaper, the *Trans-Continental.* It is no wonder James Norman Hall, author of *The Caine Mutiny,* said, "I can no more conceive of a world without railroads and trains to run on them than I can imagine wishing to live in such a world."

The living room of a private Pullman car
Pullman Negative Collection, Smithsonian Institution, Washington, D.C. (Neg. 4586).

CONNECT

What forms of travel exist today that might offer similar luxuries?

In spite of his plush surroundings, the porter's job was anything but glamorous. He was viewed as a servant. At first these travelin' men didn't mind playing the role George Pullman had cast for them. They wore the mask very well.

Dressed in well-tailored blue uniforms, the Pullman porters adhered to very specific rules of conduct issued by the Pullman Company. Although a pleasant "good morning" or "good afternoon" when greeting each boarding passenger was all that was originally required, many porters took the time to learn the names of their regular passengers and greeted them by name—"Good morning Mr. Smith"—and *always* with a broad smile.

After a while, the smile became associated with the porters, but instead of being a natural outgrowth of a pleasant situation, the Pullman Company ordered the porters to smile.

Many of George Pullman's other rules reflected the social climate of the day. For example, the white conductor was authorized to assist an unaccompanied woman traveler up the boarding steps. If the white conductor was not around, the porter could help the woman aboard, *if* she asked.

Once the passengers were comfortably seated and their bags were stored, the porter attended to special requests. He might be handing out newspapers, helping a mother with restless children, or pointing out geographic points of interest to first-time travelers or foreign visitors.

The Pullman porter's primary focus was the customer's welfare. He was instructed—and very often tested—to answer all calls promptly

---

4. **stewards:** people in charge of dining arrangements.

and courteously, no matter what time the calls were made.

When it was time to make the beds, the porter was expected to move with speed and <u>agility</u>. The company rule book was precise. According to Nathaniel Hall, a porter, the rule book specified "the proper handling of the linen closet—the proper method of folding and putting away clean linen and blankets, the correct way of stacking laundry bags and dirty, discarded bedding. A sheet, towel, or pillowcase once unfolded cannot be used again, although it may be spotless. Technically, it is dirty and must make a round trip to the laundry before it can reenter the service." Porters were not allowed to make noise. "Noise was tabooed," reported Hall. "And even a soft knock on the top of the berth [was] forbidden. A porter must gently shake the curtains on the bedding from without."

Pullman demanded that all passengers were made to feel special, and part of the Pullman trademark was being waited on by a humble, smiling black servant. Porters' salaries were deliberately kept low so they'd be dependent upon the tip to make ends meet.

The public knew that on a Pullman coach, the customer was always right. No exceptions.

A Pullman barber shaves a passenger.
Detail, Oregon Historical Society (Neg. 73453).

But in some cases, travelers took this to its illogical extreme. For example, young college students liked to chide, embarrass, and <u>harass</u> a porter to see how much he would take. It was a foolish game that the porters had no choice but to play. If the porter went along with whatever was required of him, providing laughs at the cost of his self-respect, the students rewarded him with a big tip. Also, a porter was very often the target of cruel practical jokes and <u>insensitive</u> racial slurs. But if he endured it without a word of protest, again he was rewarded for being such a "good sport."

Some passengers resorted to physical abuse: kicking, poking, and shoving. The porter could not speak up for himself or expect the company to help. In fact the company's inaction regarding the poor treatment of porters was interpreted by the public to mean the men in blue were non-humans. Taking the lead from Pullman, the

WORDS	**agility** (ə-jĭl′ĭ-tē) *n.* nimbleness; ease of movement
TO	**harass** (hăr′əs) *v.* to irritate or torment continually
KNOW	**insensitive** (ĭn-sĕn′sĭ-tĭv) *adj.* unfeeling

public disregarded the porters' feelings and crushed their manhood beneath its heel. Without company protection or job security, the early porters could either bury their pride and quietly accept their circumstances or quit. Some quit, but most had no choice but to stay.

Even under these circumstances, the porters took pride in their work, salvaging their manhood in the respect they received at home. Between 1867 and 1890, the early porters earned a reputation for being outstanding employees, highly praised for their honesty, politeness, and reliability. More than a few white passengers were shocked to learn that porters were "remarkably intelligent."

George Pullman and his "Ambassadors of Hospitality" were highly praised by both races. At the 1893 Chicago World's Fair, Pullman was honored for being the largest employer of the former slave. President Grover Cleveland cited Pullman as an example of how other businesses could use blacks in jobs of "service." Travelers all over the world praised the "smiling porter" who became the role model of the black employee—grinning and satisfied, happy and uncomplaining.

EVALUATE

How did the image of the Pullman porter compare with the basic reality of his situation?

Even Frederick Douglass, renowned black orator, newspaper publisher, and leading abolitionist,[5] praised George Pullman for his hiring practices, and thanked him for being the "best friend of the black worker." (In later years, the Pullman Company would use Douglass's quote to garner support against union porters.)

Some of those who knew George Pullman privately doubted that he ever befriended

Some of those who knew George Pullman privately doubted that he ever befriended anyone.

anyone. Described as a megalo-maniac[6] who abused power and wealth to get what he wanted, his simplistic philosophy was "my rule or your ruin." Other historians claim that Pullman was a "complex man" who was misunderstood.

While historians disagree about Pullman's character, his genius for business was never questioned. From 1869 until his death in 1897, George Mortimer Pullman managed the Pullman Company like a well-oiled machine.

In 1880, Pullman set aside thirty-six hundred acres in the southern outskirts of Chicago and built a planned community called Pullman, Illinois. Twelve thousand white Pullman employees were required to live in the company-owned town. They had to shop at company-owned stores and even worship in a company-owned church. Black employees were not permitted to live in Pullman.

Rents were high but salaries were low, and many of the employees were actually starving. All living expenses were taken out of each employee's paycheck. One man reportedly

---

5. **abolitionist** (ăb´ə-lĭsh´ə-nĭst): a person favoring an end to slavery.

6. **megalomaniac** (mĕg´ə-lō-mā´nē-ăk): a person who believes himself or herself to be all-powerful.

earned two cents after all his company debts had been deducted.

White Pullman employees rebelled by unionizing under the leadership of Eugene Debs, a socialist labor leader. Black employees were not invited to participate.

After serving in the Indiana State Legislature, Debs had helped establish and was currently serving as the president of the American Railway Union (ARU). Pullman refused to recognize the ARU and on May 11, 1894, 90 percent of the workers walked off their jobs. The rest of the employees, who were black, were laid off. The company shut down, and the historic Pullman strike was under way. A court ordered the strikers back to work. Debs and the ARU members refused to obey the court order. Police officers were sent to arrest the striking workers.

Passengers in a Pullman dining car, being served by a waiter
Detail, Oregon Historical Society (Neg. 38564).

PREDICT

How might the outcome of the strike affect the situation of the Pullman porters?

In July 1894, during a <u>confrontation</u> between the strikers and police officers, violence broke out, and during two dreadful days of rioting, seventeen people were killed and several hundred buildings were burned and looted.

The Chicago press blamed Eugene Debs and the ARU for what happened. Debs was labeled a dangerous radical. He was arrested and imprisoned for refusing to obey the court order.

Public sentiment turned against the labor movement. The Pullman workers were tired, confused, and their families were hungry. Slowly the men returned to the same low-paying jobs. Some money was better than nothing.

Pullman took some of the strikers back, but each one had to sign a pledge promising never to join a union while employed by the Pullman Company. Although porters had not participated in this strike, they were forced to sign the pledge, too.

Losing in the challenge against Pullman destroyed the ARU, and in 1897 it folded. Debs, however, organized the Social Democratic Party and ran for president of the United States five times between 1900 and 1920.

After the strike, George Pullman kept a tight rein on his company. It was said that any mention of unions or workers' rights sent him into a rage. When George Pullman died in 1897, his family covered his grave with tons of

The *Empire State Express,* among the fastest trains of the 1890s and early 1900s, was one of many that featured Pullman cars. Culver Pictures.

reinforced concrete. The family said they feared vandals might desecrate[7] his grave. Ambrose Bierce, an American journalist and writer known for his cutting wit, wrote, "It is clear the family in their bereavement[8] was making sure he wasn't going to get up and come back."

After Pullman's death, his company continued to grow. By the turn of the twentieth century, Pullman had bought out the Wagner Palace Car Company as well as T. T. Woodruff, Jerome Marbles, and Barney and Smith. The company now had a <u>monopoly</u> on sleeping cars. And every person working on a car that bore Pullman's name was a nonunion worker. ❖

---

7. **desecrate** (dĕs′ĭ-krāt′): to damage in a way that shows disrespect.
8. **bereavement** (bĭ-rēv′mĕnt): sadness at the loss of a loved one.

Night Journey

by Theodore Roethke

Now as the train bears west,
Its rhythm rocks the earth,
And from my Pullman berth
I stare into the night
5 While others take their rest.
Bridges of iron lace,
A suddenness of trees,
A lap of mountain mist
All cross my line of sight,
10 Then a bleak wasted place,
And a lake below my knees.
Full on my neck I feel
The straining at a curve;
My muscles move with steel,

15 I wake in every nerve.
I watch a beacon swing
From dark to blazing bright,
We thunder through ravines
And gullies washed with light.
20 Beyond the mountain pass
Mist deepens on the pane,
We rush into a rain
That rattles double glass.
Wheels shake the roadbed stone,
25 The pistons jerk and shove,
I stay up half the night
To see the land I love.

RESPONDING
O P T I O N S

FROM **PERSONAL RESPONSE** *TO* **CRITICAL ANALYSIS**

REFLECT   **1.** Whom were you thinking about as you finished reading this selection—George Pullman, the Pullman porters, or someone else? Record your thoughts in your notebook.

RETHINK   **2.** What do you think it would have been like to be a Pullman porter?
Consider
- the hardships the porters experienced
- the respect given to the porters by their own communities

          3. What do you think of George Pullman?
Consider
- his decision to hire ex-slaves
- his role in the Pullman strike

RELATE   **4.** If you haven't already done so, read "Night Journey" on page 338. What might the speaker of the poem have in common with a typical Pullman porter?

ANOTHER PATHWAY

How would this selection be different if it were a work of fiction rather than nonfiction? Would you learn additional information about Pullman porters and the hardships they faced? What events or ideas might be left out of a fictional work about this subject? Jot down your thoughts in your notebook to share with the class.

QUICKWRITES

1. Write an **advertisement** for porters that the Pullman Company might have placed in the help-wanted section of the *Dayton Globe-Herald* in 1897.

2. This selection opens with a ballad about the railroad. Draft a **ballad** a porter might have written about his life traveling the rails.

3. Draft a **comparison/contrast paragraph** in which you compare Pullman porters with today's transportation workers.

     📁 *PORTFOLIO Save your writing. You may want to use it later as a spring-board to a piece for your portfolio.*

LITERARY CONCEPTS

A **primary source** is one that presents direct, firsthand knowledge about a subject. For example, "My First Dive with the Dolphins" (page 65) is a primary source because it was written by Don C. Reed about his own personal experience. A **secondary source** is one that presents indirect, secondhand knowledge about a subject. The selection "Matthew Henson at the Top of the World" (page 53) is an example of a secondary source. It was written by Jim Haskins about past people and events that he had researched. In this excerpt from *A Long Hard Journey,* Patricia and Fredrick McKissack use a primary source in the form of the railroad song "Lonesome Whistle." See if you can find another example of a primary source used in the selection.

Review the Words to Know in the boxes at the bottom of the selection pages. Then, on your own paper, write the word that best completes each of the following sentences.

1. The furniture in the Pullman cars was upholstered with _____.
2. The Pullman Company was one of many that displayed cruel and _____ treatment of its African-American employees.
3. Some passengers deliberately tried to _____ the porters by using racial slurs and even physical abuse.
4. The worst part of many jobs is the _____.
5. The porters displayed their _____ in how quickly and easily they could prepare passengers' rooms.
6. Because he lived during the same time period as Eugene Debs, George Pullman was a _____ of Debs.
7. Porters and other former slaves who entered the work force found it difficult to _____ their self-respect when treated poorly.
8. Striking railroad workers had a _____ with the police that resulted in the deaths of several people.
9. Like the Pullman Company, a company with a _____ does not have to compete with other companies that make the same product.
10. The Pullman porters functioned much like an _____ club because they shared experiences that few African Americans of the time could.

PATRICIA AND FREDRICK MCKISSACK

Both born in Nashville, Tennessee, Patricia and Fredrick McKissack grew up in a time of great struggle and great opportunity for African Americans. By the time the two graduated from Tennessee State University and married in 1964, sit-ins by young African Americans had begun to force the desegregation of public places. As Fredrick explains, "Life actually changed. In a sense we climbed from the Old South to the New South. We went from segregated schools to integrated situations." They were the first generation to do so.

The couple turned to writing as a way to share with young people what they had been through as African Americans. According to Fredrick, "The reason that we write for children is to tell them about these things and to get them to internalize the information, to feel just a little of the hurt, the tremendous amount of hurt and sadness that racism and discrimination cause—for all people, regardless of race." The McKissacks have written nearly 100 books of history, historical fiction, and biography—most of them together. Patricia explains, "We try to enlighten, to change attitudes, to form new attitudes—to build bridges with books."

OTHER WORKS *Abram, Abram, Where Are We Going?; The Civil Rights Movement in America from 1865 to the Present; Taking a Stand Against Racism and Racial Discrimination; The Royal Kingdoms of Ghana, Mali, and Songhay: Life in Medieval Africa*

PREVIEWING

Barbara Frietchie

John Greenleaf Whittier

PERSONAL CONNECTION

Just what is courage? Is courage simply a willingness to fight—or can it be something else? Consider some acts of bravery that you have heard about or seen. Think of the qualities that brave people have in common. Then, in your notebook, write your own definition of *courage*. As you read this poem, decide whether the character of Barbara Frietchie fits your definition.

To me, courage is the willingness to take action in a difficult situation.

HISTORICAL CONNECTION

John Greenleaf Whittier wrote this poem to honor what he felt was an act of courage that may have occurred before a clash of Union and Confederate forces during the Civil War. On September 10, 1862, General Robert E. Lee, commander of the Confederate Army of Northern Virginia, and General Thomas J. "Stonewall" Jackson led over 55,000 soldiers through Frederick, Maryland. They were on their way to Sharpsburg and to defeat in a battle—the battle of Antietam—that would prove to be the most bloody of the war.

One citizen of Frederick was Barbara Frietchie, an elderly widow fiercely loyal to the Union. According to legend, as Jackson's troops marched through the town, she waved a Union flag defiantly at the Confederate troops.

READING CONNECTION

Poetic Language Readers rarely come across certain words except in poems. These unusual words can heighten a poem's effect, particularly when it is recited or spoken aloud. Three examples from "Barbara Frietchie" are shown in the chart on this page. Poets may also arrange words in a way different from the word order that people generally use in conversation. They do this to fit the rhyming patterns and rhythms they have chosen for their poems. You may understand a confusing line or sentence better if you rewrite the words in a more recognizable order.

Use in Poem	Standard Form
morn	morning
o'er	over
fourscore	eighty (a score is 20)

LASERLINKS
- *HISTORICAL CONNECTION*
- *VISUAL VOCABULARY*

BARBARA FRIETCHIE

BY JOHN GREENLEAF WHITTIER

Up from the meadows rich with corn,
Clear in the cool September morn,

The clustered spires[1] of Frederick stand
Green-walled by the hills of Maryland.

5 Round about them orchards sweep,
Apple and peach tree fruited deep,

Fair as the garden of the Lord[2]
To the eyes of the famished rebel horde,[3]

On that pleasant morn of the early fall
10 When Lee marched over the mountain-wall;

Over the mountains winding down,
Horse and foot, into Frederick town.

Forty flags with their silver stars,
Forty flags with their crimson bars,

---

1. **spires:** tall, pointed towers.
2. **the garden of the Lord:** the Garden of Eden, described in the opening chapters of the biblical Book of Genesis.
3. **famished rebel horde:** the ragged and hungry Confederate troops moving into Frederick.

15 Flapped in the morning wind; the sun
Of noon looked down and saw not one.

Up rose old Barbara Frietchie then,
Bowed with her fourscore years and ten;

Bravest of all in Frederick town,
20 She took up the flag the men hauled down;

In her attic window the staff[4] she set,
To show that one heart was loyal yet.

Up the street came the rebel tread,
Stonewall Jackson riding ahead.

25 Under his slouched hat[5] left and right
He glanced; the old flag met his sight.

"Halt!"—the dust-brown ranks stood fast.
"Fire!"—out blazed the rifle-blast.

It shivered[6] the window, pane and sash;
30 It rent[7] the banner with seam and gash.

Quick, as it fell, from the broken staff
Dame Barbara snatched the silken scarf.

She leaned far out on the window-sill,
And shook it forth with a royal will.

35 "Shoot, if you must, this old gray head,
But spare your country's flag," she said.

A shade of sadness, a blush of shame,
Over the face of the leader came;

The nobler nature within him stirred
40 To life at that woman's deed and word;

"Who touches a hair of yon gray head
Dies like a dog! March on!" he said.

All day long through Frederick street
Sounded the tread of marching feet:

45 All day long that free flag tossed
Over the heads of the rebel host.

Ever its torn folds rose and fell
On the loyal winds that loved it well;

And through the hill-gaps sunset light
50 Shone over it with a warm good-night.

Barbara Frietchie's work is o'er,
And the Rebel rides on his raids no more.

Honor to her! and let a tear
Fall, for her sake, on Stonewall's bier.[8]

55 Over Barbara Frietchie's grave,
Flag of Freedom and Union, wave!

Peace and order and beauty draw
Round that symbol of light and law;

And ever the stars above look down
60 On thy stars below in Frederick town!

---

4. **staff:** a pole on which a flag is displayed.
5. **slouched hat:** a soft hat with a wide brim.
6. **shivered:** caused to break into pieces.
7. **rent:** tore or split apart.
8. **bier** (bîr): a coffin and its stand.

RESPONDING
OPTIONS

FROM PERSONAL RESPONSE TO CRITICAL ANALYSIS

REFLECT
1. What are your reactions to the character of Barbara Frietchie? Discuss your ideas with a friend.

RETHINK
2. In your opinion, why might John Greenleaf Whittier have been inspired to write this tribute to Barbara Frietchie?
   Consider
   • how Whittier seems to feel about the war
   • Frietchie's age and actions
   • Stonewall Jackson's reaction

3. What do you think Stonewall Jackson's reaction reveals about him?

4. Reread the definition of *courage* you wrote for the Personal Connection on page 341. Explain whether Barbara Frietchie's actions fit your definition or you would revise your definition on the basis of your reading of the poem.

5. A pair of lines of "Barbara Frietchie" have become famous. Some people can recite these lines from memory, even if they cannot remember one other word from the poem. Which lines do you think are famous and why? In a small group, take turns reciting the lines each person identifies.

RELATE
6. A flag is only a piece of fabric attached to a staff. Yet many men and women have acted with courage to protect their national flags from dishonor and disgrace. Why do you think flags might be so important to people? Explain your opinion.

ANOTHER PATHWAY

Cooperative Learning

In a group, reread "Barbara Frietchie." How are the personalities and beliefs of Barbara Frietchie and Stonewall Jackson revealed in the course of the poem? Make a chart like this one and add to it, noting the results of your discussion.

Barbara Frietchie's Personality Traits	Stonewall Jackson's Personality Traits
courage	

QUICKWRITES

1. Imagine that the Civil War has just ended. You have been sent to conduct an **interview** with Barbara Frietchie. What will your first five questions be?

2. Write several **rhymed couplets** that might be carved on Barbara Frietchie's gravestone. Try to capture the spirit of this courageous woman so that all who see her grave marker will have some idea what she was like.

📁 *PORTFOLIO Save your writing. You may want to use it later as a spring-board to a piece for your portfolio.*

LITERARY CONCEPTS

Many readers find reading "Barbara Frietchie" aloud to be fun, partly because the simple structure of the poem allows the reader to move along at a brisk pace. The poem is divided into pairs of rhymed lines, or **couplets.** Did you enjoy the effect of the couplets? Why or why not?

Another poetic technique that makes this poem appealing is **alliteration,** the repetition of consonant sounds at the beginning of words. Poets use alliteration to emphasize certain words or to add a musical beat to their works. In "Barbara Frietchie," the words "*Forty flags*" and "*silver stars*" in line 13 show alliteration. See if you can find more examples of alliteration in the poem. Then team up with one or two other students and read the poem aloud.

CONCEPT REVIEW: Rhythm When you read the poem aloud, did you notice the strong, steady beat of the lines? Remember, a poem's beat is called its rhythm. Why might Whittier have used a regular, steady rhythm in "Barbara Frietchie"?

ALTERNATIVE ACTIVITIES

1. Imagine that Barbara Frietchie and Stonewall Jackson have survived the Civil War and meet again. With another student, create a **dialogue** between the two and present it to your class.

2. With a group of classmates, develop and present a **choral reading** of "Barbara Frietchie" for the rest of the class or for another class in your school. Choose recorded music from the Civil War period to play softly in the background for all or part of the reading. If you like, dress in clothing appropriate for the 1860s.

ACROSS THE CURRICULUM

 Social Studies Barbara Frietchie waved a Union flag out her window at the approaching Confederate troops. How did the U.S. flag of the early 1860s compare with the flag of today? Explore how the flag has changed over the years, and present your findings in a series of drawings of the flag of the United States at various points in history.

JOHN GREENLEAF WHITTIER

1807–1892

A son of Quaker farmers, John Greenleaf Whittier was born in Haverhill, Massachusetts. At 14, he discovered the poetry of the Scottish poet Robert Burns and began to write verses himself.

Whittier found the greatest meaning in his life through the abolitionist cause, a movement of people whose religious beliefs led them to demand immediate freedom for slaves. He worked hard as an abolitionist, speaking publicly and publishing pamphlets.

Whittier's first book was published in 1831, and in 1846 he published a collection of antislavery poems, *Voices of Freedom.* After the Civil War ended, Whittier turned to writing poetry about his youth, his family, and the New England countryside.

Whittier died at 85, a famous and well-loved poet, as well as a wealthy one. He never forgot his early principles, though. In his will, he left money to the Hampton Institute, a school in Virginia for African Americans and Native Americans.

OTHER WORKS *Legends of New England*

PREVIEWING

The Enchanted Raisin
Jacqueline Balcells

PERSONAL CONNECTION

As this unusual story unfolds, you will see how the actions of mischievous children lead to extraordinary consequences. With a partner, briefly discuss tales you recall that open with the phrase "Once upon a time . . ." What features of these tales—character portrayals, comical or grand language, amazing events—appealed most to you?

LITERARY CONNECTION

"The Enchanted Raisin" may seem strangely familiar to you as you read. That's because the story includes many of the same elements that traditional storytellers have used for ages. Perhaps its odd characters and startling events will take you back to the tales you enjoyed as a child. However, this story works a twist on the tales of old because it is set in our current, everyday world. This kind of modern fiction allows the writer to apply traditional storytelling features to the ideas and issues of today. Mixing old and new elements, the writer creates situations that go in both expected and unexpected directions.

Once upon a time, there was a mom who had three absolutely unbearable children. They did every bad and stupid thing imaginable, as well as the unimaginable ones.

WRITING CONNECTION

The following words and phrases refer to events in "The Enchanted Raisin." Which of them seem to suggest extraordinary consequences? Use the words to predict the plot of the story, and write one or more predictions in your notebook. Then read the story to see how your predictions match the writer's ideas.

disobedient children · raisin · cruel stepmother · attic · tears · fruitcake

shrinking · matchbox · raisin cake · hunger · laughter

The ENCHANTED Raisin

by Jacqueline Balcells

Once upon a time, there was a mom who had three absolutely unbearable children. They did every bad and stupid thing imaginable, as well as the unimaginable ones. Several times they almost burned down the house, and they flooded it a hundred times. They broke the furniture, smashed the plates, fought and screamed like crazy people, spilled ink on the white sheets, and swung from the curtains as if they were monkeys in the jungle. And why bother saying what happened when they were sent outside: they spread panic throughout the neighborhood.

Their dad was almost never home, and their poor mother couldn't manage these three little devils. She was completely exhausted at the end of the day from chasing after them.

"My children," she said to them, "please stop your foolishness, if only this once. Look at me: each one of your pranks and screams is a wrinkle on my face. I am becoming an old lady."

And it was true. This woman, who had been tall and beautiful, was wrinkling and shrinking from one day to the next.

Her children didn't notice anything. But one day, when she went to meet them after school, their friends asked with astonishment, "Why does your grandmother come to get you now?"

The children felt bad for a moment; they were upset that their mother was mistaken for their grandmother. But they didn't think about it for long—they had so much to do!

The poor woman continued to wrinkle and shrink at an incredible rate. The moment arrived when she could no longer walk: her legs had become two little sticks that were so skinny, they were like cherry stems, and her back was so curved, she could barely see in front of her. Nevertheless, her three children did not stop inventing more and more horrible pranks:

"Let's take the feathers out of the pillows!"

"Let's pull out the dog's fur!"

"Let's cut off the cat's ears!"

"Let's dig a hole in the field for the gardener to fall into!"

By now, their mother was so small that, standing, she did not reach her youngest child's knees. She sighed, "Children, enough! Look at my size, my wrinkles. If this continues, I will shrink so much that you won't even be able to see me." But she never thought this would happen.

One night after supper, she dragged herself to her room, exhausted. She put on her nightgown, which was now one hundred times too big. She climbed on her bed, rolled herself into a ball and fell deeply asleep.

The next morning when they woke up, the children did what they always did. They jumped on their beds like devils and began to yell, "Moooooommm, bring us our breakfast!"

There was no response. They yelled louder, with no success. They began to howl, once, twice, ten times, thirty times. After the fifty-first shout, with their throats sore, they decided to go to their mother's room.

Her bed was unmade, but she was nowhere to be found. The children realized that something strange was happening. Suddenly, the youngest child bent over the pillow and screamed.

"What's the matter?" his brother asked.

"Look, look there!" he shouted.

Between the folds of their mother's nightgown was a small, dark ball. It was a raisin.

The children were frightened. They called louder and louder, "Mooooommy, Mooooommy, . . . !"

Like the other times, there was no answer, but the oldest child realized that, with each shout, the raisin on the pillow moved slightly. They were quiet and watched it: the raisin didn't move. They shouted "Mom!" and the raisin shook a little.

Then they remembered their mother's words: "If this continues, I will shrink so much that you won't be able to see me." And, horrified, they realized that this raisin that moved when they yelled "Mom" was all that remained of their mother, who in that way tried to make them recognize her. How they cried and wailed!

"Poor us! What are we going to do now that Mom is a raisin? What is Dad going to say when he gets home and sees her?"

Their father had been on a business trip for several weeks, but was due to return home that very night. The children, frightened and not knowing what to do, waited for him in their room all day long. Once in a while, to <u>reassure</u> themselves, they approached the raisin and called "Mom!" The raisin invariably moved.

That evening, their father arrived home. He opened the door, dropped his briefcase, took off his hat and coat, and called his wife from the hall: "Hello, are you there? Aren't you going to welcome me home? Aren't you going to give me a hug and bring me a glass of wine?"

Instead of his wife, his children appeared walking one behind the other with their heads bowed. The oldest held a matchbox in his hands.

"What's going on? Why aren't you in bed? And where's your mother?"

"She's in this box," the oldest answered in a mournful tone. "She turned into a raisin."

His father became angry. "You know that I hate jokes! Go to bed immediately!"

He searched the house for his wife. It was useless to tell him he would not find her. He then said, "She must have gone out for a walk!" But an hour later, as she had not appeared, he began to worry.

WORDS TO KNOW **reassure** (rē′ə-shŏŏr′) *v.* to restore confidence to

Illustration by Roni Shepherd.

He put on his hat and left. He walked around the neighborhood, went to the houses of his neighbors, relatives and friends. He asked everyone, "Have you seen my wife?" Then he went to the police station. But they couldn't tell him anything either.

One night passed, a day and another night. And while the time passed and his wife continued to be missing, the father began to ask himself with great pain if his wife had died.

"She must have taken a walk by the lake and drowned! And the worst thing is, I will never know the truth!" he lamented[1] in anguish.

The months passed with no news. Feeling very lonely, the man finally decided to remarry.

"A new wife would help me take care of these wild animals . . ."

So he chose a wife who was not as pretty as the first one—so as not to say frightful—but she seemed sweet and self-sacrificing. In reality, her face was as ugly as her heart was hard: she led him to believe that she adored the children, but the truth is that she <u>detested</u> them.

The father didn't realize anything. But the three children immediately understood that their stepmother was evil, and they did not trust her. Also, they knew that their real mother was still alive in the matchbox that they guarded so carefully. They were certain she would stop being a raisin and return to her former self.

From time to time at night, the children circled the box, removed the cover and called softly, "Mom, Mom."

From time to time at night, the children circled the box, removed the cover and called softly, "Mom, Mom."

And each time, the raisin responded by rocking gently.

One day when their father was in a good mood, they again asked him to go to their room to see what happened with the raisin. Perhaps he would understand! But their father didn't want to know anything; on the <u>contrary</u>, he became furious: "How long is this stupid joke going to continue? Little devils . . . if you keep up these stories, you are going to get it. I don't want to hear you mention that raisin again!"

Frightened, the children watched over the box.

But, horrors, the stepmother overheard the conversation from behind the door, and she believed them! For a while, she had had her suspicions about the matchbox that the children watched over with such anxiety.

At the beginning, she didn't say anything. But a few days later, one afternoon when the father wasn't home, she called the children and said to them: "Children, I am going to make a raisin cake and I am short one raisin. I believe you have one. Go get it right now!" The stepmother had an evil expression on her face. The children didn't dare protest. They went to their room and asked each other, "What should we do? We can't give her our mother so she can throw her in the oven!" The oldest decided, "Let's go up to the attic. We will hide the box and tell our stepmother that we lost it."

---

1. **lamented** (lə-měn′tĭd) **in anguish** (ăng′gwĭsh): cried out in grief.

WORDS
TO
KNOW

detest (dĭ-těst′) *v.* to hate
contrary (kŏn′trĕr′ē) *n.* an exact opposite

Unfortunately, the evil woman had followed them and once again listened to their conversation from behind the door. She entered the room like a whirlwind and yelled, "Don't you dare trick me! Give me the raisin now, I already have the oven hot!"

The oldest child had just enough time to grab the box. He yelled for his brothers to follow him, and ran upstairs as fast as he could. On his way out, he pushed the stepmother, who fell to the floor with a loud rattling of her bones because she was very thin.

The children ran up to the attic, closed the door and blocked the entrance with a large bureau.[2] Meanwhile, the stepmother got up painfully, brushed herself off, and quickly headed toward the attic. "Open the door, brats! Open it up, little monsters! You'll see what will happen when your father gets home!" But the children, mute with fear, didn't budge.

Then, a cold, wicked and terrible fury invaded her.

"You don't want to open the door? Very well, you will stay locked there as long as it takes. And when you are dying from hunger . . . you will eat the raisin!" She took a key from her pocket and turned it in the lock. Then she laughed three times, "Ha, ha, ha," with a sharp and evil crackle that was unlike the musical laughs she let her husband hear.

At nightfall, her husband came home and asked, "Where are the children?"

She answered, feigning[3] surprise, "Don't you remember? They left to visit their grandmother in the country for a few days." She lied so convincingly that he said, distracted, "That's true, I had forgotten."

Meanwhile, above in the attic, the three children celebrated the victory of having escaped from the cruel woman. But as the hours passed and they became tired of being prisoners, they began to think about how they would escape. The only opening besides the sealed door was a small skylight that was difficult to reach since it was high above the floor in the rafters. And it was at least ten meters above the ground, over the garden.

"We could never jump," they said. "We would need a parachute or a rope."

But in the attic, they couldn't find anything. Suddenly, in the middle of their reflections, the three children realized with surprise that they hadn't fought, whined or played pranks for a long time. It was possible for them to behave! They were so happy with this discovery that they hugged each other and promised to continue their good behavior as long as they could.

---

2. **bureau** (byŏŏr′ō): a chest of drawers, especially one for holding clothes.

3. **feigning** (fā′nĭng): pretending.

Alborado de fiesta [Dawning of a party], Arturo Estrada. Courtesy of the artist.

knowing what else to do, the children curled up on the floor in a corner, cuddling each other, with the matchbox in the middle. They stayed like that until they fell asleep.

In the morning, the growling of their stomachs woke them. They had never been so hungry before. "We must eat something!" they said. Then they looked at the matchbox. "Oh no," said the oldest, "we are not going to eat the raisin, never!" After thinking for a moment, he continued in a serious tone, "Brothers, remember the stories of lost explorers or shipwrecked people who are left without food? They end up eating anything or anyone. . . . This must not happen to us!"

The youngest then said, "Let's separate ourselves from our mother so we can be sure we will not eat her."

"Yes," said the middle child. "If we throw her from the skylight, she will land on the grass in the garden, and since it is soft, she won't get hurt."

The children looked at the small raisin for the last time. Their eyes filled with tears. It was hard for them to separate from their mother!

But now it was vital that they find a way to escape. Night was falling, and with it, they felt the first signs of cold and hunger. The oldest sighed, "If only I had my bed and a good blanket." "And a large glass of warm milk," added the second. "And our beautiful mother," murmured the youngest. Not

But, how could they reach the skylight to throw her into the garden? They could drag over the bureau that was against the door and climb on top of it, but they ran the risk that the evil stepmother would choose that moment to search for them. No! The best thing was to try to climb on top of each other to reach the skylight. The oldest would stand on a chair, the youngest child would balance on the very top and open the skylight.

And that is what they did. Or, it is what they almost did, because the chair was broken, which did not help the operation.

"Can you reach it? Can you touch the skylight?" the older children asked the youngest, who was balancing on top of them.

"Yes . . . , I found it . . . pass me the box!"

"What? Don't you have it?"

"No! I left it on the floor . . ."

They had to start over!

There was a small argument: each accused the other of having forgotten the box. But they soon made up.

"We'll just begin again," said the oldest child.

And they climbed on top of each other again: the oldest on the chair, the middle child on top of the oldest, and the youngest on top of the middle child, like acrobats. The youngest child reached the window and was about to open it when suddenly, crack, the chair broke in two and the children fell to the floor with a great crash.

At that very moment their father was entering the house. He heard the noise and said to his wife, "Go see what is happening!"

She disappeared for a moment and returned saying, "It isn't anything, just some mice running through the attic."

Meanwhile, in the attic, the three children were crying. Large tears of pain ran down their cheeks: tears of pain, because they had hurt themselves in the fall, and of frustration, because how were they going to reach the skylight now that the chair was broken? To <u>console</u> themselves, they opened the matchbox and looked at the raisin. But just seeing the raisin made them even sadder, and they started to cry over it as hard as they could.

The children's tears fell in torrents on the matchbox, so that it flooded and the raisin was left floating in a small, warm puddle.

Suddenly, the oldest child shouted, "Look! It's growing!"

It was true. The raisin, swollen from the children's tears, had begun to grow. The more they cried, the more the raisin grew. And seeing it grow, the children cried more, but now from happiness.

The raisin continued inflating, stretching, enlarging, growing more and more. Until . . . before the children's disbelieving eyes, it changed form and . . . "Mommmmmmmm!" they yelled.

It was their mother, as tall and as beautiful as before she had shriveled up. The mother took her children in her arms and, laughing and crying, hugged them against her for a long time.

Meanwhile, on the first floor, the father was wondering about the strange noises that were

> The raisin, swollen from the children's tears, had begun to grow.

WORDS TO KNOW   **console** (kən-sōl′) v. to comfort

coming from the attic. Finally, he could stand it no longer, and he said to his wife, "Those mice in the attic have a strange way of squeaking. It is as if they were crying. Give me the keys. . . . I am going to see what is happening."

His wife tried every way to stop him, but her efforts were in vain. He went upstairs, tried to open the door with the key, and when it wouldn't open, pushed it with all his might. Imagine his surprise to find his three children in the arms of his first, beautiful wife! The four, hugging tightly, looked at him without saying anything.

Then this man, who wasn't as bad as he seemed, felt as if he would die from remorse and joy. He covered his children with kisses, and then kneeling at his wife's feet, he begged forgiveness for having doubted her.

He was immediately forgiven, and father, mother and children walked downstairs hand in hand to have dinner, with their hearts full of happiness.

The stepmother hadn't waited for them. Guessing what had happened, she had run off at full speed with her bags.

The raisin cake in the oven was completely burnt.

The mother threw it in the trash and quickly made another, delicious cake full of candied fruit.

The whole family happily and hungrily ate this new cake that didn't contain a single raisin. ❖

RESPONDING
OPTIONS

FROM *PERSONAL RESPONSE* TO CRITICAL ANALYSIS

REFLECT

1. What is your reaction to "The Enchanted Raisin"? Jot it down in your notebook.

RETHINK

2. What advice for the future would you give the mother or the children?

3. What do you think is the theme of "The Enchanted Raisin"?

Consider

- what you know about similar tales and their themes
- the extraordinary consequences of the children's actions

4. Look over any predictions you wrote before reading "The Enchanted Raisin." How well do your predictions match an actual event or the outcome of the story?

5. In your opinion, is this modern tale more or less appealing than traditional ones you have heard or read? Explain.

RELATE

6. Many traditional tales portray stepparents—especially stepmothers—as evil characters. Do you think modern tales should portray stepparents as villains? Why or why not?

LITERARY CONCEPTS

A **fantasy** is a work of fiction that contains at least one fantastic or unreal element. The setting of a fantasy might be a totally imaginary world or a familiar, realistic place where highly unusual things happen. The plot might involve magic or characters with extraordinary abilities. Fairy tales, fables, and science fiction are examples of fantasy. One unusual happening in "The Enchanted Raisin" is a raisin that moves when someone speaks to it. Describe another unusual happening in the story.

ANOTHER PATHWAY

Cooperative Learning

Form teams and have each team choose a part of the story to animate in the form of a flip book. With the members of your team, make a series of small drawings that show the progression of a single important action in the story (for example, the mother's change into a raisin). Glue the drawings into a booklet form.

QUICKWRITES

1. Imagine that the husband in this story wants to file a **missing-person report** about his wife with the police. Draft one for him. Be sure to include details about the wife's height, weight, appearance, and clothing, as well as where she was last seen and by whom.

2. Tabloid newspapers are often filled with sensational or exaggerated reports that are almost as fantastic as "The Enchanted Raisin." In the style of a tabloid, draft a **newspaper article** that tells the story of a woman who turned into a raisin.

📁 *PORTFOLIO Save your writing. You may want to use it later as a springboard to a piece for your portfolio.*

ALTERNATIVE ACTIVITIES

1. Think about the effects, or consequences, of the children's misbehavior. Copy and fill in a chart like the one below to make a **map** of the children's actions. The first part has been done for you. Remember that one consequence may lead to another.

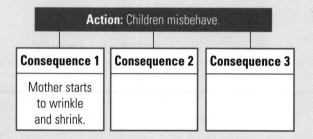

Action: Children misbehave.		
Consequence 1	**Consequence 2**	**Consequence 3**
Mother starts to wrinkle and shrink.		

2. With several other students, create **puppets** of the characters in "The Enchanted Raisin" and make backdrops of the settings. Choose one student to read or retell the story. As the story is read or told, use the puppets to perform it on a puppet stage for a class of younger students.

EXERCISE A Review the Words to Know in the boxes at the bottom of the selection pages. Then for a pair of synonyms in each group of wor below. If you find a pair of synonyms, write them on your paper. If not, write *No synony*

1. repeat, reassure, receive, resent
2. detest, deplete, hate, deprive
3. sacrifice, comfort, guard, console
4. mournful, ardent, mute, relentless
5. novelty, contrary, opposite, consequence

EXERCISE B Use the vocabulary words to complete the titles of the imaginary books listed below.

1. *I Am! I'm Not! and Other _____ Statements* by Booth Sides
2. *How to _____ Others* by U.R. Fine
3. *I've Never Been Accused of Being _____* by Raisin Cane
4. *1001 Ways to _____ a Sad Friend* by Eiffel Payne
5. *Learning to Love What You _____* by I. M. Trying

JACQUELINE BALCELLS

A Chilean-born journalist, Jacqueline Balcells (1950–) began to create stories for her children when she lived in France. "The Enchanted Raisin" was published in French in 1984. After returning to Chile, Balcells published a Spanish version of the story in 1986. Since then, Balcells has published four other books for children, including two science-fiction novels that she coauthored. Her most recent book, written in Spanish, recognizes the 500th anniversary of the discovery of the New World. "The Enchanted Raisin" was chosen for exhibition at the 1988 Children's International Book Fair in Italy.

OTHER WORKS *Adventure in the Stars, Alpha Centaur Mission, The Signs Archipelago*

FOCUS ON DRAMA

A drama is a story that is meant to be acted out for an audience. In a drama, or **play,** the plot is told through the words and actions of the characters. A drama can take place on stage, before a radio microphone, or before a TV or movie camera.

All dramas have three elements that are similar to the elements of fiction. These elements are character, plot, and setting. Unlike fiction, drama is written in a special form called a **script.** The script contains the words, or lines, that each character says as well as the type of information described below.

CAST OF CHARACTERS The script begins with a list of the characters in the play. Sometimes, the list includes brief descriptions of the characters.

DIALOGUE Most of the script consists of the **dialogue** of the play—that is, the conversation between the characters. Through the dialogue you get to know both the characters and the plot of the drama. Take a look at the following example from *The Hobbit:*

> **Thorin.** We're all hungry.
> **Ori.** And tired.
> **Oin.** I can't go any further.
> **Bilbo.** We must go on. Maybe we'll find some berries.
> **Gloin.** Find berries in the spring—that's a hobbit for you!

STAGE DIRECTIONS The script also includes **stage directions.** These are the instructions for the actors, the director, and the stage crew. Stage directions are printed in italics in this book so that you will not confuse the stage directions with the dialogue. Sometimes the stage directions are also enclosed in parentheses. The stage directions also describe the objects—called **props**—that actors need during the play.

In addition, stage directions describe the **scenery** for the play. Scenery is the painted screens, backdrops, and other materials that help a stage look like a city street or a tropical jungle. Scenery creates the setting for a drama. For example, the scenery for *The Hobbit* gives the audience the feeling that they are in a fantastical and strange world. In the following example, from *The Hobbit*, you can see how the stage directions both tell the actors what to do and describe the props and scenery.

> *At rise of curtain:* Bilbo *is discovered busily writing in his journal. He is sitting on the stoop before the cave entrance. Dragon smoke belches from under the entrance. The* Dwarves *glumly pace around the stage, hands behind their backs.*

SCENES AND ACTS Fiction or nonfiction books are usually divided into chapters. Plays, however, are divided into **scenes** and **acts.** A change in the setting or the time in a play begins a new scene. In longer plays, the scenes are grouped into larger units, called acts.

STRATEGIES FOR READING DRAMA

Drama is meant to be performed or read aloud, but since plays are written, you can also read them on your own. The following strategies will help increase your enjoyment, whether you perform a play with friends, read it aloud in class, or read it by yourself:

- **Read the play silently.** Before you perform a play or read it aloud with others, read it to yourself. This way, you will understand the entire plot and get to know the characters ahead of time.

- **Figure out what is happening.** Don't expect to understand everything about the play right away. When you read a book or watch a movie, you don't immediately understand what is going on. The same is true for drama.

- **Read the stage directions carefully.** When you watch a drama on stage, you actually see the action and the scenery. When you read a drama, however, you have to use your imagination. The stage directions tell you where and when each scene is happening and help you understand more about the characters and the plot. If you skip over the stage directions, you miss out on much of the play.

- **Get to know the characters.** In fiction, an author can describe a character's appearance and personality in great detail. In a play, the characters' own words and actions tell you what the characters are like. Read the dialogue carefully, as well as the stage directions that accompany it. In addition, try to discover the feelings behind the words.

- **Keep track of the plot.** The plot of a play usually centers on a main conflict that the characters try to resolve. When you read or watch a play, look for the conflict and get involved in the story. Notice how the characters try to work out the conflict or solve their problems.

- **Read the play aloud with others.** People of all ages and in all countries have been performing and reading plays for centuries. When you read the part of a character, you become an actor. Let yourself get into the part. For a brief while, become that character. React to what other characters say and do to you. Remember to be ready with your character's lines of dialogue and read only the words your character says. Pay attention to the stage directions so that you know how to read your lines and what to do next, but don't read these italicized instructions aloud.

Perhaps everyone wonders at times what it would be like to be someone else. Drama gives you that opportunity. When you take the part of a character in a play, you have a chance to step into someone else's feelings and experience something new.

DRAMA

A Shipment of Mute Fate

Les Crutchfield
Based on a story by Martin Storm

PERSONAL CONNECTION

In the opening speech of this play, the narrator states, ". . . a cold chill gripped me, and I shivered with sudden dread—dread of the thing I was doing, and was about to do!" The stage directions call for music that "comes up and dissolves slowly." In your notebook, sketch a scene of the sea that forms in your mind as you think about these opening words and stage directions. Choose your colors carefully. Don't worry about details; just make sure the scene portrays the atmosphere that the words *chill* and *dread* create.

CULTURAL CONNECTION

Most of this play is set aboard a ship that is sailing from Venezuela to New York City, a route you can visualize by referring to the map on this page. Understanding some of the technical terms in this play will help you enjoy it more. A ship's **captain** leads the **crew.** Various **mates** (officers) help keep order and **navigate** (steer) the ship from the **bridge** (the ship's control room). A chief **steward** (an officer in charge of supplies) directs assistants in the **galley,** or kitchen. Everyone sleeps in **bunks** or **berths** (beds). The **port** side of the ship is the side that is on the left of someone aboard who is facing the **bow,** or front.

Venezuela to New York City

New York

Miles
0 150 300

UNITED STATES

Atlantic Ocean

Caribbean Sea

VENEZUELA La Guaira

Orinoco River

Caracas

N W E S

READING CONNECTION

Sound Effects Sound effects, such as music, help convey the setting and atmosphere of a radio play. Because the audience cannot see the action, they have to imagine it. Sound effects are described in the stage directions, which are italicized and placed in parentheses throughout this play. As you read, pause when you come to a stage direction describing sound effects. Create the sound in your mind before reading on.

LASERLINKS
• READING CONNECTION

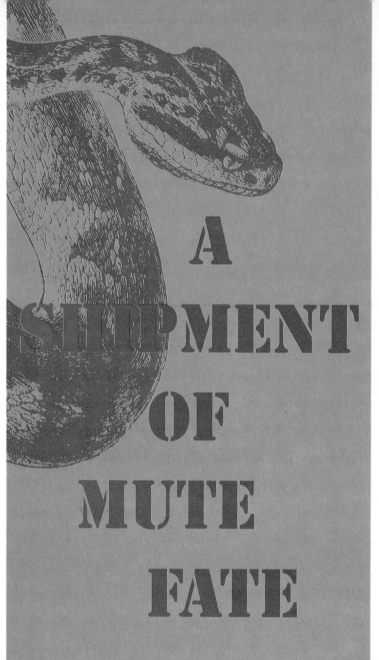

A SHIPMENT OF MUTE FATE

A RADIO PLAY
by Les Crutchfield

BASED ON A STORY
by Martin Storm

Early Morning After the Storm at Sea (1902), Winslow Homer. Oil on canvas, 76.8 cm × 127 cm, gift of J. H. Wade (24.195). Copyright © 1995 The Cleveland (Ohio) Museum of Art.

CHARACTERS

Chris Warner, a young zoologist

Captain Wood, captain of the *Chancay*

Sanchez, native guide

Mrs. Willis, stewardess

Mr. Bowman, chief steward

Other Crew Members and Passengers

Chris (*narrating*). I stopped on the wharf at La Guaira[1] and looked up the gangplank[2] toward the liner *Chancay*—standing there quietly at her moorings.[3] The day was warm under a bright Venezuela sun—and the harbor beyond the ship lay drowsy and silent. But all at once in the midst of those peaceful surroundings, a cold chill gripped me, and I shivered with sudden dread—dread of the thing I was doing, and was about to do! (*Pause. Music comes up and dissolves slowly*) But too much had happened to turn back now. I'd gone too far to stop. (*Sound: wooden box set on wooden wharf, boat whistles, etc.*)

I set the box down on the edge of the wharf, placed it carefully so as to be in plain sight—and within gunshot—of the captain's bridge. (*Sound: steps on gangplank, fade.*)

Then I turned and started up the gangplank. I knew what I was going to do—but I couldn't forget that a certain pair of beady eyes was watching every move I made. Eyes that never blinked and never closed—just watched . . . and waited!

(*Sound: shipboard commotion*)

Willis (*coming in*). Oh! You startled me, sir! I didn't hear—why . . . (*with relief*) why, it's Mr. Warner!

Chris. Hello, Mother Willis. How's the best-looking stewardess on the seven seas?

Willis (*a bit evasive*). Why, I'm . . . I'm fine, Mr. Warner. (*Hurriedly*) Nice to see you again.

Chris (*joshing*). Wait a minute! That's a fine greeting after two months.

Willis. Well—it's just that I'm so . . . so busy just now.

Chris. I don't believe a word of it—sailing day's tomorrow. And on the trip down from New York—you said I was your favorite passenger.

Willis. But—

Chris. Here—what's that you're carrying in your apron?

Willis (*obviously nervous*). Oh, it's nothing. Just . . . supplies.

Chris. Supplies? Let's have a look.

Willis. No! Please!

Chris. Why—it's a cat!

Willis (*almost in tears*). It's Clara, Mr. Warner. Mr. Bowman said I had to leave her ashore—and I just couldn't!

Chris. Who's Mr. Bowman?

Willis. The new chief steward. Clara's been aboard with me for two years—and I just can't leave her here in a foreign country. Especially with her condition so delicate and all!

Chris. Yes (*ahem*), I see! I see what you mean. Well, I hope you get away with it.

---

1. **La Guaira** (lä gwī′rä): a seaport in northern Venezuela.
2. **gangplank:** a removable ramp used to board or leave a ship docked at a pier.
3. **moorings:** a place where a ship is docked or anchored.

WORDS TO KNOW   **evasive** (ĭ-vā′sĭv) *adj.* not straightforward

Willis. You . . . you won't tell anyone?

Chris. Not a soul. As a matter of fact, if I don't get my way with the Captain, you and I may both end up smuggling!

(*Music: brief <u>transition</u>, dissolves*)

Captain (*fades in*). Most happy to have had you aboard on the trip down two months ago, Christopher, and I'm very glad you're coming along with us on the run back to New York.

Chris. Thanks, Captain Wood. There is one thing, though. I'm having a little trouble with the <u>customs</u> men here, and I wondered if you—

Captain. I can't do it, Christopher. I cabled[4] your father this morning—told him I'd have done it for you if I possibly could. He sent a request from New York, you know.

Chris. Yes, I thought he would . . . I . . . wired him from upriver last week.

Captain. I hated to refuse—but it's out of the question.

Chris. Captain Wood, I'm afraid I don't follow you.

Captain. Responsibility to the passengers, son. We'll have women and children aboard—and on a liner, the safety of the passengers comes ahead of anything else.

Chris. But with proper precautions!

Captain. Something might happen. I don't know what—but something might.

Chris. You've carried worse things!

Captain. There isn't anything worse—and any skipper afloat'll bear me out. No, son—I simply can't take the chance, and that's final!

(*Music: hit and out*)

Chris (*narrating*). Final! It wasn't final if I could do anything about it. I hadn't come down here to spend two months in that stinking back country and then be stopped on the edge of the wharf! Two months of it—heat, rain, insects, malaria—I'd gone clear into the headwaters of the Orinoco.[5] (*Fading from mike*) Traveled through country where every step along the jungle trail might be the last one. . . .

(*Music: swells and dissolves. Sound of men on a trail.*)

Chris. Oh . . . Sanchez!

Sanchez (*coming toward mike*). *Sí,* Señor Warner.

Chris. Better start looking for a place to camp. Be dark in a little while.

Sanchez. *Sí,* Señor—very soon we turn to river, camp on rocks by water. This very bad country.

Chris. This very bad country! You've been saying that for ten days now. Very bad country.

Sanchez. *Sí,* Señor Warner—this very bad country.

Chris. Oh, skip it. For all the luck we've had so far, it might as well be Central Park.[6]

Sanchez. Central Park? I no understand.

Chris. Never mind. If we don't—

(*Excited cries of "Bushmaster!" Sounds of scrambling.*)

Chris. Here—what's the matter? Quiet now! Sanchez—what's wrong?

Sanchez. There in the path! See? Bushmaster!

(*Music: loud, then fades*)

Chris (*narrating*). Bushmaster! The deadliest snake in the world! Bushmaster—its Latin name was *Lachesis mutus*—Mute Fate! It lay

---

4. **cabled:** sent a telegraph message by undersea cable.

5. **Orinoco** (ôr′ə-nō′kō): a long river in Venezuela.

6. **Central Park:** a large park in New York City.

WORDS TO KNOW

transition (trăn-zĭsh′ən) *n.* a passage from one activity or theme to another
customs (kŭs′təmz) *adj.* involved in collecting taxes on imported and exported goods

there in the center of the path—an eight-foot length of silent death—coiled loosely in an undulant[7] loop, ready to strike violently at the least movement. Here was the one snake that would go after any animal that walked—or any man. It lay there and watched us—not moving—not afraid—ready for anything. The splotch of its colors stood out like some horribly gaudy floor mat—lying there on the brown background of the jungle—waiting for someone to step on it. Here was what I'd come two thousand miles for . . . a bushmaster!

(*Sound: pistol shot. Music: up and out sharply as . . .*)

Chris. Sanchez! . . . I didn't want that snake killed!

Sanchez. He no killed, Señor—he gone. Bushmaster very smart, very quick—see bullet in time to dodge.

Chris. Anyway, he's gone! And the only one we've seen in five weeks!

Sanchez. Oh, we find other. This very bad country.

Chris. Well, lay off that gun the next time. Don't shoot—do you understand?

Sanchez. Why you say no shoot? You want bushmaster.

Chris. Sure—but I want it alive!

Sanchez. Señor Warner—you tell me you want bushmaster, but you no say "alive"!

Chris. You're getting two hundred dollars for it.

Sanchez. For dead man—what is two hundred dollars? Tomorrow we go back to Caracas.[8]

Chris (*going away from mike*). Sanchez—I'll give you a thousand dollars! (*Music swells, then fades. Chris narrates.*) It cost me fifteen hundred—but three days later, Sanchez brought me the snake in a rubber bag. He was shaking so hard I thought for a moment the thing

had struck him. . . .

Sanchez (*excitedly*). One thing you make sure, Señor Warner. No turn him loose in Venezuela. Because he know I the one who catch him—and he know where I live!

Chris. All right, Sanchez—I'll keep an eye on him.

Sanchez. He know you pay me to catch him. All the time he watch and wait. You no forget that, Señor Warner—because he no forget . . . not ever!

(*Music: loud, then under voice*)

Chris (*narrating*). Well, after going through all that trouble and danger—I wasn't going to let a pigheaded ship captain stop me at the last minute! At least not as long as the cables were still in operation between La Guaira and New York. . . .

(*Music: swells for transition, then cuts as door closes and steps come in*)

Chris (*coming in*). Morning, Captain Wood. The boy at the hotel said you wanted to see me.

Captain. That's right, Christopher. Uh . . . Sit down. (*sound of chair*) Seems you weren't willing to let matters stand the way we left them yesterday.

Chris. Sorry to go over your head, Captain Wood—but I had to. The museum sent me all the way down here for it, and I'm not going to be stopped by red tape. This'll be the only live bushmaster ever brought to the United States.

Captain. If I had my way . . . but, orders are orders. Got a cable from the head office this morning. All right. Suppose we talk about precautions.

---

7. **undulant** (ŭn′jə-lənt): wavy.

8. **Caracas** (kə-rä′kəs): the capital and largest city of Venezuela.

Chris. I'll handle it any way you say.

Captain. It's got to have a stronger box. That crate's too flimsy.

Chris. It's stronger than it looks—and that wire screen on top'd hold a wildcat. But anyway, I bought a heavy sea chest this morning. We'll put the crate inside of it.

Captain. Sounds all right. Got a lock on it?

Chris. Heavy padlock. It's fixed so the lid can be propped open a crack without unlocking it. The snake's got to have air.

Captain. But in dirty weather, that lid stays shut. I'll take no chances.

Chris. Fair enough.

Captain. We'll keep the thing in my inside cabin, where I sleep. Can't have it in the baggage room. And nobody on board's to know about it.

Chris. Whatever you say, Captain. But we won't have any trouble. After all, it's only a snake—it doesn't have any magical powers.

Captain. I saw a bushmaster in the zoo at Caracas once. Had it in a glass cage with double walls. It'd never move—just lie there and look at you as long as you were in sight. Gave a man the creeps!

Chris. I didn't know they had a bushmaster at the Caracas Zoo.

Captain. They don't now. Found the glass broken one morning, and the snake gone. The night watchman was dead. They never found out what happened.

Chris. Well . . . the watchman must've broken the glass by accident.

Captain. The way they figured it—the glass was broken from the inside! (*pause*) We . . . sail in four hours.

(*Music: transition . . . to sound of the open sea . . . music background*)

Chris (*narrating*). Into the Caribbean—with perfect weather, and a sea as smooth as an inland lake. The barometer dropped a little on the third day—but cleared up overnight, and left nothing worse than a heavy swell.[9] But in spite of the calm seas and pleasant weather, I was becoming possessed with an <u>ominous</u> anxiety. I was developing an obsessive fear of that snake! I stayed clear of the passengers pretty much—got the habit of dropping into Captain Wood's quarters several times a day. . . . (*Sound: door opens and closes. Steps.*)

He kept the heavy box underneath his berth. I'd approach it quietly and shine my flashlight through the open crack. (*Pause. Sound of two or three steps and stop.*)

Never once could I catch that eight-foot devil asleep, or even excited. He'd be lying there half-coiled, his head raised a little, staring out of those beady black eyes—waiting. He'd still be like that when I'd turn away to leave. (*slow steps*)

Maybe that's what bothered me—that horrible and constant watchful waiting. (*Sound: door opens.*) What in the name of heaven was he waiting for?

(*Sound: door closes*)

Willis (*fading in*). Well—hello there, Mr. Warner!

Chris. Oh . . . how are you, Mother Willis?

Willis. My, but you and the Captain spend an awful lot of time around this cabin. I'm beginning to think the two of you must have some guilty secret!

Chris. Oh, no, nothing like that, Mother Willis. I don't know about Captain Wood—but I . . . I certainly don't have any guilty secret!

---

9. **swell:** a large wave.

(*Music: transition into sound. Open foredeck of liner bucking a swell.*)

Chris. Well! She's running quite a swell out there, Mr. Bowman!

Bowman. Yeah—it's a little heavy, all right, Mr. Warner. Guess a storm passed through to the west of us yesterday when the glass dropped.

Chris. Think it missed us, then, huh?

Bowman. Yeah—that's what the mate figures. Sure stirred up some water, though.

Chris (*laughs*). This'll put half the passengers in their bunks.

Bowman. Make it great for my department. Two thirds of 'em will want a steward to hold their heads!

Chris. They'll keep Mother Willis so busy she'll—Hey! Look at that wave!

Bowman. Huh? . . . Great Jehoshaphat! We're taking it on the port bow! Hang on!

(*Sound: wave crashes across the foredeck . . . seems to shake the whole ship . . . and subsides*)

Chris. Whew! Not another wave that size in sight. That was a freak if there ever was one.

Bowman. You see 'em like that sometimes—even in a calm sea. (*pause*) Gotta get topside, Mr. Warner. Wave really smashed into the officers' deck. Probably did some damage. . . .

Chris. Yeah, I suppose . . . What did you say?

Bowman. Wheel companionway was open on the port side—bridge cabins musta taken a pretty bad smashing. They're right below the—Say, is something wrong, Mr. Warner?

Chris. No. No—nothing at all, Mr. Bowman. At least . . . I hope not!

(*Music: attacks and holds under voice*)

Chris (*narrating*). Of course, I knew it was only one chance in a thousand—but the chances against that freak wave were one in a thou-

sand, too! I stumbled up the companionway and along the passage to the Captain's cabin.

(*Music . . . sound of door opening*)

Willis (*surprised, affably*). Oh . . . come on in, Mr. Warner.

Chris. Mother Willis!

Willis. My, isn't this cabin a mess? I'd better get some of these things out to dry.

Chris. Yeah. Well, I just wanted to check— Where's that box that was under the Captain's bunk?

Willis. Oh, that! I just shoved it out on deck.

Chris. What!

Willis. The desk over there slid into it. It was all smashed.

Chris. But the small box inside of it! What happened to it?

Willis. Oh, they were both splintered, Mr. Warner—broken wide open.

Chris. Oh, no!

Willis. Why, Mr. Warner—you're as white as a sheet!

Chris. Mother Willis—will you go find Captain Wood? Tell him to . . . come down here immediately.

Willis. Well . . . of course, Mr. Warner. (*going*) I'll go tell him right away.

(*Sound: door closes. Sounds as cued under the following:*)

Chris (*narrating*). I pulled open the top drawer of the bureau beside me (*drawer opening*) and took out the Captain's flashlight and a loaded pistol (*drawer closing*). Mother Willis had left a mop standing by the door. I put my foot on the head of it and snapped off the handle (*snap of handle*). Every move I made turned into slow motion. I could hear my own heart beating. Slowly I started to search the cabin. (*Music: suspense motif*)

Sodden heaps of clothing were scattered around on the wet, black floor. I punched at them one at a time—holding the gun cocked—the flashlight pointing along the stick. Nothing. I worked around the room—throwing the light into the dark corners, back of the desk, under the bunk. And wherever I turned, I could feel those cold, unblinking eyes at my back—watching and waiting. (*pause*) Using the stick, I pushed open the closet door and threw the light inside. Carefully I poked at the boxes and junk on the floor. (pause) The snake was not in the closet. Inch by inch, I covered the entire cabin—and then at last I realized the horrible truth.

(*Sound: door opening. Music: up and clip off.*)

Captain. Mother Willis just told me, Christopher. (*door closes*) So it's happened!

Chris. That's right, Captain. It's happened.

Captain. I see you found the gun. We'd better start searching the cabin.

Chris. Captain Wood, I . . . just finished searching it.

Captain. Then . . . ! (*pause*) Women, kids—and that thing loose on board. A thousand places for it to hide. Heaven help us!

(*Music: establish theme for the "search"*)

Captain (*fades in*). There's no use starting to blame anybody now, gentlemen. I didn't call you officers in here to pass judgment. The thing's done—and that's that.

Mate. You're right there, Captain.

Captain. What we *have* got to do is decide how to handle it.

Bowman. It'd be easier if we didn't have to tell the passengers and crew, sir. I've seen panics aboard ship before!

Captain. Yes, I agree with you, Mr. Bowman—but I don't quite see how we can avoid it.

Mate. They gotta right to know! As long as that snake's loose, everybody on board's in the same danger—and they all oughta know about it!

Chris. Captain Wood—that thing is eight feet long. It can't simply crawl into a crack. Why don't we make a quick search of the whole ship before we spread any alarm?

Captain. Yes, I've thought of that, Christopher.

Bowman. As far as I can see, the only place it *couldn't* be is in the boilers or on top of the galley stove.

Mate. It might've crawled overboard.

Captain. We can't count on that. We've got to assume it's on the ship somewhere.

Mate. Yeah, and that could be anywhere. In a coil of rope—or in a pile of clothes.

WORDS
TO
KNOW   **sodden** (sŏd′n) *adj.* thoroughly wet

Bowman. Yes, or under some woman's berth— or a baby's crib.

Mate. Or even in—

Chris. You've already said it! That bushmaster could be anywhere. We've got to do something, and do it fast!

Captain. All right. I think the best idea's to make a quick search first. You agree to that?

(Cast *ad-libs assent.*[10])

Captain. Then if we don't find it—we'll have to warn the passengers.

Chris. We've got to find it!

(*Music: up and sustained under voice*)

Chris (*narrating*). Alone in the dim baggage room, I went through the same movements as I had earlier in the Captain's cabin—gun in one hand, flashlight in the other, poking into every dark corner, behind every trunk and box. Since there was no one in the baggage room, I could keep the gun cocked and ready. The rest of those poor devils were having to do the same thing—barehanded! All over the ship the search went on.

(*Music: up and cut off*)

Woman (*fade in*). Here, now, Steward! What on earth are you doing, rummaging through my cabin?

Bowman. Just checking up, ma'am!

Woman. Well, I'm sure there's nothing in here that has to be checked.

Bowman. Sorry, ma'am—Captain's orders. It'll only take a few minutes.

Woman. Well, I never heard of such a thing! A passenger simply doesn't have any privacy at all! (*fading back into music*) I've traveled on a lot of different lines, but I've certainly never heard of anything so completely highhanded before . . . !

(*Music: up and under voices*)

Mate. Sorry, sir. Wonder if you'd mind moving over to the other rail? I'd like to look through these lockers.

Man. Sure—go ahead. What's the matter . . . you lost something?

Mate. No. No—just looking things over.

Man. Nothing in there but life preservers.

Mate. Yeah—that's right.

Man. You must be getting ready to sink the boat. (*laughs*) Gonna collect the insurance, eh? (*fading*) Gonna send us all to the bottom! (*laughs*)

(*Music: up and out*)

Chris (*narrating*). But not one of us could find that deadly shape—coiled in some dark corner, or outstretched along a window seat. Not one of us caught a glimpse of that horrid head, with its beady black, watchful eyes. (*Fades*) It was nearly dark when we met together again in the chart room.

Captain (*fades in*). Well, gentlemen—there's no other way. We've risked all the time we can. We must warn the passengers!

Mate. How'll we do it, Captain? Call 'em all together in the lounge?

Captain. No. If we did anything like that, we'd be asking for a panic.

Bowman. We'll get one—whether we ask for it or not!

Captain. Pick a few men and go through the cabin decks. Tell 'em individually—inside their cabins. Watch for any that act like they might cause trouble—and we'll keep an eye on 'em. Handle the crew the same way.

(Officers *ad-lib agreement. Sounds of steps, chairs.*)

---

10. **ad-libs assent** (ə-sĕnt′): shows agreement in any way it pleases.

Captain (*up a bit*). As soon as you're finished—arm all the deck officers and start searching again. Our only chance of preventing a panic is to find that snake!

(*Music: sets growing tension, sustains it under voice*)

Chris (*narrating*). The slow nightmare that followed grew worse by the hour. None of us slept. All the ship's officers not on duty kept on with that endless search. Passengers locked themselves in their cabins, or huddled together in the lounges—knowing all the time that no spot on board could be called safe. Fear was a heavy fog in the lungs of all of us—and every light on the vessel burned throughout the night. Morning came and brought no relief. Terror and tension mounted by the hour.

(*Music: swells, fades. Sound of woman sobbing.*)

Willis. There now, Mrs. Crane. Go back to your cabin. The horrid thing's probably crawled overboard by now.

Woman. You're just saying that! You're paid to say it! You don't know! Nobody does!

Willis. Now, now. Everything's going to be all right.

Woman. If we could only get off the ship, they could <u>fumigate</u> it. Yes! That's what we've got to do! (*Fading from mike*) We've got to get off the ship!

Willis (*calling excitedly*). Mr. Bowman—she's going to jump.

Bowman (*in distance*). No you don't, lady.

Woman (*distance*). Let me go! (*sobbing*)

Captain (*coming in*). Nice work, Mr. Bowman. Get her down to her cabin. And whatever you do—don't turn her loose!

(*Music: up and under*)

Man (*fading in*). You never know when it might strike you. You can't put on a coat or move a chair without risking your life. Something's gotta be done. It might be right here in this lounge!

(*Sound: stir of fearful crowd*)

Mate (*coming in*). All right, mister—better quiet down and take it easy.

Man. Take it easy, huh? You're a great officer! Why don't you *do* something about it? That thing might be crawling around here right under our feet. . . .

(*Sound: rise of frightened voices*)

Mate. I said shut up! Are you trying to start a riot?

Man. I gotta right to talk! I don't want to die! Nobody's gonna tell me what—

(*Sound: sock in jaw—body falling. Music: up and back under.*)

Chris (*narrating*). The second night passed and morning came around again—a gray and rainy day that dragged by, and then night came down again—third night of the terror. Again every light burned, and the whole ship seethed in the throes of incipient panic.[11] Faced by a horror they'd never met on the sea before, crew and officers alike were on the verge of revolt. Passengers sat huddled in a trancelike <u>stupor</u>, ready to scream at the slightest unknown sound.

(*Music: dissolves slowly*)

Chris. At seven bells,[12] I made my way forward

---

11. **seethed . . . panic:** struggled with the beginnings of overpowering fear.

12. **seven bells:** the beginning of the seventh half-hour of a four-hour watch, announced by the ringing of a ship's bell.

to the chart room, and found Captain Wood bent over a desk.

(Sound: door closes. Steps.)

Captain (*wearily*). Oh . . . hello, Christopher. Come on in and sit down.

Chris (*on edge*). It's got to be *somewhere,* Captain Wood! It's got to be!

Captain. I don't know. You could search this ship for six months and never touch all the hiding places aboard. If we can only hold out for two more days—we'll be in port.

Chris. What's your home office say?

Captain. Here's the latest wireless from 'em. "Keep calm—and keep coming." Huh! What else *can* we do? How is it below?

Chris. Pretty bad. Anything could happen.

Captain. Yeah, that's why I took the guns away from the men. One pistol shot, and we'd have a riot on our hands.

Chris. The whole thing's my fault, Captain Wood! That's what I can't forget!

Captain. Take it easy, son.

Chris. If there was only some way I could pay for it myself. Alone!

Captain. No—I know how you feel. But it's no more your fault than mine, or the man who asked you to bring that snake back . . . alive. Nobody planned this. You'd better try to get a little sleep.

Chris. Sleep!

Captain. Mr. Bowman made some coffee down in the steward's galley a while ago. Better go on down and get yourself a cup—then rest for a couple hours.

Chris. Rest—I can't rest!

Captain. Christopher—it's not going to help anything if you stumble through a hatch[13] half-asleep—and break your neck. Go on and get some coffee. One way or another we've got to hold out for two more days.

(*Music: transition and dissolves. Sound: door closing and steps under . . . other sounds as cued.*)

Chris (*narrating*). The light was on in the steward's galley—and the coffeepot was standing on the stove. (*Steps stop.*) It was still warm, so I didn't bother to heat it. (*pouring*) I poured out a cup . . . (*steps*), carried it over, and set it on the porcelain table top in the center of the room. I started to light a cigarette. The door of the pan cupboard beneath the sink was standing slightly ajar, and I happened to glance toward it. I dropped the cigarette and moved slowly backward. I'd found the bushmaster!

(*Music: loud, then continues softly, movement slow and tense*)

Chris. As I moved, the snake slid out of the cupboard in a single sinuous slide—and drew back into a loose coil on the galley floor— never taking his eyes off me. I backed slowly away—waiting any moment for that deadly, slithering strike. How had he known it was me? He'd stayed quiet when Bowman was here. How had he picked the first time in five days that I was without a gun? My hands touched the wall behind me and I stopped, in terror. . . . The call button and door were on the far side of the room. I'd backed into a dead end! I stared at the snake in fascination—expecting any moment the ripping slash of those poisoned fangs. The lethal coils tightened a little—then were still again. *Homo sapiens versus Lachesis mutus*—a man against mute fate. And all the odds were on . . . fate. I knew then that I was going to die!

---

13. **hatch:** an opening in a ship's deck.

WORDS
TO
KNOW

lethal (lē'thəl) *adj.* deadly

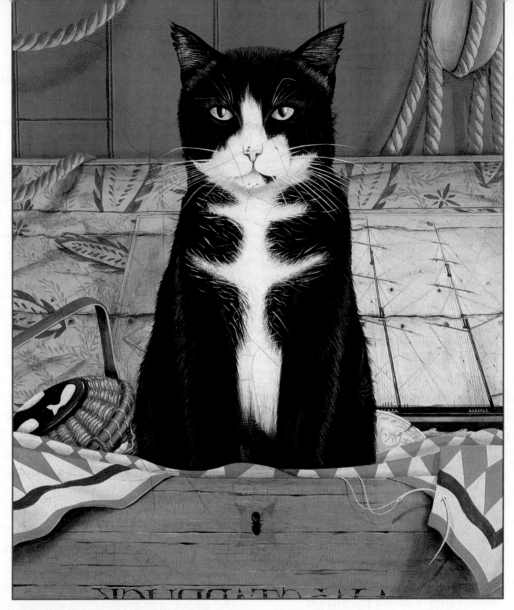

The Nantucket Cat, Paul Stagg. From *The Mardi Gras Cat Book* by Paul Stagg and Naomi Lewis, published by Heinemann Press. Copyright © The Stephanie Hoppen Picture Archive Ltd., London.

(*Music: long chord and clip off*)

Chris. I could feel the sweat run down between the wall and the palms of my hands pressing against it. My skin crawled and twitched, and the pit of my stomach was cold as ice. There was no sound but the rush of blood in my ears. The snake shifted again—drawing into a tighter coil—always tighter. Why didn't the devil get it over with? Then . . . for an instant his head veered away. Something moved by the stove. I didn't dare turn to look at it. Slowly it moved out into my line of vision. It was a cat! The scrawny cat that Mother Willis sneaked aboard in La Guaira!

Cat. (*a low, threatening growl*)

Chris. Its back was arched, and every hair stood on end. It moved stiff-legged now, walking in a half-circle around the snake. The bushmaster moved slowly and kept watching the cat. He tightened—he was going to strike at any second.

(*Sound: thud of striking snake, and scrape as it recovers*)

Cat. (*snarl and spit . . . then back to the low growl*)

Chris. He struck and missed—the cat was barely out of reach. Now she was walking back and forth again. She was asking to die.

(*Sound: thud and recovery*)

Cat. (*snarl, spit, and back to growl*)

Chris. Missed again—by a fraction of an inch. He was striking now without even going to a full coil!

(*Sound: thud and recovery*)

Cat. (*snarl, spit, growl*)

Chris. Missed! Again and again—always missing by the barest <u>margin</u>. Each time the cat danced barely out of reach—and each time she <u>countered</u> with one precise spat of a dainty paw—bracing her skinny frame on three stiff legs. And then suddenly I realized what she was doing!

(*Sound: thud and recovery*)

Cat. (*snarl, spit, growl*)

Chris. The bushmaster was tiring—and one strike was just an instant slow. But in that split second, sharp claws raked across the evil head and ripped out both the lidless eyes. The cat had deliberately blinded the snake!

(*Sound: repeated thuds of struggle*)

Cat. (*snarling, spitting*)

Chris. He didn't bother to coil now but slid after her in a fury—striking wildly but always missing. And every strike was a little slower than the last one. Until finally—

(*Sound: The thuds change to the frantic scraping of a heavy snake.*)

Chris. As the snake's neck stretched out at the end of a strike, the cat made one leap and sank her razor-sharp teeth just back of the ugly head—sank 'em until they crunched bone with tooth and claw. She clung, as the monstrous snake flailed and lashed on the floor . . . striving to get those hideous coils around her, trying to break her hold, to shake off the slow and certain paralyzing death . . . (*sound of cat out*) that gradually crept over him, and at last stilled his struggles forever!

(*Pause. Music.*)

Chris. I took a deep breath—the first in minutes—the cat lay on her side on the floor, panting—resting from the fight just over. She had a right to rest. That mangy, brave, beautiful alley cat had just saved my life—and maybe others as well. But as I turned toward the stove—I suddenly became very humble. There were three reasons why that cat had fought and killed the world's deadliest snake. And those three reasons came tottering out from under the stove on shaky little legs— three kittens with their eyes bright with wonder and their tails stiff as pokers. Up on the decks, hundreds of passengers would sigh with relief at the news that the days and nights of terror were ended. They could wait a little longer. (*pause*) I pulled open the doors of the cabinet and found a can of milk. Then I dropped down on my knees . . . on the floor of the galley.

WORDS
TO
KNOW

margin (mär′jĭn) *n.* an amount of difference or space between two things
counter (koun′tər) *v.* to respond to another's action; return a blow

RESPONDING
O P T I O N S

FROM PERSONAL RESPONSE TO CRITICAL ANALYSIS

REFLECT

1. What would be the first thing you would say to a friend about this radio play? Write your comment in your notebook or on a sheet of paper.

RETHINK

2. Do you think Chris Warner should have brought the bushmaster aboard the ship? Why or why not?
Consider
- his reason for bringing the snake
- his actions after the dangerous snake disappears
- the possible consequences for others on the ship

3. What do you think might have happened if Mrs. Willis's cat had not killed the bushmaster?

4. Did the directions for sound effects add to or detract from your enjoyment of the play? Explain your answer.

5. Take a moment to consider any changes you might want to make in the sketch you created for the Personal Connection on page 359. Now that you have read the play, what details would you add to convey its atmosphere better?

RELATE

6. Zoologists today know that the bushmaster does not survive in captivity because it refuses to eat. Do you think wild animals should be caught and placed in zoos? Give reasons for your opinion.

ANOTHER PATHWAY
Cooperative Learning

With a small group of classmates, produce *A Shipment of Mute Fate* as a radio play, complete with sound effects. Some students can read parts, and others can find creative ways to produce the sound effects. Rehearse until you can create an atmosphere that seems appropriate for the play.

QUICKWRITES

1. Write a **headline** and a draft of an accompanying **news article** about the events in this drama. Begin by asking and answering the questions *who, what, when, where, why,* and *how.* Give all the important details needed to understand what happened.

2. Pretend that you are a passenger who was not warned about the bushmaster's presence. Write a **letter of complaint** to the ship's owner.

3. A ship's captain often keeps a daily log of the ship's progress and of important events. Write a **log entry** for the day the captain learns that his orders have been overruled and the bushmaster will be on board.

📁 *PORTFOLIO Save your writing. You may want to use it later as a spring-board to a piece for your portfolio.*

Suspense is a feeling of tension and excitement that makes a reader curious about the outcome of a story. A writer creates suspense by raising questions in the reader's mind about possible endings to the conflict. Les Crutchfield begins to build suspense in the play's first speech by having Chris tell us that he felt a "cold chill" and "shivered with sudden dread" and by using sound effects like music. Find another passage in the play that you find especially effective in creating suspense.

LITERARY LINKS

Think about the selections you've read in this part of Unit Three. Which character or characters in the selections do you think most directly face the consequences of their actions? Compare your ideas with those of a classmate.

ALTERNATIVE ACTIVITIES

1. With a group of classmates, select **background music** for *A Shipment of Mute Fate*. Read the stage directions for clues to the kinds of music needed. Experiment with different types of music, such as classical, jazz, and popular (or a combination of these). Make your music reflect the atmosphere created in the play.

2. With a group of classmates, create an original **radio play** for the class. Sketch out a plot, draw up a cast of characters, and rehearse the dialogue. Create sound effects and choose appropriate background music. Make a tape of your radio play to share with the rest of the class.

ACROSS THE CURRICULUM

Science Find out more about the bushmaster and other poisonous and nonpoisonous snakes. Make a chart that compares the different features of the most common snakes. Do an oral reading of this play with some friends who haven't already read it, using the chart as a visual aid to help them distinguish a bushmaster from other types of snakes.

SNAKES

POISONOUS

King Cobra
12 to 18 feet long

NOT POISONOUS

Northern Water Snake
2 to 3½ feet long

On your paper, write the letter of the word or phrase that best completes each sentence below.

1. If the deck of a ship is **sodden,** it is (a) dirty, (b) wet, (c) rotten, (d) made of wood.

2. A **customs** official makes sure that (a) transported animals are well treated, (b) travelers know local habits, (c) taxes on imports and exports are paid, (d) passengers have tickets.

3. To **fumigate** a ship is to (a) disinfect it, (b) burn it down, (c) abandon it, (d) search it thoroughly.

4. If passengers are in a **stupor,** they might be described as (a) scared, (b) dazed, (c) angry, (d) uneducated.

5. A **lethal** grip is one that is (a) weak, (b) friendly, (c) lively, (d) deadly.

6. One example of a **transition** is (a) exchanging money for a snake, (b) moving from land to sea, (c) telegraphing the home office, (d) the engine of a ship.

7. An animal that tried to **counter** an attack would (a) strike back, (b) jump away, (c) fake death, (d) hide.

8. An **evasive** answer is one that involves (a) confessing the truth, (b) being polite, (c) avoiding the truth, (d) helping the questioner.

9. The **margin** between the snake and the cat is (a) their hatred for each other, (b) their strength and power, (c) the structure between them, (d) the space between them.

10. An **ominous** feeling makes a person (a) curious, (b) sick, (c) confident, (d) fearful.

LES CRUTCHFIELD

Les Crutchfield did not start out wanting to be a writer. He earned a college degree in engineering and became a specialist in rockets and explosives. During World War II, Crutchfield directed research programs on various secret rocket projects. He was the co-inventor of a rocket that helped heavily loaded airplanes take off.

It was only in the 1940s, when Crutchfield's wife took him to see a rehearsal for a radio show, that he became interested in writing plays. In 1946 his first radio script was accepted,

1916–1966

and his writing career was launched. Over the next 20 years Crutchfield created radio scripts for more than 20 adventure, mystery, and drama series.

In the 1950s Crutchfield started writing for a new entertainment sensation—television. He is probably best known as one of the main writers for *Gunsmoke,* a suspenseful series about law and order in the Old West. First broadcast as a radio program, *Gunsmoke* became one of the longest-running shows in television history.

WRITING TO EXPLAIN

"It's not fair!" Have you ever shouted these words?
Perhaps you felt you were treated unjustly, or maybe you
noticed a situation in your school or community that just
didn't seem right. The characters in Unit Three, "A Sense
of Fairness," face problems of all shapes and sizes. Could
you have helped them find solutions?

GUIDED ASSIGNMENT

Write a Problem-Solution Essay Often there are no
instant or perfect solutions to our problems. Still, writing
about them can help increase our understanding of them
and lead to possible solutions. This lesson will help you write
an essay that explains a problem and your solution for it.

Journal Entry

Friday, November 11

I don't know what to do. On the
way home from school yesterday, I
ran into Gordon at the park. I'm
sure he didn't expect to see me
there, because I caught him smoking.
He made me promise not to tell
Mom or Dad, and said he'd never
talk to me again if I did. But
everyone knows how bad smoking is
for you! I don't understand why he
would do it. I feel like I should do
something. After all, he is my big
brother...

1 Examine the Issues

The real world is full of all kinds of problems to solve.
Some are issues that everyone must face. Other prob-
lems are found in your own city or neighborhood.
Still others are ones you have to solve on your own.

Identify the Problem What is the problem in each
of the items on these pages? Who or what has
caused this problem? Could any of the problems
have been avoided? How?

Connect to Life All problems need solutions. What
are the issues that concern you most? Think about
unfair situations you have experienced. Look back at
dilemmas the characters in this unit faced. Consider
topics in the news. Then make a list of several
problems you might like to write about.

Almanac Statistics

Threatened and Endangered U.S. Wildlife Species

Source: U.S. Fish and Wildlife Service.

**Based on the information in this
chart, why do you think the
topic of endangered species is
so common in the media today?**

Some of the best kids in my gym class are girls. They often get picked for teams before the guys do!

Sexism and Soccer in Seattle

Twelve-year-old Eve Russell likes playing soccer with boys. She prefers their rough and competitive style of play to the girls' more passing-oriented game. So rather than join the girls' soccer team, Russell became a member of the boys' team. Her teammates are glad she did; they say they play better when she's there. They think her decision was fine.

Unfortunately, the Seattle Youth Soccer Association (SYSA) and its president, Robin Chalmers, don't agree. They believe that Russell could get roughed up by a boy angry at losing to a girl, and that she needs to bond with other females in the game. What's more, Chalmers sees her choice as a threat and an insult to the girls' program, which he has worked hard to make one of the best in the country. And he resents charges of discrimination. "Our rules are there to protect the female," he argues. He fears that if Russell is allowed to stay on the boys' team, kids all over the city will want to switch too, ultimately damaging the girls' program. So far, though, no other children have shown an interest in switching teams.

Erika Dillman
from *Women's Sport and Fitness*, April 1995

It doesn't bother other players, so she should be allowed to stay. It doesn't seem fair.

We have a problem at our school that involves fairness for both guys and girls.

2 What's Bothering You?

Look over your list of problems and mark the two or three that concern you most. You can begin to explore these ideas by freewriting for a few minutes about each. In your notebook, write down your first thoughts about each of these issues.

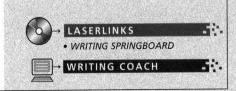

LASERLINKS
• *WRITING SPRINGBOARD*

WRITING COACH

Gathering Information

Thinking Through Problems You will want to write about a problem that has meaning for you but is not too big for you to solve. These pages will help you define your problem, look at its causes, and think about whether or not your solutions might work.

1 Choose and Investigate a Topic

Look again at your freewriting. Decide which problem you most want to write about. These activities will help you explore your topic further.

FOCUS YOUR PROBLEM

Describe the problem you'd like to take on. It might be an annoying situation you face every day or a larger issue that others are trying to solve as well. If you have strong feelings about a problem that seems too big for you to solve, such as homelessness, don't just pass it over. Try to narrow your focus, perhaps to helping out at a local soup kitchen.

ASK QUESTIONS

The first step toward solving any problem is learning as much as you can about it. The following questions may help you decide what you need to find out.

- How did the problem start?
- Whom does it affect?
- Why should something be done about it?
- Have others tried to solve this problem? How?

FIND INFORMATION

A library is often a good place to begin your search for information. There you might find

- community newspapers and magazines
- surveys and reports on issues in your area
- lists of local organizations and records of what was said during previous meetings (Check bulletin boards for future meeting dates and times.)

You might also try talking to the people who are directly involved with your problem. Use the tips in the SkillBuilder on the next page to build your interviewing techniques.

Baseball Diamond

Bedford Middle School

Basketball Court

School Building

N

② Explore Solutions

To help you find the best solution to your problem, you might make a problem-solving chart, like the one below. Begin by writing down every possible solution you can think of—even the ones you think won't work.

Now list reasons why each possible solution is a good or bad idea. The reasons supporting your idea are called pros; those against it are called cons.

Student's Problem-Solving Chart

Problem: There's only one ball diamond to play on at our school. The 7th- and 8th-grade guys always use it, so we 6th-grade guys never get to play. The girls usually get left out, too.

Possible Solutions	Pros	Cons
1. build more diamonds	• all grades could play, girls too • fair to all boys	• take too much time and money to build • games too short and girls might still get left out
2. each grade gets field for ⅓ of time it is available		• principal won't do it
3. keep field open later	• all play full games • all kids involved • students would work together as teammates	• have to do other things when your team is not playing
4. organize mixed teams; have teams play each other		

Decision Point Try out each solution in your mind. Decide which solution or solutions are the best. Think about whether using a combination of solutions might work.

③ Identify Your Audience and Goal

What are you trying to accomplish by writing about this problem? Are you just trying to understand it better or to get others to help you solve it? Who should hear your ideas? Before you begin to write, consider your audience and goal. This will help you choose the best way to present your problem and solution. See pages 382 and 383 for some ideas.

Getting Your Ideas Down

Organizing Your Draft Writing about a problem and its solution, as well as sharing your work with others, is often a first step toward making a change. The information on these pages can help you explain your problem and solution in a way that will make an impression on others.

❶ Write a Discovery Draft

One way to start organizing your information is to use headings like the ones in the model below. Start wherever you feel comfortable. You might jump from part to part, leaving holes as you go. The Writing Coach can help you with this stage.

Student's Discovery Draft

Fairness on the Field

My Discovery Draft

INTRODUCTION: ?? (maybe say something about how trying to play baseball in the field after school is dangerous?)

PROBLEM: Every day after school kids race out to the field to claim the baseball diamond. Only two teams can play at a time, and the older guys almost always get there first, so we sixth-grade boys hardly ever get to play. The girls usually get left out, no matter what grade they're in.

SOLUTION: I think there should be an after-school softball league. All kids who want to play could be put on teams and the teams would take turns playing each other. It would be fair to everybody, especially the sixth-grade boys and the girls. It might help us all get along better. The only bad thing is you'd have to find something else to do whenever your team wasn't playing. We could even have playoffs at the end of the year! That would make it even more fun!

With the free time on the diamond, maybe people would come up with new games to play and other after school leagues would start!

CONCLUSION: ?? (should ask kids to support my idea)

My Comments
My Discovery Draft

Use quote from interview?

Tell readers why they should care. (Kids get hurt running or fighting; it would be safer for teachers, too.)

Tell why we'd get along (because we'd be teammates).

Tell them what action to take.

Additional comments: Could submit my essay to school newspaper!

② Analyze Your Discovery Draft

Take a look at your draft. Have you described the problem? Does your solution make sense? To help you evaluate your draft, ask yourself the following questions:

- Have I provided enough information to help my reader understand the problem?
- Is it clear why the problem is important to solve?
- Why is my solution a good one?
- Have I explained the pros and any cons of my solution?

If you need help making your ideas clearer, see the SkillBuilder at the right for tips on elaborating.

③ Rework and Share

The guidelines below can help you make your problem-solution essay stronger and more interesting to read.

Hook Them with Your Introduction The first paragraph should grab your readers' interest. You might do this by telling how the problem affects your readers or you personally.

Explain the Problem Clearly Either in your introduction or in the main part of your draft, state the problem clearly and tell your readers why they should care about solving it.

Offer a Workable Solution Explain your solution and tell why it is workable. If you are suggesting more than one solution, list the pros and cons of each.

End with a Strong Conclusion Urge your readers to take the action necessary to help solve the problem. Another way to make your ending strong is to warn what could happen if the problem is ignored.

 PEER RESPONSE

A peer may help you see the strengths and weaknesses of your problem-solution essay. After a classmate has read your draft, ask him or her the following questions:

- Summarize the problem I explained and the solution I suggested. Does my solution sound like it might work?
- Are the pros and cons of my solution clearly explained?
- Have I provided all the information you need to understand my solution or to take the action I suggest?

SkillBuilder

 WRITER'S CRAFT

Elaborating on Ideas
Don't stop short when explaining your ideas. Use the following tips to keep your readers from becoming confused.

- Define unusual terms.
- Tell a story to illustrate the problem.
- Be specific—your audience might not be as familiar with the issue as you are.
- Describe conditions your readers may not know about.
- Give reasons for your conclusions.

APPLYING WHAT YOU'VE LEARNED
Check your essay to see whether you can make your ideas clearer or more complete.

 WRITING HANDBOOK

For more on elaboration, see page 783 of the Writing Handbook.

THINK & EVALUATE

Preparing to Revise

1. Which part of your draft do you feel is the strongest? the weakest? Why?
2. What else would you like to find out about your problem or the solution you are suggesting? Where might you go to answer remaining questions?
3. How can you improve the way you explain your solution?

Polishing Your Draft

Adding the Final Touches Your draft is almost ready to present. Here are some matters to take care of before you share your solution to the problem you have explored.

Student's Newspaper Article

Bedford Middle School
Bullfrog News
November 11

Fair Ball for All!

"Last year 24 students were hurt on the playing field, and that was before the games even started!" That's what our principal, Ms. Tailor, said when I asked her whether after-school sports at our school were dangerous. I already knew they were. I got hurt last week.

After-school sports are a problem for everyone at school: the guys, girls, and teachers. Every day when the bell rings, all the kids race out to the field to claim the baseball diamond for their team. The problem is, only two teams can play at once but there are three grades sharing the field. Usually the seventh- or eighth-grade guys beat us sixth-grade guys to the mound. Whenever we get there first, they try to kick us off. Sometimes there are fights. This is dangerous for both the students and the teachers who have to break them up. Because of this we sixth-grade guys hardly ever get to use the diamond. The girls always get left out, no matter what grade they're in.

I have an idea that will solve our problems. It won't cost a lot of money or take much time to organize. We could probably put my plan into action by next week. Here's my solution.

(continued)

If you think my idea is a good one, you should tell Ms. Tailor or write a note and put it in the suggestion box in her office. If we don't solve this problem soon, you could be the next one to get hurt!

1 Revise and Edit

Now that you've written about your problem, you probably understand it better and may see some ideas that need fixing up. Consider these points as you revise your essay.

- Peer comments may point to places where you could add facts, statistics, or examples to make your explanation stronger.
- The Standards for Evaluation on the next page will help you explain your problem and solution clearly and accurately.
- Look at the model on this page to see how one student elaborated on ideas to make his explanation clearer and more interesting.

What about the opening paragraph of this article grabs your interest and makes you want to read further?

How has this student made the conclusion to his article powerful?

Petition for After-School League

Student's Petition

We the students of Bedford Middle School would like to organize an after-school softball league. This is in order to avoid the problems we have had when lots of kids get left out or get hurt trying to claim the field for their team.

We think any 6th, 7th, and 8th graders interested in playing softball should be placed on teams so that everyone gets to play. A schedule should be made so all teams play each other. If this happens, then no "unorganized" teams can use the baseball diamond after school, only teams in the league.

To encourage teamwork, we think there should also be playoffs at the end of each quarter between the two teams with the best records. Maybe the school can even award the winning team something like a free lunch the next day.

Name	Grade	Room
1. Alice Chan	7	210
2. Lizzy Wills	7	211
3. Mario Sanchez	6	113
4. Mihi Jasinski	8	211
5. Joey Ali	6	113

2 Share Your Work

Circulating a petition like the one above is one way to help others become part of a solution. Perhaps seeing your efforts will encourage others to take action on their own.

PUBLISHING IDEAS

- Deliver a "Lunchtime Soapbox" presentation to inform your classmates about the problem and your ideas to solve it.
- Make and display posters in your school or neighborhood.

Standards for Evaluation

A problem-solution essay
- explains the problem clearly and accurately, and tells why a solution is necessary
- has a workable solution that is explained well
- uses language, details, and examples that are appropriate to the audience
- has a conclusion that provides the information necessary for the audience to take action

---

REFLECT & ASSESS

UNIT THREE: A SENSE OF FAIRNESS

By reading the selections in this unit, you have become aware of a wide range of unfair situations and an equally wide range of responses to them. Think over what you've learned. Choose one or more of the options in each of the following sections.

REFLECTING ON THEME

OPTION 1 **Role-Playing a Response** A quotation from Martin Luther King, Jr., opens this unit: "Injustice anywhere is a threat to justice everywhere." Form a discussion group, with each member taking the role of a person from one of this unit's selections. Respond to the quotation. Then pick one response that you think best reflects your own thoughts.

OPTION 2 **Making a Top-Ten List** In dealing with life's injustices, which individuals from the unit responded with hope, with wisdom, or with determination? Work with a team of classmates to brainstorm a list of the top ten personal qualities it takes to overcome an unjust situation.
Consider . . .
• what actions were taken in each case
• the outcomes of the actions
• how each person reacted to success or failure

OPTION 3 **Evaluating Causes** With a partner, look over six selections in this unit. Make a chart, writing the titles of selections that end fairly under the column heading "Fair." Under the column headings "Unfair" and "Unsettled," list the selections whose endings fit these categories. In your notebook, briefly analyze how unfair situations in the selections come about.

Self-Assessment: Now that you've considered how people sometimes treat one another, describe what you have learned about how to change an unfair situation. In your notebook, describe how you will use what you've learned the next time you or someone you know is treated unfairly.

REVIEWING LITERARY CONCEPTS

OPTION 1 **Thinking About Point of View**
Usually, a story is told either from the first-person point of view or from the third-person point of view. Compare the points of view used in the selections in this unit (not including poetry) by filling out a chart like the one shown. (One example has been done for you.) Then circle the titles in which you think the choice of point of view had a strong effect on you.

Selection Title	Main Character	First-Person Point of View	Third-Person Point of View	Effect on Selection
"Shrewd Todie and Lyzer the Miser"	Todie		✓	You know what happens to him and you know his thoughts.

OPTION 2 **Looking at Suspense** A graph that records the suspense in "User Friendly" has been started here. Copy the graph. List three more key events in the selection, and draw a dot beneath the number that shows the level of suspense in each. Do the same with two other selections. Discuss your graphs with a partner. See if you agree about the most suspenseful events.

least suspenseful ——→ most suspenseful

Suspense Scale	1	2	3	4	5	6	7	8	9	10
Louis the computer asks Kevin a question it isn't programmed to ask.			●							

Events of "User Friendly"

Self-Assessment: Along with point of view and suspense, the following literary terms were discussed in this unit. In your notebook, draw a target. Near the center or bull's-eye of the target, write the terms you understand well. Along the outer rings of the target, write the terms you don't understand or have forgotten the meanings of. Use the Handbook of Reading Terms and Literary Concepts on page 762 to review those terms.

alliteration	*description*
couplet	*humor*
sensory details	

PORTFOLIO BUILDING

- **QuickWrites** Some of the QuickWrites assignments in this unit involved writing letters. If you did these assignments, review your work to choose two letters you like. Did you do a good job of allowing your personal voice (or the voice of a character) to come through? Explain why you chose them. Then add the letters and the explanation to your portfolio.

- **Writing About Literature** Earlier in this unit, you analyzed the plot of a story. Did writing a plot analysis teach you anything new about the story? Did you enjoy the story more after analyzing it closely? Make a list of any new information that you learned, and attach it to your plot analysis.

- **Writing from Experience** In writing your problem/solution essay, you had a chance to take a step toward solving a problem that has meaning for you. Have you taken any of the steps that you proposed in your essay? What were the results? Looking back, would you now suggest any new ways of solving the problem? Include your thoughts with your problem/solution essay.

- **Personal Choice** Write a brief update of your progress to add to your portfolio. (If you began an oral log of reactions to your work in Unit One, you may prefer to update your progress orally on the audiotape.) Review your work for the Alternative Activities and Another Pathway assignments, as well as the evaluations of all the projects you did for this unit. Identify skills or strategies in which you have shown improvement (for example, taking notes, using vivid words, or speaking clearly). Put your update into your portfolio.

Self-Assessment: Compare your choices for your portfolio in Unit Three with the choices that you made in earlier units. In your notebook, write a note comparing a recent and an early piece. Point out the strengths that the recent piece shows.

SETTING GOALS

How well are you working with others, particularly in group situations? Are you willing to share your ideas? Do you listen carefully to the ideas of other group members? Do you respond sensitively? Write a suggestion or two to keep at hand as you prepare for group work in the next unit.

PROVING GROUND

All
serious
daring
starts
from
within.

EUDORA WELTY
American Writer

Out at Third, Nelson Rosenberg. Watercolor and gouache on paper, 15″ × 21 ⅞″, acquired 1939, The Phillips Collection, Washington, D.C.

SHOWING YOUR TRUE COLORS

WHAT DO YOU THINK?

REFLECTING ON THEME

Showing your true colors is showing who you really are. The activities here deal with facing a test or challenge. Keep a record in your notebook of your ideas, impressions, and results. As the characters in Part 1 of this unit show their true colors, see how their experiences compare with yours.

What are the pieces of a friend?

Design a jigsaw puzzle that conveys the qualities you seek in a true friend. The puzzle might picture an act of friendship or show phrases that express your ideas. Add your puzzle to a class display.

Do you just have to have this?

What kinds of material possessions are important to people your age? Why are they important? In your notebook, list some of these items. For each item, briefly explain why owning it is important and what it reveals to others about the person who owns it. Compare your chart with those of your classmates.

Are finders truly keepers?

Survey your classmates to see what they would do if they found a wallet containing $100 in cash but no identification. Would they turn it in? Would they keep it? Have students express their opinions on small slips of paper, fold them in half, and drop them into a box. Tabulate the results and share them with the class.

Can you compose yourself?

Work with a partner to compose a song called "Showing My True Colors." Choose a tune familiar to both of you, then write new lyrics for it. The lyrics should tell a story or give an example that illustrates the idea of the title. Sing or play your song for the class.

FICTION

The Secret of the Wall

Elizabeth Borton de Treviño (dĕ trĕ-vē'nyô)

PERSONAL CONNECTION

What are the most important qualities a friend should have? In your notebook, make a chart similar to the one shown. List the three qualities that you value most in a friend. Number them in order of importance to you. Then get together with one or two classmates and compare your charts. As you read, see whether you change your ideas about the qualities a friend should have.

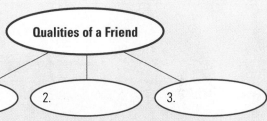

Qualities of a Friend

1.　　2.　　3.

HISTORICAL CONNECTION

The narrator and his two friends live in Guanajuato (gwä-nä-hwä'tô), a city in the rugged central highlands of Mexico. At one time, the mining of silver brought wealth to Guanajuato, but in 1821, troubled times began. Mexico had freed itself from Spanish control, but wars and revolutions shook the country for another hundred years. The desperate citizens of Mexico hid silver and other valuables from the bands of raiding soldiers and revolutionaries who battled back and forth across the country, trying to gain control.

Map of Mexico

UNITED STATES

MEXICO

Gulf
of
Mexico

N
W · E
S

• Guanajuato
• Mexico City

Miles
0　250　500

READING CONNECTION

Context Clues In describing the character Serafin's movements early in the story, the author uses the word *sauntered.* In the next sentence, she says Serafin "walked down one of the corridors slowly, looking at his feet." The second sentence provides **context clues** that can help you understand what *saunter* means—"to walk in a leisurely and casual way." Sometimes the author uses a Spanish word and then restates it or defines it in the same sentence. For example, she refers to "the *secundaria,* our high school." When you read an unfamiliar word in this or any story, look at surrounding words or sentences for clues to its meaning.

LASERLINKS
• CULTURAL CONNECTION

389

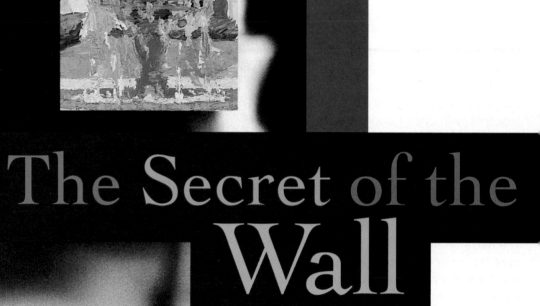

The Secret of the Wall

Wall

by Elizabeth Borton de Treviño

On a day in September, I walked down to Cantaranas Plaza and past it, along the narrow cobblestone street, and there was the great *zaguán*, the entrance to the *secundaria*,[1] our high school. Beyond I could see the broad, white, ascending steps of the university, where I would go one day.

The streets of Guanajuato smell of dried chilies, of jasmine and carnations in pots behind the iron-barred windows, of hot baked bread and of burro droppings. It is my town in central Mexico, a romantic old town that has lived days of wealth and luxury, because of the rich silver mines nearby, and days of poverty, because of the <u>turmoil</u> of revolutions and social change. Heroism has been here, in these little winding alleys and broad, fountain-centered plazas. Faith is here, in our many beautiful churches, soaring into the sky. Many artists have lived here and loved Guanajuato and painted it. My family has lived here since the days of my great-grandfather, and I always knew the legends of some of the streets, of many of the old houses, and the stories of ghosts and hauntings, some violent, some tender.

School smelled like schools everywhere, of chalk dust and disinfectant soap and boys. I found my classroom and a seat on the aisle where I could rest my leg by extending it out along my desk. Three years ago I had had polio.[2] It left me weak in the back and in one leg; I still have to take special exercises and wear a brace for some hours every day. But Dr. Del Valle, who took care of me when I was sick, had said at last that I could walk to and from school every day and that I would be getting stronger all the time. Yet I knew that I would not be able to take part in the games or play out in the court during recess. All the boys were younger than I, but almost all were taller and broader, too. The only one I knew was Serafin, Dr. Del Valle's youngest boy. He stood half a head taller than any of the others and was handsome and strong. I thought, Serafin will surely captain one of the ball teams—soccer or basketball or baseball— and he will be president of the class.

But I was wrong. When the first recess for games came, I went to sit under the arcades[3] and watch, and I saw the shouting boys choose up sides. The games professor passed out mitts and bats and balls. Serafin was a swift runner, but he didn't try very hard. He seemed uninterested and when one of the other boys jostled him, he dropped out. "Coward!" they called after him, but he just shrugged his shoulders. He came over and sat down by me, looking very <u>sullen</u>.

"It's a silly game anyhow," he said.

"I wish I could play!" I burst out.

"Why?" he asked. "You don't get anything out of it. It's just exercise. Getting knocked about and hurt sometimes. Foolishness. I play a much better game, by myself, every day."

"You do? What game?"

"I may tell you someday." Then he got up and <u>sauntered</u> off. He walked down one of the corridors slowly, looking at his feet, and then he stooped to pick up something and put it in his pocket. I turned my eyes back to the noisy fun in the school patio. I had hopes of distinguishing myself in another way. My father is a fine chess player, and groups of the

---

1. *zaguán* (sä-gwän′) . . . *secundaria* (sĕ-ko͞on-dä′ryä) *Spanish.*
2. **polio:** short for *poliomyelitis,* the name of a disease that often results in muscle weakness and crippling.
3. **arcades:** covered passageways.

WORDS
TO
KNOW

turmoil (tûr′moil′) *n.* a state of great confusion or upset; commotion

sullen (sŭl′ən) *adj.* showing irritation or unhappiness by a gloomy silence; moody

saunter (sôn′tər) *v.* to walk in a leisurely and casual way best players in our town meet at our house on Saturday evenings. During the years of my illness, Papacito[4] had taught me how to play and had bought me a small chess set that was portable and on which the pieces could be fixed so that a game might go on from where it had been left off days before. There were no gentlemen in Papacito's chess circle who were unwilling to sit down to a game with me, and once I had even beaten Don[5] Mario, the postman, who often came. He was Guanajuato's champion.

Limping home, after that first day in class, I tried to place Serafin in my chess game. A knight? Perhaps. Not a bishop or a tower. And, of course, not a pawn. He was too independent for that.

As I passed Cantaranas Plaza, I saw several country fellows with their weary burros, taking water at the fountain, and I sat there a moment, on the lip of the fountain, dipping my hand in the water and talking with them. As they went away, single file, down the street toward the country, the dusty peons,[6] who worked on buildings in the city, came tramping along. They smelled of sweat and of chili, and though they were so tired that they could scarcely lift their feet, they laughed and joked with each other. Many were boys not much older than I. I felt sorry that they could not be in school, but I knew that most of them worked to help support families.

Tía[7] Lola had made my favorite *polvorones*[8] for supper, to celebrate my first day back at school. Tía Lola is Papacito's sister, who came to live with us after my mother's death. When we had finished supper that night, we sat and talked for half an hour before Papacito went into his library to work and study.

> "That's my game," he told me suddenly one day. "Finders keepers!"

As the days went by I became more interested in all my classes. I often took my chessboard to school, and while the others were at games, Professor Morado sometimes played with me. The boys were pleasant, but careless with me; they thought me a cripple, because I had to wear my brace some days. Only one sought me out. Serafin. I took this philosophically, for I had observed him, and he, who could have done so, did not try to make friends. When the boys shoved him in the halls or pushed at him, he backed away and seemed to be afraid of them. I suppose he thought that I, so obviously outside the circle of the other boys in class, would be grateful for his company. And, in a way, that was true.

He began walking home with me afternoons, sometimes chatting, sometimes morosely making no comment on anything I said. He often leaned down to pick up a button, or a bit of cord, or a pin.

"That's my game," he told me suddenly one day. "Finders keepers!"

"How silly! You can't often find anything worthwhile."

---

4. **Papacito** (pä-pä-sē′tô) *Spanish:* dear Papa.
5. **Don** (dôn) *Spanish:* a title of respect, like *Mr.* or *sir.*
6. **peons** (pē′ŏnz′): unskilled laborers.
7. **Tía** (tē′ä) *Spanish:* aunt.
8. *polvorones* (pôl-vô-rô′nĕs) *Spanish:* cinnamon cookies.

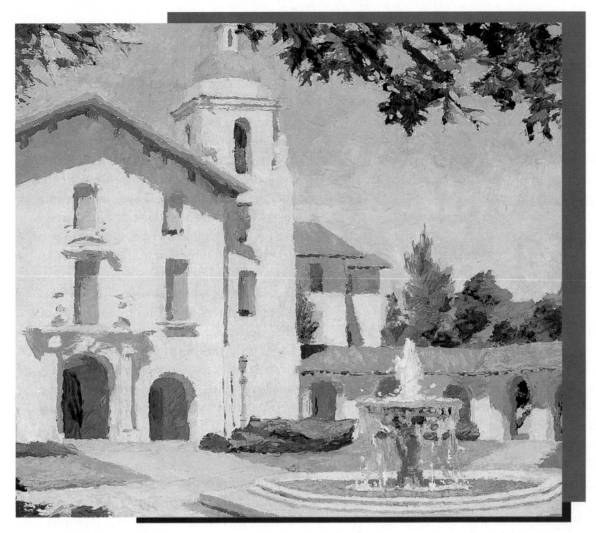

Copyright © Camille Przewodek.

"Oh, but you're wrong! I often do! I must have 100 pesos'[9] worth of stuff piled up at home that I found this way. Besides, just now we were only wandering along. But sometimes I pick out somebody and follow them.

"You'd be surprised how often they put down a package and forget it, or leave their umbrella, or even drop money!"

"But . . . but . . ." I stuttered, "if you see them drop something, you ought to give it back!"

"No," he answered stubbornly. "Finders keepers. That's the game."

"But what do your parents think about this? Tía Lola would never let me keep anything I found if it were valuable. Or my father either. I'd have to find out who it belonged to and give it back, or give it to the poor."

"Ah, my father and mother don't even know about my game, and I shan't tell them," he responded. "Papá is always out, all hours of the day or night on his calls, and Mámacita is usually in bed with a headache. They don't care what I do."

9. **pesos** (pā′sōz) *Spanish:* units of Mexican money.

I was troubled about all this, but I did not talk it over with my father or Tía Lola for a very selfish reason: I had no other friend, and I did not want to be deprived of Serafin, unsatisfactory and worrisome though he was. I knew he was cowardly, secretive, and selfish, but he was a companion. So I kept silent, though I never did go to his house. He sometimes came to mine, but only to talk or play with my dog in the patio.

I was not very lonely. I often went to Cantaranas fountain and took my chessboard. I could work out problems in chess there and watch the people passing by.

I was doing this about five o'clock of a November day when dusk was beginning to let down veils of darkness over the town. I had just closed my chessboard and was about to start home when a workman came toward me from one of the streets that led down into town. From his plaster-covered shoes and the sacking that he still wore over his shoulders, and his dusty shirt and trousers, I could tell he was probably working on one of the new buildings that were going up near the entrance of the city.

He was about nineteen, I thought. He smiled at me shyly.

"I have seen you going to high school early in the morning," he said.

He paused and shuffled his feet. "And I have seen you sitting here in the afternoons, studying."

"That's right."

"My name is Martin Gonzales," he said, suddenly, after a long pause. "I am going to ask you to do me a favor."

"Gladly, if I can." I thought he might ask for a peso.

"I want you to write a letter for me."

"But I have no paper and envelope."

"Bring them tomorrow and write a letter, please. I will pay you the fee."

That night at supper I said, "Papacito, I am going to be an evangelist."

All the men who sit at their typewriters in the big main square downtown are called, by the country people, *evangelists*, after St. John the Evangelist, I suppose. These men keep a few legal forms in their pockets and write collection letters and the like. Quite a few are busy writing personal letters for the people who cannot read or write.

"But you have no typewriter!" cried Tía Lola, serving me a big dish of *chongos*,[10] my favorite dessert.

"I will only do this one letter. It is for a nice fellow, a laborer. I suppose he is <u>illiterate</u>."

Papacito sighed. "We have too many of them," he said. "Mexico needs more schools, more teachers. We have made some progress, but not enough."

The next day Serafin wanted me to go with him rambling through the town, playing that game of finders keepers. But I told him about the letter I was to do. He made a face and would not come with me. But he said, "A workman on buildings? Maybe he will know where they plan to knock down some old places. Ask him."

I waited for Martin and wrote his letter for him. It was a note to a girl in another town. He was ashamed for her to know that he could not write, and if he had gone to one of the evangelists down in the main square, she would have suspected, knowing very well that he had no typewriter.

---

10. *chongos* (chông'gôs) *Spanish:* a custard made with eggs and milk.

WORDS
TO
KNOW

illiterate (ĭ-lĭt'ər-ĭt) *adj.* not able to read or write

I accepted the payment he offered me, so as not to wound his pride and so as to leave the door open for him should he want me to do other letters for him. Like my father, I felt very sad that this big, nice man could not read or write.

He put the letter away carefully inside his dirty shirt and turned his bright eyes toward my chessboard. I asked if he knew the game, but he shook his head. Idly I explained the moves and the names of the pieces.

Then began a curious friendship. Martin passed by the fountain every afternoon, sometimes bringing with him another big, shy workman who wanted a letter. I began to develop a small but regular business, and I looked forward to that hour in Cantaranas Plaza. It comforted me to think I was doing something useful, and I began to plan on teaching them to read a little when vacations came.

Serafin was <u>scornful</u> and did not often drop by anymore. "How stupid!" he said. "Writing silly letters for oafs."

"Martin is no oaf! I am teaching him chess, and he will be a good player!"

"I don't believe it!"

"Stay and watch then! Here he comes now."

Martin came hurrying along. I presented them, and Serafin had the grace to take Martin's calloused hand, after it had been dusted against his trousers and deferentially[11] offered.

I had the pieces set up on my little board. Martin drew the white, so he had first move. He made an opening gambit[12] I had never before seen used. I did not know the defense, and he soundly beat me. Serafin's eyes were starting from his head, for like most of us

boys in Guanajuato, he knew something of the game.

"*Caray,*[13] you stopped me in my tracks, Martin!" I cried. "Who showed you that gambit?"

"I made it up," he told me, pleased. "I thought about the chessboard all day, as I was working. I could see it in front of my eyes, and every piece, and so I played a game with myself, in imagination, and it seemed to me that the opening I used just now was a good one."

> I often went to Cantaranas fountain and took my chessboard. I could work out problems in chess there and watch the people passing by.

Martin arrived on Saturday evening in clean, freshly ironed cotton work clothes. Like all our country people, he has perfect manners, and, of course, so has my father and so have his friends. They made Martin welcome, and my father sat down to play his first game with him. To my amazement, he defeated my father in the first game, and the second one was a real struggle, finally ending in stalemate.[14] My father was perfectly delighted, and all the others crowded round to congratulate Martin.

---

11. **deferentially:** very respectfully.
12. **gambit:** in chess, an opening move designed to gain an advantage.
13. *caray* (kä-rī′) *Spanish:* an exclamation of surprise.
14. **stalemate:** in chess, a situation in which neither player can make a legal move, the results being a draw or tie.

Mexican Boy (1926), Victor Higgins. Oil on canvas, 24" × 20", private collection. Photo courtesy of Gerald Peters Gallery, Santa Fe, New Mexico.

"Young man, you are a chess genius, I think!" cried Don Mario, the postman. "You must join us every Saturday! Keep our game keen!"

After he had left, my father and his friends talked excitedly about Martin. They had in mind to train and polish him, and enter him in the state championship chess games in the spring.

The next day there was a piece in the paper about a treasure having been found by workmen when tearing down an old house in Celaya. Under the flagstones of the patio they came upon a strongbox filled with silver coins. My father read the item aloud.

"Too bad we live in a house built by my grandfather," chuckled Papacito, "and that I know he happened to die land-poor. And my father was a believer in banks."

"My friend Luisa, in Guadalajara, had a friend who found a buried treasure in the kitchen of the house they bought," contributed Tía Lola.

"Well, it happens often and it is reasonable," explained Papacito. "Mexico has gone through violent times, and insurgent[15] and revolutionary armies have swept in and out of so many towns that the people often buried or hid their valuables so as not to have to surrender them. And then, of course, sometimes they couldn't get back to retrieve them. Or they died, and nobody ever knew what had happened to their money."

I was thinking this over as I walked to school, and in the first recess Serafin sought me out, full of excitement.

"Did you read about the treasure in Celaya?" he asked me, breathless. "Let's go treasure hunting here! There must be quantities of old houses where people have buried money!"

"Well, yes. My father said there was every likelihood. But how? Which houses? And how would you start? Nobody would even let you begin!"

"Why couldn't Martin tell us where? He works with a wrecking crew, knocking down old houses, doesn't he? He could sneak us into one some night!"

"Tía Lola wouldn't let me go."

"Don't tell her!" counseled Serafin impatiently.

"Well . . ."

It is one of the joys in our town to go out in the dusk or in the evening, wandering through the narrow little alleys and streets, singing and serenading the young ladies behind their barred windows. I had never done this, because of my leg, but I was really strong enough to start out soon.

---

15. **insurgent** (ĭn-sûr′jənt): rebelling against a government.

It was the <u>deceit</u> that unnerved me. But the call of adventure was strong, and, I'll confess it, I longed to go treasure hunting. I resolved to speak to Martin.

I had my chance when he stopped by Cantaranas Plaza after work. I was waiting for him.

"We began to tear down the old house of the Lost Grandfather today," he told me. "The workmen are not happy about it. They say it is haunted."

"Yes? Tell me about it?"

"The Lost Grandfather groans and howls there on windy nights; people have heard him. He was an old gentleman who simply disappeared during the Revolution."

"Strange. Aren't you afraid to work there, Martin?"

"I? No. I am only a simple, uneducated fellow. But I do not believe in ghosts," he told me, scornfully.

Serafin was eager to go out that very night, but he decided that he had better reconnoiter[16] first. But the next day at recess, he told me, in whispers, that the situation was perfect. There was a watchman, but he was very old and deaf, and did not know anything about the ghost.

"His daughter brings him his supper at about nine o'clock, and he eats it, and then he goes to sleep on some sacks in the back. To try him out, I even pounded on the gate and struck the rocks of the patio with a small steel bar I have. The old fool did not hear a sound. We'll go tonight!"

I was scared, but terribly eager to go just the same. Little prickles of excitement ran up and down my spine all day.

Just at dusk, Serafin came by for me. He had a long, paper-wrapped parcel under his arm. "An iron bar with a pointed tip," he said, "and a candle."

As we left I had a bad time with Tuerto, my little white dog with the black spot around one eye. Tuerto whined and begged to come with us, and he got out twice and had to be brought back in and scolded before he would not try to follow me. I believe he smelled my excitement.

As we came near the haunted house, we saw the watchman's daughter just arriving.

"Good! She's early!" hissed Serafin. She left the big *zaguán* slightly ajar as she went in, and, pulled and pushed by Serafin, I followed. We were inside!

We had to wait a long time, pressed up hard against the wall where we would not be seen, while the old watchman and his daughter talked a long time over some family problem. A little wind began to rise, and I shivered with nerves and with cold.

At last she left, calling *adios,* and the old man made the sign of the cross behind her as the *zaguán* clanged to. Then he shuffled off to somewhere in the back.

"Come in now," said Serafin. "He eats and rests way back there, where they have begun taking out the rear walls. I want to try inside, around the fireplace. That's where lots of treasures have been buried."

We went cautiously into the big central hall of the house. It was quite dark and very mysterious. A little light drifted in from the street, but the shadows were deep, and there were strange noises, little scurryings and rattlings. Our eyes grew used to the dark. Soon we made out the fireplace. From it stretched out two walls, at the far ends of which there were doors into other rooms.

"Let's sound those walls," suggested Serafin.

---

16. **reconnoiter** (rē′kə-noi′tər): to scout or explore.

"You go along there, and I'll go here. See if they sound hollow to you. Like this." And he went along, giving a smart rap on the plaster. I dutifully did as I was told, almost forgetting the watchman, but the walls sounded the same along their length to me.

"We might as well open up anyhow and see how solid they are," whispered Serafin, and he went at a place in the wall not far from the chimney. I was terrified. It seemed to me that the clanging and banging would bring not only the watchman, but even people from the street, in upon us. However, Serafin labored away, to no avail.

"I'll try over here," he panted, and again he dug at the wall, but there seemed to be nothing but firmly set bricks inside.

"Here. You try." He gave me his improvised pick, and I went at a place on the other side of the fireplace. At first the plaster gave way easily. Then I came upon the same hard bricks. But as I struck and pried at them, one of them crumbled away, and another, and I put my hand in. There was an opening!

Serafin almost shouted in his joy. "I'll open it up more, and then you get inside and see what's there!" He worked away very fast and soon had a hole in the hollow wall through which I could just squeeze my shoulders.

"Get in!" he urged, and pushed me.

"It's terribly dark," I said. "Give me the candle."

He passed it in to me, and I lighted it. I stood inside the wall, in a very narrow passage. The air was still and dead, and the candle flickered along the wall.

And then suddenly there was a deep, mournful groan. I started and dropped the candle. As I struck against the wall, plaster

and bricks rained down, and I found myself cut off. I tried to scratch and scrabble my way out, but in the dark I had no way of knowing whether I would be able to get free again.

"Serafin!" I called with all my might, but there was no answer. Only, at my shout, more plaster and bricks fell.

I was scared to death. I stood there and cried, until I realized that I would have to be sensible and think.

I cannot pretend that I was able to do this immediately. I suffered from a confusion of feelings. I thought I might be buried alive; I feared our being caught in that house where we had no permission to be; I was frightened of the dark and of the sounds. But eventually I was able to control myself.

> And then suddenly there was a deep, mournful groan. I started and dropped the candle.

I was not scared by the groan. I did not believe in ghosts, and I knew there must be some natural explanation. I felt sure Serafin would go at once and bring help. And after a bit, I realized I would not smother, for there was a thin breath of air, from somewhere in the wall, that moved along my cheek.

It came to me, at last, that I might find some opening in the wall, and cautiously I started exploring. Luckily I had some matches in my pocket, and though I scrabbled around trying to find the candle, I could not. So I lit a match, and in that light went along, feeling the sides of the hollow wall close against me, until the match burned down to my fingers and I was in darkness again. In this way I passed around a bend in the wall, where it curved out around

Long Day's Shadow (1994), Marilyn Sunderman. Courtesy of the artist, Sedona, Arizona.

the fireplace I thought, and emerged into the wall beyond, which was also hollow. But there, as I lit a third match, I saw, suddenly illuminated, a skeleton fully dressed in the clothes of last century and sitting on a low bench. It was wedged between the walls, and on its knees was a box. It was a terrible figure, but even in that first moment of shock and <u>revulsion</u>, I felt pity. What had been a man must have had himself walled in here, with his treasure . . . and no one had ever come back to free him. Was it the Lost Grandfather?

I said a prayer for the soul of that pitiful skeleton man, and then tried to maneuver myself around in the wall and feel my way

back whence I had come. I decided to save my matches, and when I felt the fallen rubble, I lay down, very gingerly, to wait for rescue, saying my prayers all the while.

I may have dozed, from fear and hunger and cold, for I awoke startled to hear a dog yelping. It was my Tuerto! And, as I came to myself and realized where I was, I heard scratching and striking along the wall. I hurried back, in case some more bricks should tumble down, but before long there was an opening, the rubble was being pulled away and there was Martin, looking in, with his face all pale and drawn.

"Thank God! He's all right!" he called.

And I heard Tía Lola and my father echo, "Thank God!"

He pulled me out, and Tuerto leaped upon me and almost smothered me with doggy kisses. Then I was enclosed in my aunt's arms, and I felt my father's hand on my hair.

I can't remember much more of what happened until they got me home and to bed, and Tía Lola gave me a drink of hot lemonade.

Serafin had abandoned me. They did not know he had even been with me, until I told them.

Martin had happened to come back to our house that evening, to tell my father he could not come to play chess on Saturday, and as Tía Lola opened the *zaguán* to him, Tuerto had shot out and into the street.

Tía Lola had been crying. She was worried, for it was after eight and I had not come home. Martin said to her, "Look, the little dog is trailing him! I'll follow and bring back Carlitos."

My loyal Tuerto led Martin straight into the haunted house and to the wall. Martin had called and called, but I had been asleep and did not hear. Anyhow he rushed back to bring my father and Tía Lola, and also a pick. And so they had found me.

In bed, safe and warm, I remembered the poor skeleton. "There is a dead man in the walls," I told them, "holding a treasure on his lap. Please go back and get it, Martin!"

"Shall I?" Martin looked at my father.

"We'll go," said my father, and they left me to Tía Lola.

I tried to stay awake until they came back, but excitement and fright had taken their toll and I fell deeply asleep. I did not know until the next morning that Martin and I had a

fortune between us. The skeleton was extracted from the wall and given decent burial, and my father looked up in the old records of the city and of taxpayers on the old houses, to find out his probable identity. Then he had searched for relatives, but there seemed to be none. So, after my father paid the taxes on the treasure, it remained for us. Finders keepers.

It was not so very much, after all. The box had held silver coins and some jewels, but these were not of much intrinsic value anymore. Still, something like 20,000 pesos remained to be divided between Martin and me.

"What will you do with your part?" I asked Martin, a few days later.

> He would never be anything in the Great Chess Game but a simple pawn.

"I will take care of my mother and my little brothers, and I shall go to school," he cried.

But in the Saturday evening chess circle, my father and his friends decided among them they would teach Martin to read and write, and coach him until he could pass examinations and then go on to evening classes. Meanwhile, he was going to be their champion in chess tournaments, and he could make some money giving exhibition games.

"What will you do with your part of the treasure?" Don Mario asked me. They were all eating *enchiladas*[17] and drinking coffee, after their game. Before I could answer, there was a

---

17. *enchiladas* (ĕn-chē-lä′däs) *Spanish:* rolled tortillas filled with a seasoned mixture.

clamor at our *zaguán*. And the big knocker sounded several times. Tía Lola ushered in Dr. Del Valle, and Serafin.

Dr. Del Valle gave Serafin a push into the center of the room. "Begin," he ordered his son.

"I am sorry," stammered Serafin.

Dr. Del Valle was trembling with emotion. "I never thought I would see the day when I would feel so ashamed of my son," he told my father. "He has just now confessed to me that he induced Carlos to go with him to that house, to break into the walls and look for treasure, and that when the wall caved in he ran home and left Carlos there, perhaps to die!"

Serafin stood with drooping head, and two tears slid down his cheeks. "I am sorry," he whispered again.

"We knew," said my father. "We realized that Serafin must have been paralyzed with fear. That is why I did not speak of it to you. He is forgiven. Isn't he, Carlos?"

"Of course," I answered at once.

For what else could I say? I knew what it was to be scared senseless, almost to panic. I couldn't hate Serafin, even though Tía Lola did. I was even, in a way, sorry for him. For I knew that he would never be anything in the Great Chess Game but a simple pawn, like me. Martin would end as a knight.

"I suppose by rights," I said to Serafin, not being above heaping some coals of fire on his head, "at least part of the treasure should be yours. You started looking in the wall where it was found."

He glanced hopefully at me as I went on. "So I trust you will agree with me about what to do with it. I want to give it for a classroom in one of the new schools being built down by the highway. We could name that room." He was disappointed, I could see. But he was trapped. Or, as Tía Lola said later, he made a virtue of necessity.[18]

"Whatever you say, Carlos," he answered meekly.

"Why don't we name it for the Lost Grandfather?" I cried.

And so it will be. My father turned over the money to the education department, and a plaque will be affixed to one of the rooms, saying, "This room was built with funds left by the Lost Grandfather." The president of Mexico is coming to inaugurate[19] the school, and several others, and Serafin and I and all our relatives, and Martin, and the whole class at school and Professor Morado, and many others, will be there. All Guanajuato will be in gala dress. The day will be a great *fiesta*.

Olé, poor Lost Grandfather. Your treasure will be of good use, at last. ❖

---

18. **made a virtue of necessity:** pretended to be doing something because it was right when, in fact, doing it only because forced to.

19. **inaugurate** (ĭn-ô′gyə-rāt′): to open officially with a formal ceremony.

401

RESPONDING
O P T I O N S

FROM PERSONAL RESPONSE *TO* CRITICAL ANALYSIS

REFLECT

1. Which character made the strongest impression on you? Describe your impression to another student.

RETHINK

2. What do you think of the way Carlos treats Serafin at the end of the story?

3. Carlos thinks of life as "the Great Chess Game." Why do you think he makes this comparison?

4. What kind of person is Martin Gonzales?
   Consider
   • his first meeting with Carlos
   • his interest in chess
   • his plans for his share of the treasure

5. Review the list you made for the Personal Connection on page 389. Compare Carlos, Martin, and Serafin in terms of the qualities of friendship that you find most important.

RELATE

6. Carlos and Serafin display their "true colors" in the different opinions they have about what should be done with something valuable found in the street. Do you believe in the rule of finders keepers? Explain why or why not.

ANOTHER PATHWAY

Display a chess set if available, or draw a diagram of a chessboard with the pieces positioned and labeled. Discuss the use of chess in "The Secret of the Wall" in terms of the following:

- how the author uses the game to advance the plot of the story
- why Carlos thinks of life as "the Great Chess Game"
- the other characters' amazement at Martin's abilities
- the comparison of Serafin to a pawn and Martin to a knight

THE WRITER'S STYLE

The author skillfully creates the settings and develops the characters in this story through the use of specific details and careful word choice. Reread de Treviño's descriptions of Guanajuato, the high school, and Cantaranas Plaza. Then pay attention to detail and word choice as you write a short passage describing your neighborhood and your school.

QUICKWRITES

1. Imagine that you are present at the inauguration ceremony for the new school that Carlos and Serafin have helped fund. Draft a short **speech** for either Carlos or Serafin explaining the decision to donate the treasure to the new school.

2. Draft a **newspaper account** of Carlos's rescue. Look back over the story for facts and details that you can include.

   📁 **PORTFOLIO** *Save your writing. You may want to use it later as a springboard to a piece for your portfolio.*

LITERARY CONCEPTS

The way a writer creates and develops a character's personality is called **characterization.** A writer can make a character come alive through direct description of the character, through the character's words and actions, and through the words and actions of other characters. Martin, for example, is described as wearing "clean, freshly ironed cotton work clothes." You can infer from this information that Martin is a working person who cares about his appearance. Find examples of each method of characterization in the story. Which method of characterization do you think provides the most helpful information about the characters?

CONCEPT REVIEW: Suspense Recall that suspense is a feeling of tension and excitement that makes a reader curious about the outcome of a story. For example, in the play *A Shipment of Mute Fate,* a moment of suspense happens when Chris spots the deadly bushmaster snake in an open cupboard. Find an example of how de Treviño creates suspense in "The Secret of the Wall."

ALTERNATIVE ACTIVITIES

1. Create a **diorama** that portrays Guanajuato and one of the scenes in the story. Be sure to include some of the most prominent locations mentioned in the story: the fountain in Cantaranas Plaza, the school, Carlos's house, and the old house of the Lost Grandfather. Then create representations of the figures of Carlos, Martin, and Serafin, and place them at appropriate points in the scene. Add your diorama to an exhibit of dioramas illustrating events in the story.

2. Imagine that you are the music director for a film version of "The Secret of the Wall." Pick three or four scenes and find **music** that you think conveys the mood at those points in the story. Keep in mind the story's setting and the various events described. Use the music you pick as background for a reading of those scenes to the class.

ACROSS THE CURRICULUM

Mathematics The treasure of the Lost Grandfather amounted to about 20,000 pesos. How much money would this be today if it were converted to U.S. dollars? (Remember that the money would have had a different value during the time in which the story is set.) Research the monetary systems of Mexico and the United States, and summarize your findings on a chart. You may wish to display Mexican coins and currency with the chart.

LITERARY LINKS

Compare and contrast the character of Serafin in this selection with Mourad in "The Summer of the Beautiful White Horse."

Serafin | Mourad

EXERCISE A For each group of words below, on your paper write the letter of the word that is the best antonym for the boldfaced word.

1. **induce:** (a) discourage (b) argue (c) awaken

2. **clamor:** (a) plainness (b) grace (c) silence

3. **turmoil:** (a) calm (b) light (c) happiness

4. **saunter:** (a) whisper (b) grin (c) march

5. **illiterate:** (a) dark (b) pleasant (c) educated

6. **scornful:** (a) respectful (b) lucky (c) proper

7. **deceit:** (a) jealousy (b) truthfulness (c) beauty

8. **morosely:** (a) simply (b) happily (c) intelligently

9. **sullen:** (a) brave (b) gentle (c) cheerful

10. **revulsion:** (a) fear (b) surprise (c) admiration

EXERCISE B Working with a partner, act out the meaning of one of the following words while another pair of students guesses the word: *sullen, saunter, morosely, scornful, deceit, revulsion, induce.* Then switch so that you and your partner guess which word the other pair of students is acting out.

ELIZABETH BORTON DE TREVIÑO

As a child in California, Elizabeth Borton de Treviño was delighted by the sounds of the piano, the violin, and the Spanish language. These interests remained with her, leading her to study the literature, language, and history of Spain at Stanford University.

Her knowledge of music and Spanish helped de Treviño win her first job, as a reporter for the *Boston Herald.* While working as a music reviewer, she was asked to use her Spanish to interview a dancer and musician from Spain. From that point, her work opportunities

1904–

broadened. Traveling to Mexico on a newspaper assignment, she met Luis Treviño Gomez, who became her husband. Mexico became her adopted country, and she has lived there since 1935.

De Treviño once said, "I generally get story ideas from some true event or moment in history that fires my imagination." *I, Juan de Pareja* is her most famous novel. This story of a slave who worked for the real-life painter Diego Velázquez earned de Treviño the Newbery Medal in 1966.

OTHER WORKS *El Guero, Leona: A Love Story*

from Talking with Artists
Pat Cummings

PERSONAL CONNECTION

What does the word *talent* mean to you? In your notebook or on a sheet of paper, list some abilities you consider to be talents. What are *your* particular talents? Create a chart similar to the one shown, and fill it in with these talents, entering your strongest in the space numbered 1 and your weakest in the space numbered 4. Add more spaces if you wish. As you read this interview, see if your ideas about individual talent change.

My Talents
1.
2.
3.
4.

CULTURAL CONNECTION

This selection is from the book *Talking with Artists.* The author, Pat Cummings, interviewed artists by posing questions that students often ask when artists visit schools and libraries. All of the artists are talented illustrators of children's books, and some of them, like Cummings herself, also write the books in which their illustrations appear. In these interviews, the illustrators talk about their early art experiences and offer encouragement to young people who would like to explore their own artistic talent.

WRITING CONNECTION

Jerry Pinkney, the artist interviewed in this selection, says that he decided to develop his artistic talent because of his two older brothers who drew. In your notebook, copy and complete the sentence shown. Then go on to write a brief description of a talent you are currently developing.

> **"I first became interested in _____ because _____."**

Talking with Artists

by Pat Cummings

An Interview
with Jerry Pinkney

My story. I first became interested in art because of my two older brothers who drew. They liked to make pictures of airplanes, cars, things of that sort. I began by mimicking them, trying to draw what they drew.

I remember an incident in the first grade when I was growing up in Philadelphia that shaped the idea in my mind that I wanted to be an artist. For a Fire Prevention Week project I drew a red fire engine on a big sheet of brown paper. I received a lot of attention from that, and I liked it. I was encouraged by my teacher, and, as I kept drawing, I became the "class artist."

Probably part of the reason that I focused on my drawing so much was that I felt I wasn't very strong in other areas. I was able to escape some projects by drawing the assignments.

I was able to take private art classes when I was in junior high school. My father was a handyman who did painting, plumbing, electrical work, gardening—a bit of everything. He had several clients who knew of private art classes, and I remember taking classes in different neighborhoods. Usually they were still-life[1] painting classes.

When I was eleven or twelve years old, I had a newspaper stand on the corner of a fairly large intersection in Philadelphia. I would take my drawing pad and sketch while I was there. An artist named John Liney, who was a cartoonist for the Henry comics,[2] noticed me drawing. He took me to visit his studio, which was about a block away. From time to time I would go to see him, and he would give me different materials to work with, different art supplies. So at that early age I had a sense that it was possible to make a living doing art. Knowing him and seeing how he worked helped me understand the possibilities of using one's talents.

One early influence was the work of Arthur Rackham, who was an illustrator of children's stories. I liked the quality of his drawing and how he used color.

I later went to Dobbins Vocational High School and took commercial art classes that introduced me to lettering and technical drawing, airbrush, and all kinds of media.[3] In the twelfth grade, we even attended some figure-drawing evening classes.

There was a competition for scholarships to the Philadelphia Museum College of Art. Only four or five were available. I had to show a portfolio[4] and write a paper stating why I wanted to attend. It felt great to win a scholarship, and I began studying advertising and design. But I soon realized that I enjoyed painting and printmaking classes even more, and drawing became very important to me.

I began doing greeting cards, advertising, and textbook illustration in Boston. The textbook work made me realize I liked illustration that was tied to a story.

Book illustration seemed freer than some of the work I was doing. Working with a manuscript was very exciting. I also began to look into and research African-American artists. I admired Charles White, whose strong, graphic

---

1. **still-life:** a type of painting that uses an object or group of objects as the subject of the painting.

2. **Henry comics:** a long-running newspaper comic strip about a boy named Henry.

3. **media:** the materials or techniques with which an artist works.

4. **portfolio:** samples of an artist's work that show the range of the artist's skills.

WORDS TO KNOW

mimicking (mĭm´ĭ-kĭng) *n.* copying or imitating the actions of another **mimic** *v.*

client (klī´ənt) *n.* a customer

commercial (kə-mûr´shəl) *adj.* done for profit; having to do with a business drawings gave such dignity to the black figure. I was also impressed by the photographs of James Van Der Zee. If you look at the work of these two men, I think you'll see their influence in my book *Home Place*.

I've won a lot of awards for my art, and it feels wonderful to know that my work is appreciated. My work includes a mixture of things that I, myself, have appreciated. In some ways, it is a testimony to be able to state through my art, "Yes, these people have influenced me."

My work includes a mixture of things that I, myself, have appreciated.

1. *Where do you get your ideas from?*

Most of my work comes from the text, which I use as a sort of springboard. I try to find stories that allow me to make some kind of personal statement. For example, I'll find manuscripts that deal with the African Americans and our history in this country. So the ideas come from the story but also from my own personal <u>commitment</u>. I have just recently collaborated on two books, *Sunday Outing* and *Back Home*, with my wife Gloria Jean Pinkney.

2. *What is a normal day like for you?*

Part of the year I travel to visit schools and libraries. When I'm working in the studio, I'm at the drawing board between eight-thirty and nine o'clock in the morning. I get started easily and work straight through the day, taking a break for lunch or maybe to take a walk. Usually, my day ends between eight-thirty and ten o'clock at night. So many things that can happen during the day need to be taken care of as well. I might spend a lot of time on the phone discussing work, or packing up art that must be shipped to a gallery or publisher, running out to get photocopies of things. All of this accounts for a fairly long day.

3. *Where do you work?*

I work in my studio right in the house. I have a screened-in porch that looks out into the woods. So it's really quite a nice environment with good space and lots of light.

4. *Do you have any children? any pets?*

Yes. I have four children. Troy Bernadette Ragsdale is the director of Child Life at Jacobi Hospital and mother of our granddaughter, Gloria, who appears on the cover and inside of the book *Pretend You're a Cat*.

Brian Pinkney is an illustrator, and a very active one, in the area of children's books. He is married to Andrea Davis Pinkney, who is an author and children's book editor.

Scott Cannon Pinkney is the senior vice president and creative director of his own direct response agency. He is married to Kim Pinkney, and they live in Toronto, Canada, with their two children.

And our son Myles Carter Pinkney is a cameraman and photographer. He has just contracted to do his first children's picture book. Myles and his wife, Sandra, have three children.

WORDS TO KNOW · **commitment** (kə-mĭt'mənt) *n.* devotion to a cause or set of beliefs; feeling of responsibility

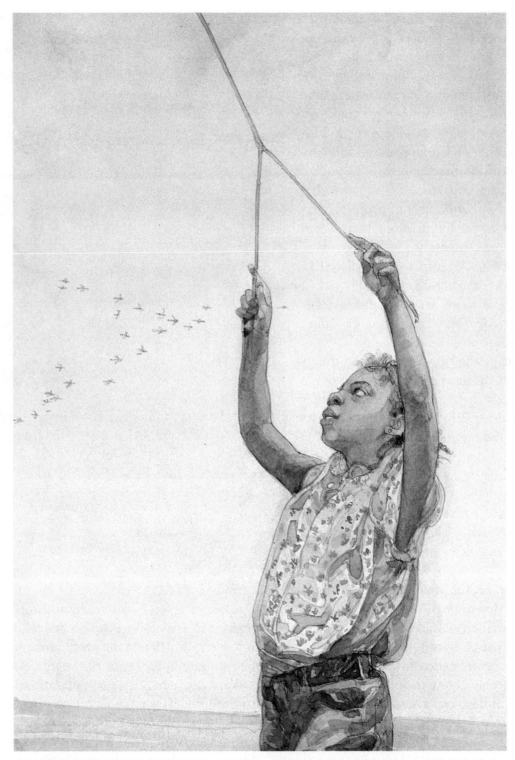

This 1992 illustration by Pinkney is from the children's book *Drylongso*, written by Virginia Hamilton.
Illustration by Jerry Pinkney. From *Drylongso* by Virginia Hamilton. Illustration Copyright © 1992 Jerry Pinkney, reproduced with permission of Harcourt Brace & Company.

5. *What do you enjoy drawing the most?*

It varies. Perhaps I most enjoy drawing animals. Next to that would be using animals in an anthropomorphic way—giving them human characteristics, like dressing them in clothes or giving them human expressions. Combining them with people fascinates me and gives me so many areas to work on that I enjoy.

I try to keep a balance in my work. If I find that I'm working on projects that include an awful lot of animals and less people, I want to balance it, so I go back and forth. When I get to a point where I've had it with drawing animals, I'll pick a project where there are more human figures involved. The variety can be quite, quite exciting.

I've always tried to focus on the things that give me the most enjoyment. Part of me always needs to try to do something that I've never done before or to bring a different point of view to my work. Often, this involves working on things that make me uncomfortable at the time. But the idea is to move through that uncomfortable stage and learn how to resolve the problem I'm having in my work and face it head on. Hopefully, that helps bring a freshness to the work.

This Pinkney illustration of the hero John Henry was created in 1994 for the book *John Henry,* written by Julius Lester. Illustration by Jerry Pinkney. From *John Henry* by Julius Lester. Illustration Copyright © 1994 Jerry Pinkney. Used with permission of Dial Books for Young Readers, a division of Penguin Books USA Inc.

For instance, for a while I showed most of the figures and animals in my paintings from a close-up point of view. There's not very much depth in those compositions, usually. Now I'm doing just the opposite of that and moving back and seeing characters in a much larger setting. That keeps me interested in what I'm doing. I like variety.

6. *Do you ever put people you know in your pictures?*

Yes—especially my family. When my children were very young, they were always turning up in my work. I think Brian has been a major character in a book, and Myles and Scott and Troy have been on covers. Gloria, my wife, models for me all the time and also helps take photographs of the models.

Very often, when I get a manuscript I have to find models for the characters in the story. They're people that I don't know or don't know very well, and, with the way I work, I like to introduce the models to the text and often have them act it out. Before it's all over, I end up knowing them very, very well because we've shared this kind of experience.

7. *What do you use to make your pictures?*

My work is done in pencil and watercolor on paper, usually. But I tend to use a lot of different media along with the watercolor: pastel,[5] color pencils, and Cray-Pas.[6] My worktable is just full of all these materials, and I use whatever I think will help me in getting the kind of effect that I want for the pictures.

8. *How did you get to do your first book?*

My first book, *The Adventures of Spider* by Joyce Arkhurst, was published by Little, Brown in 1964. The book came as a result of my being in the Boston area, where there are certainly a lot of book publishers. I had gotten some very nice recognition from art shows in which my work had appeared.

I think that it also had a lot to do with the climate of the times. There were publishers who were interested in publishing African-American writers. I think there was an awareness, if not pressure, that the African-American artist could perhaps bring something unique to a text, something more personal. The publishers were actually looking for someone black to do this particular project, which was a collection of West African folktales. I showed them my portfolio, they liked my work, and that's how I got to do my first book. ❖

---

5. **pastel:** chalklike sticks in a wide variety of colors.
6. **Cray-Pas:** a brand name for pastel-like color sticks.

Water Color
by Paul Engle

The painter puts two thin lines
On one side of the page,
And one line on the other side.
Suddenly grass grows there!

5   Between them, a wavering line.
Water is moving!

Your two eyes look at me.
You lift one hand.

Suddenly my heart is growing
    toward you.
10 Suddenly I am moving toward
    you!

Paintbox (1984), Marilyn Groch. Oil on canvas, 36″ × 48″, private collection, courtesy of the artist.

WORDS
TO   **unique** (yōō-nēk′) *adj.* one of a kind
KNOW

RESPONDING

OPTIONS

FROM PERSONAL RESPONSE TO CRITICAL ANALYSIS

REFLECT 1. Do you find Jerry Pinkney admirable? Record your reactions in your notebook.

RETHINK 2. In the interview, Pinkney reveals—directly and indirectly—some basic ideas that are important to him and his work. What would you identify as the rules or guidelines he seems to follow?

Consider

- his typical workday
- his personal commitment to African-American art and history
- his comments about the enjoyment and challenges he finds in his work

3. For Jerry Pinkney, working with John Liney provided a proving ground for his future career. On the basis of this interview and your own ideas, how necessary do you think it is for a person with a talent to look for guidance in developing it?

4. After reading Pinkney's comments, would you consider choosing book illustration as a career? Why or why not?

RELATE 5. In what ways does the Insight poem "Water Color" on page 411 help you understand Jerry Pinkney's comments about being an illustrator?

6. Thomas Edison, the famous American inventor, once wrote, "Genius is one percent inspiration and ninety-nine percent perspiration." How important do you think inspiration, hard work, and discipline are to success?

ANOTHER PATHWAY

Take the role of Jerry Pinkney and prepare a first-person monologue about yourself to deliver to the class. You might begin with a simple introduction, such as, "Hi! I'm Jerry Pinkney. Let me tell you a little bit about myself." Try to cover as much of the information presented in the interview as possible. Also, try to be true to the tone Pinkney uses in the interview.

QUICKWRITES

1. Look at the illustration by Jerry Pinkney on page 409. Write a **review** of the work for an art magazine.

2. Write a **dedication** for one of Pinkney's books in which Pinkney dedicates the book to John Liney, the illustrator who first helped him.

3. Write up a **schedule** for a typical work day in the life of Jerry Pinkney.

📁 *PORTFOLIO Save your writing. You may want to use it later as a springboard to a piece for your portfolio.*

LITERARY CONCEPTS

An **interview** is a meeting in which a person answers questions about professional or personal matters. Interviews may be tape-recorded, filmed, or recorded in written accounts. An interview allows the reader to learn information and form conclusions about a person as if the reader were asking the questions. What additional questions would you have asked Jerry Pinkney?

ART CONNECTION

The illustration from the book *John Henry* (page 410) portrays the strength of the man who could dig through a mountain faster than a steam drill could.

One critic commented that Pinkney's illustrations show John Henry's energy as "bursting from nature." If you were interviewed about Pinkney's work, what would you say about this illustration?

Detail from an illustration by Jerry Pinkney. From *John Henry* by Julius Lester.

PAT CUMMINGS

Born in Chicago, Pat Cummings (1950–) is a children's author and illustrator. She grew up in Germany and Japan, as well as Illinois, New York, Virginia, Kansas, and Massachusetts, because her father's career with the U.S. Army required frequent moves. As a child, she was often excluded because of her African-American background. She has resolved to create works that appeal to people of all races and has refused to illustrate stories containing negative stereotypes.

Pat Cummings has been both writer and illustrator of four books for young people. Two were inspired by her brother Artie's imaginary childhood friend, Jimmy Lee. Her books feature people of all races taking positive approaches to everyday problems. She says, "I feel the best stories allow a child to discover a solution or approach to their own situation." *Talking with Artists* received the *Boston Globe/Horn Book* Award for nonfiction in 1992.

OTHER WORKS *Jimmy Lee Did It; C.L.O.U.D.S.; Clean Your Room, Harvey Moon!; Petey Moroni's Camp Runamok Diary*

LASERLINKS
• AUTHOR BACKGROUND
• ART GALLERY

PREVIEWING

The White Umbrella
Gish Jen

PERSONAL CONNECTION

With a small group of classmates, discuss the idea of "keeping up appearances." What does the expression mean? How important is keeping up appearances to you? In what ways do you and people you've observed keep up appearances? Share your group's ideas with the class as a whole.

CULTURAL CONNECTION

Because the 12-year-old narrator of "The White Umbrella" wants to keep up appearances, she is embarrassed that her mother has to work outside the home. At the time the story probably takes place, relatively few mothers had entered the work force. In 1965, only 35 percent of mothers in the United States had jobs. By 1992, however, over 67 percent of mothers worked outside the home.

READING CONNECTION

Making Inferences You make inferences when you "read between the lines," or use general knowledge and your own experience to fill in details about what you are reading. In this story, for example, Miss Crosman, a piano teacher, offers her students food, a ride home, and dry towels. From this information, you can infer that Miss Crosman is a concerned and warm-hearted person. As you read, look for words or actions that will help you make inferences about the personality of the narrator, a character concerned with keeping up appearances. A chart similar to the one below might help you organize your thoughts.

Information from the Story

Miss Crosman brought a blanket and the umbrella to the narrator.

What I Know from Experience

Being wet from rain makes a person cold.

Inference

Miss Crosman is concerned, kind, and thoughtful.

The White Umbrella

by Gish Jen

When I was twelve, my mother went to work without telling me or my little sister.

"Not that we need the second income." The lilt of her accent drifted from the kitchen up to the top of the stairs, where Mona and I were listening.

"No," said my father, in a barely <u>audible</u> voice. "Not like the Lee family."

The Lees were the only other Chinese family in town. I remembered how sorry my parents had felt for Mrs. Lee when she started waitressing downtown the year before; and so when my mother began coming home late, I didn't say anything and tried to keep Mona from saying anything either.

"But why shouldn't I?" she argued. "Lots of people's mothers work."

"Those are American people," I said.

"So what do you think we are? I can do the pledge of allegiance with my eyes closed."

Nevertheless, she tried to be <u>discreet</u>; and if my mother wasn't home by 5:30, we would start cooking by ourselves, to make sure dinner would be on time. Mona would wash the vegetables and put on the rice; I would chop.

For weeks we wondered what kind of work she was doing. I imagined that she was selling perfume, testing dessert recipes for the local newspaper. Or maybe she was working for the florist. Now that she had learned to drive, she might be delivering boxes of roses to people.

"I don't think so," said Mona as we walked to our piano lesson after school. "She would've hit something by now."

A gust of wind littered the street with leaves.

"Maybe we better hurry up," she went on, looking at the sky. "It's going to pour."

"But we're too early." Her lesson didn't begin until 4:00, mine until 4:30, so we usually tried to walk as slowly as we could. "And anyway, those aren't the kind of clouds that rain. Those are cumulus clouds."[1]

We arrived out of breath and wet.

"Oh, you poor, poor dears," said old Miss Crosman. "Why don't you call me the next time it's like this out? If your mother won't drive you, I can come pick you up."

"No, that's okay," I answered. Mona wrung her hair out on Miss Crosman's rug. "We just couldn't get the roof of our car to close, is all. We took it to the beach last summer and got sand in the mechanism." I pronounced this last word carefully, as if the credibility of my lie depended on its middle syllable. "It's never been the same." I thought for a second. "It's a convertible."

"Well then make yourselves at home." She exchanged looks with Eugenie Roberts, whose lesson we were interrupting. Eugenie smiled good-naturedly. "The towels are in the closet across from the bathroom."

Huddling at the end of Miss Crosman's nine-foot leatherette couch, Mona and I watched Eugenie play. She was a grade ahead of me and, according to school rumor, had a boyfriend in high school. I believed it. . . . She had auburn hair, blue eyes, and, I noted with a particular pang,[2] a pure white folding umbrella.

"I can't see," whispered Mona.

"So clean your glasses."

"My glasses *are* clean. You're in the way."

I looked at her. "They look dirty to me."

"That's because *your* glasses are dirty."

Eugenie came bouncing to the end of her piece.

"Oh! Just stupendous!" Miss Crosman hugged her, then looked up as Eugenie's mother walked in. "Stupendous!" she said again. "Oh! Mrs. Roberts! Your daughter has a gift, a real gift. It's an honor to teach her."

Mrs. Roberts, radiant with pride, swept her daughter out of the room as if she were royalty, born to the piano bench. Watching the way Eugenie carried herself, I sat up and concentrated so hard on sucking in my stomach that I did not realize until the Robertses were gone that Eugenie had left her umbrella. As Mona began to play, I jumped up and ran to the window, meaning to call to them—only to see their brake lights flash then fade at the stop sign at the corner. As if to allow them passage, the rain had let up; a quivering sun lit their way.

---

1. **cumulus** (kyōom′yə-ləs) **clouds:** clouds with flat bottoms and fluffy, rounded tops.

2. **pang:** a sudden feeling of longing or distress.

Girl at Piano (1966), Will Barnet. Oil on canvas, 64" × 39", private collection. Copyright © 1995 Will Barnet/Licensed by VAGA, New York.

The umbrella glowed like a scepter[3] on the blue carpet while Mona, slumping over the keyboard, managed to eke out[4] a fair rendition of a cat fight. At the end of the piece, Miss Crosman asked her to stand up.

"Stay right there," she said, then came back a minute later with a towel to cover the bench. "You must be cold," she continued. "Shall I call your mother and have her bring over some dry clothes?"

"No," answered Mona. "She won't come because she . . ."

"She's too busy," I broke in from the back of the room.

"I see." Miss Crosman sighed and shook her head a little. "Your glasses are filthy, honey," she said to Mona. "Shall I clean them for you?"

Sisterly embarrassment seized me. Why hadn't Mona wiped her lenses when I told her to? As she <u>resumed</u> abuse of the piano, I stared at the umbrella. I wanted to open it, twirl it around by its slender silver handle; I wanted to dangle it from my wrist on the way to school the way the other girls did. I wondered what Miss Crosman would say if I offered to bring it to Eugenie at school tomorrow. She would be impressed with my consideration for others; Eugenie would be pleased to have it back; and I would have possession of the umbrella for an entire night. I looked at it again, toying with the idea of asking for one for Christmas. I knew, however, how my mother would react.

"Things," she would say. "What's the matter with a raincoat? All you want is things, just like an American."

Sitting down for my lesson, I was careful to keep the towel under me and sit up straight.

"I'll bet you can't see a thing either," said Miss Crosman, reaching for my glasses. "And you can relax, you poor dear. . . . This isn't a boot camp."[5]

When Miss Crosman finally allowed me to start playing, I played extra well, as well as I possibly could. See, I told her with my fingers.

---

3. **scepter** (sĕp′tər): the rod or baton a ruler holds as a sign of authority.
4. **eke out:** to get or produce with great struggle.
5. **boot camp:** a military base where new members of the armed forces receive basic training.

You don't have to feel sorry for me.

"That was wonderful," said Miss Crosman. "Oh! Just wonderful."

An entire constellation rose in my heart.

"And guess what," I announced proudly. "I have a surprise for you."

Then I played a second piece for her, a much more difficult one that she had not assigned.

"Oh! That was stupendous," she said without hugging me. "Stupendous! You are a genius, young lady. If your mother had started you younger, you'd be playing like Eugenie Roberts by now!"

I looked at the keyboard, wishing that I had still a third, even more difficult piece to play for her. I wanted to tell her that I was the school spelling bee champion, that I wasn't ticklish, that I could do karate.

"My mother is a concert pianist," I said.

She looked at me for a long moment, then finally, without saying anything, hugged me. I didn't say anything about bringing the umbrella to Eugenie at school.

The steps were dry when Mona and I sat down to wait for my mother.

"Do you want to wait inside?" Miss Crosman looked anxiously at the sky.

"No," I said. "Our mother will be here any minute."

"In a while," said Mona.

"Any minute," I said again, even though my mother had been at least twenty minutes late every week since she started working.

According to the church clock across the street we had been waiting twenty-five minutes when Miss Crosman came out again.

"Shall I give you ladies a ride home?"

> *I could not believe that I was actually holding the umbrella.*

"No," I said. "Our mother is coming any minute."

"Shall I at least give her a call and remind her you're here? Maybe she forgot about you."

"I don't think she *forgot,*" said Mona.

"Shall I give her a call anyway? Just to be safe?"

"I bet she already left," I said. "How could she forget about us?"

Miss Crosman went in to call.

"There's no answer," she said, coming back out.

"See, she's on her way," I said.

"Are you sure you wouldn't like to come in?"

"No," said Mona.

"Yes," I said. I pointed at my sister. "She meant yes too. She meant no, she wouldn't like to go in."

Miss Crosman looked at her watch. "It's 5:30 now, ladies. My pot roast will be coming out in fifteen minutes. Maybe you'd like to come in and have some then?"

"My mother's almost here," I said. "She's on her way."

We watched and watched the street. I tried to imagine what my mother was doing; I tried to imagine her writing messages in the sky, even though I knew she was afraid of planes. I watched as the branches of Miss Crosman's big willow tree started to sway; they had all been trimmed to exactly the same height off the ground, so that they looked beautiful, like hair in the wind.

It started to rain.

"Miss Crosman is coming out again," said Mona.

"Don't let her talk you into going inside," I whispered.

"Why not?"

"Because that would mean Mom isn't really coming any minute."

"But she isn't," said Mona. "She's *working*."

"Shhh! Miss Crosman is going to hear you."

"She's working! She's working! She's working!"

I put my hand over her mouth, but she licked it, and so I was wiping my hand on my wet dress when the front door opened.

"We're getting even *wetter*," said Mona right away. "Wetter and wetter."

"Shall we all go in?" Miss Crosman pulled Mona to her feet. "Before you young ladies catch pneumonia? You've been out here an hour already."

"We're *freezing*." Mona looked up at Miss Crosman. "Do you have any hot chocolate? We're going to catch *pneumonia*."

"I'm not going in," I said. "My mother's coming any minute."

"Come on," said Mona. "Use your *noggin*."[6]

"Any minute."

"Come on, Mona," Miss Crosman opened the door. "Shall we get you inside first?"

"See you in the hospital," said Mona as she went in. "See you in the hospital with *pneumonia*."

I stared out into the empty street. The rain was pricking me all over; I was cold; I wanted to go inside. I wanted to be able to let myself go inside. If Miss Crosman came out again, I decided, I would go in.

She came out with a blanket and the white umbrella.

I could not believe that I was actually holding the umbrella, opening it. It sprang up by itself as if it were alive, as if that were what it wanted to do—as if it belonged in my hands, above my head. I stared up at the network of silver spokes, then spun the umbrella around and around and around. It was so clean and white that it seemed to glow, to <u>illuminate</u> everything around it. "It's beautiful," I said.

M iss Crosman sat down next to me, on one end of the blanket. I moved the umbrella over so that it covered that too. I could feel the rain on my left shoulder and shivered. She put her arm around me.

"You poor, poor dear."

I knew that I was in store for another bolt of sympathy, and braced myself by staring up into the umbrella.

"You know, I very much wanted to have children when I was younger," she continued.

"You did?"

She stared at me a minute. Her face looked dry and crusty, like day-old frosting.

"I did. But then I never got married."

I twirled the umbrella around again.

"This is the most beautiful umbrella I have ever seen," I said. "Ever, in my whole life."

"Do you have an umbrella?"

"No. But my mother's going to get me one just like this for Christmas."

"Is she? I tell you what. You don't have to wait until Christmas. You can have this one."

"But this one belongs to Eugenie Roberts," I protested. "I have to give it back to her tomorrow in school."

"Who told you it belongs to Eugenie? It's not Eugenie's. It's mine. And now I'm giving it to you, so it's yours."

"It is?"

She hugged me tighter. "That's right. It's all yours."

---

6. **noggin:** head.

Japanese Rain on Canvas (1972), David Hockney. Acrylic on canvas, 48″ × 48″. Copyright © David Hockney.

"It's mine?" I didn't know what to say. "Mine?" Suddenly I was jumping up and down in the rain. "It's beautiful! Oh! It's beautiful!" I laughed.

Miss Crosman laughed too, even though she was getting all wet.

"Thank you, Miss Crosman. Thank you very much. Thanks a zillion. It's beautiful. It's *stupendous!*"

"You're quite welcome," she said.

"Thank you," I said again, but that didn't seem like enough. Suddenly I knew just what she wanted to hear. "I wish you were my mother."

Right away I felt bad.

"You shouldn't say that," she said, but her face was opening into a huge smile as the lights of my mother's car cautiously turned the corner. I quickly collapsed the umbrella and put it up my skirt, holding onto it from the outside, through the material.

"Mona!" I shouted into the house. "Mona! Hurry up! Mom's here! I told you she was coming!"

Then I ran away from Miss Crosman, down to the curb. Mona came tearing up to my side as my mother neared the house. We both backed up a few feet so that in case she went onto the curb, she wouldn't run us over.

"But why didn't you go inside with Mona?" my mother asked on the way home. She had taken off her own coat to put over me and had the heat on high.

"She wasn't using her noggin," said Mona, next to me in the back seat.

I should call next time," said my mother. "I just don't like to say where I am."

That was when she finally told us that she was working as a check-out clerk in the A&P. She was supposed to be on the day shift, but the other employees were unreliable, and her boss had promised her a promotion if she would stay until the evening shift filled in.

For a moment no one said anything. Even Mona seemed to find the <u>revelation</u> disappointing.

"A promotion already!" she said, finally.

I listened to the windshield wipers.

"You're so quiet." My mother looked at me in the rear view mirror. "What's the matter?"

"I wish you would quit," I said after a moment.

She sighed. "The Chinese have a saying: one beam cannot hold the roof up."

"But Eugenie Roberts's father supports their family."

She sighed once more. "Eugenie Roberts's father is Eugenie Roberts's father," she said.

As we entered the downtown area, Mona started leaning hard against me every time the car turned right, trying to push me over. Remembering what I had said to Miss Crosman, I tried to <u>maneuver</u> the umbrella under my leg so she wouldn't feel it.

"What's under your skirt?" Mona wanted to know as we came to a traffic light. My mother, watching us in the rear view mirror again, rolled slowly to a stop.

"What's the matter?" she asked.

"There's something under her skirt," said Mona, pulling at me. "Under her skirt."

Meanwhile, a man crossing the street started to yell at us. "Who do you think you are, lady?" he said. "You're blocking the whole crosswalk."

We all froze. Other people walking by stopped to watch.

"Didn't you hear me?" he went on, starting to thump on the hood with his fist. "Don't you speak English?"

My mother began to back up, but the car behind us honked. Luckily, the light turned green right after that. She sighed in relief.

"What were you saying, Mona?" she asked.

We wouldn't have hit the car behind us that hard if he hadn't been moving too but as it was, our car bucked violently, throwing us all first back and then forward.

"Uh oh," said Mona when we stopped. "Another accident."

I was relieved to have attention <u>diverted</u> from the umbrella. Then I noticed my mother's head, tilted back onto the seat. Her eyes were closed.

"Mom!" I screamed. "Mom! Wake up!"

She opened her eyes. "Please don't yell," she said. "Enough people are going to yell already."

"I thought you were dead," I said, starting to cry. "I thought you were dead."

She turned around, looked at me intently, then put her hand to my forehead.

"Sick," she <u>confirmed</u>. "Some kind of sick is giving you crazy ideas."

As the man from the car behind us started tapping on the window, I moved the umbrella away from my leg. Then Mona and my mother were getting out of the car. I got out after them; and while everyone else was inspecting the damage we'd done, I threw the umbrella down a sewer. ❖

WORDS TO KNOW

revelation (rĕv′ə-lā′shən) *n.* something made known to others
maneuver (mə-nōō′vər) *v.* to guide or direct through a series of movements
diverted (dĭ-vûr′tĭd) *adj.* turned away **divert** *v.*
confirm (kən-fûrm′) *v.* to make certain

421

RESPONDING
O P T I O N S

FROM PERSONAL RESPONSE TO CRITICAL ANALYSIS

REFLECT   1. What was your reaction as you finished reading?

RETHINK   2. Why do you think the narrator throws the umbrella down a sewer?
   Consider
   • why she admires the umbrella
   • her mixed feelings about accepting the umbrella
   • her reaction to the accident

3. How important do you think keeping up appearances is to each of the sisters?

4. What can you infer about the kind of person the girls' mother is? Explain, using examples from the story and from your own experience.

RELATE   5. When the mother in this story points out that "lots of people's mothers work," her daughter replies, "Those are American people." The family seems unsure as to how it fits into the American culture. In what ways do you think people should change when they move to a different country?

ANOTHER PATHWAY
Cooperative Learning
Work with some classmates, using a graphic image of an umbrella, to create a story map for "The White Umbrella." Pick one segment of the open umbrella in which to describe the first scene in the story. Then record each remaining scene in the story.

Event 1
Event 2
Event 3

LITERARY CONCEPTS

A **symbol** is a person, place, or object that stands for something beyond itself. In literature, objects and images are used to symbolize things that cannot actually be seen, such as an idea or feeling. In "Cricket in the Road," for example, the bat and ball might symbolize the friendship between Selo, Vern, and Amy. When the children separate for a time, Selo throws them away. When the friends are reunited, a new bat takes on the same meaning. What do you think the white umbrella in this story might symbolize?

QUICKWRITES

1. Write a **motto,** or saying, that might hang on this family's kitchen wall. Use what you have learned about the family's values to choose an appropriate motto.

2. Write the text for a **Mother's Day card** that the narrator might give to her mother. Include comments that relate directly to the events in the story.

PORTFOLIO Save your writing. You may want to use it later as a springboard to a piece for your portfolio.

CRITIC'S CORNER

A member of the student board that reviewed the stories in this book says, "I liked how the story was told by the main character. When a story is written like this, I think it makes it more interesting, because you see how the main character feels." Do you agree that having the main character as a first-person narrator makes the story more interesting? Why or why not?

WORDS TO KNOW

On your own paper, answer the following questions.

1. Which cannot be what it was before if it becomes a **revelation**—a government, a secret, or a promise?

2. With which can you **confirm** the spelling of a word—a pen, an eraser, or a dictionary?

3. With which would you **illuminate** a house—lamps, a roof, or a bulldozer?

4. What does a baseball player use to try to **divert** a thrown ball—a glove or a catcher's mask?

5. Would a **discreet** person be most likely to behave in a rude, cautious, or bold way?

6. When you are eating, is the most **audible** food a raw carrot, a cupcake, or a hamburger?

7. What do you have to do before you can **resume** something—finish it, repeat it, or pause?

8. Would a person who saw something that was truly **stupendous** be most likely to yawn, giggle, or gasp?

9. If a person is known for **credibility,** what is his or her reputation for—honesty, bravery, or sassiness?

10. If someone wanted to **maneuver** a car, what would his or her concern be—stopping it, steering it, or affording it?

GISH JEN

1956–

A daughter of immigrant Chinese parents, Gish Jen grew up just north of New York City. She remembers her family feeling the need to fit in—to be absorbed into the main culture. "We were almost the only Asian-American family in town," she recalls. "People threw things at us and called us names. We thought it was normal—it was only much later that I realized it had been hard." Jen says these experiences did not make her childhood unhappy. In fact, her writing contains a great deal of humor.

Jen's first name is really Lillian. She adopted the name Gish, the last name of the famous silent-picture actress Lillian Gish, just for fun in high school. After Jen graduated from college, she went to China to teach English and later enrolled in The Writer's Workshop, a well-known program at the University of Iowa, where she wrote "The White Umbrella."

About her writing, Jen says, "If there is one thing I hope readers come away with, it's to see Asian Americans as 'us' rather than 'other.'"
OTHER WORKS *Typical American*

POETRY

Concrete Cat
Dorthi Charles

Chang McTang McQuarter Cat
John Ciardi

PERSONAL CONNECTION

Have you heard the expression "Curiosity killed the cat"? What other qualities or traits come to mind when you think of cats? Draw a picture similar to the one shown, and write a quality you think of on each "whisker." As you read, see how your ideas about cats compare with those presented in the poems.

SCIENCE CONNECTION

Cats, which belong to the scientific family of animals called *Felidae,* have a history dating back about 55 million years. The ancestors of the cats we know today were the African wildcat, the Kaffir cat, and the European wildcat.

The Egyptians were probably the first to tame cats, which they did around 3500 B.C. Cats were useful because they protected the Egyptian storehouses of grain from rats and mice. Egyptians admired the sleek and graceful form of cats and duplicated it in sculpture, furniture, and jewelry. By 1500 B.C., the Egyptians had come to view cats as sacred. The sculpture shown is a representation of the goddess Bastet or Bast, who was also depicted by ancient Egyptians with the head of a cat and the body of a woman.

Around 900 B.C., Phoenician traders carried Egyptian cats to Europe, where they bred with European wildcats to produce the ordinary house cat. European explorers, colonists, and traders brought such cats to North and South America in the 1700s.

The goddess Bastet in the form of a cat (about 664–610 B.C.) Egyptian bronze, The Granger Collection, New York.

READING CONNECTION

Concrete Poems Although these two poems share the same subject, they are very different in form. "Chang McTang McQuarter Cat" has a regular pattern of both rhyme and rhythm. "Concrete Cat" is called a concrete poem. In concrete poetry, the poet arranges the words into a special shape or picture. The image helps reveal the poem's meaning. For example, a concrete poem about spring might be presented in the shape of a flower.

LASERLINKS
• *SCIENCE CONNECTION*

CONCRETE CAT

BY DORTHI CHARLES

eAr   eAr
eYe   eYe   stripestripestripestripe   t a i l t a i l
whisker   whisker   stripestripestripe
whisker   whisker   stripestripestripestripes
         m   h   stripestripestripe
          o U t   stripestripestripestripe

         paw paw   paw paw

                                               əsnou

     dishdish   litterbox
                                       litterbox

FROM **PERSONAL RESPONSE** *TO* **CRITICAL ANALYSIS**

REFLECT 1. What was your impression of the concrete poem "Concrete Cat"?

RETHINK 2. Why do you think the mouse is upside down?

3. What effect do you think the poet was trying to convey?

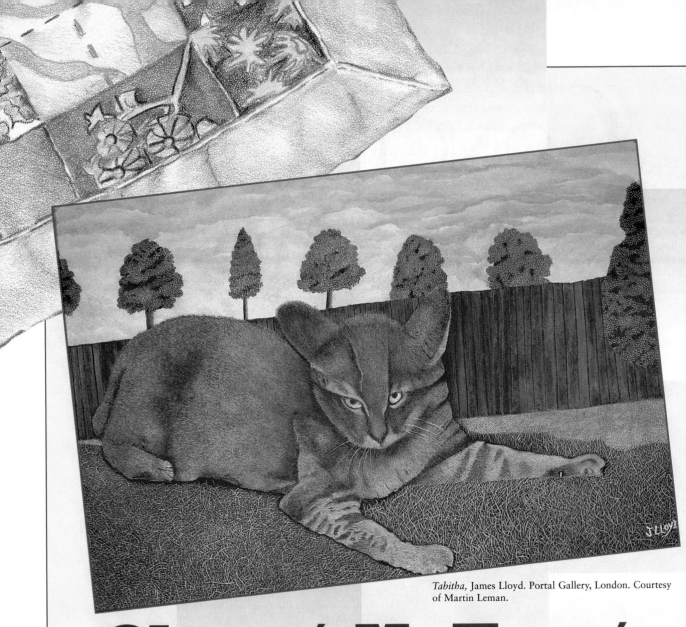

Tabitha, James Lloyd. Portal Gallery, London. Courtesy of Martin Leman.

Chang McTang
McQuarter Cat

BY JOHN CIARDI

Chang McTang McQuarter Cat
Is one part this and one part that.
One part is yowl, one part is purr.
One part is scratch, one part is fur.
5 One part, maybe even two,
Is how he sits and stares right through
You and you and you and you.
And when you feel my Chang-Cat stare
You wonder if you're really there.

10 Chang McTang McQuarter Cat
Is one part this and ten parts that.
He's one part saint, and two parts sin.
One part yawn, and three parts grin,
One part sleepy, four parts lightning,
15 One part cuddly, five parts fright'ning,
One part snarl, and six parts play.
One part is how he goes away
Inside himself, somewhere miles back
Behind his eyes, somewhere as black
20 And green and yellow as the night
A jungle makes in full moonlight.

Chang McTang McQuarter Cat
Is one part this and twenty that.
One part is statue, one part tricks—
25 (One part, or six, or thirty-six.)

One part (or twelve, or sixty-three)
Is—Chang McTang belongs to ME!

Don't ask, "How many parts is that?"
Addition's nothing to a cat.

30 If you knew Chang, then you'd know this:
He's one part everything there is.

RESPONDING
OPTIONS

FROM **PERSONAL RESPONSE** TO **CRITICAL ANALYSIS**

REFLECT 1. What phrases or lines from "Chang McTang McQuarter Cat" stand out in your mind? Jot your favorite phrases or lines in your notebook.

RETHINK 2. How do you think the speaker feels about Chang McTang?

3. In two or three words, describe your impression of Chang McTang.

4. What do you think the speaker means by saying that Chang McTang is "one part everything there is"?

RELATE 5. Look again at the qualities of cats you recorded for the Personal Connection on page 424. Has reading "Concrete Cat" and "Chang McTang McQuarter Cat" changed your ideas about cats? Why or why not?

ANOTHER PATHWAY

How would you compare the "personalities" of the two cats in these poems? Look for photographs or illustrations in magazines that match your idea of what these cats would look like and how they would act. Create a collage of these images that you could show to younger children as you read the poems to them.

LITERARY CONCEPTS

The pattern of rhyme at the end of the lines of a poem is called the poem's **rhyme scheme.** A rhyme scheme is noted by assigning letters of the alphabet to the lines of a poem. The letters show which lines end with the same sounds. Here is the rhyme scheme of the first four lines of "Barbara Frietchie":

Up from the meadows rich with corn,	**A**
Clear in the cool September morn,	**A**
The clustered spires of Frederick stand	**B**
Green-walled by the hills of Maryland.	**B**

Select one stanza from "Chang McTang McQuarter Cat" and identify the rhyme scheme of that stanza.

CONCEPT REVIEW: Repetition The use of a word or phrase over and over in a literary work to get across a certain meaning is called repetition. Find an example of repetition in "Concrete Cat" and one in "Chang McTang McQuarter Cat."

QUICKWRITES

1. Write a **poem** about your own pet or another subject of your choice, using the style of either Dorthi Charles or John Ciardi.

2. Imagine you are Chang McTang. Write a **letter** to the speaker of the poem, expressing your outlook on life.

3. Draft a brief **story,** using Chang McTang as the main character. Make up any other characters you want in your story.

📁 **PORTFOLIO** *Save your writing. You may want to use it later as a springboard to a piece for your portfolio.*

LITERARY LINKS

Choose one of the characters from an earlier selection, and depict his or her most important qualities in a concrete poem.

CRITIC'S CORNER

The poet who wrote "Concrete Cat" once said, "A poem is most likely to arise when I haven't an idea in the world. It usually begins with a promising blob of language." How does that statement affect your understanding of "Concrete Cat"?

ACROSS THE CURRICULUM

Art Cats have found their way into paintings and sculptures, both ancient and contemporary. Use art books from your school or community library to find examples of cats portrayed in fine art. Prepare a cat-lover's guide to fine art, including a list of the paintings or sculptures you find, for your classmates to use.

Who's the Fairest of Them All? Frank Paton (1856-1909). Bonhams, London, Bridgeman/Art Resource, New York.

DORTHI CHARLES (X. J. KENNEDY)

Dorthi Charles (1929–) is a pen name of the well-known author and poet X. J. Kennedy. Kennedy spent a good deal of his youth producing hand-drawn cartoons similar to *Superman* and *Batman.* When he finally concluded he wasn't talented enough to pursue cartooning as a career, he turned to writing science fiction. It was eight years before he sold a story to a magazine.

Kennedy served for four years in the navy, where he began writing poetry during off-duty time. Eventually he sold two poems to *The New Yorker,* and his career as a poet was established. Kennedy now devotes himself to his work full-time.

Kennedy credits the poet Myra Cohn Livingston and the children's book editor Margaret McElderry for the encouragement and support that led to his writing for children. He notes, "It's writing for kids that's the most fun of all."

OTHER WORKS *One Winter Night in August and Other Nonsense Jingles; The Phantom Ice Cream Man; The Owlstone Crown*

JOHN CIARDI

1916–1986

The poet and critic John Ciardi was born in Boston to Italian immigrants in an area still referred to as Little Italy. His father died when Ciardi was only three years old, and his mother spoke little English. As he grew older, he discovered the advantages of being reared in a bilingual atmosphere.

From 1939 to 1961, Ciardi taught college English. He gave up teaching to become a full-time writer, and served as poetry editor of the *Saturday Review* from 1956 to 1977. About children's poetry he once said, "I dislike most of the children's poems I see because they seem written by a sponge dipped in warm milk and sprinkled with sugar." Motivated by his young nephews and later his own children, Ciardi himself began writing poetry for children, which is considered his most important literary contribution.

OTHER WORKS *The Reason for the Pelican, Scrappy the Pup, I Met a Man, The King Who Saved Himself from Being Saved*

PREVIEWING

NONFICTION

from Gold and Silver, Silver and Gold
Alvin Schwartz

PERSONAL CONNECTION

Through the ages, people have searched for hidden treasure and for instant wealth. Columbus was seeking the fabled treasure of the Indies in 1492, not a new continent. What urge compels people to pursue buried treasure and get-rich-quick schemes? Jot down on a sheet of paper some of the motives you think inspire people to enter sweep-stakes, buy lottery tickets, and invest in various easy-money offers. As you read, see whether your ideas about the pursuit of wealth change.

HISTORICAL CONNECTION

In the late 1690s, when Captain Kidd sailed the route shown on the map, England was at war with France on two fronts: in North America, over French expansion into the colonies, and in Europe, over a similar extension of French power. At the same time, piracy was rapidly increasing, as sea thieves plundered the coasts of North and South America and Africa, searching for treasure on any ships they encountered.

King William of England demanded that the new royal governor of New York eliminate piracy. Because the war with France left few ships available to chase pirates, the governor turned to privateers. Unlike pirates, privateers were hired and licensed by governments to capture and plunder enemy and pirate ships. They did not receive regular pay, only a share of any goods they captured. The crews of privateer ships were often undisciplined and disloyal. Some even resorted to mutiny, a rebellion of sailors against superior officers.

Captain Kidd's Voyage

NORTH AMERICA — Boston, New York, Cape Cod, Long Island
Mediterranean Sea
New Jersey
St. Thomas, St. Martin
Hispaniola
Caribbean Sea
Red Sea
AFRICA
INDIA
Bombay
SOUTH AMERICA
Atlantic Ocean
Indian Ocean
Pacific Ocean
MADAGASCAR
Miles
0 800 1600
N W E S

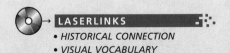

LASERLINKS
• *HISTORICAL CONNECTION*
• *VISUAL VOCABULARY*

Problem Solving

Many selections that you have read in this book involve one or more characters faced with a conflict or problem of some sort. Those problems may range from a physical challenge that must be overcome to a difficult situation that must be resolved. In any case, the selections often explore the characters' attempts to find solutions to their problems. In "Tuesday of the Other June," for example, the main character solves her problem with the "Other June" by physically standing up to her and refusing to accept her bullying.

One way to begin to understand a selection is to think about the problems it portrays and possible solutions to those problems. The chart shown provides some questions to keep in mind as you attempt to identify problems and solutions in a selection—and as you evaluate the end result.

Problem
- Who has the problem?
- What is the problem?
- Why is it a problem?

Solutions
- Which characters try to solve the problem?
- What attempts are made to solve the problem?
- How well do those possible solutions work?

End Result
- Is the problem completely resolved?
- Which attempted solution works in the end?
- Is the character with the problem satisfied with the end result?

In this selection, a number of problems are presented, along with some attempted solutions. Take advantage of the questions that you find as you read to help you understand the problems Captain Kidd and others face and their efforts to resolve them.

from

Gold and Silver, Silver and Gold

by Alvin Schwartz

Captain William Kidd was a shipmaster in New York City in the 1690s, when New York was an English colony. He lived with his wife and children in a big house on Liberty Street.

If anyone had accused Kidd of piracy, those who knew him would have laughed.

He was widely thought of as a decent, trustworthy man. In fact, he once had worked for the colonial government tracking down pirates in the waters around New York.

In those days, pirates plundered[1] British ships wherever they found them. It was such a problem that the king of England decided to crush them once and for all, and he ordered the royal governor of New York, the earl of Bellomont, to do so.

Governor Bellomont asked Kidd to take on the job. His orders were to capture as many pirates and pirate ships as he could in two years. He also was to capture any French ships he saw, because England was at war with France.

Bellomont bought Kidd a ship, the *Adventure Galley,* and armed it with thirty-four cannons. Kidd was to hire a crew. But there would be no money to pay them. Instead, they would get one-fourth of any booty[2] they took from the pirates or the French. If they took no booty, they would get no pay. Since few seamen would work under such conditions, Kidd could hire only wastrels[3] and drifters, some of whom were former pirates.

He left New York in September 1696 with one hundred and fifty-five men and sailed to the Madeira Islands off Africa. He continued south around the tip of Africa, into the Indian Ocean. Then he headed north toward the island of Madagascar, where many pirates made their headquarters. But Kidd did not find any.

In the five months since he'd left New York, he had not taken any booty, and his crew had not been paid. Frustrated and angry, they threatened to <u>mutiny</u>. But Kidd quieted them with talk of the dazzling riches that lay ahead.

---

1. **plundered:** robbed of goods by force.
2. **booty:** anything of value taken by force from an enemy, often gold, silver, and other treasures.
3. **wastrels** (wā′strəlz): loafers and good-for-nothings.

WORDS
TO
KNOW

mutiny (myōot′n-ē) *v.* to engage in open rebellion against authority

433

They set sail for the coast of India, where he hoped to find pirates.

Soon they came upon a merchant ship, the *Loyal Captain*. When she turned out to be a Dutch vessel, Kidd decided to send her on her way. But his crew had other ideas. They grabbed the guns on board and got ready to steal whatever she had.

"Let's take her!" they yelled.

"No!" Kidd cried. "She is not our enemy."

"We'll take her anyway!"

"Desert my ship," he warned, "and I'll turn my cannons on you."

CLARIFY

What problem confronts Captain Kidd at this point?

The mutiny died. But in a week or two, Kidd clashed with one of its leaders, a gunner named William Moore. Moore blamed him for not taking any ships. "You have brought us ruin," he snarled. Kidd struck him on the head with a bucket and killed him. The crew muttered and rumbled like distant thunder but did nothing. Later, the ballad writer wrote:

> *Many long leagues[4] from shore*
> *I murdered William Moore*
> *And laid him in his gore[5]*
> *when I sailed.*

The *Adventure Galley* and its crew sailed on. They came to a French ship that had been wrecked. Since France and England were at war, Kidd took what gold there was and shared it with his men. But this did not satisfy them. They continued to threaten him. They wanted him to attack every ship they saw, not just French or pirate ships.

Fearing for his life, Kidd finally gave in. He and his crew plundered several small vessels. Then they took a large merchant ship, the *November*, which was loaded with cotton and sugar. Two months later, they captured the *Quedah Merchant*, with a cargo of gold, silver, jewels, silk, and other goods.

Both were owned by the Great Mogul, the emperor of India. The Mogul traded with England, but he also traded with her enemy, France. When Kidd checked the papers of the two ships, he breathed a sigh of relief. He found that France had agreed to protect them as if they were French ships. Under his orders, it seemed that he could take them as prizes of war. Kidd kept their "French papers" as proof that he had done the right thing, even if he had done so by accident.

When the *Adventure Galley* sprung a leak, he set sail for the port of St. Marie in Madagascar and took the Mogul's ships with him. What happened to their crews is not known. But on the way, some of Kidd's crew mutinied again. They stole what they could from the *November*, then sank it.

When Kidd and his men arrived at St. Marie, the *Adventure Galley* was leaking badly. To add to his troubles, Kidd found a pirate ship, the *Mocha Frigate*, tied up there. Kidd ordered the pirates to surrender, but they fled into the woods.

He told his crew to go after them, but most decided to join the pirates. They brought the pirates back from where they were hiding, then gave Kidd his choice of also turning pirate or losing his life.

PREDICT

How do you think Captain Kidd will handle this situation?

He locked himself in his cabin on the *Adventure Galley*, loaded forty pistols, and waited for them to attack. Instead, they boarded Kidd's other ship, the *Quedah Merchant*, moved part of her cargo to the *Mocha Frigate*, and sailed away. But in their

---

4. **leagues:** units of distance equal to about three miles each.
5. **gore:** blood from a wound.

Captain Kidd on Gardiner's Island (1894), Howard Pyle. Courtesy of Nedra Matteucci's Fenn Galleries, Santa Fe, New Mexico.

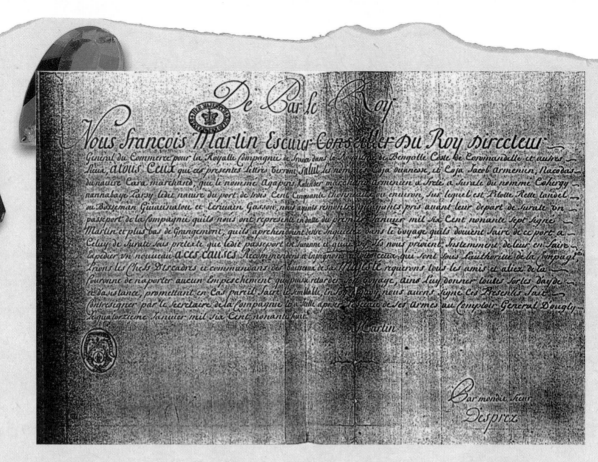

The all-important "French papers" that Kidd hoped would prove his innocence—but which mysteriously disappeared. Public Record Office, England.

haste they left behind a treasure trove of gold, silver, and jewels.

When the *Adventure Galley* began to sink where it was anchored, Kidd burned it. He then set sail for home in the *Quedah Merchant* with the seamen who had remained loyal. It was two and a half years since he had left New York.

Meanwhile, the Great Mogul had complained to England that Kidd had stolen his ships. The English quickly charged Kidd with piracy. It was a crime that carried the penalty of death, and they began to hunt him down. Only when he stopped for supplies in the West Indies did he learn that he was a hunted man.

Kidd was not sure that he could count on Governor Bellomont to help clear him. As insurance, he bought a sloop called the *San Antonio*, and with this new ship and the *Quedah Merchant*, he sailed to Hispaniola.[6] There he moved the treasure from the *Quedah Merchant* to the *San Antonio*. He hid the *Quedah Merchant* and the rest of its cargo in a small cove and left part of his crew to guard it. If he needed to, he would try to trade the ship for a pardon from the charge of piracy.

Kidd sailed north on the *San Antonio* to Delaware Bay, where he stopped for supplies. Then he moved on toward New York City, anchoring nearby at Oyster Bay. He sent a note to his wife and a letter to a lawyer named James Emmot, who had defended other men charged with piracy. Would he see Governor Bellomont for him?

---

6. **Hispaniola** (hĭs′pən-yō′lə): an island in the West Indies.

Emmot agreed to do so, and he and Kidd met on the *San Antonio*. Kidd told him that he was not a pirate, that he had taken the Mogul's ships as part of England's war with France. He gave him the French papers to show Bellomont as proof of this.

Since Bellomont was in Boston, Kidd sailed with Emmot to Rhode Island. There he put him ashore, and the lawyer made his way by land to see the governor. Kidd waited on the *San Antonio*.

PREDICT

Do you think Emmot's actions will solve Captain Kidd's problem?

Emmot returned in a few days. He had left the French papers with Bellomont as evidence of Kidd's innocence. And he had brought back a letter. Bellomont had written to Kidd: "If you are telling the truth, you will be safe from arrest. Come ashore and meet with me in Boston."

Kidd decided to see Bellomont, but he still did not completely trust him. He decided to leave the treasure aboard the *San Antonio* in a safe place. He sailed to Gardiner's Island, in Long Island Sound,[7] a hundred miles from New York City. There he left Emmot to make his way home, then he talked the owner of the island, a man named John Gardiner, into keeping part of the treasure for him. Gardiner buried it on the island. Some of Kidd's friends came aboard the *San Antonio* and took away the rest. Only then did Kidd set sail for Boston to see Bellomont.

But Bellomont had lied to him. When Kidd went ashore, he was arrested and sent to England in chains, to be tried for piracy. Bellomont told Kidd he had to arrest him. But he said he would send the French papers to England so that Kidd could use them at his trial. Whether he would keep his word this time remained to be seen.

Bellomont quickly seized the buried treasure on Gardiner's Island, as well as the treasure Kidd had given his friends to keep for him. It came to sixty-eight pounds of gold, one hundred and forty-three pounds of silver, and a pound of rubies, diamonds, and other jewels. Today the gold and silver alone would be worth half a million dollars. The governor also sent a crew to find the *Quedah Merchant* and its cargo.

At his trial in London, Kidd demanded the French papers Bellomont had promised to send. They were the only chance he had to save his life. But the government said there were no such papers, and Kidd was sentenced to hang for piracy.

It was the most famous trial of the day. As most people saw it, Kidd was a good man who had gone bad. The wildest tales were told of how wicked he had become and how much wealth he had. The ballad writer wrote of him:

I steered from sound to sound
And many ships I found
And most of them I burned
as I sailed . . .
I had ninety bars of gold
And dollars manifold[8]
With riches uncontrolled
as I sailed.

Captain Kidd rode to his execution, standing backward in a cart, a noose around his neck. Huge crowds jeered and pelted him with rubbish and rocks as he passed.

He was hanged three times. The first time the rope broke. So he was hanged a second time. Then his body was covered with tar and taken to the waterfront, where it was hung

---

7. **sound:** an inlet or arm of the ocean, surrounded on three sides by land and often used as a port or harbor for ships. Long Island Sound separates Long Island from Connecticut to the north.

8. **manifold:** many.

from another gallows[9]—a warning to seamen on passing ships not to become pirates.

There the story ends, and we return to the questions at the beginning. . . . Was Kidd really a pirate? And was there really a buried treasure?

There was a treasure, as we have seen, but it was buried for only a few weeks. Yet few knew it had been found, and people searched for it for more than two hundred years.

Whether Kidd was really a pirate is something that you must decide for yourself. Did he take the ships he captured because his crew forced him to do so? Or did he take them out of greed? Or was it both? Through song and story, Kidd became the symbol of every pirate. And his treasure, for which people searched for so long, became the symbol of every treasure. ❖

---

9. **gallows:** a platform built for the purpose of hanging a prisoner.

HISTORICAL INSIGHT

The History of Piracy

History shows that since the times of the early civilizations of the Middle East, piracy has existed wherever and whenever the rewards have outweighed the risks. Pirates plundered the ships of the Assyrian kingdoms along the coast of the Persian Gulf 3,000 years ago. Piracy appeared wherever sea trade offered tempting booty, including the ancient Mediterranean, among the Phoenicians, Greeks, Romans, and Carthaginians.

Hundreds of years later, in the Middle Ages, Vikings roamed the seas between the British Isles, Scandinavia, and the mainland of Europe. They plundered ships and murdered the crews. From the 1600s to the 1700s, piracy again flourished in the Mediterranean.

As countries competed to colonize the North American continent in the 1500s, piracy broke out in the Caribbean and lasted 300 years. Many pirates also sailed the Indian Ocean and the Red Sea, plundering the ships of the Great Mogul and bringing their booty thousands of miles to sell to colonists hungry for luxuries.

Probably the most famous of these pirates was Captain William Kidd. The increased size of merchant ships, the recognition by governments of piracy as an international offense, and action by navies of Great Britain and other countries eventually led to the end of piracy on almost all seas by the mid-1800s.

RESPONDING
OPTIONS

FROM PERSONAL RESPONSE TO CRITICAL ANALYSIS

REFLECT
1. What incident or fact in this account of William Kidd did you find most surprising? Compare your response with the responses of some of your classmates.

RETHINK
2. What conclusions have you come to about the kind of person Kidd was?

   Consider
   - his release of the Dutch ship *Loyal Captain*
   - his killing of the gunner William Moore
   - his theft of the Great Mogul's ships
   - his refusal to turn pirate with his crew at St. Marie

3. Do you sympathize with Kidd's predicament? Why or why not?

4. How would you answer the author's question "Was Kidd really a pirate?" Explain your response.

RELATE
5. After reading the selection, what, if anything, do you think today's lottery players and sweepstakes fans have in common with someone like Captain Kidd?

ANOTHER PATHWAY
Cooperative Learning

Work with a group to set up a television talk show in which Captain Kidd is the primary guest. Assign roles for the group to play, including that of the talk-show host. Present the facts from the perspective of each guest.

LITERARY CONCEPTS

Tone is an expression of the attitude a writer takes toward a subject. The writer's style and use of description help create tone. Often, understanding a writer's tone is a key factor in understanding a work of nonfiction. The writer's tone helps to establish the purpose for writing the work; it indicates how seriously the reader should accept the events in an account. For example, Don C. Reed uses an informal tone in "My First Dive with the Dolphins" because one of his purposes is to entertain. Find passages in Alvin Schwartz's account of William Kidd that reveal the tone. How would you describe the tone of this selection?

QUICKWRITES

1. Reread the ballad verses that are quoted in the selection. Write your own verse of a **ballad** about Captain Kidd.

2. Write a ship's **log entry** for the night at St. Marie when Kidd locked himself in his cabin.

3. Imagine that you are Captain Kidd. Draft the **last will and testament** that you would compose before going ashore in Boston.

   📁 *PORTFOLIO Save your writing. You may want to use it later as a springboard to a piece for your portfolio.*

ALTERNATIVE ACTIVITIES

1. Research pirate clothing or pirate ships. Design and construct **costumes** or **models** based on your research to display in your classroom.

2. *Cooperative Learning* Join a few classmates and form a legal team to defend Captain Kidd. Review the selection and come up with your own version of a **legal brief** in which you present an argument for finding Captain Kidd innocent of piracy. Present your legal brief to the class.

CRITIC'S CORNER

A number of writers, including Edgar Allan Poe and Robert Louis Stevenson, have referred to Captain Kidd in their writings. What elements of Kidd's experience do you think have made his story so popular among writers and storytellers?

WORDS TO KNOW

The name of Captain Kidd is forever linked with such words as *piracy, treasure, buccaneer,* and *mutiny.* Create a concept map for the word **mutiny,** using the model shown. *Mutiny* can be used as either a noun or a verb; be aware of which part of speech you are working with as you complete the map. Write a definition of the word, a synonym of it, and an example of its use. Compare your finished map with those of your classmates.

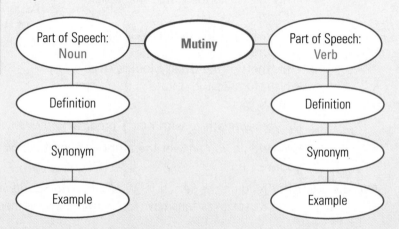

ALVIN SCHWARTZ

An author of many best-selling books for children, Alvin Schwartz (1927–1992) was born in Brooklyn, New York. He studied journalism in college and held various reporting and writing jobs until the 1960s, when he became a freelance writer. He went on to publish more than 50 books and received numerous awards and honors. Schwartz often collected folklore from the elderly and from children, whom he called "our strongest, most cohesive folk group."

Many of Schwartz's most popular books are collections of folk tales, tongue twisters, jokes, riddles, superstitions, and ghost stories. Schwartz believed that technology has caused people to rely less on themselves, and he saw folklore as a way to counter this change. He wanted readers to understand that they are all part of a living tradition, with the same joys, fears, anger, love, and need for dignity and security as people who lived long ago. His advice to students who read his books is: "Laugh when you can."

OTHER WORKS *Tomfoolery: Trickery and Foolery with Words, Kickle Snifters and Other Fearsome Critters, The Cat's Elbow and Other Secret Languages*

REFLECT
&
ASSESS

from

Champions

by Bill Littlefield

Copyright © Brooks Dodge/Sports File.

Twenty-odd years beyond required gym class, Diana Golden still remembers what it felt like to be the last one picked for the basketball team, or the volleyball team, or any other team. "Come on," she used to say under her breath as the ranks of the unpicked grew thin, "pick me, come on."

According to her recollection, nobody ever did. That was part of what led her to embrace skiing as a child. You didn't have to be picked for it. You could do it by yourself. And it wasn't a required sport.

When she'd gotten pretty good at it, somebody suggested that Diana should try out for a kids' ski racing team. She made the team but only lasted about two weeks. It was too serious. Too much competition. Too much like gym class. She returned to skiing for fun.

And then one day when she was twelve years old, Diana Golden's right leg collapsed under her. Weird, she thought. And then it happened again. When the doctors told her that the leg was cancerous and would have to be removed, she thought there had been some mistake. Cancer wasn't for twelve-year-olds. "Did you ask my grandfather?" she said. Granddaddy was a doctor, and he'd certainly tell these younger doctors they were wrong.

"He knows," they told her. "He agrees with us. We're sorry."

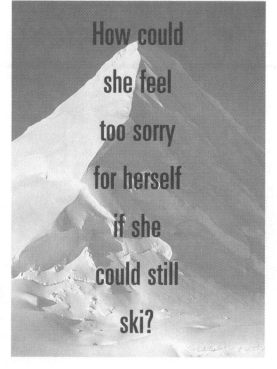

How could she feel too sorry for herself if she could still ski?

Diana Golden remembers that, after her surgery, she was brave while her parents and the doctors remained in the hospital room with her. But when they'd left her alone with her roommate, she cried for two hours. She couldn't remember ever seeing anyone with only one leg. She was sure her life would be a hopeless muddle of crutches, braces, mechanical legs, and pity from all quarters.[1] But eventually she ran out of tears, and her roommate said, "Hey, when you have a fake leg, maybe you'll be able to turn your foot around backwards." And Diana laughed.

Over the days that followed, it occurred to Diana to ask one of her doctors if she'd still be able to ski. "No reason why not," the doctor said. That helped, too. How could she feel too sorry for herself if she could still ski? And how could she feel sorry for herself when so many of the other children in the hospital with her would never enjoy that opportunity, or any other?

"I saw teenagers die," she remembered years later. "I saw a two-year-old die. *That* was the stuff that was hard to understand. Given those things, I never felt bitter, never wondered 'Why me?' I was *living*."

Within a few months after the removal of her leg, Diana Golden was back on the slopes. Of course she was still there on her own terms. She was a weekend hacker[2] who liked skiing well enough to learn how to do it on one leg, but she was hardly inclined to train or work at it.

Through her first two years in high school, Diana Golden remained a weekend skier. She didn't train for competition, but given the circumstances, she couldn't help but develop some technique. As she has said since, "It didn't take me long to figure out there'd be

---

1. **from all quarters:** from everyone everywhere.
2. **hacker:** an enthusiastic amateur.

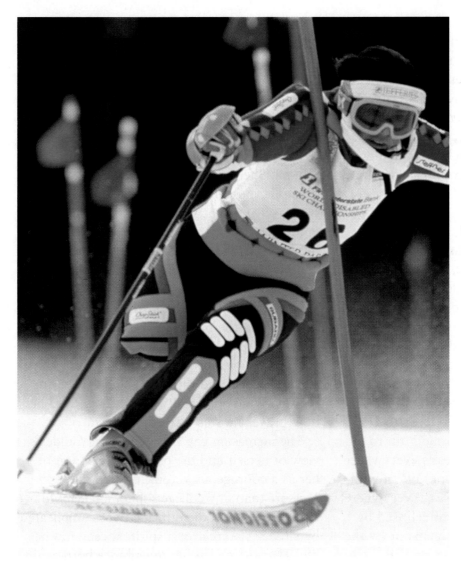

Diana Golden in action. Copyright © Brooks Dodge/Sports File.

would make a difference to me. He understood when he saw me skiing that I'd reached a point where working out, training, and pushing myself wouldn't be drudgery anymore. It wouldn't be gym class. And he was right. It was fun."

Within a few months Diana Golden, who had never done a pushup or a sit-up, was embarrassing the two-legged skiers with her workouts. "All of a sudden," as Golden remembered during a newspaper interview with Melanie Stephens years later, "I began to discover that I could train my body. It was wonderful. It was discovering the things that my body could do for me, discovering what it felt like to be strong."

By the winter of her senior year, Diana Golden had left klutziness[3] so far behind that it was hard to remember the bad old days. The rigorous training to strengthen her leg, her back, and her arms felt not only right, but indispensable. And the progress the training produced was nothing short of astonishing. Only a year after taking David Livermore up on his suggestion, Diana Golden was competing in the World Games for Disabled Athletes in Geilo, Norway. Within

no more snowplowing."

One afternoon during the winter of her junior year, a fellow in a ski parka and goggles flagged Diana Golden down on the slopes. When she'd skied up alongside him, she recognized the man as David Livermore, the skiing coach at Lincoln-Sudbury High School in Massachusetts, where Diana was a student. "Listen," Livermore said to her, "why don't you work out with the ski team?"

"He recruited me," Golden said later. "He's a perceptive man. He realized that the training

---

3. **klutziness:** clumsy awkwardness.

the same year she won the downhill event in the World Handicapped Championships and became the brightest star on the United States Disabled Ski Team. She was skiing so well that, as *Boston Globe* sportswriter Tony Chamberlain put it, "She seemed *advantaged.*" She had only one ski to worry about controlling, and she "moved back and forth down the hill with an unbroken motion as graceful as grass waving in a breeze."

That was, of course, an illusion. Skiing fast, like a lot of athletic feats, is harder than it looks. And skiing fast on one leg meant that Diana Golden had to cut from one edge of her ski to the other with more precision than most two-legged skiers could imagine. She had less margin for error because with one leg she had less opportunity to regain her balance when she lost it. Yet that sort of disadvantage never seemed to occur to Diana Golden. She was having too much fun to worry about it. She turned heads everywhere she skied, firing down the slopes like a wild bird, arms extended, snow flying everywhere. And the sense of fun was never eclipsed by the regimen of pushups and sit-ups or by the demands of competition. Once, at Vail, Colorado, when an out-of-control two-legged skier sent her sprawling and failed even to apologize, Golden bounced up, a look of mock horror spread across her face, and she shouted, "Hey, you! Look what you've done to my leg!"

By the time Diana Golden was ready to leave high school and enroll at Dartmouth College, the transformation was complete. "I was a total *anti*-klutz," she remembered. "Being a ski champion had become an image, the way I saw myself." She wasn't the only one who saw it that way. Even before she had graduated from high school, magazine and newspaper stories had begun to celebrate Diana Golden as not only a champion, but a hero, a role model, a courageous, inspirational athlete who had thumbed her nose at cancer and gone on not only to lead a full life but to win gold medals in the process.

Diana Golden didn't *feel* like a hero, though. She just felt like a skier who was doing her best to compete. Years later she would say, "What was heroic about me? People who stand up for what they believe are heroic. Martin Luther King. Nelson Mandela. Mother Theresa. Those are heroes . . . people who have done something wonderful for other people. I was just skiing fast." Sometimes the acclaim and the babbling about her courage got so strange that Golden could only laugh at it, like the time she was filling her car at a self-service station and the man behind the cash register, wide-eyed and well-meaning, told her how brave she was to be doing *that*.

The increasing gap between Diana Golden's view of herself and the public's perception of her as a courageous heroine created more pressure than any college sophomore should have to bear, and the difficulty was complicated by Golden's search for a spiritual center in her life. That search led her to embrace born-again Christianity, which in turn led to what Golden remembered as "a conflict between skiing and my desire to win on one hand, and my feeling of faith on the other. Skiing was one god, and God was another. I couldn't reconcile the demands of the two." Skiing began to make less and less sense. The praise heaped upon her in the sports columns and the magazine feature pieces rang more and more hollow. The attempt to figure out who she really was and what she wanted began to nudge training and racing out of Diana Golden's days.

Eventually Golden, who had practically defined herself through competitive skiing since David Livermore's fortuitous[4] suggestion four years earlier, gave it up entirely. Over her last two years at Dartmouth, which is smack in the heart of New Hampshire's ski country, she skied only three times, and she never raced. She studied, read, and gradually began to understand herself as a person who *had* skied, rather than as a skier.

Then during her senior year it dawned on Diana Golden that to allow the media to define her or to warp her understanding of herself might stunt her own growth. She began to feel that it was crazy to have quit doing something she loved because the papers and television spots might misrepresent her efforts, or because of her inability to reconcile her faith with her athletic ambitions. As she said in retrospect,[5] "I began to understand who I was under the roles I had taken." This isn't an easy thing for an athlete—particularly a very good athlete—to do. Young football players, basketball players, or skiers who constantly read about how brave, strong, and talented they are can have a hard time remembering that they are also fallible, entitled to goof, human.

For Diana Golden, that discovery didn't happen all at once, and when she graduated from Dartmouth, she wasn't ready to redevote herself absolutely to skiing. She took a job as a computer software salesperson. Personable, outgoing, and bright, she was good at her work. But before long she was bored. Maybe that's part of the reason she finally said "Sure" when some of her old friends proposed, for the umpteenth time, a ski weekend. Maybe they knew Diana well enough to figure that if they kept asking, she'd finally agree to go. But she surprised them once they'd all taken the lift to the top of the hill. In fact she delighted them by hopping with a giggle onto the slalom[6] course on the slope and tearing through the gates with all the joy and enthusiasm that had characterized her championship runs. By the time she reached the bottom of the mountain, she was halfway hooked on skiing again. All she needed was a gentle push from one more friend, who told her, "When you're thirty, you can do anything you want, but you won't be winning races. Go for it now."

She did. Some of her expertise came back quickly, but the layoff meant she had to work harder than ever to strengthen her knee, leg, stomach, and arms again. She trained with other so-called "disabled" skiers, but also with the two-legged variety, whom Golden called the "normies." With each group she would pick out somebody who was a little faster, a little more confident, a little more successful than she was. Then she would work at narrowing the gap between their performances, and eventually she would leave most of her rivals in a shower of snow.

She turned heads everywhere she skied, firing down the slopes like a wild bird, arms extended, snow flying everywhere.

---

4. **fortuitous:** lucky or fortunate.
5. **in retrospect:** in looking back on events.
6. **slalom** (slä'ləm): a downhill race over a zigzag course marked by poles or gates.

Soon Diana Golden realized that training was only part of the challenge. Because she wanted to compete all over the world against the best skiers she could find, she also had to work at finding a way to pay for the travel and living expenses. Sponsors! she thought, though this was an unprecedented[7] notion for a disabled athlete. She went to the Rossignol Ski Company and said, "You guys back two-legged skiers all the time. You give them equipment. You finance their trips and pay their expenses so folks will see them winning races on your skis. Do the same for me. But don't do it because I ski on one leg. Do it because I'm going to win races. And every time I do it, there'll be a picture of your ski and your company logo on the sports page." Then she'd smile to close the deal.

If Rossignol had any doubts at the outset, they vanished in the glow of the results Diana Golden posted. As had been the case when David Livermore had first invited her to join the ski team, the timing was perfect. Diana Golden was ready to focus her concentration on becoming a great skier. Within a year of her return to competition in 1985, she won four gold medals. During the eighties she ran her totals to ten World Handicapped Championship golds and nineteen national championships. From 1986 to 1990 she monopolized[8] the World Disabled skiing championships, and in 1988 she won an Olympic gold medal in the giant slalom for disabled skiers, which was a demonstration sport at the time. . . .

The titles Diana Golden won were not preceded by words like "disadvantaged" or "disabled." She had simply earned recognition as the best there was at what she did—which is what she'd been after all along. "'Courageous' is my pet peeve," she told Meg Lukens for an article in *Sports Illustrated*. "I think it belittles our ability. I never wanted to be thought of as just having courage. I wanted to be recognized as a top-notch athlete, as the best in the world."

In 1991, at twenty-seven, Diana Golden retired from competitive skiing. She'd won more gold medals than she could carry, and now other challenges beckoned. She took up rock climbing and announced her intention to coach skiers—"both the one-legged and the two-legged kind." She said she wanted to bring credibility to "disabled ski instructors—not just as teachers of other disabled people, but of anyone." She trekked off alone into the Utah desert for five days, testing herself against heat, cold, exhaustion, and loneliness, charging along on two forearm crutches until she found the reward she'd intuitively[9] known the trip would provide. "It was just beautiful," she said of that adventure. "I was out there alone, with the sun on my back, and it was as if I could smell everything around me—the cliffs, the ruins. It seemed like I was taking everything in one sensual rush. I wasn't small, frail, and vulnerable. I was tough, strong, and indomitable. I was capable."

When she returned home she had once again made an opportunity of what most people would consider an obstacle, but Diana Golden wouldn't call the trek a big deal. She'd leave that for others. And when they said she was "courageous" and even "heroic," she'd patiently sit down with them and explain why that wasn't it at all. ❖

---

7. **unprecedented** (ŭn-prĕsʹĭ-dĕnʹtĭd): never before known or experienced.

8. **monopolized:** had complete possession of.

9. **intuitively:** in a way that involves knowing something without having a specific reason or any proof.

Diana Golden in a moment of victory as a member of the United States Disabled Ski Team.
Copyright © Brooks Dodge/Sports File.

BILL LITTLEFIELD

A graduate of Yale University, Bill Littlefield (1948–) is a popular sports commentator on National Public Radio. His radio work has earned him two Associated Press broadcast awards. Littlefield was born in Montclair, New Jersey. A poet as well as a novelist and biographer, Littlefield also teaches at Curry College in Milton, Massachusetts. This excerpt about Diana Golden is from *Champions: Stories of Ten Remarkable Athletes,* which also features such well-known athletes as Satchel Paige and Muhammad Ali.

OTHER WORKS *Prospect*

WRITING ABOUT LITERATURE

JUST IMAGINE

Believe it or not, many people get just as frightened by reading about a haunted house as they would by visiting one. This is because a talented writer can create scenes that let readers use their imaginations to "see" what a haunted house is like. On the following pages you will

- see how writers create scenes that show rather than tell
- use this skill to write an extra scene for a published story
- use context clues to understand a real-life scene

Writer's Style: Show, Don't Tell Good writers don't just tell what happens in a story or what a place or person is like. They describe actions, conversations, and appearances that let readers see things for themselves.

Reading the Literature

Notice how the authors of these excerpts use descriptive details to "show" setting and emotion.

Literature Models

Showing Setting
What is Guanajuato like? Why is this passage more revealing than a telling sentence, such as "Guanajuato smelled wonderful" or "Guanajuato is an old town"?

> The streets of Guanajuato smell of dried chilies, of jasmine and carnations in pots behind the iron-barred windows, of hot baked bread and of burro droppings. It is my town in central Mexico, a romantic old town that has lived days of wealth and luxury, because of the rich silver mines nearby, and days of poverty, because of the turmoil of revolutions and social change.
>
> Elizabeth Borton de Treviño, from "The Secret of the Wall"

Showing Feelings
How does this passage show how the narrator is feeling? Which words are especially helpful in revealing her feelings?

> I could not believe that I was actually holding the umbrella, opening it. It sprang up by itself as if it were alive, as if that were what it wanted to do—as if it belonged in my hands, above my head. I stared up at the network of silver spokes, then spun the umbrella around and around and around. It was so clean and white that it seemed to glow, to illuminate everything around it.
>
> Gish Jen, from "The White Umbrella"

Connect to Life

Like storytellers, good nonfiction writers can show and not tell to describe events and experiences. Notice how this writer describes his first taste of habanero chili peppers.

Magazine Article

"*H*elado, *por favor,*" I croak, my eyes watering. His [the waiter's] return with the ice cream is mercifully quick. I shovel it in. I let it wallow on my tongue and linger against the roof and sides of my mouth and the back of my throat. The fire finally goes out.

Jim Robbins
from "It feels like your lips are
going to fall off," *Smithsonian*

**Showing
a Reaction**
What did the writer think of the peppers? Which words show you how he reacted?

Try Your Hand: Showing, Not Telling

1. **Imagine the Actions** Think about the noises, facial expressions, and physical motions that you see when someone is angry, sad, or tired. Can you act out these emotions with your body? Jot down a list of the physical clues you give people to show them how you feel.

2. **Show Me How** Add descriptive details that change these sentences so that they *show* rather than *tell*.

   - Serafin was bored.
   - Carlos heard something.
   - Martin looked like a construction worker.

3. **Try This with a Friend** With a partner, try writing a paragraph showing what makes your neighborhood or town special. Remember to use descriptive words that let readers "see" the special things you describe.

SkillBuilder

GRAMMAR FROM WRITING

Understanding Complete Subjects and Predicates
No matter how many details you add to show readers what happens, every sentence must express a complete thought. A sentence that doesn't form a complete thought is a fragment. Each sentence has a **complete subject** that includes all of the words that tell whom or what the sentence is about. Each sentence also has a **complete predicate** that includes all of the words that tell what the subject does or is or what happened to the subject. What are the complete subject and predicate in this sentence from "The White Umbrella"?

Huddling at the end of Miss Crosman's nine-foot leatherette couch, Mona and I watched Eugenie play.

APPLYING WHAT YOU'VE LEARNED
Complete each sentence by adding either a subject or predicate to each sentence fragment.

1. An old chessboard
2. sounded like a deep groan
3. The ghost in the house

GRAMMAR HANDBOOK

For more information on complete subjects and predicates, see page 812 of the Grammar Handbook.

Creative Response

After reading a story, do you ever wonder what happened before the story began, or after it ended? Do you ever try to imagine the scenes that were left out? An enjoyable way to respond to a story is to try to fill in some of these missing pieces. To respond to these questions, you can look for clues in the story and come to your own conclusions.

GUIDED ASSIGNMENT

Fill in the Blanks In this lesson, you'll write a scene showing an event that was not in the story.

Student's Sequence Chart

"The Secret of the Wall"
— a new scene —

First

The wall caves in on Carlos

Second

Serafin hears noises, then runs home

Third

Serafin talks to his mother

Fourth

Serafin climbs into his bed and cries

1 Prewrite and Explore

Here are some things to think about as you look over the selections you have read and decide on a blank that might be fun to fill in.

- What event did I really wonder about but not get to see? Which scene did I want to go on longer?
- What might have happened the week, day, or hour before the story began? If the story were to continue, what might happen next?
- What additional conversation might have taken place between two characters?

Decision Point Decide which story you want to work on and which scene you want to add. Remember two important points:

- You want your scene to fit in with the original story. That means that the characters must act and talk as they do in the story.
- Events in your scene should help explain or continue events described in the original story.

Now you can start plotting what's going to happen in your scene. A sequence chart like the one on the left can help you organize and order the new events.

❷ Freewrite

Let your mind wander as you write. Try to imagine what each character is thinking. Or, you may want to try role-playing a scene with several classmates. This student imagined what happened to Serafin after the wall caved in on Carlos in "The Secret of the Wall" and decided to write about it.

Student's Freewriting

What happened to Serafin?
shivering and afraid, cold dark room with no candle,
sounds of Carlos screaming behind the wall, he probably
feels like he should do something but he's really scared,
he just stands still and tries not to listen to the
screaming, or maybe he just starts to run

I have to show how he looks afraid, maybe puts his hands over his ears

Would dialogue help to show this scene better?

his mother wouldn't seem to mind that he had been out, she isn't worried, but he tells her that he was alone all evening anyway, because he's scared, and when he goes to bed he puts his head under the covers thinking about Carlos stuck in the wall.

❸ Draft and Share

Begin drafting your scene. As you write, try to replace all the "telling" parts with "showing" descriptions. Then share your draft with a partner and discuss whether your scene fits in with the rest of the story.

 PEER RESPONSE

- Which parts of my scene really show what's happening? Which parts do I need to improve?
- How do the events and characters in my scene fit or not fit in with the original story?
- How could I make my scene more like the original story?

4 Revise and Edit

As you revise your draft, think about these questions.

- Do the characters act appropriately?
- Does my response create an interesting scene that fits in with the original story?
- Does my response meet the Standards for Evaluation below?

When you are finished, ask a classmate to read the scene aloud to you. What makes your response unique? Then reflect on what you enjoyed or found rewarding in writing your scene.

Student's Model

Serafin's Escape

When the wall caved in on Carlos, Serafin screamed in horror. The iron bar dropped from his hands and clanged against the rock. The room was pitch black without Carlos's candle, and Serafin could hear crying. He started to shake, and he pressed his hands against his ears to block out the sound. Serafin stomped his feet, moaning, as the sounds behind the wall softened. Then he ran toward the door.

What emotions is Serafin experiencing here? How does the writer show what Serafin is feeling?

Serafin's mother sat at the kitchen table with a glass of water. She looked up calmly after a while.

"Where have you been?" she asked him.

"Nowhere," he replied. "I have been by myself."

"Go to bed," she told him. "It is too late for you."

Serafin crept into his bed and pulled the covers over his head and tried to imagine what Carlos was doing.

What does the dialogue show about Serafin's thoughts? How well does this dialogue match other conversations in the story?

Standards for Evaluation

A "fill-in-the-blanks" response

- describes a scene that is not presented in the story
- shows an understanding of story characters
- adds descriptive details that match the original story
- uses sensory details and language

Grammar in Context

Prepositional Phrases A prepositional phrase is a group of words that begins with a preposition and ends with its object, which is a noun or a pronoun. Prepositional phrases can modify a noun or a verb. Phrases like this can help you describe your scene clearly, since they show where things are and when things happened.

"Go to bed," she told him, "It is too late for you."
Serafin ~~went to~~ *crept into his* bed and pulled the covers ~~on~~ *over his head* and tried
to imagine what Carlos was doing.

Every prepositional phrase makes the sentence more specific. Notice how adding the two phrases *into his bed* and *over his head* to the second sentence makes the image more exact.

Try Your Hand: Using Prepositional Phrases

1. Combine each pair of sentences below into one sentence by using prepositional phrases.

- Carlos discovered a hole. The hole was in the wall.
- Martin asked Carlos for help because he couldn't write. Martin wanted help with a letter.

2. Number your paper from 1 to 5. Use each prepositional phrase below in a sentence.

- to and from school everyday
- on the playground
- through the streets of Guanajuato
- in the middle of Cantaranas Plaza
- around the chessboard

Understanding Objects of Prepositions

The noun or pronoun that follows a preposition is the object of the preposition. Prepositions help to show relationships between the object and another word in the sentence. What relationship is shown in each sentence below?

The money went to a new school being built down by the highway.

Carlos heard scratching and striking along the wall.

Carlos has a little white dog with a black spot around one eye.

APPLYING WHAT YOU'VE LEARNED
Choose a preposition from column A and an object of a preposition from column B to complete the sentences below.

A	B
into	cobblestone street
during	sky
on	chess match

1. Carlos's shoes clattered
2. The huge church soared
3. The crowd was silent

WHAT ON EARTH?

Just as you fill in missing information when you read a story, you'll often witness scenes in everyday life that require you to fill in the blanks. Sometimes, asking questions and then using your imagination are the only ways to try to make sense of situations you don't quite understand.

View Suppose you accidentally walked into the event in this photo and witnessed this scene. What would your first reaction be? What makes this scene puzzling?

Interpret What is going on in this photo? How might you explain why the woman is going into the pool?

Discuss In a group, share your ideas about this scene. Then use the SkillBuilder at the right to learn about formulating questions.

CRITICAL THINKING

Formulating Questions

In life, as in the photograph on these pages, some events simply do not make sense. Asking the right questions can help you begin to understand puzzling situations.

Start by writing the headings Who, What, When, Why, and How on a separate sheet of paper. Under each heading, jot down facts that you already know about the topic of the photograph. Then write down questions you have about the photo. For example, "Who is the woman in the white dress? What is she doing? *Is* she falling or diving into the pool? Why is she doing this?"

Answering such questions can help you focus your ideas. Then you can begin to develop an explanation that makes sense of the situation.

APPLYING WHAT YOU'VE LEARNED

In a small group, think of other situations or problems that are particularly confusing or unexplained. Brainstorm a list of questions about the problems you wonder about. Discuss which questions are most helpful.

TAKING NECESSARY STEPS

WHAT DO YOU THINK?

REFLECTING ON THEME

Tests of ability often take place in public settings. Tests of character, however, often take place where struggles to grow or change go unseen. Use these activities to explore some necessary steps. Jot down your thoughts in your notebook. Later you can compare them with the characters' steps.

What are the steps to adulthood?

What accomplishments prove that a young person is ready to handle grown-up responsibilities? In your notebook, copy and complete this statement:

> I think the three most important steps in becoming an adult are
>
> 1. _____
> 2. _____
> 3. _____

What does it take?

Do you ever dream of being a prima ballerina, a world-class athlete, or a top scientist? With a group of classmates, brainstorm the steps that might be necessary to develop a high level of ability. Then think of questions to ask in interviewing a successful person in your school or community.

How does one meet a challenge?

Imagine that a person you admire is to speak at your school. You are to introduce the person. Write an introduction, thinking about the steps the person took to meet a challenge and what his or her success means to you. Rehearse and present your introduction to your class.

Looking Back

On a sheet of paper, draw a big outline of a light bulb. Then look in your notebook to review your early ideas about the theme "Showing Your True Colors." Did the experiences of a character in Part 1 spark new ideas about facing tests and challenges? Did an activity lead you in a new direction? Fill in the light bulb as you share your thoughts with a partner or small group.

NONFICTION

At Last I Kill a Buffalo
Luther Standing Bear

PERSONAL CONNECTION

In the account you are about to read, the author looks back upon a childhood experience that had helped to shape his life. He had faced a test of character that challenged not only his bravery but his honesty as well. Do you recall a situation in which your character was tested—one in which you struggled with inner conflicts and remained true to yourself? Briefly describe the circumstances in your notebook or on a sheet of paper.

HISTORICAL CONNECTION

"At Last I Kill a Buffalo" portrays incidents that take place within a Sioux (soō) tribe. The Sioux nation, made up of seven tribes, can be traced to the Great Lakes, where its members built shelters called tepees, harvested crops, and hunted deer. Pushed westward by the French fur traders and the Chippewa (chĭp'ə-wô') tribe, the Sioux learned to live in new environments. The Lakota (lə-kō'tə), or Teton, Sioux were the first to move to the Great Plains, a region identified on the map shown. The Lakota Sioux traveled throughout the western Dakotas and Nebraska, following the buffalo herds they hunted.

The Sioux had a complicated code of behavior that stressed self-discipline, community involvement, and a desire to live peacefully with nature. At the same time, the Sioux valued bravery. As Sioux boys prepared to face adulthood, they participated in tests of their character. They were expected to be brave, honest, and capable of making personal sacrifices. A Sioux boy had to be unselfish, kind to older people, and always ready to help those in need.

READING CONNECTION

Setting a Purpose Think about the title "At Last I Kill a Buffalo." What guesses can you make about the test of character the narrator faces? What questions does the title raise for you ? Deciding on a reason to read a selection is called setting a purpose. As you read about a test of character, use elements such as the title and illustrations to help you answer any questions you identified.

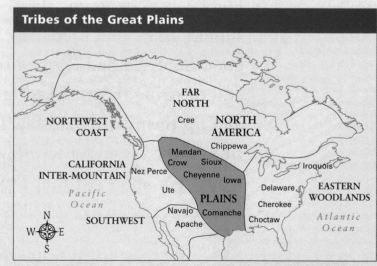

Tribes of the Great Plains

FAR NORTH

NORTHWEST COAST

Cree NORTH AMERICA

Chippewa

CALIFORNIA INTER-MOUNTAIN

Nez Perce

Mandan
Crow Sioux
Cheyenne Iowa

Iroquois

Ute

Delaware

EASTERN WOODLANDS

Pacific Ocean

PLAINS

Navajo Comanche

Cherokee

SOUTHWEST

Apache

Choctaw

Atlantic Ocean

N
W⊕E
S

LASERLINKS

- *HISTORICAL CONNECTION*
- *VISUAL VOCABULARY*

AT LAST I KILL A BUFFALO

BY LUTHER STANDING BEAR

At last the day came when my father allowed me to go on a buffalo hunt with him. And what a proud boy I was!

Ever since I could remember my father had been teaching me the things that I should know and preparing me to be a good hunter. I had learned to make bows and to string them and to make arrows and tip them with feathers. I knew how to ride my pony no matter how fast he would go, and I felt that I was brave and did not fear danger. All these things I had

Buffalo Hunter (about 1844), unknown artist. Oil on canvas, 40″ × 51 ⅛″. Santa Barbara (California) Museum of Art, gift of Harriet Cowles Hammet. Photo by Scott McClaine.

A buffalo hide illustrated (about 1835) with the acts of bravery
of Mato Tope, a famous chief of the Mandan tribe.
Bern (Switzerland) Historical Museum. Copyright © Bern Historical Museum.
Photo by Stefan Rebsamen.

learned for just this day when Father would allow me to go with him on a buffalo hunt. It was the event for which every Sioux boy eagerly waited. To ride side by side with the best hunters of the tribe, to hear the terrible noise of the great herds as they ran, and then to help to bring home the kill was the most thrilling day of any Indian boy's life. The only other event which could equal it would be the day I went for the first time on the warpath to meet the enemy and protect my tribe.

On the following early morning we were to start, so the evening was spent in preparation. Although the tepees[1] were full of activity, there was no noise or confusion outside. Always the evening before a buffalo hunt and when everyone was usually in his tepee, an old man went around the circle of tepees calling, "I-ni-la, i-ni-la," not loudly, but so everyone could hear. The old man was saying, "Keep quiet, keep quiet." We all knew that the scouts had come in and reported buffalo near and that we must all keep the camp in stillness. It was not

1. **tepees** (tē′pēz): portable dwellings of certain Native American peoples, consisting of a conical framework of poles covered with animal skins or bark.

necessary for the old man to go into each tepee and explain to the men that tomorrow there would be a big hunt, as the buffalo were coming. He did not order the men to prepare their weapons, and neither did he order the mothers to keep children from crying. The one word, "I-ni-la," was <u>sufficient</u> to bring quiet to the whole camp. That night there would be no calling or shouting from tepee to tepee, and no child would cry aloud. Even the horses and dogs obeyed the command for quiet, and all night not a horse neighed and not a dog barked. The very presence of quiet was everywhere. Such is the orderliness of a Sioux camp that men, women, children, and animals seem to have a common understanding and sympathy. It is no mystery but natural that the Indian and his animals understand each other very well both with words and without words. There are words, however, that the Indian uses that are understood by both his horses and dogs. When on a hunt, if one of the warriors speaks the word "A-a-ah" rather quickly and sharply, every man, horse, and dog will stop instantly and listen. Not a move will be made by an animal until the men move or speak further. As long as the hunters listen, the animals will listen also.

The night <u>preceding</u> a buffalo hunt was always an exciting night, even though it was quiet in camp. There would be much talk in the tepees around the fires. There would be sharpening of arrows and of knives. New bowstrings would be made, and quivers would be filled with arrows.

It was in the fall of the year, and the evenings were cool as Father and I sat by the fire and talked over the hunt. I was only eight years of age, and I know that Father did not expect me to get a buffalo at all, but only to try perhaps for a small calf should I be able to get close enough to one. Nevertheless, I was greatly excited as I sat and watched Father working in his easy, firm way.

I was wearing my buffalo-skin robe, the hair next to my body. Mother had made me a rawhide belt, and this, wrapped around my waist, held my blanket on when I threw it off my shoulders. In the early morning I would wear it, for it would be cold. When it came time to shoot, I should not want my blanket, but the belt would hold it in place.

You can picture me, I think, as I sat in the glow of the campfire, my little brown body bare to the waist, watching, and listening intently to my father. My hair hung down my back, and I wore moccasins and breechcloth of buckskin.[2] To my belt was fastened a rawhide holster for my knife, for when I was eight years of age we had plenty of knives. I was proud to own a knife, and this night I remember I kept it on all night. Neither did I lay aside my bow, but went to sleep with it in my hand, thinking, I suppose, to be all the nearer ready in the morning when the start was made.

Even the horses and dogs obeyed the command for quiet.

---

2. **breechcloth of buckskin:** a cloth, in this case one made from deer skin, used to cover the area between the waist and thighs.

Father sharpened my steel points for me and also sharpened my knife. The whetstone[3] was a long stone which was kept in a buckskin bag, and sometimes this stone went all over the camp; every tepee did not have one, so we shared this commodity[4] with one another. I had as I remember about ten arrows, so when Father was through sharpening them I put them in my rawhide quiver. I had a rawhide quirt,[5] too, which I would wear fastened to my waist. As Father worked, he knew I was watching him closely and listening whenever he spoke. By the time all preparations had been made, he had told me just how I was to act when I started out in the morning with the hunters.

We went to bed, my father hoping that tomorrow would be successful for him so that he could bring home some nice meat for the family and a hide for my mother to tan. I went to bed but could not go to sleep at once, so filled was I with the wonderment and excitement of it all. The next day was to be a test for me. I was to prove to my father whether he was or was not justified in his pride in me. What would be the result of my training? Would I be brave if I faced danger, and would Father be proud of me? Though I did not know it that night, I was to be tried for the strength of my manhood and my honesty in this hunt. Something happened that day which I remember above all things. It was a test of my real character, and I am proud to say that I did not find myself weak but made a decision that has been all these years a gratification to me.

The next morning the hunters were catching their horses about daybreak. I arose with my father and went out and caught my pony. I wanted to do whatever he did and show him that he did not have to tell me what to do. We brought our animals to the tepee and got our bows and arrows and mounted. From over the village came the hunters. Most of them were leading their running horses. These running horses were anxious for the hunt and came prancing, their ears straight up and their tails waving in the air. We were joined with perhaps a hundred or more riders, some of whom carried bows and arrows and some armed with guns.

The buffalo were reported to be about five or six miles away as we should count distance now. At that time we did not measure distance in miles. One camping distance was about ten miles, and these buffalo were said to be about one half camping distance away.

Some of the horses were to be left at a stopping place just before the herd was reached. These horses were pack animals which were taken along to carry extra blankets or weapons. They were trained to remain there until the hunters came for them.

O**n I rode through the cloud, for I knew I must keep going.**

---

3. **whetstone:** a hard stone used to sharpen knives and other metal blades.

4. **commodity:** a basic good that has useful economic value.

5. **quirt:** a small riding whip.

Though they were neither hobbled[6] nor tied, they stood still during the shooting and noise of the chase.

My pony was a black one and a good runner. I felt very important as I rode along with the hunters and my father, the chief. I kept as close to him as I could.

Two men had been chosen to scout or to lead the party. These two men were in a sense policemen whose work it was to keep order. They carried large sticks of ash wood, something like a policeman's billy,[7] though longer. They rode ahead of the party while the rest of us kept in a group close together. The leaders went ahead until they sighted the herd of grazing buffalo. Then they stopped and waited for the rest of us to ride up. We all rode slowly toward the herd, which on sight of us had come together, although they had been scattered here and there over the plain. When they saw us, they all ran close together as if at the command of a leader. We continued riding slowly toward the herd until one of the leaders shouted, "Ho-ka-he!" which means, "Ready, go!" At that command every man started for the herd. I had been listening, too, and the minute the hunters started, I started also.

Away I went, my little pony putting all he had into the race. It was not long before I lost sight of Father, but I kept going just the same. I threw my blanket back, and the chill of the autumn morning struck my body, but I did not mind. On I went. It was wonderful to race over the ground with all these horsemen about me. There was no shouting, no noise of any kind except the pounding of the horses' feet. The herd was now running and had raised a cloud of dust. I felt no fear until we had entered this cloud of dust and I could see nothing about me—only hear the sound of feet. Where was Father? Where was I going? On I rode through the cloud, for I knew I must keep going.

Then all at once I realized that I was in the midst of the buffalo, their dark bodies rushing all about me and their great heads moving up and down to the sound of their hoofs beating upon the earth. Then it was that fear overcame me and I leaned close down upon my little pony's body and clutched him tightly. I can never tell you how I felt toward my pony at that moment. All thought of shooting had left my mind. I was seized by blank fear. In a moment or so, however, my senses became clearer, and I could distinguish other sounds beside the clatter of feet. I could hear a shot now and then, and I could see the buffalo beginning to break up into small bunches. I could not see Father nor any of my companions yet, but my fear was vanishing and I was safe. I let my pony run. The buffalo looked too large for me to tackle, anyway, so I just kept going. The buffalo became more and more scattered. Pretty soon I saw a young calf that looked about my size. I remembered now what Father had told me the night before as we sat about the fire. Those instructions were important for me now to follow.

I was still back of the calf, being unable to get alongside of him. I was anxious to get a shot, yet afraid to try, as I was still very nervous. While my pony was making all speed to come alongside, I chanced a shot, and to my surprise my arrow landed. My second arrow glanced along the back of the animal and sped on between the horns, making only a slight wound. My third arrow hit a spot that made the running beast slow up in his gait. I shot a fourth arrow, and though it, too, landed, it was not a fatal wound. It seemed to me that it was taking a lot of shots, and I was not proud

---

6. **hobbled:** tied around the legs to prevent movement.

7. **billy:** a short wooden club.

Buffalo hunt (about 1884), New Bear (Hidatsa people).Charles H. Barstow Collection of Indian
Ledger Art, Montana State University-Billings Library, Special Collections.

of my marksmanship. I was glad, however, to see the animal going slower, and I knew that one more shot would make me a hunter. My horse seemed to know his own importance. His two ears stood straight forward, and it was not necessary for me to urge him to get closer to the buffalo. I was soon by the side of the buffalo, and one more shot brought the chase to a close. I jumped from my pony, and as I stood by my fallen game, I looked all around wishing that the world could see. But I was alone. In my determination to stay by until I had won my buffalo, I had not noticed that I was far from everyone else. No admiring friends were about, and as far as I could see I was on the plain alone. The herd of buffalo had completely disappeared. And as for Father, much as I wished for him, he was out of sight, and I had no idea where he was.

I stood and looked at the animal on the ground. I was happy. Everyone must know that I, Ota K'te,[8] had killed a buffalo. But it looked as if no one knew where I was, so no one was coming my way. I must then take something from this animal to show that I had killed it. I took all the arrows one by one from the body. As I took them out, it occurred to me that I had used five arrows. If I had been a skillful hunter, one arrow would have been sufficient, but I had used five. Here it was that temptation came to me. Why could I not take out two of the arrows and throw them away? No one would know, and then I should be more greatly admired and praised as a hunter. As it was, I knew that I should be praised by Father and Mother, but I wanted more. And so I was tempted to lie.

I was planning this as I took out my skinning knife that Father had sharpened for

I looked all around wishing that the world could see.

me the night before. I skinned one side of the animal, but when it came to turning it over, I was too small. I was wondering what to do when I heard my father's voice calling, "To-ki-i-la-la-hu-wo," "Where are you?" I quickly jumped on my pony and rode to the top of a little hill nearby. Father saw me and came to me at once. He was so pleased to see me and glad to know that I was safe. I knew that I could never lie to my father. He was too fond of me and I too proud of him. He had always told me to tell the truth. He wanted me to be an honest man, so I resolved then to tell the truth even if it took from me a little glory. He rode up to me with a glad expression on his face, expecting me to go back with him to his kill. As he came up, I said as calmly as I could, "Father, I have killed a buffalo." His smile changed to surprise, and he asked me where my buffalo was. I pointed to it, and we rode over to where it lay, partly skinned.

Father set to work to skin it for me. I had watched him do this many times and knew perfectly well how to do it myself, but I could not turn the animal over. There was a way to turn the head of the animal so that the body would be balanced on the back while being skinned. Father did this for me, while I helped all I could. When the hide was off, Father put

---

8. **Ota K'te** (ō'tä kə-tā'): the Lakota Sioux name of Luther Standing Bear. The name means "Plenty Kill."

it on the pony's back with the hair side next to the pony. On this he arranged the meat so it would balance. Then he covered the meat carefully with the rest of the hide, so no dust would reach it while we traveled home. I rode home on top of the load.

I showed my father the arrows that I had used and just where the animal had been hit. He was very pleased and praised me over and over again. I felt more glad than ever that I had told the truth, and I have never regretted it. I am more proud now that I told the truth than I am of killing the buffalo.

We then rode to where my father had killed a buffalo. There we stopped and prepared it for taking home. It was late afternoon when we got back to camp. No king ever rode in state[9] who was more proud than I that day as I came into the village sitting high up on my load of buffalo meat. Mother had now two hunters in the family, and I knew how she was going to make over me. It is not <u>customary</u> for Indian men to brag about their <u>exploits</u>, and I had been taught that bragging was not nice. So I was very quiet, although I was bursting with

pride. Always when arriving home I would run out to play, for I loved to be with the other boys, but this day I lingered about close to the tepee so I could hear the nice things that were said about me. It was soon all over camp that Ota K'te had killed a buffalo.

My father was so proud that he gave away a fine horse. He called an old man to our tepee to cry out the news to the rest of the people in camp. The old man stood at the door of our tepee and sang a song of praise to my father. The horse had been led up, and I stood holding it by a rope. The old man who was doing the singing called the other old man who was to receive the horse as a present. He accepted the horse by coming up to me, holding out his hands to me, and saying, *"Ha-ye,"* which means "Thank you." The old man went away very grateful for the horse.

That ended my first and last buffalo hunt. It lives only in my memory, for the days of the buffalo are over. ❖

---

9. **rode in state:** rode in a formal parade, with honors such as those given to a political leader.

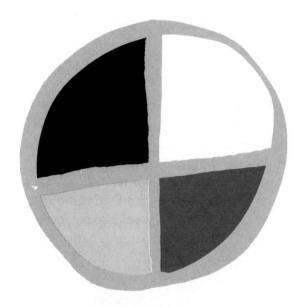

THE FLOWER-FED BUFFALOES

by Vachel Lindsay

The flower-fed buffaloes of the spring
In the days of long ago,
Ranged where the locomotives sing
And the prairie flowers lie low:—
5 The tossing, blooming, perfumed grass
Is swept away by the wheat,
Wheels and wheels and wheels spin by
In the spring that still is sweet.
But the flower-fed buffaloes of the spring
10 Left us, long ago.
They gore no more, they bellow no more,
They trundle around the hills no more:—
With the Blackfeet, lying low,
With the Pawnees, lying low,
15 Lying low.

Below Zero (1993), John Axton. Oil on canvas, 30″ × 40″, courtesy of Ventana Fine Art, Santa Fe, New Mexico.

RESPONDING
OPTIONS

FROM PERSONAL RESPONSE TO CRITICAL ANALYSIS

REFLECT

1. At what point in your reading of "At Last I Kill a Buffalo" did you most identify with Ota K'te? Jot down your ideas in your notebook.

RETHINK

2. How would you describe the test of character Ota K'te faces? Explain.

   Consider
   - the physical challenges of the hunt
   - the tribe's expectations for a young boy
   - the step Ota K'te takes concerning the arrows

3. What do you think of the relationship between Ota K'te and his father? Explain.

4. After the hunt, the father gives away a valuable horse. What does this act suggest about the values of the Sioux? Explain.

RELATE

5. What do you think the images and impressions in "The Flower-Fed Buffaloes," the Insight poem on page 467, add to Luther Standing Bear's description of the buffalo hunt?

ANOTHER PATHWAY
Cooperative Learning

In a small group, discuss the scenes or descriptions in "At Last I Kill a Buffalo" that reveal something about the character of Ota K'te. Make and fill in a chart that matches specific scenes or quotes from the story with your observations regarding what the scenes or quotes reveal about Ota K'te.

LITERARY CONCEPTS

Writers carefully choose details that appeal to a reader's sense of sight, sound, smell, touch, or taste. These details help to create an image of a scene, an event, or a character in the reader's mind. Most readers expect to find imagery presented in poetry—but writers of personal accounts use **imagery** too. For example, in "My First Dive with the Dolphins," the narrator uses imagery in describing his first sight of a certain dolphin: "There it was: a glistening, gleaming, silver bubble ring, rising . . . another ring emerged, rising faster, so that it joined its luminous relation." See if you can find an example of imagery that you think is especially effective in "At Last I Kill a Buffalo."

QUICKWRITES

1. Reread the definition of narrative poetry on page 104, and review "The Cremation of Sam McGee" (page 161) or another narrative poem in this book. Write a **narrative poem** of at least 15 lines describing the events in Luther Standing Bear's account.

2. Write a **letter** that Ota K'te might have written to his father in which he tells him what really happened during the buffalo hunt.

   📁 *PORTFOLIO Save your writing. You may want to use it later as a springboard to a piece for your portfolio.*

ALTERNATIVE ACTIVITIES

Choose some aspect of the Sioux culture—their food, shelter, hunting practices, language, or anything else you might be interested in—and conduct library research on the topic. Make a **model** of the subject you choose. For example, if you choose to study the food, make a sample of a food item. If you choose to study the shelters of the Sioux, you might make a cutaway model of a buffalo-hide tepee.

ART CONNECTION

The buffalo hide on page 460 is an example of how Native Americans, including the Sioux, used hides to record ideas or acts important to the tribe. This hide belonged to Mato Tope (Four Bears), a famous chief of the Mandan tribe. The Mandans have lived in North Dakota, along the Missouri River, for more than 500 years. The pictures and symbols on the hide show the acts of courage in battle of Mato Tope, who lived from 1800 to 1837. What acts of courage might Ota K'te draw on the hide of his buffalo?

WORDS TO KNOW

For each boldfaced word, write the letter of the situation that best demonstrates its meaning.

1. **customary**
   (a) a man taking a woman's last name after their wedding
   (b) a boy making a wish before blowing out birthday candles
   (c) a girl graduating from college before she is 12 years old
2. **preceding**
   (a) a student sitting quietly in a classroom
   (b) a page that was read just before this one
   (c) a principal telling students to walk, not run, in the halls
3. **exploit**
   (a) a parent telling a child how to do the math homework
   (b) a bully making fun of a smaller child on the playground
   (c) a soldier sneaking into the enemy camp to get information
4. **sufficient**
   (a) two children who want to play catch
   (b) two children who want to become a baseball team
   (c) two children who want to use the same baseball glove
5. **gratification**
   (a) a scolding from a person you respect
   (b) a compliment from a person you admire
   (c) a threat from a person who frightens you

LUTHER STANDING BEAR

Luther Standing Bear (1868?–1939), whose Lakota Sioux name was Ota K'te (Plenty Kill), was born about 1868. When he was 11 years old, his father sent him to Carlisle, Pennsylvania, to attend the Carlisle Indian School, which was operated by the federal government from 1879 until 1918.

OTHER WORKS *My People the Sioux, Land of the Spotted Eagle, Stories of the Sioux*

PREVIEWING

NONFICTION

Tutankhamen *from* Lost Worlds
Anne Terry White

PERSONAL CONNECTION

What words come to your mind when you think of ancient Egypt? In this selection you will get a peek at the civilization of the ancient Egyptians. In your notebook, copy a pyramid like the one shown, and fill in the words that you connect with Egypt. Compare your pyramid graphic with a classmate's.

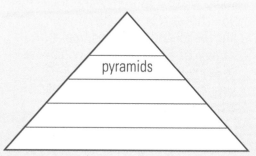

pyramids

HISTORICAL CONNECTION

Valley of the Kings

(Map showing: LEBANON, SYRIA, ISRAEL, JORDAN, SAUDI ARABIA, EGYPT, Mediterranean Sea, Red Sea, Gulf of Suez, Nile River, Cairo, Valley of the Kings, Luxor. Scale in Miles: 0, 50, 100)

From 2750 to 1784 B.C., Egyptians built great pyramids as tombs for their kings, or Pharaohs (fâr′ōz). The great treasures of these tombs were often stolen by grave robbers, and by 1570 B.C. pyramids were no longer built. Instead, to discourage grave robbing, Pharaohs began to seek secret locations for tombs. These burial places were cut into the cliffs west of their capital, Thebes. Sixty-two tombs in the form of halls and chambers have been discovered in what is called today the Valley of the Kings and in the nearby Western Valley.

One of the most famous of these tombs is that of the young Pharaoh Tutankhamen (tōōt′äng-kä′mən), who ruled Egypt from about 1347 to 1339 B.C. The discovery in his tomb of numerous artifacts—hand-crafted objects such as tools, weapons, and jewelry—has provided valuable information about life in ancient Egypt.

READING CONNECTION

Skimming and Scanning As you read about the search for the tomb of Tutankhamen, see how the information given compares to your ideas about ancient Egypt. When looking for a specific fact in a piece of writing, scanning, or sweeping your eyes across each page, can help you spot what you are looking for. If you want to understand the main idea of a piece of writing or to get an overview of its contents, use skimming instead. To skim, move your eyes rapidly over the pages. Glance at the title, highlighted words or phrases, maps and charts, and the topic sentences, which are usually the first sentences in each paragraph.

LASERLINKS
• *HISTORICAL CONNECTION*

TUTANKHAMEN

FROM

LOST

WORLDS

BY

ANNE TERRY WHITE

One of the four miniature coffins that
contained Tutankhamen's internal organs.
Copyright © Lee Boltin.

Five seasons had passed and the British archaeologist[1] Howard Carter and his financial supporter, Lord Carnarvon, had failed in their search for the tomb of the Pharaoh Tutankhamen. Howard Carter remained convinced that he was close to the 3,200-year-old tomb. Carter persuaded Lord Carnarvon that the tomb most likely lay in the center of the Valley of the Kings. In November 1922, Carter and his crew began uncovering the area near the tomb of Rameses VI—the only section that had not been dug up in the Valley of the Kings.

Now Carnarvon and Carter were not planning to dig at random in the Valley of the Tombs of the Kings. They were on the lookout for a particular tomb, the tomb of the Pharaoh Tutankhamen, and they believed they had worked out the location where it lay. To the eyes of most people their undertaking seemed absurd. Nearly everybody was convinced that Tutankhamen's tomb had already been found. But Lord Carnarvon and Mr. Carter were not to be <u>dissuaded</u>, for they believed that the pit-tomb containing the fragments bearing the figures and names of Tutankhamen and his queen was far too small and insignificant for a king's burial. In their opinion the things had been placed there at some later time and did not indicate that the Pharaoh himself had been buried on the spot. They were convinced that the tomb of Tutankhamen was still to be found, and that the place they had chosen—the center of the Valley—was the best place to look for it. In that vicinity had been unearthed something which they considered very good evidence—two jars containing broken bits of things that had been used at the funeral ceremonies of King Tutankhamen.

Nevertheless, when in the autumn of 1917 the excavators[2] came out to look over the spot they had chosen and to begin their Valley campaign in earnest, even they thought it was a desperate undertaking. The site was piled high with refuse thrown out by former excavators. They would have to remove all that before they could begin excavating in virgin soil.[3] But they had made up their minds and meant to go through with it; even though it took many seasons, they would go <u>systematically</u> over every inch of ground.

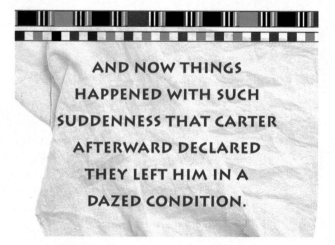

AND NOW THINGS HAPPENED WITH SUCH SUDDENNESS THAT CARTER AFTERWARD DECLARED THEY LEFT HIM IN A DAZED CONDITION.

In the years that followed, they did. They went over every inch, with the exception of a small area covered with the ruins of stone huts that had once sheltered workmen probably employed in building the tomb of Rameses VI.[4] These huts lay very near the tomb of the

---

1. **archaeologist** (är´kē-ŏl´ə-jĭst): a scientist who studies the material evidence, such as graves, buildings, tools, and pottery, remaining from past human life and culture.
2. **excavators** (ĕk´skə-vā´tərz): people who search by digging or uncovering.
3. **virgin soil:** ground that has not been dug up or explored.
4. **Rameses** (răm´ĭ-sēz´) **VI:** a Pharaoh whose tomb was built higher on the hill, above Tutankhamen's.

WORDS TO KNOW

dissuade (dĭ-swād´) *v.* to persuade someone not to do something; discourage
systematically (sĭs´tə-măt´ĭk-lē) *adv.* in an orderly, thorough manner

Howard Carter (left) and Lord Carnarvon at the entrance to Pharoah Tutankhamen's tomb, February 1923.
The Griffith Institute, Ashmolean Museum, Oxford, England.

Pharaoh on a spot which Carter and Carnarvon had not touched for reasons of courtesy. The tomb of Rameses VI was a popular show-place in the valley, and digging in the area of the huts would have cut off visitors to the tomb. They let it be, and turned instead to another site which they felt had possibilities.

The new ground proved, however, no better than the old, and now Lord Carnarvon began to wonder whether with so little to show for six seasons' work they were justified in going on. But Carter was firm. So long as a single area of unturned ground remained, he said, they ought to risk it. There was still the area of the huts. He insisted on going back to it. On November first, 1922 he had his diggers back in the old spot.

And now things happened with such suddenness that Carter afterward declared they left him in a dazed condition. Coming to work on the fourth day after the digging on the little area had started, he saw at once that something extraordinary had happened. Things were too quiet; nobody was digging and hardly anybody was talking. He hurried forward, and there before him was a shallow step cut in the rock beneath the very first hut attacked! He could hardly believe his eyes. After all the disappointments of the past six seasons, was it possible that he was actually on the threshold[5] of a great discovery? He gave the command to dig, and the

5. **threshold:** an entrance or beginning.

Some of the artifacts discovered in Tutankhamen's tomb. Note the numbered labels used to catalogue the objects. Valley of the Kings antechamber, west side with numbers (Egyptian Dynasty XVIII, Thebes). Photo by Egyptian Expedition, The Metropolitan Museum of Art. Copyright © The Metropolitan Museum of Art, all rights reserved.

diggers fell to work with a will. By the next afternoon Carter was able to see the upper edges of a stairway on all its four sides, and before very long there stood revealed twelve steps, and at the level of the twelfth the upper part of a sealed and plastered doorway.

Carter's excitement was fast reaching fever pitch. Anything, literally anything, might lie beyond. It needed all his self-control to keep from breaking the doorway down and satisfying his curiosity then and there. But was it fair to see what lay beyond that door alone? Although Lord Carnarvon was in England, was it not his discovery as much as Carter's? To the astonishment of the workmen, the excavator gave orders to fill the stairway in again, and then he sent the following cable off to Carnarvon: "At last have made wonderful discovery in Valley. A magnificent tomb with seals intact. Recovered same for your arrival. Congratulations."

As he waited for Lord Carnarvon to come,

Carter found it hard to persuade himself at times that the whole episode had not been a dream. The entrance to the tomb was only thirteen feet below the entrance to the tomb of Rameses VI. No one would have suspected the presence of a tomb so near the other. Had he actually found a flight of steps? Was it really there under the sand, waiting to conduct him to the great mystery?

In two weeks' time Lord Carnarvon and his daughter were on the spot. Carter now ordered his men to clear the stairway once more, and there on the lower part of the sealed doorway the explorers beheld what almost took their breath away— the seal of the Pharaoh Tutankhamen. Now they knew. Beyond this doorway lay either the Pharaoh's secret treasure store or else the very tomb for which they were searching. Yet one thing made them uneasy. They noticed that part of the door was patched up and that in the patched-up part there stood out clearly the seal of the cemetery. It was evident that the door had been partly broken down—by robbers, of course—and then patched up again by cemetery officials. Had the robbers been caught in time? Did at least some of Tutankhamen's glory yet remain behind that twice-sealed doorway? Or would perhaps only barren walls reward their years of <u>tedious</u> toil?

With pounding hearts they broke down the door. Beyond lay only another obstacle to their progress—a passage filled with stone. Had the robbers got beyond that? They began slowly to clear away the stone, and on the following day—"the day of days," Carter called it, "and one whose like I can never hope to see again"—they came upon a second sealed doorway, almost exactly like the first and also bearing distinct signs of opening and reclosing.

His hands trembling so that he could scarcely hold a tool, Carter managed to make a tiny hole in the door and to pass a candle through it. At first he could see nothing, but as his eyes grew accustomed to the light, "details of the room slowly emerged from the mist, strange animals, statues, and gold—everywhere the glint of gold."

"Can you see anything?" Carnarvon asked anxiously as Carter stood there dumb with amazement.

"Yes, wonderful things!" was all the explorer could get out.

And no wonder. What he saw was one of the most amazing sights anybody has ever been privileged to see. It seemed as if a whole museumful of objects was in that room. Three gilt[6] couches, their sides carved in the form of monstrous animals, and two statues of a king, facing each other like two <u>sentinels</u>, were the most prominent things in the room, but all around and between were hosts of other things—inlaid caskets, alabaster vases, shrines, beds, chairs, a golden inlaid throne, a heap of white boxes (which they later found were filled with trussed ducks and other food offerings), and a glistening pile of overturned chariots. When Carter and Carnarvon got their senses together again, they realized all at once that there was no coffin in the room. Was this then merely a hiding place for treasure? They examined the room very intently once again, and now they saw that the two statues stood one on either side of a sealed doorway. Gradually the truth dawned on them. They were but on the threshold of their discovery.

---

6. **gilt:** covered with a layer of gold.

475

What they saw was just an antechamber.[7] Behind the guarded door there would be other rooms, perhaps a whole series of them, and in one of them, beyond any shadow of doubt they would find the Pharaoh lying.

But as they thought the thing over, the explorers were by no means certain that their first wild expectations would actually come to pass. Perhaps that sealed doorway, like the two before it, had also been re-opened. In that case there was no telling what lay behind it.

On the following day they took down the door through which they had been peeping, and just as soon as the electric connections had been made and they could see things clearly, they rushed over to the doubtful door between the royal sentinels. From a distance it had looked untouched, but when they examined it more closely, they saw that here again the robbers had been before them; near the bottom was distinct evidence that a small hole had been made and filled up and re-sealed. The robbers had indeed been stopped, but not before they had got into the inner chamber.

It took almost as much self-command not to break down that door and see how much damage the robbers had done as to have filled in the staircase after it had once been cleared. But Carter and Carnarvon were not treasure-seekers; they were archaeologists, and they would not take the chance of injuring the objects within the antechamber just to satisfy their curiosity. For the moment they let that go and turned their attention to the things already before them.

There was enough there to leave them altogether bewildered. But while they were yet going crazily from one object to another and calling excitedly to each other, they stumbled on yet another discovery. In the wall, hidden behind one of the monstrous couches, was a small, irregular hole, unquestionably made by the plunderers[8] and never re-sealed. They dragged their powerful electric light to the hole and looked in. Another chamber, smaller than the one they were in, but even more crowded with objects! And everything was in the most amazing mess they had ever seen. The cemetery officials had made some attempt to clean up the antechamber after the robbers and to pile up the funeral furniture in some sort of order, but in the annex they had left things just as they were, and the robbers had done their work "about as thoroughly as an earthquake." Not a single inch of floor space remained unlittered.

Carter and Carnarvon drew a long breath and sobered down. They realized now that the job before them was going to take months and months. It would be a monumental task to photograph, label, mend, pack, and ship all this furniture, clothing, food, these chariots, weapons, walking sticks, jewels—this museumful of treasures. ❖

---

7. **antechamber** (ăn′tē-chām′bər): a small room leading to a larger one.

8. **plunderers:** people who invade a place to rob and destroy it.

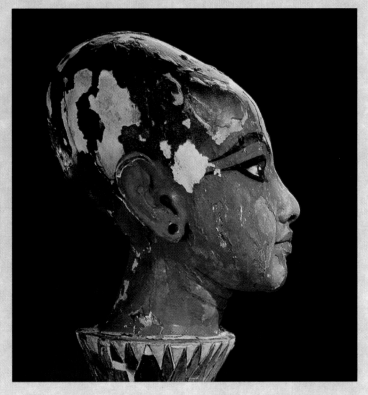

THE BOY PHARAOH

Tutankhamen, the Boy Pharaoh, ruled Egypt from about 1347 B.C. until his death, nine years later, in 1339 B.C. He became king at about the age of nine. Historians are unsure how he died and disagree on the identity of his parents. Tutankhamen, encouraged by his minister of state, Ay (ī), restored the ancient religion of Egypt, which recognized many gods and goddesses. After the Pharaoh's death, Ay directed his burial in the Valley of the Kings and also ruled briefly as king.

Tutankhamen is remembered for the treasures of his tomb, discovered by archaeologist Howard Carter in 1922. The treasures included everything a wealthy king would need in death, which the ancient Egyptians believed to be the next world. Most of the treasure is now on display in the Egyptian Museum in Cairo.

Tutankhamen's tomb may have been the most spectacular of the tombs unearthed in the Valley of the Kings, but it was not the last. In the spring of 1995, archaeologists discovered yet another tomb. This tomb, very near the site of Tutankhamen's, was designed for 50 princes—sons of Pharaoh Rameses II. Rameses II ruled Egypt from 1279 to 1212 B.C. In many ways his 67 years as a ruler were far more significant than Tutankhamen's nine years. Interestingly, the entrance to the tomb of the 50 princes lay hidden for nearly 70 years beneath the debris unearthed by Carter and Lord Carnarvon's search for the tomb of Tutankhamen.

RESPONDING OPTIONS

FROM PERSONAL RESPONSE TO CRITICAL ANALYSIS

REFLECT

1. How did you react to this account of the discovery of King Tutankhamen's tomb? Share your reactions with the class.

RETHINK

2. What personal characteristics do you think Lord Carnarvon and Howard Carter show in their efforts to locate the tomb?

Consider

- their continued work for six seasons
- their early refusal to dig near the tomb of Rameses VI
- Carter's refusal to continue excavating without Carnarvon

ANOTHER PATHWAY

Adapt the events in the selection into a **radio drama.** With a partner, improvise a scene in which Carter and Carnarvon decide to continue their search for the tomb of Tutankhamen and succeed in unearthing the Pharaoh's long-buried resting place. Tape-record your drama, and play the recording for the class.

3. Based on the artifacts found in the tomb, what can you infer about the beliefs of the Egyptians? Explain your answer.

4. After reading the account, what would you add to your pyramid graphic from the Personal Connection on page 470?

RELATE

5. The dry air and sands preserved the buried treasure of Egyptian tombs for thousands of years. Do you think those artifacts should be preserved untouched, or made available for public viewing in museums? Explain your opinion.

LITERARY CONCEPTS

Informative nonfiction is written mainly to provide factual information. Nonfiction of this type includes science and history texts, informational books, encyclopedias, pamphlets, and most of the articles in magazines and newspapers. Since the main purpose of this material is to inform, writing of this kind requires a tremendous amount of research by the author to make sure that the information is correct. Authors of informative nonfiction study primary source materials such as log entries, letters, and other documents to gather information for their writing. What are some of the sources of information that Anne Terry White might have checked before she wrote this account?

QUICKWRITES

1. Write the **log entries** that Howard Carter might have written during the two weeks he waited for Lord Carnarvon's return from England.

2. Pretend you are reporting the discovery of the tomb. Draft a **newspaper account** to accompany the following headline: "Tomb of Egyptian King Found in Valley of the Kings."

📂 *PORTFOLIO Save your writing. You may want to use it later as a springboard to a piece for your portfolio.*

ALTERNATIVE ACTIVITIES

1. Use encyclopedias and other reference materials to learn more about some aspect of ancient Egypt that you included in the Personal Connection on page 470. With a teacher's help, you might also contact an on-line information service for further details. Add the information you gather to a class **reference center** or computer **data bank** of material the class can use.

2. Create a **mural** for your classroom that illustrates the events described in Anne Terry White's account.

ART CONNECTION

The miniature coffin on page 471 is one of the many extraordinary pieces found in the tomb of Tutankhamen. The coffin, made of gold inlaid and decorated with colored glass and quartz, is one of four that contained the young Pharaoh's internal organs. Tutankhamen is shown holding objects that were symbols of his rule. The vulture and cobra on his headpiece represent his kingdom Upper Egypt and Lower Egypt. Would you visit a local museum to view such Egyptian artifacts? Why or why not?

WORDS TO KNOW

Review the Words to Know in the boxes at the bottom of the selection pages. Then write the vocabulary word that best completes each sentence.

1. People who search for objects from the past work very carefully. They often make a pattern of ropes and dig in each section to cover the ground _____.

2. They dig slowly and sift each shovelful of dirt. Yes, much of the work is just plain _____.

3. They have to make sure no one disturbs the area before they are finished. Ropes around the "dig" help to _____ people from walking over the ground.

4. At night, they may hire a lookout to work as a _____.

5. Even a broken bit of an ancient pot can be an important find. Imagine how these people feel when they find a pot that is _____!

ANNE TERRY WHITE

The first book that Anne Terry White (1896–1980) wrote was about Old Testament figures, and her second book was about William Shakespeare. Writing the books was her way of introducing her daughters to great works of literature in a manner that they would find both entertaining and easy to understand.

White came to the United States from the Ukraine when she was eight years old. She grew up in New England and attended Brown and Stanford Universities. In addition to writing books, White worked as a teacher and a social worker.

"Tutankhamen" is an excerpt from White's book *Lost Worlds: The Romance of Archaeology.* Considered one of the foremost writers of nonfiction for young people, she also produced other types of literature, including retellings of myths, legends, and Russian folktales.

OTHER WORKS *Myths and Legends, Prehistoric America, Odysseus Comes Home from the Sea*

LASERLINKS
• ART GALLERY

POETRY

Pole Vault	Analysis of Baseball
Shiro Murano	May Swenson

PERSONAL CONNECTION

In each of these poems, a sport is described in a way that reveals its unique qualities. From ancient times, people have enjoyed a wide variety of sports both as observers and as participants. What is your favorite sport? Draw a graphic with a structure that shows a characteristic of the sport. Fill it in with words that describe that sport. The baseball graphic shown is an example.

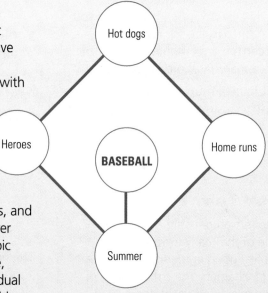

Hot dogs

Heroes

BASEBALL

Home runs

Summer

CULTURAL CONNECTION

Each sport described in the poems has its own history, rules, and characteristics. The pole vault, in some form, dates back over 2,500 years to the Olympic Games of ancient Greece, which glorified the individual athlete. This sport is a field competition in which an athlete uses a pole to propel his or her body over a crossbar set at a certain height. The vault is successful if the vaulter makes it over the crossbar without knocking it down.

A pole vaulter in action.

Baseball, often considered the national game of the United States, has a more recent origin. Sports historians generally believe that baseball developed from an old English game called rounders, which was played in the New England colonies. Many people credit Alexander Cartwright of New York as being the founder of organized baseball. Cartwright wrote a set of rules that established the distance between bases as 90 feet and set the number of players on each team as nine. He also organized the first serious baseball team, the Knickerbockers.

WRITING CONNECTION

In the Personal Connection you chose a favorite sport and listed some of its characteristics. In your notebook, explain which of its traits and which of your personal experiences have made it your favorite sport.

Pole Vault

by Shiro Murano

He is running like a wasp,
Hanging on a long pole.
As a matter of course he floats in the sky,
Chasing the ascending[1] horizon.
5   Now he has crossed the limit,
    And pushed away his support.
For him there is nothing but a descent.[2]
Oh, he falls helplessly.
Now on that runner, awkwardly fallen on the ground,
10 Once more
    The horizon comes down,
Beating hard on his shoulders.

---

1. **ascending:** moving upward; rising.
2. **descent:** the act of going downward.

FROM **PERSONAL RESPONSE** *TO* **CRITICAL ANALYSIS**

REFLECT   **1.** Draw the image you visualized as you read "Pole Vault."

RETHINK **2.** How would you describe the effect created by the description of the pole vaulter as "running like a wasp / Hanging on a long pole"?

3. What do you think would have been gained or lost if the poet had written a description of pole vaulting in paragraph form instead of in a poem?

4. Based on what you know about pole vaulting and what you have learned in the poem, why do you suppose someone would choose to participate in this sport?

Analysis of Baseball

by May Swenson

It's about
the ball,
the bat,
and the mitt.
5 Ball hits
bat, or it
hits mitt.
Bat doesn't
hit ball, bat
10 meets it.
Ball bounces
off bat, flies
air, or thuds
ground (dud)
15 or it
fits mitt.

Bat waits
for ball
to mate.
20 Ball hates
to take bat's
bait. Ball
flirts, bat's
late, don't
25 keep the date.
Ball goes in
(thwack) to mitt,
and goes out
(thwack) back
30 to mitt.

Ball fits
mitt, but
not all
the time.
35 Sometimes
ball gets hit
(pow) when bat
meets it,
and sails
40 to a place
where mitt
has to quit
in disgrace.
That's about
45 the bases
loaded,
about 40,000
fans exploded.

It's about
50 the ball,
the bat,
the mitt,
the bases
and the fans.
55 It's done
on a diamond,
and for fun.
It's about
home, and it's
60 about run.

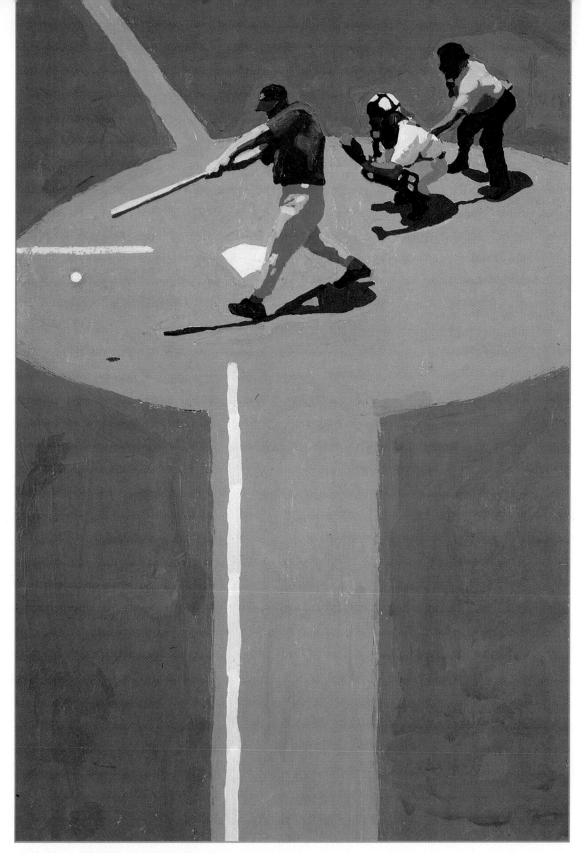

Illustration by John Ferry.

RESPONDING OPTIONS

FROM PERSONAL RESPONSE TO CRITICAL ANALYSIS

REFLECT

1. How would you describe the poem "Analysis of Baseball"? Share your observations with the class.

RETHINK

2. Why do you think the poet presents only two or three words in each line of the poem?

3. In the third stanza the poet writes, "That's about / the bases / loaded, / about 40,000 / fans exploded." What images and impressions do you form from these lines?

4. Do you think this poem would provide a newcomer to baseball with a clear sense of the game? Why or why not?

RELATE

5. Compare and contrast "Pole Vault" and "Analysis of Baseball." How well does each succeed in describing the unique characteristics of a sport?

ANOTHER PATHWAY

On your own or with some classmates, write a sports broadcast or commentary using the events described in either "Pole Vault" or "Analysis of Baseball." Perform your broadcast or commentary in front of the class.

LITERARY CONCEPTS

Onomatopoeia (ŏn'ə-măt'ə-pē'ə) is the use of words to imitate sounds. The words *boom* and *hiss* are examples of onomatopoeia. In the first stanza of "Analysis of Baseball," May Swenson uses the word *dud* partly to imitate the sound of the ball hitting the ground. Find another example of onomatopoeia in "Analysis of Baseball."

QUICKWRITES

1. Compose your own **poem** based on your favorite sport.

2. Write about your favorite sport in the form of a **cinquain** (sĭng'kān), a five-line, nonrhyming poem with a single stanza. Use the graphic and example below to help you write your own cinquain.

Line 1: A word that is the title of the poem. ····▶ **Swim,**

Line 2: Two adjectives that describe the topic. ····▶ **Sleek, fluid**

Line 3: Three "-ing" words related to the topic. ···▶ **Moving, floating, stroking**

Line 4: A phrase related to the topic. ········▶ **Swimming like a fish**

Line 5: A synonym for the topic. ···········▶ **Freedom**

📁 **PORTFOLIO** *Save your writing. You may want to use it later as a springboard to a piece for your portfolio.*

CRITIC'S CORNER

One critic remarked that May Swenson is able to make a reader see clearly what he or she has "merely looked at before." Think about the meaning of the statement. In what ways does "Analysis of Baseball" help you to see the game of baseball more clearly?

ACROSS THE CURRICULUM

Physical Education Pole vaulting remains a popular Olympic sport today. Research the sport of pole vaulting to learn more about how a pole vaulter trains for the sport, the records that have been set for the event, and the names of well-known pole vaulters. Find out why pole vaulters changed from using wooden to using fiberglass poles. Prepare a brief "how-to" presentation for the class, including a step-by-step description of the act of pole vaulting. If possible, show the class a videotape of a pole vaulter in action.

SHIRO MURANO

Interested in poetry from an early age, the Japanese poet Shiro Murano (1901–) began writing haiku when a junior high school student. He attended Keio University where he became interested in German poetry. The influence of German poetry was apparent in his first book of poetry, published in 1926.

In 1960 Murano was awarded the Yomiuri Literary Award, a highly respected Japanese literary award. This was for his poetry collection *A Strayed Sheep*, which, with the collection *Gymnastics*, is considered one of his finest works.

MAY SWENSON

1913–1989

During May Swenson's long years as an apprentice poet, she learned a valuable technique for writing poetry. She took whatever lines popped into her head and used them as the first lines of a poem. Thus the simple line "feel like a bird" became the first line of a four-stanza poem.

One of the characteristics that made Swenson's poetry unique was her practice of constructing poems in which the words are arranged in the shapes of the poems' subjects. Her award-winning poetry has been praised for the imaginative quality of her observations. Her book *Poems to Solve* presents 35 poems containing riddles, hidden meanings, and ideas to puzzle and challenge the reader. Born in Logan, Utah, May Swenson moved to New York City after graduating from college. There she lived in poverty for many years, struggling to master the craft of poetry. Eventually, she achieved her dream and became one of the best-known poets of her generation.

OTHER WORKS *Another Animal, The Guess and Spell Coloring Book, More Poems to Solve*

FICTION

My Friend Flicka

Mary O'Hara

PERSONAL CONNECTION

Have you ever made a difficult choice that you had to defend? Record the situation and your reactions to it in your notebook. Draw a graph like the one shown and fill it in with the pros and cons you thought about when you made your choice. Discover what happens in this story when a boy named Kennie makes a major choice that he has to defend.

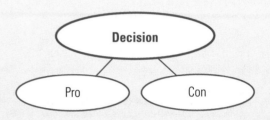

CULTURAL CONNECTION

"My Friend Flicka" takes place around 1940 on a Wyoming horse ranch where the careful breeding of horses is essential to success. A purebred horse is one that belongs to a recognized breed. Owners must make important decisions as they carefully select stallions (male horses) and mares (female horses) to produce foals that have traits the owners want, such as speed, strength, or size. The height of a horse is measured in four-inch units called hands (four inches is the width of an average adult's hand). The height is considered to be the distance from the withers (the ridge between a horse's shoulder blades) to the ground.

READING CONNECTION

Strategies for Reading As you read the following story about the difficult choice a young boy makes, keep in mind the reading strategies you have learned. At different points in the story you will encounter questions requiring you to use one of the reading strategies listed below.

Reading Strategies	
Questioning	Ask questions about the events and characters in the story.
Connecting	Think of similarities between events in the story and your own experiences.
Predicting	Predict what might happen next and how the story might end.
Clarifying	Stop occasionally for a quick review of what you understand so far.
Evaluating	Form opinions about the story.

LASERLINKS
• CULTURAL CONNECTION

My Friend Flicka

by Mary O'Hara

eport cards for the second semester were sent out soon after school closed in mid-June.

Kennie's was a shock to the whole family.

"If I could have a colt all for my own," said Kennie, "I might do better."

Rob McLaughlin glared at his son. "Just as a matter of curiosity," he said, "how do you go about it to get a *zero* in an examination? Forty in arithmetic; seventeen in history! But a *zero?* Just as one man to another, what goes on in your head?"

"Yes, tell us how you do it, Ken," chirped Howard.

"Eat your breakfast, Howard," snapped his mother.

Kennie's blond head bent over his plate until his face was almost hidden. His cheeks burned.

McLaughlin finished his coffee and pushed his chair back. "You'll do an hour a day on your lessons all through the summer."

Nell McLaughlin saw Kennie wince as if something had actually hurt him.

Lessons and study in the summertime, when the long winter was just over and there weren't hours enough in the day for all the things he wanted to do!

Kennie took things hard. His eyes turned to the wide-open window with a look almost of despair.

The hill opposite the house, covered with arrow-straight jack pines, was sharply etched in the thin air of the eight-thousand-foot altitude. Where it fell away, vivid green grass ran up to meet it; and over range and upland poured the strong Wyoming sunlight that stung everything into burning color. A big jack rabbit sat under one of the pines, waving his long ears back and forth.

Ken had to look at his plate and blink back tears before he could turn to his father and say carelessly, "Can I help you in the corral with the horses this morning, Dad?"

"You'll do your study every morning before you do anything else." And McLaughlin's scarred boots and heavy spurs clattered across the kitchen floor. "I'm disgusted with you. Come, Howard."

Howard strode after his father, nobly refraining from looking at Kennie.

"Help me with the dishes, Kennie," said Nell McLaughlin as she rose, tied on a big apron, and began to clear the table.

Kennie looked at her in despair. She poured steaming water into the dishpan and sent him for the soap powder.

"If I could have a colt," he muttered again.

"Now get busy with that dish towel, Ken. It's eight o'clock. You can study till nine and then go up to the corral. They'll still be there."

At supper that night Kennie said, "But Dad, Howard had a colt all of his own when he was only eight. And he trained it and schooled it all himself; and now he's eleven, and Highboy is three, and he's riding him. I'm nine now, and even if you did give me a colt now, I couldn't catch up to Howard, because I couldn't ride it till it was a three-year-old, and then I'd be twelve."

Nell laughed. "Nothing wrong with that arithmetic."

But Rob said, "Howard never gets less than seventy-five average at school and hasn't disgraced himself and his family by getting more demerits[1] than any other boy in his class."

Kennie didn't answer. He couldn't figure it out. He tried hard; he spent hours poring over his books. That was supposed to get you good

---

1. **demerits:** marks in a student's record for poor work or for misbehavior.

WORDS TO KNOW

despair (dĭ-spâr′) *n.* complete hopelessness
refrain (rĭ-frān′) *v.* to hold oneself back

marks, but it never did. Everyone said he was bright; why was it that when he studied he didn't learn? He had a vague feeling that perhaps he looked out the window too much or looked through the walls to see clouds and sky and hills and wonder what was happening out there. Sometimes it wasn't even a wonder, but just a pleasant drifting feeling of nothing at all, as if nothing mattered, as if there was always plenty of time, as if the lessons would get done of themselves. And then the bell would ring, and study period was over.

If he had a colt—

When the boys had gone to bed that night, Nell McLaughlin sat down with her overflowing mending basket and glanced at her husband.

He was at his desk as usual, working on account books and inventories.

Nell threaded a darning needle and thought, "It's either that whacking big bill from the vet for the mare that died or the last half of the tax bill."

It didn't seem just the auspicious moment to plead Kennie's cause. But then, these days there was always a line between Rob's eyes and a harsh note in his voice.

"Rob," she began.

He flung down his pencil and turned around.

"Damn that law!" he exclaimed.

"What law?"

"The state law that puts high taxes on pedigreed[2] stock. I'll have to do as the rest of 'em do—drop the papers."

"Drop the papers! But you'll never get decent prices if you don't have registered horses."[3]

"I don't get decent prices now."

"But you will someday, if you don't drop the papers."

"Maybe." He bent again over the desk.

Rob, thought Nell, was a lot like Kennie himself. He set his heart. Oh, how stubbornly he set his heart on just some one thing he

> Oh, how stubbornly he set his heart on just some one thing he wanted above everything else.

wanted above everything else. He had set his heart on horses and ranching way back when he had been a crack rider at West Point[4]; and he had resigned and thrown away his army career just for the horses. Well, he'd got what he wanted— She drew a deep breath, snipped her thread, laid down the sock, and again looked across at her husband as she unrolled another length of darning cotton.

To get what you want is one thing, she was thinking. The three-thousand-acre ranch and the hundred head of horses. But to make it pay—for a dozen or more years they had been trying to make it pay. People said ranching hadn't paid since the beef barons ran their

---

2. **pedigreed:** having an established, purebred line of ancestors.

3. **registered horses:** horses that have documents proving that they are purebred, which increases their value.

4. **West Point:** the U.S. Military Academy in West Point, New York, where U.S. Army officers are trained.

herds on public land; people said the only prosperous ranchers in Wyoming were the dude ranchers; people said—

But suddenly she gave her head a little rebellious, gallant shake. Rob would always be fighting and struggling against something, like Kennie; perhaps like herself, too. Even those first years when there was no water piped into the house, when every day brought a new difficulty or danger, how she had loved it! How she still loved it!

She ran the darning ball into the toe of a sock, Kennie's sock. The length of it gave her a shock. Yes, the boys were growing up fast, and now Kennie—Kennie and the colt—

After a while she said, "Give Kennie a colt, Rob."

"He doesn't deserve it." The answer was short. Rob pushed away his papers and took out his pipe.

"Howard's too far ahead of him, older and bigger and quicker and his wits about him, and—"

"Ken doesn't half try, doesn't stick at anything."

She put down her sewing. "He's crazy for a colt of his own. He hasn't had another idea in his head since you gave Highboy to Howard."

"I don't believe in bribing children to do their duty."

"Not a bribe." She hesitated.

"No? What would you call it?"

She tried to think it out. "I just have the feeling Ken isn't going to pull anything off, and"—her eyes sought Rob's—"it's time he did. It isn't the school marks alone, but I just don't want things to go on any longer with Ken never coming out at the right end of anything."

"I'm beginning to think he's just dumb."

"He's not dumb. Maybe a little thing like this—if he had a colt of his own, trained him, rode him—"

Rob interrupted. "But it isn't a little thing, nor an easy thing, to break and school a colt the way Howard has schooled Highboy. I'm not going to have a good horse spoiled by Ken's careless ways. He goes woolgathering.[5] He never knows what he's doing."

"But he'd *love* a colt of his own, Rob. If he could do it, it might make a big difference in him."

"*If* he could do it! But that's a big if."

PREDICT

How would Kennie act if he had a colt?

At breakfast next morning Kennie's father said to him, "When you've done your study, come out to the barn. I'm going in the car up to section[6] twenty-one this morning to look over the brood mares. You can go with me."

"Can I go too, Dad?" cried Howard.

McLaughlin frowned at Howard. "You turned Highboy out last evening with dirty legs."

Howard wriggled. "I groomed him—"

"Yes, down to his knees."

"He kicks."

"And whose fault is that? You don't get on his back again until I see his legs clean."

The two boys eyed each other, Kennie secretly triumphant and Howard chagrined. McLaughlin turned at the door. "And, Ken, a week from today I'll give you a colt. Between now and then you can decide what one you want."

---

5. **woolgathering:** daydreaming.

6. **section:** a square piece of land measuring one mile on each side; 640 acres.

WORDS TO KNOW **rebellious** (rĭ-bĕl′yəs) *adj.* resisting control; not giving in

My Children (1920), W. Herbert Dunton. Oil on canvas, Museum of Fine Arts, Museum of New Mexico, Santa Fe, anonymous gift.

Kennie shot out of his chair and stared at his father. "A—a spring colt,[7] Dad, or a yearling?"[8]

McLaughlin was somewhat taken aback, but his wife concealed a smile. If Kennie got a yearling colt, he would be even up with Howard.

"A yearling colt, your father means, Ken," she said smoothly. "Now hurry with your lessons. Howard will wipe."

Kennie found himself the most important personage on the ranch. Prestige lifted his head, gave him an inch more of height and a

---

7. **spring colt:** a colt born the previous spring

8. **yearling:** an animal that is a year old.

WORDS
TO
KNOW

prestige (prĕ-stēzh′) *n.* widely recognized importance; position of high honor

491

bold stare, and made him feel different all the way through. Even Gus and Tim Murphy, the ranch hands, were more interested in Kennie's choice of a colt than anything else.

Howard was <u>fidgety</u> with suspense. "Who'll you pick, Ken? Say—pick Doughboy, why don't you? Then when he grows up he'll be sort of twins with mine, in his name anyway. Doughboy, High-boy, see?"

The boys were sitting on the worn wooden step of the door which led from the tack room[9] into the corral, busy with rags and polish, shining their bridles.

Ken looked at his brother with scorn. Doughboy would never have half of Highboy's speed.

"Lassie, then," suggested Howard. "She's black as ink, like mine. And she'll be fast—"

"Dad says Lassie'll never go over fifteen hands."

Nell McLaughlin saw the change in Kennie, and her hopes rose. He went to his books in the morning with determination and really studied. A new alertness took the place of the daydreaming. Examples in arithmetic were neatly written out, and, as she passed his door before breakfast, she often heard the monotonous drone of his voice as he read his American history aloud.

Each night, when he kissed her, he flung his arms around her and held her fiercely for a moment, then, with a winsome and <u>blissful</u> smile into her eyes, turned away to bed.

He spent days inspecting the different bands of horses and colts. He sat for hours on the corral fence, very important, chewing straws. He rode off on one of the ponies for half the day, wandering through the mile-square pastures that ran down toward the Colorado border.

And when the week was up, he announced his decision. "I'll take that yearling filly of Rocket's. The sorrel[10] with the cream tail and mane."

His father looked at him in surprise. "The one that got tangled in the barbed wire? That's never been named?"

In a second all Kennie's new pride was gone. He hung his head defensively. "Yes."

"You've made a bad choice, son. You couldn't have picked a worse."

"She's fast, Dad. And Rocket's fast—"

"It's the worst line of horses I've got. There's never one amongst them with real sense. The mares are hellions and the stallions outlaws; they're untamable."

"I'll tame her."

Rob guffawed. "Not I, nor anyone, has ever been able to really tame any one of them."

Kennie's chest heaved.

"Better change your mind, Ken. You want a horse that'll be a real friend to you, don't you?"

"Yes—" Kennie's voice was unsteady.

"Well, you'll never make a friend of that

🥾 "You said she'd never been named. I've named her. Her name is Flicka."

---

9. **tack room:** a room in which saddles and other horse gear are stored.

10. **sorrel** (sôr′əl): a horse with a brownish orange color.

WORDS TO KNOW

fidgety (fĭj′ĭ-tē) *adj.* moving restlessly
blissful (blĭs′fəl) *adj.* very happy; overjoyed

filly. She's all cut and scarred up already with tearing through barbed wire after that mother of hers. No fence'll hold 'em—"

"I know," said Kennie, still more faintly.

"Change your mind?" asked Howard briskly.

"No."

Rob was grim and put out. He couldn't go back on his word. The boy had to have a reasonable amount of help in breaking and taming the filly, and he could envision precious hours, whole days, wasted in the struggle.

Nell McLaughlin despaired. Once again Ken seemed to have taken the wrong turn and was back where he had begun, stoical,[11] silent, defensive.

But there was a difference that only Ken could know. The way he felt about his colt. The way his heart sang. The pride and joy that filled him so full that sometimes he hung his head so they wouldn't see it shining out of his eyes.

He had known from the very first that he would choose that particular yearling because he was in love with her.

The year before, he had been out working with Gus, the big Swedish ranch hand, on the irrigation ditch, when they had noticed Rocket standing in a gully on the hillside, quiet for once and eyeing them cautiously.

"Ay bet she got a colt," said Gus, and they walked carefully up the draw. Rocket gave a wild snort, thrust her feet out, shook her head wickedly, then fled away. And as they reached the spot, they saw standing there the wavering, pinkish colt, barely able to keep its feet. It gave a little squeak and started after its mother on crooked, wobbling legs.

"Yee whiz! Luk at de little *flicka!*" said Gus.

"What does *flicka* mean, Gus?"

"Swedish for little gurl, Ken—"

Ken announced at supper, "You said she'd never been named. I've named her. Her name is Flicka."

The first thing to do was to get her in. She was running with a band of yearlings on the saddleback,[12] cut with ravines and gullies, on section twenty.

They all went out after her, Ken, as owner, on old Rob Roy, the wisest horse on the ranch.

Ken was entranced to watch Flicka when the wild band of youngsters discovered that they were being pursued and took off across the mountain. Footing made no difference to her. She floated across the ravines, always two lengths ahead of the others. Her pink mane and tail whipped in the wind. Her long, delicate legs had only to aim, it seemed, at a particular spot for her to reach it and sail on. She seemed to Ken a fairy horse.

He sat motionless, just watching and holding Rob Roy in, when his father thundered past on Sultan and shouted, "Well, what's the matter? Why didn't you turn 'em?"

Kennie woke up and galloped after.

Rob Roy brought in the whole band. The corral gates were closed, and an hour was spent shunting the ponies in and out and through the chutes, until Flicka was left alone in the small round corral in which the baby colts were branded. Gus drove the others away, out the gate, and up the saddleback.

But Flicka did not intend to be left. She hurled herself against the poles which walled the corral. She tried to jump them. They were seven feet high. She caught her front feet over the top rung, clung, scrambled, while Kennie held his breath for fear the slender legs would

---

11. **stoical** (stō′ĭ-kəl): showing no emotion.

12. **saddleback:** a ridge with a sunken top.

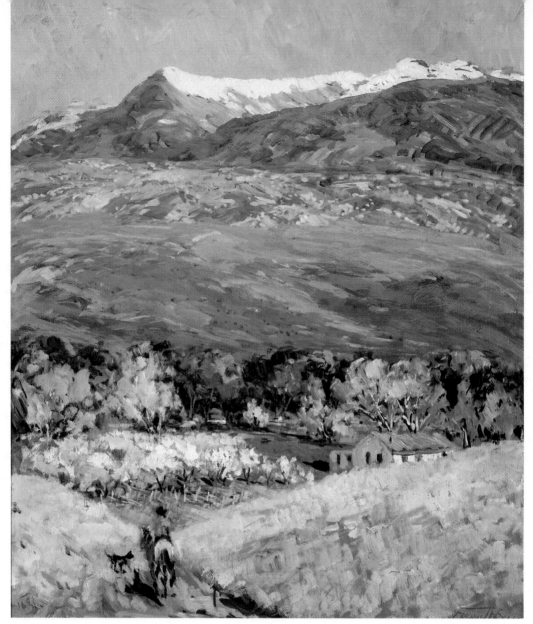

New Mexico Spring (about 1950), Fremont Ellis. Oil on canvas, 36" x 30", The Anschutz Collection, Denver. Photo by James O. Milmoe.

be caught between the bars and snapped. Her hold broke; she fell over backward, rolled, screamed, tore around the corral. Kennie had a sick feeling in the pit of his stomach, and his father looked disgusted.

One of the bars broke. She hurled herself again. Another went. She saw the opening and, as neatly as a dog crawls through a fence, inserted her head and forefeet, scrambled through, and fled away, bleeding in a dozen places.

As Gus was coming back, just about to close the gate to the upper range, the sorrel whipped through it, sailed across the road and ditch with her inimitable[13] floating leap, and went up the side of the saddleback like a jack rabbit.

---

13. **inimitable** (ĭ-nĭm′ĭ-tə-bəl): not capable of being imitated or copied.

From way up the mountain, Gus heard excited whinnies as she joined the band he had just driven up, and the last he saw of them they were strung out along the crest running like deer.

"Yee whiz!" said Gus, and stood motionless and staring until the ponies had disappeared over the ridge. Then he closed the gate, remounted Rob Roy, and rode back to the corral.

Rob McLaughlin gave Kennie one more chance to change his mind. "Last chance, son. Better pick a horse that you have some hope of riding one day. I'd have got rid of this whole line of stock if they weren't so damned fast that I've had the fool idea that someday there might turn out one gentle one in the lot—and I'd have a racehorse. But there's never been one so far, and it's not going to be Flicka."

"It's not going to be Flicka," chanted Howard.

"Perhaps she *might* be gentled," said Kennie; and Nell, watching, saw that although his lips quivered, there was <u>fanatical</u> determination in his eye.

"Ken," said Rob, "it's up to you. If you say you want her, we'll get her. But she wouldn't be the first of that line to die rather than give in. They're beautiful and they're fast, but let me tell you this, young man, they're *loco!*"[14]

Kennie flinched under his father's direct glance.

"If I go after her again, I'll not give up

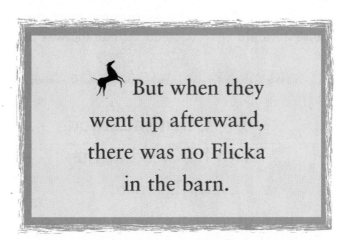

But when they went up afterward, there was no Flicka in the barn.

whatever comes; understand what I mean by that?"

"Yes."

"What do you say?"

"I want her."

They brought her in again. They had better luck this time. She jumped over the Dutch half door of the stable and crashed inside. The men slammed the upper half of the door shut, and she was caught.

The rest of the band were driven away, and Kennie stood outside of the stable, listening to the wild hoofs beating, the screams, the crashes. His Flicka inside there! He was drenched with perspiration.

"We'll leave her to think it over," said Rob when dinnertime came. "Afterward, we'll go up and feed and water her."

But when they went up afterward, there was no Flicka in the barn. One of the windows, higher than the mangers, was broken.

The window opened into a pasture an eighth of a mile square, fenced in barbed wire six feet high. Near the stable stood a wagon-load of hay. When they went around the back of the stable to see where Flicka had hidden herself, they found her between the stable and the hay wagon, eating.

At their approach she leaped away, then headed east across the pasture.

---

14. **loco** (lō′kō): a slang term meaning "crazy."

"If she's like her mother," said Rob, "she'll go right through the wire."

"Ay bet she'll go over," said Gus. "She yumps like a deer."

"No horse can jump that," said McLaughlin.

Kennie said nothing because he could not speak. It was, perhaps, the most terrible moment of his life. He watched Flicka racing toward the eastern wire.

A few yards from it, she swerved, turned, and raced diagonally south.

"It turned her! It turned her!" cried Kennie, almost sobbing. It was the first sign of hope for Flicka. "Oh, Dad! She has got sense. She has! She has!"

Flicka turned again as she met the southern boundary of the pasture, again at the northern; she avoided the barn. Without abating anything of her whirlwind speed, following a precise, accurate calculation, and turning each time on a dime, she investigated every possibility. Then, seeing that there was no hope, she raced south toward the range where she had spent her life, gathered herself, and shot into the air.

Each of the three men watching had the impulse to cover his eyes, and Kennie gave a sort of a howl of despair.

Twenty yards of fence came down with her as she hurled herself through. Caught on the upper strands, she turned a complete somersault, landing on her back, her four legs dragging the wires down on top of her, and tangling herself in them beyond hope of escape. . . .

Often she stood with her head at the south fence, looking off to the mountain.

Kennie followed the men miserably as they walked to the filly. They stood in a circle watching while she kicked and fought and thrashed until the wire was tightly wound and knotted about her, cutting, piercing, and tearing great three-cornered pieces of flesh and hide. At last she was unconscious, streams of blood running on her golden coat and pools of crimson widening and spreading on the grass beneath her.

With the wire cutter which Gus always carried in the hip pocket of his overalls, he cut all the wire away, and they drew her into the pasture, repaired the fence, placed hay, a box of oats, and a tub of water near her, and called it a day.

"I don't think she'll pull out of it," said McLaughlin.

EVALUATE

What do you think of Kennie's choice of Flicka?

Next morning Kennie was up at five, doing his lessons. At six he went out to Flicka.

She had not moved. Food and water were untouched. She was no longer bleeding, but the wounds were swollen and caked over.

Kennie got a bucket of fresh water and poured it over her mouth. Then he leaped away, for Flicka came to life, scrambled up, got her balance, and stood swaying.

Kennie went a few feet away and sat down to watch her. When he went in to breakfast, she had drunk deeply of the water and was mouthing the oats.

There began then a sort of recovery. She ate,

drank, limped about the pasture, stood for hours with hanging head and weakly splayed-out[15] legs under the clump of cottonwood trees. The swollen wounds scabbed and began to heal.

Kennie lived in the pasture too. He followed her around; he talked to her. He too lay snoozing or sat under the cottonwoods; and often, coaxing her with hand outstretched, he walked very quietly toward her. But she would not let him come near her.

Often she stood with her head at the south fence, looking off to the mountain. It made the tears come to Kennie's eyes to see the way she longed to get away.

Still Rob said she wouldn't pull out of it. There was no use putting a halter on her. She had no strength.

One morning, as Ken came out of the house, Gus met him and said, "De filly's down."

Kennie ran to the pasture, Howard close behind him. The right hind leg which had been badly swollen at the knee joint had opened in a festering wound, and Flicka lay flat and motionless, with staring eyes.

"Don't you wish now you'd chosen Dough-boy?" asked Howard.

"Go away!" shouted Ken.

Howard stood watching while Kennie sat down on the ground and took Flicka's head on his lap. Though she was conscious and moved a little, she did not struggle nor seem frightened. Tears rolled down Kennie's cheeks as he talked to her and petted her. After a few moments, Howard walked away.

other, what do you do for an infection when it's a horse?" asked Kennie.

"Just what you'd do if it was a person. Wet dressings. I'll help you, Ken. We mustn't let those wounds close or scab over until they're clean. I'll make a poultice[16] for that hind leg and help you put it on. Now that she'll let us get close to her, we can help her a lot."

"The thing to do is see that she eats," said Rob. "Keep up her strength."

But he himself would not go near her. "She won't pull out of it," he said. "I don't want to see her or think about her."

Kennie and his mother nursed the filly. The big poultice was bandaged on the hind leg. It drew out much poisoned matter, and Flicka felt better and was able to stand again.

She watched for Kennie now and followed him like a dog, hopping on three legs, holding up the right hind leg with its huge knob of a bandage in comical fashion.

"Dad, Flicka's my friend now; she likes me," said Ken.

His father looked at him. "I'm glad of that, son. It's a fine thing to have a horse for a friend."

QUESTION

Why does Kennie's father respond in this way?

Kennie found a nicer place for her. In the lower pasture the brook ran over cool stones. There was a grassy bank the size of a corral, almost on a level with the water. Here she could lie softly, eat grass, drink fresh running water. From the grass, a twenty-foot hill sloped up, crested with overhanging trees. She was enclosed, as it were, in a green open-air nursery.

Kennie carried her oats morning and evening. She would watch for him to come, eyes and ears pointed to the hill. And one evening Ken, still some distance off, came to a stop, and a wide grin spread over his face. He had heard her nicker. She had caught sight of him coming and was calling to him!

---

15. **splayed-out:** turning outward.

16. **poultice** (pōl′tĭs): a soft, pastelike mixture of mud, herbs, or medicine that is applied to a sore.

He placed the box of oats under her nose, and she ate while he stood beside her, his hand smoothing the satin-soft skin under her mane. It had a nap as deep as plush. He played with her long, cream-colored tresses, arranged her

Ken knew she heard the other colts galloping on the upland.

"You'll go back there someday, Flicka," he whispered. "You'll be three and I'll be eleven. You'll be so strong you won't know I'm on your back, and we'll fly like the wind. We'll stand on the very top where we can look over the whole world and smell the snow from the Never-summer Range. Maybe we'll see antelope—"

This was the happiest month of Kennie's life.

With the morning, Flicka always had new strength and would hop three-legged up the hill to stand broadside to the

Sweet Talkin' Man (1982), Gordon Snidow. Courtesy of The Greenwich Workshop, Inc. Copyright © 1982 The Greenwich Workshop, Inc.

forelock neatly between her eyes. She was a bit dish faced, like an Arab, with eyes set far apart. He lightly groomed and brushed her while she stood turning her head to him whichever way he went.

He spoiled her. Soon she would not step to the stream to drink but he must hold a bucket for her. And she would drink, then lift her dripping muzzle, rest it on the shoulder of his blue chambray shirt, her golden eyes dreaming off into the distance, then daintily dip her mouth to drink again.

When she turned her head to the south and pricked her ears and stood tense and listening,

early sun, as horses love to do.

The moment Ken woke he'd go to the window and see her there, and when he was dressed and at his table studying, he sat so that he could raise his head and see Flicka.

After breakfast, she would be waiting for him and the box of oats at the gate, and for Nell McLaughlin with fresh bandages and buckets of disinfectant; and all three would go together to the brook, Flicka hopping along ahead of them, as if she was leading the way.

But Rob McLaughlin would not look at her.

One day all the wounds were swollen again. Presently they opened one by one, and Kennie and his mother made more poultices.

Still the little filly climbed the hill in the early morning and ran about on three legs. Then she began to go down in flesh and almost overnight wasted away to nothing. Every rib showed; the glossy hide was dull and brittle and was pulled over the skeleton as if she were a dead horse.

Gus said, "It's de fever. It burns up her flesh. If you could stop de fever she might get vell."

McLaughlin was standing in his window one morning and saw the little skeleton hopping about three-legged in the sunshine, and he said, "That's the end. I won't have a thing like that on my place."

Kennie had to understand that Flicka had not been getting well all this time; she had been slowly dying.

"She still eats her oats," he said mechanically.

They were all sorry for Ken. Nell McLaughlin stopped disinfecting and dressing the wounds. "It's no use, Ken," she said gently. "You know Flicka's going to die, don't you?"

"Yes, Mother."

Ken stopped eating. Howard said, "Ken doesn't eat anything anymore. Don't he have to eat his dinner, Mother?"

But Nell answered, "Leave him alone."

Because the shooting of wounded animals is all in the day's work on the Western plains, and sickening to everyone, Rob's voice, when he gave the order to have Flicka shot, was as flat as if he had been telling Gus to kill a chicken for dinner.

"Here's the Marlin, Gus. Pick out a time when Ken's not around and put the filly out of her misery."

Gus took the rifle. "*Ja,* boss—"

Ever since Ken had known that Flicka was to be shot, he had kept his eye on the rack which held the firearms. His father allowed no firearms in the bunkhouse. The gun rack was in the dining room of the ranch house, and, going through it to the kitchen three times a day for meals, Ken's eye scanned the weapons to make sure that they were all there.

That night they were not all there. The Marlin rifle was missing.

When Kennie saw that, he stopped walking. He felt dizzy. He kept staring at the gun rack, telling himself that it surely was there—he counted again and again—he couldn't see clearly—

Then he felt an arm across his shoulders and heard his father's voice.

"I know, son. Some things are awful hard to take. We just have to take 'em. I have to, too."

Kennie got hold of his father's hand and held on. It helped steady him.

Finally he looked up. Rob looked down and smiled at him and gave him a little shake and squeeze. Ken managed a smile too.

"All right now?"

"All right, Dad."

They walked in to supper together.

Ken even ate a little. But Nell looked thoughtfully at the ashen color of his face and at the little pulse that was beating in the side of his neck.

After supper he carried Flicka her oats, but

> "I know, son. Some things are awful hard to take. We just have to take 'em. I have to, too."

he had to coax her, and she would only eat a little. She stood with her head hanging, but when he stroked it and talked to her, she pressed her face into his chest and was content. He could feel the burning heat of her body. It didn't seem possible that anything so thin could be alive.

Presently Kennie saw Gus come into the pasture carrying the Marlin. When he saw Ken, he changed his direction and sauntered along as if he was out to shoot some cottontails.

Ken ran to him. "When are you going to do it, Gus?"

"Ay was goin' down soon now, before it got dark—"

"Gus, don't do it tonight. Wait till morning. Just one more night, Gus."

"Vell, in de morning, den, but it got to be done, Ken. Yer fader gives de order."

"I know. I won't say anything more."

An hour after the family had gone to bed, Ken got up and put on his clothes. It was a warm moonlit night. He ran down to the brook, calling softly, "Flicka! Flicka!"

But Flicka did not answer with a little nicker; and she was not in the nursery nor hopping about the pasture. Ken hunted for an hour.

At last he found her down the creek, lying in the water. Her head had been on the bank, but as she lay there, the current of the stream had sucked and pulled at her, and she had had no strength to resist; and little by little her head had slipped down, until when Ken got there only the muzzle was resting on the bank, and the body and legs were swinging in the stream.

Kennie slid into the water, sitting on the bank, and he hauled at her head. But she was heavy, and the current dragged like a weight; and he began to sob because he had no strength to draw her out.

Then he found a leverage for his heels against some rocks in the bed of the stream, and he braced himself against these and pulled with all his might; and her head came up onto his knees, and he held it cradled in his arms.

He was glad that she had died of her own accord, in the cool water, under the moon, instead of being shot by Gus. Then, putting his face close to hers and looking searchingly into her eyes, he saw that she was alive and looking back at him.

And then he burst out crying and hugged her and said, "Oh, my little Flicka, my little Flicka."

The long night passed.

The moon slid slowly across the heavens.

The water rippled over Kennie's legs and over Flicka's body. And gradually the heat and fever went out of her. And the cool running water washed and washed her wounds.

When Gus went down in the morning with the rifle, they hadn't moved. There they were, Kennie sitting in water over his thighs and hips, with Flicka's head in his arms.

Gus seized Flicka by the head and hauled her out on the grassy bank and then, seeing that Kennie couldn't move, cold and stiff and half paralyzed as he was, lifted him in his arms and carried him to the house.

"Gus," said Ken through chattering teeth, "don't shoot her, Gus."

"It ain't fur me to say, Ken. You know dat."

"But the fever's left her, Gus."

"Ay wait a little, Ken—"

Rob McLaughlin drove to Laramie to get the doctor, for Ken was in violent chills that would not stop. His mother had him in bed wrapped in hot blankets when they got back.

He looked at his father imploringly as the doctor shook down the thermometer.

"She might get well now, Dad. The fever's left her. It went out of her when the moon went down."

"All right, son. Don't worry. Gus'll feed her, morning and night, as long as she's—"

"As long as I can't do it," finished Kennie happily.

The doctor put the thermometer in his mouth and told him to keep it shut.

All day Gus went about his work, thinking of Flicka. He had not been back to look at her. He had been given no more orders. If she was alive, the order to shoot her was still in effect. But Kennie was ill, McLaughlin making his second trip to town, taking the doctor home, and would not be back till long after dark.

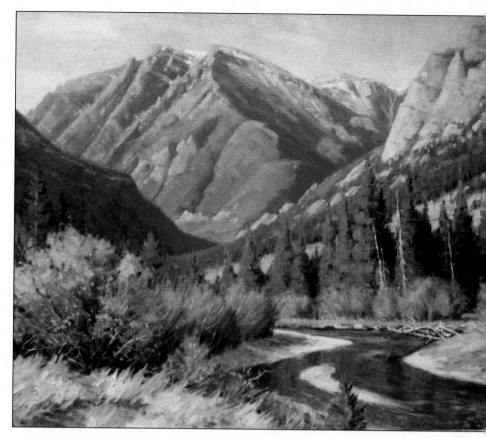

In the Valley of the Rosebud (1992), Ralph E. Oberg. Oil on canvas, 24″ x 30″. Copyright © Ralph E. Oberg.

After their supper in the bunkhouse, Gus and Tim walked down to the brook. They did not speak as they approached the filly, lying stretched out flat on the grassy bank, but their eyes were straining at her to see if she was dead or alive.

She raised her head as they reached her.

"By the powers!" exclaimed Tim. "There she is!"

She dropped her head, raised it again, and moved her legs and became tense as if struggling to rise. But to do so she must use her right hind leg to brace herself against the earth. That was the damaged leg, and at the first bit of pressure with it she gave up and fell back.

"We'll swing her onto the other side," said Tim. "Then she can help herself."

"*Ja*—"

Standing behind her, they leaned over, grabbed hold of her left legs, front and back, and gently hauled her over. Flicka was as lax and willing as a puppy. But the moment she found herself lying on her right side, she began to scramble, braced herself with her good left leg, and tried to rise.

"Yee whiz!" said Gus. "She got plenty strength yet."

"Hi!" cheered Tim. "She's up!"

But Flicka wavered, slid down again, and lay flat. This time she gave notice that she would not try again by heaving a deep sigh and closing her eyes.

Gus took his pipe out of his mouth and thought it over. Orders or no orders, he would try to save the filly. Ken had gone too far to be let down.

"Ay'm goin' to rig a blanket sling fur her, Tim, and get her on her feet and keep her up."

There was bright moonlight to work by. They brought down the posthole digger and set two aspen poles deep into the ground either side of the filly, then, with ropes attached to the blanket, hoisted her by a pulley.

Not at all disconcerted, she rested comfortably in the blanket under her belly, touched her feet on the ground, and reached for the bucket of water Gus held for her.

Kennie was sick a long time. He nearly died. But Flicka picked up. Every day Gus passed the word to Nell, who carried it to Ken. "She's cleaning up her oats." . . . "She's out of the sling." . . . "She bears a little weight on the bad leg."

Tim declared it was a real miracle. They argued about it, eating their supper.

"Na," said Gus. "It was de cold water, washin' de fever outa her. And more dan dat—it was Ken—you tink it don't count? All night dot boy sits dere and says, 'Hold on, Flicka, Ay'm here wid you. Ay'm standin' by, two of us togedder'—"

Tim stared at Gus without answering, while he thought it over. In the silence, a coyote yapped far off on the plains, and the wind made a rushing sound high up in the jack pines on the hill.

Gus filled his pipe.

"Sure," said Tim finally. "Sure, that's it."

Then came the day when Rob McLaughlin stood smiling at the foot of Kennie's bed and said, "Listen! Hear your friend?"

Ken listened and heard Flicka's high, eager whinny.

"She don't spend much time by the brook anymore. She's up at the gate of the corral half the time, nickering for you."

"For me!"

Rob wrapped a blanket around the boy and carried him out to the corral gate.

Kennie gazed at Flicka. There was a look of marveling in his eyes. He felt as if he had been living in a world where everything was dreadful and hurting but awfully real; and *this* couldn't be real; this was all soft and happy, nothing to struggle over or worry about or fight for any more. Even his father was proud of him! He could feel it in the way Rob's big arms held him. It was all like a dream and far away. He couldn't, yet, get close to anything.

But Flicka—Flicka—alive, well, pressing up to him, recognizing him, nickering—

Kennie put out a hand—weak and white—and laid it on her face. His thin little fingers straightened her forelock the way he used to do, while Rob looked at the two with a strange expression about his mouth and a glow in his eyes that was not often there.

"She's still poor, Dad, but she's on four legs now."

"She's picking up."

Ken turned his face up, suddenly remembering. "Dad! She did get gentled, didn't she?"

"Gentle—as—a kitten—"

They put a cot down by the brook for Ken, and boy and filly got well together. ❖

RESPONDING
OPTIONS

FROM PERSONAL RESPONSE TO CRITICAL ANALYSIS

REFLECT

1. What image from the story had the greatest impact on you? In your notebook, briefly describe the image and how you reacted to it.

RETHINK

2. Do you think Kennie's decision to choose Flicka was a good one? Explain your answer.

3. How would you describe Kennie's relationships with the different members of his family?

4. In your opinion, how does Kennie change during the story?

   Consider
   - his feelings about himself
   - his care of Flicka
   - the personal traits he exhibits

5. If Flicka had died, do you think the lessons Kennie learned from her would have died too? Why or why not?

RELATE

6. At one point, Rob McLaughlin says about his son, "Ken doesn't half try, doesn't stick at anything." How important do you think it is for a nine-year-old to persist at an activity?

ANOTHER PATHWAY
Cooperative Learning

Present a Readers Theater performance of "My Friend Flicka" for your class. With a group, adapt one or two scenes. Look at the story for dialogue, but feel free to add lines of your own. Try to convey the mood of the scenes you choose through the expression in your voice and the interaction of the characters.

THE WRITER'S STYLE

One reviewer of the novel version of *My Friend Flicka* commented that Mary O'Hara's description "makes you smell the grass and feel the coolness of the wind." Choose a description of the setting or a character from the short story version. Explain how well you think the description appeals to either the sense of sight, hearing, touch, smell, or taste.

QUICKWRITES

1. Write a **diary entry** that Kennie might write during the period when Flicka is sick.

2. Based on Kennie's experiences with Flicka, write some **guidelines** on choosing and taking care of a colt or filly.

📁 *PORTFOLIO Save your writing. You may want to use it later as a springboard to a piece for your portfolio.*

LITERARY CONCEPTS

To create a story that readers can understand and enjoy, a writer connects the events carefully. The **plot** consists of the actions or events that make up a story. The plot is the writer's plan for what happens, when it happens, and to whom it happens. Make and fill out a story map for "My Friend Flicka" similar to the one shown.

CONCEPT REVIEW: Suspense As you know, suspense is the feeling of excitement that grows when the reader wants to know how a situation will turn out. Flicka's attempt to jump over the fence, for example, is a moment of suspense. Locate and describe another suspenseful part of the story.

Main Character:	Setting:
Conflict or Story Problem:	
Major Events:	
Event 1	
Event 2	
Event 3 (add more as needed)	
Solution:	
	Theme:

ALTERNATIVE ACTIVITIES

1. Design a **poster** to advertise a new movie version of "My Friend Flicka." Using either hand-drawn art or magazine pictures, try to capture the mood of the story in an illustration.

2. The word *yearling* is one of many special terms in the story that relate to horses. Review the story, and make a list of the specialized vocabulary words. Using reference materials, define the words and list them alphabetically. Combine your definitions with illustrations to create a **pocket dictionary** of horse terms to accompany the story.

CRITIC'S CORNER

Mary O'Hara said of Kennie, the main character of "My Friend Flicka," "I don't know where Ken came from. He just walked into my heart and mind one day ready-made." Do you think O'Hara is successful in making Kennie McLaughlin seem like a real-life person? Write your opinions in your notebook, taking into account the way in which Kennie speaks, feels, and acts throughout the story.

EXERCISE A Answer the following questions.

1. Would a person who was **fanatical** about watching TV watch none, a little, or a lot?

2. If a father asked a **rebellious** child to do something, would that child be most likely to say "Yes, sir!" "Do I have to?" or "No!"?

3. Would a person who is feeling **despair** most likely sigh, giggle, or yawn?

4. Does a person with a lot of **prestige** usually get treated with scorn, respect, or amusement?

5. If you **envision** an event, do you see it in a photograph, in your mind, or in a movie?

EXERCISE B For each phrase in the first column, write the letter of the phrase from the second column that means the same thing.

1. a vague uneasiness   (a) a jumpy ump

2. resist the urge to whine   (b) pursue the crew

3. a fidgety referee   (c) a blurry worry

4. a blissful father   (d) refrain from complaining

5. follow the sailors   (e) a glad dad

MARY O'HARA

The author of "My Friend Flicka," the beloved children's classic, began her writing career as a scriptwriter in the 1920s, during the early days of motion pictures. In 1931, Mary O'Hara Alsop traded screen writing for story writing and moved with her husband to a sheep ranch in Wyoming. There she found herself in a "different world. . . . Vast. Empty. Glowing with heavenly colors." She used her maiden name, O'Hara, as her pen name.

1885–1980

One day, as O'Hara struggled with a story idea that was not working out, she recalled that when she told stories about her many animals, people always seemed to listen. "How easy it would be," she thought, to write a story "about that little filly, for instance, the one that got caught in the barbed wire." Within 24 hours, she had written the notes and a few scenes for a short story called "My Friend Flicka." In 1941, O'Hara expanded the short story into a novel and continued the story of the McLaughlin family in other works. Three of her books were made into movies in the 1940s.

OTHER WORKS *Thunderhead, Green Grass of Wyoming, The Son of Adam Wyngate, The Catch Colt*

WRITING TO EXPLAIN

As you learned in Unit Four, "Proving Ground," the challenges we face in life often bring out either the best or the worst in us. Would you have reacted in the same way as the characters in the stories if you had been in their shoes? Comparing people, places, things, and ideas can help you better understand a subject, make a decision, or prove a point. In this way, comparing and contrasting may help you get through your own personal proving ground.

GUIDED ASSIGNMENT

Write a Compare-Contrast Essay In this lesson you will have the opportunity to explore the similarities and differences between two subjects.

Cartoon
Humor often comes from comparing people and situations.

1 Why Make Comparisons?

The world is filled with things to compare. What do you and your best friend have in common? How are the two of you different? Would you rather play the trumpet or the trombone? You might find yourself making comparisons to help you do the following things.

Explain the Unfamiliar Sometimes the best way to understand or explain something unusual is to compare it to something familiar. The food described in the book excerpt on the next page may be new to you. How might a comparison help you decide whether you'd like it?

Make a Decision Studying the differences between two or more things can help you make choices. Based on the information in the ad and the announcement on the opposite page, would you rather have a paper route or be in a play?

2 What Will You Compare?

Make some notes about possible topics.

- Is there a person you wish your friends knew, a place you'd like them to imagine, or an idea you want to show? How could you help them understand the topic through a comparison?
- Do you have a difficult decision to make? Jot down your possible choices.

Decision Point Freewrite for a few minutes to see what thoughts you uncover, and then choose the comparison that interests you most.

Buttra, Oudom, and Richard Prek moved to the United States from Cambodia with their mother, Sohka, and grandmother, Sok Eng. The food they eat is a daily reminder of the Cambodian culture they left behind.

For dinner, the boys eat the kind of food their grandmother knew as a child in Cambodia and that she learned to cook as a young bride and mother. It is nothing like the bread or the spaghetti or the other foods they see and some- times eat at school, but it is the kind of food they have eaten all their lives, and they love it. Each evening, their grandmother's pots simmer and sizzle with spicy fried rice and rice noodles; warm white rice; spring rolls; *bawbaw*, a chicken soup with rice; or any of the other traditional Asian vegetables; or any of the other traditional dishes that Sok Eng manages to make using the foods she and Sohka find in the Asian markets of Boston. Everyone eats in the living room, sitting on the couch or floor, as they would in Cambodia, using the silverware they were introduced to here.

Nancy Price Graff

from *Where the River Runs: A Portrait of a Refugee Family*

W a n t e d :

The Huronville Daily News is seeking responsible students to deliver afternoon weekday papers. Routes range from four to eight blocks. (More cus- tomers, higher pay!) Will be expected to deliver in all weather conditions. Must provide own transportation. Required to collect payments monthly. Must be reliable! Call 555-NEWS for an application.

Mom wants me to find something to do after school. Maybe get a job?

Be a ST★R!

Tryouts for *The Phantom Tollbooth*

When:	March 6th, 3:30 P.M.
Where:	In the school auditorium
How:	Those interested in reading for a part can pick up a script in the drama room (#118) this week.
Rehearsals:	Mondays and Wednesdays 3:30–5:30 P.M. and Saturdays 9–11 A.M.
Performances:	June 1st and 2nd

Or I could try out for this play. . . . Which activity should I choose?

▶ **LASERLINKS**
• *WRITING SPRINGBOARD*

▶ **WRITING COACH**

Working Through Ideas

Maps of Your Notes Now that you've chosen two subjects to compare, you're ready to discover ways they are similar and different. The steps on these pages will help you recognize the differences and organize your observations.

① Choose Features to Compare

To compare your subjects, you'll need to decide which characteristics, or features, you want to examine. The student writer is comparing being in a play with having a paper route. He identified the key points that would affect his decision:

- time commitment
- enjoyment
- skills he'd learn
- others who would be involved

List three or four features of your subjects that you'd like to compare.

② Find and Diagram the Details

Now look at each feature you listed. How are your two subjects similar and different? List all the details you can. Do research if necessary. You may want to use a chart like the one below to help you organize your observations.

In the first column, list the features you chose to compare. Then, under each of your subjects, write down details that show how the subjects are similar or different. The SkillBuilder will show you how to make another type of organizer—a Venn diagram.

Student's Comparison Chart

features	school play: The Phantom Tollbooth	job: paper route
Time commitment	- practice twice a week and Saturdays for 2 hours	- every weekday for about 1 1/2 hours
Enjoyment Skills I'd learn	- fun to act on stage - help me with memorizing - make me better at speaking	- have money to spend - learn how to handle money
Others who would be involved	- old friends, plus meet new people	- be on my own, except for talking to customers

3 Know Your Audience

Who will your audience be: your classmates, your parents, or members of your community? You may want to write just for yourself, as the student trying to decide between the job and the play is doing. If you are writing for others, how can you best reach them? What might they already know about your subjects?

Decision Point Will you want to include diagrams or illustrations in your presentation to help you show your comparison?

4 Think Before You Draft

Before you begin writing your draft, think about how you will organize your comparison. Here are two methods you might try.

Subject-by-Subject One way to organize is to cover all the features of one subject first, and then describe the second subject, explaining how each feature is similar to or different from the first subject.

Feature-by-Feature Another method is to examine one feature at a time, comparing both subjects and then moving on to the next feature.

Page 791 of the Writing Handbook provides more information on organizing your comparison-contrast essay.

**Student's
Organizational Notes**

Thinking on the Page

A Clearer Focus Now you're ready to begin drafting your comparison. What have you discovered by studying the features of your subjects? Do you have a better understanding of something or someone? Are you now able to make a decision? Get ready to tell your readers what you have learned.

❶ Draft to Discover

Start by writing the part of the comparison you feel most comfortable with. Don't limit yourself to the information in your charts, diagrams, or other prewriting notes. New ideas or features may occur to you while you're writing.

Student's Discovery Draft

Workspace

My Draft	Kwok's Comments on My Draft
A Difficult Decision	
(Decision I have to make) My mom said I had to choose something to do after school. She works and doesn't want me to be home alone. So: school play, or paper route?	You've really thought this through! Maybe Ms. R. would let you present this to our class orally. Then we could help you decide.
(PLAY) First, the features of doing a play. **(Time)** Play rehearsals are held only two days a week after school, but we'd also practice on Saturdays. This part is not that great. **(Skills)** I'd have to learn lines for a part. Maybe this would help me become better at memorizing for tests too! I'd probably also get better at speaking in front of big groups. **(Others involved)** Lots of my friends are going to try out, and I'd meet new people too. **(Enjoyment)** We'd have to work hard for the play, but it would be a fun kind of work.	You may have to give up some things to get what you want.
(JOB) Although the paper route doesn't seem as much fun, there are some good reasons to choose it. **(Time)** I would get weekends off, but I'd have to deliver papers every weekday, which could become a drag! **(Skills)** I would become better at working with money. **(Others involved)** I'd mostly be on my own, which could be nice, but it could also be lonely. I would have to talk to my customers when I collected money. That kind of makes me nervous. **(Enjoyment)** I'd have extra money to buy stuff with. That's the best part of the job!	This is an interesting point. Yes, and this might help you do better on math tests!

---

② Evaluate Your Draft

Check to make sure you have explained your ideas thoroughly to your readers by asking yourself the following questions:

- Do the details I include show both how my subjects are similar and how they are different?
- Would my comparison be clearer if I organized my information differently?
- How might I publish my comparison to best reach and teach my audience? (See page 513 for publishing ideas.)

③ Rework Your Comparison

Once you have evaluated your draft, you may want to change a few things. The following tips can help you rework your essay.

Introduction Be sure you introduce at the beginning of your essay what you will be comparing. Your introduction should also make it clear why you are making a comparison.

Body To help readers follow your comparison, begin a new paragraph for each subject (when using subject-by-subject organization) or for each feature (when using feature-by-feature organization).

Conclusion You may have learned something surprising or formed new ideas as you compared your subjects. You might want to mention these discoveries in your conclusion.

 PEER RESPONSE

Here are some questions to ask a peer reviewer so that you can get helpful feedback on your essay. If you are using the Writing Coach, comments can be typed into the side column.

- Why do you think I chose to compare these subjects?
- Which points of comparison did you find most interesting? least interesting?
- What other features might I have compared?
- Have I strayed from my organizational pattern? Where?

SkillBuilder

 WRITER'S CRAFT

Using Transitions
Transition words and phrases can help you to draw attention to similarities and differences between subjects or features.

> **Both** the play and paper route take time after school, **but** play rehearsals are on Saturdays too.

Transitions that signal	
similarities	**differences**
• both	• but
• also	• instead
• neither	• however
• in addition	• yet
• similarly	• unlike
• likewise	• on the other hand

WRITING HANDBOOK

For more information on using transitions, see page 781 of the Writing Handbook.

APPLYING WHAT YOU LEARNED
Where might you add transitions in your comparison to make it stronger or clearer?

RETHINK & EVALUATE

Preparing to Revise

1. Would reorganizing your comparison make it easier to follow? Why?
2. What do you like about your draft? What parts do you still need to work on?

Pulling It All Together

The Final Stages Before sharing your comparison with others, use the guidelines on these pages to help you improve your essay. If you've decided to present your explanation in a special format, you may want to make some additional changes. For example, the student writer decided to take his peer reader's advice and get his classmates' help with his decision.

Student's Oral Presentation Notes

> 1
>
> What I am comparing and why:
> My mom works. She asked me to find something to get involved with after school so that I won't be home alone.
>
> I compared working on the school play to delivering papers for the Huronville Daily News to help me decide which I'd rather spend my time doing.

> 3
> Feature Two: Skills I'd Learn

> 2
> Feature One: Time Commitment
> Both activities would take lots of time.
> (play) Rehearsals for The Phantom Tollbooth last two hours and are held three times a week. Practices are held on Saturday, which is not so cool.
> (job) The time it takes to deliver papers each day is shorter than play rehearsals (1 1/2 hours instead of 2). The paper route would keep me busier more days during the week, but I'd be free on weekends.

> 4
> Feature Three: Others Involved

> 5
> Feature Four: Enjoyment

> 6
> After comparing these two activities, I discovered they are more alike than I thought. I guess that's why I liked them both to begin with. Now I see that working at a job can be fun, and a play is not only fun but hard work too. So which should I choose? Can you help me decide?

What transition words or phrases did the student writer use in his comparison?

1 Revise and Edit

Give yourself and your draft a rest and then read it again. How well have you examined your subjects?

- See how one student created note cards to help him remember important points he wanted to present orally.
- Use the SkillBuilder on page 513 to check your use of comparatives and superlatives.
- Refer to the Standards for Evaluation to improve each part of your comparison.

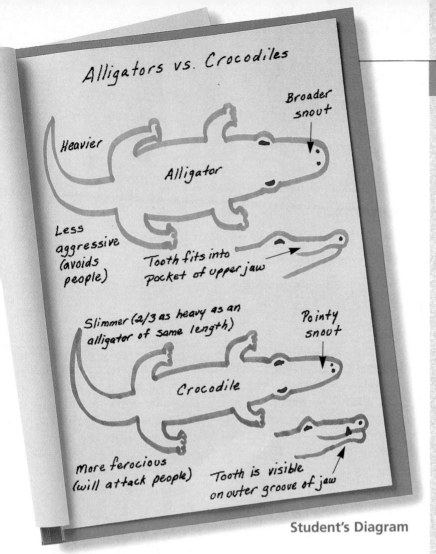

Alligators vs. Crocodiles

Broader snout

Heavier

Alligator

Less aggressive (avoids people)

Tooth fits into pocket of upper jaw

Slimmer (2/3 as heavy as an alligator of same length)

Pointy snout

Crocodile

More ferocious (will attack people)

Tooth is visible on outer groove of jaw

Student's Diagram

❷ Share Your Comparison

You may want to include photographs or drawings of your subjects to help show their similarities and differences. The example above shows how another student added diagrams with captions to his essay to highlight the features he was comparing.

Standards for Evaluation

A comparison-contrast essay
- states clearly the subjects being compared and shows how they are alike and different
- is easy to follow, using either feature-by-feature or subject-by-subject organization
- uses transitions to signal similarities and differences
- ends with a conclusion that explains the decision made or a new understanding of the subjects compared

GRAMMAR FROM WRITING

Using Comparatives and Superlatives

Use the **comparative** form when you are comparing or contrasting two subjects.

*Play rehearsals are **more fun** than delivering papers.*

Use the **superlative** form when you are comparing or contrasting three or more subjects.

*I would like the **fastest** bike of all for my paper route.*

GRAMMAR HANDBOOK

For more help with comparatives and superlatives, see pages 831–832 of the Grammar Handbook.

Editing Checklist Check these points as you revise your draft.

- Did you use transitions?
- Have you used the correct form of comparatives and superlatives?

REFLECT & ASSESS

Evaluating Your Experience

1. What did you learn about your subjects by comparing them?
2. How did your prewriting notes or diagrams help you write your essay?

PORTFOLIO What did you accomplish by writing this essay? Add your answer and assignment to your portfolio.

REFLECT & ASSESS

UNIT FOUR: PROVING GROUND

In this unit, individuals discover what really matters—in growing up, in making friends, and in meeting physical challenges. Which of their discoveries meant the most to you? See what doing one or more of the options in each of the following sections can reveal.

REFLECTING ON THEME

OPTION 1 **Comparing Qualities** What qualities are shared by people who attempt to prove themselves? Make a chart, like the one shown, to record the qualities of three people in this unit. A section for Carlos (in "The Secret of the Wall") has been started for you. Color or shade in the boxes for the qualities you think each character has, adding more qualities if you wish. Compare diagrams with a partner. Then circle the name of the quality you think is the most necessary for success.

Character	Determined	Fearless	Generous	Honest
Carlos				

OPTION 2 **Giving Characters Report Cards** What personal qualities do you think "prove" or reveal a person's true nature? Make a list of the qualities that are shown by characters in the selections, as well as other qualities that you think are signs of personal growth or maturity. Use the list to evaluate four characters in this unit. In your opinion, which character grows the most as the events of the story unfold? Discuss your choice with a partner.

Self-Assessment: One character may have come to your mind often as you completed one of these activities. If you could follow the example set by one person in the unit, which person would it be? In your notebook, write a short character sketch of that person and tell what he or she means to you.

REVIEWING LITERARY CONCEPTS

OPTION 1 **Thinking About Characterization** You know that the way an author creates and develops a character's personality is called characterization. Choose one character from each selection. Then using a chart like the one shown here, analyze how each character is developed. Which character do you think you came to know best? Why?

What does the character look like?	What are the character's thoughts?
What do others think about the character?	How does the author describe the character's personality?

OPTION 2 **Looking at Symbols** You have learned that in literature, objects and images are used to symbolize things—such as ideas or feelings—that cannot be seen. Copy this diagram and work with a partner to identify a symbol in each of the three selections listed. Discuss what you think each symbol stands for.

Uses of Symbols in Selections		
"The Secret of the Wall"	"The White Umbrella"	"At Last I Kill a Buffalo"

Self-Assessment: Besides characterization *and* symbol, *this unit also introduced the terms* interview, rhyme scheme, onomatopoeia, *and* tone. *On a page in your notebook, draw a large arrow pointing upward. Near the top of the arrow, write the terms that you understand best. Near the middle and the bottom, write the terms you don't understand as well. To clarify the meanings of terms, check The Handbook of Reading Terms and Literary Concepts on page 762.*

PORTFOLIO BUILDING

- **QuickWrites** Two of the QuickWrites assignments in this unit gave you opportunities to write speeches. Choose the speech that you think would be more interesting to present to a group. Use a pencil to lightly underline the parts of the speech that you think are the strongest. In a cover note, explain why you think it presents your ideas so well. Then add the speech and the note to your portfolio.

- **Writing About Literature** In your essay, you had a chance to write an additional scene for a story. Reread your scene. Then write a letter to the author of the story, telling him or her why that scene should be added to the story. Explain why you think your scene fits with what he or she wrote. Attach a copy of your letter to your essay if you decide to include it in your portfolio.

- **Writing from Experience** Earlier in this unit, you compared and contrasted two subjects. Did you find any similarities between the subjects that you didn't expect? Did you find differences that you didn't know about before? Write down your thoughts and attach them to your compare-contrast essay.

- **Personal Choice** Look over the notes, graphics, and records you created for projects in this unit. In addition, review your work for Personal Connections, Writing Connections, and alternative and cross-curricular activities. Choose a piece of writing or an activity in which you made an experience come alive for your audience through vivid language or strong presentation. Write a note explaining how you achieved this result. Attach the note to the piece of writing or the project evaluation, and place them in your portfolio.

Self-Assessment: Look over and compare the earliest work in your portfolio with your more recent work. Write a note to yourself, describing what you now see as your strengths and weaknesses.

SETTING GOALS

What reading or writing strategies do you want to work on as you complete the next unit? Write at least three of your goals on a sheet of paper, then exchange papers with a classmate. Agree on a time in the near future to evaluate each other's progress toward the goals.

The Pursuit of a Goal

Before

proceeding,

one must

reach.

WOLOF
(West African) proverb

Gathering at Blue Waters (1989), Floyd E. Newsum, Jr., artist/professor of art, University of Houston, Downtown. Courtesy of the artist and Lynn Goode Gallery, Houston.

FACING INNER FEARS

WHAT DO YOU THINK?

REFLECTING ON THEME

Has fear ever kept you from pursuing a dream? Some of the greatest obstacles to reaching goals may lie within us. The activities on this page will help you to explore ways of overcoming inner fears. Keep a record of your impressions, to compare with those of the characters in Part 1 as they pursue their goals.

What do you fear?

Use a questionnaire to survey your classmates anonymously about their fears. Do they fear heights? darkness? snakes? Create a chart showing the students' top five fears. Then ask them to suggest ways of facing each fear.

Top Fears
1.
2.
3.
4.
5.

How would you cope?

Think about these situations: (1) You are switched to a different homeroom; (2) You return to soccer practice after an injury; (3) A parent loses his or her job. What fears would each situation create? Create a visual display, such as a storyboard, with images that explain what you would do.

What is the price of beauty?

Bring to class a list of the names and prices of the beauty products used in your home every day. Work with other students to determine which products are most popular and which are most expensive. Do a rough calculation of the total cost of the products listed by the students in your class. With your classmates, discuss whether people depend on beauty products to mask inner fears about appearance.

How could you help?

How do you stop in a pair of in-line skates? How do you budget your weekly allowance? With a partner, create a "how-to" pamphlet or video that outlines steps a person can follow to operate a new device or handle a new situation. Make the pamphlet or video available to the class.

FICTION

Flowers and Freckle Cream

Elizabeth Ellis

PERSONAL CONNECTION

Who is handsome? Who is beautiful? Standards of beauty vary from one culture to another and from one generation to the next. In a small group, discuss with your classmates the differences in standards of beauty. As you read, notice the main character's ideas about beauty.

CULTURAL CONNECTION

Each year in the United States, spending for beauty products increases, supporting the opinion of some people that Americans place great importance on physical appearance. Manufacturers of beauty products attempt to attract customers through advertisements on TV and radio, and in newspapers and magazines. In 1990, about 10 percent of all magazine advertising was bought by manufacturers of cosmetics, perfume, and similar products. Refer to the chart shown to see how spending for magazine advertisements of beauty products has increased.

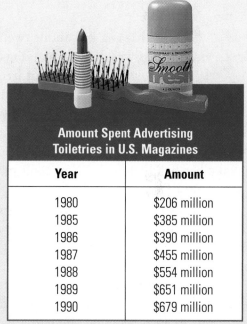

Year	Amount
Amount Spent Advertising Toiletries in U.S. Magazines	
1980	$206 million
1985	$385 million
1986	$390 million
1987	$455 million
1988	$554 million
1989	$651 million
1990	$679 million

Source: Publishers Information Bureau

WRITING CONNECTION

Over a century ago, an author wrote, "Beauty is in the eye of the beholder." In your notebook or on a sheet of paper, explain what you think this statement means. Write about an instance you may recall that either proves or disproves this statement.

beauty

Flowers and Freckle Cream

by Elizabeth Ellis

When I was a kid about twelve years old, I was already as tall as I am now, and I had a lot of freckles. I had reached the age when I had begun to really look at myself in the mirror, and I was underwhelmed.[1] Apparently my mother was too, because sometimes she'd look at me and shake her head and say, "You can't make a silk purse out of a sow's ear."[2]

I had a cousin whose name was Janette Elizabeth, and Janette Elizabeth looked exactly like her name sounds. She had a waist so small that men could put their hands around it . . . and they did. She had waist-length naturally curly blond hair too, but to me her unforgivable sin was that she had a flawless peaches-and-cream complexion. I couldn't help comparing myself with her and thinking that my life would be a lot different if I had beautiful skin too—skin that was all one color.

And then, in the back pages of Janette Elizabeth's *True Confessions* magazine, I found the answer: an advertisement for freckle-remover cream. I knew that I could afford it if I saved my money, and I did. The ad assured me that the product would arrive in a "plain brown wrapper." Plain brown freckle color.

For three weeks I went to the mailbox every day precisely at the time the mail was delivered. I knew that if someone else in my family got the mail, I would never hear the end of it. There was no way that they would let me open the box in private. Finally, after three weeks of scheduling my entire day around the mail truck's arrival, my package came.

I went to my room with it, sat on the edge of my bed, and opened it. I was sure that I was looking at a miracle. But I had gotten so worked up about the magical package that I couldn't bring myself to put the cream on. What if it didn't work? What would I do then?

I fell asleep that night without even trying the stuff. And when I got up the next morning and looked at my freckles in the mirror, I said, "Elizabeth, this is silly. You have to do it now!" I smeared the cream all over my body. There wasn't as much of it as I had thought there would be, and I could see that I was

---

1. **underwhelmed:** not impressed.

2. **a silk purse out of a sow's ear:** something beautiful and of high quality from something inferior or ugly.

going to need a part-time job to keep me in freckle remover.

Later that day I took my hoe and went with my brother and cousins to the head of the holler[3] to hoe tobacco, as we did nearly every day in the summer. Of course, when you stay out hoeing tobacco all day, you're not working in the shade. And there was something important I hadn't realized about freckle remover: if you wear it in the sun, it seems to have a reverse effect. Instead of developing a peaches-and-cream complexion, you just get more and darker freckles.

By the end of the day I looked as though I had leopard blood in my veins, although I didn't realize it yet. When I came back to the house, my family, knowing nothing about the

---

3. **head of the holler:** dialect for "head of the hollow," the end of a small valley.

Siri (1970), Andrew Wyeth. Tempera on panel, 30″ × 30½″, collection of the Brandywine River Museum, Chadds Ford, Pennsylvania. Copyright © 1970 Andrew Wyeth.

freckle-remover cream, began to say things like, "I've never seen you with that many freckles before." When I saw myself in the mirror, I dissolved into tears and hid in the bathroom.

y mother called me to the dinner table, but I ignored her. When she came to the bathroom door and demanded that I come out and eat, I burst out the door and ran by her, crying. I ran out to the well house[4] and threw myself down, and I was still sobbing when my grandfather came out to see what was wrong with me. I told him about how I'd sent for the freckle remover, and he didn't laugh—though he did suggest that one might get equally good results from burying a dead black cat when the moon was full.

It was clear that Grandpa didn't understand, so I tried to explain why I didn't want to have freckles and why I felt so inadequate when I compared my appearance with Janette

Elizabeth's. He looked at me in stunned surprise, shook his head, and said, "But child, there are all kinds of flowers, and they are all beautiful." I said, "I've never seen a flower with freckles!" and ran back to my room, slamming the door.

When my mother came and knocked, I told her to go away. She started to say the kinds of things that parents say at times like that, but my grandfather said, "Nancy, leave the child alone." She was a grown-up, but he was her father. So she left me alone.

I don't know where Grandpa found it. It isn't at all common in the mountains where we lived then. But I know he put it in my room because my mother told me later. I had cried myself to sleep that night, and when I opened my swollen, sticky eyes the next morning, the first thing I saw, lying on the pillow next to my head, was a tiger lily. ❖

---

4. **well house:** a shed covering a deep hole from which water is drawn.

Superb Lilies #2 (1966), Alex Katz. Oil on canvas, 72″ × 144″. Courtesy of Robert Miller Gallery, New York. Copyright © 1996 Alex Katz/Licensed by VAGA, New York.

SAME SONG
by Pat Mora

While my sixteen-year-old son sleeps,
my twelve-year-old daughter
stumbles into the bathroom at six a.m.
plugs in the curling iron
5   squeezes into faded jeans
curls her hair carefully
strokes Aztec Blue shadow on her eyelids
smooths Frosted Mauve blusher on her cheeks
outlines her mouth in Neon Pink
10   peers into the mirror, mirror on the wall
frowns at her face, her eyes, her skin,
not fair.

At night this daughter
stumbles off to bed at nine
15   eyes half-shut while my son
jogs a mile in the cold dark
then lifts weights in the garage
curls and bench presses
expanding biceps, triceps, pectorals,
20   one-handed push-ups, one hundred sit-ups
peers into that mirror, mirror and frowns too.

RESPONDING
OPTIONS

FROM PERSONAL RESPONSE TO CRITICAL ANALYSIS

REFLECT
1. What reactions does Elizabeth's experience trigger in you? Describe your reactions briefly in your notebook.

RETHINK
2. What thoughts do you imagine go through Elizabeth's mind when she sees the tiger lily?

3. What kind of person is Grandpa?
   Consider
   - his comments about beauty
   - his action at the end of the story

4. Suppose the freckle cream had worked. Would Elizabeth's life have changed? Why or why not?

RELATE
5. The narrator in this story and the son and daughter described in the Insight poem "Same Song" on page 523 are all concerned with appearance. Prepare a comparison chart of the ways in which each tries to improve his or her looks.

ANOTHER PATHWAY

Imagine that Elizabeth had thought about the pros and cons of investing in the freckle cream before she sent away for it. Create the list she might have made, using a diagram similar to the one shown. Then look at her list from the grandfather's point of view. Add his cons—and pros, if any—to Elizabeth's list.

| To Buy or Not to Buy ||
Pros	Cons

LITERARY CONCEPTS

The **style** of a piece of literature refers to the way it is written. Style is not *what* is said, but rather *how* it is said. Style involves the combination of various elements, such as sentence length, word choice, imagery, and tone. The choices a writer makes about all these elements can determine how a reader responds to a piece of writing. For example, early in this story you might have been amused by the line, "I was underwhelmed." Elizabeth Ellis's choice of a humorous term to describe her main character's feelings immediately alerts the reader to a writer with a style all her own. Find another example in the story that you think reveals the writer's style and explain why you think as you do.

QUICKWRITES

1. Write the **magazine advertisement** that persuades Elizabeth to order the freckle cream.

2. Imagine that Grandpa left a note with the tiger lily on Elizabeth's pillow. Write the **note** he might have written.

   📁 *PORTFOLIO Save your writing. You may want to use it later as a springboard to a piece for your portfolio.*

LITERARY LINKS

Both Elizabeth in "Flowers and Freckle Cream" and Laurence Yep in "Chinatown" from *The Lost Garden* consider themselves outsiders within their own families. What goals does each pursue in an attempt to "belong," either by appearance or actions?

ACROSS THE CURRICULUM

Science An old saying maintains that "a face without freckles is like a heaven without stars." What are freckles? What causes them to appear? Find out more about these "stars," and present your information in an informative brochure that could be made available at the school nurse's office.

WORDS TO KNOW

WORDPLAY An acrostic is a series of lines in which the first letters of the lines form a word or message when read vertically. Complete the acrostic of the word *freckles* below, creating words that relate to Elizabeth or some part of the story.

F
R
E
C
K
L
E
S

ELIZABETH ELLIS

A professional storyteller, Elizabeth Ellis was born in Kentucky and grew up in Tennessee, amid the Applachian Mountains. After graduating from East Tennessee State University, she moved to Dallas, Texas, where she worked for 10 years as a children's librarian in the city's public library system. There, she says, "I realized it was the storytelling part of my job that I enjoyed the most—and the card-filing part that I liked the least."

In 1979, after attending the National Storytelling Festival in Jonesborough, Tennessee, for the first time and realizing that people made their living telling stories, Ellis left the library and became a professional storyteller. For the past 16 years, she has charmed audiences of all ages with her repertoire of more than 500 stories including several about Texas, Appalachia, personal experiences, and—her favorite—unknown heroic women. Ellis performs throughout North

1943–

America at festivals, workshops, schools, and libraries where she is described as "spellbinding with a relaxed style, warm delivery, and a beautiful voice."

Many of Ellis's stories she heard from her grandfather, a circuit-riding minister who collected stories as he traveled and whom Ellis credits with giving her an ability to see the beauty in everyone. The story "Flowers and Freckle Cream" is based on experiences she had while spending summers with her grandfather in Kentucky. She resides in Dallas, where she continues to share her stories. "It's a charming way to make a living. Sometimes I feel guilty because I have so much fun."

OTHER WORKS *Homespun Tales, Tales of Wit and Humor, Best Loved Stories Told at the National Storytelling Festival;* available on audiocassette: "Like Meat Loves Salt," "Tales of Ancient Egypt," "I Will Not Talk in Class"

NONFICTION

The First Emperor
from The Tomb Robbers
Daniel Cohen

PERSONAL CONNECTION

In the account you are about to read, an early Chinese ruler tries to achieve immortality, the ability to live forever. What would be the advantages and disadvantages of being immortal? Record your thoughts about immortality in your notebook. As you read, think about how the ruler's determination to live forever affects his daily life.

HISTORICAL CONNECTION

Three dynasties, or ruling families, known as the Xia (shyä), the Shang (shäng), and the Zhou (jō), controlled ancient China from about 2000 to 256 B.C. The Zhou dynasty ruled by *feudalism* (fyōōd'l-ĭz'əm), an economic system in which people of the noble class own the land and peasants perform the labor on it. In 256 B.C., the feudal state of Qin (chĭn), also spelled Ch'in, defeated the last Zhou ruler. Ten years later a man named Cheng, the subject of this selection, became king of Qin. By 221 B.C., he had united all of China under the Qin dynasty.

Believing in immortality, the new ruler thought that his family's reign would last 10,000 generations, and he created a new title. He added *shih* (shē), meaning "first," to *huang ti* (hwäng-dē), meaning "emperor," and called himself Ch'in Shih Huang Ti, sometimes spelled Qin Shihuangdi. The Qin dynasty survived only 15 years, but it began 2,100 years of rule by emperors. Throughout the following seven dynasties, Chinese emperors were called *huang ti,* until 1912, when China became a republic.

Qin Dynasty

Miles
0 | 250 | 500

Gobi
(Desert)

Sea
of
Japan

Beijing

Huang He

Qin Dynasty

Xianyang • Luoyang

Yellow
Sea

Himalayas

East
China
Sea

TAIWAN

South
China
Sea

Pacific
Ocean

Extent of Qin Dynasty, 221 B.C.
Present-day boundary of China.
Great Wall

LASERLINKS
• HISTORICAL CONNECTION

The Techniques of SQ3R

SQ3R is a step-by-step strategy to help you study a nonfiction selection more effectively. SQ3R stands for the steps Survey, Question, Read, Recite, Review. The chart shown explains the five steps:

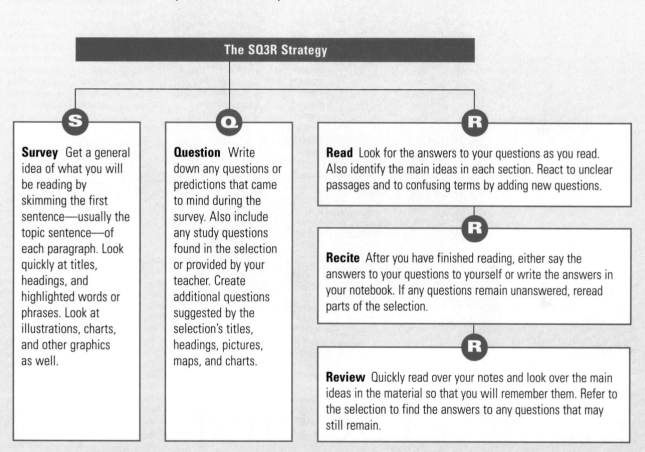

The SQ3R Strategy

S

Survey Get a general idea of what you will be reading by skimming the first sentence—usually the topic sentence—of each paragraph. Look quickly at titles, headings, and highlighted words or phrases. Look at illustrations, charts, and other graphics as well.

Q

Question Write down any questions or predictions that came to mind during the survey. Also include any study questions found in the selection or provided by your teacher. Create additional questions suggested by the selection's titles, headings, pictures, maps, and charts.

R

Read Look for the answers to your questions as you read. Also identify the main ideas in each section. React to unclear passages and to confusing terms by adding new questions.

R

Recite After you have finished reading, either say the answers to your questions to yourself or write the answers in your notebook. If any questions remain unanswered, reread parts of the selection.

R

Review Quickly read over your notes and look over the main ideas in the material so that you will remember them. Refer to the selection to find the answers to any questions that may still remain.

The SQ3R study method may be helpful as you read "The First Emperor." If you encounter any difficulty with a particular section, use the appropriate strategy to help you approach the section. Questions that appear within the selection may also help direct your reading.

AMBITION 志

DESTINY 命

永 ETERNITY

忠 LOYALTY

The First
EMPEROR

from *The Tomb Robbers* by Daniel Cohen

Terra cotta statues from the tomb of Ch'in Shih Huang Ti.
Copyright © An Keren/PPS/Photo Researchers.

There is what may turn out to be the greatest archaeological[1] find of modern times, one that may ultimately outshine even the discovery of the tomb of Tutankhamen.[2] It is the tomb of the emperor Ch'in Shih Huang Ti. Now admittedly the name Ch'in Shih Huang Ti is not exactly a household word in the West. But then neither was Tutankhamen until 1922. The major difference is that while Tutankhamen himself was historically <u>insignificant</u>, Ch'in Shih Huang Ti was enormously important in Chinese history. In many respects he was really the founder of China.

The future emperor started out as the king of the small state Ch'in. At the time, the land was divided up among a number of small states, all constantly warring with one another. Ch'in was one of the smallest and weakest. Yet the king of Ch'in managed to overcome all his rivals, and in the year 221 B.C. he proclaimed himself emperor of the land that we now know as China. From that date until the revolution of 1912, China

---

1. **archaeological** (är'kē-ə-lŏj'ĭ-kəl): having to do with archaeology, the scientific study of the life and culture of ancient peoples.
2. **Tutankhamen** (tōōt'äng-kä'mən): a Pharaoh, or king, of Egypt from 1347 to 1339 B.C. He is not considered an important king, partly because he was very young and ruled for only about nine years. His tomb was found almost intact by the British archaeologist Howard Carter in 1922.

A soldier and his horse, one of many remarkable statues found in the tomb of the Emperor Shih Huang Ti.
Copyright © Laurie Platt Winfrey, Inc.

was always ruled by an emperor. The name China itself comes from the name Ch'in.

Shih Huang Ti ruled his empire with ferocious efficiency. He had the Great Wall of China built to keep out the northern barbarians. The Great Wall, which stretches some fifteen hundred miles, is a building project that rivals and perhaps <u>surpasses</u> the Great Pyramid[3]. The Great Wall took thirty years to build and cost the lives of countless thousands of laborers. Today the Great Wall remains China's number one tourist attraction.

As he grew older, Shih Huang Ti became <u>obsessed</u> with the prospect of his own death. He had survived several assassination attempts

and was terrified of another. He traveled constantly between his 270 different palaces, so that no one could ever be sure where he was going to be. He never slept in the same room for two nights in a row. Anyone who revealed the emperor's whereabouts was put to death along with his entire family.

Shih Huang Ti searched constantly for the secret of <u>immortality</u>. He became prey to a

---

3. **Great Pyramid:** one of the largest pyramids built by the ancient Egyptians. It is made of more than 2 million stone blocks, each weighing about two tons. Each side of its base is longer than two football fields.

WORDS
TO
KNOW

surpass (sər-păs′) v. to be better or greater than
obsessed (əb-sĕst′) adj. concerned too much with a single emotion or idea **obsess** v.
immortality (ĭm′ôr-tăl′ĭ-tē) n. endless life or existence

host of phony magicians and other fakers who promised much but could deliver nothing.

The emperor heard that there were immortals living on some far-off islands, so he sent a huge fleet to find them. The commander of the fleet knew that if he failed in his mission, the emperor would put him to death. So the fleet simply never returned. It is said that the fleet found the island of Japan and stayed there to become the ancestors of the modern Japanese.

In his desire to stay alive, Shih Huang Ti did not neglect the probability that he would die someday. He began construction of an immense tomb in the Black Horse hills near one of his favorite summer palaces. The tomb's construction took as long as the construction of the Great Wall—thirty years.

PREDICT

What special plans do you think the emperor will make for his tomb?

The emperor, of course, did die. Death came while he was visiting the eastern provinces. But his life had become so secretive that only a few high officials were aware of his death. They contrived to keep it a secret until they could consolidate their own power. The imperial procession headed back for the capital. Unfortunately, it was midsummer and the emperor's body began to rot and stink. So one of the plotters arranged to have a cart of fish follow the immense imperial chariot to hide the odor of the decomposing corpse. Finally, news of the emperor's death was made public. The body, or what was left of it, was buried in the tomb that he had been building for so long.

Stories about that tomb sound absolutely incredible. It was said to contain miniature reproductions of all the emperor's 270 palaces. A map of the entire empire with all the major rivers reproduced in mercury, which by some mechanical means was made to flow into a miniature ocean, was also part of the interior of the tomb. So was a reproduction of the stars and planets. According to legend, the burial chamber itself was filled with molten copper so that the emperor's remains were sealed inside a gigantic ingot.[4]

It was also said that loaded crossbows were set up all around the inside of the tomb and that anyone who did manage to penetrate the inner chambers would be shot full of arrows. But just to make sure that no one got that far, the pallbearers who had placed Shih Huang Ti's remains in the tomb were sealed inside with it. They were supposed to be the only ones who knew exactly how to get in and out of the intricate tomb. All of this was done to preserve the emperor's remains from the hands of tomb robbers. Did it work? We don't really know yet.

CLARIFY

Summarize some of the precautions taken supposedly to protect the emperor's remains.

There are two contradictory stories about the tomb of Ch'in Shih Huang Ti. The first says that it was covered up with earth to make it resemble an ordinary hill and that its location has remained unknown for centuries.

But a more accurate legend holds that there never was any attempt to disguise the existence of the tomb. Ch'in Shih Huang Ti had been building it for years, and everybody knew

---

4. **ingot** (ĭng'gət): a mass of metal shaped as a bar or block.

WORDS	**consolidate** (kən-sŏl'ĭ-dāt') v. to make strong or secure
TO	**reproduction** (rē'prə-dŭk'shən) n. a copy; an imitation
KNOW	**intricate** (ĭn'-trĭ-kĭt) adj. full of complicated details

where it was. After his death the tomb was surrounded by walls enclosing an area of about five hundred acres. This was to be the emperor's "spirit city." Inside the spirit city were temples and all sorts of other sacred buildings and objects dedicated to the dead emperor.

Over the centuries the walls, the temples, indeed everything above ground was carried away by vandals. The top of the tomb was covered with earth and eventually came to resemble a large hill. Locally the hill is called Mount Li. But still the farmers who lived in the area had heard stories that Mount Li contained the tomb of Ch'in Shih Huang Ti or of some other important person.

In the spring of 1974 a peasant plowing a field near Mount Li uncovered a life-sized clay statue of a warrior. Further digging indicated that there was an entire army of statues beneath the ground. Though excavations are not yet complete, Chinese authorities believe that there are some six thousand life-sized clay statues of warriors, plus scores of life-sized statues of horses. Most of the statues are broken, but some are in an absolutely remarkable state of preservation. Each statue is finely made, and each shows a distinct individual, different from all the others.

This incredible collection is Shih Huang Ti's "spirit army." At one time Chinese kings practiced human sacrifice so that the victims could serve the dead king in the next world. Shih Huang Ti was willing to make do with the models. Men and horses were arranged in a military fashion in a three-acre underground chamber. The chamber may have been entered at some point. The roof certainly collapsed. But still the delicate figures have survived surprisingly well. Most of the damage was done when the roof caved in. That is why the Chinese archaeologists are so hopeful that when the tomb itself is excavated, it too will be found to have survived surprisingly well.

The Chinese are not rushing the excavations. They have only a limited number of trained people to do the job. After all, the tomb has been there for over two thousand years. A few more years won't make much difference.

Though once denounced as a tyrant, Ch'in Shih Huang Ti is now regarded as a national hero. His name is a household word in China. The Chinese government knows that it may have an unparalleled ancient treasure on its hands, and it wants to do the job well. Over the next few years we should be hearing much more about this truly remarkable find.

WORDS
TO
KNOW
preservation (prĕz′ər-vā′shən) *n.* the condition of being kept perfect or unchanged
tyrant (tī′rənt) *n.* a cruel, unjust ruler
unparalleled (ŭn-păr′ə-lĕld′) *adj.* having no equal; unmatched

THE EMPEROR

Ch'in Shih Huang Ti came to power in China in 246 B.C., at the age of 13, when he became king of the state of Qin. The new ruler set out to extend his power throughout the empire. Shih Huang Ti divided the empire into 36 provinces and created a system of government that would allow him to maintain firm control. Each province had two officials—one governor and one defender. This brought unity to the empire and allowed the emperor to establish standard systems of money, measurement, and writing. Taking the land away from thousands of noble families, he put an end to the feudal system and allowed anyone who could pay taxes to own land.

To protect his empire from possible invasion from the north, Shih Huang Ti used a forced-labor crew of 700,000 to build the Great Wall of China. This massive hand-built wall was lengthened and repaired over the centuries, and by the time of the Ming dynasty (1368–1644) stretched for 4,000 miles.

Much of the emperor's burial site remains to be uncovered. In addition to the clay army—which when discovered was arranged in a military formation including bowmen, archers, and charioteers—archaeologists found chariots, iron farm tools, objects of silk, linen, jade, and bone, and weapons such as spears and swords that remain shiny today. Archaeologists anticipate that it will take many years to complete the excavation of the emperor's burial site. Four separate dig areas have been covered with roofing and serve as an on-site museum, even as excavation of the area continues.

Shih Huang Ti became a national hero to many modern-day Chinese when the clay army and other artifacts were uncovered. He is recognized and honored for bringing a national unity to China that lasted over 2,000 years. Though he did not live forever, Shih Huang Ti may indeed have achieved a degree of immortality: the tomb and the many astounding objects found at the burial site promise to fascinate many generations to come.

The Great Wall stands today as the longest structure ever built.
Copyright © D. E. Cox/Tony Stone Images.

RESPONDING
O P T I O N S

FROM PERSONAL RESPONSE TO CRITICAL ANALYSIS

REFLECT

1. What were your thoughts as you finished reading this selection? Record them in your notebook.

RETHINK

2. How would you describe Ch'in Shih Huang Ti?

   Consider
   • his attempts to achieve immortality
   • his accomplishments
   • his effects on those he ruled

3. Review the ideas about immortality you recorded in the Personal Connection on page 526. In your opinion, are the advantages of immortality worth the efforts Ch'in Shih Huang Ti made to try to achieve it? Explain your answer.

4. What information from the selection do you find most interesting or surprising? Share your thoughts with a classmate.

RELATE

5. Many people would like to achieve a certain kind of immortality—that of having their name and achievements live on after their death. If you could choose what to be remembered for centuries from now, what would you choose? Share your ideas with your classmates.

ANOTHER PATHWAY
Cooperative Learning

Work with a group to develop a catalog for an exhibit about Ch'in Shih Huang Ti. Refer to encyclopedias for additional details about the emperor and the excavation of his tomb. Combine the information into one catalog that you might add to the school library's reference materials.

LITERARY CONCEPTS

An **author's purpose** may be to entertain, to inform, to express an opinion, or to persuade. A writer may combine two or three purposes, but one is usually of more importance. Think about the purposes Daniel Cohen may have had for writing this selection. Which purpose do you think was most important to him? Why?

QUICKWRITES

1. Daniel Cohen offers two different explanations of why the tomb had remained hidden for so long. Draft your own **legend** about the location of the emperor's body and tomb.

2. Imagine that you are a Chinese archaeologist in 1974. Draft a **log entry** you might make describing your reactions to this discovery.

3. Write an **epitaph** that could be engraved on the tomb of Ch'in Shih Huang Ti.

   ☐ *PORTFOLIO Save your writing. You may want to use it later as a springboard to a piece for your portfolio.*

ALTERNATIVE ACTIVITIES

1. From the selections in this book, choose a historical figure or a character who you believe is truly immortal. With a partner, do a **talk-show interview** with one of you playing the person or character and the other playing the host. Invite the class members to be the audience for the show.

2. Construct a **model** of the Great Wall, the tomb of Ch'in Shih Huang Ti, or another artifact mentioned in the selection. Review Cohen's account to be sure that your model fits his description.

LITERARY LINKS

Now that you have read "The First Emperor," review the story "The Dog of Pompeii" (page 124) and the nonfictional excerpt "Tutankhamen" from *Lost Worlds* (page 470). Compare the ancient cultures of Pompeii, Egypt, and China as revealed by the artifacts described in the selections.

ACROSS THE CURRICULUM

History The imperial rule of China begun by the Qin dynasty lasted until 1912. Research the dynasties that followed the Qin. Create a time line to summarize your findings. Present the time line to the class with a brief description of each dynasty.

ART CONNECTION

The clay figures of a soldier and his horse shown on page 530 were among those discovered at the burial site of Ch'in Shih Huang Ti. The military dress of the figure suggests that it was meant to help protect the emperor's tomb from invaders. Look carefully at the figures in the photograph to see what details you can observe. Does this image help you to understand or appreciate the enormous task that making over 6,000 of these statues must have been? Why or why not?

EXERCISE A For each group of words below, write the letter of the word that is the best antonym, or opposite, for the boldfaced word.

1. **consolidate** (a) buy (b) honor (c) separate

2. **unparalleled** (a) straight (b) common (c) simple

3. **preservation** (a) freedom (b) destruction (c) delay

4. **intricate** (a) plain (b) strong (c) flat

5. **reproduction** (a) original (b) question (c) enemy

EXERCISE B Review the Words to Know at the bottom of the selection pages. For each phrase in the first column, write the letter of the synonymous phrase from the second column.

1. an insignificant restaurant

2. outdo the girl

3. the fact of deathlessness

4. haunted by thoughts of a visitor

5. the tardier tyrant

a. surpass the lass

b. obsessed with a guest

c. a minor diner

d. the later dictator

e. the reality of immortality

DANIEL COHEN

An extremely productive author, Daniel Cohen has written more than 130 books, most of which are young-adult nonfiction. His science books, studies of animals and their relationships with humans, and historical introductions to ancient civilizations have been highly praised.

A native of Chicago, Cohen earned a degree in journalism from the University of Illinois in 1959. After a decade spent working his way from the position of proofreader for *Time* magazine to the position of managing editor of *Science Digest,* he left the editorial field to pursue a career as a freelance writer.

Research for his popular books on ghost stories and the supernatural has led Cohen to creep around haunted houses and spend "a damp and chilly night in an English churchyard," but he admits that he has never seen a ghost. One of the author's most popular books is *The Body Snatchers,* an informal history of grave robbing, which includes information about the Egyptian tombs.

Cohen and his wife, Susan, have cowritten several popular books for teens. Their topics range from movies and television to dinosaurs. He defends his choice of material, especially the supernatural: "I don't really 'believe in' most of the subjects I write about, and I don't pretend to."

OTHER WORKS *Young and Famous: Sports' Newest Superstars, Phantom Animals, Railway Ghosts and Other Highway Horrors, Prophets of Doom*

LASERLINKS
• *ART GALLERY*

POETRY

Message from a Caterpillar
Lilian Moore

Chrysalis Diary
Paul Fleischman

PERSONAL CONNECTION

Think about your various experiences with the natural world. What changes in nature have you observed? In your notebook, jot down some of your observations of change. As you read, be aware of the changes in nature described in the poems.

SCIENCE CONNECTION

The upcoming poems share a common theme—the transformation of a caterpillar into a butterfly or moth. This process of change is called metamorphosis (mĕt′ə-môr′fə-sĭs) and includes four stages, which are shown in the illustration below.

Once the caterpillar hatches, it grows rapidly, molting, or shedding its outer skin, several times. When the butterfly caterpillar reaches the third stage, it molts again to become a pupa (pyoo′pə), which quickly develops a hard shell. This shell often has a gold sheen and therefore is called a *chrysalis* (krĭs′ə-lĭs) from the Greek word *chrysos,* meaning "gold." Moth caterpillars do not form a chrysalis. Instead, most of them spin a silken cocoon around themselves. During the pupal stage, the wings, legs, and body of the adult moth or butterfly develop. Then the case splits open and the adult emerges. The exact moment when the case opens is determined by instinct, an inborn pattern of behavior that is often a response to the conditions in an environment.

READING CONNECTION

Choral Reading You may notice the unusual way that the words of "Chrysalis Diary" are arranged. This poem is designed to be read aloud by two readers, one reading the lines on the left side of the page, the other reading the lines on the right side. The oral interpretation of poetry by two or more voices is called choral reading. "Chrysalis Diary" is read from top to bottom, with some parts assigned to a single reader and some lines meant to be spoken together. Take the opportunity to read this poem aloud with a partner. Notice the effect created by two voices.

1 Eggs
2 Larva (caterpillar)
3 Pupa (chrysalis)
4 Adult

Message from a Caterpillar

by Lilian Moore

Don't shake this
bough.
Don't try
to wake me
5   now.

In this cocoon
I've work to
do.
Inside this silk
10   I'm changing
things.

I'm worm-like now
but in this
dark
15   I'm growing
wings.

FROM **PERSONAL RESPONSE** *TO* **CRITICAL ANALYSIS**

REFLECT   1. What were you left thinking at the end of the poem? Discuss your reactions with a classmate.

RETHINK   2. How would you describe the caterpillar's feelings about change?
     Consider
     • the tone of the caterpillar's statements
     • the active role the caterpillar seems to take in changing

3. What theme, or message about life, do you think is presented in this poem?
     Consider
     • to whom this message may be directed
     • the last stanza

Chrysalis Diary

by Paul Fleischman

November 13:

Cold told me
to fasten my feet
to this branch,

5

to shed my skin,

and I have obeyed.

to dangle upside down
from my perch,

to cease being a caterpillar
and I have obeyed.

10 December 6:

the color of leaves and life,
has vanished!

15 lies in ruins!
I study the
brown new world around me.

I hear few sounds.

20

Swinging back and forth
in the wind,
I feel immeasurably alone.

25

I can make out snow falling.

I find I never tire of
30 watching the flakes
in their multitudes
passing my window.

Astounding.
35 I enter these
wondrous events
in my chronicle[2]

Green,

has vanished!
The empire of leaves
lies in ruins!

I fear the future.

Have any others of my kind
survived this cataclysm?[1]

January 4:

For five days and nights
it's been drifting down.

The world is now white.
Astounding.

knowing no reader
would believe me.

---

1. **cataclysm** (kăt′ə-klĭz′əm): any sudden, violent change; disaster.
2. **chronicle** (krŏn′ĭ-kəl): record; diary.

40 February 12:

Unable to see out
at all this morning.

45 and branches falling.

ponder their import,[3]

50

and wait for more.

An ice storm last night.

Yet I hear boughs cracking

Hungry for sounds
in this silent world,
I cherish these,

miser[4] them away
in my memory,
and wait for more.

---

3. **ponder their import:** think deeply about their meaning.

4. **miser:** to gather up and save in a greedy way.

I wonder whether
55　I am the same being
who started this diary.

like the weather without.

60　my legs are dissolving,

my body's not mine.
This morning,
a breeze from the south,
65　strangely fragrant,

a faint glimpse of green
In the branches.

March 28:

I've felt stormy inside

My mouth is reshaping,

wings are growing
my body's not mine.

a red-winged blackbird's
call in the distance,

70　And now I recall
that last night
I dreamt of flying.

RESPONDING
O P T I O N S

FROM **PERSONAL RESPONSE** TO **CRITICAL ANALYSIS**

REFLECT **1.** What images does "Chrysalis Diary" bring to mind? Sketch an image from the poem in your notebook.

RETHINK **2.** What did the poem bring to mind about your own experiences of facing inner fears?

Consider
- the diary form of the poem
- the speaker's comments at different stages of change

3. Reread the definition of instinct in the Science Connection on page 537. How important a role do you think instinct plays in the changes described in "Chrysalis Diary"?

RELATE **4.** At one point the speaker of "Chrysalis Diary" says, "my body's not mine." How do you think the speaker of "Message from a Caterpillar" would react to this statement?

ANOTHER PATHWAY

With a partner, explore the way each of these speakers feels about the changes taking place. Each of you represent one of the speakers and discuss your reactions to what is happening to you. In what ways are your reactions to change similar or different? Be sure that you refer to the poems to make your responses true to the speaker you represent.

LITERARY CONCEPTS

Language that communicates ideas beyond the dictionary meaning of the words is called **figurative language.** Poets and other writers use figurative language to paint vivid images in the minds of readers. Two kinds of figurative language are **simile** and **metaphor.** Both simile and metaphor are comparisons of two things that are basically unlike yet have something in common. While a simile contains the word *like* or *as,* a metaphor makes the comparison more directly. In "Chrysalis Diary," for example, the speaker uses a metaphor to compare the autumn leaves to a destroyed empire: "The empire of leaves / lies in ruins!" Identify another metaphor or simile from "Chrysalis Diary" or "Message from a Caterpillar."

CONCEPT REVIEW: Form The shape of the words and lines of a poem on the page is called **form.** In a class discussion, compare the forms used in these poems. Does one form appeal to you more than another? Explain.

QUICKWRITES

1. Everything in nature undergoes change of some sort—including human beings. Write a **poem** that conveys your reactions to changing as you get older.

2. Pretend it is spring and the speakers of the two poems meet after their changes are complete. Write the **dialogue** the two might have. You may create a humorous or a serious conversation.

📁 *PORTFOLIO Save your writing. You may want to use it later as a springboard to a piece for your portfolio.*

LILIAN MOORE

"To me," Lilian Moore says, "a poem is like a balloon on a string. What you get out of it depends on how tall you are, how long the string is. Something there for everyone."

Born in New York City, where she graduated from Hunter College, Lilian Moore (1909–) is a poet, editor, and reading specialist. The author of more than 35 children's books, she says that one of the most satisfying things she has done was to found the Arrow Book Club at Scholastic Book Services—"the first quality paperback book program for elementary school children."

Believing that "children who read will often begin naturally to write," Moore has written numerous easy-to-read books, including several about Little Raccoon. "Message from a Caterpillar" is from *Little Raccoon and Poems from the Woods,* a collection of poems that describe a young raccoon's discoveries in the woods—day and night, throughout the year. In recognition of her poetry, Moore received the National Council of Teachers of English Award for Poetry for Children in 1985.

OTHER WORKS *Catch Your Breath: A Book of Shivery Poems, Think of Shadows, Something New Begins, To See the World Afresh, Go with the Poem*

PAUL FLEISCHMAN

An award-winning author of young-adult novels, poetry, short stories, and picture books, Paul Fleischman (1952–) earned a bachelor's degree from the University of New Mexico and has worked as a bagel baker, bookstore clerk, and proofreader. Fleischman learned the importance of sound from his father, a children's author, as he read aloud his own books. Fleischman's emphasis on sound also reflects an intense love for music. Listening to classical music helped him learn how to shape his writing.

The writer claims that his greatest pleasure is the actual writing, trying to "please my readers' ears while telling my tale." His two poetry collections, *I Am Phoenix: Poems for Two Voices* and *Joyful Noise: Poems for Two Voices,* are written to be spoken by two readers. The first collection praises a variety of birds; the second is written from the viewpoint of various insects. *Joyful Noise* was named as a *Boston Globe-Horn Book* Award honor book in 1988 and received the Newbery Medal in 1989.

OTHER WORKS *The Half-a-Moon Inn, Graven Images: Three Stories, Path of the Pale Horse*

LASERLINKS
• *SCIENCE CONNECTION*

FICTION

The Circuit
Francisco Jiménez   (hē-mĕ′nĕs)

PERSONAL CONNECTION

By this time in your life, you probably have moved to a new neighborhood or town at least once, or you may have shared another's experience of moving. Imagine some of the effects that frequent moves might have on your life. How would frequently moving affect your emotions, your experiences in school, and your friendships? Jot down these reactions in your notebook or on a sheet of paper.

> I moved to a new neighborhood when I was 8 and I remember how strange it seemed

CULTURAL CONNECTION

This story is about the problems that frequent moves cause for Panchito, a young Mexican boy in a family of migrant farm workers in California. Migrant farm workers are laborers who migrate, or move, from one agricultural area to another in search of work. The workers often move in a circuit—a regular route of travel—that follows the harvest seasons in different places. Most migrant workers work hard for low pay. Children as well as adults work in the fields. The many hours of work and constant moving make regular attendance at school difficult.

California

Santa Rosa
San Francisco
Fresno
CALIFORNIA
Pacific Ocean
Los Angeles

N W E S

Miles
0   80   160

READING CONNECTION

Evaluating When you evaluate literature, you form opinions about it. As you read the following story, think about the author's purpose. Why do you think Jiménez wrote about the difficulties a young migrant worker has with moving? After you have read the story, decide how well Jiménez uses character, setting, plot, and theme to achieve his purpose.

The Circuit

by Francisco Jiménez

It was that time of year again. Ito, the strawberry sharecropper, did not smile. It was natural. The peak of the strawberry season was over and the last few days the workers, most of them *braceros*[1], were not picking as many boxes as they had during the months of June and July.

As the last days of August disappeared, so did the number of *braceros*. Sunday, only one—the best picker—came to work. I liked him. Sometimes we talked during our half-hour lunch break. That is how I found out he was from Jalisco[2], the same state in Mexico my family was from. That Sunday was the last time I saw him.

When the sun had tired and sunk behind the mountains, Ito signaled us that it was time to go home. "*Ya esora*[3]," he yelled in his broken Spanish. Those were the words I waited for twelve hours a day, every day, seven days a week, week after week. And the thought of not hearing them again saddened me.

As we drove home, Papa did not say a word. With both hands on the wheel, he stared at the dirt road. My older brother, Roberto, was also silent. He leaned his head back and closed his eyes. Once in a while he cleared from his throat the dust that blew in from outside.

Yes, it was that time of year. When I opened the front door to the shack, I stopped. Everything we owned was neatly packed in cardboard boxes. Suddenly I felt even more the weight of hours, days, weeks, and months of work. I sat down on a box. The thought of having to move to Fresno and knowing what was in store for me there brought tears to my eyes.

---

1. *braceros* (brä-sĕ′rôs) *Spanish:* Hispanic farm workers.
2. **Jalisco** (hä-lēs′kô).
3. **Ya esora:** a made-up spelling for the sharecropper's pronunciation of the Spanish expression *Ya es hora* (yä′ĕs-ô′rä), which means "It is time."

The Dry Ditch (1964), Kenneth M. Adams. Copyright © Eiteljorg Museum of American Indians and Western Art, Indianapolis, Indiana.

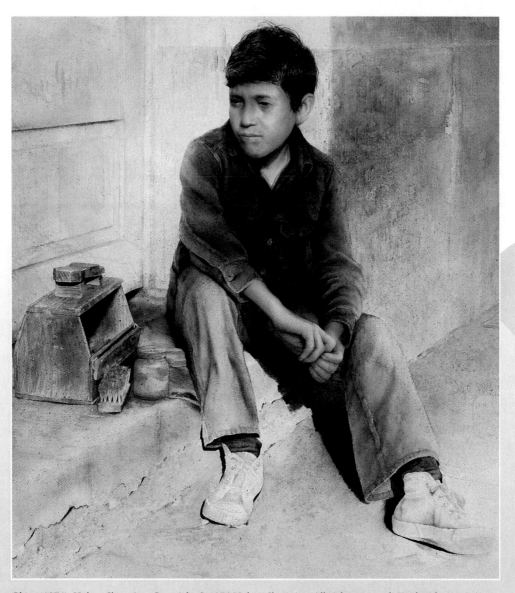

Chico (1974), Hubert Shuptrine. Copyright © 1974 Hubert Shuptrine. All rights reserved. Used with permission.

That night I could not sleep. I lay in bed thinking about how much I hated this move.

A little before five o'clock in the morning, Papa woke everyone up. A few minutes later, the yelling and screaming of my little brothers and sisters, for whom the move was a great adventure, broke the silence of dawn. Shortly, the barking of the dogs accompanied them.

While we packed the breakfast dishes, Papa went outside to start the "Carcanchita." That was the name Papa gave his old '38 black Plymouth. He bought it in a used-car lot in Santa Rosa in the winter of 1949. Papa was very proud of his car. *"Mi Carcanchita,"*[4] my little jalopy, he called it. He had a right to be proud of it. He spent a lot of time looking at other cars before buying this one. When he finally chose the "Carcanchita," he checked it thoroughly before driving it out of the car lot.

---

4. *Mi Carcanchita* (mē kär-kän-chē′tä) Spanish.

He examined every inch of the car. He listened to the motor, tilting his head from side to side like a parrot, trying to detect any noises that spelled car trouble. After being satisfied with the looks and sounds of the car, Papa then insisted on knowing who the original owner was. He never did find out from the car salesman. But he bought the car anyway. Papa figured the original owner must have been an important man, because behind the rear seat of the car he found a blue necktie.

Papa parked the car out in front and left the motor running. *"Listo,"*[5] he yelled. Without saying a word, Roberto and I began to carry the boxes out to the car. Roberto carried the two big boxes and I carried the smaller ones. Papa then threw the mattress on top of the car roof and tied it with ropes to the front and rear bumpers.

Everything was packed except Mama's pot. It was an old large galvanized pot she had picked up at an army surplus store in Santa Maria the year I was born. The pot was full of dents and nicks, and the more dents and nicks it had, the more Mama liked it. *"Mi olla,"*[6] she used to say proudly.

I held the front door open as Mama carefully carried out her pot by both handles, making sure not to spill the cooked beans. When she got to the car, Papa reached out to help her with it. Roberto opened the rear car door, and Papa gently placed it on the floor behind the front seat. All of us then climbed in. Papa sighed, wiped the sweat off his forehead with his sleeve, and said wearily: *"Es todo."*[7]

As we drove away, I felt a lump in my throat. I turned around and looked at our little shack for the last time.

As we drove away, I felt a lump in my throat.

At sunset we drove into a labor camp near Fresno. Since Papa did not speak English, Mama asked the camp foreman if he needed any more workers. "We don't need no more," said the foreman, scratching his head. "Check with Sullivan down the road. Can't miss him. He lives in a big white house with a fence around it."

When we got there, Mama walked up to the house. She went through a white gate, past a row of rose bushes, up the stairs to the front door. She rang the doorbell. The porch light went on and a tall husky man came out. They exchanged a few words. After the man went in, Mama clasped her hands and hurried back to the car. "We have work! Mr. Sullivan said we can stay there the whole season," she said, gasping and pointing to an old garage near the stables.

The garage was worn out by the years. It had no windows. The walls, eaten by termites, strained to support the roof full of holes. The loose dirt floor, populated by earthworms, looked like a gray road map.

That night, by the light of a kerosene lamp, we unpacked and cleaned our new home. Roberto swept away the loose dirt, leaving the hard ground. Papa plugged the holes in the walls with old newspapers and tin can tops. Mama fed my little brothers and sisters. Papa and Roberto then brought in the mattress and placed it in the far corner of the garage. "Mama, you and the little ones sleep on the mattress. Roberto, Panchito, and I will sleep outside under the trees," Papa said.

---

5. *listo* (lē′stô) *Spanish:* ready.
6. *mi olla* (mē ô′yä) *Spanish:* my pot.
7. *Es todo* (ĕs tô′dô) *Spanish:* That's everything.

Early next morning Mr. Sullivan showed us where his crop was, and after breakfast, Papa, Roberto, and I headed for the vineyard to pick.

Around nine o'clock the temperature had risen to almost one hundred degrees. I was completely soaked in sweat, and my mouth felt as if I had been chewing on a handkerchief. I walked over to the end of the row, picked up the jug of water we had brought, and began drinking. "Don't drink too much; you'll get sick," Roberto shouted. No sooner had he said that than I felt sick to my stomach. I dropped to my knees and let the jug roll off my hands. I remained motionless with my eyes glued on the hot, sandy ground. All I could hear was the drone of insects. Slowly I began to recover. I poured water over my face and neck and watched the black mud run down my arms and hit the ground.

I still felt a little dizzy when we took a break to eat lunch. It was past two o'clock and we sat underneath a large walnut tree that was on the side of the road. While we ate, Papa jotted down the number of boxes we had picked. Roberto drew designs on the ground with a stick. Suddenly I noticed Papa's face turn pale as he looked down the road. "Here comes the school bus," he whispered loudly in alarm. Instinctively, Roberto and I ran and hid in the vineyards. We did not want to get in trouble for not going to school. The yellow bus stopped in front of Mr. Sullivan's house. Two neatly dressed boys about my age got off. They carried books under their arms. After they crossed the street, the bus drove away. Roberto and I came out from hiding and joined Papa. "*Tienen que tener cuidado,*"[8] he warned us.

Suddenly I noticed Papa's face turn pale as he looked down the road.

After lunch we went back to work. The sun kept beating down. The buzzing insects, the wet sweat, and the hot dry dust made the afternoon seem to last forever. Finally the mountains around the valley reached out and swallowed the sun. Within an hour it was too dark to continue picking. The vines blanketed the grapes, making it difficult to see the bunches.

"*Vámonos,*"[9] said Papa, signaling to us that it was time to quit work. Papa then took out a pencil and began to figure out how much we had earned our first day. He wrote down numbers, crossed some out, wrote down some more. "*Quince,*"[10] he murmured.

When we arrived home, we took a cold shower underneath a waterhose. We then sat down to eat dinner around some wooden crates that served as a table. Mama had cooked a special meal for us. We had rice and tortillas with *carne con chile,*[11] my favorite dish.

The next morning I could hardly move. My body ached all over. I felt little control over my arms and legs. This feeling went on every morning for days, until my muscles finally got used to the work.

It was Monday, the first week of November. The grape season was over and I could now go to school. I woke up early that morning and lay in bed, looking at the stars and savoring the thought of not going to work and of starting

---

8. ***Tienen que tener cuidado*** (tyĕ-nĕn′ kĕ tĕ-nĕr′ kwē-dä′dô) *Spanish:* you have to be careful.
9. ***Vámonos*** (vä′mô-nôs) *Spanish:* Let's go.
10. ***Quince*** (kēn′sĕ) *Spanish:* fifteen.
11. **tortillas** (tôr-tē′yäs) with ***carne con chile*** (kär′nĕ kôn chē′lĕ) *Spanish:* flat, round cornmeal cakes and a mixture of meat and spicy red peppers.

sixth grade for the first time that year. Since I could not sleep, I decided to get up and join Papa and Roberto at breakfast. I sat at the table across from Roberto, but I kept my head down. I did not want to look up and face him. I knew he was sad. He was not going to school today. He was not going tomorrow, or next week, or next month. He would not go until the cotton season was over, and that was sometime in February. I rubbed my hands together and watched the dry, acid-stained skin fall to the floor in little rolls.

When Papa and Roberto left for work, I felt relief. I walked to the top of a small grade next to the shack and watched the "Carcanchita" disappear in the distance in a cloud of dust.

Two hours later, around eight o'clock, I stood by the side of the road waiting for school bus number twenty. When it arrived I climbed in. No one noticed me. Everyone was busy either talking or yelling. I sat in an empty seat in the back.

When the bus stopped in front of the school, I felt very nervous. I looked out the bus window and saw boys and girls carrying books under their arms. I felt empty. I put my hands in my pants pockets and walked to the principal's office. When I entered I heard a woman's voice say: "May I help you?" I was startled. I had not heard English for months. For a few seconds I remained speechless. I looked at the lady who waited for an answer. My first instinct was to answer her in Spanish, but I held back. Finally, after struggling for English words I managed to tell her that I wanted to enroll in the sixth grade. After answering many questions, I was led to the classroom.

Mr. Lema, the sixth-grade teacher, greeted me and assigned me a desk. He then intro-

He looked up at me and smiled. I felt better.

duced me to the class. I was so nervous and scared at that moment when everyone's eyes were on me that I wished I were with Papa and Roberto picking cotton. After taking roll, Mr. Lema gave the class the assignment for the first hour. "The first thing we have to do this morning is finish reading the story we began yesterday," he said enthusiastically. He walked up to me, handed me an English book, and asked me to read. "We are on page 125," he said politely. When I heard this, I felt my blood rush to my head; I felt dizzy. "Would you like to read?" he asked hesitantly. I opened the book to page 125. My mouth was dry. My eyes began to water. I could not begin. "You can read later," Mr. Lema said understandingly.

For the rest of the reading period, I kept getting angrier and angrier with myself. I should have read, I thought to myself.

During recess I went into the restroom and opened my English book to page 125. I began to read in a low voice, pretending I was in class. There were many words I did not know. I closed the book and headed back to the classroom.

Mr. Lema was sitting at his desk correcting papers. When I entered he looked up at me and smiled. I felt better. I walked up to him and asked if he could help me with the new words. "Gladly," he said.

The rest of the month I spent my lunch hours working on English with Mr. Lema, my best friend at school.

One Friday during lunch hour, Mr. Lema asked me to take a walk with him to the music room. "Do you like music?" he asked me as we entered the building.

"Yes, I like Mexican *corridos*,"[12] I answered. He then picked up a trumpet, blew on it and handed it to me. The sound gave me goose bumps. I knew that sound. I had heard it in many Mexican *corridos*. "How would you like to learn how to play it?" he asked. He must have read my face, because before I could answer, he added: "I'll teach you how to play it during our lunch hours."

That day I could hardly wait to get home to tell Papa and Mama the great news. As I got off the bus, my little brothers and sisters ran up to meet me. They were yelling and screaming. I thought they were happy to see me, but when I opened the door to our shack, I saw that everything we owned was neatly packed in cardboard boxes. ❖

---

12. *corridos* (kô-rē′dôs) *Spanish:* slow, romantic songs.

LITERARY INSIGHT

the 1st

by Lucille Clifton

what I remember about that day
is boxes stacked across the walk
and couch springs curling through the air
and drawers and tables balanced on the curb
5 and us, hollering,
leaping up and around
happy to have a playground;

nothing about the emptied rooms
nothing about the emptied family

RESPONDING
O P T I O N S

FROM **PERSONAL RESPONSE** *TO* **CRITICAL ANALYSIS**

REFLECT   1. How did you react to the end of the story? Record your reactions in your notebook.

RETHINK   2. How would you describe Panchito, the narrator of the story?
   Consider
   • his attitude toward school and work
   • his feelings about his brother
   • his feelings about frequent moves

   3. Do you think the narrator's friendship with Mr. Lema will have a lasting effect? Why or why not?

   4. Compare and contrast the feelings about moving that are communicated in "The Circuit" and the Insight poem "the 1st" on page 552.

RELATE   5. Recent statistics show that only about 20 percent of migrant workers go beyond sixth grade in school, partly for reasons made clear in this story. How do you think this situation could be changed?

ANOTHER PATHWAY

Review Panchito's experiences in "The Circuit." Plan and rehearse a speech you might give as the narrator if you were attempting to convince the members of a state committee that living conditions for migrant workers must be improved.

LITERARY CONCEPTS

Sensory details are words and phrases that help the reader see, hear, taste, smell, and feel what the writer is describing. Jiménez uses many sensory details that help paint a vivid picture of the hardships of migrant life. One example is the phrase "the drone of insects," which appeals to the reader's sense of sound. Find other sensory details in the story and add them to a chart similar to the one shown.

Sensory Details	
Smell	hot grits and sausage
Sight	
Hearing	
Touch	
Taste	

QUICKWRITES

1. Write a **prediction** of what life will be like for the narrator of "The Circuit" ten years later. Give reasons for your prediction.

2. Review the Reading Connection on page 545. Then write an **evaluation** of "The Circuit."

3. Write the **letter** that Panchito might send to Mr. Lema from the next town along "the circuit."

   PORTFOLIO *Save your writing. You may want to use it later as a springboard to a piece for your portfolio.*

ALTERNATIVE ACTIVITIES

1. Imagine that Panchito's family earns $9,000 a year. Create a monthly **family budget** based on details about their lives revealed in the story. Be sure to account for such items as groceries, clothing, gasoline, medicine, a fund for emergencies such as car repairs or doctor visits, and any other monthly expenses you think they might have.

2. Prepare a **dramatic reading** of this story to present to the class. Working with a few classmates, assign the roles of the narrator, Papa, Mama, the foreman in Fresno, and any other character who has a line of dialogue in the story. When the narrator, in reading the story, comes to a passage of dialogue spoken by another character, the student playing that character speaks the lines himself or herself.

3. Panchito might find that photographs of the important people and events in his life would help him to remember them. Using magazines, art postcards, or other sources, collect photos that could represent people and events in the story. Create a **photographic display** including captions that will help explain the significance of the photos.

THE WRITER'S STYLE

Jiménez sprinkles the story with words from the original language of Panchito and his family. Panchito frequently uses a Spanish word and then goes on to explain its meaning. What do you think the use of the original language adds to the story?

ACROSS THE CURRICULUM

Social Studies Who was Cesar Chavez and how did he affect the lives of migrant farm workers? Refer to books about him or to an encyclopedia. (If you have access to a CD-ROM encyclopedia or an on-line service, you might use your computer to start your research.) Summarize your information either in a report that can be distributed to the class or on an in-classroom computer data base to which students have access.

FRANCISCO JIMÉNEZ

Born in Mexico, Francisco Jiménez immigrated to the United States with his parents in 1947. His mother worked in a factory, and his father was a farm worker. Jiménez is now a literature professor at the University of Santa Clara in California. He has written articles and stories for periodicals and has cowritten two textbooks on Spanish.

Jiménez says that his primary goal in writing "is to fill the need for cultural and human understanding, between the United States and

1943–

Mexico in particular. I write in both English and Spanish. The language I use is determined by what period in my life I write about. Since Spanish was the dominant language in my childhood, I generally write about those experiences in Spanish." (He translated "The Circuit" from the original Spanish.) Jiménez considers it a privilege to be able to write stories in both languages. Jiménez's most recent book, *Migrant Child,* is a collection of autobiographical short stories.

LASERLINKS
- *AUTHOR BACKGROUND*
- *SOCIAL SCIENCE CONNECTION*

The Scribe

by Kristin Hunter

Copyright © Michael Paraskevas.

*W*e been living in the apartment over the Silver Dollar Check Cashing Service five years. But I never had any reason to go in there till two days ago, when Mom had to go to the Wash-a-Mat and asked me to get some change.

And man! Are those people who come in there in some bad shape.

Old man Silver and old man Dollar, who own the place, have signs tacked up everywhere:

NO LOUNGING, NO LOITERING[1]

THIS IS NOT A WAITING ROOM

and

MINIMUM CHECK CASHING FEE, 50¢

and

LETTERS ADDRESSED, 50¢

and

LETTERS READ, 75¢

and

LETTERS WRITTEN, ONE DOLLAR

And everybody who comes in there to cash a check gets their picture taken like they're some kind of criminal.

After I got my change, I stood around for a while digging the action. First comes an old lady with some kind of long form to fill out. The mean old man behind the counter points to the "One Dollar" sign. She nods. So he starts to fill it out for her.

"Name?"

"Muskogee Marie Lawson."

"SPELL it!" he hollers.

"M, m, u, s—well, I don't exactly know, sir."

"I'll put down 'Marie,' then. Age?"

"Sixty-three my last birthday."

"Date of birth?"

"March twenty-third"—a pause—"I think, 1900."

"Look, Marie," he says, which makes me

mad, hearing him first-name a dignified old gray-haired lady like that, "if you'd been born in 1900, you'd be seventy-two. Either I put that down, or I put 1910."

"Whatever you think best, sir," she says timidly.

He sighs, rolls his eyes to the ceiling, and bangs his fist on the form angrily. Then he fills out the rest.

"One dollar," he says when he's finished. She pays like she's grateful to him for taking the trouble.

Next is a man with a cane, a veteran who has to let the government know he moved. He wants old man Silver to do this for him, but he doesn't want him to know he can't do it himself.

"My eyes are kind of bad, sir. Will you fill this thing out for me? Tell them I moved from 121 South 15th Street to 203 North Decatur Street."

Old man Silver doesn't blink an eye. Just fills out the form, and charges the crippled man a dollar.

And it goes on like that. People who can't read or write or count their change. People who don't know how to pay their gas bills, don't know how to fill out forms, don't know how to address envelopes. And old man Silver and old man Dollar cleaning up on all of them. It's pitiful. It's disgusting. Makes me so mad I want to yell.

And I do, but mostly at Mom. "Mom, did you know there are hundreds of people in this city who can't read and write?"

Mom isn't upset. She's a wise woman. "Of course, James," she says. "A lot of the older people around here haven't had your advantages. They came from down South, and they had to quit school very young to go to work.

"In the old days, nobody cared whether our

---

1. **loitering** (loi′tər-ĭng): staying around without purpose.

people got an education. They were only interested in getting the crops in." She sighed. "Sometimes I think they *still* don't care. If we hadn't gotten you into that good school, you might not be able to read so well either. A lot of boys and girls your age can't, you know."

"But that's awful!" I say. "How do they expect us to make it in a big city? You can't even cross the streets if you can't read the 'Walk' and 'Don't Walk' signs."

"It's hard," Mom says, "but the important thing to remember is it's no disgrace. There was a time in history when nobody could read or write except a special class of people."

And Mom takes down her Bible. She has three Bible study certificates and is always giving me lessons from Bible history. I don't exactly go for all the stuff she believes in, but sometimes it *is* interesting.

"In ancient times," she says, "no one could read or write except a special class of people known as scribes. It was their job to write down the laws given by the rabbis and the judges.[2] No one else could do it.

"Jesus criticized the scribes," she goes on, "because they were so proud of themselves. But he needed them to write down his teachings."

"Man," I said when she finished, "that's something."

My mind was working double time. I'm the best reader and writer in our class. Also it was summertime. I had nothing much to do except go to the park or hang around the library and read till my eyeballs were ready to fall out, and I was tired of doing both.

So the next morning, after my parents went to work, I took Mom's card table and a folding chair down to the sidewalk. I lettered

"There was a time in history when nobody could read or write except a special class of people."

a sign with a Magic Marker, and I was in business. My sign said:

PUBLIC SCRIBE—ALL SERVICES FREE

I set my table up in front of the Silver Dollar and waited for business. Only one thing bothered me. If the people couldn't read, how would they know what I was there for?

But five minutes had hardly passed when an old lady stopped and asked me to read her grandson's letter. She explained that she had just broken her glasses. I knew she was fibbing, but I kept quiet.

I read the grandson's letter. It said he was having a fine time in California but was a little short. He would send her some money as soon as he made another payday. I handed the letter back to her.

"Thank you, son," she said, and gave me a quarter.

I handed that back to her too.

The word got around. By noontime I had a whole crowd of customers around my table. I was kept busy writing letters, addressing envelopes, filling out forms, and explaining official-looking letters that scared people half to death.

---

2. **the rabbis and the judges:** the teachers and rulers of the ancient Hebrews.

Afternoon Glare—Main Street (1991), Carl J. Dalio. Collection of the artist. Copyright © 1991 Carl J. Dalio.

I didn't blame them. The language in some of those letters—"Establish whether your disability is one-fourth, one-third, one-half, or total, and substantiate[3] in paragraph 3 (b) below"—would upset anybody. I mean, why can't the government write English like everybody else?

Most of my customers were old, but there were a few young ones too. Like the girl who had gotten a letter about her baby from the Health Service and didn't know what "immunization"[4] meant.

At noontime one old lady brought me some iced tea and a peach, and another gave me some fried chicken wings. I was really having a good time when the shade of all the people standing around me suddenly vanished. The sun hit me like a ton of hot bricks.

Only one long shadow fell across my table. The shadow of a tall, heavy, blue-eyed cop. In our neighborhood, when they see a cop, people scatter. That was why the back of my neck was burning.

"What are you trying to do here, sonny?" the cop asks.

---

3. **substantiate** (səb-stăn′shē-āt): to give evidence to prove a claim.

4. **immunization** (ĭm′yə-nĭ-zā′shən): medicine given to protect against disease.

"Help people out," I tell him calmly, though my knees are knocking together under the table.

"Well, you know," he says, "Mr. Silver and Mr. Dollar have been in business a long time on this corner. They are very respected men in this neighborhood. Are you trying to run them out of business?"

"I'm not charging anybody," I pointed out.

"That," the cop says, "is exactly what they don't like. Mr. Silver says he is glad to have some help with the letter writing. Mr. Dollar says it's only a nuisance to them anyway and takes up too much time. But if you don't charge for your services, it's unfair competition."

Well, why not? I thought. After all, I could use a little profit.

"All right," I tell him. "I'll charge a quarter."

"Then it is my duty to warn you," the cop says, "that it's against the law to conduct a business without a license. The first time you accept a fee, I'll close you up and run you off this corner."

He really had me there. What did I know about licenses? I'm only thirteen, after all. Suddenly I didn't feel like the big black businessman anymore. I felt like a little kid who wanted to holler for his mother. But she was at work, and so was Daddy.

"I'll leave," I said, and did, with all the cool I could muster. But inside I was burning up, and not from the sun.

One little old lady hollered "You big bully!" and shook her umbrella at the cop. But the rest of those people were so beaten down they didn't say anything. Just shuffled back on inside to give Mr. Silver and Mr. Dollar their hard-earned money like they always did.

I was so mad I didn't know what to do with myself that afternoon. I couldn't watch TV. It was all soap operas anyway, and they seemed

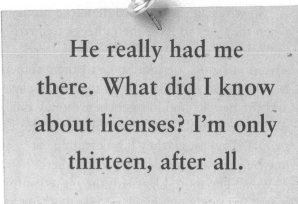

He really had me there. What did I know about licenses? I'm only thirteen, after all.

dumber than ever. The library didn't appeal to me either. It's not air-conditioned, and the day was hot and muggy.

Finally I went to the park and threw stones at the swans in the lake. I was careful not to hit them, but they made good targets because they were so fat and white. Then after a while the sun got lower. I kind of cooled off and came to my senses. They were just big, dumb, beautiful birds and not my enemies. I threw them some crumbs from my sandwich and went home.

"Daddy," I asked that night, "how come you and Mom never cash checks downstairs in the Silver Dollar?"

"Because," he said, "we have an account at the bank, where they cash our checks free."

"Well, why doesn't everybody do that?" I wanted to know.

"Because some people want all their money right away," he said. "The bank insists that you leave them a minimum balance."

"How much?" I asked him.

"Only five dollars."

"But that five dollars still belongs to you after you leave it there?"

"Sure," he says. "And if it's in a savings account, it earns interest."

"So why can't people see they lose money when they *pay* to have their checks cashed?"

"A lot of *our* people," Mom said, "are scared of banks, period. Some of them remember the Depression,[5] when all the banks closed and the people couldn't get their money out. And others think banks are only for white people. They think they'll be insulted, or maybe even arrested, if they go in there."

Wow. The more I learned, the more pitiful it was. "Are there any black people working at our bank?"

"There didn't use to be," Mom said, "but now they have Mr. Lovejoy and Mrs. Adams. You know Mrs. Adams, she's nice. She has a daughter your age."

"Hmmm," I said, and shut up before my folks started to wonder why I was asking all those questions.

The next morning, when the Silver Dollar opened, I was right there. I hung around near the door, pretending to read a copy of *Jet* magazine.

"Psst," I said to each person who came in. "I know where you can cash checks *free*."

It wasn't easy convincing them. A man with a wine bottle in a paper bag blinked his red eyes at me like he didn't believe he had heard right. A carpenter with tools hanging all around his belt said he was on his lunch hour and didn't have time. And a big fat lady with two shopping bags pushed past me and almost knocked me down, she was in such a hurry to give Mr. Silver and Mr. Dollar her money.

*B*ut finally I had a little group who were interested. It wasn't much. Just three people. Two men—one young, one old—and the little old lady who'd asked me to read her the letter from California. Seemed the grandson had made his payday and sent her a money order.

"How far is this place?" asked the young man.

To tell the truth, the bank did look kind of scary. It was a big building with tall white marble pillars.

"Not far. Just six blocks," I told him.

"Aw shoot. I ain't walking all that way just to save fifty cents."

So then I only had two. I was careful not to tell them where we were going. When we finally got to the Establishment Trust National Bank, I said, "This is the place."

"I ain't goin' in there," said the old man. "No sir. Not me. You ain't gettin' me in *there*." And he walked away quickly, going back in the direction where we had come.

To tell the truth, the bank did look kind of scary. It was a big building with tall white marble pillars. A lot of Brink's armored trucks and Cadillacs were parked out front. Uniformed guards walked back and forth inside with guns. It might as well have a "Colored Keep Out" sign.

Whereas the Silver Dollar is small and dark and funky and dirty. It has trash on the floors and tape across the broken windows. People going in there feel right at home.

I looked at the little old lady. She smiled back bravely. "Well, we've come this far, son," she said. "Let's not turn back now."

---

5. **Depression:** the Great Depression, a period of slow business activity and high unemployment from 1929 through the 1930s, before bank deposits were insured.

So I took her inside. Fortunately Mrs. Adams's window was near the front.

"Hi, James," she said.

"I've brought you a customer," I told her.

Mrs. Adams took the old lady to a desk to fill out some forms. They were gone a long time, but finally they came back.

"Now, when you have more business with the bank, Mrs. Franklin, just bring it to me," Mrs. Adams said.

"I'll do that," the old lady said. She held out her shiny new bankbook. "Son, do me a favor and read that to me."

"Mrs. Minnie Franklin," I read aloud. "July 9, 1972. Thirty-seven dollars."

"That sounds real nice," Mrs. Franklin said. "I guess now I have a bankbook, I'll have to get me some glasses."

Mrs. Adams winked at me over the old lady's head, and I winked back.

"Do you want me to walk you home?" I asked Mrs. Franklin.

"No thank you, son," she said. "I can cross streets by myself all right. I know red from green."

And then she winked at both of us, letting us know she knew what was happening.

"Son," she went on, "don't ever be afraid to try a thing just because you've never done it before. I took a bus up here from Alabama by myself forty-four years ago. I ain't thought once about going back. But I've stayed too long in one neighborhood since I've been in this city. Now I think I'll go out and take a look at *this* part of town."

Then she was gone. But she had really started me thinking. If an old lady like that wasn't afraid to go in a bank and open an account for the first time in her life, why should *I* be afraid to go up to City Hall and apply for a license?

Wonder how much they charge you to be a scribe? ❖

KRISTIN HUNTER

1931–

Known for her realistic descriptions of urban life, Kristin Hunter has set many of her stories in cities similar to the one she describes in "The Scribe." At 14, Hunter was a columnist and feature writer for the Philadelphia edition of the Pittsburgh Courier. She earned a bachelor's degree from the University of Pennsylvania, where she later returned to teach writing.

Hunter says that "the bulk of my work has dealt—imaginatively, I hope—with relations between the white and black races in America." Hunter's stories about ghetto life suggest that individuals can change and improve their lives, however difficult, by believing in themselves and the power that lies within them.

The author has received numerous awards for her work from such respected organizations as the National Council on Interracial Books for Children, the National Conference of Christians and Jews, and the Pennsylvania Council on the Arts. Hunter has produced novels, short stories, poems, and magazine articles for a wide audience.

OTHER WORKS *The Soul Brothers and Sister Lou, Boss Cat, Guests in the Promised Land, Lou in the Limelight*

WRITING ABOUT
LITERATURE

A New Spin on Things

Each of us sees the world from a unique perspective. Talented poets use their writing skills and imaginations to describe in new and interesting ways how they see the world. That's why poetry is so personal. In the following pages, you will

- explore how writers use sensory language
- write a poem of your own
- look beyond appearances to find significance and value

Writer's Style: Sensory Language All good writers are good observers. They notice the tiniest details and use carefully chosen words to describe the look, feel, smell, taste, and sound of what they observe.

Read the Literature

Sensory language is language that appeals to the senses. Notice the words these writers use to appeal to the senses and make their writing lively.

Literature Models

Appealing to Touch
Pick out the words that appeal to the sense of touch. What other senses does this paragraph appeal to?

After lunch we went back to work. The sun kept beating down. The buzzing insects, the wet sweat, and the hot dry dust made the afternoon seem to last forever. Finally the mountains around the valley reached out and swallowed the sun. Within an hour it was too dark to continue picking. The vines blanketed the grapes, making it difficult to see the bunches.

Francisco Jiménez, from "The Circuit"

Appealing to Sight
Which words help you see what this writer is describing? What kinds of images does this passage create in your mind?

what I remember about that day
is boxes stacked across the walk
and couch springs curling through the air
and drawers and tables balanced on the curb

Lucille Clifton, from "the 1st"

Connect to Life

Poets aren't the only writers who use sensory language. Sensory words can help any writer create precise, interesting descriptions. Notice how these students describe homemade candy.

Consumer Magazine

Sweet and frothy at first, then tart and fizzy—like pop rocks without any pop.

—Zach

They're supposed to be like Gummi Worms, but taste like thick, grainy, sour gelatin instead.

—Cameron

from *Zillions* magazine

Appealing to Taste
Which words give you an idea of what the candy tastes like? How would you describe your favorite candy?

Try Your Hand: Using Sensory Language

1. **Choosing the Right Words** Finish each sentence by choosing a word or phrase that appeals to the senses. The first sentence has been done.

   - The trumpet, shrill and piercing, made my ears ring.
   - The insects in the fields . . .
   - The taco . . .
   - The sun on my neck . . .
   - The flowers . . .

2. **Sensory Phrases** With a classmate, write sensory descriptions of one or more of the following experiences.

   - taking a bite of a hot pepperoni pizza
   - a ride on a roller coaster
   - a tour of a chocolate factory

3. **Spicing It Up** Make the following scene more interesting and lifelike by using sensory language.

   Many people lined the streets. Marching bands went past me. Floats made out of flowers were pretty. Cowboys on horses rode by. I smelled popcorn and I got hungry. I couldn't see, so I moved toward the front.

SkillBuilder

 WRITER'S CRAFT

Using Compound Sentences
Writers often use compound sentences to help build their descriptions and images. A compound sentence is made up of two or more simple sentences joined together. The following compound sentences come from "Flowers and Freckle Cream."

But child, there are all kinds of flowers, and they are all beautiful.

I had a cousin whose name was Janette Elizabeth, and Janette Elizabeth looked exactly like her name sounds.

The parts of compound sentences can be joined by a semicolon or by a comma and a coordinating conjunction.

APPLYING WHAT YOU'VE LEARNED
On a sheet of paper, turn each pair of sentences into a compound sentence.

1. The freckle cream arrived in three weeks. It came in a plain brown package.
2. Wearing the freckle cream in the sun gave me more freckles. It made the freckles darker.

 GRAMMAR HANDBOOK

For more information on compound sentences, see page 843 of the Grammar Handbook.

Creative Response

People sometimes respond to a poem by writing one of their own. As you've seen, the poems in Unit Five are about very different topics. You, too, can write a poem about *anything*. You can describe something interesting, important, or trivial. The only limit to what you say in a poem—and how you say it—is your imagination.

GUIDED ASSIGNMENT

Write a Poem Writing your own poem may help you understand poetry a little better. On the following pages, you will explore your responses to the poems in Unit Five. Then you'll create a poem that only you could write.

❶ Prewrite and Explore

A poem can be about anything that strikes you as interesting, strange, funny, sad, or important. Look at the world around you. Pay attention to what you see, feel, and hear—a bright sunny day, a bumpy car ride, a baby's giggle.

The following list of ideas might help you to discover a poem inside you.

- Listen to the conversations around you.
- Reread the poems or stories in Unit Five, or elsewhere, that stir a memory.
- Recall events, experiences, and images.

Decision Point Based on your responses to the suggestions above, what is your poem going to be about?

Student's Concept Web

BEGINNING SMALL

Don't try to plan your poem too formally. Instead, start with a phrase, a feeling, an image, or an idea and write down what you think or feel. Sometimes, what you remember most about an experience are sensory impressions. Try to capture those impressions as accurately as you can by using sensory language.

The notebook below shows how one student got ideas for a poem by using personal mementos and a concept web.

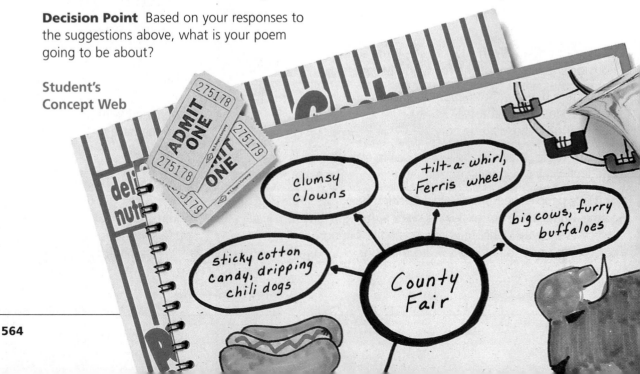

clumsy clowns

tilt-a-whirl, Ferris wheel

big cows, furry buffaloes

sticky cotton candy, dripping chili dogs

County Fair

② Freewrite

Now you can freewrite. Experiment with images, ideas, words, and meanings. Keep the ones you like best and try new ones. Sometimes the best way to begin a poem is simply to start writing. Then mark the words and phrases that you like the best and want to keep working with.

Student's Freewriting

The county fair smelled liked <u>charcoal grills</u> and my Uncle Del's barn. There were hundreds of <u>animals</u>; we liked them the best.
We rode on the <u>Ferris wheel and the tilt-a-whirl.</u>
We saw clowns, a sharpshooter, and a <u>buffalo.</u> I played arcade games and even won a <u>colorful</u> stuffed animal.

What do I remember most about the fair?

I picked popcorn and <u>corn-on-the-cob</u> from my teeth. But the hot dogs and <u>barbecue smells</u> were the greatest of all.

What words can I use to make the fair seem real to others?

③ Draft and Share

Experiment with the words you choose. Try arranging them differently. Try short lines, long lines, or an unusual arrange-ment of words. You might even experiment with your poem to see if rhyming the last words of lines makes your poem seem more musical. When your poem starts to take shape, share it with a classmate.

 PEER RESPONSE

- What was your first reaction to my poem?
- What ideas or meanings did you get from my poem?
- Which words helped you picture what I was describing?

SkillBuilder

 WRITER'S CRAFT

Using Sound Devices
Poets and writers choose words for their meanings and some-times for the sounds they make. As you write, read your work aloud and listen to the sounds of the words. Try choosing words that use sound in an interesting way. One sound device is **alliteration**. Alliteration is the repetition of beginning sounds, such as *wild wind*.

Other methods you can try include

- using words that have the same vowel sound (*blue shoes*)
- using words that sound like what they mean (*plop, hiss*)

APPLYING WHAT YOU'VE LEARNED
Use one of the sound devices discussed above to write a description of each of the items in this list.

1. an ocean wave
2. a car horn
3. a shark
4. a parade
5. a flock of birds
6. a hat
7. a parade
8. a train
9. a pair of socks
10. a school bell

4 Revise and Edit

Most poets rework their poems many times before they are satisfied. Before you work on your final draft, read your poem aloud and listen carefully to decide whether each word you have used adds to the poem's effect. Think about how you arranged the words and sentences on the page. Then check the questions next to the poem and consider the Standards for Evaluation as you finish your poem.

Student's Final Draft

Which words or phrases seem unique and interesting? Which senses does this poem appeal to?

How did the poet arrange words and lines to reflect the content?

The County Fair

Running back and forth and forth and back,
From the tilt-a-whirl to the Ferris wheel,
We BumpedPushedScrunched.
(Crowds are no fun!)

In the air floated smells of charcoal grills and barbecue sauce.
Hot dogs sizzled and corn-on-the-cob bobbed.
(Our bellies felt like bursting.)

We stared at clowns, a strongman, and a grouchy old buffalo.
And in the hot barns we petted whale-sized cows, cloudlike sheep,
    and bunnies curled like balls.
Then we tiptoed through the barns crunching straw—watching
                              where
              we
                                        stepped.

Standards for Evaluation

The poem
• describes a memorable or interesting experience, person, or event
• has descriptive and fresh language
• has sensory language and sound devices that make the poem interesting and fun to read

Grammar in Context

Inverted Sentences Experimenting with the word order in your sentences can help you write interesting poems. In most sentences, the subject comes before the verb.

The trumpet's blast echoed down the hall.

Sometimes writers *invert* the order of a sentence to create a special tone or to make their writing more interesting.

Down the hall echoed the trumpet's blast.

Notice that the same rules of subject-verb agreement apply to inverted sentences. The model below shows how one student used inverted sentences in a poem.

~~Smells of charcoal grills and barbecue sauce float~~
~~in the air.~~
In the air float smells of charcoal grills and
barbecue sauce.

Try Your Hand: Using Inverted Sentences

Rewrite each sentence as an inverted sentence. Be sure the subject and verb in each sentence agree.

1. The sun (sink) behind the mountains.
2. Papa whispers, "Here comes the school bus."
3. Pesky insects (buzz) in our ears.
4. Our dinner of rice and tortillas with *carne con chile* (sit) atop some wooden crates.
5. Papa's '38 Plymouth (disappear) into the distance.

GRAMMAR FROM WRITING

Understanding Subject-Verb Agreement

In every sentence, the verb and the subject must still agree in number. If the subject is singular, the verb must be singular. If the subject is plural, so is the verb. For example, look at this part of Paul Fleischman's "Chrysalis Diary":

My mouth is reshaping,
my legs are dissolving,
wings are growing
my body's not mine.

When writing, keep in mind that the verb and its subject may be separated by other words or phrases. Make sure that the verb agrees with its subject, which may not be the nearest noun.

APPLYING WHAT YOU'VE LEARNED
Write the following sentences, changing the verb in parentheses to the present tense.

1. Freckles (appeared) overnight on Elizabeth's body.
2. Elizabeth (squeezed) freckle-remover cream from the tube.
3. Elizabeth and her cousins (worked) in the fields in the summer.

 GRAMMAR HANDBOOK

For more information on subject-verb agreement and inverted sentences, see page 815 of the Grammar Handbook.

READING
THE WORLD

HIDDEN VALUES

Everybody sees the world differently. That's why your poem was different from your classmates' poems. Understanding and appreciating what other people value can teach you much about them, the world, and even yourself.

View In your notebook, write down your first impressions of the bear in the photograph.

Interpret Would you want this stuffed bear? Do you see anything special about it? What value might it have?

Discuss With a small group, take turns describing objects valued by you and no one else. Then use the SkillBuilder at the right to help you look beyond appearances.

CRITICAL THINKING

Looking Beyond Appearances

You've seen that each of us finds value, beauty, and significance in different objects and experiences. For example, what was your opinion of the stuffed bear pictured here? To some people, this stuffed animal is just an old, worthless child's toy. Other people may look deeper and see a treasured family memento with high personal value.

This particular bear was one of the first teddy bears ever. It was named for Theodore "Teddy" Roosevelt, the 26th president of the United States. The directors of the Smithsonian Institution, a group of museums in Washington, D.C., thought this teddy bear was valuable enough to include in one of the collections. Teddy bears, the directors thought, are a part of American culture. One of the first teddy bears ever made, therefore, has historical value to many people.

APPLYING WHAT YOU'VE LEARNED
In a small group, discuss how your opinion of this teddy bear changed when you learned more about it. Then discuss other objects that you gained a better understanding of when you looked beyond appearances.

RELUCTANT HEROES

WHAT DO YOU THINK?

REFLECTING ON THEME

What qualities come to mind when you think about heroes? Bravery? Daring? Sometimes a hero may at first appear cowardly. Use these activities to examine what it takes to become a hero or heroine. Then, as you read *The Hobbit*, compare your ideas about heroism with those of Bilbo Baggins, a character who says, "No adventures, thank you."

Can you be persuaded?

Have you ever been coaxed into riding a roller coaster, speaking in front of a group, or participating in some other activity that you might not have the courage to do on your own? Perform a monologue in which you share your reactions to such a situation.

What can a goal reveal?

Think about a goal you have worked to achieve. What did pursuing your goal teach you about yourself? Was all the effort worth it? Draw a before-and-after picture of yourself in your notebook.

Looking Back

What do you remember most about your experience with the readings and activities in Part 1, "Facing Inner Fears"? In your notebook, complete the sentence shown. Be sure to give reasons for your response.

What danger lurks?

Create a board game in which a hero or heroine must overcome obstacles to reach a goal. Use a web similar to the one shown here to help with your planning. Then play the game with a group of classmates.

Characters · Name of Game · Obstacles · Object · Rules

Part 1 of this unit was memorable to me because . . .

REFLECT & ASSESS

PREVIEWING

DRAMA

The Hobbit

J.R.R. Tolkien (tōl′kēn′)

dramatized by Patricia Gray

PERSONAL CONNECTION

You are about to meet Bilbo Baggins, a hairy-footed, gnomelike creature called a hobbit. Bilbo embarks on an astonishing adventure, a journey of discovery—a quest. What images or ideas does the word *quest* bring to your mind? Can ordinary people go on quests, or are quests just gone on by characters in myths, fairy tales, and fantasies? Discuss quests with a few classmates; then list your ideas in a graphic like the one shown. As you read, compare your diagram with the events and images of Bilbo Baggins's quest.

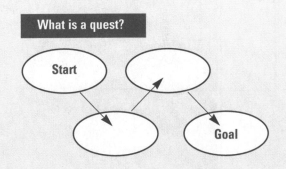

What is a quest?

Start

Goal

LITERARY CONNECTION

John Ronald Reuel (rōō′əl) Tolkien was a respected English scholar who became famous as the author of *The Hobbit* (1937) and *The Lord of the Rings* (1954–1955), a trilogy, or set of three novels, about the kingdom of Middle Earth. Though an imaginary place, Middle Earth has similarities to the England of Tolkien's time. In fact, the fantasy writer poked gentle fun at the habits and manners of many types of English people. Bilbo Baggins, Esquire, for example, is a typical sort of country gentleman. He is pleased with the comforts of home, a bit stuffy, less than brilliant, yet a determined defender of his family's honor.

READING CONNECTION

Stage Directions The stage directions for this play, which are printed in italic type, describe the scenery, props, and sound and light effects. They also tell where the actors enter, how they speak or move, and where they exit the stage. Stage directions help the reader picture exactly what is going on and where it is happening. The diagram shown identifies the parts of the stage and the abbreviations used in *The Hobbit*. Before you begin reading, become familiar with the parts of the stage and with the terms used.

Key
D = Downstage
U = Upstage
C = Center
R = Right
L = Left

Bilbo Comes to the Huts of the Raft Elves (1966), J.R.R. Tolkien. Illustration from *The Hobbit* by J.R.R. Tolkien. Copyright © 1966 J.R.R. Tolkien. Reprinted by permission of Houghton Mifflin Co. All rights reserved.

The Hobbit

A play by Patricia Gray 🦋 *Based on a story by J.R.R. Tolkien*

CAST OF CHARACTERS

Bilbo Baggins	a Hobbit
Gandalf	a great Wizard
Dwalin and **Balin**	
Kili and **Fili**	
Dori, Nori and **Ori**	Dwarves
Oin and **Gloin**	
Bifur and **Bofur**	
Bombur	
Thorin	Leader of the Dwarves
Grocery Boy	a Hobbit lad
Bert	
Essie	Trolls
Tom	
The Great Goblin	
Attendant Goblin	Goblins
Gollum	a slimy creature
The Elven-Queen	
Two Elf Guards	Wood-elves
Smaug	the Dragon

Other Hobbits, Goblins, Elves, etc., may be added as desired, or the number may be easily reduced.

Place: *From Underhill, through the Wilderland, to the Lonely Mountain.*

Time: *Long ago in the quiet of the world.*

The hill : hobbiton-across-the Water

The Hill: Hobbiton-Across-the-Water (1966), J.R.R. Tolkien. Illustration from *The Hobbit* by
J.R.R. Tolkien. Copyright © 1966 J.R.R. Tolkien. Reprinted by permission of Houghton Mifflin
Co., all rights reserved.

Act One ⚜ Scene One

Scene: *The houselights dim. The lights come up in front of the curtain, revealing an imaginary part of the world called Middle Earth. We are in the Shire,[1] Underhill, home of the Hobbits. It is a pleasant morning. The Shire is the picture of rural perfection.*

At left sits a well-appointed[2] little Hobbit by the name of Bilbo Baggins, Esq.[3] *He is sitting on the stoop outside his round green door, which has a shiny yellow brass doorknob in the exact middle. At the side is a mailbox with several letters in it. Before him is a turntable or lazy Susan, laid with four complete breakfasts. Bilbo has just eaten the first of these and lets out a deep sigh of satisfaction. He carefully dabs his mouth with a huge napkin. Emitting another sigh, he turns the table so that breakfast number two is before him. He digs in with determination after a brief hesitation over which jam to spread his muffin with.*

From right an extraordinary old man, Gandalf, *enters. He is tall, with a flowing white beard and bushy black brows, out of which gleam deep, piercing eyes. On his head is a tall, peaked hat covered with strange designs. He wears a long gray cloak, a silver scarf, and immense black boots and carries a staff.*

Gandalf (*regarding the scene with relish, taking a deep breath of the sparkling air*). Ah, the Shire! How delicious the morning is in this part of the world! The air is *stuffed* with comfort! It feels like nothing exciting has happened here for ages—all green and still— (*crosses to* Bilbo, *who is well into his third breakfast*)—rather like the inside of one of those fresh eggs you're eating—don't you think?

Bilbo (*looking up, startled*). Oh! I wouldn't know. It's hard to look at a place from the outside when you live in the inside! But then you're a stranger here. Welcome! I still have a breakfast or two left if you'd care for some.

Gandalf. Thank you, I haven't the time—and I am not a stranger anywhere unless, of course, I choose to be.

(*A Hobbit with a green, pointed cap peeks down at them from a window flap in the curtain. Immediately, two more Hobbits pop out from the two sides of the curtain.*)

Bilbo (*confused*). Oh, yes? Well, how do you do, sir— (*offering his hand*)

Gandalf (*ignoring the gesture*). Magnificently, of course! (*slowly and deliberately*) But at the

---

1. **Shire:** a county or district.
2. **well-appointed:** neat and well-dressed.
3. **Esq.:** abbreviation of Esquire, an honorary title for a country gentleman.

moment, I am looking for someone to share a great adventure— (*pauses to see* Bilbo's *reaction, which is sheer horror*) —a stupendous adventure that I'm arranging—and it's very difficult to find anyone— (*The three* Hobbits *who have been listening suddenly vanish. We hear sounds of doors and shutters slamming offstage.*) What was that?

Bilbo (*standing up, taking from his pocket a long wooden pipe and tapping it impatiently*). That was neighbors slamming doors and shutters.

Gandalf (*sadly*). On adventure. Tch, tch.

Bilbo. You, sir, are in the neighborhood of Hobbits.

Gandalf (*feigning ignorance*). Hobbit? Hobbit? What's a Hobbit?

Bilbo. We're just plain folk—have no use for adventures. (*shudders*) Nasty, uncomfortable things! Adventures make you late for dinner! Can't think what anybody sees in them! (Gandalf *continues to stare at* Bilbo *with a strangely disturbing gleam in his eye.* Bilbo *nervously crosses to the mailbox and removes some letters. He sits on the stoop and examines them.*) Good morning, we don't want any adventures here. You might try across The Hill or over The Water. (Bilbo *devotes himself to his letters.*)

Gandalf. You should be ashamed of yourself, *Bilbo Baggins!*

Bilbo (*sitting up alertly*). That's my name! How did you know—

Gandalf (*cutting in*). You know mine, too, although you don't know that I belong to it. I am Gandalf, and Gandalf means me! To think that I should have lived to be good-morninged by Belladonna Took's son—as if I were selling buttons at the door!

Bilbo (*beside himself with excitement*). Gandalf! Gandalf! Good gracious! Not the wandering wizard who used to tell such wonderful tales at parties about dragons and giants and goblins—

Gandalf (*merely yawning*). The same, dear boy.

Bilbo. And about the rescue of princesses and the unexpected luck of widows' sons! And the fireworks! I remember those! Old Grandpa Took used to send them up on Midsummer's Eve. What a display!

Gandalf. Naturally.

Bilbo. Up they rose, like great lilies and snapdragons, and hung in the twilight all evening, falling at last like silver and gold rain! . . . Dear me! Are you the same Gandalf who led so many of our quiet lads and lasses off on mad adventures? Bless me, life used to be quite inter— I mean, you used to upset things quite badly in these parts! I beg your pardon, but I had no idea you were still in the business.

Gandalf. Where else should I be? Tch, tch. Well, for your grandfather Took's sake and for the sake of your poor mother, Belladonna, I'll give you what you asked for.

Bilbo. But I haven't asked for anything!

Gandalf. Yes, you have. My pardon—I give it to you. In fact, I will be so kind as to send you on an adventure—very amusing for me, very good for you—and profitable, *if* you live through it.

Bilbo. *If I live through it?* Sorry. No adventures, thank you. Good morning! (*starts for his door, then remembers his manners*) I'd ask you in to tea, but—

Gandalf. How kind of you to ask me—I hate to think alone! (*propelling him through the door*) You go along in and fix the tea. I'll be in shortly—I have a little business to attend to. (*Gives* Bilbo *a final shove through the door, then chuckles slyly to himself, rubs his hands, and hangs a large, colorful sign on the door. The sign reads* BURGLAR WANTS GOOD JOB, PLENTY OF EXCITEMENT AND REASONABLE REWARD. *He looks off right*) Ah, here they come! (*goes through door*)

(*The curtain opens to reveal the main hall at Bag-End, residence of* B. Baggins, Esquire. *Upstage center is a large round door with a mat in front. To the left of it is a pegged coat-rack. Downstage is a long table, with benches. To the right of the table is a fireplace with a stool before it.* Gandalf, *at center, looking around the room, calls off to* Bilbo.)

Gandalf. A fine place you have here, Bilbo.

(Bilbo *bustles on left with tea trolley.*)

Bilbo. Yes, I love my quiet home.

Gandalf. I haven't been this way for a long time—not since your grandfather Took passed on—

Bilbo. Yes, well, I don't expect there's much to amuse you around here—

Gandalf. True—but you Hobbits make a relaxing change from those dwarves and elves with their hardheaded hustle and lightheaded bustle. Do you know the most amazing thing

about Hobbits?

Bilbo. No, what?

Gandalf. That you remain gentlefolk in spite of everything. I mean I just dropped in and yet you *insisted* I stay to tea.

Bilbo (*protesting weakly*). Well—(*Doorbell rings.* Bilbo *starts in surprise.*)

Gandalf. You expecting someone?

Bilbo (*crossing to door*). No—oh, maybe the groceries.

(Bilbo *opens the door upstage center, and in pops a dwarf,* Dwalin, *with a blue beard neatly tucked into his golden belt. He wears a dark green hood.*)

Dwalin (*executing a low, sweeping bow*). Dwalin, at your service!

Bilbo (*baffled, looking for groceries*). Why—Bilbo Baggins, at yours! Ummm—I was expecting groceries.

Dwalin. I was told you set a great table.

Gandalf. Ask the fellow in to tea, why don't you?

Bilbo. Yes, yes, certainly. Uh, would you care to join us? The kettle's on the boil—

Dwalin. Delighted! (*hangs his hood on a peg and seats himself expansively at table*)

Bilbo (*sitting down beside* Dwalin). Well, now! (*laughs nervously*) Tell me—(*The doorbell rings again.*) Oops, excuse me. (*goes to the* *door, saying while opening it*) I have no idea *who* it could—Oh!

(*There stands an elderly dwarf,* Balin, *with a white beard and scarlet hood.*)

Balin (*hobbling inside, gesturing at the coat rack with his cane*). Ha! I see they have begun to arrive already! (*hangs his hood next to* Dwalin's) Balin, at your service! (*It is difficult for him to execute a bow. He groans.*)

Bilbo. Thank you. Uh, you said "*They* have begun to arrive"?

Gandalf (*calling*). Groceries, Bilbo?

Bilbo. Actually, no— (*taking a deep breath, to* Balin) Won't you join us for tea?

Balin. A glass of buttermilk would suit me better, if it's all the same to you, my good sir. But I don't mind some cake—seed cake, if you have any. (*crosses to table*)

Bilbo (*automatically*). Oh, lots! Excuse me. (*hurries off left to get cake*)

Dwalin. No hurry. (*to* Balin) Fine lodgings here, eh, brother?

Balin (*seating himself*). Ummm. These Hobbits have the cream.[4] A big thing this is we're setting out for.

(*Doorbell rings, bringing on* Bilbo *from left with platter of cakes.*)

Dwalin. But dangerous. Terribly dangerous!

Bilbo. Not again!

Gandalf (*crossing to* Bilbo). Allow me to unburden you— (*Takes platter from* Bilbo *and passes platter to others.* Dwalin *takes two cakes and downs them rapidly and is shortly back for more.* Balin *takes one and nibbles at it and puts it down on small table. Later* Balin *eats it unnoticed.*)

(*Bell rings again.* Bilbo *rushes to the door and*

opens it. There stand two dwarves, Kili *and* Fili, *look-alikes with blue hoods, silver belts and yellow beards. Each carries a bag of tools and spades.*)

Kili. Kili!

Fili. Fili! (*Both sweep off their hoods and bow.*)

Kili and **Fili** (*together*). At your service!

Bilbo. Baggins, here— (*weakly*) At yours . . . uh, and your families'!

Kili. Dwalin and Balin here already, I see. Let us join the <u>throng</u>! (Kili *and* Fili *hang up their hoods, cross to table and sit down.*)

Bilbo (*horrified*). *Throng!*

Gandalf. Why, Bilbo, I really am surprised! I didn't think that Hobbits mixed with dwarves.

Bilbo. They don't!

Gandalf. No? That's odd, since you have so many dwarf friends.

Bilbo (*confidentially, to* Gandalf). I've never laid eyes on them before! If my neighbors knew, they'd be scandalized![5] Dwarves here! At Bag-End! (*Bell rings, and then there is the lively rat-a-tat of a stick on the door.*)

Dwalin. That'll be Dori, Nori, Ori, Oin and Gloin!

Bilbo (*horrified, crossing to door*). Who? (*hurrying to the door as the rat-a-tat continues*) The nerve!

(Bilbo *opens the door, and there stand no less than five dwarves,* Dori, Nori, Ori, Oin *and* Gloin, *their broad hands stuck in their gold and silver belts. They bow upon introducing themselves.*)

Dori (*has a blond beard, dark purple hood, and*

---

4. **the cream:** the best or choicest of things.

5. **scandalized:** shocked.

WORDS		
TO	**throng** (thrông) *n.* a large gathering of people; crowd
KNOW		

gold belt; *doffing his hood*). Dori!

Nori (*has a blond beard, pale purple hood, and silver belt; doffing his hood*). Nori!

Ori (*has a brown beard, orange hood, and gold belt; doffing his hood*). Ori!

Oin (*has an auburn beard, brown hood, and a gold belt; doffing his hood*). Oin!

Gloin (*has a gray beard, gray hood, and a silver belt; doffing his hood*). Gloin!

Bilbo. Oh!

Dori, Nori, Ori, Oin, and **Gloin** (*together*). At your service! (*They hang up their hoods.*)

Bilbo. Where do you all come from? (*crossing to Gandalf, frantically*) There's just no end to them! I must be having a nightmare! (*Gandalf pinches Bilbo.*) Ouch!

Gandalf. You're awake. (*Dwarves have been whispering among themselves.*)

Bilbo (*coughing importantly to get the Dwarves' attention*). Ahem, ahem. Honored Dwarves, I'm sorry, but I'm afraid you've mistaken this for a restaurant. This is a private home. (*Dwarves laugh politely at what they think is an attempt at humor.*)

Dori (*slapping Bilbo on the back good-naturedly*). Oh-ho, jolly good! Bring out the food.

Ori. Hot cocoa for me, please.

Dwalin (*from the table*). And more cakes! We're fresh out. Please! (*Shows empty plate. There is a terrific banging on the door.*)

Bilbo (*fuming*). Stop that pounding! What are you trying to—

(*Bilbo pulls the door open with a jerk, and in tumble four dwarves,* Bifur, Bofur, Bombur, *and* Thorin, *one on top of the other.*)

Gandalf (*laughing*). Careful. Careful! It's not like you, Bilbo, to keep friends waiting on the mat and then open the door like a popgun! (*The* Dwarves *pick themselves up and bow as they announce themselves, except for* Thorin, *who was at the bottom of the heap, directly under* Bombur, *the fattest of the lot.*)

Bifur (*Has a very slight chestnut beard and pale yellow hood; he is the youngest of the dwarves.*) I'm Bifur!

Bofur (*has a gray beard and a dark yellow hood and a silver belt*). Bofur!

Bifur and **Bofur** (*together*). At your service!

Bombur (*Has a light blue beard and a pale green hood. He is the fattest of the dwarves and is a natural clown. He scrambles off* Thorin *and bows deeply.*) Bombur, at your service! (*He indicates* Thorin, *who was at the bottom of the heap and who stands apart brushing himself off indignantly.*) Our great leader, Thorin. (*Thorin has a black beard and a sky blue hood with a long silver tassel.*)

Thorin (*snarling at* Bombur). Sir! (*Bombur cringes. They all hang up their hoods.*)

Bilbo (*interceding*). My fault. I'm terribly sorry.

Thorin (*grunting*). Don't mention it. (*gazes regally up at the ceiling, looking at row of thirteen hoods*) I see we are all here.

Gandalf. Quite a merry gathering! (*Doorbell rings.*)

Thorin. Who can *that* be?

Bilbo. Well, *I* certainly wouldn't know!

(*Bilbo crosses to door and opens it, and there stands a Hobbit Boy with a box of groceries.*)

Grocery Boy. Your groceries, Mr. Baggins.

Bilbo (*quickly*). Thank you, lad. I'll take them— (*takes box and attempts to shut door on boy*)

Grocery Boy (*peering over* Bilbo's *shoulder*). Having a party, Mr. Baggins?

Bilbo. Humph.

Grocery Boy. *Dwarves!* Cheez, Mr. Baggins—hundreds of 'em. Wait till they hear of this down the road. Dwarves! Like locusts! (Bilbo *shuts the door rudely on the boy.*)

Bilbo (*sadly*). Oh, dear!

Thorin (*crossing to table with new arrivals*). I trust there's food for the latecomers.

Bilbo (*tight as a coil*). Well—I may have a *little* tea left.

Gandalf. Tea? No, no, thank you. A little red wine and some cold chicken and pickles.

Thorin. And for me.

Bifur. Apple pie—and coffee, if you don't mind.

Bofur. And mince pie with cheese!

Bombur (*already seated at the table, drumming on it with zest*). Pork pie and salad! (Thorin *gives* Bombur *a disgusted look.*)

Bifur. And raspberry jam and muffins.

Gandalf. Put on a few eggs, there's a good fellow.

Dori (*from table*). Cold tongue!

Nori. A side of ham!

Ori. Cupcakes!

Oin. Assorted cheeses—if you please!

Dwalin. More cakes and ale!

Bilbo (*dumbfounded*). More! (*sarcastic*) Oh, certainly, dig in, dig in! (*heading left for the kitchen with box of groceries*) Don't stint yourselves! (*grumbling to himself as he goes off*) Seem to know as much about the inside of my kitchen as I do! (*calling back*) I could use some help!

Thorin. Bifur! Nori! (Bifur *and* Nori *go off left to help* Bilbo.) Now! Lower the lamp, Balin. (Balin *pulls down the lamp, which hangs over the table. The lights dim.*)

Dwalin (*rubbing his palms together*). Dark for dark business!

Balin. Hush! Let Thorin speak!

Thorin (*at head of table; standing and clearing his throat importantly*). Gandalf, dwarves, and Mr. Baggins!

(Bilbo, Bifur *and* Nori *bustle on left, laden with huge platters of food and drink.*)

Bilbo. Why so dark?

Fili. We *like* the dark. (Fili *notices* Bilbo *is not serving himself and begins to fill a plate for him.*)

Dwarves. Shh—

Thorin. We are met together in the house of our friend and fellow conspirator—

WORDS TO KNOW **conspirator** (kən-spîr'ə-tər) *n.* someone who takes part in a plot

580

Bilbo (*protesting*). No, no!

Thorin. —this wise and brave Hobbit—

Bilbo (*flattered*). Dear me!

Thorin. May the hair on his toes never fall out! All praise to his food. (*The* Dwarves *raise their mugs.*)

Dwarves (*toasting*). Hear, hear! (Bilbo *has slunk over to his stool in front of the fire where he sits clutching his toes protectively. Fili* brings *him a plate of food, but* Bilbo *shakes his head. His appetite is completely gone. Fili returns to his own place.*)

Thorin. We are met to discuss our plans. We shall start before dawn on a long, hard journey, so dangerous that some may not live through it or they may reach the misty mountain only to be eaten by the dragon— (Bilbo *lets out a piercing shriek, falling off the stool to the floor, where he lies shaking and twitching wildly. The* Dwarves *spring up and stare at him in dismay.*)

Gandalf (*producing a blue light [created by camera flash equipment] at end of his staff and crossing to* Bilbo, *prodding him with his foot*). Come, come. He's an excitable little fellow. He gets these queer fits, but he's fierce as a dragon in a pinch!

Bilbo (*shrieking*). I'm struck by lightning! Struck by lightning! (Dwarves *circle* Bilbo *curiously.*)

Gloin (*the doubter, snorting*). Humph! It's all very well for you to talk . . . but one shriek like that in a moment of danger might wake the dragon and all his kin. They'd eat the lot of us fast as you'd swallow a dozen cupcakes.

Thorin. It *did* sound more like fright than excitement. In fact, but for the sign on the door, I'd have thought we'd come to the wrong house.

Balin. Why, he just turned to jelly right before our eyes! He looks more like a grocer than a burglar!

Bilbo (*raising himself up with all the dignity he can muster*). Pardon me, but I couldn't help overhearing your insults. Am I allowed a few words?

Thorin (*condescendingly*). By all means.

Bilbo. First, I don't know what you're talking about. There isn't any sign on my door—unless, of course, you're referring to the dents from all your banging!

Gandalf. Of course there's a sign. I put it there myself.

Thorin. My good sir, the sign says: "Burglar wants good job, plenty of excitement and reasonable reward." Read it yourself. (*opens door and shows sign*)

Bilbo. So! I've been deceived!

Gandalf (*to* Thorin). You asked me to find a fourteenth man for your expedition—and I chose Mr. Baggins here—

Bilbo (*incensed*). Oh, you *did*, did you? Well, if you think that I—

Gandalf. —*but* I'm afraid I've made a sad mistake. This can't be the chap! No, no, I was looking for a member of the famous Took family. Imagine! I mistook *him* for a *Took!* (*glowers at* Bilbo)

Bilbo (*stung*). But I *am* a Took!

Gandalf. Really? Tch, tch, the blood must have thinned then.

Bilbo. Why, my great-uncle, Bull-Roarer Took—

Gloin (*cutting in*). Yes, yes, but we're talking about you!

Gandalf (*melodramatically*). I said to myself, now *here* is a Hobbit with desires beyond his next cup of tea—but alas, he's just an ordinary run-of-the-Shire Hobbit. When adventure knocks, he locks his door and hides under the bed.

Bilbo (*highly insulted, standing up*). Really, this is too much!

Gandalf (*to* Dwarves). Well, dwarves, you can go back to shoveling coal. The Hobbit is afraid to go, and you certainly can't set out with thirteen! That's too unlucky!

Bilbo (*with great dignity*). Sir, I must tell you that to uphold the honor of the Took family, I would cross mountains and deserts and fight a hundred dragons! I would—

Gandalf (*cutting in*). Splendid! Mr. Baggins is with us! (*shakes* Bilbo's *hand*) Now, Thorin—(*crosses to* Thorin)

Bilbo (*mumbling to himself*). Now why did I say that? Bilbo, you're a fool! Now you *have* put your foot in it!

Thorin (*to* Gandalf). But are you sure he'll do? You yourself said that he—

Gandalf (*interrupting*). If I say he's a burglar, a burglar he is—or will be when the time comes. There's more to him than you guess or he has any idea of himself. You'll live to thank him, and to thank him that you live.

Thorin. Let us hope so! (*turns to others*) Well, now to get on with the plans. It's late. (*All walk over to the table and sit with* Thorin *at the head,* Bilbo *at his right and* Bombur *next to* Bilbo.)

Gandalf (*spreading a large map on the table before* Thorin). Let's have some light on this. (Bombur *adjusts the overhanging lamp. Lights come up. To* Thorin.) This is a map of the Lonely Mountain. It was left by your grandfather, King Thrain.

Thorin. Ah, yes?

Bilbo. What mountain?

Bombur (*giving* Bilbo *a friendly nudge*). Where the *treasure* is! *And* the dragon. (*makes a gruesome face and hisses alarmingly at* Bilbo)

Thorin (*studying the map*). I don't see that this will help much—I remember the mountain well enough and the lands about it— (*pointing them out*) Mirkwood—the Withered Heath—

Bombur. That's where the great dragons breed! (*makes clawlike, threatening gestures and hisses at* Bilbo, *who manages a sickly smile in spite of being terrified*)

Thorin. There's the dragon—marked in red. Well, we're not likely to miss *him,* are we! (*Laughter from company.* Bilbo's *laughter lingers on.* Dwarves *look at him curiously.*)

Bilbo (*nervously*). Oh ho ho ha! The— (*stops, embarrassed*) Dragon! I'm not overfond of dragons, but then I've never actually known any.

Gandalf (*dismissing* Bilbo's *chatter*). You will, you will. (*to* Thorin) Look here, Thorin. This circle on the map marks the secret entrance in the mountain—here! (*points to spot on map*)

Thorin. Ha! But is it still secret? That's the question!

Balin. By now the dragon must know these caves from top to bottom.

Gandalf. Not the secret entrance. It's so well hidden it looks exactly like the side of the mountain. And by the way, I've a key that goes with the map. Here it is. (*hands* Thorin *a key*) Keep it safe!

Thorin. Indeed I will! (*fastens it on a gold chain that hangs about his neck and speaks with great satisfaction*) Well, now, things begin to look more hopeful. A secret entrance! What luck!

Bombur (*to* Bilbo). Arrrgh! Hear him roar? It's almost dinner time. The dragon's hungry for some nice roasted burglar! (Bilbo *hides his face in his hands and moans. The other* Dwarves *chuckle and nudge each other.*)

Thorin (*turning to* Bilbo *with mock politeness*). Suppose we ask our burglar expert to give us his ideas and suggestions—

Bilbo (*confused and shaky*). Well, first off I should like some information. I mean, about the dragon and the treasure and how it got there and who it belongs to, and so on—

Thorin (*wearily*). Oh, very well—

Bilbo. And I'd also like to know about risks, out-of-pocket expenses, time required, wages, et cetera.

Balin. He wants to know his chances of coming back alive and how much gold he'll get.

Thorin. His chances are as good as ours. The circumstances are briefly these: Long ago when my grandfather was king, the dwarves settled here— (*points at map*) —under the Lonely Mountain, and they built the merry town of Dale. Those were the happy days! They made beautiful things just for the fun of it. Not to sell, as we do now. When they needed more gold or emeralds or rubies, they just dug them out of the mountain. There was no end to the supply. But that brought the dragon. Good times always bring dragons. History illustrates—

Gandalf (*interrupting*). Be brief, won't you?

Thorin (*insulted*). Very well. There was an especially wicked dragon called Sm-sm-sm— (*apologetically*) —his name seems to stick in my throat—

Gandalf (*helpfully*). Smaug!

Thorin. Yes, curse him! He flew from the east and burned the town. Only a few escaped,

my father among them.

Bilbo (*thrilled*). And then?

Thorin. The dragon ate all the dwarves and took their treasure. The <u>fiend</u>! (*pounds on the table*) So now we mean to get back what is rightfully ours and bring our curses home to Sm-sm-sm—

Gandalf (*helping*). Smaug!

Thorin. Death to all dragons—especially Sm-sm-sm—

Dwarves (*banging their mugs and roaring it out*). Smaug!

Bilbo (*weakly*). Hear, hear!

Dwarves. Hear what?

Bilbo (*flustered*). Hear what I've got to say!

Gandalf. Go ahead. Say it!

Bilbo. I think you ought to go first to the secret entrance and look around—dragons must sleep sometimes. And now I'm off to bed. You have my blessing. Uh—is there anything I can get you before you go?

Thorin. Before *we* go, I suppose you mean. You're the burglar and getting inside the entrance is *your* job.

Dwarves (*thundering applause*). Thorin!

Bilbo. But—but, you see, I may have spoken a little hastily just now. It's an inconvenient time to—

Gandalf (*dismissing it*). It's nearly dawn. Time to clear up and start. (Bilbo *tries to attract his attention by pulling at his sleeve, but* Gandalf *ignores him, and he is equally unsuccessful in attracting* Thorin's *attention.* Bilbo *finally gives up, shaking his head gloomily. The* Dwarves *jump up and begin to make tall stacks of the plates and glasses.* Gandalf *and* Thorin *remain seated, looking over the map.*)

Bilbo (*squeaking with fright*). Please be careful! (*spinning around the room*) Please don't trouble! I can take care of everything after you've all gone!

Dwarves (*chanting while clearing table*).
Chip the glasses, and crack the plates!
Blunt the knives and bend the forks!
That's what Bilbo Baggins hates—
Smash the bottles and burn the corks!

Bilbo (*shrieking*). My best china! Please be careful!

Dwarves (*chanting*).
Cut the cloth and tread on the fat!
Pour the milk on the pantry floor!
Leave the bones on the bedroom mat!
Splash the wine on every door!
That's what Bilbo Baggins hates!
So, carefully! carefully with the plates!

(*The Dwarves exit with the glasses, platters, etc., Bilbo whirling around madly. Offstage there is a tremendous clatter as the curtain falls.*)

(*Lights come up in front of the curtain. The Dwarves are lined up on the apron, sticks with bundles over their shoulders, ready to start. Thorin is at the head.*)

Thorin (*pacing impatiently*). Well, where's the Hobbit? Where's our burglar?

(*Bilbo runs on left, puffing profusely.*)

Bifur. Here he is! Bravo!

Thorin. Humph!

Bilbo (*very put out, catching his breath*). Oh, my! Oh, my! The way the morning starts decides the day! It's going to be a miserable day! Hunting dragons! At my age! What a fool I am. Everyone expecting me to be ready at the drop of a hat! (*Feels his head. No hat.*) My *hat!* My coat, my brolly,[6] my pocket hanky—my purse—

Thorin (*cutting in*). Stop fussing!

Bilbo (*searching his pockets*). Where's my diary? If the dragon eats me, there'll be no record! My friends back home won't know what happened! And I've got no money—

Thorin (*disgusted*). Get a grip on yourself, Baggins!

Dwalin (*grimly*). You'll learn to do without small comforts before we reach journey's end.

Gloin (*disgusted, acting it out*). Where's his money? Imagine! Our burglar hasn't any money! (*Capers about, imitating* Bilbo's *fluster. The* Dwarves *laugh derisively.*)

Bombur (*helpful but mocking*). I've a spare hood. The lining is fireproof. It'll keep your hair from being burned when Smaug spits fire at you.

Bilbo (*politely*). Thank you, Bombur, much obliged. (*Tries it on. It is very large.*) I wish it fitted closer, but the fireproof lining is great. Very great.

(Gandalf *strides on from left.*)

Gandalf. Are we all ready to start? Ah, Bilbo, I believe you forgot these. (*hands* Bilbo *a handkerchief, a pipe and tobacco pouch, a leather-bound journal and a hat*)

Bilbo (*delighted, stowing them away*). Oh, thank you! And my diary! How kind of you! (*Bilbo is puzzled by the hat. He replaces the hood with the hat and looks regretfully at the lining of the hood. Then with decision he replaces the hood on his head, looks uncertainly at the hat and then tosses it offstage.*)

Dwarves (*approvingly*). Bilbo! Long live our burglar!

Gandalf. And I remembered you, Bombur. (*hands over a string bag of small, hard cakes*)

---

6. **brolly:** a British term for umbrella.

Bombur. Cakes! Thank you! Where did you get them?

Gandalf. From a friend of mine. He lives far from here. You may yet meet him.

Bombur (*eating one*). It tastes of honey.

Gandalf. Yes, my friend keeps bees. (Bombur *starts to take another.*) You'll need these cakes. Don't eat them right away.

Bombur (*stowing the cakes away*). Need them? With all the food we're taking! But, as you say, Gandalf.

Thorin. Our marching song! (Thorin *leads the* Dwarves *off left. They march off heavily, in* step, *chanting in gloomy tones.*)

> Far over the misty mountains cold
> To dungeons deep and caverns old
> We must away, ere break of day,
> To seek the pale enchanted gold!

(Gandalf *and* Bilbo *follow closely after* Dwarves.)

Bilbo (*to* Gandalf). Couldn't they sing something cheery?

Gandalf. Such as—

Bilbo (*firmly*). Such as "Home, Sweet Home."

(*As they exit,* Gandalf *puts his arm around* Bilbo *and laughs.*)

FROM **PERSONAL RESPONSE** *TO* **CRITICAL ANALYSIS**

REFLECT 1. What do you think of Bilbo Baggins, Esquire? Share your impressions with your class.

RETHINK 2. Why do you suppose Gandalf chooses Bilbo to join the quest?
   Consider
   - Gandalf's comment to Bilbo, "I'll give you what you asked for."
   - that Gandalf says to the dwarves, "There's more to him than you guess or he has any idea of himself."
   - why Bilbo agrees to get involved

   3. Bilbo says, "It's hard to look at a place from the outside when you live in the inside." Do you agree? Why or why not?

   4. Based on what you have learned about Bilbo so far, do you think he will be a successful burglar? Explain your opinion.

Scene Two

Scene: *In the forest several months later. The curtain rises to reveal a nearly bare stage that is divided into three playing areas. At right there is a platform approximately a foot-and-a-half high that extends in from the right side to about one-quarter of the way across the stage. A similar platform extends the same distance from left.*

At rise of curtain: Lights come up on the platform at left. Bilbo *is discovered sitting on a log at the edge, legs crossed, writing thoughtfully in his journal with a long quill pen. Behind him, the* Dwarves, *except for* Fili *and* Kili, *are sprawled out, resting. The only sound is that of* Bombur's *heavy snoring.* Bilbo *finishes with a flourish, blows on script,[7] holds it off admiringly and reads aloud:*

Bilbo (*reading his entry*). "Have just stopped to rest and let Fili and Kili water our ponies. Thought for today: Adventures are not all Sunday strolls in May sunshine." That's really well put. (*lays down book and massages his feet*) Covered with burrs! (*picks at burrs*) And soaked with these nasty May rains. Bother burgling! I wish I was home with the kettle just beginning to sing!

Bofur (*rousing and leaning on an elbow*). You'll wish that again before we're out of this mess. But go on, I like to hear you read about our adventures.

Bilbo. Thanks. (*resumes reading*) "At first I thought adventures were much like picnics. We traveled past pretty farms, and the people seemed friendly. But things have changed lately.

See thought for today. We've seen no one all day, and there's nothing ahead but black, rainy mountains. As soon as Fili and Kili are back, we should move ahead and make an early camp and have some hot supper."

Bombur. Sound idea! (*Takes out bag of honey cakes and looks at them. He glances about to see if anyone is noticing, and then slips a cake in his mouth.*)

Bifur (*rousing*). Did someone say supper?

Thorin (*rousing*). We should be going on. Where are Fili and Kili? (*Offstage cries are heard.*)

Bilbo (*jumping up*). I hear something.

Dori (*rising*). It's Fili.

Nori (*rising*). And Kili.

Bifur (*struggling to his feet*). They're shouting for help!

(Fili *and* Kili *enter. They are drenched, breathless, and gasping.*)

Thorin. Where are the ponies? What's happened?

Kili. We lost them. (*The* Dwarves *press forward around them, excitedly ad-libbing[8] questions: "Lost them!" "How could you?" "Did they run away?" etc.*)

Thorin (*sternly*). Silence, dwarves. Kili, what happened?

Kili. We took them down to water like you said. But the streambed was almost dry, and they wandered out into it drinking at some of the little pools. (*pauses, gulping breath*)

Thorin (*sternly*). Did you stay with them?

Kili (*uncomfortably*). I did, until they were settled drinking water. Then I—well, I went along the bank looking for mushrooms to eat.

---

7. **script:** Bilbo's journal, not the script of the play.

8. **ad-libbing:** in a play, making up one's own lines rather than speaking words written by the playwright.

Thorin. You mean you left them!

Kili. But Fili was watching them from the bank, and I ran back the minute I heard him shout.

Thorin. What happened, Fili?

Fili. A great wall of water came thundering out of the mountains. I shouted, but it was over the ponies in a moment. They just tumbled over and over like logs and were gone!

Thorin. All of them!

Fili. Yes.

Thorin. And the food bags?

Kili. On the ponies. (Thorin *turns away with a gesture of despair.*)

Bilbo. But then we've nothing to eat.

Bifur. We've got the honey cakes.

Dwalin. Wise Gandalf. He knew we'd need them!

Thorin. But maybe we'll have a greater need of them later. This isn't a real emergency. We're not starving.

Bombur. I am.

Thorin. After all, we've got our burglar here. (*to* Bilbo) It's up to you, burglar. Burgle us some food.

Bilbo. Up to me. I like that! Out here in the middle of nowhere! It needs a magician to find food here. Besides, maybe this is the time Gandalf meant us to eat the honey cakes. Why don't you ask him?

Balin. He's right. Ask Gandalf. (*There is a general murmur of agreement from the* Dwarves.)

Thorin. You may be right. (*glances around*) Where's Gandalf?

Balin. Asleep, probably. I'll wake him up. (*calls*) Gandalf! (*No answer. Louder.*) Gandalf!

Dori. He's gone!

Ori. Gone! Oh, no!

Gloin. Smartest thing he ever did!

Balin. If I was a wizard, I'd vanish, too.

Thorin. Yes—well, I'm sure he had his reasons. We'll have to go on without him.

Dwarves (*ad-libbing groans, etc.*) Oh, no!

Thorin (*proudly*). We dwarves have always stood alone. Our forefathers didn't depend on magic.

Gloin. And look what happened—a dragon ate them!

Bifur. Speaking of eating—

Thorin (*crossly*). Oh, very well! Bombur, share out the cakes. (Bombur *rapidly passes out the cakes, starting with* Thorin. *He comes to* Bilbo *last.* Bilbo *takes the cake* Bombur *hands him. He sees the bag is empty.*)

Bilbo. But there's none left for you! (*All the* Dwarves *turn to look at* Bombur.)

Bombur (*embarrassed*). Never mind. I had mine.

Bilbo. But you didn't. You just passed them out.

Bombur. I ate mine before.

Bilbo. You mean that time when Gandalf gave them to you? That doesn't count.

Bombur (*blurting it out miserably*). I ate one just before Fili and Kili came back. I'm sorry!

Gloin (*indignant*). You broke into our supplies?

Bilbo (*calmly*). They weren't ours, they were Bombur's. Gandalf gave the cakes to him. Besides, we thought we still had our supplies then.

Gloin. I still think—

Bilbo. After all, I'm the only one concerned. You all had your share, and I say Bombur had the right to eat all the cakes if he wanted to. They were his. (*breaks his cake in two*) Take half of this one, Bombur.

Bombur. I couldn't. . . .

Bilbo (*thrusting it in his hand*). Then you'll be wasting food as well as the time we're all wasting, for the cake will just crumble away. Come on—together. (Bilbo *and* Bombur *each pop the half cake in their mouths, smile and clasp hands in a brief handshake.*)

Balin. The burglar's right. We're wasting time. What's your plan, Thorin?

Thorin. Look over there— (*Gestures left. All look off.*)

Bilbo. Is that where Smaug, the dragon—

Thorin (*cutting in*). Of course not. But fierce trolls live there. (*All shudder.*)

Bilbo. What are trolls?

Thorin. Huge creatures, too big for us to fight! They eat dwarves— and Hobbits.

Bilbo (*aghast*). But shouldn't we run? Do we go on right up to where they are?

Thorin. We have to. That's the only way. (*encouragingly*) But there's one way to get the better of a troll. They're night creatures. Sunlight kills them. Turns them to stone.

Balin. I've heard of that. The thing to do is trick them into staying out of their cave until a ray of sunlight hits them.

Bilbo (*more cheerfully*). That shouldn't be so hard.

Gloin. But the trolls know this will happen. They're hard to fool. Chances are, they've got you frying in a pan while you're still trying to trick them. (Bombur *has been sneaking up on* Bilbo *from the rear. He grabs him.*)

Bombur. Got you! I'm a troll. (Bilbo *lets out a shriek.*)

Thorin (*sharply*). Order. (*to* Bombur) No more tricks till we're safely out of here! (*to* Bilbo) Be quiet. Do you want to bring a band of trolls down on us?

Balin (*pointing to platform right*). Look, there's a light over there!

(*The platform right is now dimly lit with a reddish glow. We can make out three large figures. They are trolls:* Bert, Tom, *and* Essie. *They are seated on the ground, toasting mutton on long spits of wood and licking the gravy off their fingers. There is a large wine jug.*)

Thorin. So there is! Fili, Kili, you look. Your eyes are sharpest. (Fili *and* Kili *strain to see.*)

Fili. It looks like—

Kili. It's trolls. Three of them.

Dwarves (*ad-lib*). Trolls! Ugh! Ich! Oh! (*The* Dwarves *huddle together, except* Thorin, *who stands apart.*)

Bombur (*sniffing the air deliciously*). I can smell

mutton cooking! (*All sniff the air.*)

Thorin. It *does* smell like mutton.

Dwarves (*ad-lib*). Ummm! Sure does! I could do with some mutton! With mint.

Bombur. Mutton with garlic. I'm *never* wrong about that!

Oin. It's a pity it belongs to the trolls.

Gloin. Yeh. But . . . wait a minute . . . we have a *burglar* with us!

Bilbo (*sarcastically*). Ah! So you've finally noticed!

Gloin (*rubbing his hands together*). Yes, indeed, a burglar! Bilbo, your chance has come at last!

Bilbo (*warily*). It has?

Oin (*to* Thorin). It's the burglar's turn.

Bilbo. It is?

Gloin. Now you can show your stuff. (*moves closer to* Bilbo, *until they are nose to nose*) Gandalf said that Hobbits were especially clever at quietly sneaking *up*—

Bilbo (*incredulously*). You can't mean—the trolls? You want *me* to burgle trolls?

Thorin (*nodding*). Exactly.

Bilbo (*desperately*). But I—I thought I was only supposed to burgle the *dragon!*

Thorin. Later, later. Bring back as much mutton as you can carry. We're hungry, remember. If you run into any difficulty, hoot twice like a barn owl, and we'll come.

Bilbo (*exploding*). *What!* Are you out of your mind?

Thorin (*icily*). I beg your pardon?

Bilbo (*indignantly*). Hobbits never hoot! But, no matter. No matter. Forward, Bilbo! (*He draws himself up to his full height and walks grandly off the platform.*)

Dwarves. Careful, now! Don't come back empty-handed! Good luck!

Bilbo (*crawling stealthily toward the* Trolls; *turning his head toward* Dwarves). Hush! Stop the racket! You'll spoil everything. (*Muttering to himself, he continues to crawl toward the* Trolls.) Dwarves!

(*Lights dim on platform left and come up on platform right as* Bilbo *approaches the* Trolls' *campfire.*)

Bert (*disgusted*). Ugh! I'm sick to death o' mutton, Essie! It's coming out me ears! Mutton yesterday, mutton today, and blimey[9], if it don't look like mutton again tomorrer! (*turns his back to the fire and tosses his mutton over his shoulder in* Bilbo's *direction*)

Tom. Never a blinking bit o' manflesh or a nice shoulder of dwarf have we had for a long time! (*faces front, also tossing his mutton over his shoulder*)

Essie. Aw, git off! Times been up our way when yer'd have said "Thank yer, Essie" for a nice bit o' fat valley mutton like what this is.

Bert (*taking a healthy pull at the jug*). Ugh! No more'n a dribble o' drink left! (Tom *grabs the jug.*) What the 'ell we was a-thinkin' of to come into these parts beats me! (Tom *takes a pull at the jug.* Bert *gives him a jab in the ribs, causing* Tom *to choke.*)

Tom (*coughing*). We ain't done badly. We've et a village and a half between us since we come.

Bert (*whining*). Them villages was barely bite-sized. (Bilbo *has made his way to the fire and is just about to make off with the discarded mutton when* Essie *spots him.*)

Essie (*wheeling around, catching* Bilbo *by the scruff of his neck and holding fast*). Blimey,

---

9. **blimey:** a British expression similar to "golly."

boys, look what I've copped!¹⁰

Bert (*jumping up*). 'Ere, wot's it?

Tom (*eying* Bilbo). Lumme¹¹ if I know. (to Bilbo, prodding him in the belly) What are yer? Man? (Bilbo *shakes his head wildly.*)—dwarf? (Bilbo *shakes his head again.*)

Bilbo (*stuttering*). Ha—ha—ha—Hobbit!

Tom. A hahahahobbit? Can't say I tasted 'em. Can yer cook 'em, Essie?

Essie (*pinching* Bilbo *like a soup chicken*). Yer can try. Won't make above a mouthful, though—not once he's skinned and boned. Now if there was four and twenty of 'em, I might make a pie!

Bert. Hey, you! Any more o' your sort a-sneakin' in these here woods, yer nasty little rabbit?

Bilbo (*correcting him politely*). Hobbit, not rabbit. Yes, lots—no—none at all!

Bert (*scratching his head*). What d'yer mean?

Bilbo (*collecting his scattered wits*). What I say. (*to* Essie) There's no need to pinch me, madam.

Essie. Shut yer mouth! I can always serve you on toast—minced!

Bilbo (*pleading*). Oh, please don't cook me, kind ma'am and sirs! I'm a good cook myself and cook better than I cook, if you see what I mean. Besides I like it here with you.

Bert (*suspiciously*). What's 'e say? (*grabs* Bilbo *by the hair*)

Bilbo. Ow!

Essie (*softening*). Ah, poor little blighter,¹² let him go.

Tom. Not till 'e says what 'e means by *lots* and *none at all*. I don't want me throat slit in my sleep! (*grabs for* Bilbo's *feet*) I'll hold his toes in the fire till 'e talks!

(Gandalf's *head appears from behind a tree.*

There is a flash of blue fire from his staff, which the Trolls *do not notice.*)

Tom. No! There isn't time. We have to get back to our cave before sunup.

Essie (*hanging on*). Give him back. He's mine.

Tom. Well, I'm boss.

Gandalf (*sticking his head out and calling in a voice mimicking* Essie's). Tom, yer a fat fool!

Tom (*taken aback*). Essie! Watch what you say!

Gandalf (*sticking his head out, mimicking* Tom). Yer a swag-belly, Essie!

Essie (*shrieking*). What? I'll give you what for! (*kicks* Tom *in the shins*)

Tom (*howling*). Oww! (*Releases* Bilbo *and hops about.* Bilbo *runs and hides behind a tree.*)

Bert (*scratching his head; slow on the uptake*). You insult the missus, Tom? (a*dvancing menacingly on* Tom)

Tom (*baffled*). Wha'? I didn't say nothing—

Bert (*putting his fist in* Tom's *eye*). Liar!

Tom (*hopping around in pain*). Yeow!

Gandalf (*mimicking* Tom). Big skunk!

Essie (*coming up behind* Tom *and hitting him on the head with a dummy club*). Take *that!*

Tom (*howling and rubbing his head*). Ow! Ow! What did you do that for? (*picks up club and hits* Bert *on the head*)

Bert (*stunned*). Gosh! Ouch! (*A bird calls, and other birds chime in.*)

Gandalf (*stepping out from behind tree, holding his staff high with blue fire coming from it; loudly*). Dawn take you all, and be stone to you! (*The* Trolls *look at one another agape*

---

10. **copped:** taken or stolen.

11. **Lumme** (lŭm′ē): a slang expression short for "Lord love me!" Here it is similar to "darned."

12. **blighter:** a British term for a fellow held in low regard.

and turn toward the voice. The twittering of birds rises to a climax of bird calls, and a great shaft of light strikes the Trolls.)

Trolls. Wha'? Huh? Ugh! (*Suddenly they freeze into statues.*)

Gandalf (*walking around the* Trolls, *waving his hand in front of their faces, touching* Bert's *hair, etc.*). Excellent! Museum pieces!

Bilbo (*capering wildly*). They're stone! They've turned to stone!

Gandalf. Where are the dwarves?

Bilbo. Waiting for me to return with some food or to hoot like an *owl.*

Gandalf (*hooting*). Whoo! Whoo!

Thorin (*at platform left, springing up*). The signal! To the rescue, dwarves! (*They all groan and follow reluctantly.* Thorin *runs up to* Bert *with bravado, brandishing his sword.*) On guard, Troll! (Bert *does not stir;* Thorin *lunges fiercely.*) Aha! (*Still no reaction;* Thorin, *completely baffled, kicks* Bert *in the knee.*) Yeow! (*Holds his foot, hopping in pain.* Bilbo *and* Gandalf *laugh uproariously.* Thorin *is startled.*) Gandalf!

Dwarves (*circling the* Trolls *curiously; ad-lib*). Stone! Horrid! What a trio! Solid rock! (*and so on*)

Gandalf. A fine pickle you left your burglar in, Thorin!

Thorin. And where were you, if I may ask?

Gandalf. I went to look ahead.

Thorin. And what brought you back?

Gandalf. Looking behind—

Thorin. Exactly! But could you be more plain?

Gandalf. I went on to spy out our road. It will soon become much more dangerous. I had not gone very far when I met some elf friends—they were hurrying along for fear of trolls. I had a feeling I was needed here, and I hurried back. So now you know.

Thorin. We thank you! Pack up the food, dwarves—

Gandalf (*picking up two swords from the ground*). And don't leave these behind! Hmmm, these were not made by the trolls—the workmanship is much too good. The trolls must have stolen these. Why, these are elvish blades—with the ancient runes[13] engraved on them. The elves have cleaved many a goblin with these, I'll warrant.[14] (*hands one to* Thorin *and one to* Bilbo)

Bilbo. For me? Why, thank you!

Thorin. I will keep this sword in honor. May it soon cleave goblins again!

Bilbo. Oh, dear!

Gandalf. A wish that will soon be granted.

Bilbo. I didn't wish a thing!

Gandalf. Come, let's head for the Misty Mountains. You must keep to the proper path, or you'll get lost and have to come back. Remember that: stick to the path!

Thorin. We will, Gandalf.

Elves (*offstage, burst of laughter, then singing*).
O! Where are you going
With beards all a-wagging?
No knowing, no knowing
What brings Mister Baggins,
And Balin and Dwalin
down into the valley
in June
ha! ha!

Thorin. Elves! Humph!

(First Elf *peeks around the curtain left.*)

---

13. **runes:** symbols used in writing that are sometimes believed to have magic powers.

14. **warrant:** to guarantee.

First Elf. Well, well! Just look! Bilbo, the Hobbit, on an adventure with dwarves! Isn't it delicious!

(Second Elf *peeks around the curtain right.*)

Second Elf. Most astonishingly wonderful!

Thorin. Silly fools!

Third Elf (*off*). Mind you don't step on your beard, Thorin! (*burst of laughter from* Elves, *off*)

Gandalf. Hush, hush, my friends! Valleys have ears, and some elves have over-merry tongues. We must go quietly. There is grave danger ahead.

(*They all exit as curtain falls.*)

Scene: *A cave in the Misty Mountains. Lightning flashes. Sounds of thunder.*

At rise of curtain: Lights come up on platform at stage left. The Dwarves *and* Gandalf *are huddled together, talking in hushed tones.* Bilbo *sits downstage on platform, writing in his diary. He scribbles industriously, then holds book off and reads impressively.*

Bilbo (*reading his entry*). "This is the first chance I've had to write in ages. We've been driven before the storm for twelve days and nights." (*There is a distant roll of thunder and more lightning.*) "The mountain path is steep and long. We are now resting in a smelly cave." (*He again scribbles rapidly.*)

Thorin (*in a low voice*). This is awful!

Gloin (*holding his nose*). Phew!

Balin. At least it's dry!

Gandalf (*to* Thorin). If you know a better place, take us there!

Bilbo (*holding his script off and reading again*). "We don't dare to talk too loud—there are goblins in these mountains. All this misery for their gold—and my pride—hardly seems worthwhile. The next time anyone calls me a coward, I'll agree with him and stay home. I'd gladly trade my share of the treasure this minute for a steaming bowl of mutton soup!"

Gandalf. Keep your voices down! Thorin, look, your blade glows—that means goblins are nearby. Keep your eyes and ears open. Goblins are swift as weasels in the dark and make no more noise than bats. (*They huddle to-*

gether, *peering in all directions; lightning flashes and sounds of thunder.*) Are your guards posted?

Thorin (*nodding*). Four of them, Gloin north, Bofur south, Oin east and Ori west.

(*Lights dim on platform left and come up on platform right. Drumbeats are heard off. The Great Goblin steps out on the platform, followed by an Attendant.*)

Great Goblin (*bellowing in a stony voice*). Who are those miserable persons?

Attendant Goblin (*bowing and scraping*). Dwarves, I believe, O Truly Tremendous One.

Great Goblin. What are they doing in my <u>domain</u>?

Attendant Goblin (*shaking*). I'll go and ask them, O Truly Tremendous One.

Great Goblin (*with an awful howl of rage*). Ask them? (*kicks the Attendant Goblin and bats him over the head*) Beat them! Gnash them! Squash them! Smash them! (*gesturing left*) After them!

(*The drumbeats increase as many Goblins rush on right with bloodcurdling cries. As they reach center, the lights come up on platform left.*)

Oin (*reporting*). Goblins coming.

Ori. I think they're going to rush us!

Goblins (*chanting and cracking whips*).
Swish, smack! Whip, crack!
Clash, crash! Crush, smash!

Thorin (*drawing his sword*). Ready, my goblin-cleaver! (*He stands on the edge of the platform.*) Ready, dwarves—and Mr. Baggins. (Gandalf, *arms folded, stands aloof watching intently. The Goblins rush at the Dwarves. Thorin stabs one with his blade. The other* Dwarves *back up* Thorin, *and there are hand-to-hand conflicts.* Bilbo *trips up a Goblin who is about to stab* Thorin *from behind.* Thorin *stabs another. All conflicts must be rehearsed with extra care so that the tempo is very fast. The Goblins fall, howling.*)

Goblins (*ad-lib*). Aie! He's got a goblin-cleaver! Watch out! Stay back! (*The Goblins back off in terror.*)

Gandalf (*to Dwarves and Bilbo*). Quick. Now's our chance! Everyone follow me! (*Runs off left. Others follow,* Bilbo *last. From off.*) Quicker, quicker! (Goblins *run after them, howling and hooting.*)

(*Blackout*)

(*Lights come up very dimly in a cave. Bilbo is discovered[15] lying on the ground downstage center.*)

Bilbo (*sitting up, holding his head in pain*). Oooh! My head! Where am I? My head—I must have run into a tree! (*groping*) It's so dark in here I can't see a thing. (*calls loudly*) Anyone here?

Echo (*getting progressively fainter*). Here— here—here.

Bilbo (*getting frightened*). Who's that?

(*Now gleams appear in the darkness. They prove to be always in pairs, of yellow or green or red eyes. They seem to stare awhile and then slowly fade out and disappear and shine out again in another place. Sometimes they shine down from above. Some of them are bulbous.*)

Bilbo. Now I remember. The goblins!

Echo. 'Oblins, 'oblins—'oblins— 'oblins.

Bilbo. And what are those awful eyes watching

---

15. **discovered:** revealed or found when the lights brighten.

me for? (*lowers voice*) I was on Dori's back and someone tackled him and he dropped me!

Echo. 'Opped me—'opped me—'opped me— 'opped me.

Bilbo (*frightened, to the eyes*). Keep away from me, eyes! I wonder what happened to the dwarves? I hope the goblins didn't get them! (*gasps*) My sword! (*holding it up*) It hardly glows. That means the goblins aren't near and yet they're still around. Ugh! What a nasty smell! Go away, you horrible eyes! (*realizing, stage whisper*) I know where I am. I'm still in the goblins' cave! They smell that way, and these may be just the eyes of bats and mice and toads and slimy things like that. (*more naturally*) Cheer up, Bilbo. Fear always helps the thing you're afraid of. You're alive and you've been in holes before. You live in one. This is just an ordinary, black, foul, disgusting hole. So blah! (*The eyes begin to flicker out, pair by pair, until all are gone. Bilbo brightens further.*) If this place were aired and decorated, it would be nice and cozy. So now I'll just figure out how to get out of here. (Bilbo *crawls around on his hands and knees toward stage right.*) Seems to be a

lake over here—no use heading that way. Ouch! Something hurt my knee— (*picks up a small object*) It's a ring! Someone's lost a ring. Well, finders keepers. I'll just stick it in my pocket so I don't lose it myself. (*Pockets ring. Lights come up a little.*) I can see better now. (*stands and turns toward stage left*)

(*An unobtrusive black rubber float is pulled on stage right. On it sits a slimy creature, dressed in black tights or a shiny rubber diving suit touched up with Vaseline to make it glisten, complete with cap, goggles painted a pale watery green. He sits with a leg dangling over each side of the raft, or with knees bent, and holds a short paddle as if rowing.*)

Gollum (*making a swallowing sound as he is pulled on*). Gollum! Gollum!

Bilbo (*whirling around*). What's that!

Gollum. It's me—Gollum!

Bilbo (*peering nervously in* Gollum's *direction*). Who's there?

Gollum (*in full view now*). Bless us and splash us, my preciousss! Here's something to eat! (*guttural*) Gollum!

Bilbo (*brandishing his blade, while shaking and backing off*). Stay back!

Gollum (*swaying his head from side to side as he talks*). What's he got in his handses, hmmm?

Bilbo (*as fiercely as possible*). A sword, an elvish blade! It came out of Gondolin.

Gollum (*taken aback, hissing*). S-s-s-s-s. What *iss* he, my preciousss? Hic! (*more politely*) Whom have we the pleasure of meeting?

Bilbo (*rapidly*). I am Mr. Bilbo Baggins, a Hobbit. I've lost the dwarves and the wizard and I don't know where I am—but then I don't want to know where I am. The only thing I want to know is how to get out of here!

Gollum (*hissing*). S-s-s-s-s s'pose we sits here and chats with it a bitsy, my preciousss—A Bagginsess! (*rubs his stomach*) It likes riddles, p'raps[16] it does, does it? S-s-s-s-s.

Bilbo. You mean me?

Gollum. Yesssss—

Bilbo. Well, I'd love to, but I'm expected somewhere else— (*to himself*) I hope. (*to* Gollum) So if you'd kindly direct me to the nearest exit—

Gollum (*cutting in*). S-s-s-s-s stop. First a riddle, yesss?

Bilbo (*resigned*). Very well, if you insisssst! After you—

Gollum. S-s-s-s-s say,
What has roots as nobody sees,
Is taller than trees,
Up, up it goes,
And yet never grows?

Bilbo. Easy! Mountain. Now if you'll kindly—

Gollum (*cutting in*). S-s-s-s-s so does it guess easy? It must have a competition with us, my preciouss. If we wins, we eats it—it tastes better if we earns it. If it wins, we shows it the way out. Yessss.

Bilbo (*resigned*). Well—all right. Only, how many of them are you? Who's this "Precious" you keep talking to?

Gollum. Our Preciousss Self! We has to talk to someone, doesn't we? We are alone here—forever.

Bilbo. So, I see. It's a dreadful place.

Gollum. We likes it! We generally passes the time feasting on fishesss and gobbling goblins. S-s-s-s-s.

Bilbo. Goblins! Ick! I didn't think anyone ate *them!*

Gollum. We acquired the taste. Hic! S-s-s-s-s. (*impatient*) Your turn. Riddle! Riddle!

Bilbo. Just a minute— (*thinking hard*) Ah!—
Thirty white horses on a red hill,
First they champ,
Then they stamp,
Then they stand still.

Gollum. Easy! Teethes! Teethes! My preciouss, but we has only *six*. Now! Ssssss.
Voiceless it cries,
Wingless flutters,
Toothless bites,
Mouthless mutters.

Bilbo. Half a moment! (*straining*) *Wind!* Wind, of course!

Gollum (*disappointed*). Ssssssss. Your turn!

Bilbo. Uh—
A box without hinges, key or lid,
Yet golden treasure inside is hid.

Gollum (*having great difficulty*). S-s-s-s-s. (*whispers*) What iss it? Sssssss. (*takes a fish out of his pocket and wipes his brow with it*)

Bilbo. Well—what is it? The answer's not a kettle boiling over, as you seem to think from the noise you are making!

Gollum. Give us a chance; let it give us a chance, my preciousss—

Bilbo. Well?

---

16. **p'raps:** perhaps.

Gollum (*wiping his brow with fish; suddenly*). *Eggses!* Eggses it is! Ssssssss—here's a choice one!
Alive without breath,
As cold as death;
Never thirsty, ever drinking,
All in mail,[17] never clinking!

Bilbo (*stumped*). Ahem—ahem—well now. Just a minute—

Gollum (*starting to emerge from the raft*). S-s-s-s-s-s.

Bilbo (*panic-stricken*). Wait! I gave you a long time to guess!

Gollum (*settling back in raft, hissing with pleasure*). Is it nice, my preciousss? Is it juicy? Is it crunchable?

Bilbo (*stalling for time*). Actually, I never gave a thought to how I'd taste cooked until I set out on this horrid adventure. But I'm sure I'd be terribly indigestible. (*false laughter*) Ha, ha!

Gollum. S-s-s-s-s—the riddle, answer it! It must make haste. We is hungry! (*wipes his brow with the fish*)

Bilbo (*pointing wildly at the fish*). *Fish!* That's the answer! Fish!

Gollum (*angry*). S-s-s-s-s—rotten luckses! It's got to ask us a question, my preciouss, yes, yess, just *one* more, yesss. Ask uss!

Bilbo (*frantic*). Oh, dear! I can't think— (*Grabs for his sword, puts his hand in his pocket. To himself.*) What have I got in my pocket?

Gollum (*taking this for the question*). Ssss—not fair! Not fair, my preciouss, to ask us what it's got in its nassty little pocketses!

Bilbo (*explaining*). But I— (*thinks better of it*) Well, why not? (*boldly*) What have I got in my pocket?

Gollum. S-s-s-s-s. It must give us three guesseses, my preciouss, three!

Bilbo. Very well! Guess away!

Gollum. Handses!

Bilbo. Wrong. Guess again!

Gollum. S-s-s-s-s—knife!

Bilbo. Wrong! Last guess!

Gollum (*wiggling and squirming, hissing and sputtering, rocking sideways and slapping his feet on the floor*). S-s-s-s-s-s.

Bilbo (*trying to sound bold and cheerful*). Come on! I'm waiting! Time's up!

Gollum (*shrieking*). String or nothing!

Bilbo (*relieved*). Both wrong. (*brandishes his sword*)

Gollum (*eying the sword*). S-s-s-s-s-s.

Bilbo (*shivering*). Well? Show me the way out. You promised!

Gollum. Did we say so, preciouss? Show the nassty little Baggins the way out, yes, yess. But what's it got in its pocketses, eh? (*starts to get up*) Not string, preciouss, but not *nothing*. Oh, no! Gollum!

Bilbo. Never you mind. A promise is a promise!

Gollum. Cross it is. The Baggins is getting cross, preciouss, but it must wait, yes, it must. We can't go up the tunnels so hasty. We must go and get somethings first, yess, things to help us. My birthday present, that's what we wants now—then we'll be quite safe! (*He steps out of his raft and waddles upstage right.*) We slips it on, and it won't see us, will it, my preciouss. No, it won't see us, and its nassty little sword will be useless, yess—Ssssss. (*exits right*)

Bilbo (*calling*). Hurry up!

Gollum (*off, letting out a horrible shriek*).

---

17. **mail:** flexible armor made up of overlapping metal rings or scales.

Aaaaaah! Where iss it! Lost! Lost!

Bilbo. What's the matter?

Gollum (*offstage, wailing*). Gone—must find it! Lost! Lost!

Bilbo. Well, so am I!

(Gollum *waddles on from right, on his hands and knees, searching wildly.*)

Gollum. Cursesss! Must find it!

Bilbo. You can look for whatever it is later. You never guessed my riddle. You promised!

Gollum. Never guessed—never guessed— (*Light dawns.*) What has it got in its pocketses? Tell us! (*advances toward* Bilbo)

Bilbo. What have you lost?

Gollum. We guesses, we *guesses,* precious, only guesses. He's got it, and the goblinses will catch it and take the present from it. (*makes a lunge at* Bilbo) They'll find out what the present can do. It'll just keep it in its pocketses. It's lost itself, the nassty, nosey thing.

Bilbo. I better put that ring on or I'll lose it. (*puts his hand into his pocket and slips the ring on his finger and holds it up*) This?

Gollum (*rushing right past* Bilbo, *wailing*). Cursess, the Baggins is *gone*—my precious. It has my ring! The ring of *power!*

Bilbo (*alone on stage*). He ran right past—as if he didn't see me—as if I weren't there. . . .

Maybe I'm not! The ring! I wonder if it made me invisible? (*inspects himself*) I can still see me.

(Gollum *rushes on again from left.*)

Gollum. Give it back like a good Baggins! Where isss it? (*rushes off right*)

Bilbo. A magic ring! I've heard of such things in Gandalf's stories—but to *find* one! What luck!

Gollum (*offstage, shrieking*). Thief!

Bilbo. I could stab him with my blade, but that would be wrong when he can't see me.

(Gollum *waddles on right, worn out and weeping.*)

Gollum (*sitting downstage*). It's gone! (*guttural sobs*) Gollum! Gollum! Thief! Thief Baggins! We hates it, we hates it, hates it forever! S-s-s-s-s. (*recovering*) But he doesn't know the way out—he said so. (Bilbo *nods silently and sits beside him.*) But he's tricksy. He doesn't say what he means—like what was in his pocketses—he knows! He knows a way *in.* He must know a way *out!* Yesss—he's off to the back door, that's it! (*springs up*) After him! Make haste! (*runs off left*) Gollum! Gollum!

Bilbo. I'll follow him to the exit. Then with luck I can slip out the door! (*runs off left after* Gollum)

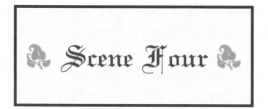

Scene Four

In front of curtain: Outside the cave entrance. Bilbo's head pops out of the center of the curtain. He looks around warily.

Bilbo. Whew! A narrow escape! (*comes downstage center, looking himself over*) Torn my cloak! Burst my buttons! But I've got spare buttons at home. I wonder where I am? (*looks off*) Good heavens. This must be the other side of the Misty Mountains! I don't see Gandalf and the dwarves. Maybe the goblins got them. I'd have to go back in there after them . . . I guess—(*shudders*) But at least I have Gollum's ring— (*holds finger up*) Why, I must be invisible this very moment! Fancy!

Balin (*calling, from offstage*). Mr. Baggins! Mr. Baggins! Where are you?

Bilbo (*overjoyed*). Balin!

(*Balin pops his head around curtain, right. Bilbo goes to greet him with outstretched arms; of course he is invisible.*)

Balin. He's not here. But I'm sure I heard him call my name!

Thorin (*offstage*). Are you certain? (*Bilbo puts his hand to his mouth and doubles up with silent laughter.*)

(*Balin walks in right, followed by Thorin, Gandalf and the Dwarves.*)

Thorin. Confound the Hobbit! Still lost!

Gandalf. Keep looking. We can't go on without him. I feel responsible for him.

Ori. Pity you didn't pick someone with more sense!

Thorin. He's been more trouble than he's worth.

(*Bilbo draws himself up, offended.*)

Oin. Why couldn't he stick with us?

Gloin (*testily*). That's right. I refuse to go back into those awful tunnels to look for the little blighter, drat him! (*Bilbo kicks his leg.*) Ouch!

Thorin. What's the matter?

Gloin. Dunno—felt as if someone kicked my leg!

Gandalf (*to Gloin*). Serves you right if someone did. (*angrily, to all*) Now either you help me look for him or I leave you here to get out of this mess as best you can. Why didn't you stay with him, Dori?

Dori. Good heavens! Can you ask? Goblins fighting and biting—everybody falling over bodies and hitting one another! You shouted "Follow me, everybody!"—I thought everybody had—

Thorin. And here we are, minus a burglar. Drat him! (*Bilbo steps down in the middle of them and slips off the ring. He is now visible.*)

Bilbo. And here's the burglar!

Dwarves (*jumping; ad-lib*). What! Bilbo! Mr. Baggins! Where did you come from?

Gandalf. Bilbo, my boy! What a relief!

Thorin (*to Balin*). A fine lookout you are, Balin!

Balin. Well, it's the first time that even a mouse has crept by me. I take my hood off to you, Mr. Baggins! (*He does, and bows.*) You're a great burglar. Balin, at your service—

Bilbo (*bowing*). Your servant, Baggins.

Dwarves (*ad-lib*). How'd you escape? What happened? Tell us!

Gandalf. He can tell us on the way. We must leave at once. (*Dwarves groan.*)

Bilbo. But I'm so dreadfully hungry—

Fili. Me, too—

Kili. And me—

Bombur. Me most of all!

Gandalf. Forget it. Hundreds of goblins will be out after us as soon as it gets dark. So tighten your belts and let's go. Better no supper than *be* supper.

Dwarves. Hear, hear!

Thorin. But where are we going? (*takes out his map*)

Gandalf. Through Mirkwood Forest. (*groans from the* Dwarves) It is dark and dangerous, but it won't be too bad if you can only remember one thing: the path is clearly marked and you *must stay on it.* Don't let anything tempt you to leave it even for a moment.

Thorin. But aren't you coming with us?

Gandalf. Impossible. I have pressing business in the South.

Thorin. But you *can't* desert us now!

Gandalf. We may meet again before all is over, and then again we may not. That depends on your luck and courage and good sense. But I am sending Mr. Baggins with you, and there's more to him than meets the eye. (Bilbo *groans.*) Cheer up, Bilbo, don't

look so glum. Cheer up, Thorin and Company. Think of the treasure at the end!

Bilbo. Do we really have to go through Mirkwood? Isn't there some safer way round it?

Gandalf. There are no safe ways in this part of the world. You are over the Edge of the Wild now, and there's danger everywhere.

Thorin (*studying map, irritably*). You said something about a forest path—

Gandalf. Yes. Straight through the forest is your way now. Don't stray off the path. If you do, it's a thousand to one you'll never find it again and never get out of Mirkwood. And then, I suppose, you'll all be eaten by goblins, and I shall never see you again!

Thorin (*sourly*). Very con<u>soling</u> you are, to be sure.

Gandalf. Come now, enough delay. These woods will soon be thick with goblins! (Gandalf *exits right. His voice is heard faintly in the distance.*) Don't leave the path! (*The* Dwarves *and* Bilbo *trudge glumly off left.*)

FROM **PERSONAL RESPONSE** *TO* **CRITICAL ANALYSIS**

REFLECT

1. What scenes or events in the play so far have had the greatest impact on you? Write your ideas in your writing notebook.

RETHINK

2. At this point in the play do you think Bilbo is more helpful or harmful to the progress of the adventure?

   Consider
   - what happens when he tries to steal food from the trolls
   - what happens after the fight with the goblins
   - his encounter with Gollum

3. Bilbo keeps a journal of his adventure. What do you think Bilbo's journal entries reveal about him and about the adventure?

4. Later, when Bilbo finds himself in a dark, smelly cave, he tells himself, "Fear always helps the thing you're afraid of." What do you think he means by this?

5. How would you describe Gandalf's role in the quest? Explain.

6. At the end of Act One, Gandalf again cautions the group not to stray from the path through Mirkwood Forest. Do you think they will follow his advice? Why or why not?

Illustration by Frank Gargiulo.

Act Two ⟡ Scene One

Scene: *Mirkwood Forest, weeks later. The stage is dimly lit. On the platform at stage left are huge gnarled tree trunks. Vines trail the forest floor. On a tree a sign is posted reading* MIRK-WOOD. PROCEED AT YOUR OWN RISK. *Along the front, signs are placed at intervals: the path. The* Dwarves *and* Bilbo *trudge on left in single file, with* Thorin *at their head.*

Thorin (*pausing on the path*). There's just no end to this accursed forest. (*shakes his fist*) I hate Mirkwood more than I hate the goblin tunnels.

Balin. Misery me! It goes on forever!

Oin. And ever!

Gloin. And ever.

Bofur. Gandalf said, "Cheer up, I'm sending Mr. Baggins with you. He has more about him than you guess. You'll find that out before long." (*turns sharply to* Bilbo) Well, Mr. Baggins? It's been long enough—

Gloin (*angrily*). What good's a Hobbit? Gandalf left us with a Hobbit to help us! Hah!

Bilbo. That's right, Gloin. Blame it all on me! I wanted to come on this adventure! I begged you to let me come!

Thorin (*placatingly*). Now, now, this won't do. We must all stick together.

Bombur (*slapping his own face*). Ouch! Mosquitos biting! Sticky vines wrapping round my throat, roots pulling at my feet! I can't go another step. Go on if you must. I'm going to lie down here and *sleep*— (*sits*) —and dream of food, if I can't get it any other way. (*curls up, yawns sleepily*) The treasure? I'll be too starved to enjoy it— (*Swats at a mosquito. There is a sudden flash of light.*)

Bifur (*jumping*). What was that?

Balin. Those flashes of light again! We'd better circle away from them.

Bilbo. But if we circle away, we'll have to leave the path!

Thorin. So?

Bilbo. Gandalf warned us not to.

Balin. Bilbo's right.

Kili. So he is.

Nori. Gandalf did say we mustn't leave the path. But he didn't know all that was going to happen.

Bilbo. I think he had a pretty good idea, all the same.

Thorin. We're all hungry.

Ori. And tired.

Oin. I can't go any further.

Bilbo. We must go on. Maybe we'll find some berries.

Gloin. Find berries in the spring—that's a Hobbit for you!

Dori. It's time to rest and eat.

Bilbo. Let's stick to the path a while longer. (*The lights flash again.*)

Bombur. I can smell meat roasting.

Thorin. Fili and Kili, go and investigate. But *be careful.*

Fili and **Kili.** Yes, sir. (Fili *and* Kili *go out right.*)

Bilbo. They've left the path. Gandalf said—

Thorin. Gandalf should have stayed with us if he expected to run things.

Balin. But he did say don't leave the path.

Thorin. Well, we haven't left it. Only Fili and Kili have.

Bilbo. Curious—it's so quiet—as horribly quiet as it is before something awful happens.

Balin (*looking off right*). Fili and Kili are coming back.

(Fili *and* Kili *come on right and rush up to* Thorin.)

Fili and **Kili** (*together*). It's elves! They've got food!

Others. Elves! (*The following speeches are said in such rapid succession it is as if one person were talking.*)

Fili. We crept up—

Kili. To the lights—

Fili. What a sight!

Kili. In a clearing—

Fili. Lots of elves sitting round a fire.

Balin. What luck!

Kili. Laughing!

Fili. Eating!

Kili. We couldn't bear it. We ran up to beg some food and poof! The lights went out.

Fili. As if by magic!

Kili. Somebody kicked the fire, and it went up— (*gestures widely*) —in glittering sparks—

Fili. And they all vanished!

Thorin. Those were wood-elves.

Bombur. Friendly elves! And they've got food!

Thorin. No, no, the wood-elves aren't very friendly. They don't like strangers. Mirkwood breeds distrust. (*There is another flash of light.*)

Bilbo. The lights again!

Bombur. Let's all go to the feast!

Dwarves (*ad-lib*). Whoopee! Let's go! (*They start to go, leaving the path at an angle.*) Come on, Bilbo.

Bilbo (*standing fast*). Wait! A feast will be no good if we don't get back alive from it.

Bombur. Well, I'm going. We won't last much longer without food anyway.

Bilbo. That's true—I guess.

Bifur. Come on, Bilbo. (Bilbo *reluctantly follows the others off the path.*)

(*The* Elven-Queen *and several of her attendant* Lords *and* Ladies *enter from left. The* Queen *wears a trimly fitted garment of forest green and a crown of oak leaves and berries. She carries a wand of carved oak. Her attendant* Ladies *carry bows and arrows.*)

Elven-Queen. Halt! (Dwarves *and* Bilbo *freeze in surprise.*)

Thorin. By whose authority do you bid us halt?

Elven-Queen. I am the Elven-Queen. Who are you that trespass on my domain?

Thorin (*stage whisper to* Bilbo). Quick, Bilbo, make yourself invisible. Put on your ring.

(Bilbo *does so, and from then on he is ignored by all.*)

Elven-Queen (*imperiously*). Speak.

Thorin (*stepping forward proudly*). I am Thorin Oakenshield, son of Thrain, son of Thror, King under the Mountain!

Elven-Queen (*disdainfully*). A dwarf all the same. Why did you and your folk attack my people?

Thorin. We did not attack them, Your Majesty. We came to beg because we are starving.

Elven-Queen. What are you doing in Mirkwood?

Thorin. We are looking for food and drink.

Elven-Queen (*impatiently*). But why are you here at all? (Thorin *remains silent.*) Come now! (Thorin *remains silent.*). Very well! You shall all go to my dungeons where you shall remain until you tell me the truth—if it takes a thousand years! Seize them! *The* Elf Guards *grab* Thorin *and surround the others. To the* Guards.) How many are there?

Guard. Thirteen, O Queen.

Elven-Queen. Away with them. (*She exits left.*)

First Guard. Step lively, dwarves!

Second Guard. March! (*The* Elves *march the* Dwarves *off left.*)

Bilbo (*taking off his ring and speaking to it*). Well, my friend, thanks to you I'm still free. We should have stayed on the path as Gandalf warned us. And now they'll all be shut up in a stone dungeon. That's a hard thing! Somehow I must get them out! (Bilbo *runs off left.*)

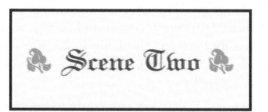

Scene Two

Scene: *The dungeon of the Elven-Queen's palace. At rise, the* Dwarves *are discovered behind the bars of a large prison cell in the center section of the stage. They are seated on wooden stools in attitudes of despondency.*[18] *Thorin occupies a private cell to their right. On the platform at right there are a table and chairs. On the platform left are a pile of straw and four wine barrels. Also in this section, somewhere in the background, are various possessions of the dwarves: bags containing tools (drills and hammers), jackets, pad and pencil.*

At rise of curtain: Bilbo *sits against one of the barrels, writing busily in his journal. As lights come up on platform left,* Bilbo *finishes writing and holds up his diary to see better.*

Bilbo (*reading impressively*). "Well, so far I haven't come up with a plan of escape. I might as well be locked up with my friends. Being invisible day after day is driving me mad. This is without a doubt the dreariest, dullest part of this wretched adventure. At least the dwarves are eating well. I have to steal my scraps of food from the kitchen." (*nods approval and scribbles again*)

Thorin (*calling softly to* Bilbo). Psst!

Bilbo (*ignoring him, reading again, impressively*). "I'm like a burglar that can't get away but must go on miserably burgling the same house day after day!" (*snaps journal shut*)

Thorin (*louder*). Psst, Mr. Baggins!

---

18. **attitudes of despondency:** positions that show loss of courage or hope.

Bilbo. Shhh— (*gets up, looks around and crosses cautiously to* Thorin's *cell*) What is it, Thorin? The guards will be coming any minute with your food.

Thorin. Then put on your ring. Why aren't you wearing it?

Bilbo. I don't like to wear it when I don't have to. It makes me feel funny. What did you want?

Thorin. Did you get off the message to Gandalf?

Bilbo. I don't know where to send it.

Thorin. Of course. I get more stupid every day.

Bilbo. Me, too. It's hard to concentrate when I'm invisible so much. It's as if I'm not all there.

Thorin. At least do *something*. You're a burglar. Steal! (*The other* Dwarves *have gathered at the front of their cage and are listening eagerly.*)

Bilbo. Well, I could steal the keys—that's not so hard.

Thorin (*brightening*). You could? Wonderful!

Dwarves. Bilbo!

Bilbo. But how would we get past the guards? One invisible ring isn't much good among fourteen.

Thorin. We might escape—somehow.

Bilbo. But we couldn't possibly get out of the main gate.

Thorin. Why not?

Bilbo. Sealed by elf magic.

Thorin (*deflated*). Oh. (*There is the sound of a key turning in a lock.*)

Bilbo (*hushed tones*). The guards are coming. Talk up and distract them! I'll see what I can do about the keys.

Thorin (*urgently*). Put on your ring, you stupid Hobbit! (Bilbo *smites his brow at his forgetfulness, pulls out ring and puts it on.*)

(*The* Guards *enter from right. The* First Guard *has a large ring of keys fastened by a chain to her belt. The* Second Guard *carries a tray with a bowl of soup and end of a loaf of bread. The* First Guard *takes up her stand by the door, guarding it. The* Second Guard *brings the tray of food to* Thorin.)

Second Guard. Food for you, Thorin Oakenshield. Thanks to our gracious Queen. (Bilbo, *walking on tiptoe, begins to cross very cautiously toward the* First Guard.)

Thorin (*taking the tray*). I thank the Elven-Queen and hope to return her hospitality when I have recaptured my castle. Its dungeons are deep.

First Guard. What's that he says?

Second Guard. He threatens our Queen.

First Guard. That's treason! Write it down! Write down every word he says!

Second Guard. I've nothing to write with.

First Guard (*rushing forward and barely missing colliding with the tiptoeing* Bilbo, *who leaps aside to avoid her*). Here, take this. (*gives him a pencil*)

Second Guard. Now, are you ready to answer the questions of our Elven-Queen?

Thorin. I refuse to answer questions under duress.[19]

First Guard (*leaning forward, excitedly*). More treason. Write that down! (Bilbo *is now crouched by the side of the* First Guard, *ready to start removing keys from her key ring.*)

Second Guard (*writing busily on pad*). Prisoner defies our Elven-Queen.

Thorin. *Now*, Bilbo!

First Guard. What's that he's saying?

---

19. **duress** (dŏŏ-rĕs′): the use of force or threats.

Second Guard. Sounded like he said Bilbo. Dwarves are stupid. Let's get out of here. (Bilbo *has begun removing the key ring. He is very cautious, but his hands are shaking and the keys clink. The* First Guard *moves uneasily, and* Bilbo *freezes. The* First Guard *fumbles for her keys. Doesn't find them. She fumbles again.* Bilbo *extends the keys so that she touches them. She is satisfied and returns her attention to* Second Guard.)

First Guard. He hasn't eaten yet, and the others haven't had their food.

Second Guard. Let them do without. (*to* Thorin) The tray. Let me have it.

Thorin (*throwing it at her feet*). Gladly.

Dwarves (*roaring approval*). Thorin!

Second Guard. If it weren't forbidden, I'd make you suffer for that! But wait and see how you like your dinner—*when* it comes! It'll be *well salted.* I promise you that.

First Guard. There's a big feast tonight, and *we'll* be eating like kings! (*The* Guards *stalk out with a clanking of the door.*)

Thorin (*excitedly*). Did you get the keys?

Bilbo. I did. (*He unlocks the cage door.*)

Thorin. My word! Gandalf spoke true. You're a fine burglar when the time comes! We're all forever in your service! (Thorin *steps out and bows as* Bilbo *unlocks the door.*)

Dwarves. Bravo! Mr. Baggins— (*All bow.*) — at your service!

Bilbo. Thank you. At yours. (*He bows.*) But now what? We're still stuck here in the dungeon, and if we go out, the guards will grab us and put us right back in! (Bilbo *crosses despondently and sits on one of the barrels.*)

Dwarves (*ad-lib, uneasily*). That's true. He's got a point there, all right. (*and so on*)

Dwalin (*prodding* Balin). Speak to him, Balin.

Balin. Why me?

Dwalin. You're the oldest.

Balin. Uh, Thorin—

Thorin (*warily*). Yes, Balin?

Balin. We were thinking that—umm, maybe it might be best to tell the Elven-Queen about our quest—the treasure and all that.

Dwalin (*putting in*). Maybe if she knew, she might even help us. After all, the dragon has stolen elf treasure, too. They took the Elven crown jewels even!

Thorin (*outraged*). Tell the Queen? And right away she'd ask for a share! Just because you're cowards you want me to ransom you all with *my* treasure! A share? What's to stop her from taking it all?

Gloin. Let's not fight about who gets the treasure until we're out of here.

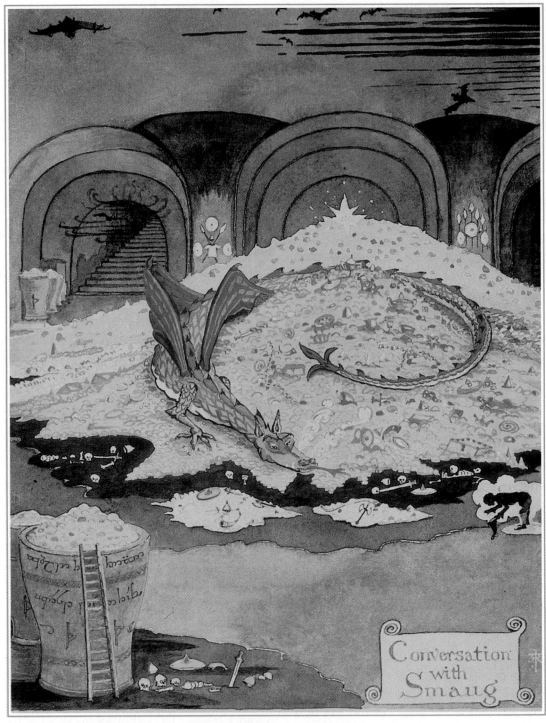

Conversation with Smaug (1966), J.R.R. Tolkien. Illustration from *The Hobbit* by J.R.R. Tolkien.
Copyright © 1966 J.R.R. Tolkien. Reprinted by permission of Houghton Mifflin Co.,
all rights reserved.

Bilbo (*suddenly jumping up, excitedly*). I've got it! (*taps the wine barrel*) And to think they've been here all the time! (*crosses to* Thorin) I've got a plan! You won't like it, but it's our only chance! (*to the others*) Follow me and all keep together. (*The* Dwarves *look at each other blankly.*)

Bofur. We can't see you, Bilbo.

Thorin. Take off your ring.

Bilbo (*slipping off ring*). Sorry.

Bifur. There he is.

Bilbo. Over here! (Dwarves *ascend platform left.*) Balin, guard the door in case anyone comes.

Balin. Right. (*crosses and listens at door*) Not a sound. (*takes up watch, his back against door*)

Bilbo. Now. (*coming down eagerly to* Thorin) As you know, we can't escape through the gates. But there is another way out.

Thorin. There is?

Bilbo. There's a stream under the wine cellar that joins the river further east, and when the wine barrels are empty like these— (*taps one*) —the guards dump them through a trap door just outside here— (*gestures left*) —and they float away.

Bifur. How do you know?

Bilbo. I've watched them. Lots of times. They go bobbing down the river, and the current carries them along to Lake-town. (*excitedly*) And where is Lake-town?

Thorin. At the foot of the Lonely Mountain.

Bilbo (*triumphantly*). Our exact destination.

Thorin. Interesting, but it doesn't help us.

Bilbo. Can't you see? We hide ourselves in the empty barrels, and the elves dump us through the trap door along with the empties. We sim- ply ride down to Lake-town. (*The* Dwarves *hear this with complete dismay.*)

Dwarves (*ad-lib*). No, no. Not me.

Thorin. Bilbo, no! This is madness!

Gloin. We'd be battered to pieces!

Nori. Or drowned like kittens!

Dwalin. Who'll let us out? We'll starve to death nailed up in those things. (*kicks a barrel scornfully*)

Bilbo. No, no! Don't worry! We'll pack the barrels with straw and seal them airtight, and I'll see that everyone gets out.

Thorin. Great! And just how do we breathe?

Bilbo. Air holes.

Bombur. You're not getting *me* into one of those! I won't fit, thank goodness!

Bilbo. Yes, you will, Bombur. We'll shove you in. (Dwarves *all turn away, muttering among themselves.* Bilbo *is annoyed and downcast.*) Oh, very well! Then go back to your cozy cells. I'll lock you all in again, and you can figure out a better plan for escape.

Thorin (*soothingly*). Now, Mr. Baggins, be rea- sonable.

Bilbo. But I doubt I can ever get hold of the keys again. (Dwarves *groan.*)

Thorin. It seems we have no choice. We'll try your plan. It just might work.

Balin. But there aren't enough barrels.

Bilbo. Most of them are piled out there. (*ges- tures offstage left*)

Dwalin. I still feel the risk is too great—

Bilbo (*ignoring him*). We'll have to act at once. Time's passing.

Balin (*excitedly*). I hear them. Hurry!

Bilbo. Are they coming?

Balin. Not yet. They're down the corridor. Hear

them singing? (Balin *slightly opens door right*.)

Elves (*chanting offstage right*).
Roll—roll—roll—roll,
Roll-roll-rolling down the hole!
Heave ho! Splash plump!
Down they go, down they bump!
Down the swift dark stream you go
Back to lands you once did know.

Balin. They'll be along for our barrels soon.

Thorin. Line up the barrels. Kili and Fili, bore holes. Gloin, make a list and check every dwarf off as he goes in. Bifur, collect straw from our cells to pad the barrels. Bofur, collect jackets and stuff them with straw to leave in the cells.

Bofur. Whatever for?

Thorin. Make it look as if we're all asleep. They'll finally figure out how we got away, but the longer they think we're still here, the better for us.

Nori (*approvingly*). Pretty smart! (*A scene of great activity follows. Kili and Fili pull tools out of their bags and go from barrel to barrel pretending to bore holes in them while Bifur brings out armfuls of straw and pokes them into the barrels. Gloin, with pad and pencil, checks off the Dwarves as they go into the barrels. Oin has gone off left.*)

Oin (*speaking from offstage*). Fili, Kili, don't forget we've got barrels off here, too.

Fili and **Kili.** In a minute. We're coming.

Bofur (*busily stuffing jackets with straw*). I hate to leave these good jackets behind.

Thorin. Nori, you and Ori start packing dwarves in. Start with Bombur. He'll be the hardest. (*Nori and Ori march the protesting Bombur to a barrel.*)

Bombur. Not me! Let someone else go first!

Thorin. Dwalin, Dori, Oin, you're after Bombur. Line up the rest. Into those barrels fast! Kili and Fili, as soon as you finish boring air holes, head up[20] barrels. Close those outside first.

Kili and **Fili** (*putting aside their drills and picking up hammers*). But who'll head up our barrels?

Bilbo. I'll do it! (*There is a frantic scene of Dwarves hopping into barrels. Some of this supposedly goes on offstage, to make the process faster. Bilbo is everywhere at once. Fili and Kili go out left, and there is a sound of hammering.*)

Balin (*warningly*). I think they're coming. They just said, "That's the last of that lot."

Thorin. Leave the door. Over here, quick. Into your barrel.

Bilbo. Balin, outside. (*Balin goes out left.*) You're next, Thorin.

Thorin. The leader should go last.

Bilbo. No time to argue. Into the barrel, Thorin! (*calling offstage*) Everybody in out there? Hurry!

Kili. Just heading up Balin.

Fili. We're coming!

Thorin. But who'll be last?

(*Kili and Fili enter left and thrust the protesting Thorin into a barrel.*)

Bilbo. I'll be last. Hurry, Kili and Fili. (*They put the barrel head in place. Offstage shouts are heard.*) In with you, Kili and Fili.

Fili. But we can't both fit in one barrel.

Bilbo. Into it. (*Bilbo pushes the protesting pair in and closes the barrel. Suddenly he realizes that there is no one to close his.*) But what

---

23. **head up:** to seal or close up.

about me? Well, I'll just have to catch a loose barrel and ride on it. (*At the very last he suddenly remembers his journal. He dashes back and grabs it.*) Now into the river! (*holds his nose firmly*)

(*As* Bilbo *seems to leap off into the river, the* Guards *come surging through the door chanting:*)

Guards. Roll—roll—roll—roll—

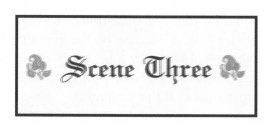

Scene Three

In front of curtain: Lights come up in front of curtain to reveal Dwalin, Bofur, Bifur, Dori, Ori, Nori, Oin, *and* Gloin *in various stages of exhaustion and saturation.*[21] Thorin *and* Bilbo *are sitting at center stage, back to back. Behind them are three of the wine barrels (fronts, indicated by cardboard props). They contain* Balin, Kili, Fili, *and* Bombur.

Thorin (*groaning*). I've never felt worse than at this moment!

Bilbo (*nudging* Thorin). But are you alive or dead?

Thorin. Achoo!

Bilbo. Are you still in prison or are you free? If you want food and if you want to get on with this silly adventure of yours, you'd better slap your arms and legs and try to help me get the others out while there's a chance! (*stands up*)

Thorin. Uh-huh— (*gets up painfully*) Ooooh! My knees! My elbows! (Thorin *goes over to a barrel and removes the lid.*) It's Balin! Come on, old friend.

(Balin's *head pops out. He pulls some straws from his draggled beard.*)

Balin (*groaning*). Ooooh! I'm too old for this sort of thing.

Bilbo (*removing lid from another barrel*). It's Kili—and Fili! (*Their heads pop out, and then* Kili *and* Fili *crawl out of the barrel.*)

Kili. Aaaa—

Fili. Choo!

Thorin (*removing the lid from the last barrel*). This one's packed solid—must be Bombur.

Bombur (*wailing from inside*). Pull me out!

Thorin. I need help over here. (Bilbo, Bofur, *and* Bifur go *over to barrel. They all reach in and pull.*) Push, Bombur.

Bombur (*still inside*). Oooooh! Ugh!

(Bombur *pops out of the barrel.*)

Bombur. Ah! I hope I never smell the smell of apples again! My barrel was full of it. To smell apples when you can scarcely move and are sick and cold with hunger is torture! I could eat anything in this wide world now for hours on end—but not an apple!

Thorin. Well, that's all of us. It could be worse—and then again, it could be a good deal better.

Bilbo. I'm going into Lake-town for food.

Bombur. Good thinking!

Thorin. Then, we'll make camp and wait for you here. In the morning we can start for the Lonely Mountain to drive the dragon from his cave. (Bilbo *slips his ring on his finger and goes off.*)

Gloin. Maybe he's dead by now. (*There is a tremendous distant, bellowing roar.*)

Dwarves (*ad-lib*). He's alive. That's Smaug. Now our burglar will steal the treasure for us! (*Again the dragon roars.*)

---

21. **saturation:** wetness.

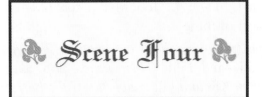

Scene Four

Scene: *The Lonely Mountain, outside the entrance to the dragon's cave. The stage is barren except for a few blackened tree stumps. A few broken mining tools may be lying about at stage right. The mountain is indicated by a **3/4** frame drop,[22] with a practical doorway left of center. Left of the door, the remaining quarter of the drop is scrim[22] gauze so that when lights are brought in front and up behind the scrim portion, you can play the scene in the cave. If this is not possible, travelers[22] may be employed to the same purpose. A scrim, of course, lends more magic to the scene. It is almost sunset, and the sky is reddening in the west.*

At rise of curtain: Bilbo is discovered busily writing in his journal. He is sitting on the stoop before the cave entrance. Dragon smoke belches from under the entrance. The Dwarves glumly pace around the stage, hands behind their backs.

Bilbo (*holding script off and reading it*). "And so we have come at last to the Lonely Mountain. What a <u>desolate</u> spot! But Thorin remembers when it was green and fair. According to his map, I am now sitting on the very doorstep of the secret entrance to the dragon's cave. But despite our best efforts, the door remains mysteriously sealed." (*resumes writing silently*)

Thorin (*stopping before the door, shaking his fist passionately*). Come out and get us then! I'd rather face ten thousand of you than stand here doing nothing.

Bilbo (*reading from journal again*). "I don't say so, but our <u>predicament</u> may be a blessing in disguise. I'm not looking forward to burgling old Smaug. No, actually, I prefer just sitting—" (*stops writing and hums pleasantly to himself*)

Gloin. All that treasure in there! Just waiting to be burgled, and *what* is our burglar doing for us?

Thorin (*approaching* Bilbo). Just what *are* you doing, Mr. Baggins?

Bilbo (*who has been humming happily*). Hmmm? You said sitting on the doorstep and thinking would be my job, so I'm sitting and thinking. Come join me. This is certainly the warmest spot on the mountain.

Thorin (*angry*). Mr. Baggins!

Bilbo. That certainly is a fine-looking key Gandalf gave you, Thorin.

Thorin. But there's no keyhole! (*flicks at the key about his neck*)

Bilbo. Let's have another look at your map.

Thorin. Again! What for?

Bilbo. I just thought maybe—

Thorin. Oh, very well. (*Pulls out and opens map. Bilbo joins him in scanning it. Droning:*) The runes tell us to stand by the gray stone—we've been doing *that,* all right! And the setting sun by the last light of Durin's Day will—

Thorin and **Bilbo** (*together*). —shine upon the keyhole—

---

22. **3/4 frame drop . . . scrim . . . travelers:** These are all curtains or cloths used for different purposes. A drop is lowered from above the stage to serve as a background. In this case, it is stretched on a frame that is three-fourths as wide as the stage and has a cutout doorway. A scrim is a loosely woven fabric used with the lighting to create a special effect. Travelers are curtains hung from a track and moved onstage from the sides.

Bilbo (*cheerily*). Well, perhaps today is Durin's Day.

Bombur. Wake me when something happens. (*lies down*)

Thorin. Durin's Day! I never heard of it. I've lost track of time altogether . . .

Dwalin. Our beards will grow 'til they hang down the cliff into the valley before anything happens here! (*Suddenly a red ray of sunset light falls upon the cave entrance.*)

Dwarves. Look! The setting sun shines on the door!

Bilbo. This must be the sign!

Thorin. Push! Hard! (*The Dwarves push against the door.*)

Nori. It won't budge!

Bilbo. The keyhole! Look for the keyhole! (*spots it*) *Here* it is! The key! Quick, Thorin, try your key while the light still shines on the keyhole.

Thorin (*removing the key from around his neck and trying it*). It fits! It fits! (*turns the key*) The door is unlocked.

Dwarves. Hooray!

Thorin (*standing on the stoop and addressing company*). And now is the time for our <u>esteemed</u> Mr. Baggins to perform the service for which he was included in our company.

Now is the time for him to earn his reward—by being first to enter the secret door.

Dwarves. Hear! Hear! Bilbo first!

Bilbo. Well, I don't think I'll refuse. Perhaps I've begun to trust my luck more than I used to.

Gloin. Well, well, look at our burglar now! Is this the same safe fellow who was lost without his pocket hanky?

Thorin. Mr. Baggins, this is your opportunity.

Bilbo. I have no doubt it's an opportunity, but who's coming with me? (*The* Dwarves *look the other way, embarrassed. They cough self-consciously and shuffle their feet. Bilbo stands to one side.*) Any volunteers?

Thorin. Now, that isn't quite fair of you, Mr. Baggins. You know we would go with you if it would do any good. But the moment the dragon sees us he will kill us. Since he can't see you, you'll be safe.

Bilbo. I'll lend you the ring.

Thorin. But then you'd be seen. No, no, you better wear it. We'll stand by out here.

Bilbo. Hmmmm! In that case, stand by the door. (*slips his ring on*)

Thorin. Good luck, Bilbo, my friend! (*reaches for Bilbo's hand but winds up shaking the air;*

WORDS TO KNOW

esteemed (ĭ-stēmd′) *adj.* highly thought of; respected **esteem** *v.*

tries again and misses) Mr. Baggins?

Bilbo (*clasping* Thorin's *hand*). Here I am, Thorin.

Thorin (*laughing and shaking* Bilbo's *hand*). Oh! Good luck!

(*The* Elven-Queen, *accompanied by two* Attendants, *rushes on from right. She is followed by a number of her* Elves *armed with bows and arrows.*)

First Attendant. Halt! In the name of the Elven-Queen. (*The* Dwarves *groan as the* Elves *surround them.*)

Elven-Queen (*stepping forward*). So, Thorin Oakenshield, we meet again! Of course I knew I would find you here. Where is the burglar?

Thorin. What burglar?

Elven-Queen. Don't try to deceive me. *He* may be invisible, but the treasure isn't! Well, now that we are all here, we can discuss matters. How shall we divide the treasure?

Thorin. No elf has a claim to the treasure of my people! I will not parley[23] with armed elves.

Elven-Queen. But the wealth of the elves is mingled in Smaug's <u>hoard</u>. Let us discuss that.

Thorin. We will give you nothing! Not a single gold coin. We look on you as foes and thieves!

Elven-Queen. So you claim treasure that is not really yours. Then how are you better than Smaug? Besides, you need my aid.

Bilbo (*stepping up to the* Elven-Queen *and removing his ring*). Have you a better plan than ours, Your Majesty?

Elven-Queen (*startled*). Ah, the burglar has decided to show himself! But you're not a dwarf—what are you?

Bilbo. A Hobbit, ma'am. Allow me to introduce myself. Bilbo Baggins, Esquire, companion to Thorin Oakenshield. At your service. (*bows cordially*)

Thorin (*furious*). Mr. Baggins! Will you please not interfere—

Elven-Queen. A Hobbit? Then maybe you'll listen to reason. Certainly I have a better plan. Dragons have to be *slain.* Then we should share the treasure. Part of it belongs to us. The dragon stole it from us.

Bilbo. Well, slaying dragons is not at all in my line. I was engaged as a burglar. But if part of the treasure belongs to you, I favor giving it to you.

Thorin. I will not share the treasure. I, myself, will slay the dragon.

Elven-Queen. With what?

Thorin. With this! (*draws his battered sword*)

Elven-Queen. You ruined that sword when you struck the troll, not knowing he had turned to stone. Behold the sword of the elves. (*claps her hands*)

(*Two* Elves *enter carrying a gleaming sword on a purple pillow. They stand before the* Elven-Queen.)

Elven-Queen. This blade was forged to slay Smaug. Agree to give us our rightful share of the treasure and you shall use it.

Thorin. I will not give up so much as one gold piece of the treasure. All of it belongs to me.

Bilbo. But, Thorin, if part of it is really hers—

Thorin (*thrusting him aside*). Silence, traitor!

Balin. Thorin, we know the crown jewels of the elves are in the hoard.

---

23. **parley:** to have a discussion, especially with an enemy.

Thorin. I no longer call you friend, Balin.

Bilbo. It's a bitter thing if our adventure ends this way. I wish Gandalf could help us now!

(Gandalf *enters behind* Bilbo.)

Gandalf (*lifts his staff majestically, with the blue light shining*). Gandalf is here!

Bilbo. Gandalf!

Thorin (*sourly*). Well, I never expected to see you again. I expect you're coming around for a share, too?

Gandalf. You are not cutting a very splendid figure, Thorin. But things may change yet. Instead of destroying each other, you should destroy Smaug together so that Middle Earth can again <u>thrive</u> in peace and plenty. I bring with me certain knowledge that you will need in order to <u>vanquish</u> him. But I will not reveal it unless you and the Elven-Queen agree to join forces. (*The* Elven-Queen *and* Thorin *hesitate and then approach one another and clasp hands, at first reluctantly and then with warmth.*)

Dwarves. Hurrah for the wood-elves! (*They toss their hats into the air.*)

Elves. Hurrah for the dwarves! (*They drum with their arrows on their bows.*)

Gandalf. Excellent!

Dwarves (*bowing to* Elves). At your service!

Elves (*returning the bows*). At yours! (*elvish laughter*)

Gandalf. The dragon cannot be wounded except for one spot! He wears a diamond waistcoat[27] that protects him from danger, but there is a bare spot just over his heart.

Thorin (*excited*). Then that's the place to strike.

Gandalf. Quite so. You will only have one chance—if any—and you must use the Elven blade and no other.

Elven-Queen. He shall have it. (*Claps her hands. The* Attendants *offer* Thorin *the sword.*)

Thorin (*taking it*). Many thanks, O Elven-Queen. (*brandishes sword*) Blade! I shall not disgrace you! I shall drive you home to your <u>destiny</u>! (*suddenly realizing*) But how?

Gandalf. Quite simple. Bilbo, you will go in first, wearing your ring. Thorin, you follow, but only as far as the inside of the door, and don't move a muscle or Smaug will see you. Once inside, Bilbo must somehow get Smaug to expose his bare patch.

Bilbo. How?

Gandalf. You'll find a way.

Bilbo. But—

Gandalf (*cutting in*). And when you do, signal to Thorin, who will fall upon Smaug and slay him. Good luck to you both. (Bilbo *slips on his ring and is no longer visible to them.*)

Bilbo. I'm going now, Thorin.

Thorin (*gesturing to* Bilbo). I follow, Mr. Baggins. (Bilbo *steps inside the door, followed by* Thorin.)

(*Lights dim down in front as they come up in the cave behind the scrim. The den is bathed in a golden red light. The walls and ceiling are covered with every kind of treasure: crowns, coats of silver mail, jeweled goblets, shields, etc.* Smaug *lies asleep on a vast pile of precious gems. Bubbling noises and vapors emanate from him.* Bilbo *enters from right. He is dazzled*

---

24. **waistcoat:** a short, vestlike garment with no sleeves or collar.

WORDS
TO
KNOW

thrive (thrīv) *v.* to grow strong and rich; be successful; do well

vanquish (văng′kwĭsh) *v.* to conquer; defeat

destiny (dĕs′tə-nē) *n.* what will necessarily happen to a person or thing; fate *by the light and glittering jewels and rubs his eyes. Suddenly he sees* Smaug *and jumps.*)

Smaug (*stirring, in a thundering voice*). Thief! I know you're there. I smell you and I hear your breath. Thought you'd catch me napping, did you? (*Vapors and bubbles increase.*)

Bilbo (*summoning up all his courage*). Oh, no, O Smaug. I did not come to rob you. I only wished to have a look at you and see if you were truly as great as tales say. I did not believe them—

Smaug (*somewhat flattered*). Do you now?

Bilbo. Truly, songs and tales fall far short of the reality! You are the greatest of calamities.[25]

Smaug. Nice manners for a thief and a liar. Come closer so I can eat—I mean, see you.

Bilbo. I don't think that would be wise, O Smaug.

Smaug. Hmmm, you seem familiar with my name, but I don't remember smelling you before. Who are you? Where do you come from?

Bilbo (*trying to sound formidable*). I come from under the hill and over the hills. I am he that walks unseen. I am Barrel-rider and Ring-bearer and Luckwearer, and I am here to reclaim the rightful treasure of the King under the Mountain.

Smaug (*snorting and belching smoke*). The King under the Mountain is dead, and I have eaten his people as a wolf eats sheep. I laid low the warriors of old, when I was young and tender. Now I am old and strong! Thief in the shadows!

Bilbo. I am the clue finder. I am he that buries his friends alive and drowns them and draws them alive again from the water. I am Ring-winner and Luckwearer and Barrel-rider!

Smaug (*gloating*). My armor is like tenfold shields, my teeth are swords, my claws spears, the shock of my tail is a thunderbolt, my wings are as a hurricane, and my breath is death!

Bilbo (*in a frightened squeak*). I have always understood that dragons are softer underneath, especially in the region of the, er, chest, but that you are guarded by a diamond waistcoat, if those are real diamonds. I hear they are only fakes.

Smaug (*snapping*). Your information is false and the jewels are real. Look at them, fool. My waistcoat is made entirely of diamonds, which no blade can pierce! (Smaug *rears up and displays the glittering waistcoat. There is a black spot over the heart, bare of diamonds.*)

Bilbo (*calling off*). Now, Thorin!

(Thorin *rushes on from right and plunges his sword into* Smaug's *chest.* Smaug *thrashes about wildly, emitting bubbling noises and thick smoke, then collapses and lies still.*)

Bilbo. Well done, Thorin, well done!

Thorin. What a treasure! (*He looks at it and removes a magnificent golden coat from the wall.*) Mr. Baggins, here is the first payment of your reward! Cast off your old cloak and put on this! It was my grandfather's. (Bilbo *removes his cloak, and* Thorin *helps him into the gold coat.*)

Bilbo. Thank you! My, my, I feel magnificent! But I expect I look rather <u>absurd</u>. How they would laugh back home in the Shire. Still, I wish there was a looking glass handy!

Thorin (*surveying the treasure*). Dividing all this

---

25. **calamities:** disasters; troubles; misfortunes.

WORDS
TO
KNOW   **absurd** (əb-sûrd′) *adj.* laughable; ridiculous

will be a long task.

Bilbo. I'll miss all that. I must be going home.

Thorin. But yours is a large share. Very large. Wait for it.

Bilbo. How would I get a large share safely back to the Shire, and what would I do with it when I got there? The coat is enough for me.

Thorin. At least take this casket of gold coins. No one can question your right to that. Perhaps you may find good use for it on your return. Things change, and not always for the better.

Bilbo (*accepting the small casket* Thorin *offers*). I thank you, Thorin Oakenshield, and await the day when you rap again on the door of your faithful burglar.

Thorin. And the Queen— (*glances around, and his eyes light on a richly encrusted robe of state*) This robe is not dwarf treasure. (*takes it up*) And here is the ancient Crown of the Elves! (*picks up a jeweled crown*) Help carry them, Bilbo.

Bilbo. Now let us leave this place. (*They leave the cave and join the others. Lights come up again in front.*)

Dwarves and **Elves** (*ad-lib*). Thorin! Mr. Baggins! Hooray!

Thorin. Rejoice, my friends! Smaug is dead!

All. Bravo, Thorin. Bravo, Mr. Baggins!

Thorin (*to the* Elven-Queen). Madam, your robe. (*He puts it over her shoulders. Her ladies adjust it.*) Your crown. (*places it on her head*)

Dwarves and **Elves.** Hail Queen of the Elves!

Elven-Queen. I thank you all. You have grown in <u>stature</u>, Thorin Oakenshield. Dwarves, you have a brave and honorable chief.

Thorin. It was your sword that felled the dragon, Great Queen.

Elven-Queen (*smiling*). But your hand that wielded it!

Gandalf. Excellent! (*crosses right and slips out unnoticed*)

Elven-Queen. I must return to my kingdom. Farewell, and may dwarves and elves ever live in friendship. And you, Bilbo Baggins, I name Elf Friend forever. (*All bow as* Thorin, *holding her hand high, escorts her off right.*)

Bilbo. I, too, must start the long journey home. Farewell, friends. (*smiles at them*) Remember, a certain burglar will always be listening for the sound of a dwarf staff beating on his door! (*He exits right.*)

Dwarves (*waving and laughing*). Good-bye, Mr. Baggins. We shall miss you!

WORDS TO KNOW	**stature** (stăch′ər) *n.* level of achievement, especially when thought to be worthy of respect

DRAGON FRIENDS AND FOES

Evidence has led researchers to conclude that belief in dragons began with snakes. The word *dragon* comes from the ancient Greek word *drakon,* used to describe any large snake or serpent.

Dragons or dragonlike creatures appear frequently in the ancient myths and legends of Asian and European cultures. In Babylonian legend, the hero Marduk captured the dragon Tiamat, slaying her with a fork of lightning. The Egyptian dragon Apepi, the ruler of darkness, tried to destroy Ra, the god of the sun. The Hydra, a swamp dragon with nine or more heads, viciously battled heroes in several Greek myths. In India, Ananta, an 11-headed dragon, was thought to support the world on its back.

The mythical dragons of the Far East — particularly of China and Japan—are usually wise, friendly creatures who promise good luck and possible wealth. The most powerful group of Chinese dragons was the Shen Lung, whose image was believed to prevent evil spirits from spoiling the new year. Dragons appear on Chinese artifacts dating from the 10th and 11th centuries B.C. The five-clawed dragon (as pictured here) was used as the emblem of Chinese emperors and their families.

In legends of the Western world, dragons are usually portrayed as terrifying, fire-breathing monsters with batlike wings, scaly bodies, and spiky tails. The typical dragon could be found in a distant, desolate place, where it devoured countless people, burned countrysides to cinders, and stole gold and jewels. It made its den in a mountain cave that few dared to approach. It is likely that J.R.R. Tolkien, an expert in medieval literature, had tales such as these in mind when creating his dragon, Smaug.

Dragon, detail of Chinese silk robe. Minneapolis (Minnesota) Institute of Arts.

RESPONDING
OPTIONS

FROM PERSONAL RESPONSE TO CRITICAL ANALYSIS

REFLECT

1. Which scene or incident in the play did you find the most exciting? Why?

RETHINK

2. One reader had this comment about the play: "Gandalf planned the whole adventure. He knew everything would come out all right." Tell whether you agree or disagree, and why.

3. How has this adventure changed Bilbo?

   Consider
   • how he felt about adventure at the beginning of the play
   • his comment that "a certain burglar will always be listening for the sound of a dwarf staff beating on his door!"
   • the feats he accomplishes along the way

4. Based on the events described in *The Hobbit*, do you think you would like to go on a quest? Why or why not?

RELATE

5. A quest is often thought of as something noble—an attempt to right a wrong, such as Bilbo and the dwarves undertook, or an attempt to help others through some effort or mission. Would you consider space missions, deep-sea exploration, and similar activities to be quests? What modern-day quests can you think of?

ANOTHER PATHWAY

Cooperative Learning

Work with a couple of classmates to create a map of the journey. Label every location mentioned in the play, beginning at Bilbo's home, the Shire. Beside each location write a description of the events that occurred and the outcome of those events. Display your map in the classroom.

QUICKWRITES

1. Create a record of the quest for the stolen riches in the form of a **ballad,** a song that describes a famous character or event.

2. Suppose that Gandalf had to advertise for volunteers to regain the treasure from the terrifying Smaug. Write a **newspaper advertisement** for Gandalf.

3. Imagine that Gandalf's wizard supervisor has ordered Gandalf to write a **progress report** on the adventure. Choose a point in the action. Write a report describing what is happening and how well Gandalf thinks the effort is going.

📁*PORTFOLIO Save your writing. You may want to use it later as a springboard to a piece for your portfolio.*

ADVENTURERS WANTED

Do you have an itch to be rich? A hunger for heroism? Join an exciting quest for treasure. Must deal with dwarves, trolls, elves, and a dragon.

Dialogue is conversation between characters. A play is made up almost entirely of dialogue, which reveals the plot, the characters' personalities, and the theme. Playwrights rely on dialogue to move along the action and to develop their characters. As they speak, characters often state how they feel about others; however, they usually reveal their own personalities as well. Find a passage from the play that is especially revealing of Bilbo's or another character's personality.

ALTERNATIVE ACTIVITIES

1. Using clay or some other material, make **sculptures** of some of the characters in the play. Refer to the stage directions for descriptions of what the characters look like and what they are wearing.

2. Make a **dramatic recording** of the events of the play. Assign roles and find ways to produce sound effects. You might want to write passages for a narrator to describe the settings of the action in the drama.

CRITIC'S CORNER

The poet W. H. Auden (a student of Tolkien's) wrote, "I suppose readers exist who do not enjoy Heroic Quests, but I have never met them." Auden was fascinated by Tolkien's detailed description of an imaginary world inhabited by hobbits and other creatures in which the forces of good eventually triumphed over those of evil. Based on your impressions of *The Hobbit,* would you be interested in reading other tales of quest and adventure? Why or why not?

ART CONNECTION

The illustration "The Hill: Hobbiton-Across-the-Water" on page 574 is one of many depictions of Middle Earth that J.R.R. Tolkien created. In the process of writing *The Hobbit,* Tolkien made a number of drawings of the settings, characters, and actions.

"The Hill: Hobbiton-Across-the-Water" and the illustration of Smaug in his treasure-filled den (page 608) were used as the front and back dust-jacket illustrations for the first American edition of *The Hobbit,* published in 1938. Some recent editions of *The Hobbit* include others of Tolkien's original illustrations. A collection of his drawings, entitled *Pictures by J.R.R. Tolkien,* was published in 1979.

EXERCISE A Review the Words to Know in the boxes at the bottom of the selection pages. Then write the vocabulary word that best completes each rhyme. One word appears twice in the same sentence.

1. Bilbo, the Hobbit, thinks something is wrong when his home becomes filled with a loud, noisy _____.

2. The dwarves make him nervous. He's *not* reassured when they tell him their plan, which he thinks is _____.

3. But he goes off with Thorin and all of the rest, off on a dangerous, difficult _____.

4. The trolls get so angry (as each one is beaned) that they fight one another—it's _____ against _____!

5. Bilbo decides he will be a key snatcher, and success at this effort increases his _____.

6. They all get quite seasick from bobbing and rolling, at least they are free (which is very _____).

7. There is danger of death, or at least of great pain, when our heroes sneak into the dragon's _____.

8. A casket of gold becomes Bilbo's reward. There is treasure aplenty in Smaug's secret _____!

9. Bilbo's much cleverer than he first seemed. The dwarves all admire him. He is _____.

10. For the ring that he found helped them all to survive, and the treasure will now surely help them to _____.

EXERCISE B Answer the questions.

1. Is a **conspirator** in a plan of yours someone who works with you, against you, or in spite of you?

2. If you were in a **predicament**, would you be happy, bored, or worried?

3. Which color would a person be most likely to use to make a scene look **desolate**—yellow, gray, or red?

4. Does your **destiny** usually have to do with the past, the present, or the future?

5. If you and your teammates **vanquish** another team, have you won, lost, or tied?

J.R.R. TOLKIEN

Neither one world nor one career satisfied J.R.R. Tolkien. As a young child, Tolkien made up his own alphabet and language and grew up to become a respected professor of Old English and Middle English. The author of dragon stories at age seven, the adult Tolkien wrote *The Hobbit; or There and Back Again*, a fantasy drawn from the bedtime stories he had made up for his children. The novel, published in 1937, was instantly popular.

The three books that make up the *Lord of the Rings* trilogy, published 17 years after *The Hobbit*,

1892–1973

became popular worldwide. Readers of these books found in their pages an entire world—complete with its own languages, races, and histories. Tolkien societies, clubs organized to read and discuss Tolkien's books, were formed, and scholarly studies were written about the trilogy. Tolkien's tales of Middle Earth continue to attract and captivate readers.

OTHER WORKS *The Silmarillion; The Lord of the Rings* trilogy: *The Fellowship of the Ring, The Two Towers, The Return of the King*

WRITING TO EXPLAIN

Photograph

Some of the characters you met in Unit Five, "The Pursuit of a Goal," went to great lengths to get what they wanted. Do you agree with what they did? In your opinion, was their reaching the goal worth the price they paid? Writing about a complex issue can help you think about your opinion and figure out why you feel the way you do.

GUIDED ASSIGNMENT

Write an Opinion Essay In this lesson, you'll write an essay explaining and supporting your position on an issue that's important to you.

① What's Your Opinion?

Do you have a strong opinion about something? Do your friends or family members share your feelings? Would writing about your opinions help people to see your side?

The items on these pages present situations you may or may not agree with. In your notebook, describe what the issue is in each example. How do you feel about each situation? Why?

② What's Important to You?

People often work toward goals that do not involve material rewards. Pride, good health, or fun may be the payoff.

Connect to Life Do any of the examples on these pages remind you of situations in your own life? Are you or any of your friends going after goals that call for you to give up something? Do you think others would agree with this sacrifice? Do a brief QuickWrite describing your thoughts.

Look for Ideas The following suggestions can help you think of other issues to explore. List your writing ideas in your notebook.

- Search through your journal for issues you feel strongly about.
- Think about people or topics in the news that have caused arguments or discussions between you and your friends.
- Brainstorm a list of things you might try to change if you were president.

School Survey

Olympic hopefuls spend 40 hours a week in the gym training, which leaves little time for fun, friends, or a full day in school. Is it worth it?

QUESTION OF THE WEEK:

Have you ever been a winner in an art contest, a band competition, a science fair, or a sporting event? Do you have a ribbon, trophy, medal, or plaque to show as a result?

Some schools in our area have stopped giving out awards. They say they don't want any student to feel better or worse than any other.

The school newspaper staff would like to hear your opinion! Do you think our school should do away with awards, or do you think it's important to reward winners? We'll print the results of this survey in next month's paper.

How do you feel?
(check one) () Award the winners!
() Equal treatment for all!

If you like, write us a brief note telling us why you feel the way you do.

Magazine Article

PacificKid Magazine

Don't Skate Here, Dude!

Signs along boardwalks and sidewalks throughout the state have left skateboarders complaining they have no place to go. Boulder Beach city officials explain that skateboarding in public places is not just an annoyance to drivers and pedestrians, but also dangerous to the skateboarders. "And if someone gets hurt, the city will have a lawsuit on its hands," Mayor Jackson is quick to point out.

Since the signs have gone up, many serious sidewalk surfers have moved to vacant lots, turning them into cement playgrounds. Ramps, platforms, and old drainage pipes create courses for those who have mastered the streets, curbs, and even steps of city buildings.

Area business owners are concerned about graffiti, safety, and abusive behavior, and have asked police to crack down on these "parks."

PacificKid has an e-mail address. I wonder if they'd print my opinion if I sent it to them.

I can see that the business owners might be nervous at first, but I think they should give the kids a chance.

LASERLINKS
• *WRITING SPRINGBOARD*
WRITING COACH

Finding a Focus

A Thoughtful Opinion Why do you have the opinions you do? Are they based on facts, feelings, or experiences you have had? These pages will help you discover how to learn about other viewpoints and how to use this information to help support your own opinion.

❶ Pick an Issue

Do you have an especially strong opinion about one of the topics you listed earlier? You will have an easier time supporting ideas that you really care about. Your topic should also be interesting to other people and have at least two clear sides.

Choose the issue that stands out the most and freewrite for several minutes on the topic. Try listing the key ideas involved, and then state your position in one sentence.

Student's Freewriting Notes

- Kids built a skateboard park because it is now illegal to skate where they normally skated.

- City might tear down park because business owners are worried kids will cause trouble or get hurt.

- I heard it's a pretty safe place (no fights, drugs, or serious injuries).

- At least these kids are out trying to get better at something and not just lying around watching TV.

My opinion: I think the city should help kids keep their park and make it safer.

❷ Make It Clear for Yourself

Before you can state your opinion, you have to make sure you understand the issue completely. The following methods may help you find out more about your topic.

Discuss Talk over the issue with classmates or family members to hear their opinions. Listen carefully to ideas that are different from your own.

Test In a small group, challenge each others' opinions to find holes in them. Ask "Why?" and "What's your proof?" You can then strengthen your argument by adding more examples or facts that plug the holes.

Read Some libraries have computerized periodical indexes such as *Infotrac*. By typing in your subject, you'll get a listing of articles from most major magazines and newspapers.

Call an Expert Phone someone who is involved in the issue or knows a lot about it.

Evening Edition

FINAL

The Boulder Beach Gaze

InfoTrac * General Periodical Index (BACKFILE) 1988 - present

Heading: SKATEBOARDING
- parks
3. Is it safe to skate? (city's skate parks built by youth are examined) by Carin McGiffin il v. 48
Boulder Beach Gazette March 23
11. To skate or not

③ Gather Support

When writing an opinion essay, you must not only state your position but back it up. The following types of information can help you support your viewpoint.

- Facts are statements that can be proved true. Solid facts, such as statistics and examples, strengthen your case.
- Opinions are personal feelings, attitudes, or beliefs. Quoting the opinions of experts can be an effective way to support your ideas. For example, *One skateboarder who has ridden ramps all over the world said this park was "The best by far! It flows!"*
- Observations that you or others have made can also be used to support your opinion.

You may want to list under one of these three heads the information you are gathering. See how one student did this in the chart below. (The SkillBuilder offers additional help.)

Student Research Notes

Facts:	Opinions:	Observations:
- Kids worked to clean up area. - No rules about using protective gear. - Park built by kids in Portland, Ore, is now the most successful in the world. At first their city was against it, too.	- "It's the wrong place for a skateboard park," said one store owner. - "The problems are caused by the gangs or other outsiders, not us," said one skateboarder.	- Older kids often help younger kids learn new tricks. - Kids respect one another's skills. - Different types of people go there (girls, guys, honor students, kids in college).

④ Think About Your Audience

Will you aim your writing at a certain audience? Will any of them hold a different opinion? Which of your arguments would work best with these readers?

Pulling It Together

Support for Your Opinion Writing a discovery draft may help you clarify your thoughts about your issue. As you write, you will find your ideas taking shape and maybe even changing. That's fine. Just as you might sway others' opinions with convincing information, your own opinion may be changed as you learn more about an issue.

❶ Write a Discovery Draft

You may need to refer to your notes as you write to help you back up your opinion. Ask yourself, Why do I believe this is true? Then list the reasons. Use facts, observations, and opinions of experts to support your ideas. Use the SkillBuilder to help you make your writing more precise.

Student's Discovery Draft

Dear PacificKid,

I think the skateboarding park that the kids across town built is great! I don't think the city should close it down, because

You might want to start by saying that you read the article in their magazine. — JM

Put these together

1. The kids who skate there don't cause any trouble. They go there to have fun and skate. They should be left alone!

2. Kids came together and worked hard to build this. They all pitched in their time and money. (information found in <u>The Boulder Beach Gazette</u>) ←Add how it is free for others to use

~~3~~. Lots of types of people are learning from each other and getting along.

The article mentions safety. Maybe you should talk about injuries. — JM

3 ~~4~~. If the city tears down the park, where will the kids go? What will they do? (Might go back to skating in the streets)

Will you give reasons why the Portland park is good? Then tell how ours could work too. — JM

4 ~~5~~. Portland, Oregon, has a successful park that was built by kids. Ours can be too. (credit information to <u>The Oregonian</u>)
     ^successful

I think the city officials should go out there and see for themselves what a good place the kids' park is. They wouldn't tear it down, because they'd see how important it is to the kids.

② Analyze Your Draft

Did any of your views change as you found out more about your issue? The facts that affected you could also affect your reader. Be sure to include those details in your final draft.

③ Choose a Form

To help you decide how to present your opinion, think about the best ways to reach your audience. If you want your whole community to read your essay, you might write a letter to the editor of your local newspaper. To reach the students in your school, you might make and distribute pamphlets. Keep your publishing form in mind as you rework your draft.

④ Rework and Share

Use the following suggestions to make your essay stronger.

Present Your Reasons Effectively One way to organize your essay is to first state your opinion and then order the supporting reasons from the weakest to the strongest, saving your best point for last. Using a different paragraph for each reason will make your essay easy to follow.

Finishing Strong You might end your essay with a recommendation. Asking your audience to think about the issue and come to their own conclusion is another way to finish strong.

The Writing Handbook gives additional tips on organizing persuasive writing on pages 796–797.

 PEER RESPONSE

Comments from a peer reader may help you decide how to revise your essay. Invite a classmate to read your draft and respond to the following.

- Restate my opinion in one or two sentences.
- Which parts were most effective? Which were not convincing?
- What other examples would support my opinion?
- What is your own opinion on the issue? How did my writing affect it?

SkillBuilder

 WRITER'S CRAFT

Using Precise Language
As you write your opinion essay, be careful to use words that say exactly what you mean. Avoid vague words like *good, bad, right,* and *wrong.* They may mean different things to different people. Also stay away from words like *huge* and *few.* Be specific whenever possible, giving the actual size, cost, or number. Using precise language will help make your opinion and supporting reasons more convincing.

 WRITING HANDBOOK

For more on using precise language, see page 784 of the Writing Handbook.

APPLYING WHAT YOU'VE LEARNED
Look over your draft and replace vague words or phrases with precise language.

THINK & EVALUATE

Preparing to Revise

1. What do your readers need to know to understand your opinion? Have you presented this information?
2. Will you reorganize your revised draft? How?
3. How can you best get your message to others?

Adding Final Touches

An Opinion Worth Sharing A well-written opinion paper can influence a reader's beliefs and actions. To make your essay as powerful as possible, take time to make some final revisions.

① Revise and Edit

Give your draft a rest. Then use the Standards for Evaluation, the Editing Checklist, and the following tips to help you finalize your opinion paper.

- Decide which of your peer readers' suggestions will help you make changes that strengthen your argument.
- Have you presented your ideas in the strongest way possible? The SkillBuilder can help you make your writing more powerful.
- Notice how one student states her viewpoint and backs it up with facts, observations, and opinions in the model below.

Student's E-Mail

Skateboarders

Send Print File Help Trash e-Mail

Dear PacificKid,

The article you printed about closing skateboarding parks in Boulder Beach really got my attention. I feel strongly that the city should keep the parks open. If city officials learned the facts, as I have, they'd realize that the parks are valuable for many reasons.

First, the parks bring out the best in the skaters. Girls and guys from all over the city help one another and teach each other new stunts. The skateboard parks are not just places for kids to go to practice the sport they love. They are places for making friends.

Second, even though just four skaters spent their time and money turning the empty lots into parks, the parks are free to everyone. According to one professional skateboarder, the parks are some of the best in the state. Our city should thank the builders, not punish them by closing their parks.

Third, although many people think that skate parks are unsafe, this is just not true. My research shows that there have been no serious injuries at any Boulder Beach skate parks. If they are closed, the kids might go back to skating in the streets, which is dangerous for everyone.

What examples of precise language can you find?

Why do you think the student ordered her reasons the way she did?

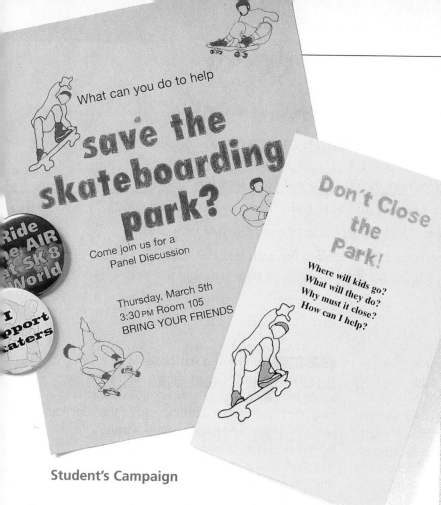

What can you do to help

save the skateboarding park?

Come join us for a
Panel Discussion

Thursday, March 5th
3:30 PM Room 105
BRING YOUR FRIENDS

Don't Close the Park!

Where will kids go?
What will they do?
Why must it close?
How can I help?

Ride the AIR at SK8 World

I support aters

Student's Campaign

② Share Your Opinion

Your opinion could take many forms. The materials above show how one student acted on her opinion. She and her friends made pamphlets and buttons to distribute at school, then invited others to join together to help. The following are some additional publishing ideas.

- Hold a class debate between opposing teams.
- Send your essay to friends or selected groups on the Internet.

Standards for Evaluation

An opinion essay
- states clearly the issue and the writer's opinion
- supports ideas with observations, facts, or expert opinions
- presents ideas logically
- concludes by summing up reasons, making a recommendation, or asking readers to rethink their opinion

 GRAMMAR FROM WRITING

Using Active Voice
The **active voice** focuses on the doer of the action: *Kids of all ages built the park.* (Focus is on *kids*.)

The **passive voice** stresses the person or thing being acted upon: *The park was built by kids of all ages.* (Focus is on the *park*.)

Use the active voice to strengthen your position and make readers feel more involved.

GRAMMAR HANDBOOK

For more on using verbs, see page 835 of the Grammar Handbook.

Editing Checklist
- Use precise words and phrases.
- Double-check numbers and statistics for accuracy.
- State ideas in the active voice.

REFLECT & ASSESS

Evaluating Your Experience

1. How did your opinion change or develop as you researched and wrote about your topic?
2. What did you learn about getting other people to see your point?

📁 **PORTFOLIO** How did writing this paper help you understand the issue better? Add your answer and essay to your portfolio.

REFLECT & ASSESS

UNIT FIVE: THE PURSUIT OF A GOAL

By reading the selections in this unit, you have seen how goals can be reached or missed and how trying to reach goals can shape people's lives. Now your goal is to complete one or more of the options in each of the following sections. Use the activities to help you reflect on what you've learned.

REFLECTING ON THEME

OPTION 1 **Predicting the Future** What impact can an early experience have on a person's future? Imagine that ten years have passed in the lives of Elizabeth (in "Flowers and Freckle Cream"), Panchito (in "The Circuit"), and James (in "The Scribe"). Draft a brief description of each character's new situation. Share opinions about how the characters' experiences may have affected their ability to reach their goals.

OPTION 2 **Finding Inspiring Thoughts** Working with a partner, skim this unit's selections to find ways in which characters encourage themselves or are encouraged by others. Then, with the rest of your classmates, create a chart titled "How to Get What You Want." In it, list ten tips for pursuing goals, based on the experiences of the characters. Copy the chart in your notebook, placing a star by any tip that might apply to pursuing your own goals.

OPTION 3 **Comparing Attitudes** With a group of classmates, copy the chart shown. Complete the chart, indicating each character's attitudes at the beginning, the middle, and the end of the selection. Use the symbol + to show a positive attitude and the symbol − to show a negative attitude. Then refer to the chart as you draft a persuasive essay about how attitude can affect the ability to achieve a goal.

Attitude Chart			
Character	**Beginning**	**Middle**	**End**
Elizabeth	+		

Self-Assessment: What do you now think is the most important thing to remember about pursuing a goal? How does your idea compare with what you thought before you started working on one of the activities? Answer these questions in your notebook.

REVIEWING LITERARY CONCEPTS

OPTION 1 **Noticing Sensory Details** Words and phrases that help the reader see, hear, taste, smell, and feel what a writer is describing are called sensory details. Review five of the selections in this unit. Then make a chart, like the one shown, to record details that helped you "experience" the action.

Sensory Details					
Selection	**Sight**	**Sound**	**Touch**	**Taste**	**Smell**
"Flowers and Freckle Cream"	"... she had a flawless peaches-and-cream complexion"	"I burst out the door"			

OPTION 2 **Looking at Style** As you know, the style of a work of literature is the way it is written. Style involves such elements as sentence length, word choice, use of dialogue, and tone. Look through this unit's selections to find examples of three or four very different styles. Copy this chart in your notebook, and use it to record your examples. Then, with a few classmates, discuss what makes the styles different.

Selection	Example of Style	Description of Style

Self-Assessment: Besides sensory details and style, the following literary terms were discussed in this unit. With a partner, take turns finding examples (in this unit or in other units of this book) to illustrate each concept. If necessary, look up the terms in the Handbook of Reading Terms and Literary Concepts on page 762.

figurative language

simile

metaphor

PORTFOLIO BUILDING

- **QuickWrites** In this unit, some of the QuickWrites assignments asked you to create newspaper accounts of events in selections. If you did these, select the two accounts you're proudest of. What do you think would draw readers into your accounts? How well do the accounts answer the questions *who, what, when, where, why,* and *how?* Write a short note to describe what you like about your work. Then add your accounts and the note to your portfolio.

- **Writing About Literature** You now have written a poem of your own. After rereading your poem, try drawing a picture to go with it. In your picture, try to capture the feelings and actions that you presented in the poem. Attach a copy of the picture to the poem, and place both in your writing portfolio.

- **Writing from Experience** When you wrote your opinion essay, you had a chance to express your views on an issue that you feel strongly about. Make a list of the people that you would like to share your opinion with. Whom would you like to persuade to see your side of the issue? How could you best reach your audience? Include your list with your opinion essay if you decide to keep it in your portfolio.

- **Personal Choice** Review everything you created while working on this unit—including charts, drawings, writings, and recordings. Pick one piece of work that stands out as your best. Write a note explaining how the writing or activity affected your ideas about pursuing a goal. Attach the note to your choice, and add both to your portfolio.

Self-Assessment: If the pieces in your portfolio are arranged in chronological order, try arranging them in a different way. You might file your pieces according to how much you like them, according to their themes, or according to the types of writing they represent.

SETTING GOALS

By now you have done a number of Across the Curriculum projects. In completing them, what did you discover to be your greatest strength? In your notebook, describe how that strength can be helpful to you as you work on future projects.

Across Time and Place

The Oral Tradition

"You can learn through the laughter. You can learn through the tears."

Diane Ferlatte
storyteller

Diane Ferlatte lives in California, where she keeps the ancient traditions of her African ancestors alive through storytelling.

STORYTELLERS PAST AND PRESENT

DIANE FERLATTE

A Present-Day Storyteller Speaks

Diane Ferlatte performs stories from the African-American tradition. Like storytellers from ancient times, she uses gestures, props, and facial expressions to engage listeners in the drama of the story.

When I was 10, my parents moved to California, looking for work. Every summer they drove me back to New Orleans. I would complain, "Why won't you take me back to Disneyland?" But my parents knew what they were doing. They took me back to my roots. They took me back to Grandpa and Grandma, to homemade biscuits, singing on the porch, and stories when there was no TV or video. I heard many stories at my grandparents' home. Sitting on the big porch in a swing, that's what

we'd do. The old folks would always be talking about family, about fishing, about true stories, about ghost stories, or about something that happened at church. As a little kid, I heard lots of stuff. If I had known I was going to be a storyteller, I sure would have listened more carefully.

My stories come from anywhere and everywhere. Most of the African stories I tell are from West Africa. In the old days, stories served to pass along information. That was part of the job of the *griots* (grē-ōz´) who kept alive the oral tradition of a village or family. They could tell you about your whole family line—where your mother came from, who your father was, what they did. It's important to keep alive the history of where you come from and what you are about.

Stories also told about people's adventures, their fears, their hopes.

An *umnqwazi* (ŏŏm-ən-kwä′zē), a headdress made of many pieces of cloth, was worn by Xhosa women.

A Xhosa storyteller might begin with a phrase that means "Now for a tale."

The hands are nearly as important as the voice in the telling of a tale, or *ntsomi* (ən-tsō′mē). Hands act out major actions, express emotions, and stress ideas.

An Ancient Storyteller
For over 500 years the Xhosa (kō′sä) people have lived and shared their stories in southern Africa.

Stories were a way of answering questions. That's where a lot of our "why" and "how" stories come from—how the lion got his roar, for example. People were curious. In African cultures, storytelling is not pure narration, or speaking. There is also music and dance and singing and religion connected with storytelling. All the arts are connected.

Stories come from the conditions in which people live. When the Africans came here as slaves, they weren't allowed to speak their own language, to play their drums, even to learn to read or write. But they could still tell their stories. The oral tradition was very strong in the world of the slaves because that was all they had. A lot of African-American stories have humor in them too. Life was so brutal for the slaves they had to laugh to keep from crying.

That's the power of communication, of the oral tradition. Once you hear somebody else's problem, it makes you think, "I'm not alone in this. Somebody else is going through the same thing." When you hear a story, you can see more of a common thread that goes through all of us. With so many cultures in this country today, we need to talk to each other. And the best way to learn about a people and a culture is to know their stories.

KEEPING THE PAST ALIVE

For nearly as long as words have been spoken, there have been tellers of stories and listeners eager to hear them. When they told stories well, they inspired others to retell the stories. From generation to generation, stories were passed from teller to listener within families, villages, and cultures. The tellers and listeners were taking part in what came to be called the oral tradition. The types of stories in the oral tradition appear in the chart below.

Known as folklore, the stories of the oral tradition continue to be told. Folklore brings the past to life for tellers, listeners, and readers of today. Like thread connecting colorful pieces of cloth, folklore connects people's lives across time and place, revealing our similarities and differences. The time line at the right presents important events of the past in cultures around the world. The folklore in this unit reflects those cultures. By reading it, you can discover for yourself how folklore links people and keeps the past alive.

AFRICA

Why Monkeys Live in Trees 654

. . .

3000–2500 B.C. *First Egyptian pyramid and Great Sphinx of Giza built*

MYTHS
- *attempt to answer basic questions about the world*
- *are considered truthful by their originators*

FOLK TALES
- *are told primarily for entertainment*
- *feature human beings or humanlike animals*

COMMON ELEMENTS
- **keep the past alive**
- **teach lessons about human behavior**
- **reveal the values of the society**

FABLES
- *are short tales that illustrate morals*
- *have characters that are animals*

LEGENDS
- *are considered factual by those who tell them*
- *may be based on facts*
- *are usually set in the past*

THE AMERICAS

The White Buffalo Calf Woman and the Sacred Pipe 723

Sister Fox and Brother Coyote 735

The Disobedient Child 694

. . .

2750–2000 B.C. *Farmers begin to settle in region between modern-day Mexico and Nicaragua*

. . .

700s B.C. *Destruction of Minoan civilization; First Olympic Games in Greece; Founding of Rome*

. . .

215 B.C. *Reign of Ch'in Shih Huang Ti (The First Emperor); Construction of Great Wall begins; Rise of Buddhist religion in China*

. . .

A.D. 1492 *Carib Indians on various Caribbean islands have first contact with Europeans after the arrival of Christopher Columbus*

. . .

549 B.C. *Foundations of Persian Empire under Cyrus the Great*

. . .

50 B.C. *German tribes practice agriculture and have contact with the Roman Empire*

LINKS TO UNIT ONE

Running Risks

The selections in Unit One reveal certain challenges that people face in life. Some of those challenges involve making risky choices and accepting what the choices bring. In each of the tales that follow, a character responds to a challenge—and must live with the consequences.

AFRICA

Why Monkeys Live in Trees

retold by Julius Lester

In the 1400s B.C., the African kingdom of Kush often included exotic animals such as monkeys in its yearly tribute to Egypt. Most African folk tales have animals as their characters. This folk tale, which recounts Monkey's attempt to outwit the other animals, is a good example of the humorous trickster tales found in most cultures. Told to entertain, "Why Monkeys Live in Trees" is a "why" story that attempts to explain an animal's characteristics.

The Red Lion

retold by Diane Wolkstein

"The Red Lion" comes from the vast Persian empire, which at its height extended from Egypt to the Indus River. Part of the land that was once Persia is modern-day Iran. In ancient Persia, the son of a tribal leader did not automatically inherit his father's rank. In this folk tale, the King of Persia dies, and his son, Prince Azgid (ăz′gēd), before he can be crowned, must prove his courage by fighting the Red Lion.

Wings

retold by Jane Yolen

Many Greek myths focus on individuals and the way they interact with other people. Ancient Greeks placed a great deal of importance on treating others fairly and with kindness. Set mainly on the ancient island of Crete in the Aegean (ĭ-jē′ən) Sea, "Wings" retells the Greek myth of a brilliant inventor named Daedalus (dĕd′l-əs) and his son, Icarus (ĭk′ər-əs). Daedalus is described as clever but not always kind. According to this retelling, "The gods always punish such a man."

AS YOU READ . . .

Discover what lessons about human behavior are taught.

Notice which human weaknesses are seen as humorous.

Find out what mysteries of nature are explained.

See how the consequences of characters' choices unfold.

WINGS

retold by Jane Yolen

Once in ancient Greece, when the gods dwelt on a high mountain overseeing the world, there lived a man named Daedalus who was known for the things he made.

He invented the axe, the bevel,[1] and the awl.[2] He built statues that were so lifelike they seemed ready to move. He designed a <u>maze</u> whose winding passages opened one into another as if without beginning, as if without end.

But Daedalus never understood the labyrinth[3] of his own heart. He was clever but he was not always kind. He was full of pride but he did not give others praise. He was a maker—but he was a taker, too.

The gods always punish such a man.

---

1. **bevel:** tool for measuring and marking angles.
2. **awl:** pointed tool for making holes in materials.
3. **labyrinth** (lăb′ə-rĭnth′): maze.

WORDS TO KNOW

maze (māz) *n.* a confusing set of winding pathways through which it is difficult to find one's way

Illustration Copyright © 1991 Dennis Nolan. From *Wings* by Jane Yolen, reproduced by permission of Harcourt Brace & Company.

Athens was the queen of cities and she had her princes. Daedalus was one. He was a prince and he was an artist, and he was proud of being both.

The very elements were his friends, and the people of Athens praised him.

"The gods will love you forever, Daedalus," they cried out to him as he walked through the city streets.

The gods listened and did not like to be told what to do.

A man who hears only praise becomes deaf. A man who sees no <u>rival</u> to his art becomes blind. Though he grew rich and he grew famous in the city, Daedalus also grew lazy and careless. And one day, without thought for the consequences, he caused the death of his young nephew, Prince Talos, who fell from a tall temple.

Even a prince cannot kill a prince. The king of Athens punished Daedalus by sending him away, away from all he loved: away from the colorful pillars of the temples, away from the noisy, winding streets, away from the bustling shops and stalls, away from his smithy,[4] away from the sound of the dark sea. He would never be allowed to return.

And the gods watched the <u>exile</u> from on high.

Many days and nights Daedalus fled from his past. He crossed strange lands. He crossed strange seas. All he carried with him was a goatskin flask, the clothes on his back, and the knowledge in his hands. All he carried with

him was grief that he had caused a child's death and grief that Athens was now dead to him.

He traveled a year and a day until he came at last to the island of Crete,[5] where the powerful King Minos[6] ruled.

The sands of Crete were different from his beloved Athens, the trees in the meadow were different, the flowers and the houses and the little, dark-eyed people were different. Only the birds seemed the same to Daedalus, and the sky—the vast, open, empty road of the sky.

But the gods found nothing below them strange.

Daedalus knew nothing of Crete, but Crete knew much of Daedalus, for his reputation had flown on wings before him. King Minos did not care that Daedalus was an exile or that he had been judged guilty of a terrible crime.

"You are the world's greatest builder, Daedalus," King Minos said. "Build me a labyrinth in which to hide a beast."

"A cage would be simpler," said Daedalus.

"This is no ordinary beast," said the king. "This is a monster. This is a prince. His name is Minotaur[7] and he is my wife's own son. He

---

4. **smithy:** workshop of a person who makes or repairs metal objects.

5. **Crete:** island about 200 miles southeast of Athens and the scene of many adventures in Greek literature.

6. **King Minos** (mī′nəs).

7. **Minotaur** (mĭn′ə-tôr′).

WORDS TO KNOW

rival (rī′vəl) *n.* a person who tries to do as well as or better than another
exile (ĕg′sīl′) *n.* a person forced to live outside his or her country

642

has a bull's head but a man's body. He eats human flesh. I cannot kill the queen's child. Even a king cannot kill a prince. And I cannot put him in a cage. But in a maze such as you might build, I could keep him hidden forever."

Daedalus bowed his head, but he smiled at the king's praise. He built a labyrinth for the king with countless corridors and winding ways. He devised such cunning passages that only he knew the secret pathway to its heart—he, and the Minotaur who lived there.

Yet the gods marked the secret way as well.

For many years Daedalus lived on the island of Crete, delighting in the praise he received from king and court. He made hundreds of new things for them. He made dolls with moving parts and a dancing floor inlaid with wood and stone for the princess Ariadne.[8] He made iron gates for the king and queen wrought[9] with cunning designs. He grew fond of the little dark-eyed islanders, and he married a Cretan wife. A son was born to them whom Daedalus named Icarus. The boy was small like his mother, but he had his father's quick, bright ways.

Daedalus taught Icarus many things, yet the one Daedalus valued most was the language of

> HE DEVISED SUCH CUNNING PASSAGES THAT ONLY HE KNEW THE SECRET PATHWAY TO ITS HEART.

his lost Athens. Though he had a grand house and servants to do his bidding, though he had a wife he loved and a son he adored, Daedalus was not entirely happy. His heart still lay in Athens, the land of his youth, and the words he spoke with his son helped keep the memory of Athens alive.

One night a handsome young man came to Daedalus' house, led by a lovesick Princess Ariadne. The young man spoke with Daedalus in that Athenian tongue.

"I am Theseus,[10] a prince of Athens, where your name is still remembered with praise. It is said that Daedalus was more than a prince, that he had the gods in his hands. Surely such a man has not forgotten Athens."

Daedalus shook his head. "I thought Athens had forgotten me."

"Athens remembers and Athens needs your help, O prince," said Theseus.

"Help? What help can I give Athens, when I am so far from home?"

"Then you do not know . . . ," Theseus began.

"Know what?"

---

8. **Ariadne** (ăr′ē-ăd′nē): daughter of King Minos.

9. **wrought** (rôt): decorated.

10. **Theseus** (thē′sē-əs): legendary Greek hero.

"That every seven years Athens must send a tribute[11] of boys and girls to King Minos. He puts them into the labyrinth you devised, and the monster Minotaur devours them there."

Horrified, Daedalus thought of the bright-eyed boys and girls he had known in Athens. He thought of his own dark-eyed son asleep in his cot. He remembered his nephew, Talos, whose eyes had been closed by death. "How can I help?"

"Only you know the way through the maze," said Theseus. "Show me the way that I may slay the monster."

"I will show you," said Daedalus thoughtfully, "but Princess Ariadne must go as well. The Minotaur is her half-brother. He will not hurt her. She will be able to lead you to him, right into the heart of the maze."

The gods listened to the plan and nodded gravely.

Daedalus drew them a map and gave Princess Ariadne a thread to tie at her waist, that she might unwind it as they went and so find the way back out of the twisting corridors.

Hand in hand, Theseus and Ariadne left, and Daedalus went into his son's room. He looked down at the sleeping boy.

"I am a prince of Athens," he whispered. "I did what must be done."

If Icarus heard his father's voice, he did not stir. He was dreaming still as Ariadne and Theseus threaded their way to the very center of the maze. And before he awakened, they

had killed the Minotaur and fled from Crete, taking the boys and girls of Athens with them. They took all hope of Daedalus' safety as well.

Then the gods looked thoughtful and they did not smile.

When King Minos heard that the Minotaur had been slain and Ariadne taken, he guessed that Daedalus had betrayed him, for no one else knew the secret of the maze. He ordered Daedalus thrown into a high prison tower.

"Thus do kings reward traitors!" cried Minos. Then he added, "See that you care for your own son better than you cared for my wife's unfortunate child." He threw Icarus into the tower, too, and slammed the great iron gate shut with his own hand.

The tiny tower room, with its single window overlooking the sea, was Daedalus' home now. Gone was Athens, where he had been a prince; gone was Crete, where he had been a rich man. All he had left was one small room, with a wooden bench and straw pallets[12] on the floor.

Day after day young Icarus stood on the bench and watched through the window as the seabirds dipped and soared over the waves.

"Father!" Icarus called each day. "Come and watch the birds."

But Daedalus would not. Day after day, he leaned against the wall or lay on a pallet

---

11. **tribute:** forced payment.
12. **pallets:** thin mattresses laid directly on the floor.

WORDS TO KNOW   **gravely** (grāv′lē) *adv.* in a very serious manner bemoaning[13] his fate and cursing the gods who had done this thing to him.

The gods heard his curses and they grew angry.

One bright day Icarus took his father by the hand, leading him to the window.

"Look, Father," he said, pointing to the birds. "See how beautiful their wings are. See how easily they fly."

Just to please the boy, Daedalus looked. Then he clapped his hands to his eyes. "What a fool I have been," he whispered. "What a fool. Minos may have forbidden me sea and land, but he has left me the air. Oh, my son, though the king is ever so great and powerful, he does not rule the sky. It is the gods' own road, and I am a favorite of the gods. To think a child has shown me the way!"

Every day after that, Daedalus and Icarus coaxed the birds to their windows with bread crumbs saved from their <u>meager</u> meals. And every day gulls, gannets, and petrels, cormorants and pelicans, shearwaters and grebes, came to the sill. Daedalus stroked the feeding birds with his clever hands and harvested handfuls of feathers. And Icarus, as if playing a game, grouped the feathers on the floor in order of size, just as his father instructed.

"MINOS MAY HAVE FORBIDDEN ME SEA AND LAND, BUT HE HAS LEFT ME THE AIR."

But it was no game. Soon the small piles of feathers became big piles, the big piles, great heaps. Then clever Daedalus, using a needle he had shaped from a bit of bone left over from dinner and thread pulled out of his own shirt, sewed together small feathers, overlapping them with the larger, gently curving them in great arcs. He fastened the ends with molded candle wax and made straps with the leather from their sandals.

At last Icarus understood. "Wings, Father!" he cried, clapping his hands together in delight. "Wings!"

At that the gods laughed, and it was thunder over water.

They made four wings in all, a pair for each of them.

Icarus had the smaller pair, for he was still a boy. They practiced for days in the tower, slipping their arms through the straps, raising and lowering the wings, until their arms had grown strong and used to the weight. They hid the wings beneath their pallets whenever the guards came by.

At last they were ready. Daedalus kneeled before his son.

"Your arms are strong now, Icarus," he said, "but do not forget my warning."

---

13. **bemoaning:** complaining about.

WORDS TO KNOW

meager (mē′gər) *adj.* of poor quality or inadequate amount

645

The boy nodded solemnly, his dark eyes wide. "I must not fly too low or the water will soak the feathers. I must not fly too high or the sun will melt the wax."

"Remember," his father said. "Remember."

The gods trembled, causing birds to fall through the bright air.

Daedalus climbed onto the sill. The wings made him clumsy but he did not fall. He helped Icarus up.

First the child, then the man, leaped out into the air. They pumped once and then twice with their arms. The wind caught the feathers of the wings and pushed them upward into the Cretan sky.

Wingtip to wingtip they flew, writing the lines of their escape on the air. Some watchers below took them for eagles. Most took them for gods.

As they flew, Daedalus concentrated on long, steady strokes. He remembered earlier days, when the elements had been his friends: fire and water and air. Now, it seemed, they were his friends once more.

But young Icarus had no such memories to steady his wings. He beat them with <u>abandon</u>, glorying in his freedom. He slipped away from his father's careful pattern along a wild stream of wind.

"Icarus, my son—remember!" Daedalus cried out.

But Icarus spiraled higher and higher and higher still. He did not hear his father's voice.

He heard only the music of the wind; he heard only the sighing of the gods.

He passed the birds. He passed the clouds. He passed into the realm of the sun. Too late he felt the wax run down his arms; too late he smelled the singe of feathers. Surprised, he hung solid in the air. Then, like a star in nova,[14] he tumbled from the sky, down, down, down into the waiting sea.

And the gods wept bitterly for the child.

"Where are you, my son?" Daedalus called. He circled the water, looking desperately for some sign. All he saw were seven feathers afloat on the sea, spinning into different patterns with each passing wave.

Weeping, he flew away over the dark sea to the isle of Sicily. There he built a temple to the god Apollo, for Apollo stood for life and light, and never grew old but remained a beautiful boy forever. On the temple walls Daedalus hung up his beautiful wings as an offering to the bitter wisdom of the gods.

So Daedalus' story ended—and yet it did not. For in Sicily he was received kindly by King Cocalus,[15] who was well pleased with his skills.

Meanwhile, back in Crete, enraged at his prisoners' escape, King Minos was determined to find and punish them. He <u>proclaimed</u> a great reward for anyone skilled enough to pass

---

14. **a star in nova:** a star that fades away after a period of unusual brilliance.

15. **King Cocalus** (kŏk′ə-ləs).

WORDS
TO
KNOW

abandon (ə-băn′dən) *n.* a wildness; unrestricted freedom of action
proclaim (prō-klām′) *v.* to announce officially

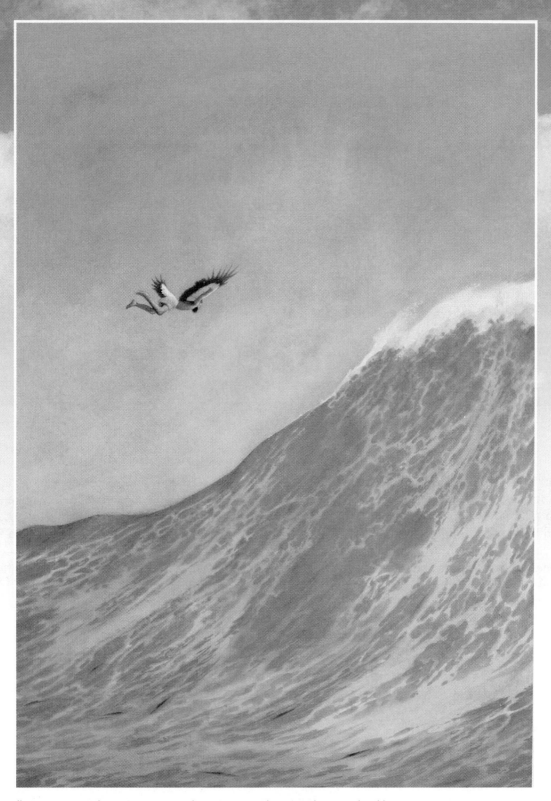

Illustration Copyright © 1991 Dennis Nolan. From *Wings* by Jane Yolen, reproduced by permission of Harcourt Brace & Company.

a silken thread through the closed spiral of a seashell. He knew that if Daedalus was alive, he could not resist the lure of such a game.

Daedalus was sure he could easily solve the puzzle. He bored a small hole in one end of a shell, moistened it with a bit of honey, then closed up the hole. Fastening a thread to an ant, he put the insect into the shell. The ant scurried through the twisting labyrinth toward the sweet smell, running as easily as Princess Ariadne had run through the maze with the thread unwinding at her waist. When the ant emerged from the other end, it had pulled the silken thread through the spirals of the shell.

Though he used a false name to claim the prize, Daedalus did not fool King Minos. Minos knew the winner was his old enemy. So, with a mighty army, Minos sailed to Sicily to bring Daedalus back.

But King Cocalus would not give up Daedalus to the foreign invaders, and a great battle was fought. With Daedalus' help, King Cocalus was victorious and King Minos was killed. Minos was clever but he was not kind. He had a heart scabbed over with old remembered wounds. ❖

JANE YOLEN

1939–

A storyteller, lecturer, and mother of three, Jane Yolen grew up in New York City in a family of writers. Yolen is best known for her folk and fairy tales. She is particularly interested in stories that have been passed from one storyteller to another for hundreds of years. Yolen's style is to give modern twists to familiar stories or to create original stories based on the feel and structure of classic tales. She reads aloud everything she writes to be sure her work reflects the flavor of the oral tradition. *Wings,* her version of the myth of Daedalus and Icarus, won a 1992 Children's Choice award. Yolen is also known for her science fiction and fantasy stories, such as *Dragon's Blood,* the first volume of a three-part fantasy about dragons.

OTHER WORKS *The Girl Who Cried Flowers and Other Tales, Owl Moon, Ring of Earth, Favorite Folktales from Around the World, The Devil's Arithmetic*

WORDS
TO
KNOW

scurry (skûr′ē) *v.* to run quickly; scamper

THE RED LION

retold by Diane Wolkstein

When the King of Persia[1] died, there was great
weeping, for he had been a brave and wise leader.
Yet in little more than a month the mourning would be over,
and the King's son, Azgid, would be crowned. But before the
Prince could be crowned, he would have to prove his
courage, just as every Prince before him had done, by fighting
the Red Lion.

One day during this time the Vizier[2] went to the young
Prince and urged him to prepare himself for the contest.
Azgid trembled. He had always been afraid of lions, and the
Red Lion was the most <u>ferocious</u> of lions. He decided to run
away.

That night, when it was very dark, he crept out of his
bedroom, mounted his horse, and rode off. He rode two days
and nights. On the morning of the third day he entered a

---

1. **Persia:** ancient empire of southwest Asia.
2. **Vizier** (vĭ-zîr′): in Moslem countries, a high officer in the
   government.

WORDS
TO
KNOW   **ferocious** (fə-rō′shəs) *adj.* fierce; savage; violently cruel

649

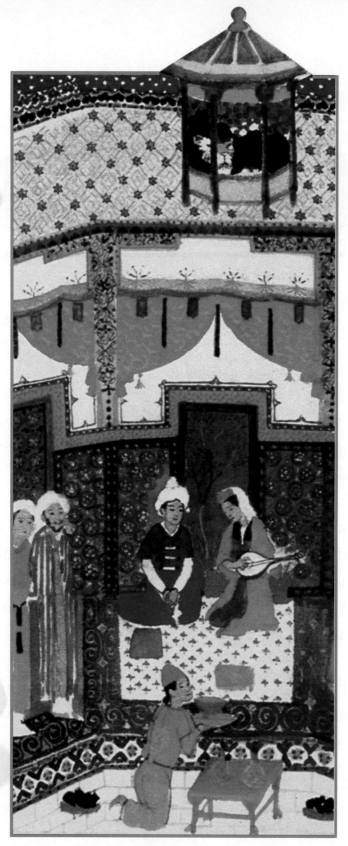

Copyright © 1977 Ed Young. Reprinted by permission of McIntosh and Otis, Inc.

grove of trees and heard a sweet melody. Dismounting, he walked quietly until he saw a shepherd sitting in a clearing and playing a flute. All about the shepherd the sheep stood listening.

"God be with you," said the shepherd to the stranger.

"And with you," the Prince replied, "but please do not stop your song."

The shepherd took up his flute and played for the clouds, for the winds, for his sheep, and for the stranger.

When he finished, Azgid spoke: "Surely you are wondering who I am. I wish I could tell you my name. But it is a secret that must stay locked in my heart. I beg you to believe me; I am no enemy. I am an honorable youth who has been forced to flee from his home."

"You are welcome to stay with me," the shepherd answered. "I would be glad of your company, and I can show you a place that will cause you to forget your troubles."

Hour after hour the Prince and the shepherd walked, the Prince leading his horse and the sheep following behind the shepherd. As the sun was setting, they came to the most beautiful valley Azgid had ever seen. It was perfectly quiet, and Azgid and the shepherd sat and gazed in wonder at the hills in front of them. Then suddenly the shepherd jumped up.

"Time to go!" he said.

"But why must we leave so quickly?" asked the Prince. "Can there be any place on earth more lovely?"

"It *is* beautiful," the shepherd agreed. But then he raised his sleeve, revealing a long, cruel red scar. He traced his finger along the scar and said: "Lions! Once I was late returning to the village, and the village gates were closed. This is the result. I do not want it to happen a second time."

"Then return to the village with the sheep,"

the Prince said, "but I cannot stay with you." He mounted his horse and rode north. He rode two days and nights, and on the third morning he came to a desert.

He and his horse were tired and hungry and thirsty. The wind blew sand in the Prince's face, and he was riding with his eyes half-shut when suddenly his horse neighed. Through the streaming sands Azgid saw the tents of an Arab camp. His horse began to prance, but he pulled back on the bridle and continued to ride slowly to show that his was a peaceful visit.

An Arab Sheik[3] greeted him with courtesy. He offered the Prince food and had his horse fed and cared for. After the Prince had eaten, he said to the Sheik: "Forgive me if I do not reveal my name. Because of certain troubles it is a secret that must stay locked in my heart. But I have jewels and precious stones I would gladly give you if you would allow me to remain with you."

"You are our guest," the Sheik replied, and he refused to accept any of the Prince's treasures.

I WISH I COULD TELL YOU MY NAME. BUT IT IS A SECRET THAT MUST STAY LOCKED IN MY HEART.

The following morning the Sheik provided the Prince with a magnificent stallion, and for the next three days the Prince rode with the Sheik and his companions, hunting antelope.

---

3. **Sheik** (shēk): the leader of an Arab family, tribe, or village.

Copyright © 1977 Ed Young. Reprinted by permission of McIntosh and Otis, Inc.

On the third evening the Sheik spoke to the Prince. "My men are pleased with your spirit," he said, "and with your skill at hunting. But there will soon be a battle. My men want to know if they can rely on your strength and courage. To the south lies a range of hills known as the Red Hills. It is lion country. Ride there tomorrow on the stallion. Take your sword and spear, and bring us back the hide of one of these fierce lions to show us we can count on you on the day of battle."

That night, when it was very still, the Prince slipped out of his tent. He stroked the beloved stallion he had ridden and whispered good-bye in his ear. Then he mounted his own horse and rode west.

After two days and nights he came to a country of rolling meadows and green fields. There in the distance he saw a splendid red sandstone palace.

At the gates the Prince took off his ring and asked the guard to present it to the Emir.[4] Immediately the Prince was invited to enter the palace.

As the Prince was explaining his situation to the Emir, Perizide,[5] the Emir's daughter, appeared. The Emir, who was impressed with Azgid's good manners and fine speech, said to his daughter, "My child, show this young man our palace and gardens, and be certain he is invited to the entertainment this evening."

Perizide led the Prince through room after room and then out into the garden. There were flowers and trees of every kind in the garden, and in the middle was an oval-shaped pool filled with rose water. In the water floated one perfect lily. It was perfect and yet not as beautiful as Perizide.

After dinner in the cool evening air, Perizide herself provided the entertainment. She played the lute[6] and sang. As Azgid listened, he felt his soul rising higher and higher. "This is why I have run away," he thought, "so I might find Perizide."

"RRRAAGGGGGH!"

"What was *that*?" cried the Prince, jumping to his feet.

"Oh, that's just our guard Boulak.[7] He's yawning."

"*Yawning*?" repeated the Prince.

"Yes," said Perizide. "He does that when it is late. I will say goodnight now."

After Perizide left, the Emir stood up. "It is late for me, too. Come, I will show you to your bedroom."

They had just begun to climb the staircase when Azgid looked up. His hand froze on the banister. There at the top of the landing was an enormous lion.

"Oh, that's just Boulak," said the Emir. "He's perfectly harmless. He never attacks unless someone is afraid of him."

"Oh, I'm not, ah, quite r-r-eady for, ah, I'm not r-ready for s-s-sleep," faltered[8] the Prince.

"Well, then, come up when you wish," said the Emir. "Yours is the first bedroom on the right."

Azgid backed down the stairs. He backed

---

4. **Emir** (ĭ-mîr´): in Moslem countries, a ruler or prince.

5. **Perizide** (pār´ĭ-zēd´).

6. **lute**: an early stringed instrument, similar to a guitar.

7. **Boulak** (boo´läk).

8. **faltered**: said in a weak or hesitant way.

down the corridor and into the music room and locked the doors. He sat on a chair and waited. Soon he heard the lion padding down the stairs. He heard him claw at the door. The door shook. The lion roared: "RRAAAGGGH!"

Azgid thought the lion would tear down the door and <u>devour</u> him, but he just sat there. He did not try to run away. The lion roared again: "RRAAAAAAGGH!"

Azgid listened. The lion roared a third time. Suddenly the Prince realized that the roars were not threats. They were warnings. They were telling him: Three times you have run away. If you run away again—wherever you may go—a lion will be waiting.

A lion would always be waiting for the Prince until he went home to fight his own lion.

Azgid listened. Boulak did not roar again. Then he heard the lion padding back up the stairs.

Early the next morning the Prince explained that he had to return home at once.

He mounted his horse and, thinking only of the Red Lion, rode day and night until he reached his palace.

At the appointed time, Azgid entered the crowded arena. The Emir, Perizide, the Sheik, and the shepherd were all there, seated in the stands. But the Prince did not look up. No, his eyes were on the doors from which the Red Lion would emerge. He waited.

The doors opened. The lion sprang out. Azgid stood firm, his spear in his hand. The lion roared and leapt—right over the head of Azgid. When Azgid whirled around to throw his spear, he saw the Red Lion lying on his back, playfully waving his paws in the air like a happy puppy. Then the lion trotted up to Azgid and affectionately licked his hands.

The Red Lion was tame. Every lion that had ever fought a Prince of Persia had been tame. Only fear would make him ferocious.

And so Azgid was crowned King of Persia. And in due time he married Perizide, and the two lived together happily and ruled their kingdom wisely and well. ❖

DIANE WOLKSTEIN

An award-winning author and storyteller, Diane Wolkstein was born in New York City. After attending Smith College, she studied pantomime in Paris for a year. From 1968 to 1980, she hosted a weekly radio show, *Stories from Many Lands,* that led one newspaper writer to describe her as "New York City's official storyteller."

Wolkstein's interest in world folklore is reflected in her books and recordings of stories, which range from myths of the Hopi Indians to

1942–

Biblical stories, from Haitian folk tales to Estonian fairy tales. *The Red Lion: A Tale of Ancient Persia* is based on an old Persian story, probably a Sufi (Moslem) "teaching tale." In addition to writing books for children and young adults, Wolkstein teaches mythology and children's literature and leads storytelling workshops throughout the United States.

OTHER WORKS *The Banza, Esther's Story, Little Mouse's Painting, The Magic Orange Tree and Other Haitian Folk Tales*

WORDS
TO   **devour** (dĭ-vour') *v.* to eat up hungrily; swallow up
KNOW

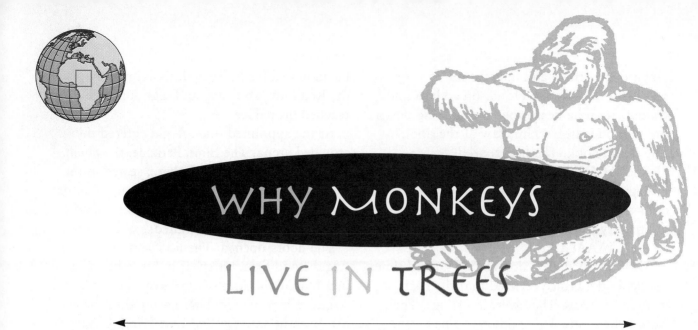

WHY MONKEYS
LIVE IN TREES

retold by Julius Lester

One day Leopard was looking at his reflection in a pool of water. Looking at himself was Leopard's favorite thing in the world to do. Leopard gazed, wanting to be sure that every hair was straight and that all his spots were where they were supposed to be. This took many hours of looking at his reflection, which Leopard did not mind at all.

Finally he was satisfied that nothing was disturbing his handsomeness, and he turned away from the pool of water. At that exact moment, one of Leopard's children ran up to him.

"Daddy! Daddy! Are you going to be in the contest?"

"What contest?" Leopard wanted to know. If it was a beauty contest, of course he was going to be in it.

"I don't know. Crow the Messenger just flew by. She said that King Gorilla said there was going to be a contest."

Without another word, Leopard set off. He went north-by-northeast, made a right turn at the mulberry bush and traveled east-by-south-by-west until he came to a hole in the ground. He went around in a circle five times and headed north-by-somersault until he came to a big clearing in the middle of the jungle, and that's where King Gorilla was.

King Gorilla sat at one end of the clearing on his throne. Opposite him, at the other side of the clearing, all the animals sat in a semicircle. In the middle, between King Gorilla and the animals, was a huge mound of what looked like black dust.

Leopard looked around with calm dignity. Then he strode regally[1] over to his friend, Lion.

---

1. **strode regally:** walked in a grand manner, like a king or queen.

Exotic Landscape (1910), Henri Rousseau. Oil on canvas, 51 ¼″ × 64″. The Norton Simon Foundation, Pasadena, California.

"What's that?" he asked, pointing to the mound of black dust.

"Don't know," Lion replied. "King Gorilla said he will give a pot of gold to whoever can eat it in one day. I can eat it in an hour."

Leopard laughed. "I'll eat it in a half hour."

It was Hippopotamus's turn to laugh. "As big as my mouth is, I'll eat that mound in one gulp."

Tthe time came for the contest. King Gorilla had the animals pick numbers to see who would go in what order. To everybody's dismay, Hippopotamus drew Number 1.

Hippopotamus walked over to the mound of black dust. It was bigger than he had thought. It was much too big to eat in one gulp. Nonetheless, Hippopotamus opened his mouth as wide as he could, and that was very wide indeed, and took a mouthful of the black dust.

He started chewing. Suddenly he leaped straight into the air and screamed. He screamed so loudly that it knocked the ears off the chickens, and that's why to this day chickens don't have ears.

Hippopotamus screamed and Hippopotamus yelled. Hippopotamus roared and Hippopotamus bellowed. Then he started sneezing and crying, and tears rolled down his face like he was standing in the shower. Hippopotamus ran to the river and drank as much water as he could, and that was very much, indeed, to cool his mouth and tongue and throat.

The animals didn't understand what had happened to Hippopotamus, but they didn't care. They were happy because they still had a chance to win the pot of gold. Of course, if they had known that the mound of black dust was really a mound of black pepper, maybe they wouldn't have wanted the gold.

Nobody was more happy than Leopard

HIPPOPOTAMUS ROARED AND HIPPOPOTAMUS BELLOWED. THEN HE STARTED SNEEZING AND CRYING.

because he had drawn Number 2. He walked up to the black mound and sniffed at it.

"AAAAAAAAACHOOOOOOO!" Leopard didn't like that, but then he remembered the pot of gold. He opened his mouth wide, took a mouthful and started chewing and swallowing.

Leopard leaped straight into the air, did a back double flip and screamed. He yelled and he roared and he bellowed and, finally, he started sneezing and crying, tears rolling down his face like a waterfall. Leopard ran to the river and washed out his mouth and throat and tongue.

Lion was next, and the same thing happened to him as it did to all the animals. Finally only Monkey remained.

Monkey approached King Gorilla. "I know I can eat all of whatever that is, but after each mouthful, I'll need to lie down in the tall grasses and rest."

King Gorilla said that was okay.

Monkey went to the mound, took a tiny bit of pepper on his tongue, swallowed, and went into the tall grasses. A few minutes later,

Monkey came out, took a little more, swallowed it, and went into the tall grasses.

Soon the pile was almost gone. The animals were astonished to see Monkey doing what they had not been able to do. Leopard couldn't believe it either. He climbed a tree and stretched out on a sturdy limb to get a better view. From his limb high in the tree Leopard could see into the tall grasses where Monkey went to rest. Wait a minute! Leopard thought something was suddenly wrong with his eyes because he thought he saw a hundred monkeys hiding in the tall grasses.

He rubbed his eyes and looked another look. There wasn't anything wrong with his eyes. There were a hundred monkeys in the tall grasses, and they all looked alike!

Just then, there was the sound of loud applause. King Gorilla announced that Monkey had won the contest and the pot of gold.

Leopard growled a growl so scary that even King Gorilla was frightened. Leopard wasn't thinking about anybody except the monkeys. He took a long and beautiful leap from the tree right smack into the middle of the tall grasses where the monkeys were hiding.

The monkeys ran in all directions. When the other animals saw monkeys running from the grasses, they realized that the monkeys had tricked them, and started chasing them. Even King Gorilla joined in the chase. He wanted his gold back.

The only way the monkeys could escape was to climb to the very tops of the tallest trees where no one else, not even Leopard, could climb.

And that's why monkeys live in trees to this very day. ❖

JULIUS LESTER

Julius Lester connects his interest in folklore to his father, who was a minister and a good storyteller. Lester says, "As a child, I loved it when my father got together with other ministers on a summer evening, because I knew that I would be treated to stories for as long as I was allowed to stay up, which was never long enough." Lester's work has received numerous awards, including a 1969 Newbery Honor award for *To Be a*

1939–

Slave. "Why Monkeys Live in Trees" is from the book *How Many Spots Does a Leopard Have?*, which contains tales that reflect both African and Jewish story traditions. Lester currently divides his time between writing and serving as a professor at the University of Massachusetts.

OTHER WORKS *Long Journey Home: Stories from Black History, The Tales of Uncle Remus: The Adventures of Brer Rabbit*

RESPONDING
O P T I O N S

LITERATURE CONNECTION PROJECT 1

Design a Board Game or Video Game
Working in a small group, design a video game or a board game based on one of the tales you've just read. Research popular games to become familiar with the types of graphics and illustrations currently used. Here are some things to consider:

Decide on an appropriate age level to target for the game.

Determine the goal of the game. For example, the goal of a game based on the well-known Cinderella story might be to get Cinderella safely through the trials of the wicked stepsisters to the Prince's ball. Brainstorm details such as which characters will be involved—in this example, Cinderella, the stepsisters and stepmother, the Prince, and the fairy godmother—as well as the rules of the game.

Write a brief instruction manual. The instructions should make it clear to your classmates how the game is played.

Draw sample video screens or a sample game board to show how the game will look. A sample gameboard is shown here.

Add your game to a class display of student-designed games.

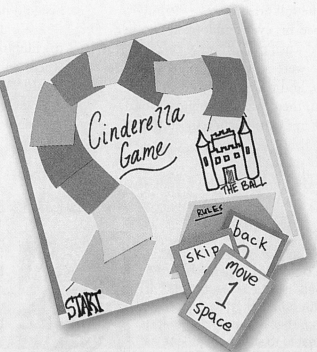

SOCIAL STUDIES CONNECTION PROJECT 2

 Design a Labyrinth Discoveries made by archaeologists suggest that the labyrinth of the Minotaur may actually exist in the ruins of the ancient palace at Knossos on Crete. The palace covered some five acres and contained hundreds of rooms, modern plumbing, and brilliantly colored frescoes (art painted on fresh, wet plaster). Research the archaeological work that began on Crete in the early 1900s. Use information from your research and details from "Wings" to draw or construct a model of the labyrinth Daedalus built for the Minotaur. Arrange a display of the drawings and models so that students may try to solve the mazes.

Map the Spice Routes Trade in spices flourished between ancient Egypt and the African kingdoms of Kush and Punt. By 80 B.C., Alexandria, Egypt, had become the greatest spice-trading port of the eastern Mediterranean, with one of its entrances known as Pepper Gate. Pepper was considered the king of spices because it could disguise the taste and odor of tainted meat before meat was preserved properly. Investigate the spices of ancient Africa. Which spices made their way by trade to other lands and continents? On a map like the one shown, trace Egyptian trade routes in the period 1570–1070 B.C. Use lines, arrows, and captions to identify and trace the movement of the various spices traded in ancient Africa.

Mediterranean Sea

Alexandria

EGYPT

Kush

N
W—E
S

Miles
0   500   1000

Punt

ACROSS CULTURES MINI-PROJECTS

Try Calligraphy The ancient Persians regarded calligraphy as an art equal to, if not more important than, painting. Experiment with calligraphy, using it to write one of the following items based on "The Red Lion": an announcement of the King's death, an invitation to the contest between Prince Azgid and the Red Lion, a proclamation of Azgid's crowning ceremony, or an announcement of Azgid and Perizide's marriage.

Create a Time Line In "The Red Lion," Perizide entertains Azgid by playing a lute, probably an ancestor of a stringed instrument made from a gourd and played with a bow. Research the lute and design an illustrated time line of its development from ancient times in Babylonia to modern times.

Present a Tableau Design a tableau (tăb′lō′)—a stop-action scene—of the major gods and goddesses of Greek and Roman mythology. Work in pairs to identify a Greek god or goddess and his or her Roman counterpart. For each god or goddess, create a costume and a symbol (for example, a trident for Poseidon) and design a backdrop or setting (for example, for Zeus, a stormy sky with thunderbolts). Then present your tableau to the class, with one partner assuming the role of the Greek god or goddess and the other partner the role of the Roman version. As a class, develop a competition involving identification of the figures portrayed.

> ### MORE ABOUT THE CULTURES
>
> - *The Kingdom of the Bulls* by Paul Capon
> - *Pompeii* by Ron and Nancy Goor
> - *Digging Up the Bible Lands* by Ronald Harker
> - *Life in Ancient Greece* by Pierre Miguel

LINKS TO UNIT TWO

The Need to Belong

In Unit Two, the selections explore the conflicting emotions that often occur when an individual is striving to find his or her place in the community. The need to belong is a basic human urge that has been expressed within the folklore of many cultures. The tales you will read next reveal how different people go about meeting this universal need.

PUERTO RICO

The Legend of the Hummingbird

retold by Pura Belpré (po͞o′rä bĕl-prā′)

Puerto Rico, an island in the Caribbean Sea, is a commonwealth of the United States. The U.S. Congress is responsible for the government of Puerto Rico, but Congress usually allows the Puerto Rican people to make their own decisions. The folklore of Puerto Rico reflects a mixture of cultures, with roots in the Orient, Arabia, Spain, and West Africa. This legend, like other legends, incorporates elements of magic and the supernatural as it explains the origin of the many-colored hummingbird.

In the Land of Small Dragon

retold by Dang Manh Kha (däng′män′kä′)
to Ann Nolan Clark

Similar stories often appear in different cultures because they focus on values that the cultures hold in common. For example, hundreds of versions of the Cinderella story can be found, from Canada to Africa to Japan. This version comes from Vietnam, a country in Indonesia that has fought for independence throughout much of its long history. This variation of the Cinderella story includes a jealous stepmother, a fairy godmother, and a magical fish.

The Bamboo Beads

by Lynn Joseph

This folk tale comes from Trinidad, a small tropical island off the coast of Venezuela. African, Indian, Spanish, and French influences are reflected in the dialect of Trinidad. The tale features Papa Bois, one of the island's most popular folklore characters. His duty is to protect the trees and animals of the woods, which include the scarlet ibis, the iguana, and such poisonous snakes as the fer-delance. However, Papa Bois sometimes chooses to make contact with humans.

AS YOU READ . . .

See how attitudes regarding power are portrayed.

Evaluate how much humans are allowed to control their own fates.

Notice which powers are connected to gods or other supernatural beings.

In the LAND of SMALL DRAGON

As told by
Dang Manh Kha
to **Ann Nolan Clark**

1

Man cannot know the whole world,
But can know his own small part.

In the Land of Small Dragon,
In the Year of the Chicken,[1]
In a Village of No-Name,
In the bend of the river,
There were many small houses
Tied together by walkways.
Mulberry and apricot,
Pear tree and flowering vine
Dropped their delicate blossoms
On a carpet of new grass.
  In a Village of No-Name
Lived a man and two daughters.
Tấm[2] was the elder daughter;
Her mother died at her birth.

---

1. **Year of the Chicken:** the name of a year in the old Chinese calendar; commonly called Year of the Rooster. Every year in the Chinese calendar has 1 of 12 animal names. For example, 1911 was a Year of the Pig, which next occurred 12 years later, in 1923.
2. **Tấm** (tăm).

A jewel box of gold and jade
Holds only jewels of great price.

Tầm's face was a golden moon,
Her eyes dark as a storm cloud,
Her feet delicate flowers
Stepping lightly on the wind.
No envy lived in her heart,
Nor bitterness in her tears.
Cám[3] was the younger daughter,
Child of Number Two Wife.
Cám's face was long and ugly,
Scowling and discontented,
Frowning in deep displeasure.
Indolent, slow and idle,
Her heart was filled with hatred
For her beautiful sister.

An evil heart keeps records
On the face of its owner.

The father loved both daughters,
One not more than the other.
He did not permit his heart
To call one name more dearly.

He lived his days in justice,
Standing strong against the wind.

Father had a little land,
A house made of mats and clay,
A grove of mulberry trees
Enclosed by growing bamboo,
A garden and rice paddy,[4]
Two great water buffalo,[5]
A well for drinking water,
And twin fish ponds for the fish.
Cám's mother, Number Two Wife,
Cared only for her own child.
Her mind had only one thought:
What would give pleasure to Cám.

Her heart had only one door
And only Cám could enter.

Number Two Wife was jealous
of Tầm, the elder daughter,
Who was beautiful and good,
So the mother planned revenge
On the good, beautiful child.
To Cám she gave everything,
But nothing but work to Tầm.
Tầm carried water buckets,
Hanging from her bamboo pole.
Tầm carried forest fagots[6]
To burn in the kitchen fire.
Tầm transplanted young rice plants
From seed bed to rice paddy.
Tầm flailed[7] the rice on a rock,
Then she winnowed and gleaned it.[8]
Tầm's body ached with tiredness,
Her heart was heavy and sad.
She said, "Wise Father, listen!
I am your elder daughter;
Therefore why may I not be
Number One Daughter, also?
"A Number One Daughter works,
But she works with dignity.
If I were your Number One
The honor would ease my pain.
As it is, I am a slave,
Without honor or dignity."
Waiting for wisdom to come,
Father was slow to give answer.

---

3. **Cám** (cäm).

4. **rice paddy:** flooded field used for growing rice.

5. **water buffalo:** slow, powerful oxlike animal used for pulling loads.

6. **fagots** (făg′əts): bundles of sticks or twigs; also spelled *faggots*.

7. **flailed:** beat out grain from its husk, or dry outer casing.

8. **winnowed and gleaned it:** separated out the useless parts of the rice and collected the remaining good parts.

"Both of my daughters share my heart.
I cannot choose between them.
One of you must earn the right
To be my Number One child."

*A man's worth is what he does,
Not what he says he can do.*

"Go, Daughters, to the fish pond;
Take your fish baskets with you.
Fish until night moon-mist comes.
Bring your fish catch back to me.
She who brings a full basket
Is my Number One Daughter.
Your work, not my heart, decides
Your place in your father's house."
Tầm listened to her father
And was quick to obey him.
With her basket, she waded
In the mud of the fish pond.
With quick-moving, graceful hands
She caught the quick-darting fish.
Slowly the long hours went by.
Slowly her fish basket filled.
Cám sat on the high, dry bank
Trying to think of some plan,
Her basket empty of fish,
But her mind full of cunning.
"I, wade in that mud?" she thought.
"There must be some better way."
At last she knew what to do
To be Number One Daughter.
"Tầm," she called, "elder sister,
Our father needs a bright flower,
A flower to gladden his heart.
Get it for him, dear sister."
Tầm, the good, gentle sister,
Set her fish basket aside
And ran into the forest
To pick the night-blooming flowers.
Cám crept to Tầm's fish basket,
Emptied it into her own.
Now her fish basket was full.

Illustration Copyright © 1982 Vo-Dinh Mai. From *The Brocaded Slipper and Other Vietnamese Tales* by Lynette Dyer Vuong. Reprinted by permission of HarperCollins Publishers.

Tầm's held only one small fish.
Quickly Cám ran to Father,
Calling, "See my full basket!"
Tầm ran back to the fish pond
With an armload of bright flowers.
"Cám," she called, "what has happened?
What has happened to my fish?"
Slowly Tầm went to Father
Bringing him the flowers and fish.
Father looked at both baskets.
Speaking slowly, he told them,
"The test was a full basket,
Not flowers and one small fish.

Take your fish, Elder Daughter.
It is much too small to eat.
Cám has earned the right to be
Honorable Number One."

2

Tầm looked at the little fish.
Her heart was filled with pity
At its loneliness and fright.
"Little fish, dear little fish,
I will put you in the well."
At night Tầm brought her rice bowl,
Sharing her food with the fish—
Talked to the thin fish, saying,
"Little fish, come eat with me"—
Stayed at the well at nighttime
With the stars for company.
The fish grew big and trustful.
It grew fat and not afraid.
It knew Tầm's voice and answered,
Swimming to her outstretched hand.
Cám sat in the dark shadows,
Her heart full of jealousy,
Her mind full of wicked thoughts.
Sweetly she called, "Tầm, sister.
Our father is overtired.
Come sing him a pretty song
That will bring sweet dreams to him."
Quickly Tầm ran to her father,
Singing him a nightbird song.
Cám was hiding near the well,
Watching, waiting and watching.
When she heard Tầm's pretty song
She crept closer to the fish,
Whispering, "Dear little fish,
Come to me! Come eat with me."
The fish came, and greedy Cám
Touched it, caught it and ate it!
Tầm returned. Her fish was gone.
"Little fish, dear little fish,
Come to me! Come eat with me!"
Bitterly she cried for it.

The stars looked down in pity;
The clouds shed teardrops of rain.

3

Tầm's tears falling in the well
Made the water rise higher.
And from it rose Nang Tien,
A lovely cloud-dressed fairy.
Her voice was a silver bell

"Little fish,

dear little fish,

I will put you

in the well."

Ringing clear in the moonlight.
"My child, why are you crying?"
"My dear little fish is gone!
He does not come when I call."
"Ask Red Rooster to help you.
His hens will find Little Fish."
Soon the hens came in a line
Sadly bringing the fish bones.
Tầm cried, holding the fish bones.
"Your dear fish will not forget.
Place his bones in a clay pot
Safe beneath your sleeping mat.
Those we love never leave us.
Cherished bones keep love alive."
In her treasured clay pot, Tầm
Made a bed of flower petals
For the bones of Little Fish
And put him away with love.
But she did not forget him;

When the moon was full again,
Tâm, so lonely for her fish,
Dug up the buried clay pot.
Tâm found, instead of fish bones,
A silken dress and two jeweled *hai*.[9]
Her Nang Tien spoke again.
"Your dear little fish loves you.
Clothe yourself in the garments
His love has given you."
Tâm put on the small jeweled *hai*.
They fit like a velvet skin
Made of moonlight and stardust
And the love of Little Fish.
Tâm heard music in her heart
That sent her small feet dancing,
Flitting like two butterflies,
Skimming like two flying birds,
Dancing by the twin fish ponds,
Dancing in the rice paddy.
But the mud in the rice paddy
Kept one jeweled *hai* for its own.
Night Wind brought the *hai* to Tâm.
"What is yours I bring to you."
Water in the well bubbled,
"I will wash your *hai* for you."
Water buffalo came by.
"Dry your *hai* on my sharp horn."
A blackbird flew by singing,
"I know where this *hai* belongs.
In a garden far away
I will take this *hai* for you."

4

What is to be must happen
As day follows after night.

In the Emperor's garden,
Sweet with perfume of roses,
The Emperor's son, the Prince,
Walked alone in the moonlight.
A bird, black against the moon,
Flew along the garden path,

Dropping a star in its flight.
"Look! A star!" exclaimed the Prince.
Carefully he picked it up
And found it was the small jeweled *hai*.
"Only a beautiful maid
Can wear this beautiful *hai*."
The Prince whispered to his heart,
And his heart answered, "Find her."

In truth, beauty seeks goodness:
What is beautiful is good.

The Prince went to his father:
"A bird dropped this at my feet.
Surely it must come as truth,
Good and fair the maid it fits.
Sire,[10] if it is your pleasure
I would take this maid for wife."
The Great Emperor was pleased
With the wishes of his son.
He called his servants to him,
His drummers and his crier,[11]
Proclaiming a Festival
To find one who owned the *hai*.
In the Village of No-Name
The Emperor's subjects heard—
They heard the Royal Command.
There was praise and rejoicing.
They were pleased the Royal Son
Would wed one of their daughters.

5

Father's house was filled with clothes,
Embroidered *áo-dài*[12] and *hai*
Of heavy silks and rich colors.

---

9. **hai** (hī): shoes.

10. **Sire**: title of respect for a superior, in this case, an
    emperor.

11. **crier**: person who makes public announcements in the
    streets of a village or town.

12. **embroidered *áo-dài*** (ou′dī): robes decorated with fancy
    needlework.

"Stay at home, you Number Two!"

Father went outside to sit.
Cám and her mother whispered
Their hopes, their dreams and their plans.
Cám, Number One Daughter, asked,
"Mother, will the Prince choose me?"
Mother said, "Of course he will.
You will be the fairest there!
When you curtsy to the Prince
His heart will go out to you."
Tâm, Daughter Number Two, said,
"May I go with you and Cám?"
Cám's mother answered <u>curtly</u>,
"Yes, if you have done this task:
Separating rice and husks
From one basket into two."
Tâm knew Cám's mother had mixed
The cleaned rice with rice unhusked.
She looked at the big basket
Full to brim with rice and husks.
Separating the cleaned rice
From that of rice unhusked
Would take all harvest moon time,
When the Festival would end.
A cloud passed over the moon.
Whirring wings outsung the wind.
A flock of blackbirds lighted

On the pile of leaves and grain.
Picking the grain from the leaves,
They dropped clean rice at Tâm's feet.
Tâm could almost not believe
That the endless task was done.
Tâm, the elder daughter, said,
"May I go? May I go, too,
Now that all my work is done?"
Cám <u>taunted</u>, "How could you go?
You have nothing fit to wear."
"If I had a dress to wear
Could I go to the Palace?"
"If wishes were dresses, yes,
But wishes are not dresses."
When Mother left she said,
"Our dear Cám is <u>ravishing</u>.
Stay at home, you Number Two!
Cám will be the one to wed."
Tâm dug up the big clay pot.
The dress and one *hai* were there—
As soft as misty moon clouds,
Delicate as rose perfume.
Tâm washed her face in the well,
Combed her hair by the fish pond.
She smoothed down the silken dress,
Tied one *hai* unto her belt
And, though her feet were bare,
Hurried, scurried, ran and ran.
She ran to the Festival
In the King's Royal Garden.
At the Palace gates the guards
Bowed before her, very low.
Pretty girls stood in a line
With their mothers standing near;
One by one they tried to fit
A foot into a small, jeweled *hai*.
Cám stood beside her mother,
By the gilded[13] throne-room door.

---

13. **gilded:** covered with a thin layer of gold.

WORDS	**curtly** (kûrt′lē) *adv.* in a way that uses so few words it is either rude or almost rude
TO	**taunt** (tônt) *v.* to make fun of in a mean way
KNOW	**ravishing** (răv′ĭ-shĭng) *adj.* unusually beautiful; delightfully pleasing

Her face was dark and angry
Like a brooding monsoon[14] wind.
Cám, wiping her tears away,
Sobbed and whimpered and complained,
"My small foot fits his old shoe—
Everything but my big toe."
Tấm stood shyly by the door
Looking in great wonderment
While trumpeters and drummers
Made music for her entrance.
People looked at gentle Tấm.
Everyone was whispering,
"Oh! She is so beautiful!
She must be a Princess fair
From some distant foreign land."
Then the Prince looked up and saw
A lady walking toward him.
Stepping from his Royal Throne,
He quickly went to meet her,
And taking her hand led her
To His Majesty the King.
What is to be must happen
As day happens after night.

Real beauty mirrors goodness.
What is one is the other.

Kneeling, the Prince placed the *hai*
On Tấm's dainty little foot.
Tấm untied the *hai* she wore
And slid her bare foot in it.

Beauty is not painted on.
It is the spirit showing.

The Prince spoke to his father.
"I would take this maid for wife."
His Royal Highness nodded.
"We will have a Wedding feast."
All the birds in all the trees
Sang a song of happiness:
"Tấm, the Number Two Daughter,
Is to be Wife Number One."

What is written in the stars
Cannot be changed or altered.

---

14. **monsoon:** in south Asia, a wind that begins the rainy season.

DANG MANH KHA

Dang Manh Kha was born in Vietnam. After attending St. John's University in Minnesota, he taught school in El Paso, Texas, for four years. In 1975 he worked for the Southeast Asian Resettlement Program to aid Vietnamese refugees. Dang Manh Kha now lives in Tucson, Arizona.

ANN NOLAN CLARK

Born in New Mexico, Ann Nolan Clark (1896–) served for many years as a teacher and writer for the Bureau of Indian Affairs and the U.S. Department of Education in Latin America. Clark has written numerous books about children in various countries, including *The Secret of the Andes,* set in Peru, which won the Newbery Medal in 1952. Clark has said, "All of my books are based upon actual experiences, knowing the people and places I write about, having been there." She lives near Tucson, Arizona.
OTHER WORKS *In My Mother's House, To Stand Against the Wind, Little Navajo Bluebird, Santiago, Tia Maria's Gardens*

The Bamboo Beads

by Lynn Joseph

Illustration Copyright © 1991 Brian Pinkney. Cover from *A Wave in Her Pocket* by Lynn Joseph, reprinted by permission of Clarion Books/Houghton Mifflin Co. All rights reserved.

Last year during the planting season, I helped Mama plant seeds on our hill. "One seed for each of my brothers and sisters," she said, and she covered up seven seeds with dark dirt. Mama's family lives on the other side of the island, so we hardly ever see them.

Each day I watched Mama water the dark mounds of dirt and weed around them. Soon, flowers grew up. They were red as the evening sun. But one day the floods came and swept them to the sea.

"Poor Mama," I said.

"They'll grow again," she replied.

She looked at her gardening gloves hanging on a nail. "If they don't grow back, we'll plant some more." And she smiled.

That night the moon was round and white as my Sunday hat. I told Daddy how Mama's flowers had drowned in the flood rains. He said, "Did I ever show you how *I* count my brothers and sisters?"

"No," I answered.

Then Daddy showed me the fisherman stars. "They point fishermen to the way home," he said. "There are eight of them. I named one each for my brothers and sisters."

"How do you know which is which?" I asked.

Daddy pointed again to the bright stars. "Well, there's Rupert and Hazel, Anthony and Derek, Peter, Janet, and Neil."

"You forgot Auntie Sonia," I said.

Daddy smiled and pointed to a tiny star. "That one's her."

I nodded my head as Daddy moved his finger around, although I couldn't tell which star was who.

After that, Daddy and I looked for the fisherman stars each night. Some nights when the sea breezes blew dark clouds in the sky, we couldn't see them. But Daddy would say, "They'll come back." And he'd smile.

"I wish I had brothers and sisters to plant flowers for or to count stars on," I told Mama and Daddy one day. "I'm tired of having only myself."

"What about all your cousins?" asked Mama.

"You can count them on something," said Daddy.

"What can I count them on?" I wondered.

"Maybe Tantie can help find you something," said Mama. "She's the one who keeps track of all yuh."

So, the next time Tantie came to visit, I said, "Tantie, Mama said you keep track of me and my cousins."

"That's right, chile," said Tantie. "And is plenty of all yuh to keep track of, too."

"I know," I said, "but how you do it? I want something that I can name after each one of my cousins. Something I can count them on. Like Mama has flowers and Daddy has his fisherman stars."

Well, Tantie looked me in the eye for a long time. Then from underneath the neck of her dress she pulled out a brown string full of bright, colorful beads.

"Tantie, where you get those pretty beads from?" I asked.

"These, my dear, is a story by itself, and if you have de time to listen, I'll tell it to you."

I nodded and sat down on the porch swing next to Tantie. As Tantie told her story, I kept trying to push the swing with my foot. But

Tantie was too heavy. The swing sat quiet. The only sound was Tantie's voice.

"A long, long time ago," she began, "when I was in my bare feet still, I went to market with a basket of bread and red-currant buns to sell. Market day was de busiest time. There was plenty to see as I set up my little stall and tucked cloths around de bread and buns so de flies wouldn't get them.

"I hadn't sold one thing yet when an old man came up. His clothes were ragged and he didn't have on no shoes. His feet didn't look like no ordinary feet. They looked like cow hooves. I didn't stare, though, because it rude to do that.

"He asked for a piece of bread. Well, I remember Mama telling me that morning to get good prices for de bread, but I was sure Mama hadn't meant from this man too. So, I cut off a hunk of bread, wrapped it in brown paper, and handed it to him. He looked so hungry that I reached for a bun and gave him that too. De man smiled and bowed his head at me. Then he went his way.

"After that I was busy selling bread. De buns went even faster. By afternoon, I had sold them all. Then I saw de old man coming over again. He didn't look so ragged anymore. His hair was combed and he had on a new shirt.

"'I'm sorry,' I said. 'No more bread left.'

"He didn't answer. Instead he handed me something. It was a piece of brown string. It looked like an ordinary old string, but I didn't tell him that.

"'Thank you for de bread, child,' he said. Then he shuffled off and was gone.

"I looked at de string for a while. I could use it to tie up my bread cloths, I thought. Or I could use it as a hair ribbon. But I decided I would put de string around my neck and wear it like a necklace."

"This de same string, Tantie?" I asked, fingering Tantie's bead necklace.

"De very same," she answered.

"Well, that evening, Mama was so proud I had sold all de bread that she gave me a treat. It was a small blue bamboo bead. It was de exact color of Mama's best blue head scarf.

"'Where you get this bead, Mama?' I asked.

"'Found it in de yard,' she replied.

"I wondered how it got there, but it didn't matter. I pulled out my brown string and untied it. Then I slipped de blue bead on and tied it around my neck again. It looked like a real necklace now that it had Mama's bead on it."

Then I slipped de blue bead on and tied it around my neck again.

"Is this your mama's bead?" I asked, touching a bright blue bead on Tantie's string.

"Yes, that's it, chile," said Tantie.

"And it shines more now than de day I got it.

"Two days later, Daddy found a smooth black bead down by de sea. He brought it home in his pocket.

"'I thought you might like this,' he said, and handed it to me. It sparkled like a black sun. I untied my necklace and slipped it on next to de blue bead. Now my string was beautiful with Mama's and Daddy's bamboo beads on it.

"During de next few days, Mama and Daddy and I kept finding shiny bamboo beads in de strangest places. I found a red one under de bed. Mama found a green one in de garden, and Daddy found a yellow one in his shoe. Mama and Daddy didn't think nothing of it, but as I added each new bead to my necklace, I got a strange, trembly feeling.

"De next week when I took Mama's bread and currant buns to market, I saw de old man who had given me my string. His clothes were still ragged and he clumped around on his hooves.

"'Hello, mister,' I said when he came over. I wrapped up a chunk of bread and two buns this time and gave them to him. He smiled and shuffled off.

"Again my day of selling flew by. Before lunchtime I had sold everything. Mama hugged me hard when I got home. But then she sat down at de kitchen table and looked serious.

"'What's wrong?' I asked.

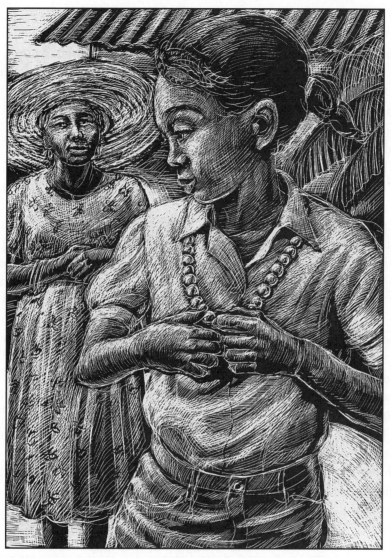

"'Look,' she said, pointing to a bowl on the table. I looked inside and there were de most beautiful, shiny bamboo beads I'd ever seen. Lots and lots of them. I put my hand in and touched de smooth wood.

"'Where they come from?' I asked.

"'Don't know,' said Mama. 'They were here when I turned around from de sink this morning. I thought you might know something about them, since you're collecting beads.'

"'No,' I said. 'I don't know about these.'

"Then Mama said, 'Let me see that string of beads around your neck, girl.'

"I showed it to Mama. She looked and looked at de beads and tugged on de string until I thought she'd break it. Then she looked at me and said, 'You've met Papa Bois.'[1]

"'Papa who?'

"'Papa Bois,' she murmured. 'He lives in de

---

1. **Papa Bois** (pä-pä-bwä′) *French:* Father Forest.

forest and protects de trees and forest animals from hunters. He spends his time whittling bamboo beads from fallen bamboo shoots. He's de only one who could make these beads. They're priceless.'

"Mama looked at me and gave me back de necklace. 'Have you met an old man without any feet?' she asked.

"I immediately thought of de old man from de market. 'Yes, Mama, I met him last week at de market. An old man in ragged clothes and no feet. He had cow hooves instead.'

"Mama closed her eyes and nodded her head. 'That's Papa Bois,' she said. 'He can be dangerous. Once he meets someone, he keeps track of them by counting their sins, their blessings, even their teeth, on his whittled beads. You never know with Papa Bois just what he's counting for you. The last time Papa Bois gave someone beads, the beads represented de number of days he had left to live. These beads on de table must be for you. He's counting something for you.'"

"'What?' I whispered, almost too frightened to speak.

"'We won't know till he's ready to say. Were you kind or mean to him?'

"'I gave him some bread to eat because he looked hungry,' I said.

"'Good,' said Mama, and she pulled me into her arms. 'That was very kind. Now you might as well put de beads on de string and wait until Papa Bois comes back and tells you what he's counting.'

"I put de pretty beads on de string. I didn't think they would all fit, but no matter how many I put on, de string never filled up. When every bead was on, I counted thirty-three beads. Then I tied it around my neck once

more. It wasn't any heavier than when I wore de string empty.

"As de days passed, Mama, Daddy, and I kept our eyes open for Papa Bois. We thought he might come by any time. I wondered over and over what Papa Bois could be counting on my beads."

"Were you scared, Tantie?" I interrupted.

"A little," she answered. "But I knew I had been kind to Papa Bois, and that was all that mattered.

"De next time I went to market for Mama, she wanted to come with me. I told her Papa Bois might not come to our stall if she was there.

"At the stall I laid de bread and buns out nicely and covered them with cloths. I saw de old man shuffling up to my table.

"'Bonjour, vieux Papa,'[2] I said. Mama had told me that to say hello in French was de polite way to greet Papa Bois. She also said not to look at his feet no matter what.

"'Bonjour,' said de old man.

"'Would you like some bread?' I asked. Papa Bois nodded.

"As I cut him a chunk of bread, I said, 'Thank you for de pretty necklace.'

"'It's for you to wear always,' he said. 'Until you find someone who should wear it instead.'

"Papa Bois's eyes looked kind in his wrinkled face. I decided I go ask him what de beads were for.

"'De beads,' he answered, 'are for all de

> "That was de last time I ever see Papa Bois."

---

2. **Bonjour, vieux Papa** (bôn-zhōōr′ vyœ′ pä-pä′) *French:* Hello, old Father.

little children you'll one day have.'

"'Thirty-three children?' I asked.

"'Yes, they'll be yours, but they won't be yours,' he said mysteriously. But then he smiled a big smile.

"'All right,' I said, and I handed him de bread and buns.

"That was de last time I ever see Papa Bois. Mama said he only comes out of his forest when he's lonely for human company. Otherwise his friends are de deer, de squirrels, and de trees. The first person he meets when he leaves his forest early in de morning is de one who counts. If that person stares at his feet or laughs at him—watch out!"

"But Tantie, what happen to de thirty-three children?" I asked.

"You're one of them," she said. "Ever since your oldest cousin Jarise was born, I been de one helping to take care of all yuh. I have thirty grandnieces and nephews now. That mean three more to come. And all yuh are my children, just like Papa Bois said."

Tantie reached up and unhooked her bamboo bead necklace. Then she laid it in my hands.

"Oh," I said, looking at Tantie's necklace again. "I'd like to be de red bead."

Tantie took the necklace out of my hands and put it around my neck. She tied the string. The necklace felt cool and smooth against my skin.

"I wish I had a mirror," I said.

"It looking beautiful," said Tantie. "And it for you now. You can count your cousins on them beads."

"You're giving this to me, Tantie?" I asked, not believing what I had heard.

"Papa Bois said I go find someone who should wear it."

"Thank you," I said. I ran my fingers over the bamboo smoothness of the beads and admired the pretty colors.

"And since you wear Papa Bois's beads, you can start helping me tell these stories," said Tantie. "I been doing de work alone for too long."

Tantie reached over and adjusted the bead string on my neck.

I looked down at the shiny red bead that was me and smiled and smiled. ❖

LYNN JOSEPH

Lynn Joseph recalls: "When I was a little girl in Trinidad, I could not imagine anywhere else but my beautiful island, with its tall coconut trees, sandy beaches, and happy sounds of steel-band music. I've lived in many other places since then, but I've never forgotten the smells, sounds, and foods of my island." Joseph moved to the United States with her

family and graduated from the University of Colorado. She currently lives in New York City. Joseph says she remembers listening to stories like "The Bamboo Beads" when she was growing up.

OTHER WORKS *Coconut Kind of Day: Island Poems, A Wave in Her Pocket, The Mermaid's Twin Sister: More Stories from Trinidad*

Hummingbirds in Thistle (1955), Walter Anderson. Watercolor. Walter Anderson Museum of Art, Ocean Springs, Mississippi, courtesy of the family of Walter Anderson.

The Legend of the Hummingbird

retold by Pura Belpré

etween the towns of Cayey and Cidra,[1] far up in the hills, there was once a small pool fed by a waterfall that tumbled down the side of the mountain. The pool was surrounded by pomarosa trees,[2] and the Indians used to call it Pomarosa Pool. It was the favorite place of Alida, the daughter of an Indian chief, a man of power and wealth among the people of the hills.

---

1. **Cayey** (kä-yä′) . . . **Cidra** (sē′drä): towns in Puerto Rico.
2. **pomarosa** (pô-mä-rô′sä) **trees:** trees, found in the West Indies, that bear an applelike fruit; also spelled *poma rosa*.

One day, when Alida had come to the pool to rest after a long walk, a young Indian came there to pick some fruit from the trees. Alida was surprised, for he was not of her tribe. Yet he said he was no stranger to the pool. This was where he had first seen Alida, and he had often returned since then to pick fruit, hoping to see her again.

And the great god Yukiyú took pity on her and changed her into a delicate red flower.

He told her about himself to make her feel at home. He confessed, with honesty and frankness, that he was a member of the dreaded Carib[3] tribe that had so often attacked the island of Boriquen.[4] As a young boy, he had been left behind after one of those raids, and he had stayed on the island ever since.

Alida listened closely to his story, and the two became friends. They met again in the days that followed, and their friendship grew stronger. Alida admired the young man's courage in living among his enemies. She learned to call him by his Carib name, Taroo, and he called her Alida, just as her own people did. Before long, their friendship had turned into love.

Their meetings by the pool were always brief. Alida was afraid their secret might be discovered, and careful though she was, there came a day when someone saw them and told her father. Alida was forbidden to visit the Pomarosa Pool, and to put an end to her romance with the stranger, her father decided to marry her to a man of his own choosing. Preparations for the wedding started at once.

Alida was torn with grief, and one evening she cried out to her god: "O *Yukiyú*,[5] help me! Kill me or do what you will with me, but do not let me marry this man whom I do not love!"

And the great god Yukiyú took pity on her and changed her into a delicate red flower.

Meanwhile Taroo, knowing nothing of Alida's sorrow, still waited for her by the Pomarosa Pool. Day after day he waited. Sometimes he stayed there until a mantle[6] of stars was spread across the sky.

One night the moon took pity on him. "Taroo," she called from her place high above the stars. "O Taroo, wait no longer for Alida! Your secret was made known, and Alida was to be married to a man of her father's choosing. In her grief she called to her god, Yukiyú; he heard her plea for help and changed her into a red flower."

"Ahee, ahee!" cried Taroo. "O moon, what is the name of the red flower?"

"Only Yukiyú knows that," the moon replied.

---

3. **Carib** (kăr′ĭb): a Native American people of the West Indies.

4. **Boriquen** (bô-rē′kĕn): an early name for Puerto Rico.

5. *Yukiyú* (yōō-kē-yōō′).

6. **mantle:** covering.

Then Taroo called out: "O Yukiyú, god of my Alida, help me too! Help me to find her!"

And just as the great god had heard Alida's plea, he listened now to Taroo and decided to help him. There by the Pomarosa Pool, before the moon and the silent stars, the great god changed Taroo into a small many-colored bird.

"Fly, *Colibrí,*[7] and find your love among the flowers," he said.

Off went the Colibrí, flying swiftly, and as he flew, his wings made a sweet humming sound.

In the morning the Indians saw a new bird darting about among the flowers, swift as an arrow and brilliant as a jewel. They heard the humming of its wings, and in amazement they saw it <u>hover</u> in the air over every blossom, kissing the petals of the flowers with its long slender bill. They liked the new bird with the music in its wings, and they called it Hummingbird.

Ever since then the little many-colored bird has hovered over every flower he finds, but returns most often to the flowers that are red. He is still looking, always looking, for the one red flower that will be his lost Alida. He has not found her yet. ❖

---

7. *Colibrí* (kô-lē-brē′).

PURA BELPRÉ

1899–1982

Pura Belpré, author and puppeteer-storyteller, was born in Puerto Rico and came to the United States in the 1920s. Working, beginning in 1921, as the first Hispanic librarian in the New York Public Library, she realized there was no folklore from Puerto Rico and set about expanding Puerto Rican folklore programs. Belpré grew up in a family of storytellers and was fluent in Spanish, English, and French. She incorporated her Spanish ancestry into her puppet shows as well as her books and thus provided young people a way of learning more about the Puerto Rican culture. In 1978 Belpré was honored for her distinguished contribution in Spanish literature by the Bay Area Bilingual Education League and the University of San Francisco.

OTHER WORKS *Juan Bobo and the Queen's Necklace: A Puerto Rican Folk Tale, Dance of the Animals: A Puerto Rican Folk Tale, Once in Puerto Rico*

RESPONDING OPTIONS

LITERATURE CONNECTION PROJECT 1

Dramatize a Tale Working in a small group, dramatize one of the tales you've just read. First, organize the plot elements of your adaptation by designing and preparing a storyboard, a series of drawings to illustrate the tale's events. An example of a storyboard for "Why Monkeys Live in Trees" is shown here. Include props, sound effects, and costumes. Next, write a script for a narrator and dialogue for the characters. Then assign roles, rehearse, and perform your

adaptation. If equipment is available, you can videotape the performance and share it with another class or a group of parents.

This storyboard shows how the action of a tale unfolds.

SOCIAL STUDIES CONNECTION PROJECT 2

 Create a Museum Display In the 1800s, hummingbirds became important in the trade between Europe and tropical America. In one year alone, a single London dealer imported more than 400,000 hummingbird skins from the West Indies.

Hummingbirds are a familiar feature in legends of Native American cultures. For example, the Aztec war god wears a bracelet of hummingbird feathers, and Puerto Rican natives believe that hummingbird nests cure asthma. With a small group of classmates, explore the role of the hummingbird in the Aztec and Puerto Rican cultures and set up a display on this topic in your classroom. Here are some ideas to pursue:

Writers Use encyclopedias, computer databases, and other reference materials to gather information. Then choose a format, such as an informative brochure or a poster, to include in the display.

Artists Hopi hummingbird kachinas, or spirit dolls, often feature sharp beaks and colored feathers. Use colored pencils or a drawing software program to design a hummingbird kachina. Then work in a group to build a kachina for the display.

Curators Prepare the exhibit space in which to display your group's materials. Write informative cards for the exhibit and act as a museum guide for visitors.

SCIENCE CONNECTION PROJECT 3

Investigate Bamboo The beads that Papa Bois gave Tantie were whittled from bamboo, a type of huge woody grass that grows in the Eastern and Western Hemispheres. There are about 200 kinds of bamboo, and the plants are used for many purposes. Research the bamboo plant and its uses in Trinidadian and other cultures. Then, as a class, combine your research on a large chart similar to the one shown. Add drawings or pictures to the chart to illustrate some of the products derived from bamboo.

Uses of Bamboo		
Country	**Products**	**Other Uses**

ACROSS CULTURES MINI-PROJECTS

Compare Cinderella Tales Compare "In the Land of Small Dragon" with similar Cinderella-like tales from other cultures, such as China and Germany. Get together with other classmates and take turns sharing your findings. Then arrange a book display of the various picture-book versions of Cinderella you may have found.

Explore Flight Hummingbirds are unique in their ability to fly upside down and in reverse and to hover, as Taroo does in "The Legend of the Hummingbird." Investigate the laws of aerodynamics (âr′ō-dī-năm′ĭks) that explain this ability. Then draw a diagram to demonstrate those laws.

Make a Kite In Asian folklore, dragons were honored. Images of dragons appeared on common objects, including the dragon kites that remain popular in the culture of Vietnam. Find out how kites are constructed. Learn more about kite celebrations in Asian cultures. Then organize a kite day, during which students can build their own kites and display them to their classmates.

Write Proverbs Proverbs, such as those found in "In the Land of Small Dragon," are old and familiar sayings that express a basic truth. For example, you may recognize "A man's worth is what he does, / Not what he says he can do" as "Actions speak louder than words." Write proverbs for "The Bamboo Beads" and "The Legend of the Hummingbird." Compile the class proverbs on a poster.

MORE ABOUT THE CULTURES

- *The Dorling Kindersley History of the World* by Plantagenet Somerset Fry
- *Exploration and Conquest: The Americas after Columbus* by Betsey and Giulio Maestro
- *The Children's Atlas of Civilizations* by Anthony Mason
- *Street Smart! Cities of the Ancient World* published by Runestone

LINKS TO UNIT THREE

A Sense of Fairness

Who is fairest of us all? What is just and what is unjust? These questions were raised in the selections presented in Unit Three. Many folk tales also have explored these issues. Each of the tales you are about to read illustrates a lesson in justice.

GUATEMALA

The Disobedient Child

retold by Victor Montejo (môn-tĕ´hô)

Guatemala is one of the seven countries that form Central America, the narrow land bridge that connects North and South America. One of the first civilizations in the Americas, the Mayan Empire, thrived in Central America from about A.D. 250 to 900. Ancient Mayan culture is reflected in this Guatemalan fable about a boy who disregards warnings. The boy seems unteachable until he is put to the test by someone with super-natural powers.

Damon and Pythias: A Drama

retold by Fan Kissen

According to legend, Damon and Pythias lived in the city of Syracuse, on the island of Sicily, in the fourth century B.C. In ancient times, Sicily was a part of the Greek world. Syracuse, one of the most powerful cities in the ancient world, was ruled at that time by a tyrant named Dionysius. Only Damon and Pythias dared to question the king's laws—and lived to talk about it.

The Three Wishes

retold by Ricardo E. Alegría
(ä-lĕ-grē′ä)

The island of Puerto Rico—which means "rich port" in Spanish—was named by its Spanish settlers for the abundance of treasures from the fields and forests that were loaded on ships bound for Spain. This Puerto Rican tale takes place in the forest of a distant past. Like many folk tales that involve the granting of wishes, the story illustrates what is most important in life and what brings the greatest happiness.

AS YOU READ . . .

Consider the way humor is used.

Find out which elements of magic and the supernatural are feared or accepted.

Discover what human faults are seen as common to everyone.

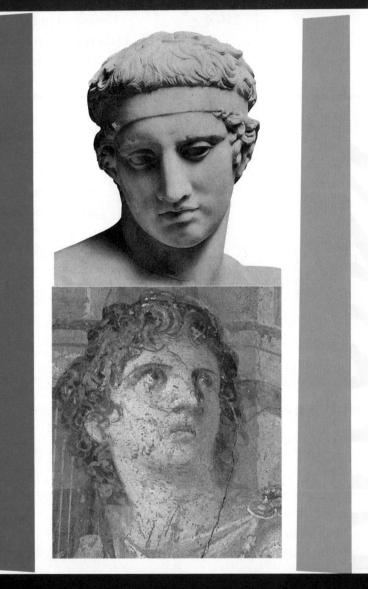

Top: Detail of statue of Diadoumenos (440 B.C.), unknown artist. Roman copy of Greek original, pentelic marble, The Metropolitan Museum of Art, Fletcher Fund, 1925 (25.78.56). Copyright © The Metropolitan Museum of Art. Bottom: Detail of Chiron the centaur teaching Achilles to play the lyre (first to third century A.D.), Roman fresco from Pompeii, Museo Archeologico Nazionale, Naples, Italy. Photo Copyright © Erich Lessing/Art Resource, New York.

CAST OF CHARACTERS

Damon	Mother
Pythias	Narrator
King	First Voice
Soldier	Second Voice
First Robber	Third Voice
Second Robber	

DAMON AND PYTHIAS: A DRAMA

RETOLD BY

FAN KISSEN

(*Sound: Iron door opens and shuts. Key in lock.*)

(*Music: Up full and out.*)

Narrator. Long, long ago there lived on the island of Sicily[1] two young men named Damon and Pythias.[2] They were known far and wide for the strong friendship each had for the other. Their names have come down to our own times to mean true friendship. You may hear it said of two persons:

First Voice. Those two? Why, they're like Damon and Pythias!

Narrator. The king of that country was a cruel tyrant. He made cruel laws, and he showed no mercy toward anyone who broke his laws. Now, you might very well wonder:

Second Voice. Why didn't the people rebel?

Narrator. Well, the people didn't dare rebel because they feared the king's great and powerful army. No one dared say a word against the king or his laws—except Damon and Pythias. One day a soldier overheard Pythias speaking against a new law the king had proclaimed.

Soldier. Ho, there! Who are you that dares to speak so about our king?

Pythias (*unafraid*). I am called Pythias.

Soldier. Don't you know it is a crime to speak against the king or his laws? You are under

---

1. **Sicily** (sĭs′ə-lē): large island off the southern tip of Italy.
2. **Damon** (dā′mən) . . . **Pythias** (pĭth′ē-əs).

arrest! Come and tell this opinion of yours to the king's face!

(*Music: A few short bars in and out.*)

Narrator. When Pythias was brought before the king, he showed no fear. He stood straight and quiet before the throne.

King (*hard, cruel*). So, Pythias! They tell me you do not approve of the laws I make.

Pythias. I am not alone, Your Majesty, in thinking your laws are cruel. But you rule the people with such an iron hand that they dare not complain.

King (*angry*). But you have the daring to complain for them! Have they appointed you their champion?[3]

Pythias. No, Your Majesty. I speak for myself alone. I have no wish to make trouble for anyone. But I am not afraid to tell you that the people are suffering under your rule. They want to have a voice in making the laws for themselves. You do not allow them to speak up for themselves.

King. In other words, you are calling me a tyrant! Well, you shall learn for yourself how a tyrant treats a rebel! Soldier! Throw this man into prison!

Soldier. At once, Your Majesty! Don't try to resist, Pythias!

Pythias. I know better than to try to resist a soldier of the king! And for how long am I to remain in prison, Your Majesty, merely for speaking out for the people?

King (*cruel*). Not for very long, Pythias. Two weeks from today, at noon, you shall be put to death in the public square as an example to anyone else who may dare to question my laws or acts. Off to prison with him, soldier!

(*Music: In briefly and out.*)

Narrator. When Damon heard that his friend Pythias had been thrown into prison and the severe punishment that was to follow, he was heartbroken. He rushed to the prison and persuaded the guard to let him speak to his friend.

Damon. Oh, Pythias! How terrible to find you here! I wish I could do something to save you!

Pythias. Nothing can save me, Damon, my dear friend. I am prepared to die. But there is one thought that troubles me greatly.

Damon. What is it? I will do anything to help you.

Pythias. I'm worried about what will happen to my mother and my sister when I'm gone.

Damon. I'll take care of them, Pythias, as if they were my own mother and sister.

Pythias. Thank you, Damon. I have money to leave them. But there are other things I must arrange. If only I could go to see them before I die! But they live two days' journey from here, you know.

Damon. I'll go to the king and beg him to give you your freedom for a few days. You'll give your word to return at the end of that time. Everyone in Sicily knows you for a man who has never broken his word.

Pythias. Do you believe for one moment that the king would let me leave this prison, no matter how good my word may have been all my life?

Damon. I'll tell him that I shall take your place in this prison cell. I'll tell him that if you do

---

3. **champion:** one who fights to help or defend a person or group.

not return by the appointed day, he may kill me in your place!

Pythias. No, no, Damon! You must not do such a foolish thing! I cannot—I will not—let you do this! Damon! Damon! Don't go! (*to himself*) Damon, my friend! You may find yourself in a cell beside me!

(*Music: In briefly and out.*)

Damon (*begging*). Your Majesty! I beg of you! Let Pythias go home for a few days to bid farewell to his mother and sister. He gives his word that he will return at your appointed time. Everyone knows that his word can be trusted.

King. In ordinary business affairs—perhaps. But he is now a man under sentence of death. To free him even for a few days would strain his honesty—any man's honesty—too far. Pythias would never return here! I consider him a traitor, but I'm certain he's no fool.

Damon. Your Majesty! I will take his place in the prison until he comes back. If he does not return, then you may take my life in his place.

King (*astonished*). What did you say, Damon?

Damon. I'm so certain of Pythias that I am offering to die in his place if he fails to return on time.

King. I can't believe you mean it!

Damon. I do mean it, Your Majesty.

King. You make me very curious, Damon, so curious that I'm willing to put you and Pythias to the test. This exchange of prisoners will be made. But Pythias must be back two weeks from today, at noon.

Damon. Thank you, Your Majesty!

King. The order with my official seal[4] shall go by your own hand, Damon. But I warn you, if your friend does not return on time, you shall surely die in his place! I shall show no mercy!

(*Music: In briefly and out.*)

Narrator. Pythias did not like the king's bargain with Damon. He did not like to leave his friend in prison with the chance that he might lose his life if something went wrong. But at last Damon persuaded him to leave, and Pythias set out for his home. More than a week went by. The day set for the death sentence drew near. Pythias did not return. Everyone in the city knew of the condition on which the king had permitted Pythias to go home. Everywhere people met, the talk was sure to turn to the two friends.

First Voice. Do you suppose Pythias will come back?

Second Voice. Why should he stick his head under the king's axe once he's escaped?

Third Voice. Still, would an honorable man like Pythias let such a good friend die for him?

First Voice. There's no telling what a man will do when it's a question of his own life against another's.

Second Voice. But if Pythias doesn't come back before the time is up, he will be killing his friend.

Third Voice. Well, there's still a few days' time. I, for one, am certain that Pythias will return in time.

Second Voice. And I am just as certain that he will not. Friendship is friendship, but a man's own life is something stronger, I say!

Narrator. Two days before the time was up, the king himself visited Damon in his prison cell.

---

4. **official seal:** mark or stamp that shows that the order came from the king.

Detail of Procession of the court of Emperor Augustus (about 13–9 B.C.), unknown Roman artist. Museum of the Ara Pacis, Rome, Nimatallah/Art Resource, New York.

(*Sound: Iron door unlocked and opened.*)

King (*mocking*). You see now, Damon, that you were a fool to make this bargain. Your friend has tricked you! He will not come back here to be killed! He has deserted you!

Damon (*calm and firm*). I have faith in my friend. I know he will return.

King (*mocking*). We shall see!

(*Sound: Iron door shut and locked.*)

Narrator. Meanwhile, when Pythias reached the home of his family, he arranged his business affairs so that his mother and sister would be able to live comfortably for the rest of their years. Then he said a last farewell to them before starting back to the city.

Mother (*in tears*). Pythias, it will take you only two days to get back. Stay another day, I beg you!

Pythias. I dare not stay longer, Mother. Remember, Damon is locked up in my prison cell while I'm gone. Please don't make it harder for me! Farewell! Don't weep for me. My death may help to bring better days for all our people.

Narrator. So Pythias began his return journey in plenty of time. But bad luck struck him on the very first day. At twilight, as he walked along a lonely stretch of woodland, a rough voice called:

First Robber. Not so fast there, young man! Stop!

Pythias (*startled*). Oh! What is it? What do you want?

Second Robber. Your money bags.

Pythias. My money bags? I have only this small bag of coins. I shall need them for some last favors, perhaps, before I die.

First Robber. What do you mean, before you die? We don't mean to kill you, only to take your money.

Pythias. I'll give you my money, only don't delay me any longer. I am to die by the king's order three days from now. If I don't return to prison on time, my friend must die in my place.

First Robber. A likely story! What man would be fool enough to go back to prison ready to die?

Second Robber. And what man would be fool enough to die for you?

First Robber. We'll take your money, all right. And we'll tie you up while we get away.

Pythias (*begging*). No! No! I must get back to free my friend! (*fade*) I must go back!

Narrator. But the two robbers took Pythias' money, tied him to a tree, and went off as fast as they could. Pythias struggled to free himself. He cried out for help as loud as he could for a long time. But no one traveled through that lonesome woodland after dark. The sun had been up for many hours before he finally managed to free himself from the ropes that had tied him to the tree. He lay on the ground, hardly able to breathe.

(*Music: In briefly and out.*)

Narrator. After a while Pythias got to his feet. Weak and dizzy from hunger and thirst and his struggle to free himself, he set off again. Day and night he traveled without stopping, desperately trying to reach the city in time to save Damon's life.

(*Music: Up and out.*)

Narrator. On the last day, half an hour before noon, Damon's hands were tied behind his back, and he was taken into the public square. The people muttered angrily as Damon was led in by the jailer. Then the king entered and seated himself on a high platform.

(*Sound: Crowd voices in and hold under single voices.*)

Soldier (*loud*). Long live the king!

First Voice (*low*). The longer he lives, the more miserable our lives will be!

King (*loud, mocking*). Well, Damon, your lifetime is nearly up. Where is your good friend Pythias now?

Damon (*firm*). I have faith in my friend. If he has not returned, I'm certain it is through no fault of his own.

King (*mocking*). The sun is almost overhead. The shadow is almost at the noon mark. And still your friend has not returned to give you back your life!

Damon (*quiet*). I am ready, and happy, to die in his place.

King (*harsh*). And you shall, Damon! Jailer, lead the prisoner to the—

(*Sound: Crowd voices up to a roar, then under.*)

First Voice (*over noise*). Look! It's Pythias!

Second Voice (*over noise*). Pythias has come back!

Pythias (*breathless*). Let me through! Damon!

Damon. Pythias!

Pythias. Thank the gods I'm not too late!

Damon (*quiet, sincere*). I would have died for you gladly, my friend.

Crowd Voices (*loud, demanding*). Set them free! Set them both free!

King (*loud*). People of the city! (*crowd voices out*) Never in all my life have I seen such faith and friendship, such loyalty between men. There are many among you who call me harsh and cruel. But I cannot kill any man who proves such strong and true friendship for another. Damon and Pythias, I set you both free. (*roar of approval from crowd*) I am king. I command a great army. I have stores of gold and precious jewels. But I would give all my money and my power for one friend like Damon or Pythias!

(*Sound: Roar of approval from crowd up briefly and out.*)

(*Music: Up and out.*)

FAN KISSEN

For 17 years, Fan Kissen (1901–1989?) was a radio scriptwriter. In her radio series, *Tales from the Four Winds,* she dramatized world folk tales and legends. Her plays, which are written as radio scripts, always include instructions for music and sound effects. Kissen also has taught elementary school in her hometown of New York City. In addition to writing plays, she writes biographies for young people.

OTHER WORKS *The Crowded House and Other Tales, They Helped Make America, The Straw Ox and Other Plays, The Bag of Fire and Other Plays*

THE THREE WISHES

retold by Ricardo E. Alegría

Many years ago, in the days when the saints walked on earth, there lived a woodsman and his wife. They were very poor but very happy in their little house in the forest. Poor as they were, they were always ready to share what little they had with anyone who came to their door. They loved each other very much and were quite content with their life together. Each evening, before eating, they gave thanks to God for their happiness.

One day, while the husband was working far off in the woods, an old man came to the little house and said that he had lost his way in the forest and had eaten nothing for many days. The woodsman's wife had little to eat herself, but, as was her custom, she gave a large portion of it to the old man. After he had eaten everything she gave him, he told the woman that he had been sent by God to test her and that, as a reward for the kindness she and her husband showed to all who came to their house, they would be granted a special grace.[1] This pleased the woman, and she asked what the special grace was.

The old man answered, "Beginning immediately, any three wishes you or your husband may wish will come true."

When she heard these words, the woman was overjoyed and exclaimed, "Oh, if my husband were only here to hear what you say!"

The last word had scarcely left her lips

HE HAD NO SOONER SAID THE WORDS THAN HIS WIFE'S EARS BEGAN TO GROW.

when the woodsman appeared in the little house with the ax still in his hands. The first wish had come true.

The woodsman couldn't understand it at all. How did it happen that he, who had been cutting wood in the forest, found himself here in his house? His wife explained it all as she embraced him. The woodsman just stood there, thinking over what his wife had said. He looked at the old man who stood quietly, too, saying nothing.

Suddenly he realized that his wife, without stopping to think, had used one of the three wishes, and he became very annoyed when he remembered all of the useful things she might have asked for with the first wish. For the first time, he became angry with his wife. The desire for riches had turned his head, and he scolded his wife, shouting at her, among other things, "It doesn't seem possible that you could be so stupid! You've wasted one of our wishes, and now we have only two left! May you grow ears of a donkey!"

He had no sooner said the words than his wife's ears began to grow, and they continued to grow until they changed into the pointed, furry ears of a donkey.

When the woman put her hand up and felt them, she knew what had happened and began to cry. Her husband was very ashamed and

---

1. **special grace:** gift from God.

sorry, indeed, for what he had done in his temper, and he went to his wife to comfort her.

The old man, who had stood by silently, now came to them and said, "Until now, you have known happiness together and have never quarreled with each other. Nevertheless, the mere knowledge that you could have riches and power has changed you both. Remember, you have only one wish left. What do you want? Riches? Beautiful clothes? Servants? Power?"

The woodsman tightened his arm about his wife, looked at the old man, and said, "We want only the happiness and joy we knew before my wife grew donkey's ears."

No sooner had he said these words than the donkey ears disappeared. The woodsman and his wife fell upon their knees to ask God's forgiveness for having acted, if only for a moment, out of covetousness[2] and greed. Then they gave thanks for all the happiness God had given them.

The old man left, but before going, he told them that they had undergone this test in order to learn that there can be happiness in poverty just as there can be unhappiness in riches. As a reward for their <u>repentance</u>, the old man said that he would bestow upon them the greatest happiness a married couple can know. Months later, a son was born to them. The family lived happily all the rest of their lives. ❖

---

2. **covetousness** (kŭv′ĭ-təs-nəs): a greedy desire for wealth or possessions, especially for something that another person has.

RICARDO E. ALEGRÍA

Ricardo E. Alegría lives and writes in the city in which he was born—San Juan, Puerto Rico. "The Three Wishes" is taken from Alegría's collection of Puerto Rican folk tales, which is also called *The Three Wishes*. His works are written in Spanish; this story was translated by Elizabeth Culbert. Alegría also is the author of several books and numerous

1921–

articles on folklore, history, and archaeology. He has taught history at the University of Puerto Rico, and he has served as the director of the Institute of Puerto Rican Culture.

OTHER WORKS *History of the Indians of Puerto Rico*

693

Effigy vessel (about A.D. 1000–1250), unknown Mayan artist.
Ceramic, painted red, blue, and white, 31.7 cm in height,
Museo Nacional de Antropología, Mexico. Photo Copyright © Stuart Rome.

THE DISOBEDIENT CHILD

RETOLD BY VICTOR MONTEJO

In old times in *Xaqla'* Jacaltenango[1] there was a very disobedient child who often disappointed his parents. No matter how hard they tried to teach him, he never changed.

One afternoon the boy ran away from home, looking for someone who would <u>tolerate</u> his mischief. Walking through the woods he discovered a lonely little house and ran up to it. On the porch of the straw-covered house sat an old man, smoking peacefully. The boy stood before him without saying hello or any other word of greeting.

When the old man noticed the boy's presence, he stopped smoking and asked him, "Where do you want to go, boy?"

"I am looking for someone who can give me something to eat," the boy answered.

The wise old man, who already knew the boy's story, said, "No one will love you if you continue being so bad."

The boy did not respond except to laugh.

---

1. *Xaqla'* **Jacaltenango** (chäk-lä' häk´äl-tĕ-nän´gô): town in the mountains of Guatemala.

WORDS
TO
KNOW
tolerate (tŏl′ə-rāt′) *v.* to put up with

Then the old man smiled and said, "You can stay with me. We will eat together."

The boy accepted his offer and stayed in the old man's house. On the following day before going to work, the old man told the boy: "You should stay in the house, and the only duty you will have is to put the beans to cook during the afternoon. But listen well. You should only throw thirteen beans in the pot and no more. Do you understand?"

The boy nodded that he understood the directions very well. Later, when the time arrived to cook the beans, the boy put the clay pot on the fire and threw in thirteen beans as he had been directed. But once he had done that, he began to think that thirteen beans weren't very many for such a big pot. So, disobeying his orders, he threw in several more little fistfuls.

When the beans began to boil over the fire, the pot started to fill up, and it filled up until it overflowed. Very surprised, the boy quickly took an empty pot and divided the beans between the two pots. But the beans overflowed the new pot, too. Beans were pouring out of both pots.

When the old man returned home, he found piles of beans, and the two clay pots lay broken on the floor.

"Why did you disobey my orders and cook more than I told you to?" the old man asked angrily.

The boy hung his head and said nothing. The old man then gave him instructions for the next day. "Tomorrow you will again cook the beans as I have told you. What's more, I forbid you to open that little door over there. Do you understand?"

The boy indicated that he understood very well.

The next day the old man left the house after warning the boy to take care to do exactly what he had been told. During the afternoon the boy put the beans on the fire to cook. Then he was filled with curiosity. What was behind the little door he had been forbidden to open?

Without any fear, the boy opened the door and discovered in the room three enormous covered water jars. Then he found three capes inside a large trunk. There was one green cape, one yellow cape and one red cape. Not satisfied with these discoveries, the boy took the top off the first water jar to see what it contained.

Immediately the water jar began to <u>emit</u> great clouds that quickly hid the sky. Frightened and shivering with cold, the boy opened the trunk and put on the red cape. At that instant a clap of thunder exploded in the house. The boy was turned into thunder and lifted to the sky, where he unleashed a great storm.

When the old man heard the thunder, he guessed that something extraordinary had happened at home, and he hurried in that direction. There he discovered that the forbidden door was open and the top was

IMMEDIATELY THE WATER JAR BEGAN TO EMIT GREAT CLOUDS THAT QUICKLY HID THE SKY.

WORDS TO KNOW   **emit** (ĭ-mĭt´) v. to send out; give forth off the jar of clouds, from which churning mists still rose toward the sky. The old man covered the jar and then approached the trunk with the capes. The red cape, the cape of storms, was missing. Quickly the old man put on the green cape and regained control over the sky, calming the great storm. Little by little the storm <u>subsided</u>, and soon the man returned to the house, carrying the unconscious boy in his arms.

A little while later the old man uncapped the same jar, and the clouds which had blackened the sky returned to their resting place, leaving the heavens bright and blue again. When he had done this, the old man capped the jar again and put away the red and green capes.

Through all of this the boy remained stunned and soaked with the rains until the kind old man restored his spirit and brought him back to normal. When the boy was alert again and his fear had left, the old man said, "Your disobedience has almost killed you. You were lucky that I heard the storm and came to help. Otherwise you would have been lost forever among the clouds."

The boy was quiet and the old man continued.

"I am Qich Mam,[2] the first father of all people and founder of *Xaqla',* he who controls the rain, and waters the community's fields when they are dry. Understand, then, that I wish you no harm and I forgive what you have done. Promise me that in the future you will not disobey your parents."

The boy smiled happily and answered, "I promise, Qich Mam, I promise." Qich Mam patted him gently and said, "Then return to your home and be useful to your parents and to your people."

From that time on the boy behaved differently. He was very grateful for the kindness of the old man who held the secret of the clouds, the rains, the wind and the storms in his hands. ❖

---

2. **Qich Mam** (kēch′ mäm′): a thunder spirit of the Mayan people.

VICTOR MONTEJO

Victor Montejo was born and raised in Guatemala and later taught primary school in Jacaltenango, the setting of "The Disobedient Child." Unfortunately, because of the political climate in Guatemala, Montejo was forced to flee to the United States in 1982. Since then, he has published a number of stories, fables, and poems and has worked as a

1952–

writer-in-residence at Bucknell University in Pennsylvania. He has also done doctoral work in anthropology at the University of Connecticut. "The Disobedient Child" is from Montejo's book *The Bird Who Cleans the World.*
OTHER WORKS *Testimony: Death of a Guatemalan Village*

RESPONDING
OPTIONS

Create a Picture Book Working with a few classmates, make a picture-book version of one of the stories you've read in this part of the unit to share with a class of younger students. In determining which story to choose, consider the age level of your audience. Then think about these possibilities:

Illustrations Select characters and settings that retell the story. Then use simple drawings, photographs, or pictures from magazines, and present events in chronological order. "Clip art" from a computer program may provide ideas.

Pop-up Choose a character or an event and create a pop-up feature by following the steps shown here. For example, a pop-up feature for "Wings" might show Icarus rising toward the clouds.

Book jacket Design a colorful cover for your book that will make younger readers want to open it.

Share the book with a primary class or with a group of children during a story hour in the library.

Explore Pottery Making Of the cultures represented in these three stories, the ancient Greeks were the first to elevate the making of pottery, one of the oldest human crafts, to an art form. On Crete, the Minoans began using a hand-turned wheel around 2500 B.C. The pottery of the ancient cultures that existed in what is now Puerto Rico and Guatemala reflects the influences of the Arawak, Carib, and Mayan civilizations. The basic steps used in making pottery are almost the same today as they were hundreds of years ago; only the tools have changed.

Explore ancient methods of making pottery, and compare how different cultures practiced the art. Begin by organizing your information in a chart similar to the one shown. Then, for each culture you study, use the information to create illustrations that could be used to make a slide show on pottery as an art form in ancient cultures.

Culture	Date	Materials	Designs

SOCIAL STUDIES CONNECTION PROJECT 3

Construct a Stage The roots of modern drama can be traced to ancient Greece. As early as the fifth century B.C., citizens of Athens gathered at religious festivals in the *agora,* or marketplace, to watch performances of stories about Greek gods or heroes. These early dramas combined religion and history with entertainment.

Create a diorama of a scene from *Damon and Pythias* or another Greek myth. Refer to an encyclopedia or to books about Greece for information on ancient Greek amphitheaters. Some, like the Theater of Epidaurus in Argolis, are still in use today. Use a simple box to create a stage against a painted background, or construct a more elaborate model of an amphitheater. Be sure to include masked figures to represent the actors.

Display your diorama in the classroom.

ACROSS CULTURES MINI-PROJECTS

Make Your Own Hieroglyphics Ancient Mayans used hieroglyphics (hī′ər-ə-glĭf′ĭks), a system of writing in which pictures are used to represent meaning or sounds. Research Mayan hieroglyphics, and then make your own copies of the Mayan symbols, using potato or clay prints or some other method. Compare Mayan hieroglyphics with those of ancient Egypt. See if you can communicate with a classmate by using only hieroglyphics.

Compare Tales In "The Three Wishes," a woodsman and his wife are allowed three wishes. What other stories can you recall in which characters are granted wishes? In a small-group discussion, compare and contrast those stories with this Puerto Rican tale. Then present some of the stories to the class.

Map Hurricanes The Caribbean lands of Guatemala and Puerto Rico are subject to hurricanes, tropical storms that are more devastating than the one unleashed by the boy in "The Disobedient Child." The word *hurricane*

comes from the name of the Carib god of evil, Juracán. Find out more about the hurricanes that affect these countries, and use a map to chart the typical formation and movement of hurricanes in that region.

Build a Fresco The rooms in Minoan palaces were decorated with colorful frescoes, pictures painted on damp plaster walls. Explore the frescoes of the ancient Greeks, and draw samples to share.

MORE ABOUT THE CULTURES

- *Fired Up! Making Pottery in Ancient Times* by Rivka Gonen
- *The Hispanic Americans* by Milton Meltzer
- *Ancient Greece* by Robert Nicholson
- *Discovering Our Past* by Peter Seymour

WRITING ABOUT LITERATURE

A LESSON LEARNED

What did you learn from "In the Land of Small Dragon"? What is the moral of "The Three Wishes"? There are many lessons to be learned from folk tales, but not all of the lessons carry the same importance. Each of us must evaluate the lessons we learn and decide which are valuable. On the next few pages, you will

- see how writers and storytellers vary their sentences to hold their readers' interest
- evaluate the lesson in a folk tale
- see how lessons are taught and judged in the real world

The Writer's Style: Sentence Composing Experienced writers vary the way their sentences are arranged. You can add variety to your writing by changing the order of subjects, verbs, and other sentence parts.

Read the Literature

Study the sentences in the following passages and note how the writers added variety.

Literature Models

Variety in Sentence Beginnings
What have the authors done to add interest to the sentence "Tâm . . . dug up the buried clay pot"?

> When the moon was full again,
> Tâm, so lonely for her fish,
> Dug up the buried clay pot.
> Tâm found, instead of fish bones,
> A silken dress and two jeweled *hai*.
>
> Dang Manh Kha and Ann Nolan Clark
> from "In the Land of Small Dragon"

Subject-Verb Splits
What information is given between the subject and the verb in the first sentence?

> Meanwhile Taroo, knowing nothing of Alida's sorrow, still waited for her by the Pomarosa Pool. Day after day he waited.
>
> Pura Belpré
> from "The Legend of the Hummingbird"

Connect to Life

Writers of nonfiction books must take special care not to let their writing become boring. Notice how the writer arranges the sentences in the passage shown below.

Nonfiction Book

N*uoc mam,* a brown sauce made from fermented fish, is the trademark of Vietnamese cooking. It is the main ingredient in *nuoc cham,* a dressing and table sauce that the Vietnamese eat with all foods, probably more often than you use ketchup!

Phyllis Shalant
from *Look What We've Brought You from Vietnam*

Variety in Sentence Endings
Notice the definition that the writer has given between the subject and the verb in the first sentence. What interesting note has she included at the end of this passage?

Try Your Hand: Sentence Composing

1. **Unscrambling Sentences** How many ways can you write a complete sentence from each set of scrambled sentence parts?
Example: *grew big and trustful / the little fish / loved by T'âm*

   The little fish, loved by T'âm, grew big and trustful.
   Loved by T'âm, the little fish grew big and trustful.

   - mistreated T'âm / Cám / the youngest sister
   - The emperor's son / found the jeweled *hai* / a young Prince

2. **Adding Interest** Add information to each sentence by adding an interesting beginning.
Example: (*Meeting by the pool every day,*) *Alida and Taroo became good friends.*

   - . . . his wings made a swift humming sound.
   - . . . he waited by the Pomarosa Pool.
   - . . . he is always looking for red flowers.

3. **Revising Your Writing** Look at some of the other writing you've done so far. Choose a piece that you think needs greater sentence variety. Revise the piece, using what you've learned.

SkillBuilder

 GRAMMAR FROM WRITING

Understanding Pronouns and Their Antecedents
In careful sentence composing, sometimes you combine sentences. This means you may have to replace nouns with pronouns. An **antecedent** is the word or words a pronoun stands for. Use a singular pronoun when the antecedent is singular. Use a plural pronoun when the antecedent is plural. Notice the pronouns the authors of "In the Land of Small Dragon" use in this passage:

*Pretty girls stood in a line
With their mothers
    standing near;
One by one they tried to fit
A foot into a small,
    jeweled hai.*

APPLYING WHAT YOU'VE LEARNED
Rewrite this paragraph, using pronouns in place of the words in boldface type.

*I loved this story because **this story** was like "Cinderella." T'âm was the main character. T'âm lived with a stepmother and half sister. **T'âm's stepmother and half sister** made T'âm's life miserable.*

 GRAMMAR HANDBOOK

For more information on pronouns and their antecedents, see page 826 of the Grammar Handbook.

Criticism

Long ago, people discovered that a story could be a powerful way to teach a lesson. Some stories have lessons that are timeless. Other stories, however, have lost their power over the years. What kinds of lessons do you think are timeless and valuable?

GUIDED ASSIGNMENT

Evaluate the Lesson of a Story In this assignment, you will revisit a folk tale from Unit Six. Then you will write a critical review of the literature, explaining whether you agree or disagree with the moral of the tale.

Student's Prewriting Chart

"In the Land of Small Dragon"	
lesson or moral "Beauty is not painted on./It is the spirit showing."	*my thoughts* I think this is true. It's like "beauty is only skin deep."
"An evil heart keeps records / On the face of its owner."	At first I thought this meant that evil people are ugly. But that's too simple. Maybe evil people get caught because they give themselves away.
"A man's worth is what he does,/Not what he says he can do."	This is very important. This is like the old saying "actions speak louder than words."
"Real beauty mirrors goodness / What is one is the other." ←	This seems like the most important idea in the tale to me!

① Prewrite and Explore

Think about the stories you read in Unit Six. If you need help remembering, discuss them with classmates. Jot down comments about the ideas the writers present or any questions you have. Then consider the following questions to help you pick a story to write about.

- Which stories do you have strong feelings about, either positive or negative? Why?
- Was there a moral or lesson taught in one of the stories that you agree with or disagree with or are confused about?

FOCUS ON THE LESSON

Based on your answers to the questions above, choose a story to concentrate on. What is the message of this story? A chart like the one on the left can help you think through your notes and figure out what the lesson is.

② Freewrite to Answer Questions

In some stories, the lesson or moral is not clear. Sometimes a story may have more than one lesson. If this is true of the story you've chosen, try freewriting about your thoughts.

Student's Freewrite

> I think there are a couple of lessons in "In the Land of Small Dragon." The story is about beauty and goodness. But what is the most important message? Tẩm is the good daughter and Cám is the bad daughter. Tẩm is beautiful and she also does good things for others. Is "What is beautiful is good" the main lesson? That's not right.

I think I should tell why I don't like this idea. I could use something from my own life.

> I like the part that says "A man's worth is what he does, / Not what he says he can do." I've heard the saying "Actions speak louder than words." That means the same thing. It says in the story that "real beauty mirrors goodness." I think the most important message is that real beauty comes from being nice to others, not from how a person looks.

The last sentence is what I should focus on.

③ Draft and Share

In a review, you must convince readers that you have good reasons for your opinions. Use examples from the story or incidents from personal experience to help support your opinions. Ask yourself these questions as you write your draft:

- What story events support or contradict my opinions?
- How can I organize my review to help my reader understand my opinions better?

 PEER RESPONSE

Ask a partner to read and comment on your review.

- Do you agree or disagree with my ideas? Why?
- What parts of my review convinced you or changed your mind about the value of the lesson?
- Where might story events or details help support my review?

SkillBuilder

🖊 **WRITER'S CRAFT**

Organizing Your Review
A well-organized critical review clearly presents your opinions and allows readers to understand your thinking. As you write your draft, remember that a critical response to literature contains three main parts.

- An introduction gives a brief description of the story. The introduction will help familiarize your reader with the story you are writing about.
- The body contains an in-depth discussion of at least one element of the literature, such as the lesson or moral.
- A conclusion states your opinion about the value of the literature.

APPLYING WHAT YOU'VE LEARNED
Use the guidelines above as you revise your freewriting. Organize your ideas so that you have an introduction, a body, and a conclusion.

 WRITING HANDBOOK

For more information on writing introductions, see page 778 in the Writing Handbook. For information on writing conclusions, see page 786. For information on how to write effective paragraphs, see page 779.

4 Revise and Edit

Now you are ready to revise your draft. Make sure your review contains an introduction, a body, and a conclusion. Consider whether you can find and use additional information to help support your opinions. After you complete your final draft, reflect on what you discovered about yourself or the story from writing a critical review.

Student's Final Draft

Notice that the introduction clearly states the focus of the essay. What is this writer's opinion of the lesson in this tale?

"In the Land of Small Dragon" teaches several lessons, but one valuable lesson stands out. In this Vietnamese version of "Cinderella," a beautiful peasant girl teaches us that looks aren't as important as how somebody acts. Real beauty comes from goodness, not from how a person looks. I agree strongly with this moral. Important qualities, such as kindness and loyalty, can't be seen. You have to get to know people and observe how they act.

What examples and evidence support the writer's opinion?

The lesson of this tale is valuable because everybody knows people like Cám and Tâm. Some people who are good-looking are really mean and nobody likes them. Some people are not considered beautiful, but everybody likes them because they treat people nicely and respect others. In the story, Tâm marries the Prince because she is a kind, good person, not simply because she is beautiful.

Standards for Evaluation

A critical review
- identifies the literature by title and author
- gives a brief summary of the literature
- gives a supported evaluation of an element of the story
- states opinions clearly and provides reasons and evidence from the story for those opinions

Grammar in Context

Compound Subjects and Predicates Writers often add variety to a sentence by using two or more subjects and verbs. Using compound subjects and verbs can help you avoid short, choppy sentences. When a subject has two or more parts, it is called a **compound subject.**

Tấm went fishing. _Cám_ went fishing.

Tấm and Cám went fishing.

When the predicate has two or more parts, it's called a **compound predicate.**

Tấm _put on the_ hai. Tấm _danced in the rice paddy._

Tấm _put on the_ hai and _danced in the rice paddy._

When a compound subject or predicate has three or more parts, use commas to separate the parts.

Tấm _put on the_ hai, _danced in the rice paddy,_ and then _went fishing_.

The writer of the passage below combined verbs to add variety and to make the passage easier to read.

Important qualities, such as kindness and loyalty, can't be seen. You have to get to know people _and_ ~~You have to~~ observe how they act.

Try Your Hand: Using Compound Subjects and Predicates

From the first group of sentences, create a single sentence with a compound subject. Create a single sentence with a compound predicate from the second group of sentences.

- Alida's favorite place was the Pomarosa Pool. Taroo's favorite place was the Pomarosa Pool.
- Alida admired the young man's courage. Alida learned to respect him.

SkillBuilder

 GRAMMAR FROM WRITING

Making Compound Subjects and Verbs Agree
When two or more parts of a compound subject are joined by the conjunction _and_, use the plural form of the verb.

The Prince and his Father **are** looking for a princess.

When the parts are joined by _or,_ _either/or,_ or _neither/nor,_ use the form of the verb that agrees with the subject closest to the verb.

Tấm's father or stepmother **is** running to the pond.

Either Cám or Tấm **has** a chance to become the princess.

Neither Cám's meanness nor her lies **change** Tấm.

APPLYING WHAT YOU'VE LEARNED
Read the paragraph below, correcting any errors in subject-verb agreement. Then rewrite the paragraph in present tense.

The towns of Cayey and Cidra sits far atop the hills. Alida swim and rest by the banks of a beautiful pool. Alida and Taroo fell in love and wants to get married. Neither Alida's father nor the village people wants Alida to marry Taroo.

GRAMMAR HANDBOOK

For more information on subject-verb agreement, see page 815 in the Grammar Handbook.

READING THE WORLD

BELIEVE IT OR NOT

Every day we are exposed to morals or lessons on television and in movies. As you learned by reading the folk tales in Unit Six, some lessons are more valuable than others. With so many messages being sent, can you evaluate every one you see or hear?

View Jot down what you know about the shows or movies shown here. Then list other TV shows or movies that these images remind you of.

Interpret Describe what is likely to be going on in each scene. What kinds of lessons do you think are being presented? How valuable are lessons that are presented on TV or in movies?

Discuss In a small group, discuss the kinds of lessons that are often presented in movies or television shows. Then use the SkillBuilder at the right to help you make judgments about the lessons.

 CRITICAL THINKING

Evaluating the Message

You know that television shows and movies often present lessons or morals. But how valuable are those lessons to you? Television shows and movies are limited in the way they present information. They can only last a set length of time, sometimes as little as 30 minutes. Just as in written stories, TV shows and movies have to leave out information, which can make them seem predictable. To help you judge the worth of a lesson presented in a TV show, it is useful to ask questions such as these:

- Do people in real life act like the characters on the show?
- Are problems in real life always resolved?
- Do real-life problems always have happy endings, as in many TV shows and movies?

APPLYING WHAT YOU'VE LEARNED

With a partner or a small group discuss specific television shows that presented a message. Talk about your reactions to each show and the value of the message. Describe the reasons behind your opinions.

LINKS TO UNIT FOUR

Proving Ground

In the selections in Unit Four, characters are forced to prove themselves—and in the process reveal some of their strengths and weaknesses. Those with something to prove sometimes go beyond the limits of acceptable behavior. Each tale you're about to read contains a message or lesson on staying within those limits.

UNITED STATES

The White Buffalo Calf Woman and the Sacred Pipe

retold by Joseph Bruchac (broo'chäk')

The Lakota Sioux are Native Americans who lived on the plains of Nebraska and the Dakotas. Although the Sioux at first relied on agriculture, prolonged warfare with the Ojibwa people eventually forced the Sioux to become hunters and follow buffalo herds across the plains. This Lakota Sioux legend describes the outcome of a fateful meeting between two young men and a holy person called the White Buffalo Calf Woman.

Three Strong Women

retold by Claus Stamm

Formed by ancient volcanic eruptions, the islands of Japan stretch about 1,500 miles from north to south. If those islands ran along the eastern coast of the United States, they would stretch from Maine to Florida. Mountains are mentioned often in this Japanese folk tale, perhaps because nearly two-thirds of Japan is covered by them. The character Forever-Mountain finds unexpected challenges on his way to a big wrestling match.

Arachne

retold by Olivia E. Coolidge

In ancient Greece, the rule of the gods and goddesses was to be unquestioned. Many Greek myths are about characters who do not stay within limits set by the gods or who ignore their warnings. In this myth, a weaver, Arachne, pits herself against Athena, the goddess of wisdom and of all crafts, particularly weaving.

AS YOU READ . . .

See how the values and customs of the cultures are presented.

Find out what virtuous behavior is and how it is rewarded.

See which traits are admired and respected and which are seen as negative.

ARACHNE

Illustration by Arvis Stewart, from *The Macmillan Book of Greek Gods and Heroes* by Alice Low. Copyright © 1985 Macmillan Publishing Company, reprinted with the permission of Simon & Schuster Books for Young Readers, an imprint of Simon & Schuster Children's Publishing Division.

retold by Olivia E. Coolidge

rachne[1] was a maiden who became famous throughout Greece, though she was neither wellborn[2] nor beautiful and came from no great city. She lived in an <u>obscure</u> little village, and her father was a humble dyer of wool. In this he was very skillful, producing many varied shades, while above all he was famous for the clear, bright scarlet which is made from shellfish and which was the most glorious of all the colors used in ancient Greece. Even more skillful than her father was Arachne. It was her task to spin the fleecy wool into a fine, soft thread and to weave it into cloth on the high-standing loom[3] within the cottage. Arachne was small and pale from much working. Her eyes were light and her hair was a dusty brown, yet she was quick and graceful, and her fingers, roughened as they were, went so fast that it was hard to follow their flickering movements. So soft and even was her thread, so fine her cloth, so gorgeous her embroidery, that soon her products were known all over Greece. No one had ever seen the like of them before.

---

1. **Arachne** (ə-răk′nē).
2. **wellborn:** of a high social class.
3. **high-standing loom:** a tall frame used to hold threads in a vertical position as other threads are woven through horizontally.

t last Arachne's fame became so great that people used to come from far and wide to watch her working. Even the graceful nymphs[4] would steal in from stream or forest and peep shyly through the dark doorway, watching in wonder the white arms of Arachne as she stood at the loom and threw the shuttle[5] from hand to hand between the hanging threads or drew out the long wool, fine as a hair, from the distaff[6] as she sat spinning. "Surely Athena herself must have taught her," people would murmur to one another. "Who else could know the secret of such marvelous skill?"

EVALUATE

What do you think of Arachne's pride?

Arachne was used to being wondered at, and she was immensely proud of the skill that had brought so many to look on her. Praise was all she lived for, and it displeased her greatly that people should think anyone, even a goddess, could teach her anything. Therefore, when she heard them murmur, she would stop her work and turn round indignantly to say, "With my own ten fingers I gained this skill, and by hard practice from early morning till night. I never had time to stand looking as you people do while another maiden worked. Nor if I had, would I give Athena credit because the girl was more skillful than I. As for Athena's weaving, how could there be finer cloth or more beautiful embroidery than mine? If Athena herself were to come down and compete with me, she could do no better than I."

One day when Arachne turned round with such words, an old woman answered her, a grey old woman, bent and very poor, who stood leaning on a staff and peering at Arachne amid the crowd of onlookers.

"Reckless girl," she said, "how dare you claim to be equal to the immortal gods themselves? I am an old woman and have seen much. Take my advice and ask pardon of Athena for your words. Rest content with your fame of being the best spinner and weaver that mortal eyes have ever beheld."

"Stupid old woman," said Arachne indignantly, "who gave you a right to speak in this way to me? It is easy to see that you were never good for anything in your day, or you would not come here in poverty and rags to gaze at my skill. If Athena resents my words, let her answer them herself. I have challenged

> "STUPID OLD WOMAN," SAID ARACHNE INDIGNANTLY, "WHO GAVE YOU A RIGHT TO SPEAK IN THIS WAY TO ME?"

---

4. **nymphs** (nĭmfs): in Greek mythology, minor goddesses of nature.
5. **shuttle:** a piece of wood holding the thread that is to be woven horizontally through the vertical threads on a loom.
6. **distaff:** a short rod for holding wool that is to be spun into thread.

WORDS
TO
KNOW

indignantly (ĭn-dĭg′nənt-lē) *adv.* in a way that is angry, because of an insult or an attack on one's self-respect

immortal (ĭ-môr′tl) *adj.* living or lasting forever

her to a contest, but she, of course, will not come. It is easy for the gods to avoid matching their skill with that of men."

At these words the old woman threw down her staff and stood <u>erect</u>. The wondering onlookers saw her grow tall and fair and stand clad in long robes of dazzling white. They were terribly afraid as they realized that they stood in the presence of Athena. Arachne herself flushed red for a moment, for she had never really believed that the goddess would hear her. Before the group that was gathered there she would not give in; so pressing her pale lips together in <u>obstinacy</u> and pride, she led the goddess to one of the great looms and set herself before the other. Without a word both began to thread the long woolen strands that hung from the rollers and between which the shuttle would move back and forth. Many skeins[7] lay heaped beside them to use, bleached white, and gold, and scarlet, and other shades, varied as the rainbow. Arachne had never thought of giving credit for her success to her father's skill in dyeing, though in actual truth the colors were as remarkable as the cloth itself.

oon there was no sound in the room but the breathing of the onlookers, the whirring of the shuttles, and the creaking of the wooden frames as each pressed the thread up into place or tightened the pegs by which the whole was held straight. The excited crowd in the doorway began to see that the skill of both in truth was very nearly equal but that, however the cloth might turn out, the goddess was the quicker of the two. A pattern

of many pictures was growing on her loom. There was a border of twined branches of the olive, Athena's favorite tree, while in the middle, figures began to appear. As they looked at the glowing colors, the spectators realized that Athena was weaving into her pattern a last warning to Arachne. The central figure was the goddess herself, competing with Poseidon[8] for possession of the city of Athens; but in the four corners were mortals who had tried to strive with gods and pictures of the awful <u>fate</u> that had overtaken them. The goddess ended a little before Arachne and stood back from her marvelous work to see what the maiden was doing.

> **PREDICT**
>
> How do you think the weaving contest will end?

Never before had Arachne been matched against anyone whose skill was equal, or even nearly equal, to her own. As she stole glances from time to time at Athena and saw the goddess working swiftly, calmly, and always a little faster than herself, she became angry instead of frightened, and an evil thought came into her head. Thus, as Athena stepped back a pace to watch Arachne finishing her work, she saw that the maiden hād taken for her design a pattern of scenes which showed evil or unworthy actions of the gods, how they had deceived fair maidens, resorted to trickery, and appeared on earth from time to time in the form of poor and humble people. When the goddess saw this insult glowing in bright colors on Arachne's loom, she did not wait while the cloth was judged but stepped

---

7. **skeins** (skānz): rolls of thread or yarn.
8. **Poseidon** (pō-sīd'n): in Greek mythology, the god of the sea.

WORDS **erect** (ĭ-rĕkt') *adj.* firmly straight in posture; not bending or slumping
TO **obstinacy** (ŏb'stə-nə-sē) *n.* unreasonable stubbornness
KNOW **fate** (fāt) *n.* a final outcome that cannot be avoided

forward, her grey eyes blazing with anger, and tore Arachne's work across. Then she struck Arachne across the face. Arachne stood there a moment, struggling with anger, fear, and pride. "I will not live under this insult," she cried, and seizing a rope from the wall, she made a noose and would have hanged herself.

The goddess touched the rope and touched the maiden. "Live on, wicked girl," she said. "Live on and spin, both you and your descendants. When men look at you, they may remember that it is not wise to strive with Athena." At that the body of Arachne shriveled up; and her legs grew tiny, spindly, and <u>distorted</u>. There before the eyes of the spectators hung a little dusty brown spider on a slender thread.

All spiders descend from Arachne, and as the Greeks watched them spinning their thread wonderfully fine, they remembered the contest with Athena and thought that it was not right for even the best of men to claim equality with the gods. ❖

OLIVIA E. COOLIDGE

Olivia E. Coolidge (1908–) grew up in England, where her father was a journalist and historian. After completing her studies at Oxford University, Coolidge came to the United States and taught English for several years.

Coolidge has written a number of biographies for young people in which she needed to carefully separate facts from opinions. As Coolidge says, "Facts are the bricks with which a biographer builds. . . . The more facts I have to work with, the freer I am to design my own book." Coolidge carefully researches her subjects and then forms her own opinions.

OTHER WORKS *Greek Myths, Gandhi, The Apprenticeship of Abraham Lincoln, Legends of the North, The Trojan War, Egyptian Adventures, Roman People*

WORDS TO KNOW

distorted (dĭ-stôr′tĭd) *adj.* twisted out of shape **distort** *v.*

THREE STRONG WOMEN

retold by Claus Stamm

Upper right: Figure of a woman (late 1600s), unknown Japanese artist. Arita ware, Kakiemon porcelain with overglaze polychrome enamel, Edo period, 14¼″ × 5½″, Asian Art Museum of San Francisco, The Avery Brundage Collection (B62 P5+).

Long ago, in Japan, there lived a famous wrestler, and he was on his way to the capital city to wrestle before the Emperor.

He strode down the road on legs thick as the trunks of small trees. He had been walking for seven hours and could, and probably would, walk for seven more without getting tired.

The time was autumn, the sky was a cold, watery blue, the air chilly. In the small, bright sun, the trees along the roadside glowed red and orange. The wrestler hummed to himself, "Zun-zun-zun," in time with the long swing of his legs. Wind blew through his thin brown robe, and he wore no sword at his side. He felt proud that he needed no sword, even in the darkest and loneliest places. The icy air on his body only reminded him that few tailors would have been able to make expensive, warm clothes for a man so broad and tall. He felt much as a wrestler should—strong, healthy, and rather conceited.

A soft roar of fast-moving water beyond the trees told him that he was passing above a riverbank. He "zun-zunned" louder; he loved the sound of his voice and wanted it to sound clearly above the rushing water.

He thought, They call me Forever-Mountain because I am such a good strong wrestler—big, too. I'm a fine, brave man and far too modest ever to say so. . . .

Just then he saw a girl who must have come up from the river, for she steadied a bucket on her head.

Her hands on the bucket were small, and there was a dimple on each thumb, just below the knuckle. She was a round little girl with red cheeks and a nose like a friendly button. Her eyes looked as though she were thinking of ten thousand funny stories at once. She clambered up onto the road and walked ahead of the wrestler, jolly and bounceful.

"If I don't tickle that fat girl, I shall regret it all my life," said the wrestler under his breath. "She's sure to go 'squeak' and I shall laugh and laugh. If she drops her bucket, that will be even funnier—and I can always run and fill it again and even carry it home for her."

He tiptoed up and poked her lightly in the ribs with one huge finger.

"Kochokochokocho!" he said, a fine, ticklish sound in Japanese.

The girl gave a satisfying squeal, giggled, and brought one arm down so that the wrestler's hand was caught between it and her body.

"Ho-ho-ho! You've caught me! I can't move at all!" said the wrestler, laughing.

"I know," said the jolly girl.

He felt that it was very good-tempered of her to take a joke so well, and started to pull his hand free.

Somehow, he could not.

He tried again, using a little more strength.

> *Her hands on the bucket were small, and there was a dimple on each thumb, just below the knuckle. She was a round little girl with red cheeks and a nose like a friendly button.*

716

Twenty-Second Station, Okabe, Utsu no Yama [Utsu Mountain] (1834), Hiroshige. Color woodcut from *Fifty-Three Stations of the Tokaido,* Print Collection, Miriam and Ira D. Wallach Division of Art, Prints and Photographs, The New York Public Library, Astor, Lenox and Tilden Foundations.

"Now, now—let me go, little girl," he said. "I am a very powerful man. If I pull too hard I might hurt you."

"Pull," said the girl. "I admire powerful men."

She began to walk, and though the wrestler tugged and pulled until his feet dug great furrows in the ground, he had to follow. She couldn't have paid him less attention if he had been a puppy—a small one.

Ten minutes later, still tugging while trudging helplessly after her, he was glad that the road was lonely and no one was there to see.

"Please let me go," he pleaded. "I am the famous wrestler Forever-Mountain. I must go and show my strength before the Emperor"— he burst out weeping from shame and confusion—"and you're hurting my hand!"

The girl steadied the bucket on her head with her free hand and dimpled sympathetically over her shoulder. "You poor, sweet little Forever-Mountain," she said. "Are you tired? Shall I carry you? I can leave the water here and come back for it later."

"I do not want you to carry me. I want you to let me go, and then I want to forget I ever saw you. What do you want with me?" moaned the pitiful wrestler.

"I only want to help you," said the girl, now pulling him steadily up and up a narrow mountain path. "Oh, I am sure you'll have no more trouble than anyone else when you come up against the other wrestlers. You'll win, or else you'll lose, and you won't be too badly hurt either way. But aren't you afraid you might meet a really *strong* man someday?"

Forever-Mountain turned white. He stumbled. He was imagining being laughed at throughout Japan as "Hardly-Ever-Mountain."

She glanced back.

"You see? Tired already," she said. "I'll walk more slowly. Why don't you come along to my mother's house and let us make a strong man of you? The wrestling in the capital isn't due to begin for three months. I know, because Grandmother thought she'd go. You'd be spending all that time in bad company and wasting what little power you have."

"All right. Three months. I'll come along," said the wrestler. He felt he had nothing more to lose. Also, he feared that the girl might become angry if he refused, and place him in the top of a tree until he changed his mind.

"Fine," she said happily. "We are almost there."

She freed his hand. It had become red and a little swollen. "But if you break your promise and run off, I shall have to chase you and carry you back."

Soon they arrived in a small valley. A simple farmhouse with a thatched[1] roof stood in the middle.

"Grandmother is at home, but she is an old lady and she's probably sleeping." The girl shaded her eyes with one hand. "But Mother should be bringing our cow back from the field—oh, there's Mother now!"

She waved. The woman coming around the corner of the house put down the cow she was carrying and waved back.

She smiled and came across the grass, walking with a lively bounce like her daughter's. Well, maybe her bounce was a little more solid, thought the wrestler.

"Excuse me," she said, brushing some cow hair from her dress, and dimpling, also like her daughter. "These mountain paths are full of stones. They hurt the cow's feet. And who is the nice young man you've brought, Maru-me?"

The girl explained. "And we have only three months!" she finished anxiously.

"Well, it's not long enough to do much, but it's not so short a time that we can't do something," said her mother, looking thoughtful. "But he does look terribly feeble. He'll need a lot of good things to eat. Maybe when he gets stronger he can help Grandmother with some of the easy work about the house."

"That will be fine!" said the girl, and she called her grandmother—loudly, for the old lady was a little deaf.

"I'm coming!" came a creaky voice from inside the house, and a little old woman leaning on a stick and looking very sleepy tottered out of the door. As she came towards them, she stumbled over the roots of a great oak tree.

"Heh! My eyes aren't what they used to be. That's the fourth time this month I've stumbled over that tree," she complained and, wrapping her skinny arms about its trunk, pulled it out of the ground.

"Oh, Grandmother! You should have let me pull it up for you," said Maru-me.

"Hm. I hope I didn't hurt my poor old back," muttered the old lady. She called out, "Daughter! Throw that tree away like a good girl, so no one will fall over it. But make sure it doesn't hit anybody."

"You can help Mother with the tree," Maru-me said to Forever-Mountain. "On second thought, you'd better not help. Just watch."

Her mother went to the tree, picked it up in her two hands and threw it. Up went the tree, sailing end over end, growing smaller and smaller as it flew. It landed with a faint crash far up the mountainside.

"Ah, how clumsy," she said. "I meant to throw it *over* the mountain. It's probably

---

1. **thatched:** covered with a plant material, usually straw.

WORDS TO KNOW **feeble** (fē′bəl) *adj.* weak; not strong

blocking the path now, and I'll have to get up early tomorrow to move it."

The wrestler was not listening. He had very quietly fainted.

"Oh! We must put him to bed," said Maru-me.

"Poor, feeble young man," said her mother.

"I hope we can do something for him. Here, let me carry him; he's light," said the grandmother. She slung him over her shoulder and carried him into the house, creaking along with her cane.

The next day they began the work of making Forever-Mountain into what they thought a strong man should be. They gave him the simplest food to eat, and the toughest. Day by day they prepared his rice with less and less water, until no ordinary man could have chewed or digested it.

Every day he was made to do the work of five men, and every evening he wrestled with Grandmother. Maru-me and her mother agreed that Grandmother, being old and feeble, was the least likely to injure him accidentally. They hoped the exercise might be good for the old lady's rheumatism.[2]

H e grew stronger and stronger but was hardly aware of it. Grandmother could still throw him easily into the air—and catch him again—without ever changing her sweet old smile.

He quite forgot that outside this valley he was one of the greatest wrestlers in Japan and was called Forever-Mountain. His legs had

> *The next day they began the work of making Forever-Mountain into what they thought a strong man should be. They gave him the simplest food to eat, and the toughest.*

been like logs; now they were like pillars. His big hands were hard as stones, and when he cracked his knuckles, the sound was like trees splitting on a cold night.

Sometimes he did an exercise that wrestlers do in Japan—raising one foot high above the ground and bringing it down with a crash.

Then people in nearby villages looked up at the winter sky and told one another that it was very late in the year for thunder. Soon he could pull up a tree as well as the grandmother. He could even throw one—but only a small distance. One evening, near the end of his third month, he wrestled with Grandmother and held her down for half a minute.

"Heh-heh!" she chortled, and got up, smiling with every wrinkle. "I would never have believed it!"

Maru-me squealed with joy and threw her arms around him—gently, for she was afraid of cracking his ribs.

"Very good, very good! What a strong man," said her mother, who had just come home from the fields, carrying, as usual, the cow. She put the cow down and patted the wrestler on the back.

They agreed that he was now ready to show some *real* strength before the Emperor.

"Take the cow along with you tomorrow when you go," said the mother. "Sell her and

---

2. **rheumatism** (rōō′mə-tĭz′əm): painful condition in which joints and muscles become swollen and stiff.

buy yourself a belt—a silken belt. Buy the fattest and heaviest one you can find. Wear it when you appear before the Emperor, as a souvenir from us."

"I wouldn't think of taking your only cow. You've already done too much for me. And you'll need her to plough the fields, won't you?"

They burst out laughing. Maru-me squealed; her mother roared. The grandmother cackled so hard and long that she choked and had to be pounded on the back.

"Oh, dear," said the mother, still laughing. "You didn't think we used our cow for anything like *work!* Why, Grandmother here is stronger than five cows!"

"The cow is our pet," Maru-me giggled. "She has lovely brown eyes."

"But it really gets tiresome having to carry her back and forth each day so that she has enough grass to eat," said her mother.

"Then you must let me give you all the prize money that I win," said Forever-Mountain.

"Oh, no! We wouldn't think of it!" said Maru-me. "Because we all like you too much to sell you anything. And it is not proper to accept gifts of money from strangers."

"True," said Forever-Mountain. "I will now ask your mother's and grandmother's permission to marry you. I want to be one of the family."

"Oh! I'll get a wedding dress ready!" said Maru-me.

The mother and grandmother pretended to consider very seriously, but they quickly agreed.

Next morning Forever-Mountain tied his hair up in the topknot[3] that all Japanese wrestlers wear, and got ready to leave. He thanked Maru-me and her mother and bowed very low to the grandmother, since she was the oldest and had been a fine wrestling partner.

Then he picked up the cow in his arms and trudged up the mountain. When he reached the top, he slung the cow over one shoulder and waved good-bye to Maru-me.

At the first town he came to, Forever-Mountain sold the cow. She brought a good price because she was unusually fat from never having worked in her life. With the money, he bought the heaviest silken belt he could find.

When he reached the palace grounds, many of the other wrestlers were already there, sitting about, eating enormous bowls of rice, comparing one another's weight and telling stories. They paid little attention to Forever-Mountain, except to wonder why he had arrived so late this year. Some of them noticed that he had grown very quiet and took no part at all in their boasting.

All the ladies and gentlemen of the court

---

3. **topknot:** a small bunch of hair on the top of the head.

Parade Before a Sumo Tournament (1796), Katsukawa Shun'ei. Triptych print, 37.5 cm × 25.5 cm.
Copyright © British Museum.

were waiting in a special courtyard for the wrestling to begin. They wore many robes, one on top of another, heavy with embroidery and gold cloth, and sweat ran down their faces and froze in the winter afternoon. The gentlemen had long swords so weighted with gold and precious stones that they could never have used them, even if they had known how. The court ladies, with their long black hair hanging down behind, had their faces painted dead white, which made them look frightened. They had pulled out their real eyebrows and painted new ones high above the place where eyebrows are supposed to be, and this made them all look as though they were very surprised at something.

Behind a screen sat the Emperor—by himself, because he was too noble for ordinary people to look at. He was a lonely old man with a kind, tired face. He hoped the wrestling would end quickly so that he could go to his room and write poems.

The first two wrestlers chosen to fight were Forever-Mountain and a wrestler who was said to have the biggest stomach in the country. He and Forever-Mountain both threw some salt into the ring. It was understood that this drove away evil spirits.

Then the other wrestler, moving his stomach somewhat out of the way, raised his foot and brought it down with a fearful stamp. He glared fiercely at Forever-Mountain as if to say, "Now *you* stamp, you poor frightened man!"

Forever-Mountain raised his foot. He brought it down.

There was a sound like thunder, the earth

shook, and the other wrestler bounced into the air and out of the ring, as gracefully as any soap bubble.

He picked himself up and bowed to the Emperor's screen.

"The earth god is angry. Possibly there is something the matter with the salt," he said. "I do not think I shall wrestle this season." And he walked out, looking very suspiciously over one shoulder at Forever-Mountain.

Five other wrestlers then and there decided that they were not wrestling this season, either. They all looked annoyed with Forever-Mountain.

From then on, Forever-Mountain brought his foot down lightly. As each wrestler came into the ring, he picked him up very gently, carried him out, and placed him before the Emperor's screen, bowing most courteously every time.

The court ladies' eyebrows went up even higher. The gentlemen looked disturbed and a little afraid. They loved to see fierce, strong men tugging and grunting at each other, but Forever-Mountain was a little too much for them. Only the Emperor was happy behind his screen, for now, with the wrestling over so quickly, he would have that much more time to write his poems. He ordered all the prize money handed over to Forever-Mountain.

"But," he said, "you had better not wrestle anymore." He stuck a finger through his screen and waggled it at the other wrestlers, who were sitting on the ground weeping with disappointment like great fat babies.

Forever-Mountain promised not to wrestle anymore. Everybody looked relieved. The wrestlers sitting on the ground almost smiled.

"I think I shall become a farmer," Forever-Mountain said, and left at once to go back to Maru-me.

Maru-me was waiting for him. When she saw him coming, she ran down the mountain, picked him up, together with the heavy bags of prize money, and carried him halfway up the mountainside. Then she giggled and put him down. The rest of the way she let him carry her.

Forever-Mountain kept his promise to the Emperor and never fought in public again. His name was forgotten in the capital. But up in the mountains, sometimes, the earth shakes and rumbles, and they say that is Forever-Mountain and Maru-me's grandmother practicing wrestling in the hidden valley. ❖

CLAUS STAMM

Claus Stamm, a U.S. citizen, was a Japanese-language specialist for the United States during World War II. Following the war, he attended the Institute of Eastern Studies at Columbia University in New York. Stamm's interest in the Japanese culture led to the 1962 publication of *Three Strong Women,* his retelling, in English, of the Japanese folk tale. He has also published two other books of Japanese tales. In addition, he writes haiku for children and translates them into Japanese. Stamm now lives in Japan.

OTHER WORKS *The Dumplings and the Demons, The Very Special Badgers: A Tale of Magic from Japan*

Buffalo Calf Woman, Oscar Howe. U.S. Department of the Interior, Indian Arts and Crafts Board, Sioux Indian Museum and Crafts Center, Rapid City, South Dakota.

THE WHITE BUFFALO CALF WOMAN
AND ● THE
SACRED PIPE

RETOLD BY JOSEPH BRUCHAC

It was a time when there was little food left in the camp and the people were hungry.

Two young men were sent out to scout for game. They went on foot, for this was a time long before the horses, the great Spirit Dogs, were given to the people. The two young men hunted a long time but had no luck. Finally, they climbed to the top of a hill and looked to the west.

"What is that?" said one of the young men.

"I cannot tell, but it is coming toward us," said the other.

And so it was. At first they thought that it was an animal, but as the shape drew closer, they saw it was a woman. She was dressed in white buffalo skin and carried something in her hands. She walked so lightly that it seemed as if she was not walking at all, but floating with her feet barely touching the Earth.

Then the first young man realized that she must be a Holy Person, and his mind filled with good thoughts. But the second young man did not see her that way. He saw her only as a beautiful young woman, and his mind filled with bad thoughts. She was now very close and he reached out to grab her. As soon as he did so, though, there was a sound of lightning, and the young man was covered by a cloud. When it cleared away, there was nothing left of the second young man but a skeleton.

Then the White Buffalo Calf Woman spoke. "Go to your people," she said, holding up the bundle in her hands so that the first young man could see it. "Tell your people that it is a good thing I am bringing. I am bringing a holy thing to your nation, a message from the Buffalo People. Put up a medicine lodge[1] for me and make it ready. I will come there after four days have passed."

The first young man did as he was told. He went back to his people and gave them the message. Then the crier went through the camp and told all the people that something <u>sacred</u> was coming and that all things should be made ready. They built the medicine lodge and made an earth altar which faced the west.

> AT FIRST THEY THOUGHT THAT IT WAS AN ANIMAL, BUT AS THE SHAPE DREW CLOSER, THEY SAW IT WAS A WOMAN.

Four days passed and then the people saw something coming toward them. When it came closer, they saw it was the White Buffalo Calf Woman. In her hands she carried the bundle and a bunch of sacred sage.[2] The people welcomed her into the medicine lodge and gave her the seat of honor. Then she unwrapped the bundle to show them what was inside. It was the Sacred Pipe. As she held it out to them, she told them what it meant.

"The bowl of the Pipe," she said, "is made of the red stone. It represents the flesh and blood of the Buffalo People and all other Peoples. The wooden stem of the Pipe represents all the trees and plants, all the things green and growing on this Earth. The

---

1. **medicine lodge:** a building, hut, or tent used by Native Americans for religious ceremonies.

2. **sage:** an herb having a strong pinelike odor.

WORDS TO KNOW   **sacred** (sā′krĭd) *adj.* having to do with religion; holy smoke that passes through the Pipe represents the sacred wind, the breath that carries prayers up to Wakan Tanka, the Creator."

When she finished showing them the Pipe, she told the people how to hold it and how to offer it to Earth and Sky and the Four Sacred Directions. She told them many things to remember.

"The Sacred Pipe," said the White Buffalo Calf Woman, "will show you the Good Red Road. Follow it and it will take you in the right direction. Now," she said, "I am going to leave, but you will see me again."

Then she began to walk toward the setting sun. The people watched her as she went, and they saw her stop and roll once on the Earth. When she stood up, she was a black buffalo. Then she went farther and rolled again on the Earth. This time when she stood up, she was a brown buffalo. She went farther and rolled a third time and stood up. Now the people saw that she was a red buffalo. Again she walked farther and for a fourth and final time she rolled upon the Earth. This time she became a white buffalo calf and continued to walk until she disappeared over the horizon.

As soon as the White Buffalo Calf Woman was gone, herds of buffalo were seen all around the camp. The people were able to hunt them, and they gave thanks with the Sacred Pipe for the blessings they had been given. As long as they followed the Good Red Road of the Sacred Pipe and remembered, as the White Buffalo Calf Woman had taught them, that all things were as connected as parts of the Pipe, they lived happily and well. ❖

JOSEPH BRUCHAC

1942–

The poet, novelist, and storyteller Joseph Bruchac began hearing Native American legends as a small child. A descendant of Native Americans, Bruchac says he likes to share stories from Native American traditions because "they have messages, sometimes very subtle, which can help show young people the good paths to follow." Born in the Adirondack Mountains, Bruchac also has drawn upon the legends of those mountains for his stories.

Before becoming a writer and a scholar, Joseph Bruchac taught English and literature in Ghana, West Africa, and creative writing and African-American literature at Skidmore College in New York. Bruchac has received numerous awards for his writing, including a fellowship from the National Endowment for the Arts and a Rockefeller Foundation Humanities Fellowship.

OTHER WORKS *The Wind Eagle and Other Abenaki Folk Stories; Flying with the Eagle, Racing the Great Bear*

RESPONDING OPTIONS

LITERATURE CONNECTION PROJECT 1

Present a Puppet Show Develop a puppet show based on one of the stories you have just read. Form teams to carry out the following tasks: adapting the story into a script; working as puppet makers, costumers, set designers, and stage builders; serving as puppeteers. These suggestions may help:

Writers Identify the characters to be included. Map out the events in the tale in outline form or on storyboards.

Stage builders Make the stage as simple or as complex as time allows. Three different arrangements are shown here.

Puppet makers Research techniques in puppet making. Choose to construct paper-bag, sock, glove, fabric, or stick puppets.

Present your puppet show as part of an arts program at your school or as a performance for a class of first graders or second graders.

Three simple puppet-show stages you can make.

SCIENCE CONNECTION PROJECT 2

Explore Textiles and Looms Two of the three cultures represented in these stories— the ancient Greeks and the Japanese—made use of woven textiles. Both cultures used some version of the loom, a device used to weave thread or yarn into cloth.

Find out more about the textiles and textile-making tools of different civilizations. Visit museums and conduct library research to plan and make your own simple loom, which you might use to weave a piece of cloth. Study the designs and patterns used in textiles of a civilization of your choosing. Then, using colored pencils or construction paper—or even a paint program on a personal computer—draw or make a collage of different examples of the designs and patterns you found.

A simple loom you can make yourself

SOCIAL STUDIES CONNECTION PROJECT 3

 Research the Buffalo How important a resource was the American bison, popularly called the buffalo, to the Lakota Sioux and other Native American groups? In a cluster diagram like the one shown, record the ways in which the buffalo was important to Native Americans. Make drawings to illustrate these ways, and write a caption for each drawing. As a class, collect your findings to create a visual encyclopedia.

ACROSS CULTURES MINI-PROJECTS

Compare and Contrast Characters Use a diagram, like the one shown, to compare and contrast Arachne and Forever-Mountain. Where the ovals overlap, write the qualities that are common to both characters. In the larger section of each oval, write the qualities that are unique to the character.

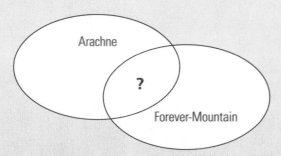

Design Trading Cards Make trading cards of the Roman gods and goddesses. Find out if the members of this god "family" had different names or abilities in Greek mythology.

Follow the Buffalo Graph the changes in the American buffalo population from 1850, when it was about 20 million, to the present.

Try Wrestling Wrestling was a popular sport in many ancient cultures, including those of Egypt, Greece, and Japan. The three most common wrestling styles today are Japanese sumo, Greco-Roman, and freestyle. Research any one of the three styles, describe the rules, and demonstrate it for the class.

MORE ABOUT THE CULTURES

- *A History of Art from 25,000 B.C. to the Present* by Marshall Davidson
- *The Magic Weaver of Rugs: A Tale of the Navajo* by Jerrie Oughton, illustrated by Lisa Desimini
- *The Greek World* by Anton Powell

PREVIEWING

The Pursuit of a Goal

The selections in Unit Five explore how an individual's interactions with others can help or hinder that person's efforts to reach a goal. Treating people with kindness and respect is an important theme in folklore. These three selections feature characters who are rewarded or punished because of their actions toward others.

UNITED STATES

Sister Fox and Brother Coyote

retold by Robert D. San Souci
(săn sōō′sē)

Tales from the American Southwest reflect a mixture of cultures, including the Hispanic and the Native American. In both cultures, celebrations and communal gatherings are an important way of passing on traditions. In this Mexican-American trickster tale, Sister Fox and her less sensible cousin, Brother Coyote, engage in a contest between brains and physical strength. Sister Fox uses the promise of good food from a fiesta, or festival, to trick her foolish cousin.

The Living Kuan-yin

*retold by Carol Kendall
and Yao-wen Li (you'wən' lē')*

China is bounded on every side by mountains, deserts, or ocean. These geographical features have helped to preserve a civilization that dates back nearly 4,000 years. Buddhism, one of the world's major religions, was established in China about 500 B.C. In Buddhism, Kuan-yin (gwän'yĭn') is the goddess of mercy who works for the salvation of people. This folk tale tells about a man named Chin Po-wan. His generosity gets him into trouble as he journeys to see Kuan-yin and is asked for help by people along the way.

King Thrushbeard

retold by the brothers Grimm

This tale was written by the famous brothers Grimm, whose stories continue to be told to children today. In the early 1800s, inspired to capture in writing some of the classic stories that made up early German literature, the brothers collected and recorded stories that had been told orally in Germany for generations. In this story, a proud princess who finds fault with all of her suitors learns through hardship to recognize a person's most valuable qualities.

AS YOU READ . . .

Notice the common threads that appear in different cultures.

Identify traits that vary from one culture to another.

Think about why certain values endure.

Consider ways in which the past is preserved.

THE LIVING KUAN-YIN

RETOLD BY

CAROL KENDALL AND YAO-WEN LI

Even though the family name of Chin means "gold," it does not signify that everyone of that name is rich. Long ago, in the province of Chekiang,[1] however, there was a certain wealthy Chin family of whom it was popularly said that its fortune was as great as its name. It seemed quite fitting, then, when a son was born to the family, that he should be called Po-wan, "Million," for he was certain to be worth a million pieces of gold when he came of age.

With such a happy circumstance of names, Po-wan himself never doubted that he would have a never-ending supply of money chinking through his fingers, and he spent it accordingly —not on himself, but on any unfortunate who came to his attention. He had a deep sense of compassion for anyone in distress of body or spirit: a poor man had only to hold out his hand, and Po-wan poured gold into it; if a destitute widow and her brood of starvelings[2] but lifted sorrowful eyes to his, he provided them with food and lodging and friendship for the rest of their days.

In such wise did he live that even a million gold pieces were not enough to support him. His resources so <u>dwindled</u> that finally he scarcely had enough food for himself, his clothes flapped threadbare[3] on his wasted frame, and the cold seeped into his bone marrow[4] for lack of a fire. Still he gave away the little money that came to him.

One day, as he scraped out half of his bowl of rice for a beggar even hungrier than he, he began to ponder on his destitute state.

"Why am I so poor?" he wondered. "I have never spent <u>extravagantly</u>. I have never, from the day of my birth, done an evil deed. Why, then, am I, whose very name is A Million Pieces of Gold, no longer able to find even a copper[5] to give this unfortunate creature, and have only a bowl of rice to share with him?"

---

1. **province of Chekiang** (chŭ'kyäng'): a region on the eastern coast of China.
2. **brood of starvelings** (stärv'lĭngz): starving children.
3. **threadbare:** so worn down that the threads show.
4. **marrow:** the soft tissue that fills the middle of most bones.
5. **copper:** a coin of little value.

Bodhisattva Guanyin (Song Dynasty, 960–1279), unknown Chinese artist. Wood, 30″ × 36″ × 64″, Eugene Fuller Memorial Collection, Seattle (Washington) Art Museum. Photo by Paul Macapia.

He thought long about his situation and at last determined to go without delay to the South Sea. Therein, it was told, dwelt the all-merciful goddess, the Living Kuan-yin, who could tell the past and future. He would put his question to her, and she would tell him the answer.

Soon he had left his home country behind and traveled for many weeks in unfamiliar lands. One day he found his way barred by a wide and furiously flowing river. As he stood first on one foot and then on the other, wondering how he could possibly get across, he heard a commanding voice calling from the top of an overhanging cliff.

"Chin Po-wan!" the voice said. "If you are going to the South Sea, please ask the Living Kuan-yin a question for me!"

The Living Kuan-yin allowed but three questions.

"Yes, yes, of course," Po-wan agreed at once, for he had never in his life refused a request made of him. In any case, the Living Kuan-yin permitted each person who approached her three questions, and he had but one of his own to ask.

Craning his head towards the voice coming from above, he suddenly began to tremble, for the speaker was a gigantic snake with a body as large as a temple column. Po-wan was glad he had agreed so readily to the request.

"Ask her, then," said the snake, "why I am not yet a dragon, even though I have practiced self-denial[6] for more than one thousand years."

"That I will do, and gl-gladly," stammered Po-wan, hoping that the snake would continue to practice self-denial just a bit longer. "But, your . . . your Snakery . . . or your Serpentry, perhaps I should say . . . that is . . . you see, don't you . . . first I must cross this raging river, and I know not how."

"That is no problem at all," said the snake. "I shall carry you across, of course."

"Of course," Po-wan echoed weakly. Overcoming his fear and his reluctance to touch the slippery-slithery scales, Chin Po-wan climbed onto the snake's back and rode across quite safely. Politely, and just a bit hurriedly, he thanked the self-denying serpent and bade him good-bye. Then he continued on his way to the South Sea.

By noon he was very hungry. Fortunately, a nearby inn offered meals at a price he could afford. While waiting for his bowl of rice, he chatted with the innkeeper and told him of the Snake of the Cliff, which the innkeeper knew well and respected, for the serpent always denied bandits the crossing of the river. Inadvertently, during the exchange of stories, Po-wan revealed the purpose of his journey.

"Why, then," cried the innkeeper, "let me prevail upon your generosity to ask a word for me." He laid an appealing hand on Po-wan's ragged sleeve. "I have a beautiful daughter," he said, "wonderfully amiable[7] and pleasing of disposition. But although she is in her twentieth year, she has never in all her life

---

6. **self-denial:** the giving up of desires or pleasures.
7. **amiable** (āʹmē-ə-bəl): good-natured and likable.

Detail of *Beneficent Rain* (Yüan Dynasty, China; about 1300), Chang Yu-ts'ai. Ink on silk, 10⅝″ × 106¾″, The Metropolitan Museum of Art, gift of Douglas Dillon, 1985 (1985.227.2). Copyright © 1985 The Metropolitan Museum of Art.

"For twenty years," he said, "from the time this house was built, my garden has been cultivated with the utmost care; yet in all those years, not one tree, not one small plant, has bloomed or borne fruit, and because of this, no bird comes to sing, nor bee to gather nectar. I don't like to put you to a bother, Chin Po-wan, but as you are going to the South Sea anyway, perhaps you would not mind seeking out the Living Kuan-yin and asking her why the plants in my garden don't bloom."

"I shall be delighted to put the question to her," said Po-wan. For after all, the Living Kuan-yin allowed each person three questions, and he had but . . .

Traveling onward, Po-wan examined the quandary[8] in which he found himself. The Living Kuan-yin allowed but three questions, and he had somehow, without quite knowing how, accumulated four questions. One of them would have to go unasked, but which? If he left out his own question, his whole journey would have been in vain.[9] If, on the other hand, he left out the question of the snake, or the innkeeper, or the kind host, he would break his promise and betray their faith in him.

uttered a single word. I should be very much obliged if you would ask the Living Kuan-yin why she is unable to speak."

Po-wan, much moved by the innkeeper's plea for his mute daughter, of course promised to do so. For after all, the Living Kuan-yin allowed each person three questions, and he had but one of his own to ask.

Nightfall found him far from any inn, but there were houses in the neighborhood, and he asked for lodging at the largest. The owner, a man obviously of great wealth, was pleased to offer him a bed in a fine chamber but first begged him to partake of a hot meal and good drink. Po-wan ate well, slept soundly, and, much refreshed, was about to depart the following morning when his good host, having learned that Po-wan was journeying to the South Sea, asked if he would be kind enough to put a question for him to the Living Kuan-yin.

PREDICT

Which question will Po-wan leave out?

"A promise should never be made if it cannot be kept," he told himself. "I made the promises and therefore I must keep them. Besides, the journey will not be in vain, for at least some of these problems will be solved by the Living Kuan-yin. Furthermore, assisting others must certainly be counted as a good deed, and the more good deeds abroad in the land, the better for everyone, including me."

At last he came into the presence of the Living Kuan-yin.

---

8. **quandary** (kwŏn′də-rē): confusing situation.

9. **in vain**: useless.

First, he asked the serpent's question: "Why is the Snake of the Cliff not yet a dragon, although he has practiced self-denial for more than one thousand years?"

And the Living Kuan-yin answered: "On his head are seven bright pearls. If he removes six of them, he can become a dragon."

Next, Po-wan asked the innkeeper's question: "Why is the innkeeper's daughter unable to speak, although she is in the twentieth year of her life?"

And the Living Kuan-yin answered: "It is her fate to remain mute until she sees the man destined[10] to be her husband."

Last, Po-wan asked the kind host's question: "Why are there never blossoms in the rich man's garden, although it has been carefully cultivated for twenty years?"

And the Living Kuan-yin answered: "Buried in the garden are seven big jars filled with silver and gold. The flowers will bloom if the owner will rid himself of half the treasure."

Then Chin Po-wan thanked the Living Kuan-yin and bade her good-bye.

On his return journey, he stopped first at the rich man's house to give him the Living Kuan-yin's answer. In gratitude the rich man gave him half the buried treasure.

Next, Po-wan went to the inn. As he approached, the innkeeper's daughter saw him from the window and called out, "Chin Po-wan! Back already! What did the Living Kuan-yin say?"

Upon hearing his daughter speak at long last, the joyful innkeeper gave her in marriage to Chin Po-wan.

Lastly, Po-wan went to the cliffs by the furiously flowing river to tell the snake what the Living Kuan-yin had said. The grateful snake immediately gave him six of the bright pearls and promptly turned into a magnificent dragon, the remaining pearl in his forehead lighting the headland[11] like a great beacon.[12]

And so it was that Chin Po-wan, that generous and good man, was once more worth a million pieces of gold. ❖

---

10. **destined** (dĕs′tĭnd): determined beforehand, as by fate.
11. **headland:** a point of land reaching out into the water.
12. **beacon:** a light for signaling or guiding.

CAROL KENDALL

Carol Kendall (1917–) says the things she likes to do best are writing, reading, studying Chinese, and "climbing to the tops of things."

Kendall is best known for *The Gammage Cup,* a 1960 Newbery Honor Book, which was adapted as an animated film for television in 1987. Kendall now lives in Lawrence, Kansas, where she met Yao-wen Li.

OTHER WORKS *The Firelings, The Wedding of the Rat Family*

YAO-WEN LI

"The Living Kuan-yin" is from *Sweet and Sour,* one of two collections of Chinese folk tales that Yao-wen Li (1924–) has coauthored with Carol Kendall. Born and raised in Canton, China, Li left China in 1947 and has lived in the United States ever since.

A return visit to China in 1973 inspired Li (whose first name means "literary brilliance") to begin collecting traditional Chinese tales.

OTHER WORKS *Cinnamon Moon*

Sister Fox
and

Brother Coyote

retold by Robert D. San Souci

In the desert country of the Southwest, there was once a very clever fox. She had been stealing a chicken every night from a certain *ranchero*,[1] Don Perez. After having failed many times to trap the sly vixen,[2] the man finally hit upon the idea of creating a manlike figure of soft, sticky wax to guard his hen house and capture her.

When Sister Fox saw the little figure sitting in the moonlight outside the hen house, she paused to size up the stranger. Always cautious, she watched for a long time, finally deciding that the small creature, looking so pale and still, posed no threat to her. Boldly she approached the mannikin[3] and said, "*¡Buenas noches, amigo!*"[4]

Of course, the little wax figure did not answer back. Several times the fox spoke to him, and always the <u>insufferable</u> person ignored her pleasantries. At last, angered by so much rudeness, Sister Fox grabbed him with her paws. She intended to shake some manners into him. Instead, she found herself stuck fast. The more she struggled to free herself, the more firmly she found her paws and fur wed to the sticky wax.

At that moment, Brother Coyote, who also had a hunger for the *ranchero*'s chickens, came by.

"*¡Hola, amiga!*"[5] called the coyote. "*¿Qué tal?*"[6]

Now the fox and coyote were cousins, but they were also rivals. They often found themselves after the same prize, and each such meeting became a contest between them. Sometimes Brother Coyote won, because he was bigger and stronger. But more often Sister Fox won, because she was clever and knew that brains could often get the better of brawn.[7]

"Hello, dear cousin," replied Sister Fox in her most honeyed voice. "You have come just in time to help me. If you do this, you will also help yourself to a nice fat chicken." She knew only too well that the coyote would more likely help her because of hunger in his belly rather than goodness in his heart.

Licking his chops at the thought of a tasty hen, Brother Coyote asked his cousin, "Please, explain yourself."

"Oh," said the <u>wily</u> fox, "Don Perez has agreed to let me have one chicken each night. This is to thank me for a certain small favor I did for him."

"And what favor is that?" asked the coyote.

"A personal matter. I promised the good *señor*[8] I would not tell. But let us return to my present difficulty. Here I am, come to collect my nightly payment according to my contract with the *ranchero*, and this little creature prevents me. Grab him by the shoulders so that I can pull myself free. Then I will go and get two chickens—one for you—and pass up my dinner tomorrow night."

The greedy coyote was excited at the thought of getting one of the *ranchero*'s celebrated[9] hens without running the risk of being shot. He walked behind the wax figure and grabbed its shoulders with his paws.

Straightaway, Sister Fox pulled free of the wax. "Now you wait here while I get a

---

1. *ranchero* (rän-chĕ′rô) *Spanish:* rancher.
2. **vixen:** a female fox.
3. **mannikin:** a lifelike model of the human body.
4. *¡Buenas noches, amigo!* (bwĕ′näs nô′chĕs ä-mē′gô) *Spanish:* Good evening, friend!
5. *¡Hola, amiga!* (ô′lä ä-mē′gä) *Spanish:* Hello, friend!
6. *¿Qué tal?* (kĕ′ täl′) *Spanish:* What's up?
7. **brawn:** well-developed muscles; physical strength.
8. *señor* (sĕ-nyôr′) *Spanish:* gentleman (also used as a title, like *Mister*).
9. **celebrated:** famous.

WORDS TO KNOW	**insufferable** (ĭn-sŭf′ər-ə-bəl) *adj.* hard to put up with; unbearable
	wily (wī′lē) *adj.* clever and skillful in a tricky way

chicken for each of us. Of course, I insist that you take the fatter one!"

So the foolish coyote waited, his paws on the wax figure and his mind on the fat hen that his cousin would soon bring him.

But the only one who came was Don Perez. He had been awakened by the squawking in his hen house when Sister Fox snatched his finest hen and ran off into the night.

When he saw the coyote, he cried, "*¡Bandido!*"[10] Then he fired his rifle. The shot went amiss and the wax figure exploded, allowing Brother Coyote to escape. But the unhappy creature had bits of wax stuck to his fur for days afterward. He vowed revenge upon Sister Fox for her scheming that had cost him a fine dinner, and—very nearly—his life.

N ot long after this, it happened that Sister Fox stole a freshly baked loaf of bread from a house on the edge of town. As she was running away into the desert with her still-warm prize, she met her cousin in a little *arroyo*.[11]

Brother Coyote was still very angry about the business with the wax man. He pounced upon the fox and bared his fangs at her. "Little cousin," he snarled, "if you do not give me that loaf of bread, I will gobble you up on the spot!"

"Oh," said the fox, thinking quickly, "this bread is not to eat. It is to lure the roosters—*¡Hay muchos!*[12] There are so many!—that are kept in a certain *hacienda*[13] I have discovered. Tonight I am going to steal as many as I have crumbs of bread."

"Well," said the gullible coyote, "let me go with you."

"No," said Sister Fox, "those roosters are so fat and lazy that they can barely move. Why should I share the secret with you?"

"Because," said the coyote unpleasantly, "I

will devour you if you do *not* let me go with you."

"Well, all right," said the fox, "I will take the bread and run home now. When the moon has set, I will meet you here. *¡Adiós!*"[14]

But Brother Coyote slapped a heavy paw

Sister Fox stole a freshly baked loaf of bread from a house on the edge of town.

across her tail. "To be certain that you do not run away, we will stay here together until the moon has set. And I am warning you: If we do not come away with ten times ten fat roosters tonight, you will not see the dawn."

So they lay side by side in the *arroyo* as the moon rose and set. By starlight, Sister Fox led her cousin to a huge wooden gate set in a high adobe wall.

"Here," she whispered.

"Hand over the bread *pronto*,"[15] Brother Coyote ordered.

The fox took a bit of the bread and

---

10. *bandido* (bän-dē′dô) *Spanish:* bandit; thief.

11. *arroyo* (ä-rô′yô) *Spanish:* a gully or large ditch.

12. *¡Hay muchos!* (ī′ mōō′chôs) *Spanish:* There are many.

13. *hacienda* (ä-syĕn′dä) *Spanish:* ranch house.

14. *adiós* (ä-dyôs′) *Spanish:* goodbye.

15. *pronto* (prŏn′tô) *Spanish:* at once; quickly.

> # To his surprise, he saw what seemed to be a huge round cheese just below the surface of the water.

crumbled it into his paw, telling him, "The roosters are just inside this gate. Push open the latch. That will be easy for you because you are bigger and stronger than I am. As soon as you are inside, scatter these bread crumbs and call, 'Here, here, *Señor* Rooster, see what I have brought you.' Then you will get a reward beyond your wildest imagining. Just be sure your greediness does not make you forget your cousin who brought you here."

Eagerly Brother Coyote took the bread crumbs, stood up on his hind legs, and tugged and pushed until he opened the big latch on the gate. Then, slipping through, he began to toss bread crumbs right and left, calling softly, "Here, here, *Señor* Rooster, see what I have for you."

But, once again, his clever cousin had tricked him. The courtyard inside held sleeping dogs, not roosters! In a moment, Brother Coyote, crying "¡Ay! Ay! Ay!" fled through the gate with the hounds snapping at his heels. "Sister Fox!" he howled, but she did not hear. She had long since returned to her lair to finish the loaf of bread and plan more mischief.

As it happened, the coyote <u>eluded</u> the dogs—but not before he had received several painful bites on his flank and left a tuft of his tail in the jaws of the lead hound.

Licking his wounds in his own den, he once again vowed to make his cousin suffer tenfold[16] for the pain and humiliation she had caused him.

Many nights later, he chanced upon Sister Fox as she sat crouched beside a deep pool of water in the foothills near the town.

"Without a doubt, I am going to eat you this time," he growled.

"Well, if it must be so, then it must be so," she said, sounding not in the least worried. "I just hope that when you have swallowed my miserable bones and stringy meat, you still have room for this cheese I am guarding. Behold what a beautiful cheese it is!"

Brother Coyote looked in the direction she was facing. To his surprise, he saw what seemed to be a huge round cheese just below the surface of the water. Of course, it was only the reflection of the full moon, riding high overhead. But the greedy coyote saw only what Sister Fox—and his own stomach—wanted him to see.

"Who left such a fine cheese in the water?" he asked suspiciously.

Sister Fox answered, "The family who lives in the grand *hacienda* not far from here. They are giving a *fiesta*[17] soon. Because the cheese is so big, and the *fiesta* is five days away, they put it in this cool water to keep it from spoiling. I found it quite by accident."

---

16. **tenfold:** ten times as much.
17. *fiesta* (fyĕs′tä) *Spanish:* party; celebration.

WORDS TO KNOW

elude (ĭ-lood′) *v.* to avoid or escape, especially by means of cleverness or skill

"Well, now you have lost it," said Brother Coyote. "With all that good cheese in easy reach, I will wait and gobble you up another time. *¡Vete!*[18] Scram!"

"*¡Gracias!*"[19] called Sister Fox as she scampered away. Then the greedy coyote jumped into the pond to pull out the cheese. But all he got for his efforts was wet fur and a bone-deep chill.

Shivering, his sopping tail dragging in the dust, he returned to his cave to plot a terrible revenge on his cousin.

Their final, fatal meeting came when Brother Coyote chased Sister Fox into a canebrake[20] and cornered her there.

"Now I am going to kill you and eat you, for all the misery you have caused me."

"That is fair," the fox replied. "But, listen! Let me help set things right, so that I can go to heaven with a clear conscience. I had not planned to tell anyone, but I was headed for this very place when you surprised me. You see," she said, lowering her voice to a whisper, "I have learned that a wedding party is coming this way. To reach the church, they must pass through this canebrake. The bride and groom are the children of very wealthy *hacendados*.[21] Their servants carry chickens to roast, *tortillas, frijoles,*[22] sweet cakes, and every manner of good thing to eat. Hidden beside the path here, I thought it would be easy to steal the best of what passes by."

"*¿De veras?*"[23] asked the ever-hungry coyote, wanting to believe her wild story.

"*Sí,*[24] it is true. Would I dare to tell you a lie," Sister Fox asked, "when you are going to send me to heaven today? San Pedro would not let me through the gate of pearls[25] with a fresh sin on my soul."

"That's true enough," agreed Brother Coyote.

"My only fear," said the fox, "is that the people will take the second path through the canebrake while we are watching this one. I will go and watch the other path. Then we must both listen for fireworks. That will mean the wedding party is coming. Whichever of us hears this must right away go and call the other, so that we will be ready for them."

"*¡Bueno!*" said the coyote, settling down to watch the path that wound through the

---

18. *¡Vete!* (vě'tě) *Spanish:* Get out of here!

19. *¡Gracias!* (grä'syäs) *Spanish:* Thank you!

20. **canebrake:** a dense growth of thick-stemmed grasses or reeds.

21. *hacendados* (ä-sěn-dä'dôs) *Spanish:* landowners; ranchers.

22. *tortillas* (tôr-tē'yäs), *frijoles* (frē-hô'lěs) *Spanish:* thin, round cakes of corn or wheat bread, and beans.

23. *¿De veras?* (dě' vě'räs) *Spanish:* Are you telling the truth?

24. *sí* (sē) *Spanish:* yes.

25. **San Pedro . . . gate of pearls:** Some Christians believe that Saint Peter (called San Pedro in Spanish) stands at the gates of heaven and decides who will be allowed to enter.

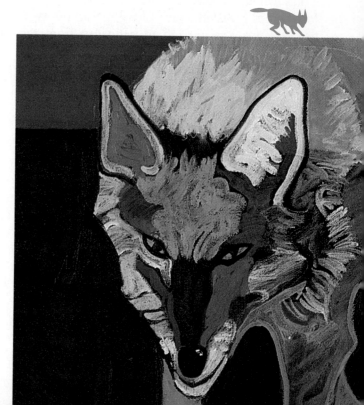

tall, tinder-dry[26] cane. He kept his ears up to listen for the sound of fireworks or Sister Fox's call.

"*¡Adiós!*" cried the sly fox, as she slipped out of the canebrake. Soon she returned, carrying in her jaws a burning brand from the kitchen of the *hacienda*. Using this, she set the canebrake on fire. When the blazing cane began to go *Pop! Popple! Pop!* the coyote mistook the sound for the noise of the wedding party's fireworks. He began to dance for joy, thinking of all the good food that he would soon have. He planned to take what he could for himself alone, and then he would punish his cousin.

The nearer the fire came and the louder the crackling and popping grew, the more wildly the coyote leaped and capered.[27] "Ah, here they come, here they come!" he sang.

Too late, the foolish creature discovered that he was dancing not at a wedding, but at a funeral—his own! ❖

---

26. **tinder-dry:** dry as the material used to light a fire.
27. **capered** (kā′pərd): jumped about in a happy, playful way.

ROBERT D. SAN SOUCI

An author of books for both young people and adults, Robert D. San Souci (1946–) has a deep interest in folklore that is reflected in much of his work. When his research into legendary American folk heroes revealed a lack of written accounts of heroines, he was inspired to write *Cut from the Same Cloth*. In that book, from which "Sister Fox and Brother Coyote" is taken, the author celebrates 15 strong-willed women of American folklore. San Souci worked five years on this collection and calls it "a labor of love."

San Souci was born in San Francisco. He worked for several bookstores until 1974, when he became a freelance writer, editor, and consultant. He also writes short stories, book reviews, and theater criticism for newspapers and magazines. San Souci has teamed with his illustrator brother Daniel on several books, including two award winners, *The Legend of Scarface: A Blackfeet Indian Tale* and *Song of Sedna: Sea-Goddess of the North.*

OTHER WORKS *The Talking Eggs, Sukey and the Mermaid, The Tsar's Promise*

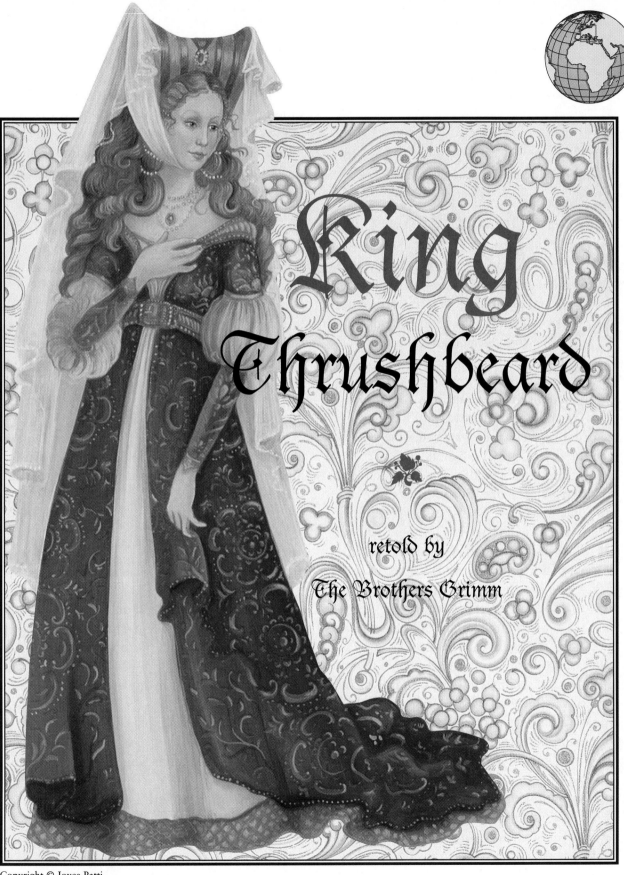

King Thrushbeard

retold by

The Brothers Grimm

king had a daughter who was unequaled for beauty, but she was so proud and thought so much of herself that no suitor[1] was good enough for her. She rejected one after another and to make matters worse poked fun at them. Once the king gave a great feast and invited all the marriageable young men from far and near. They were all lined up in the order of their rank: first came the kings, then the dukes, princes, counts, and barons, and last of all the knights. The king's daughter was led down the line, but to each suitor she had some objection. One was too fat and she called him a "wine barrel." The next was too tall: "Tall and skinny, that's a ninny." The third was short: "Short and thick won't do the trick." The fourth was too pale: "As pale as death." The fifth too red: "A turkey." The sixth wasn't straight enough: "Green wood, dried behind the stove." She found some fault with every one of them, but she made the most fun of a kindly king who was standing at the head of the line, and whose chin was slightly crooked. "Heavens above!" she cried. "He's got a chin like a thrush's bill!" And from then on he was known as Thrushbeard.

When the old king saw that his daughter did nothing but make fun of people and rejected all the suitors who had come to the feast, he flew into a rage and swore to make her marry the first beggar who came to his door. A few days later a wandering minstrel[2] came and sang under the window in the hope of earning a few coins. When the king heard him, he said: "Send him up." The minstrel appeared in his ragged, dirty clothes, sang for the king and his daughter, and asked for a gift when he had finished. The king said: "Your singing has pleased me so well that I'll give you my daughter for your wife." The princess was horrified, but the king said: "I swore I'd give you to the first beggar who came by, and I'm going to abide by my oath."

All her pleading was in vain; the priest was called, and she was married to the minstrel then and there. After the ceremony the king said: "Now that you're a beggar woman, I can't have you living in my palace. You can just go away with your husband."

The beggar took her by the hand and led her out of the palace, and she had to go with him on foot. They came to a large forest, and she asked:

"Who does that lovely forest belong to?"
"That forest belongs to King
    Thrushbeard.
If you'd taken him, you could call it your
    own."
"Alas, poor me, if I'd only known,
If only I'd taken King Thrushbeard!"

Next they came to a meadow, and she asked:

"Who does that lovely green meadow
    belong to?"
"That meadow belongs to King
    Thrushbeard.
If you'd taken him, you could call it your
    own."
"Alas, poor me, if I'd only known,

---

1. **suitor:** a man seeking to marry a woman.
2. **minstrel** (mĭn′strəl): traveling poet or singer.

If only I'd taken King Thrushbeard!"

Then they passed through a big city, and she asked:

"Who does this beautiful city belong to?"

"This city belongs to King Thrushbeard.
If you'd taken him, you could call it
    your own."

"Alas, poor me, if only I'd known,
If only I'd taken King Thrushbeard!"

"You give me a pain," said the minstrel, "always wishing for another husband. I suppose I'm not good enough for you!" At last they came to a tiny little house, and she said:

"Heavens, this shack is a disgrace!
Who could own such a wretched place?"

"If you want something done, you'll have to do it for yourself."

The minstrel answered, "It's my house and yours, where we shall live together." The king's daughter had to bend down to get through the low doorway. "Where are the servants?" she asked. "Servants, my foot!" answered the beggar. "If you want something done, you'll have to do it for yourself. And now make a fire and put on water for my supper because I'm dead tired." But the king's daughter didn't know the first thing about fires or cooking, and the beggar had to help her

or he wouldn't have had any supper at all. When they had eaten what little there was, they went to bed. But bright and early the next morning he made her get up and clean the house.

They worried along for a few days, but then their provisions were gone, and the man said: "Wife, we can't go on like this, eating and drinking and earning nothing. You'll have to weave baskets." He went out and cut willow withes[3] and brought them home. She began to weave but the hard withes bruised her tender hands. "I see that won't do," said the man. "Try spinning; maybe you'll be better at it." She sat down and tried to spin, but the hard thread soon cut her soft fingers and drew blood. "Well, well!" said the man. "You're no good for any work. I've made a bad bargain. But now I think I'll buy up some earthenware pots and dishes. All you'll have to do is sit in the marketplace and sell them."

"Goodness gracious!" she thought. "If somebody from my father's kingdom goes to the marketplace and sees me sitting there selling pots, how they'll laugh at me!" But there was no help for it; she had to give in or they would have starved.

The first day, all went well: people were glad to buy her wares because she was beautiful; they paid whatever she asked, and some didn't even trouble to take the pots they had paid for. The two of them lived on the proceeds as long as the stock held out, and then the husband

---

3. **withes** (wĭths): tough, bendable twigs.

bought up a fresh supply of crockery. She took a place at the edge of the market, set out her wares around her and offered them for sale. All of a sudden a drunken hussar[4] came galloping through, upset her pots and smashed them all into a thousand pieces. She began to cry; she was worried sick. "Oh!" she wailed. "What will become of me? What will my husband say!" She ran home and told him what had happened. "What did you expect?" he said. "Setting out earthenware pots at the edge of the market! But stop crying. I can see you're no good for any sensible work. Today I was at our king's palace. I asked if they could use a kitchen maid, and they said they'd take you. They'll give you your meals."

So the king's daughter became a kitchen maid and had to help the cook and do the most disagreeable work. She carried little jars in both her pockets, to take home the leftovers they gave her, and that's what she and her husband lived on.

It so happened that the marriage of the king's eldest son was about to be celebrated. The poor woman went upstairs and stood in the doorway of the great hall, looking on. When the candles were lit and the courtiers[5] began coming in, each more magnificent than the last, and everything was so bright and full of splendor, she was sad at heart. She thought of her miserable life and cursed the pride and arrogance that had brought her so low and made her so poor.

Succulent dishes were being carried in and out, and the smell drifted over to her. Now and then a servant tossed her a few scraps, and she put them into her little jars to take home.

"I can see you're no good for any sensible work."

And then the king's son appeared; he was dressed in silk and velvet and had gold chains around his neck. When he saw the beautiful woman in the doorway, he took her by the hand and asked her to dance with him, but she refused. She was terrified, for she saw it was King Thrushbeard, who had courted her and whom she had laughed at and rejected. She tried to resist, but he drew her into the hall. Then the string that kept her pockets in place snapped, the jars fell to the floor, the soup spilled and the scraps came tumbling out. The courtiers all began to laugh and jeer, and she

---

4. **hussar** (hə-zär′): a cavalry soldier—that is, a soldier who fights on horseback.

5. **courtiers** (kôr′tē-ərz): attendants at a royal palace.

would sooner have been a hundred fathoms[6] under the earth. She bounded through the door and tried to escape, but on the stairs a man caught her and brought her back, and when she looked at him, she saw it was King Thrushbeard again. He spoke kindly to her and said: "Don't be afraid. I am the minstrel you've been living with in that wretched shack; I disguised myself for love of you, and I was also the hussar who rode in and smashed your crockery. I did all that to humble your pride and punish you for the <u>insolent</u> way you laughed at me." Then she wept bitterly and said: "I've been very wicked and I'm not worthy to be your wife." But he said: "Don't cry; the hard days are over; now we shall celebrate our wedding." The maids came and dressed her magnificently, her father arrived with his whole court and congratulated her on her marriage to King Thrushbeard, and it was then that the feast became really joyful. I wish you and I had been there. ❖

---

6. **fathoms** (făth′əmz): units of measurement, each equal to six feet.

JAKOB AND WILHELM GRIMM

1785–1863 1786–1859

The brothers Grimm, born in Hanau, Germany, trained to be lawyers. However, an early exposure to old German romantic poems eventually led them to become interested in the language and literature of the German past. Jakob wrote, "It is high time that these old traditions were collected and rescued before they perish like dew in the hot sun."

Happier collecting local folk tales than practicing law, the brothers began a search for folk tales, particularly ones passed along orally to children, that was to become their lifelong commitment. They were always very close; according to Jakob, "Up to the very end, we worked in two rooms next to each other, always under one roof." *Grimm's Fairy Tales* has remained popular to this day.

OTHER WORKS *German Popular Tales, Grimm's Tales for Young and Old: The Complete Stories*

RESPONDING OPTIONS

LITERATURE CONNECTION PROJECT 1

Hold a Storytelling Festival Work with your classmates to present a storytelling festival for other classes in your grade or for a group of younger students. First decide which stories from Unit Six and which other tales from world folklore to include. Then, with the class divided into the following groups, prepare the story presentations:

Storytellers Rehearse each story before a mirror or in front of friends. Practice using gestures and tones of voice to make the stories come alive. If necessary, take turns telling some stories so that each person has an opportunity to perform.

Publicity Agents Create flyers to advertise the festival. Design and deliver invitations containing the date, time, and location. Produce illustrated programs to hand out at the festival.

Designers Locate or construct appropriate props, and provide costumes for the storytellers.

Producers Arrange each storyteller in a different location with a sign that announces the story title so that guests can choose among the stories. Producers might also locate audiotapes or videotapes of professional storytellers to set up for viewing in a separate area.

Camera Crew Locate video equipment and videotape the performances to share with other classes.

SOCIAL STUDIES CONNECTION PROJECT 2

Learn More About Money In "The Living Kuan-yin," Chin Po-wan's name foretells the million pieces of gold that will be his—and that he will eventually spend. Throughout history, money has taken various forms, from the salt used in ancient Rome to the seashells once commonly accepted as money in the South Pacific. Research the kinds of objects that served as money in the cultures represented in these stories. Use a chart similar to the one shown to organize your findings.

Culture: ___

Objects used as money:
___
___
___

Country: ___

Objects used as money:
___
___
___

Money Across Cultures

Celebrate Festivals Celebrations, feasts, and festivals are important events in ancient and modern cultures. The ancient Greeks held many celebrations, such as the Olympic games honoring Zeus and the drama festivals honoring Dionysus. Modern Vietnamese continue to celebrate the Dong Ky Fireworks Festival. Identify and research the festivals of the cultures represented in Unit Six. As a class, combine your research by painting a large mural that illustrates these celebrations. Include brief captions that explain the festivals.

ACROSS CULTURES MINI-PROJECTS

Build on the Oral Tradition Ask an older family member or friend to share a story that he or she remembers hearing as a child. As he or she tells the story, take notes or use a tape recorder or video camera. With your classmates, gather the written stories in a scrapbook along with photographs of the storytellers. Share the scrapbook with the individuals who told the stories.

Play "What's the Story?" Work with three or four other students to write, on small slips of paper, as many trivia questions about these three stories as you can. For example, one question might be, In which story does a snake play an important role? ("The Living Kuan-yin") Then exchange questions with another team, and see which team can answer the most questions correctly. If time permits, expand the game to include all the selections in this unit.

Read More About Minstrels In the Middle Ages and the Renaissance, minstrels—along with acrobats, puppeteers, and jugglers—wandered through Europe, performing in castles. Find out more about these minstrels and the kind of entertainment they provided. Share your information with the class, playing some recorded examples of the minstrels' music if possible.

Find the Trickster Almost every culture has trickster tales that were passed from one generation to the next through the oral tradition. Find out more about tricksters in world folklore. Then create a "Wanted" poster for your favorite trickster. Include an illustration, a description of the suspect, the charges against the suspect, and the amount of the reward.

MORE ABOUT THE CULTURES

- *The Great Wall of China* by Leonard Everett Fisher
- *See Inside an Ancient Chinese Town* by Penelope Hughes-Stanton
- *Passport to Mexico* by Carmen Irizarry

WRITING FROM EXPERIENCE

WRITING A REPORT

The stories in Unit Six, "The Oral Tradition," gave you a glimpse of the land, government, culture, and wonderings of people in other countries. Some of the stories may have left you with questions. Through research, you can answer your questions and begin a journey of discovery.

GUIDED ASSIGNMENT
Write an I-Search Report The next few pages will help you write an I-Search report—a report that includes facts about both your topic and your research process.

1 Think About Folk Tales

Which stories from this unit were your favorites? Do they remind you of other folk tales you have read or heard, perhaps from your own or a friend's culture? Would you like to learn about the country a particular folk tale came from? What else would you like to know?

Examining the Stories Think about how the details in the unit's folk tales are related to culture—arts, language, customs, or beliefs. Are these details you would like to explore about a country?

Analyzing the Examples The items on these pages were gathered by a student who became interested in finding out more about Japan after reading "Three Strong Women." What ideas do the items make you want to investigate? What kinds of information could you learn from each item?

Main Course

1.	SUKIYAKI	$12.95
2.	YAKI-NIKU	12.95
3.	YOSE-NABE	13.95
4.	TEMPURA	11.95
5.	TERIYAKI	12.95
6.	SASHIMI	15.95
7.	CHIRASHI	14.95
8.	HAMACHI-DON	14.95
9.	UNAGI-DON	16.95
10.	TEKKA-DON	14.95
11.	SUSHI COMBINATION	

    A. 8 pcs. of Sushi and 1 Roll of California Maki

    B. 6 pcs. of Sushi and Tekka Roll

Japanese meals sometimes look more like art than like food!

Japanese Menu

How would the items on this page compare with similar items from your own culture? In what ways are the two cultures different? How are they the same?

Japanese Doll

The Quake's *Shaken* Lives

KOBE, Japan, Jan. 21—The 1.4 million people who live in this city used to devote themselves to activities such as making steel, building ships, designing computers, running a port and raising children. But at 5:46 a.m. last Tuesday, in one horrifying instant, the fabric of their lives was torn.

The earthquake that rocked western Japan forced hundreds of thousands of people in this sleek city, an important commercial center, to confront scenes of chaos and destruction they never dreamed they would face. Residents of Kobe, who almost universally believed their region to be safe from the quakes that regularly hit many parts of the Japanese archipelago, found themselves heaved into a world of crushed buildings, raging fires and death on an appalling scale.

Paul Blustein, William Branigin, and Shigehiko Togo
from *The Washington Post*

I wonder how often Japan has earthquakes. Probably a lot, since there's a folk tale about them.

Travel Brochure

I heard that some of Japan's mountains are actually volcanoes.

❷ Choose Your Own Topic

Decide on the topic you want to explore—perhaps a country or culture featured in the unit or from your own background. You may even want to research one of the folk tales you read. Take a few minutes to freewrite what you already know about your topic. Then write what you'd like to learn.

LASERLINKS
• *WRITING SPRINGBOARD*
WRITING COACH

Researching Your Topic

The "I" in "I-Search" In an I-Search report, the experiences you have while researching are just as important as the information you are gathering. The steps on these pages will help you locate answers to the questions you have and to chart your progress along the way.

① Find a Focus

You may need to narrow the focus of your topic—for example, you can't cover *everything* about a country in a short report. To help you focus, try reading an encyclopedia article about your topic. Skim the sections to help you find subjects to zero in on.

Set a Purpose Why do you care about your topic? Jot down your purpose for writing. This information can help you focus your research and will be included in your I-Search report.

Make a Research Plan Review your freewriting and list questions you want to answer. Let the list guide your research efforts.

② Dig for Information

The research process can uncover information you never thought to ask about. Below are some good sources.

- Check on-line services for information about your topic.
- Newspaper travel sections often describe the culture of a country.
- Your teacher or librarian can help you identify private organizations and government agencies with information about your country.
- Museums provide a great deal of cultural information about countries.
- Neighbors, friends, or family members from the country you're exploring can also provide you with valuable information.

③ Keep Track of Your Progress

What steps are you taking to find out what you need to know? What are you discovering along the way? To help you keep track of your experiences, you might record your ideas, accomplishments, and questions in an I-Search diary like the one on the opposite page.

Source cards for a magazine or newspaper article (top), for a book (middle), for an encyclopedia entry (bottom)

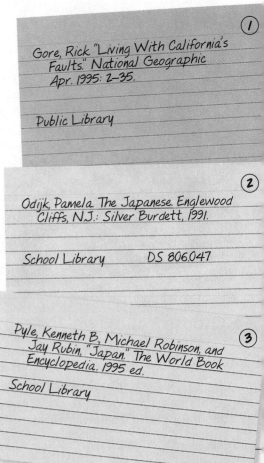

① Gore, Rick "Living With California's Faults." *National Geographic* Apr. 1995: 2–35.

Public Library

② Odijk, Pamela. *The Japanese.* Englewood Cliffs, N.J.: Silver Burdett, 1991.

School Library   DS 806.047

③ Pyle, Kenneth B., Michael Robinson, and Jay Rubin. "Japan." *The World Book Encyclopedia.* 1995 ed.

School Library

④ Create Source Cards

Source cards, like the ones on page 750, can help you keep track of the sources you use in your research. List the publishing information as shown for each book or article on a separate index card, then number each card. The cards will help you create your List of Sources, which you will attach to the end of your report.

⑤ Take Notes

Many writers record the information they plan to use in their report on index cards like the ones below. Write the main idea of the note at the top of each card, along with the number you assigned the source on its source card. As you take notes, rewrite the information in your own words to avoid plagiarizing, or using other people's words without giving them credit. The SkillBuilder gives more tips on taking notes.

Note Cards

Clothing ②

"During the Ashikaga period (fourteenth to fifteenth centuries), the kimono—a long, flowing robe worn with a sash—became the standard garment for both men and women." 23

(Quote)

Clothing ②

Numbers and colors of robes showed a person's status. Emperor and government officials wore the fanciest clothing.

(Paraphrase)

Student's I-Search Diary

May

Mon	Tue	Wed
7	1 Talked to Mr. Izu about his parents, who live in Japan. What a find!	2 Saw costumes from all different periods of history at City Museum.
	8	9

Sharing Your Experience

A Personal Touch What fascinating information did you learn? Which sources helped you the most, and which let you down? These pages will show you how to set up your report and combine the information you learned with your research experiences, both good and bad.

1 Organize Your Ideas

Before beginning your draft, you might want to sort your cards into groups of similar ideas and then use the groups to create an outline. This outline can help you see where you need more information and what notes don't really fit. The SkillBuilder on page 753 can help you create an outline.

Student's Rough Draft

Student's Outline

Good details about your purpose and personal experience! A.C.

Introduction (purpose for writing about Japan)

I. Country's Size
   A. Number of islands
   B. Number of people (?)

II. Earthquakes
   A. Why they happen
   B. How many per year

III. Sumo Wrestling
   A. National heroes
   B. ?????

IV. Clothing
   A. Influence of West (?)
   B. Traditional costumes
      1. kimonos
      2. makeup

V. Government
   A. Emperor
   B. How it's like the U.S.

Conclusion (summary)

Exploring Japan

"Three Strong Women" is a really funny Japanese folk tale that is as enjoyable as a movie. After reading the story, I could picture what everything looked like: the countryside, the clothing, and the makeup the rich people wore. I wondered if I had imagined it right. I was curious if an emperor still ruled the country. I wondered how often Japanese people felt earthquakes. I really wanted to learn more about Japan, but I wasn't too excited about writing a paper on it. *leave this out*

The first place I looked was the encyclopedia. I learned that the country of Japan is actually made up of thousands of islands, which form a curve that extends for about 1,200 miles, not just one big one, as I always thought! The encyclopedia article also explained that Japan has about 1,500 earthquakes a year! Most of them are so small they don't cause any damage, but bad ones happen every few years.

This doesn't sound like you. Have you paraphrased your source or is this a quote? A.C.

I had to find other sources to get more information on the subject I was most curious about: sumo wrestling.
— *explain this after sumo wrestling*

② Write a Rough Draft

Let your outline guide you as you write your draft. Refer to your note cards for specific information about your topic, and your I-Search diary for details about your researching experiences. One student's rough draft is shown on the left.

Introduction You might begin by telling why you wanted to learn more about your topic. A brief anecdote or story explaining why you care about the topic is one way to do this.

Body As you present what you learned, explain the steps of your research as well. You might tell where you found information and what you felt like when you did or didn't locate answers to important questions. Focus on the experiences where you learned interesting things or had a strong reaction. Your writing can be personal and informal in this type of a report, but be sure your draft flows logically from one subject to the next.

Conclusion End your I-Search report by summarizing what this personal research experience meant to you. Did you come to a new understanding or appreciation of your topic? How did your feelings or ideas about the topic change?

③ Rework and Share Your Draft

You chose your topic because it had special meaning for you. Be sure this meaning comes through in your report.

 PEER RESPONSE

When you feel ready for feedback, trade drafts with a classmate and ask questions like the following.

- Why do you think I chose to write about this topic?
- Does my report read smoothly from beginning to end? How might I rearrange parts to make it more logical?
- Do you now know more than you did about this topic? Which parts need more explanation?
- Could any part of my research process have been improved? How?

SkillBuilder

 RESEARCH SKILLS

Outlining Your Ideas
An outline like the one on page 752 can make drafting your report easier, because you have a plan to follow. To make an outline, look for main ideas, such as *earthquakes* and *clothing,* in the notes you have taken. List these ideas as headings next to Roman numerals. Then, beneath each main idea, list the details you want to include. Use capital letters for the more general details, then numbers and lowercase letters for finer details.

APPLYING WHAT YOU'VE LEARNED
Try using your note cards to create an outline. You might want to do some follow-up research to fill in any holes.

 WRITING HANDBOOK

For more information on outlining, see page 798 of the Writing Handbook.

RETHINK & EVALUATE

Preparing to Revise

1. Did your outline help you as you wrote your draft? Why or why not?
2. Did you have enough information as you drafted? Did you have too much? What would you change about the way you research next time?

Pulling It All Together

The Final Product Think about your purpose for writing about your topic. What changes do you need to make to get that purpose across to your readers? Will you add personal experiences, or take out information that's not related? Do you want to include photographs, maps, graphs, or illustrations? Now's your chance to polish your draft.

① Revise and Edit

The following points will help you finalize your I-Search report.

- Think about which of your peer suggestions you will use to make improvements to your report.
- Be sure you have used your own words or given credit to the proper source if you have included quotes.
- Use the Standards for Evaluation to help you balance information with personal experiences in your report.

② Prepare Your Final Copy

Use the student model and the SkillBuilder on the opposite page to turn your source cards into a List of Sources. Attach the list to the end of your report.

Where did this student find information about his topic?

What other graphics might you add to this report to give more information?

Student's Final Draft

Exploring Japan

Keith Jensen

Mrs. Miller

Room 206

12 May 1997

Jensen 1

Exploring Japan

I read "Three Strong Women," a Japanese folktale that was as good as a movie. I had a picture in my mind of what everything looked like: the countryside, the clothing, and the makeup the rich people wore. I wondered if I had imagined it right. I was curious to know whether an emperor still ruled the country, and why the people did certain things like paint their faces white. I wondered how often Japanese people felt earthquakes, especially since there was a bad one in Kobe, Japan, two years ago.

The first place I looked for information was the encyclopedia, where I found some quick answers. For example, through an article in <u>The World Book</u>

<u>Encyclopedia</u>, I learned that the country of Japan is actually four big islands and thousands of smaller islands. The four main islands are 1,200 miles long. Over 120 million people live on the islands of Japan!

Next, I went to the library at my school to find out about sumo wrestling. Most of the books about Japan didn't give much information on this sport except to say that almost all Japanese people are big fans. I tried calling places that teach judo to see if they knew where I could find information on the subject. Then my sister showed me an article about sumo wrestlers in a health magazine. It was really helpful. It told how all the wrestlers live and train together. They eat a traditional sumo stew made of rice, fish, and greens. Many wrestlers weigh over 400 pounds!

List of Sources

Langone, John. <u>In the Shogun's Shadow: Understanding a Changing Japan</u>. Boston: Little, Brown, 1994.

Odijk, Pamela. <u>The Japanese</u>. Englewood Cliffs, N.J.: Silver Burdett, 1991.

Pyle, Kenneth B., Michael Robinson, and Jay Rubin. "Japan." <u>The World Book Encyclopedia</u>. 1995 ed.

Standards for Evaluation

An I-Search report
- shows the writer's strong personal interest in the topic
- presents information from several sources
- includes an account of the writer's research experiences
- concludes with the writer's personal reactions and observations

---

SkillBuilder

 GRAMMAR FROM WRITING

Creating a List of Sources
Include a List of Sources with your I-Search report to show the sources of your information. To create your list, gather only the source cards you actually used in your report and alphabetize them by the authors' last names. The student model at the left shows how to record and punctuate the information on your List of Sources.

GRAMMAR HANDBOOK

For help with creating and editing a List of Sources, see page 842 of the Grammar Handbook and page 798 of the Writing Handbook.

Editing Checklist

- Have you correctly listed and punctuated the information on your List of Sources?
- Have you checked quotes to make sure they are accurate?

REFLECT & ASSESS

Evaluating Your Experience

1. How is an I-Search report different from other writing?
2. What did you learn about yourself from this assignment?

📁 **PORTFOLIO** Describe the research skills you used in this assignment. Attach your notes to your report and add them to your portfolio.

REFLECT & ASSESS

UNIT SIX: ACROSS TIME AND PLACE: THE ORAL TRADITION

In this unit, you discovered that tales from the past continue to delight, teach, and inspire readers and listeners. To show what you've learned, complete one or more of the options in each of the following sections.

REFLECTING ON THEME

OPTION 1 **Creating a Book Cover** Pretend that the selections in this unit are going to be bound together as a separate book. Design a book cover reflecting as much of the folklore you've read as possible. Include your work in a class exhibit of covers.

Consider . . .
• what cultures are represented in the unit
• which selections have memorable main characters
• what themes or other elements the selections share

OPTION 2 **Watching Behavior** Many characters in this unit have to consider or change their behavior. Use a chart like this one to analyze the actions of four of the characters. In a discussion with your classmates, point out lessons taught in the selections that are still being learned today.

Character	Behavior	Outcome of Behavior	What I Learned

OPTION 3 **Studying Heroes** With a partner, review the folklore you have read, identifying at least five characters who act as heroes. Use a web like this one to list qualities you consider heroic—such as bravery, wisdom, and unselfishness. Choose the character who you think displays the most heroic qualities, and write a brief essay explaining your choice.

Self-Assessment: What themes—messages about human nature—were present in much of the folklore you've read? What one lesson in the folklore stands out the most for you? What similarities do you see between tales of past heroes and tales about heroes of today? Respond to these questions in your notebook.

REVIEWING LITERARY CONCEPTS

OPTION 1 **Looking at Folklore** This unit has introduced you to different types of folklore. Working with a small group of classmates, choose six selections that you think are most suitable for storytelling. Determine what tones of voice might be used for their characters, as well as what gestures, costumes, and props might be used in telling these selections. In diagrams like the one shown, list at least two storytelling suggestions for each selection. Combine your suggestions with your classmates' in a book of storytelling tips.

OPTION 2 **Looking at Cultures** What insights into different cultures did you gain as you read the folklore in this unit? What did you learn about different customs? What similarities and differences between cultures did you see? For at least two pairs of selections in this unit, create Venn diagrams to compare the cultures represented in the selections. Then discuss the similarities and differences between the cultures with a small group of classmates. Present your group's conclusions to the entire class.

Self-Assessment: What do you understand about types of folklore that you didn't realize before completing these activities? What has reading about other cultures revealed to you about your own culture? Answer these questions in your notebook. Also explain why you think the oral tradition continues today.

PORTFOLIO BUILDING

- **Connecting to the Literature** Select an example of your work for a Literature Connection that you would like to talk about. Perhaps you wrote a script based on a tale, wrote an instruction manual for a board game, or created a storyboard. In a note, comment on what you enjoyed about creating the work, and explain how the folklore you read inspired you. Add the example and the note to your portfolio.

- **Writing About Literature** Earlier in this unit, you wrote a literary review to explain what you liked and disliked about a story. Imagine that a local bookstore has asked you to design a poster to let people know about the story. What images might you draw to show how you felt about the story? What written information might you include? Attach your ideas and a rough design of the poster to your literary review.

- **Writing from Experience** In writing your I-search report, you had a chance to investigate a topic that is interesting to you. Think about your research process. Where did you find the best information? If you had to do another I-search report, which sources would you return to? Are there other places you might look for information? Include your thoughts with your report if you decide to keep it in your portfolio.

- **Personal Choice** Review all of your work for this unit, including Literature Connections, Social Studies Connections, Art Connections, and Comparing Cultures projects. Select written work or project that you think best captures your response to the folklore you read. Write a note explaining what you learned from the writing or project. Attach the note to the writing or project evaluation, and place both in your portfolio.

Self-Assessment: At this point, your portfolio must be bulging with all of the material you've collected. Which pieces best reflect how you've grown as a writer? Look through your portfolio and identify the pieces that show the greatest development of your writing skills. Clip them together with a note in which you review your portfolio.

SETTING GOALS

As you completed the reading and writing activities in this unit, you probably found certain selections and types of writing that you really liked. Which author's work would you like to find out more about? Which cultures are you curious enough about to continue to explore? Write any goals you have on an index card. Display the card on a bulletin board with those of your classmates.

Student Resource Bank

Words to Know: Access Guide

abandon (646)
absurd (616)
admonishingly (325)
aggression (70)
agility (334)
anxiety (99)
apt (58)
ardent (58)
audacious (220)
audible (415)
banish (26)
bazaar (24)
blissful (492)
bondage (265)
camouflage (67)
chaos (260)
clamber (716)
clamor (401)
clan (24)
client (407)
coexistence (68)
commercial (407)
commitment (408)
compassion (730)
compressed (67)
confirm (421)
confrontation (336)
consequently (294)
console (353)
consolidate (531)
consoling (599)
conspirator (580)
consume (231)
contemporary (331)
contrary (350)
counter (372)
credibility (416)
cunning (324)
curtly (668)
customary (466)
customs (363)
debris (230)
deceit (397)
decree (24)
depleted (33)
deprivation (56)
deprive (217)

descendant (294)
desolate (612)
despair (488)
destiny (615)
destitute (730)
detest (350)
devise (217)
devour (653)
discreet (415)
dislodging (131)
dispense (219)
dissuade (472)
distorted (714)
diverted (421)
domain (593)
dominant (72)
dread (217)
drudgery (331)
dumbfounded (239)
dwindle (730)
dynasty (260)
elegant (71)
elude (738)
embrace (237)
emit (696)
endure (97)
envision (493)
erect (713)
eruption (129)
esteemed (613)
evasive (362)
exceed (231)
exclusive (332)
exile (642)
expedition (44)
exploit (466)
extravagantly (730)
fanatical (495)
fate (713)
feeble (718)
ferocious (649)
fidgety (492)
fiend (583)
frenzied (186)
fume (239)
fumigate (369)
gratification (462)

gravely (644)
grudging (96)
harass (334)
harpoon (41)
hoard (614)
hover (679)
hurtle (69)
illiterate (394)
illuminate (419)
immortal (712)
immortality (530)
inadvertently (732)
indifferent (219)
indignantly (712)
indolent (664)
induce (401)
infinite (232)
inhabitant (260)
insensitive (334)
insignificant (528)
insolent (745)
insufferable (736)
intact (474)
intricate (531)
intrusion (217)
laden (219)
lagoon (41)
lethal (370)
luminous (71)
magnification (68)
maneuver (421)
margin (372)
mascot (188)
maze (640)
meager (645)
menace (121)
menial (57)
mimicking (407)
mocking (688)
monopoly (337)
morosely (392)
mortally (231)
mute (351)
muting (433)
novelty (120)
obscure (711)
obsessed (530)

obstinacy (713)
oceanarium (67)
ominous (365)
peal (238)
phosphorus (45)
pious (218)
plush (332)
pompous (218)
ponder (27)
possess (322)
poverty-stricken (293)
practical (295)
preceding (461)
predator (119)
premise (266)
preservation (532)
prestige (491)
procedure (266)
proclaim (646)
prop (33)
properly (321)
proposition (58)
prosper (266)
pursue (493)
quest (607)
quiver (33)
ravishing (668)
rear (295)
reassure (348)
rebellious (490)
reef (41)
refrain (488)
relentless (33)
repentance (693)
reproduction (531)
resentful (57)
reservation (267)
restore (134)
resume (417)
reunion (152)
revelation (421)
revulsion (399)
rival (642)
rummaging (121)
sacred (724)
salvaging (335)
saunter (391)

savoring (98)
scavenging (119)
scornful (395)
scurry (648)
sedately (99)
sentinel (475)
shrine (128)
smirk (33)
sodden (367)
stamina (54)
stature (617)
status (261)

stereotype (172)
stoop (187)
stupendous (416)
stupor (369)
subside (697)
succulent (744)
sufficient (461)
sullen (391)
surpass (530)
surveyor (57)
systematically (472)
taunt (668)

tedious (475)
tenement (192)
thrashing (186)
thrive (615)
throng (578)
tolerate (695)
torrent (238)
trade (321)
transition (363)
trek (262)
tumult (238)
turmoil (391)

tyranny (57)
tyrant (532)
unique (411)
unparalleled (532)
vague (489)
validate (61)
vanquish (615)
vapor (133)
wily (736)

Pronunciation Key

Symbol	Examples	Symbol	Examples	Symbol	Examples
ă	at, gas	m	man, seem	v	van, save
ā	ape, day	n	night, mitten	w	web, twice
ä	father, barn	ng	sing, anger	y	yard, lawyer
âr	fair, dare	ŏ	odd, not	z	zoo, reason
b	bell, table	ō	open, road, grow	zh	treasure, garage
ch	chin, lunch	ô	awful, bought, horse	ə	awake, even, pencil,
d	dig, bored	oi	coin, boy		pilot, focus
ĕ	egg, ten	ŏŏ	look, full	ər	perform, letter
ē	evil, see, meal	ōō	root, glue, through		
f	fall, laugh, phrase	ou	out, cow		**Sounds in Foreign Words**
g	gold, big	p	pig, cap	KH	*German* ich, auch;
h	hit, inhale	r	rose, star		*Scottish* loch
hw	white, everywhere	s	sit, face	N	*French* entre, bon, fin
ĭ	inch, fit	sh	she, mash	œ	*French* feu, cœur;
ī	idle, my, tried	t	tap, hopped		*German* schön
îr	dear, here	th	thing, with	ü	*French* utile, rue;
j	jar, gem, badge	*th*	then, other		*German* grün
k	keep, cat, luck	ŭ	up, nut		
l	load, rattle	ûr	fur, earn, bird, worm		

Stress Marks

′   This mark indicates that the preceding syllable receives the primary stress. For example, in the word *language,* the first syllable is stressed: lăng′gwĭj.

′   This mark is used only in words in which more than one syllable is stressed. It indicates that the preceding syllable is stressed, but somewhat more weakly than the syllable receiving the primary stress. In the word *literature,* for example, the first syllable receives the primary stress, and the last syllable receives a weaker stress: lĭt′ər-ə-chŏŏr′.

Adapted from *The American Heritage Dictionary of the English Language, Third Edition;* Copyright © 1992 by Houghton Mifflin Company. Used with the permission of Houghton Mifflin Company.

Reading Terms and Literary Concepts

Act An act is a major unit of action in a play. *The Hobbit,* for example, has two acts. An act may be divided into smaller sections, called **scenes.**

Alliteration Alliteration is a repetition of consonant sounds at the beginning of words. Poets and songwriters use alliteration to emphasize certain words. Alliteration can also add a musical quality. Note the repetition of the *l* and *r* sound in this line from "The Cremation of Sam McGee":

> In the long, long night, by the lone firelight, while the huskies, round in a ring . . .

Analysis Analysis is a process of breaking something down into its parts so that they can be studied individually. In analyzing a poem, for example, one might look at such elements as form, rhyme, rhythm, figurative language, imagery, mood, and theme.

Anecdote An anecdote is a short, entertaining account of a person or an event. Anecdotes are often included in larger works to amuse or to make a point. In the excerpt from *Woodsong,* Gary Paulsen tells an anecdote about his encounter with a bear to point out that humans must respect the wildness of nature.

Audience The audience of a piece of writing is the particular group of people that the writer is addressing. A writer considers his or her audience when deciding on a subject, a purpose for writing, and a style in which to write.

Author's Purpose An author's purpose is his or her reason for creating a particular work. The purpose may be to entertain, to inform, to express an opinion, or to persuade readers to do or believe something. An author may have more than one purpose for writing, but usually one is the most important.

Autobiography An autobiography is the true story of a person's life, told by that person. Because autobiographies are written about real people and events, they are a form of nonfiction. Autobiographies are normally written from the first-person point of view. The excerpts from *Woodsong* and *The Lost Garden* are examples of autobiography. Shorter autobiographical writings include journals, diaries, and memoirs.

Biography A biography is the true story of a person's life, written by someone else. Biographies are usually written from the third-person point of view. "Matthew Henson at the Top of the World" is an example of biography.

Cast of Characters In the script of a play, a cast of characters is a list of all the characters in the play. It is usually found at the beginning of the script, and the characters are usually listed in the order they appear. There is a cast of characters at the beginning of *A Shipment of Mute Fate.*

Cause and Effect Two events are related as cause and effect if one brings about, or causes, the other. The event that happens first is the cause; the one that follows is the effect. Writers sometimes signal cause-and-effect relationships with words and phrases such as *because, next, therefore, since, so that,* and *in order that.* This sentence from Woodsong deals with a cause and its effect: "Because we feed processed meat to the dogs, there is always the smell of meat over the kennel."

Character Each person, animal, or imaginary creature in a work of literature is called a character. The most important characters are called **main characters.** Less important characters are called **minor characters.** In "The School Play," Robert is the main character, and Belinda and the other characters are minor characters.

Characterization The ways in which writers create and develop characters' personalities are known as characterization. A writer can develop a character in four basic ways: (1) by physically describing the character, (2) by presenting the character's thoughts, speech, and actions, (3) by presenting the thoughts, speech, and actions of other characters, and (4) by directly commenting on the character's nature.

Chronological Order Chronological order is the order in which events happen in time. In some stories, events are related in chronological order; other stories move forward and backward in time.

Clarifying The process of stopping while reading, to quickly review what has happened and to look for answers to questions, is called clarifying. It helps readers draw conclusions about what is suggested but not directly stated in the writing.

Climax In the plot of a story or play, the climax is the point of greatest interest. At the climax, the outcome of the story becomes clear. The climax of "Tuesday of the Other June," for example, occurs when June T. says "No" to the Other June with such forceful determination that the astonished bully leaves her alone.
See also **Plot.**

Comparison To point out what two or more things have in common is to make a comparison. Writers use comparisons to make ideas and details clearer to readers. In "Eleven," for example, the process of growing older is compared to little wooden dolls that fit together, one inside another.
See also **Metaphor** *and* **Simile.**

Concrete Poetry. *See* **Form.**

Conflict Conflict is a struggle between opposing forces. Almost every story and play is built around a conflict that the main character faces. A conflict may be external or internal. **External conflict** is a struggle between a character and an outside force, such as society, a force of nature, or another character. In the excerpt from *Woodsong,* for example, Gary Paulsen faces an external conflict with a bear. **Internal conflict,** on the other hand, is a struggle within a character's mind. It may occur when the character has to make a difficult decision or deal with opposing feelings. Selo's uncertainty, in "Cricket in the Road," about whether to make up with his friends is an example of internal conflict.
See also **Plot.**

Connecting When readers relate the content of a literary work to what they already know or have experienced, they are making connections.

Connecting helps readers identify with the experiences of the characters. For example, when they read Sandra Cisneros's story "Eleven," readers may remember times when they were embarrassed or falsely accused.

Context Clues Unfamiliar words are often surrounded by context clues—words or phrases that can help readers infer their meaning. A context clue may be a definition, a synonym, an example, or a comparison or contrast.

Contrast To contrast is to point out differences between things. Note how the narrator of "The All-American Slurp" contrasts Chinese and American eating habits in the following sentence: "In fact we didn't use individual plates at all but picked up food from the platters in the middle of the table and brought it directly to our rice bowls."

Couplet A couplet is a rhymed pair of lines in a poem. The poem "Barbara Frietchie" consists entirely of couplets.

Description Description is the process by which a writer creates a picture, in words, of a scene, an event, or a character. To create descriptions, writers choose details carefully— usually details that appeal to readers' senses of sight, sound, smell, touch, and taste. Note the details in this passage from "My Friend Flicka," which describes the view outside Kennie's window:

> The hill opposite the house, covered with arrow-straight jack pines, was sharply etched in the thin air of the eight-thousand-foot altitude. Where it fell away, vivid green grass ran up to meet it; and over range and upland poured the strong Wyoming sunlight that stung everything into burning color.

Dialogue The words that characters speak aloud are called dialogue. Dialogue moves a plot forward and reveals the personalities of the characters. In a play, dialogue is the main way the writer tells the story. The dialogue in fiction is usually set off with quotation marks. No quotation marks are used for the dialogue in plays.

Drama A drama, or play, is a form of literature meant to be performed before an audience. The story is presented through the dialogue and the actions of the characters. The written form of a play is known as a **script.** A script usually includes **dialogue,** a **cast of characters,** and **stage directions** that give specific instructions about performing the play.

Essay An essay is a short work of nonfiction that deals with a single subject. Essays are often found in newspapers and magazines. The purpose of an essay may be to express ideas or feelings, to analyze a topic, to inform, to entertain, or to persuade. "The Mushroom" is an essay that expresses ideas.

Evaluating Evaluating is the process of judging the worth of something or someone. In evaluating a literary work, you might focus on the elements found in that type of work—for example, the plot, setting, characters, and theme of a work of fiction. You can also evaluate a work by comparing and contrasting it with similar works.

External Conflict. *See* **Conflict.**

Fable A fable is a brief story that teaches a lesson about life. In many fables, the characters are animals that act and speak like human beings. A fable often ends with a moral—a statement that summarizes its lesson. "The Disobedient Child" is an example of a fable.

Fact and Opinion A fact is a statement that can be proved, such as "Mars is the fourth planet from the sun." An opinion, in contrast, is a statement that expresses a person's feelings, such as "Mars is the most beautiful planet." Opinions cannot be proved.

Fantasy Literature that contains at least one fantastic or unreal element is called fantasy. The setting of a work of fantasy might be a totally imaginary world, or it might be a realistic place where very unusual or impossible things happen. "The Enchanted Raisin" is an example of fantasy because it presents a person who turns into a raisin.

Fiction Literature that tells about imaginary people, places, or events is called fiction. In some works of fiction, the entire story is made up; in others, the story is based in part on real people or events. Fiction includes both **short stories** and **novels.** A short story can usually be read in one sitting. Novels are longer and tend to be more complex.

Figurative Language In figurative language, words are used to express more than their dictionary meaning. Figurative language conveys vivid images to the minds of readers. In this passage from "The Circuit," note how the figurative language helps create a picture of working in the fields:

> The sun kept beating down. The buzzing insects, the wet sweat, and the hot dry dust made the afternoon seem to last forever. Finally the mountains around the valley reached out and swallowed the sun.

See also **Metaphor, Personification,** *and* **Simile.**

Folk Tale A folk tale is a simple story that has been passed down from generation to generation by word of mouth. Folk tales are usually about people, animals, or occurrences in nature and are usually set in times long past. Their plots often include supernatural elements, like the talking animals in "Why Monkeys Live in Trees" or the granting of wishes in "The Three Wishes."

Foreshadowing A hint about an event that will occur later in a story is called foreshadowing. An example of foreshadowing occurs in the opening lines of *A Shipment of Mute Fate,* when the main character, Chris, warns the audience that a disturbing event will take place: "But all at once in the midst of those peaceful surroundings, a cold chill gripped me, and I shivered with sudden dread—dread of the thing I was doing, and was about to do!"

Form The form of a poem is the shape the words and lines make on the page. Occasionally, a poet uses the form of a poem to emphasize the poem's meaning. In **concrete poetry,** for example, the poem's shape reflects its subject. Note how the lines in Dorthi Charles's poem "Concrete Cat" resemble the parts of a cat.

Free Verse Poetry without regular patterns of rhyme or rhythm is called free verse. Free verse often sounds like conversation. "Another Mountain" is an example of a poem written in free verse.

Generalization A generalization is a statement about a whole group. Generalizations may be untrue if they are too broad or not based on fact. In "The All-American Slurp," for example, Meg's statement "All Americans slurp" is a generalization. The word *all* in this generalization makes the statement untrue.

Genre Literature is normally divided into four main categories, or genres: **fiction, nonfiction, poetry,** and **drama.**

Haiku Haiku is a traditional form of Japanese poetry. A haiku normally has three lines and describes a single moment, feeling, or thing. In a traditional haiku, the first and third lines contain five syllables each, and the second line contains seven syllables.

Humor The quality that makes something seem funny or amusing is called humor. Writers can create humor by using exaggeration, amusing descriptions, sarcasm, witty dialogue, and other devices. For example, Isaac Bashevis Singer uses Lyzer's ridiculous economies to create humor in "Shrewd Todie and Lyzer the Miser."

Imagery Words and phrases that appeal to readers' senses are referred to as imagery. Writers usually try to describe characters, places, and events in ways that help readers imagine how they look, feel, smell, sound, and taste. Note the imagery in Raymond R. Patterson's haiku "Glory, Glory . . .":

> Across Grandmother's knees
> A kindly sun
> Laid a yellow quilt.

Inference An inference is a logical guess based on evidence. A good reader makes inferences, or draws conclusions, as he or she reads—trying to figure out more than the words say. The evidence may be facts the writer provides, or it may be experiences from the reader's own life. The end of "The Adoption of Albert," for example, requires readers to make an inference about what the coffee contains.

Internal Conflict. *See* **Conflict.**

Interview An interview is a meeting in which one person asks another about personal matters, professional matters, or both. Interviews may be tape-recorded, filmed, or recorded in writing. The excerpt from *Talking with Artists* is based on an interview.

Legend A legend is a story that is handed down from the past and tells about something that really happened or someone who really lived. Legends often mix fact and fiction. "The White Buffalo Calf Woman and the Sacred Pipe" is an example of a Native American legend.

Main Character. *See* **Character.**

Main Idea A main idea is a central idea that a writer is trying to get across. It may be the central idea of an entire work or the thought expressed in the topic sentence of a paragraph. (A topic sentence may be found at the beginning, middle, or end of a paragraph.) A writer may need to use several paragraphs to develop a main idea. In one paragraph of "Chinatown," Laurence Yep begins by stating the paragraph's main idea in a topic sentence and, after supporting the idea with examples, concludes with a restatement of it:

> Moreover, my lack of Chinese made me an outsider in Chinatown—sometimes even among my friends. . . . It was as if we belonged to two different worlds.

Memoir. *See* **Autobiography.**

Metaphor A metaphor is a comparison of two things that have some quality in common. Unlike a simile, a metaphor does not contain a word such as *like, as, than,* or *resembles.* For example, in *A Shipment of Mute Fate,* Chris uses the following metaphor: "Fear was a heavy fog in the lungs of all of us."

Minor Character. *See* **Character.**

Mood A mood is a feeling that a literary work conveys to readers. Writers carefully choose words and phrases to create moods like sadness, excitement, and anger. In "My Friend Flicka," for example, a mood of deep sadness is created when it appears that Flicka will die in the stream.

Myth A myth is a traditional story that explains how something came to be. Some myths explain the origin of the world or of people. Others explain elements of nature or social customs. The characters in myths are often gods and human heroes with supernatural abilities. Because myths have been handed down from one generation to the next for a long time, their original authors are unknown. "Wings" is a retelling of a myth of ancient Greece.

Narrative Writing that tells a story is called a narrative. The events in a narrative may be real or imagined. Narratives that deal with real events include autobiographies and biographies. Fictional narratives include myths, short stories, novels, and narrative poems.

Narrative Poetry Narrative poetry is poetry that tells a story. Like any story, a narrative poem contains a setting, characters, and a plot. It may also contain such elements of poetry as rhyme, rhythm, imagery, and figurative language. "The Walrus and the Carpenter" is an example of a narrative poem.

Narrator A narrator is the teller of a story. Sometimes a story's narrator is a character who takes part in the action; in other cases, the narrator is an outside voice. In "The Scribe," for example, the narrator is James, the main character. "The School Play," in contrast, is narrated by an outside voice.
See also **Point of View.**

Nonfiction Writing that tells about real people, places, and events is called nonfiction. There are two main types of nonfiction. **Informative nonfiction** provides factual information. Newspaper and magazine articles, pamphlets, history and science textbooks, and encyclopedia articles are examples of informative nonfiction. **Literary nonfiction** reads much like fiction, except that the characters, setting, and plot are real rather than imaginary.
See also **Autobiography, Biography,** *and* **Essay.**

Novel A novel is a work of fiction that is longer and more complex than a short story. In a novel, the setting, the plot, and the characters are developed in detail. The plot usually focuses on the actions and personalities of a group of characters.

Onomatopoeia Onomatopoeia is the use of words whose sound suggests their meaning. The words *bang* and *hiss* are examples of onomatopoeia. The onomatopoetic words in "Analysis of Baseball" include *thuds, pow,* and *thwack.*

Personification The giving of human qualities to an animal, object, or idea is known as personification. In "Why Monkeys Live in Trees," the animals are personified, since they act and speak like human beings.

Play. *See* **Drama.**

Plot The series of events in a story is called the story's plot. A plot usually centers around a conflict—a problem faced by the main character. In a typical plot, the action that the characters take to solve the problem builds toward a **climax,** the turning point of the story. At that point, or shortly afterward, the problem is solved and the story ends.

Poetry Poetry is a type of literature in which ideas, images, and feelings are expressed in few words. Poets carefully select words for their sounds and meanings, combining the words in imaginative ways to present feelings, pictures, experiences, and themes vividly. In poetry, the images appeal to readers' senses, as do elements of sound, such as alliteration, rhythm, and rhyme. Most poetry is written in lines, which may be grouped in stanzas.

Point of View Every story is told from a particular point of view, or perspective. Usually, a story is told from either the **first-person** or the third-person point of view. In a story told from the first-person point of view, the narrator is a character in the story and uses pronouns like *I, me,* and *we.* "Eleven" is an example of a story told from the first-person point of view. A story told from the **third-person** point of view has a narrator who is outside the story and uses pronouns such as *he, she,* and *they.* "Aaron's Gift" is told from the third-person point of view.

Predicting Using what you already know to guess what might happen in the future is called predicting. Good readers gather information as they read. They combine that information with their own knowledge and experience to predict what might happen next.

Primary Source The information that writers of nonfiction present comes from various kinds of sources. A primary source conveys direct, first-hand knowledge. "My First Dive with the Dolphins" is a primary source because it is an account of Don C. Reed's own personal experience.
See also **Secondary Source.**

Questioning The process of asking questions when reading is called questioning. As they read, good readers ask questions in an effort to understand characters and events. They then look for answers to their questions.

Radio Play A radio play is a drama that is written specifically to be broadcast over the radio. Because the audience cannot see a radio play, sound effects are used to help listeners imagine the setting and action. The stage directions in the play's script indicate the sound effects. *A Shipment of Mute Fate* is an example of a radio play.

Repetition Repetition is the use of a sound, word, or phrase more than once. Writers use repetition to bring certain ideas, sounds, or feelings to readers' attention. For example, in the poem "Chang McTang McQuarter Cat," the speaker repeats the words *one part* frequently as he presents the qualities of the cat.
See also **Alliteration** *and* **Rhyme.**

Rhyme Rhyme is a repetition of sounds at the ends of words. In poetry, rhyme that occurs within a line is called **internal rhyme.** Rhyme that occurs at the end of lines is called **end rhyme.** Note both the internal rhymes and the end rhyme in these lines from "The Cremation of Sam McGee":

> Now a promise <u>made</u> is a debt <u>unpaid,</u> and the
>   trail has its own stern <u>code.</u>
> In the days to <u>come,</u> though my lips were <u>dumb,</u>
>   in my heart how I cursed that <u>load.</u>

Rhyme Scheme The pattern of rhymes in a poem is called the poem's rhyme scheme. A rhyme scheme can be described by using a different letter of the alphabet to represent each rhyming sound. Note the rhyme scheme of the first four lines of "The Quarrel":

I quarreled with my brother,	*a*
I don't know what about,	*b*
One thing led to another	*a*
And somehow we fell out.	*b*

Rhythm The rhythm of a line of poetry is the pattern of stressed and unstressed syllables in the line. When a rhythm is repeated throughout a poem, the poem is said to have a regular beat. Note the regular rhythm in the following lines from "The Walrus and the Carpenter." (The ´ mark indicates a stressed syllable. The ˘ mark indicates an unstressed syllable.)

> The Walrus and the Carpenter
>   Were walking close at hand:
> They wept like anything to see
>   Such quantities of sand

Scene In a play, a scene is a section that presents events taking place in a single setting. A new scene begins whenever the story calls for a change in time or place. In *The Hobbit,* for example, each act contains four scenes.

Science Fiction Science fiction is fiction that is based on real or possible scientific developments. Although much science fiction is set in the future, the problems that the characters face may be similar to real problems that people face today. "User Friendly," a story about a computer that has a mind of its own, is an example of science fiction.

Secondary Source The information that writers of nonfiction present comes from various kinds of sources. A secondary source is one that conveys indirect, secondhand knowledge. "Matthew Henson at the Top of the World" is a secondary source, since the information it contains comes from Jim Haskins's reading and research.

See also **Primary Source.**

Sensory Details Words and phrases that help readers see, hear, taste, smell, and feel what a writer is describing are called sensory details. Note the sensory details used to present the fall of Icarus in this passage from "Wings":

> He passed into the realm of the sun. Too late he felt the wax run down his arms; too late he smelled the singe of feathers. Surprised, he hung solid in the air. Then, like a star in nova, he tumbled from the sky, down, down, down into the waiting sea.

See also **Description** *and* **Imagery.**

Sequence The order in which events occur or ideas are presented is called a sequence. In a narrative, events are usually presented in chronological order—the order in which they happened. A writer may use clue words and phrases—such as *then, until, after a while,* and *finally*—to help readers understand the sequence of events.

Setting The setting of a story, poem, or play is the time and place of the action. The time may be past, present, or future. The place may be real or imaginary. In some stories, including many fables, settings may not be clearly defined. In other stories, however, settings play an important part. For example, the desert setting of "Nadia the Willful" plays an important part in the story's action and helps to create its mood.

Setting a Purpose The process of establishing specific reasons to read a work is called setting a purpose. Readers can look at a work's title, headings and subheadings, and illustrations to guess what the work may be about. Then they can use their guesses to guide their reading, discovering whether their ideas match the actual content of the work.

Short Story A short story is a work of fiction that can generally be read in one sitting. Like other works of fiction, short stories contain characters, plots, settings, and themes. The plot of a short story usually involves one main conflict. "The Secret of the Wall" is an example of a short story.

Simile A simile is a comparison of two things that have some quality in common. Unlike a metaphor, a simile contains a word such as *like, as, resembles,* or *than.* Note the simile in this sentence from "The Bamboo Beads": "That night the moon was round and white as my Sunday hat."

Skimming Skimming is the process of reading quickly to get the general idea of a work. It involves reading titles, headings, words in special print, and the first sentence of each paragraph.

Speaker In a poem, the speaker is the voice that talks to the reader—like the narrator in a work of fiction. The speaker is not always the poet, but the speaker may express the feelings of the poet.

Stage Directions In the script of a play, the instructions to the performers, director, and stage crew are called stage directions. They usually appear in italic type and within parentheses. Stage directions provide suggestions about such things as scenery, lighting, music, and sound effects. They may also tell performers how to move and how to speak their lines. Note the stage directions in this passage from *Damon and Pythias.*

Damon (*calm and firm*). I have faith in my friend. I know he will return.

King (*mocking*). We shall see!
(Sound: Iron door shut and locked.)

Stanza A group of lines within a poem is called a stanza. Stanzas are somewhat like paragraphs in stories. "The Walrus and the Carpenter," for example, contains 18 stanzas.

Style A style is a particular way of writing. It involves *how* something is said rather than *what* is said. Word choice, sentence length, tone, imagery, and use of dialogue contribute to a writer's style.

Summarizing Summarizing is telling the main ideas of a piece of writing briefly, in one's own words. When you summarize, you condense a writer's ideas into precise statements, leaving out unimportant details.

Suspense Suspense is a feeling of growing tension and excitement that makes a reader curious about the outcome of a story or an event within a story. In "The Secret of the Wall," for example, suspense is created when Carlos is trapped within the walls of the old house.

Symbol A symbol is a person, a place, or an object that stands for something other than itself. In literature, objects and images may be used to symbolize things that cannot actually be seen, such as ideas or feelings. In "Flowers and Freckle Cream," for example, the tiger lily Elizabeth receives from her grandfather may symbolize the beauty he sees in her freckled appearance.

Theme A theme is a message about life or human nature that is conveyed by a work of literature. Sometimes themes are stated directly, but often readers must figure them out. Any lessons learned by the main character of a story can be clues to a theme. For example, a theme of "The Scribe" might be that helping people is not a simple matter.

Tone The tone of a work conveys the writer's attitude toward his or her subject. A work may have one tone throughout, such as the humor-ous attitude shown in "The Adoption of Albert." Sometimes, however, the tone may change sev-eral times in the course of a work.

Visualizing The process of forming a mental picture based on a written description is called visualizing. Readers use details of sight, sound, touch, taste, and feeling to visualize the charac-ters, settings, and events in works of literature. Mentally picturing writers' descriptions makes reading more enjoyable and memorable.

The Writing Process

The writing process consists of four stages: prewriting, drafting, revising and editing, and publishing and reflecting. As the graphic to the right shows, these stages are not steps that you must complete in a set order. Rather, you may return to any one at any time in your writing process, using feedback from your readers along the way.

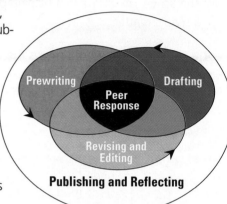

1.1 Prewriting

In the prewriting stage, you explore your ideas and discover what you want to write about.

Choosing a Topic

Ideas for writing can come from just about anywhere: experiences, memories, conversations, dreams, or imaginings. The following techniques can help you to generate ideas for writing and to choose a topic you care about.

Personal Techniques
Make a list of people, places, and activities that have had an effect on you.
Ask who, what, when, where, and why about an important event.
Ask what-if questions about everyday life.
Browse through magazines, newspapers, and on-line bulletin boards for ideas.

Sharing Techniques
With a group, brainstorm a topic by trying to come up with as many ideas as you can. Do not stop to evaluate your ideas for at least five minutes.
With a group, discuss a topic in depth, sharing your questions and ideas.

Writing Techniques
Use a word or picture as a starting point for freewriting.
Freewrite for a short time and then circle the ideas you would like to explore.
Pick a topic and list all the related ideas that occur to you.

Graphic Techniques
Create a time line of memorable events in your life.
Make a cluster diagram of subtopics related to a general topic.

Determining Your Purpose

At some time during your writing process, you need to consider your purpose, or general reason, for writing. For example, your purpose may be one of the following: to express yourself, to entertain, to explain, to describe, to analyze, or to persuade. To clarify your purpose, ask yourself questions like these:

- Why did I choose to write about my topic?
- What aspects of the topic mean the most to me?
- What do I want others to think or feel after they read my writing?

Identifying Your Audience

Knowing who will read your writing can help you clarify your purpose, focus your topic, and choose the details and tone that will best communicate your ideas. As you think about your readers, ask yourself questions like these:

- What do my readers already know about my topic?
- What will they be most interested in?
- What language is most appropriate for this audience?

1.2   Drafting

In the drafting stage, you put your ideas on paper and allow them to develop and change as you write.

There's no right or wrong way to draft. Sometimes you might be adventuresome and just dive right into your writing. At other times, you might draft slowly, planning carefully beforehand. You can combine aspects of these approaches to suit yourself and your writing projects.

 LINK TO LITERATURE

Some of the best ideas for writing can come from your own experiences. Isaac Bashevis Singer, the author of "Shrewd Todie and Lyzer the Miser," on page 319, says, "I prefer to write about the world which I knew, which I know, best. . . . I write about the things where I grew up, and where I feel completely at home."

Often what you write in your first draft of a paper may not appear in the final version, but that doesn't mean you have to throw that material away. Keep a folder of drafts or parts of drafts that never became finished papers; you may find an idea in them for future writing projects.

Discovery drafting is a good approach when you've gathered some information on your topic or have a rough idea for writing but are not quite sure how you feel about your subject or what exactly you want to say. You just plunge into your draft and let your ideas lead you where they will. After finishing a discovery draft, you may decide to start another draft, do more prewriting, or revise your first draft.

Planned drafting may work better for reports and other kinds of formal writing. Try thinking through a writing plan or making an outline before you begin drafting. Then, as you write, you can develop your ideas and fill in the details.

1.3 Using Peer Response

The suggestions and comments your peers or classmates make about your writing are called peer response.

Talking with peers about your writing can help you discover what you want to say or how well you have communicated your ideas. You can ask a peer reader for help at any point in the writing process. For example, your peers can help you develop a topic, narrow your focus, discover confusing passages, or organize your writing.

Questions for Your Peer Readers

You can help your peer readers provide you with the most useful kinds of feedback by following these guidelines:

- Tell readers where you are in the writing process. Are you still trying out ideas, or have you completed a draft?
- Ask questions that will help you get specific information about your writing. Open-ended questions that require more than yes-or-no answers are more likely to give you information you can use as you revise.
- Give your readers plenty of time to respond thoughtfully to your writing.
- Encourage your readers to be honest when they respond to your work. It's OK if you don't agree with them—you always get to decide which changes to make.

The chart on the following page explains different peer-response techniques you might use when you're ready to share your work with others.

Technique	When to Use It	Questions to Ask
Sharing	Use this when you are just exploring ideas or when you want to celebrate the completion of a piece of writing by sharing it with another person.	Will you please read or listen to my writing without criticizing it or making suggestions afterward?
Summarizing	Use this when you want to know if your main idea or goals are clear to readers.	What do you think I'm trying to say? What's my main idea?
Telling	Use this to find out which parts of your writing are affecting readers the way you want and which parts are confusing.	What did you think or feel as you read my words? Which passage were you reading when you had that response?
Replying	Use this when you want to get some new ideas to use in your writing.	What are your ideas about my topic? What do you think about what I have said in my piece?
Identifying	Use this when you want to identify the strengths and weaknesses of your writing.	Where do you like the wording? Where can it be improved? Does the organization make sense? What parts were confusing?

Tips for Being a Peer Reader

Remember these guidelines when you act as a peer reader:

- Respect the writer's feelings.
- Make sure you understand what kind of feedback the writer is looking for before you respond, and then limit your comments accordingly.
- Use "I" statements, such as "I like . . .," "I think . . .," and "It would help me if. . . ." Remember that your impressions and opinions may not be the same as someone else's.

1.4   Revising and Editing

In the revising and editing stage, you improve your draft, choose the words that best express your ideas, and proofread for mistakes in spelling, grammar, usage, and punctuation.

 WRITING TIP

You may want to ask peer readers questions if their comments are not clear or helpful to you. For example, if a reader says, "This part is confusing," you can probe to find out why. Ask, What are you confused about? What do you think might make it clearer?

The changes you make in your writing during this stage usually fall into three categories: revising for ideas, revising for form, and editing to correct mistakes. Use the questions and suggestions that follow to help you assess problems in your draft and determine what kinds of changes would improve it.

Revising for Ideas

- Have I discovered the main idea or focus of my writing? Have I expressed it clearly in my draft?
- Have I accomplished my purpose?
- Do my readers have all the information they need, or would adding more details help?
- Are any of my ideas unnecessary?

Revising for Form and Language

- Is my writing unified? Are all the ideas directly related to my main idea or focus?
- Is my writing organized well? Are the relationships among ideas clear?
- Is my writing coherent? Is the flow of sentences and paragraphs smooth and logical?

Editing to Improve Your Writing

When you are satisfied with your draft, proofread and edit it, correcting any mistakes you might have made in spelling, grammar, usage, and punctuation. You may want to proofread your writing several times, looking for different types of mistakes each time. The following checklist may help you proofread your work.

Proofreading Checklist	
Sentence Structure and Agreement	Are there any run-on sentences or sentence fragments? Do all verbs agree with their subjects? Do all pronouns agree with their antecedents? Are verb tenses correct and consistent?
Forms of Words	Do adverbs and adjectives modify the appropriate words? Are all forms of *be* and other irregular verbs used correctly? Are pronouns used correctly? Are comparative and superlative forms of adjectives correct?
Capitalization, Punctuation, and Spelling	Is any punctuation mark missing or not needed? Are all words spelled correctly? Are all proper nouns and all proper adjectives capitalized?

Use the proofreading symbols shown below to mark your draft with the changes that you need to make. See the Grammar Handbook for models in which these symbols are used.

Proofreading Symbols	
∧ Add letters or words.	/ Make a capital letter lowercase.
⊙ Add a period.	¶ Begin a new paragraph.
≡ Capitalize a letter.	— or ℘ Take out letters or words.
⌒ Close up space.	⌒ Switch the positions of letters, words, or punctuation marks.
∧ Add a comma.	

1.5   Publishing and Reflecting

After you've completed a writing project, consider sharing it with a wider audience—even when you've produced it for a class assignment. Reflecting on your writing process is another good way to bring closure to a writing project.

Creative Publishing Ideas

Following are some ideas for publishing and sharing your writing.

- Display your writing on a school bulletin board.
- Working with other students in your class, create an anthology, or collection, of stories, poems, plays, and other writing.
- Give a dramatic reading of your work for another class or group.
- Submit your writing to a local newspaper or a magazine that publishes student writing.
- Enter your work in a writing contest.
- Read your work at a school assembly.
- Create a multimedia presentation and share it with classmates.

Reflecting on Your Writing

Think about your writing process and consider whether you'd like to add your writing to your portfolio. You might write yourself a note answering questions like these and attach it to your work:

- What did I learn about myself and my subject?
- Which parts of the writing process did I most and least enjoy?
- As I wrote, what was my biggest problem? How did I solve it?
- What did I learn that I can use the next time I write?

 WRITING TIP

Consider going on-line with your writing by posting it on an electronic bulletin board or sending it to others via e-mail.

2 Building Blocks of Good Writing

A good introduction catches your reader's interest and often presents the main idea of your writing. To introduce your writing effectively, try one of the following methods.

Share a Fact

Beginning with an interesting fact can make your reader think, I'd like to learn more about that. In the example below, impressive facts about Kodiak bears capture the reader's interest.

> A male Kodiak bear may weigh 1,500 pounds, measure ten feet long, and run 35 miles an hour. Protected within Alaska's Kodiak National Wildlife Refuge, nearly 3,000 of these bears share 100-mile-long Kodiak Island, where they feast on fish, berries, and whale and seal carcasses.

Present a Description

A vivid description sets a mood and brings a scene to life. The description below sets a mood of quiet concentration.

> In the pale morning light, the shadowy track was still. With the soft thump of her feet the only sound, the athlete focused on the race that would take place the next day. Rounding the curve, she locked her eyes on the single floodlight at the far end of the track, her every muscle straining toward it.

Ask a Question

Beginning with a question can make your reader want to read on to find out the answer. Note how the introduction that follows invites the reader to learn more about an unusual sporting event.

WRITING TIP

Writing the introduction does not need to be your first task when you begin a writing project. Instead, start with any part you feel ready to write. Once your ideas come into better focus, you'll probably get a good idea about how to introduce your piece.

> Why does Danielle Del Ferraro hold a special place in the history of the Soap Box Derby? Since the Derby began in 1934, she has been the only participant ever to win twice. Her success is noteworthy because girls were not allowed to enter the gravity-powered car race until 1970.

Relate an Incident

An engaging story that includes sensory details or dialogue can help catch your reader's attention. The anecdote below leads into a discussion about safety rules for in-line skating.

> All dressed in my best clothes, I rushed outside, late for my sister's wedding. I waited impatiently for the light to change at the corner so that I could cross. Then, from out of nowhere an out-of-control in-line skater came hurtling toward me. The result was a head-on collision.

Use Dialogue

Creating fictional dialogue can be an effective way to draw your reader into your piece.

> "What's the score?" Seth called across the room.
> "Cougars 12, Tigers 6, at the end of the second quarter," Laura responded dejectedly. "What's wrong with our team?"
> "Well, the Cougars are only a touchdown ahead," her friend offered encouragingly, "and we still have half the game to go."

WRITING TIP

When writing nonfiction and quoting from a source, be sure the words appear in the same order as they do in the original. For help with punctuation and capitalization in quotations, see page 850 of the Grammar Handbook.

2.2   Paragraphs

A paragraph is made up of sentences that work together to develop an idea or accomplish a purpose. Whether or not it contains a topic sentence stating the main idea, a good paragraph must have both unity and coherence.

LINK TO LITERATURE

Notice the clear topic sentence at the beginning of page 260 of Walter Dean Myers's "Abd al-Rahman Ibrahima" from *Now Is Your Time!* The opening sentence states that it was a dangerous time in Africa, and the sentences that follow give details to support this idea.

WRITING TIP

When you are revising your writing, be sure to delete any details that do not relate to the main idea of each paragraph. If a paragraph contains two main ideas, you may break it into two separate paragraphs.

Topic Sentences

A topic sentence makes the main idea or purpose of a paragraph clear to your reader. A topic sentence can appear anywhere in a paragraph, but when it is the first sentence, it can capture the reader's attention and clearly suggest what will follow.

> *The most important rule for a beginning photographer is this: check before you click.* Do you know how to operate the camera? Is the film loaded? Is your subject well lighted—with the light source on the subject and not behind it—or will you need a flash? Have you framed your picture carefully? (You don't want a picture of your friend to be missing a head!) Are you holding the camera still? Checking the basics will go a long way toward making your snapshots memorable.

Unity

A paragraph has unity if every sentence in it supports the same main idea or purpose. One way to achieve unity in a paragraph is to state the main idea in a topic sentence and be sure that all the other sentences support that idea, as in the example above. You can create unity in a paragraph without using a topic sentence, however. Decide on a goal for your paragraph and make sure that each sentence supports that goal. Sentences should logically flow from one to the next, as shown in the paragraph below.

> The sun sank into the billowy cushions of clouds. The house, which had been brilliant white in the noonday sun, assumed a pale pink glow. The rocks and even the eerie piñon trees were enveloped in a rosy glow. I sat on the front steps, surveying the transformation and watching the light deepen from rose to mauve to purple to the deepest indigo.

Coherence

In a coherent paragraph, details are presented in a clear, sensible order. Notice that the following paragraph is coherent because the changes in the earth are related in chronological order.

Most scientists believe that all of the earth's land once formed one supercontinent. About 200 million years ago, this supercontinent, which scientists have called Pangaea, began to divide into two large masses of land. Laurasia was the northern mass; Gondwanaland was in the south. Since that time the plates on which continents rest have continued to move. The plates move toward each other, away from each other, or past each other.

2.3 Transitions

Transitions are words that show the connections between details, such as relationships in time and space, order of importance, causes and effects, and similarities or differences.

Chronological Order

Some transitions help to clarify the order in which events take place. To arrange details chronologically, as in the example below, use transitional words such as *first, second, always, then, next, later, soon, before, finally, after, earlier, afterward,* and *during.*

During the Revolutionary War, many of the colonists who remained loyal to the British monarchy lost their houses and land by force. *After* the war, almost 80,000 of these Loyalists went to England or emigrated elsewhere.

Spatial Order

Transitional words and phrases such as *across, behind, next to, nearest, lowest, above, below, underneath, on the right,* and *in the middle* can help show where items are located. The following example describes the bleachers from the point of view of a skater.

As I waited, I stared at the bleachers *across* the rink. My family was lined up *in the front* row. *Behind* the group and *to the right* were friends from school, and *next to* my friends were three of my teachers.

LINK TO LITERATURE

In the selection from Anne Terry White's "Tutankhamen" from *Lost Worlds*, on page 470, notice how transitions, such as *nevertheless, in the years that followed,* and *however,* link paragraphs together smoothly.

WRITING TIP

When you begin a sentence with a transition such as *most important, therefore, nevertheless, still,* or *instead,* set the transition off with a comma.

Degree

Transitional words and phrases such as *mainly, strongest, weakest, first, second, most important, least important, worst,* and *best* show degree of importance or rank order of details, as in the model below.

> Why do I read mysteries? *Mainly* because I enjoy the atmosphere of suspense. *Second*, I like meeting characters who are different from anybody I know in real life. *Least important*, but still a reason, is that I enjoy reading about places that interest me.

Compare and Contrast

Words and phrases such as *similarly, likewise, also, like, as, neither . . . nor,* and *either . . . or* show similarity, or likeness, between details. *However, by contrast, yet, but, unlike, instead, whereas,* and *while* show contrast, or difference. Note the use of both types of transitions in the model below.

> Matthew Henson was not recognized as the codiscoverer of the North Pole until 1944, although Robert Peary and he had reached it on April 6, 1909. *By contrast*, the achievement of Roald Amundsen's team, which made it to the South Pole in December 1911, was recognized almost immediately.

Cause and Effect

To show that details are linked in a cause-and-effect relationship, use transitional words and phrases such as *since, because, in order to, so that,* and *as a result.* Transitions in the following example show the relationship between the cotton gin and slavery.

> *Because* Eli Whitney's cotton gin decreased the processing time for cotton, plantation owners in the South planted more cotton. *As a result*, Whitney's labor-saving invention actually led to an increase in slave labor to pick the cotton.

2.4   Elaboration

To develop the main idea of a paragraph or a longer piece, you need to provide elaboration, or details, so that your readers aren't left with unanswered questions.

Facts and Statistics

A fact is a statement that can be proved, while a statistic is a fact expressed in numbers. As in the model below, the facts and statistics you use should support the statements you make.

> Women have been part of the United States' military efforts for more than a hundred years. Since the 1860s, more than 11 million women have served in the armed forces. Today approximately 350,000 women are on active or reserve duty in the military.

Sensory Details

By showing how something looks, sounds, smells, tastes, and feels, sensory details like the ones in the model below can help your readers more fully experience your subject.

> Anna Hawk got off her bike and sat beside the muddy road. The rain on her poncho made the only sound, and nothing on the prairie moved. Anna took a sip of warm, sweet cocoa from her thermos bottle.

Incidents

Describing a brief incident can help to explain or develop an idea. The writer of the model below includes an incident to explain the consequences of leaving a child alone.

> Jason left his three-year-old brother Josh alone in the kitchen while he ran upstairs to get his homework. When he returned, Jason found his brother and the kitchen covered with flour. He never finished his homework, but he learned that small children mustn't be left alone.

WRITING TIP

Facts and statistics are especially useful in supporting opinions. Be sure that you double-check in your original sources the accuracy of all facts and statistics you cite.

Examples

The model below shows how using an example can help support or clarify an idea. A well-chosen example often can be more effective than a lengthy explanation.

> Throughout history, people have used observations about nature to predict the weather. For example, you may have heard that a ring around the moon means rain the next day, or that "a red sky at night is a sailor's delight."

Quotations

Choose quotations that clearly support your points and be sure that you copy each quotation word for word. Always remember to credit the source.

> The narrator of "Thanksgiving in Polynesia" thinks that Polynesian children's lives must be great, and she can't imagine what they would find interesting about her life in Massapequa, New York. She states, "I wonder if when they're in school, they have a unit called 'The Peoples of Massapequa.'"

LINK TO LITERATURE

Notice in the excerpt from *A Long Hard Journey* how the authors Patricia and Fredrick McKissack include a quotation as elaboration on page 332. To explain the environment of a Pullman car, the writers quote a description from an 1867 issue of *Western World* magazine.

2.5   Description

Descriptive writing conveys images and impressions of a person, a place, an event, or a thing.

Descriptive writing appears almost everywhere, from cookbooks to poems. You might use a description to introduce a character in a narrative or to create a strong closing to a persuasive essay. Whatever your purpose and wherever you use description, the following guidelines for good descriptive writing will help you.

Include Plenty of Details

Vivid sensory details help the reader feel like an on-the-scene observer of the subject. The sensory details of the following scene appeal to the senses of sight, sound, touch, and even taste.

Andrew slumped against the wall outside the gym. His calves ached more than his stomach, empty and tense. He replayed the last minutes of the game—tasting sweat, hearing cheers, feeling the seams of the basketball with his fingers—but he couldn't visualize missing the shot.

Organize Your Details

Details that are presented in a logical order help the reader form a mental picture of the subject. Descriptive details may be organized chronologically, by order of importance, spatially, or by order of impression, as in the model below.

Mike descended the stairs slowly, so we saw his shoes first—polished to a gleaming black so that they looked almost like patent leather. The satin stripe on each trouser leg told us he was dressed for a formal event. The white bow tie, just below the grin, was the clincher.

LINK TO LITERATURE

Note the careful organization of details in "My First Dive with the Dolphins," on page 65. Don C. Reed describes the dive by starting at the surface of the water, noting the sensations during his descent, and finishing with a description of the floor of the oceanarium.

Show, Don't Tell

Instead of just telling about a subject in a general way, provide details and quotations that expand and support what you want to say and that enable your readers to share your experience. The following example just tells and doesn't show.

My little sister was scared by the movie *Snow White*.

The paragraph below uses descriptive details to show how the little girl reacted to the movie.

Somebody should have warned me about *Snow White*. My little sister, Caroline, liked Sleepy, Doc, Bashful, and the rest. In fact, I had to name them every time they appeared. When the evil queen came back, however, Caroline whimpered. Then she cried very loudly. I still haven't seen the end of the movie.

WRITING TIP

Metaphors and similes can help you create more vivid, memorable descriptions. Remember that a metaphor compares things directly (*The burglar was a cat slinking through the alley*), while a simile is a comparison using *like* or *as* (*The drawbridge rose as slowly as a drowsy giant waking up after a long nap*).

Use Precise Language

To create a clear image in your reader's mind, use vivid and precise words. Instead of using general nouns, verbs, and adjectives (*car, walk, tired*), use specific ones (*convertible, shuffle, exhausted*). Notice what happens when vague, general words are replaced with precise words, as in the examples below.

> The dish broke.
> The dish shattered into dozens of tiny pieces.
>
> The wind was strong and caused damage.
> The wind blew fiercely, flattening bushes and flowers.

2.6 Conclusions

A conclusion should leave readers with a strong final impression. Try any of the following approaches for concluding a piece of writing.

Restate the Main Idea

Close by returning to your central idea and stating it in a new way. If possible, link the beginning of your conclusion with the information you have presented, as the model below shows.

> As these examples show, the expansion of nature preserves will protect the wildlife of our state. The preserves allow animals to live in an area that is rarely disrupted by the activities of people. The animals, from the smallest insects to the largest mammals, need to be protected in order for them all to survive.

Ask a Question

Try asking a question that sums up what you have said and gives readers something to think about. The following example from a piece of persuasive writing ends with a question that suggests a course of action.

> More and more people are biking to school and work and are riding for exercise. Doesn't it make sense to create safe bike lanes throughout our city?

Make a Recommendation

When you are writing to persuade, you can use your conclusion to tell readers what you want them to do. The conclusion below is from an article on the important role of animal shelters.

> If you want to help animals who are waiting for new homes and to help people find the right pets for them, volunteer your time after school to care for dogs and cats at an animal shelter.

End with the Last Event

If you're telling a story, you may end with the last thing that happens. Here, a story ends with an important moment of understanding.

> Len grinned at me, eager for approval. Suddenly I understood why he had made up all those wild stories about his life.

Generalize About Your Information

The model below concludes by making a specific statement about the importance of the subject.

> At 64, Denise St. Aubyn Hubbard sailed alone across the Atlantic. Bill Pinkney was in his fifties when he sailed around the world by himself. And Tristan Jones, in his sixties and having lost a leg, sailed solo from California to Thailand. Don't ever think courage and the spirit of adventure die with middle age or old age.

LINK TO LITERATURE

In his conclusion of "Chinatown," on page 177, Laurence Yep uses a question that effectively closes his narrative. He asks, "How could I pretend to be somebody else when I didn't even know who I was?"

Narrative Writing

Narrative writing tells a story. If you write a story from your imagination, it is called a fictional narrative. A true story is called a nonfictional narrative.

Key Techniques of Narrative Writing

Writing Standards

Good narrative writing

▶ includes descriptive details and dialogue to develop the characters, setting, and plot

▶ has a clear beginning, middle, and end

▶ maintains a consistent tone and point of view

▶ uses language that is appropriate for the audience

▶ demonstrates the significance of the events or ideas

Define the Conflict

The conflict of a narrative is the problem that the main character faces. In the example below, the conflict is between a girl and her aunt.

Example

Aunt Jessica knew I didn't want that mean white horse! I'd been begging for a horse to train for almost a year, but I never meant *that* horse.

Clearly Organize the Events

Choose the important events and explain them in an order that is easy to understand. In a fictional narrative, this series of events is the story's plot.

Example

• Aunt Jessica gives me my first horse to train

• he's a horse I don't like; he's stubborn, and when I try to train him nothing works

• I see the horse running in the field; he looks proud and independent

• my aunt asks me if I'd like a different horse to train, but I say no

Depict Characters Vividly

Use vivid details to show your readers what your characters look like, what they say, and what they think.

Example

I forced myself to smile. "Thanks, Aunt Jessica, I know I can train him like you taught me."

Organizing Narrative Writing

One way to organize a piece of narrative writing is to arrange the events in chronological order, as shown in Option 1 below.

Option 1

Focus on Events
• Introduce characters and setting
• Show event 1
• Show event 2
• End, perhaps showing the significance of the events

Example

Aunt Jessica gave me my first horse to train.

He was a horse I didn't like. He was stubborn, and when I tried to train him, nothing worked.

One day I saw the horse running in the field. Instead of looking stubborn, he looked proud and independent.

Aunt Jessica offered me another horse to train, and when I said I'd like to keep the one I had, she smiled warmly at me.

You may prefer to focus on characters, especially if a change in character—the way someone thinks, feels, or behaves—is important to the outcome of the story. In that case, try organizing your story according to Option 2. Try Option 3 if you plan to focus on a conflict that a character experiences within himself or herself or with society, nature, or another character.

Option 2

Focus on Character
• Introduce the main character
• Describe the conflict the character faces
• Relate the events and the changes the character goes through as a result of the conflict
• Present the final change or new understanding

Option 3

Focus on Conflict
• Present the characters and setting
• Introduce the conflict
• Describe the events that develop from the initial conflict
• Show the struggle of the main character with the conflict
• Resolve the conflict

Remember: Good narrative writing is organized logically, with clues to help the reader understand the order of events.

WRITING TIP

Introductions Try hooking your reader's interest by opening a story with an exciting event. After your introduction, you may need to go back in time and relate the incidents that led up to the exciting event.

Explanatory Writing

4

LINK TO LITERATURE

Explanatory writing techniques provide tools for exploring the issues presented by or in literature. The examples on the following pages use explanatory writing techniques to examine Elizabeth Ellis's narrative "Flowers and Freckle Cream," starting on page 519.

Explanatory writing is writing that informs and explains. For example, you can use it to explain how to cook spaghetti, to explore the origins of the universe, or even to compare two different pieces of literature.

Types of Explanatory Writing

Analysis

Analysis explains how something works, how it is defined, or what its parts are.

Example

Unlike the narrator, I believe beauty is made up of a good appearance, self-confidence, and character.

Compare and Contrast

Compare-and-contrast writing explores the similarities and differences between two or more subjects.

Example

The narrator and her grandfather have different standards of beauty.

Cause and Effect

Cause-and-effect writing explains why something happened, why certain conditions exist, or what resulted from an action or a condition.

Example

Because she wears freckle remover in the sun, the narrator's freckles grow darker.

Problem-Solution

Problem-solution writing examines a problem and proposes a solution to it.

Example

Some people, like the narrator, wish they could look like someone else. The best solution is learning to appreciate your appearance as it is.

4.1　Compare and Contrast

Compare-and-contrast writing explores the similarities and differences between two or more subjects.

Organizing Compare-and-Contrast Writing

When you compare and contrast, you can organize your information in different ways. Two options are shown below.

Option 1　　　　　　　　　　**Example**

Feature by Feature
Feature 1
• Subject A
• Subject B
Feature 2
• Subject A
• Subject B

The characters' standards of beauty

The narrator's standard of beauty is based on her cousin's appearance.

The grandfather thinks beauty can take many forms.

The characters' ideas about attaining beauty

The narrator thinks she will be beautiful if she loses her freckles.

The grandfather thinks she is already beautiful.

Option 2　　　　　　　　　　**Example**

Subject by Subject
Subject A
• Feature 1
• Feature 2
Subject B
• Feature 1
• Feature 2

The narrator

The narrator's standard of beauty is based on her cousin's appearance.

The narrator thinks she will be beautiful if she loses her freckles.

The grandfather

The grandfather thinks beauty can take many forms.

The grandfather thinks she is already beautiful.

WRITING TIP

To help your audience understand something that is unfamiliar to them, try comparing and contrasting it with something they already know about.

WRITING TIP

See page 781 for information on using transitions in your compare-and-contrast writing.

WRITING TIP

You may want to include in your essay a diagram or chart that visually portrays the cause-and-effect relationship explained in your writing.

Cause-and-effect writing explains why something happened, why certain conditions exist, or what resulted from an action or a condition.

Organizing Cause-and-Effect Writing

Your organization will depend on your topic and purpose for writing. If you want to explain the causes of an event like the closing of a factory, you can first state the effect and then examine its causes (Option 1). If your focus is on explaining the effects of an event such as passage of a law, you might start by stating the cause and then proceed to explain the effects (Option 2). If you want to explore a topic such as the disappearance of tropical rain forests or the development of home computers, you might describe a chain of cause-and-effect relationships (Option 3).

Option 1   **Example**

Effect to Cause
Effect
• Cause 1
• Cause 2
• Cause 3

The narrator's face becomes covered with dark freckles.

She doesn't know that freckle remover should never be worn in the sun.

She applies freckle remover to her face.

She spends a day hoeing tobacco in the sun.

Option 2

Cause to Effect
Cause
• Effect 1
• Effect 2
• Effect 3

Option 3

Cause-and-Effect Chain
Cause
↓
effect (cause)
↓
effect (cause)
↓
effect (cause)

Remember: Don't assume that a cause-and-effect relationship exists simply because one event follows another. Be sure facts show that the effect couldn't have happened without the cause.

4.3 Problem-Solution

Problem-solution writing clearly states a problem, analyzes the problem, and proposes a solution to the problem.

Organizing Problem-Solution Writing

Your organization will depend on the goal of your problem-solution piece, your intended audience, and the specific problem you choose to address. The organizational methods outlined below are effective for different kinds of problem-solution writing.

Option 1

Example

Simple Problem-Solution	
Description of problem	Some people, like the narrator, wish they could look like someone else.
Recommended solution	You should learn to appreciate your own unique beauty, as the narrator's grandfather taught her.
Explanation of solution	Learning to like yourself would make you happier than trying to look like someone else.
Conclusion	The story offers a good solution to a common problem.

Option 2

Example

Deciding Between Solutions	
Description of problem	Some people, like the narrator, wish they could look like someone else.
Solution A	You can try, as the narrator did, to change the way you look.
• Pros	You might like your new appearance.
• Cons	You can never look like someone else, and you might become frustrated if you try to.
Solution B	
• Pros	
• Cons	As the narrator did, you can learn to appreciate your appearance because it is unique.
Recommendation	

Good problem-solution writing

▶ gives a clear and concise explanation of the problem and its significance

▶ proposes a workable solution and includes details that explain and support it

▶ concludes by restating the problem

WRITING TIP

Think of possible objections to your solution. You can strengthen your arguments by including possible objections and responding to them in a clear, reasonable way.

4.4 Analysis

In an analysis you try to help your readers understand a subject by explaining how it works, how it is defined, or what its parts are.

The details you include will depend upon the kind of analysis you're writing.

- A **process analysis** should provide background information, such as definitions of terms and a list of needed equipment, and then explain each important step or stage in the process. For example, you might explain the steps to program a VCR or the stages in a plant's growth cycle.
- A **definition** should include the most important characteristics of the subject. To define a rain forest, you might include such characteristics as rainfall, vegetation, and animal life.
- A **parts analysis** should describe each of the parts, groups, or types that make up the subject. For example, you might analyze the parts of the human brain, the groups affected by a new law, or the styles of jazz music.

Organizing Your Analysis

Organize your details in a logical order appropriate for the kind of analysis you're writing. A process analysis is usually organized chronologically, with steps or stages in the order they occur.

Option 1   **Example**

Process Analysis

Preview analysis

- Response 1
- Response 2
- Response 3

My response to Elizabeth Ellis's story "Flowers and Freckle Cream" changed when I reread it.

The first time I read the story, I thought the narrator acted like a baby, because she made a big deal about having freckles and wanting to be like her cousin.

The second time, I understood that she bought the freckle remover to feel more comfortable about herself.

In the third reading, I liked the way her grandfather told her to accept herself as beautiful by giving her a tiger lily.

You can organize the details in a definition or a parts analysis in order of importance or impression. Below, qualities in a definition of beauty, are organized from least to most important.

Option 2

Definition	Example
Introduce term	The narrator of "Flowers and Freckle Cream" sees beauty in terms of appearance.
General definition	I believe beauty consists of a good appearance, self-confidence, and character.
• Quality 1	A good appearance means looking your best. People who exercise and eat right are beautiful.
• Quality 2	Self-confidence draws others to you and is even more important than appearance.
• Quality 3	Good character is beauty's most important quality. People who are kind and help others are beautiful.

The following parts analysis explores the different ideas of beauty in the story "Flowers and Freckle Cream."

Option 3

Parts Analysis	Example
Introduce subject	The characters in "Flowers and Freckle Cream" have different ideas about beauty.
Explain how subject can be broken into parts	The mother believes her daughter will never attain beauty, the narrator hopes she can, and the grandfather believes she already has.
• Part 1	The mother says of the narrator, "You can't make a silk purse out of a sow's ear."
• Part 2	The narrator hopes freckle-remover cream will give her the same flawless complexion as her cousin.
• Part 3	Her grandfather tells her "there are all kinds of flowers, and they are all beautiful." He leaves a tiger lily, a freckled flower, on her pillow.

WRITING TIP

Introductions You may want to begin with a vivid description of the subject to capture the reader's attention. For example, you might describe why the narrator in "Flowers and Freckle Cream" is jealous of her cousin.

WRITING TIP

Conclusions Try ending an analysis by stating the importance of the subject to the reader. The analysis of the narrative "Flowers and Freckle Cream" could conclude with a statement about the importance of recognizing different kinds of beauty.

Persuasive Writing

Persuasive writing allows you to use the power of language to inform and influence others.

Key Techniques of Persuasive Writing

Writing Standards

Good persuasive writing

▶ has a strong introduction

▶ clearly states the issue and the writer's position

▶ presents ideas logically

▶ answers opposing viewpoints

▶ ends with a strong argument or summary or a call for action

State Your Opinion

Taking a stand on an issue and clearly stating your opinion are essential to every piece of persuasive writing you do.

Example
Our city should create bike lanes on all major streets to encourage safety.

Know Your Audience

Knowing who will read your writing will help you decide what information you need to share and what tone you should use to communicate your message. In the example below, the writer has used a formal tone that is appropriate for a petition or a letter to the editor.

Example
We, the undersigned, believe the creation of bike lanes is necessary for public safety.

Support Your Opinion

Using reasons, examples, facts, statistics, and anecdotes to support your opinion will show your audience why you feel the way you do. Below, the writer uses a statistic to support his opinion.

Example
According to the National Safe Kids Campaign, over 50,000 children are injured in bicycle accidents every year, many on major streets.

Organizing Persuasive Writing

In persuasive writing, you need to gather information to support your opinions. Here are some ways you can organize that material to convince your audience.

Option 1

Reasons for Your Opinion

Your opinion
- Reason 1
- Reason 2
- Reason 3

Example

Our city should create bike lanes on all major streets to encourage safety.

Bicycle accidents often result in serious injuries.

Bicycle lanes would separate bike traffic from car traffic, making travel safer for everyone.

Safe bike paths would encourage people to ride bicycles for recreation and transportation.

Depending on the purpose and form of your writing, you may want to show the weaknesses of other opinions as you explain the strengths of your own. Two options for organizing writing that include more than just your side of the issue are shown below.

Option 2

Why Your Opinion Is Stronger

Your opinion
- your reasons

Other opinion
- evidence refuting reasons for other opinion and showing strengths of your opinion

Option 3

Why Another Opinion Is Weaker

Other opinion
- reasons

Your opinion
- reasons supporting your opinion and pointing out the weaknesses of the other side

Remember: Effective persuasion often builds from the weakest argument to the strongest. Keep this in mind when you organize the reasons that support your opinion.

6 Research Report Writing

In research report writing, you can find answers to questions about a topic you're interested in. Your writing organizes information from various sources and presents it to your readers as a unified and coherent whole.

Writing Standards

Good research report writing

▶ clearly states the purpose of the report in a thesis statement

▶ contains only accurate and relevant information

▶ documents sources correctly

▶ develops the topic logically

▶ reflects careful research on the topic

Key Techniques of Research Report Writing

Clarify Your Thesis

Your thesis statement explains to your reader what question your report will answer. In the example below, the writer's thesis statement answers the question "How are stories of dragons from around the world similar and different?"

Example
Folk tales and myths about dragons exist in cultures all over the world, but dragons symbolize good in some cultures and bad in others.

Support Your Ideas

You need to support your ideas with specific details. In the example below, the writer supports the idea that dragon images still exist in cultures today.

Example
During the Chinese New Year, the elaborate dragon dance is used in the celebrations to drive away bad luck and bring people good luck for the coming year.

Document Your Sources

You need to document, or credit, the sources where you find your information. In the example below, the writer paraphrases and documents a passage from David Passes's book about dragons.

Example
In Mordiford, England, people tell the legend of a wyvern, a two-legged dragon with wings. The wyvern terrorized the village until a prisoner named Garston gave his life saving the community from the fire-breathing monster (Passes 30–31).

Finding and Evaluating Sources

Begin your research by looking for information on your topic in books, magazines, newspapers, and computer databases. In addition to using your library's card or computer catalog, look up your subject in indexes, such as the *Readers' Guide to Periodical Literature* or the *New York Times Index*. The bibliographies in books that you find during your research may also lead to additional sources. The following checklist will help you evaluate the reliability of the sources you find.

Checklist for Evaluating Your Sources	
Authoritative	Someone who has written several books or articles on your subject or whose work has been published in a well-respected newspaper or journal may be considered an authority.
Up-to-date	Check the publication dates to see if the source reflects the most current research on your subject.
Respected	In general, tabloid newspapers and popular-interest magazines are not reliable sources. If you have questions about whether you are using a respected source, ask your librarian.

Making Source Cards

For each source you find, record the bibliographic information on a separate index card. You will need this information to give credit to the sources you use in your paper. The samples at the right show how to make source cards for encyclopedia entries, magazine articles, and books. You will use the source number on each card to identify the notes you take during your research.

Taking Notes

As you find material that suits the purpose of your report, record each piece of information on a separate note card. You will probably use all three of the note-taking methods listed on the following page.

WRITING TIP

Your reading can inspire ideas for research topics. The title of the story "In the Land of Small Dragon," on page 662, might lead you to explore the importance of dragons in Vietnamese traditions as well as in other cultures.

Encyclopedia Entry

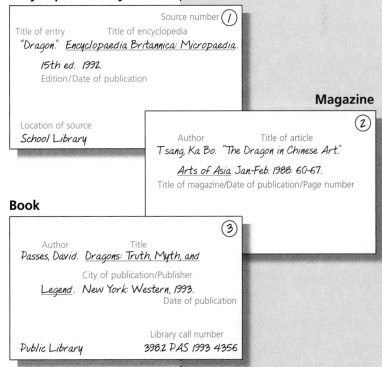

Source number ①
Title of entry   Title of encyclopedia
"Dragon." *Encyclopaedia Britannica: Micropaedia.*
     15th ed. 1992.
     Edition/Date of publication

Location of source
School Library

Magazine

②
Author   Title of article
Tsang, Ka Bo. "The Dragon in Chinese Art."
     Arts of Asia Jan-Feb. 1988: 60-67.
     Title of magazine/Date of publication/Page number

Book

③
Author   Title
Passes, David. *Dragons: Truth, Myth, and*
     City of publication/Publisher
Legend. New York: Western, 1993.
          Date of publication

     Library call number
Public Library   398.2 PAS 1993 4356

- Paraphrase, or restate in your own words, the main ideas and supporting details from a passage.
- Summarize, or rephrase the original material in fewer words, trying to capture the key ideas.
- Quote, or copy the original text word for word, if you think the author's own words best clarify a particular point. Use quotation marks to signal the beginning and the end of the quotation.

Writing a Thesis Statement

A thesis statement in a research report defines your main idea, or overall purpose, of your report. A clear one-sentence answer to your main question will result in a good thesis statement.

Question: How are stories of dragons from around the world similar and different?

Thesis Statement: Folk tales and myths about dragons exist in cultures all over the world, but dragons symbolize good in some stories and bad in others.

Making an Outline

To organize your report, group your note cards into main ideas and arrange them in a logical order. With your notes, make a topic outline, beginning with a shortened version of your thesis statement. Key ideas are listed after Roman numerals, and sub-points are listed after uppercase letters and Arabic numerals, as in the following example.

WRITING TIP

Use the same form for items of the same rank in your outline. For example, if A is a noun, then B and C should be nouns.

Dragons Around the World

Introduction—Dragons symbolize good and bad

I. Origin of dragon stories

II. Dragon stories around the world

  A. Asia

  B. Europe

    1. Beowulf and the fire dragon

    2. The Mordiford Wyvern

  C. North America

III. Dragon images in cultures today

Documenting Your Sources

When you quote one of your sources or write in your own words information you have found in a source, you need to credit that source, using parenthetical documentation.

Guidelines for Parenthetical Documentation	
Work by One Author	Put the author's last name and the page reference in parentheses: **(Passes 19)**. If you mention the author's name in the sentence, put only the page reference in parentheses: **(19)**.
Work by Two or Three Authors	Put the authors' last names and the page reference in parentheses: **(Guise, Gushwa, and Donnelly 99)**.
Work by More Than Three Authors	Give the first author's last name followed by *et al.* and the page reference: **(Park et al. 233)**.
Work with No Author Given	Give the title or a shortened version and the page reference: **("Dragon" 209)**.
One of Two or More Works by Same Author	Give the author's last name, the title or a shortened version, and the page reference: **(Guccione, "On Dragons' Wings" 71)**.

WRITING TIP

Plagiarism Presenting someone else's writing or ideas as your own is plagiarism. To avoid plagiarism, you need to credit sources as noted at the left. However, if a piece of information is common knowledge—information available in several sources—you do not need to credit the source.

Creating a List of Sources Page

At the end of your research report, you need to include a List of Sources page. Any source that you have documented needs to be listed alphabetically by the author's last name. If there is no author, use the editor's last name or the title of the work. Note the guidelines for spacing and punctuation on the model page.

Student's last name · Page number

Center heading · 1″

½″ Jensen 14

List of Sources

"Dragon." <u>Encyclopaedia Britannica: Micropaedia</u>.

15th ed. 1992.

⊢1″⊣ Passes, David. <u>Dragons: Truth, Myth, and Legend</u>. ⊢1″⊣

New York: Western, 1993.

Tsang, Ka Bo. "The Dragon in Chinese Art." <u>Arts of</u>

2 spaces after periods

<u>Asia</u> Jan.-Feb. 1988: 60-67.

Double-space between all lines

Indent additional lines ½″

1 Getting Information Electronically

Electronic resources provide you with a convenient and efficient way to gather information.

1.1 On-line Resources

When you use your computer to communicate with another computer or with another person using a computer, you are working "on-line." On-line resources include commercial information services and information available on the Internet.

Commercial Information Services

You can subscribe to various services that offer information such as the following:

- up-to-date news, weather, and sports reports
- access to encyclopedias, magazines, newspapers, dictionaries, almanacs, and databases (collections of information)
- electronic mail (e-mail) to and from other users
- forums, or ongoing electronic conversations among users interested in a particular topic

Internet

The Internet is a vast network of computers. News services, libraries, universities, researchers, organizations, and government agencies use the Internet to communicate and to distribute information. The Internet includes two key features:

- **World Wide Web,** which provides you with information on particular subjects and links you to related topics and resources (such as the Web pages shown at the left)
- **Electronic mail** (e-mail), which allows you to communicate with other e-mail users worldwide

1.2   CD-ROM

A CD-ROM (compact disc–read-only memory) stores data that may include text, sound, photographs, and video.

Almost any kind of information can be found on CD-ROMs, which you can use at the library or purchase, including

- encyclopedias, almanacs, and indexes
- other reference books on a variety of subjects
- news reports from newspapers, magazines, television, or radio
- museum art collections
- back issues of magazines
- literature collections

WHAT YOU'LL NEED

- To access on-line resources, you need a computer with a modem linked to a telephone line. Your school computer lab or resource center may be linked to the Internet or to a commercial information service.
- To use CD-ROMs, you need a computer system with a CD-ROM player.

1.3   Library Computer Services

Many libraries offer computerized catalogs and a variety of other electronic resources.

Computerized Catalogs

You may search for a book in a library by typing the title, author, subject, or key words into a computer terminal. If you enter the title of a book, the screen will display the kind of information shown at right, including the book's call number and whether it is on the shelf or checked out of the library. When a particular work is not available, you may be able to search the catalogs of other libraries.

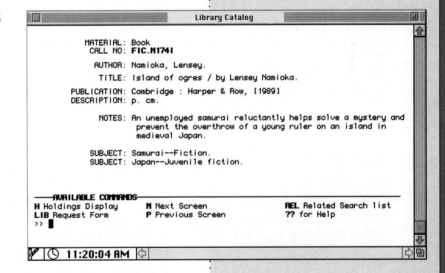

```
                        Library Catalog

       MATERIAL: Book
       CALL NO: FIC.N174I

        AUTHOR: Namioka, Lensey.
         TITLE: Island of ogres / by Lensey Namioka.
   PUBLICATION: Cambridge : Harper & Row, [1989]
   DESCRIPTION: p. cm.

         NOTES: An unemployed samurai reluctantly helps solve a mystery and
                prevent the overthrow of a young ruler on an island in
                medieval Japan.

       SUBJECT: Samurai--Fiction.
       SUBJECT: Japan--Juvenile fiction.


  ─AVAILABLE COMMANDS
  H Holdings Display       N Next Screen            REL Related Search list
  LIB Request Form         P Previous Screen        ?? for Help
  >>

  | 11:20:04 AM
```

Other Electronic Resources

In addition to computerized catalogs, many libraries offer electronic versions of books or other reference materials. They may also have a variety of indexes on CD-ROM, which allow you to search for magazine or newspaper articles on any topic you choose. Ask your librarian for assistance in using these resources.

2

Word Processing

Word-processing programs allow you to draft, revise, edit, and format your writing and to produce neat, professional-looking papers. They also allow you to share your writing with others.

2.1 Revising and Editing

Improving the quality of your writing becomes easier when you use a word-processing program to revise and edit.

Revising a Document

Most word-processing programs allow you to make the following kinds of changes:

- add or delete words
- move text from one location in your document to another
- undo a change you have made in the text
- save a document with a new name, allowing you to keep old drafts for reference
- view more than one document at a time, so you can copy text from one document and add it to another

Editing a Document

Many word-processing programs have the following features to help you catch errors and polish your writing:

- The **spell checker** automatically finds misspelled words and suggests possible corrections.
- The **grammar checker** spots possible grammatical errors and suggests ways you might correct them.
- The **thesaurus** suggests synonyms for a word you want to replace.
- The **dictionary** will give you the definitions of words so you can be sure you have used words correctly.
- The **search and replace** feature searches your whole document and corrects every occurrence of something you want to change, such as a misspelled name.

WRITING TIP

Even if you use a spell checker, you should still proofread your draft carefully to make sure you've used the right words. For example, you may have used *there* or *they're* when you meant to use *their*.

2.2   Formatting Your Work

Format is the layout and appearance of your writing on the page. You may choose your formatting options before or after you write.

Formatting Type

You may want to make changes in the typeface, type size, and type style of the words in your document. For each of these, your word-processing program will most likely have several options to choose from. These options allow you to

- change the typeface to create a different look for the words in your document
- change the type size of the entire document or of just the headings of sections in the paper
- change the type style when necessary; for example, use italics or underline for the titles of books and magazines

Typeface	Size	Style
Geneva	7-point Times	*Italic*
Times	10-point Times	**Bold**
Chicago	12-point Times	<u>Underline</u>
`Courier`	14-point Times	

Formatting Pages

Not only can you change the way individual words look; you can also change the way they are arranged on the page. Some of the formatting decisions you make will depend on how you plan to use a printout of a draft or on the guidelines of an assignment.

- Set the line spacing, or the amount of space you need between lines of text. Double spacing is commonly used for final drafts.
- Set the margins, or the amount of white space around the edges of your text. A one-inch margin on all sides is commonly used for final drafts.
- Create a header for the top of the page or a footer for the bottom if you want to include such information as your name, the date, or the page number on every page.
- Determine the alignment of your text. The screen at the left shows your options.

Centered

Bake Sale

The 6th Grade Bake Sale will be held after lunch on Tuesday, May 9th. The money we raise will go to funding the fall party. Here is what will be on sale:

Cookies (1 doz.) $3
Muffins (1/2 doz.) $2
Pie..............$6
Cake..............$5
Brownies (1 doz.) $3

Left-aligned

Right-aligned

Computers allow you to share your writing electronically. Send a copy of your work to someone via e-mail or put it in someone's drop box if your computer is linked to other computers on a network. Then use the feedback of your peers to help you improve the quality of your writing.

Peer Editing on a Computer

The writer and the reader can both benefit from the convenience of peer editing "on screen," or at the computer.

- Be sure to save your current draft and then make a copy of it for each of your peer readers.
- You might have your peer readers enter their comments in a different typeface or type style from the one you used for your text, as shown in the the example below.
- Ask each of your readers to include his or her initials in the file name.

- If your computer allows you to open more than one file at a time, open each reviewer's file and refer to the files as you revise your draft.

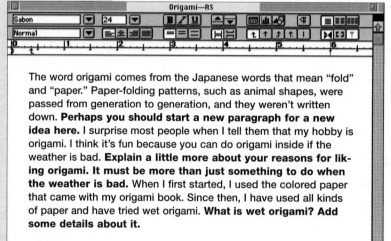

The word origami comes from the Japanese words that mean "fold" and "paper." Paper-folding patterns, such as animal shapes, were passed from generation to generation, and they weren't written down. **Perhaps you should start a new paragraph for a new idea here.** I surprise most people when I tell them that my hobby is origami. I think it's fun because you can do origami inside if the weather is bad. **Explain a little more about your reasons for liking origami. It must be more than just something to do when the weather is bad.** When I first started, I used the colored paper that came with my origami book. Since then, I have used all kinds of paper and have tried wet origami. **What is wet origami? Add some details about it.**

Peer Editing on a Printout

Some peer readers prefer to respond to a draft on paper rather than on the computer.

- Double-space or triple-space your document so that your peer editors can make suggestions between the lines.
- Leave extra-wide margins to give your readers room to note their reactions and questions as they read.
- Print out your draft and photocopy it if you want to share it with more than one reader.

Using Visuals

3

Charts, graphs, diagrams, and pictures often communicate information more effectively than words alone do. Many computer programs allow you to create visuals to use with written text.

3.1 When to Use Visuals

Use visuals in your work to illustrate complex concepts and processes or to make a page look more interesting.

Although you should not expect a visual to do all the work of written text, combining words and pictures or graphics can increase the understanding and enjoyment of your writing. Many computer programs allow you to create and insert graphs, tables, time lines, diagrams, and flow charts into your document. An art program allows you to create border designs for a title page or to draw an unusual character or setting for narrative or descriptive writing. You may also be able to add clip art, or premade pictures, to your document. Clip art can be used to illustrate an idea or concept in your writing or to make your writing more appealing for young readers.

3.2 Kinds of Visuals

The visuals you choose will depend on the type of information you want to present to your readers.

Tables

Tables allow you to arrange facts or numbers into rows and columns so that your reader can compare information more easily. In many word-processing programs, you can create a table by choosing the number of vertical columns and horizontal rows you need and then entering information in each box, as the illustration shows.

Graphs and Charts

You can sometimes use a graph or chart to help communicate complex information in a clear visual image. For example, you could use a line graph to show how a trend changes over time, a bar graph to compare statistics, or a pie chart, like the one at the right, to compare percentages. You might want to explore ways of displaying data in more than one visual format before deciding which will work best for you.

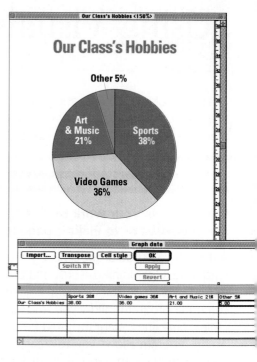

Other Visuals

Art and design programs allow you to create visuals for your writing. Many programs include the following features:

- drawing tools that allow you to draw, color, and shade pictures, such as the drawing below
- clip art that you can copy or change with drawing tools
- page borders that you can use to decorate title pages, invitations, or brochures
- text options that allow you to combine words with your illustrations
- tools for making geometric shapes in flow charts, time lines, and diagrams that show a process or sequence of events

Creating a Multimedia Presentation

A multimedia presentation is a combination of text, sound, and visuals such as photographs, videos, and animation. Your audience reads, hears, and sees your presentation at a computer, following different "paths" you create to lead the user through the information you have gathered.

4.1 Features of Multimedia Programs

To start planning your multimedia presentation, you need to know what options are available to you. You can combine sound, photos, videos, and animation to enhance any text you write about your topic.

Sound

Including sound in your presentation can help your audience understand information in your written text. For example, the user may be able to listen and learn from

- the pronunciation of an unfamiliar or foreign word
- a speech
- a recorded news interview
- a musical selection
- a dramatic reading of a work of literature

Photos and Videos

Photographs and live-action videos can make your subject come alive for the user. Here are some examples:

- videotaped news coverage of a historical event
- videos of music, dance, or theater performances
- charts and diagrams
- photos of an artist's work
- photos or video of a geographical setting that is important to the written text

 WHAT YOU'LL NEED

- Individual programs to create and edit the text, graphics, sound, and videos you will use
- A multimedia authoring program that allows you to combine these elements and create links between the screens

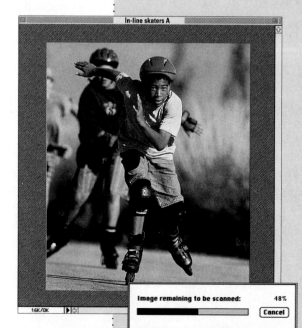

In-line skaters A

Image remaining to be scanned: 48%

Cancel

16K/OK

Animation

Many graphics programs allow you to add animation, or movement, to the visuals in your presentation. Animated figures add to the user's enjoyment and understanding of what you present. You can use animation to illustrate

- what happens in a story
- the steps in a process
- changes in a chart, graph, or diagram
- how your user can explore information in your presentation

4.2 Planning Your Presentation

To create a multimedia presentation, first choose your topic and decide what you want to include. Then plan how you want your user to move through your presentation.

Imagine that you are creating a multimedia presentation about in-line skating. You know that you want to include the following items:

- photo of in-line skaters
- a text history of how in-line skating was developed
- a diagram of an in-line skate
- text on "how to skate" for beginners
- a video of a skating demonstration
- a glossary of in-line skating terms
- an audio description of safety tips

You can choose one of the following ways to organize your presentation:

- step by step with only one path, or order, in which the user can see and hear the information
- a branching path that allows users to make some choices about what they will see and hear, and in what order

A flow chart can help you figure out the path a user can take through your presentation. Each box in the flow chart on the following page represents something about in-line skating for the user to read, see, or hear. The arrows on the flow chart show a branching path the user can follow.

When boxes branch in more than one direction, it means that the user can choose which item to see or hear first.

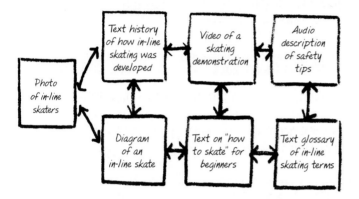

4.3 Guiding Your User

Your user will need directions to follow the path you have planned for your multimedia presentation.

Most multimedia authoring programs allow you to create screens that include text or audio directions that guide the user from one part of your presentation to the next. In the example below, the user can choose between several paths, and directions on the screen explain how to make the choice.

If you need help creating your multimedia presentation, ask your school's technology adviser. You may also be able to get help from your classmates or your software manual.

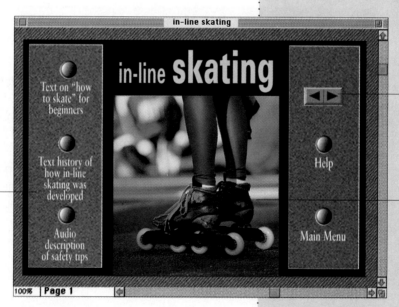

WRITING TIP

You usually need permission from the person or organization that owns the copyright on materials if you want to copy them. You do not need permission, however, if you are not making money from your presentation, if you use it only for educational purposes, and if you use only a small percentage of the original material.

Navigational buttons take the user back and forth, one screen at a time.

The user clicks on a button to select any of these options.

This screen shows a video of a skating demonstration.

Writing Complete Sentences

1

1.1 Sentence Fragments

A sentence fragment is a group of words that does not express a complete thought. It may be missing a subject, a predicate, or both. A sentence fragment makes you wonder *What is this about?* or *What happened?*

Missing Subject or Predicate

You can correct a sentence fragment by adding the missing subject or predicate to complete the thought.

"The School Play" is a story about sixth graders who
          The students
put on a play. Rehearse their parts for three weeks.
              ∧   *forget their lines.*
Even then some students.
                        ∧

APPLY WHAT YOU'VE LEARNED

Rewrite these sentences, correcting the sentence fragments.

1. "The School Play."
2. Is based on a tragedy of the winter of 1846–1847.
3. Late in October, George and Jacob Donner.
4. Led a party through the Sierra Nevada in California.
5. A terrible snowstorm.
6. Blocked the pass.
7. By April almost half of the 82 members of the original party.
8. Had died of starvation.
9. Some of the survivors.
10. Resorted to eating the corpses of those who had died.

1.2 Run-On Sentences

A run-on sentence consists of two or more sentences written incorrectly as one. A run-on sentence occurs because the writer either used no end mark or used a comma instead of a period to end the first complete thought. A run-on sentence may confuse readers because it does not show where one thought ends and the next begins.

Forming Separate Sentences

One way to correct a run-on sentence is to form two separate sentences. Use a period or other end punctuation after the first sentence, and capitalize the first letter of the next sentence.

> *Damon and Pythias* retells an ancient Greek legend this version is in the form of a play. The story is about two great friends each shows his devotion by being willing to die for the other.

Forming Compound Sentences

You can also correct a run-on sentence by rewriting it to form a compound sentence. One way to do this is by using a comma and a coordinating conjunction.

Never join simple sentences with a comma alone, or a run-on sentence will result. You need a comma followed by the conjunction *and, but,* or *or* to hold the sentences together.

> Damon and Pythias lived on the island of Sicily every- *and*
> one knew what friends they were. Their king was cruel
> *but* no one dared to criticize him. Pythias spoke against the
> king the punishment for this offense was death. *and*

LINK TO LITERATURE

In *Damon and Pythias*, on page 684, Fan Kissen writes long sentences that sometimes look like run-ons. These sentences may appear complicated, but they are clear and easy to understand. They present conversation as it usually sounds. Kissen's logical grouping of thoughts, careful use of punctuation, and play format ensure that the reader will understand.

You may use a semicolon to join two ideas that are closely related.

In addition, you can correct a run-on sentence by using a semicolon and a conjunctive adverb. Commonly used conjunctive adverbs are *however, therefore, nevertheless,* and *besides.*

Pythias had to settle his affairs; he wanted to say good-

bye to his mother. Damon took his friend's place for a

nevertheless,
while; Pythias planned to come back. Damon would

however,
have taken Pythias' punishment; Pythias returned just in

time.

APPLY WHAT YOU'VE LEARNED

Rewrite this paragraph, correcting the run-on sentences in different ways.

1. In *Damon and Pythias* the friendship of two young men helps them face death another story about friends is found in the Bible.

2. David and Jonathan were friends who protected each other they warned each other of danger.

3. Young David was a musician his songs soothed Saul, the king of Israel.

4. Jonathan was the son of Saul he remained David's closest friend throughout his life.

5. David's brave acts made him a national hero Saul became jealous of him.

6. On more than one occasion Jonathan warned David of Saul's plots Saul tried to kill David with a dagger that barely missed its mark.

7. David had opportunities to kill Saul he always refused to do bad things.

8. Such honorable conduct shamed Saul Jonathan defended David even against his own father.

Making Subjects and Verbs Agree

2

2.1 Simple and Compound Subjects

A verb must agree in number with its subject. *Number* refers to whether a word is singular or plural. When a word refers to one thing, it is singular. When a word refers to more than one thing, it is plural.

Agreement with Simple Subjects

Use a singular verb with a singular subject.

When the subject is a singular noun, you use the singular form of the verb. The present-tense singular form of a regular verb usually ends in *-s* or *-es*.

> The selection "Tutankhamen" tell^s the true story of a
>
> famous archaeological discovery.

Use a plural verb with a plural subject.

> Two determined men looks for the tomb of Pharaoh
>
> Tutankhamen.

Agreement with Compound Subjects

Use a plural verb with a compound subject whose parts are joined by *and*, regardless of the number of each part.

> Howard Carter and Lord Carnarvon exclaims when
>
> they find "wonderful things" in November of 1922.

LINK TO LITERATURE

Notice the agreement of subjects and verbs throughout "Tutankhamen" by Anne Terry White, on page 470. The selection is a historical piece about discoveries made in the 1920s.

REVISING TIP

To find the subject of a sentence, first find the verb. Then ask *who* or *what* the verb refers to. Say the subject and the verb together to see whether they agree.

When the parts of a compound subject are joined by *or* or *nor*, make the verb agree in number with the part that is closer to it.

> Neither Lord Carnarvon nor the Egyptians knows⁹
>
> where to look for the rich tomb. A frequent problem
>
> for archaeologists is that grave robbers or time cause⁵
> ∧
> great damage.

APPLY WHAT YOU'VE LEARNED

Rewrite the correct form of the verb given in parentheses.

1. "Tutankhamen" (tell, tells) the story of a great archaeological discovery in Egypt.
2. Many wonderful discoveries also (take, takes) place in our part of the world.
3. A recent discovery (excite, excites) archaeologists in Mexico.
4. This great trade center (look, looks) ancient.
5. The city (seems, seem) to have been abandoned suddenly about A.D. 1000.
6. Neither floods nor war (help, helps) city dwellers.
7. One archaeologist (think, thinks) that this city hit its peak in the Classic Period, from A.D. 300 to A.D. 600.
8. S. Jeffrey, K. Wilkerson, and other archaeologists (wonder, wonders) what brought about such growth.
9. Several smaller settlements (date, dates) from about that time.
10. Research (suggest, suggests) that El Pital was a center of trade and culture more complex than that of most other towns.
11. Earth or stone (form, forms) more than a hundred dwellings, ball courts, temples, and long platforms.
12. Some buildings (measure, measures) 130 feet in height.
13. A banana, sugar-cane, or citrus plantation (produces, produce) growth dense enough to hide even these.
14. Either vegetation or flood sediment (keep, keeps) an ancient city hidden.
15. The city of El Tajín (appear, appears) to be more recent than El Pital.

2.2　Pronoun Subjects

When a pronoun is used as a subject, the verb must agree with it in number.

Agreement with Personal Pronouns

When the subject is a singular personal pronoun, use a singular verb. When the subject is a plural personal pronoun, use a plural verb.

Even though *I* and *you* are singular, they take the plural form of the verb.

> I believes that "Abd al-Rahman Ibrahima" is the true story of an enslaved African prince. We likes that story.

When *he, she,* or *it* is the part of the subject closer to the verb in a compound subject containing *or* or *nor*, use a singular verb. When a pronoun is part of a compound subject containing *and,* use a plural verb.

> The other captives and he trusts the slaver. Their past experience makes them trusting. Neither the others nor he prepare⁺ˢ for treachery.

Agreement with Indefinite Pronouns

When the subject is a singular indefinite pronoun, use the singular form of the verb.

The following are singular indefinite pronouns: *another, either, nobody, anybody, everybody, somebody, no one, anyone, everyone, someone, one, nothing, anything, everything, something, each,* and *neither.*

> During Ibrahima's time with the Irish doctor John Coates Cox, everything go⁺ᵉˢ well. Nothing arouse⁺ˢ Ibrahima's suspicion about foreigners.

LINK TO LITERATURE

Notice how the agreement of pronoun subjects with verbs in the excerpt from Walter Dean Myers's *Now Is Your Time!,* on page 257, makes it easy for him to discuss complex events. Correct grammatical constructions give readers a clear view of the incidents the author describes.

When the subject is a plural indefinite pronoun (*both, few, many,* or *several*), use the plural form of the verb.

> Few fears what they have not been taught to fear.
>
> Ibrahima learns from his experience that many deceives
>
> or betrays others.

The indefinite pronouns *some, all, any, none,* and *most* can be either singular or plural. When the pronoun refers to one thing or part, use a singular verb. When the pronoun refers to more than one thing, use a plural verb.

> Of the captives Ibrahima meets, many die on the trip
>
> over, and most suffers on landing. Some of the food
>
> seem inedible, and some of the people gets sick.

APPLY WHAT YOU'VE LEARNED

Write the correct form of the verb given in parentheses.

1. Of the peoples in the world, many (live, lives) in the huge continent of Africa.
2. Some (appear, appears) in the selection "Abd al-Rahman Ibrahima" from *Now Is Your Time!*.
3. Each group has its own culture and customs, and each (speak, speaks) in its own language or dialect.
4. Ibrahima speaks Fulani because he (belong, belongs) to the Fula people.
5. Most of the Fula (wear, wears) their silky hair long.
6. They are a pastoral people, so many (raise, raises) livestock.
7. In the selection, we (meet, meets) the Mandingo, enemies of the Fula.
8. They (come, comes) from West Africa and belong to many independent kingdoms.
9. One (trace, traces) its dynasty back 13 centuries with hardly a break.
10. Africans and we (know, knows) this group as the Kangaba.
11. The Mandingo are an agricultural people; they (grow, grows) grain crops such as millet; and they (tend, tends) cattle.
12. We (hear, hears) of another group, the Songhai, in Myers's account.
13. They (speak, speaks) an independent language.
14. Of the Songhai traders, all (prosper, prospers) from caravan commerce.

2.3 | Common Agreement Problems

Several other situations can cause problems in subject-verb agreement.

Agreement with Irregular Verbs

Use the singular forms of the irregular verbs *do, be,* and *have* with singular subjects. Use the plural forms of these verbs with plural subjects.

	Do	Be	Have
Singular Subjects	I do you do the car does each does it doesn't	I am/was you are/were Jane is/was she isn't/wasn't either is/was	I have you have Juan hasn't he has anybody has
Plural Subjects	we do cars do they do many don't	we are/were girls are/were they are/were both are/were	we have boys have they haven't few have

> The story "The All-American Slurp" do~~es~~ a good job of
> describing our manners. The story ~~have~~ has examples of
> Chinese and American mistakes. They ~~is~~ are both funny.

Interrupting Words

Be sure the verb agrees with its subject when a word or words come between them.

A word or words that come between the subject and its verb do not affect the number of the verb.

> Many of the girls in the group feels embarrassed. A dip of
> sour cream and onion flakes cause~~s~~ a problem for the Lins.

REVISING TIP

Look carefully at words that come before the verb to find the subject. Remember that the subject may not be the noun or pronoun closest to the verb.

LINK TO LITERATURE

In "The All-American Slurp,"
on page 6, notice how
Lensey Namioka makes sub-
jects and verbs agree in spite
of words or phrases that separate them. This skill allows
her to add more information
to each sentence and to vary
the rhythm of the sentences.

Interrupting Phrases

**Be certain that the verb agrees with its subject when a
phrase comes between them.**

The subject of a verb is never found in a prepositional phrase,
which may follow the subject and come before the verb.

> The members of the Gleason family offers snacks to
>
> the Lins. A cooked vegetable, according to many
>
> Chinese people, taste better than a raw one.

Phrases beginning with *including, as well as, along with,* and *in
addition to* are not part of the subject.

> The Lins learn that celery, as well as radishes and
>
> carrots, count as a finger food. Each guest, including
>
> the parents and the children, skip the dip.

The subject of a verb is never found in an appositive, which may
follow the subject and come before the verb.

> Meg, daughter of the Gleasons, struggle to eat a tradi-
>
> tional Chinese meal. Pot stickers, a Chinese delicacy, is
>
> enjoyed by almost everyone.

Inverted Sentences

**When the subject comes after the verb, be sure the verb
agrees with the subject in number.**

A sentence in which the subject follows the verb is called an
inverted sentence.

From knowing the rules of courtesy come ^s confidence.
From breaking them, however, comes ^g ^ the most fun and
laughter.

Questions are usually in inverted form, as are sentences that begin with *here is, here are, there is,* and *there are.* (For example: *Where is the fire? There are people rushing outside.*)

"What kind of food does ^do^ ^g you enjoy?" the families
might have asked. Why were ^was^ ^g each worrying about what
to eat? There are ^is^ ^g a good choice of restaurants. Here is ^are^ ^g a
few of my favorites.

 REVISING TIP

To check subject-verb agreement in inverted sentences, place the subject before the verb. For example, change *Here is an idea* to *An idea is here.*

APPLY WHAT YOU'VE LEARNED

Write the correct form of each verb given in parentheses.

1. The story "The All-American Slurp" (does, do) readers a favor; it helps us not take ourselves too seriously.
2. Most of us, at some time or another, (has, have) wondered about rules of polite behavior.
3. What (is, are) the right things to do?
4. Dip, including things like sour cream, (was, were) difficult for the Lins.
5. (Does, Do) you handle similar problems in another country as well as the Lins?
6. The difficulties for a traveler (is, are) often greater.

7. Roast gorilla, along with side dishes, (is, are) a delicacy in one African country.
8. A Saudi Arabian (has, have) sheep's eyeballs as a delicacy.
9. (Is, Are) there a gracious way to deal with a disgusting dish? Here (is, are) some ways.
10. Swallowing fast, telling yourself that it "tastes just like chicken," (is, are) a good way.
11. Some, to disguise the form or texture of a food, (slice, slices) the item thinly.
12. Finally, a burp or a belch at the end of a meal, in some places, highly (compliment, compliments) the cook.

3 Using Nouns and Pronouns

3.1 Plural and Possessive Nouns

Nouns refer to people, places, things, and ideas. A noun is plural when it refers to more than one person, place, thing, or idea. Possessive nouns show who or what owns something.

Plural Nouns

Follow these guidelines to form noun plurals.

Nouns	To Form Plural	Examples
Most nouns	add -s	eye—eyes
Most nouns that end in s, sh, ch, x, or z	add -es	chorus—choruses bench—benches
Most nouns that end in ay, ey, oy, or uy	add -s	day—days donkey—donkeys
Most nouns that end in a consonant and y	change y to i and add -es	lily—lilies folly—follies
Most nouns that end in o	add -s	piano—pianos radio—radios solo—solos
Some nouns that end in a consonant and o	add -es	mango—mangoes ginkgo—ginkgoes potato—potatoes
Most nouns that end in f or fe	change f to v and add -es or -s	leaf—leaves wife—wives but roof—roofs

Some nouns have the same spelling in both singular and plural forms: *deer, moose, shrimp,* and *salmon.* Some nouns have irregular plurals that do not follow any rule: *mice, feet.*

LINK TO LITERATURE

In "Shrewd Todie and Lyzer the Miser," on page 319, Isaac Bashevis Singer uses vocabulary that may be unfamiliar to the reader. Some examples are *borscht,* referring to a soup made of beets, spinach, or cabbage, and *gulden,* the name of a type of coins. These nouns help capture the flavor of the setting, an old Russian village.

REVISING TIP

The plurals of many musical terms that end in *o* preceded by a consonant are formed by adding -s. These nouns include *rondos, falsettos,* and *pianos.*

In "Shrewd Todie and Lyzer the Miser" Todie has trouble fulfilling his family ~~dutys~~. *duties* Firewood and ~~potatos~~ *potatoes* are very expensive. ~~Loafs~~ *Loaves* of bread are rare.

Possessive Nouns

Follow these guidelines to form possessive nouns.

Nouns	To Form Possessive	Examples
Singular nouns	add apostrophe and -*s*	team—team's
Plural nouns ending in *s*	add apostrophe	workers—workers' members—members'
Plural nouns not ending in *s*	add apostrophe and -*s*	people—people's men—men's

Because of his childrens needs, Todie approaches the rich miser Lyzer for loans. Lyzers own goat must beg the neighbors for the peelings of potatoes.

REVISING TIP

The dictionary usually lists the plural form of a noun if the plural is formed irregularly or if it might be formed in more than one way. Dictionary listings are especially helpful for nouns that end in *o, f,* and *fe.*

APPLY WHAT YOU'VE LEARNED

Write the correct noun given in parentheses.

*1*Isaac Bashevis (Singers', Singer's) (storys, stories) are known and loved the world over. *2*Often set in Russia or Poland, they usually focus on the funny (traits, traites) and problems of the (characters, characters'). *3*Most of the (tales, tale's) are simple, yet in 1978 they won Singer a Nobel Prize in literature. *4*Often the stories have to do with the daily (temptationes, temptations) that everyone faces. *5*The way (peoples', people's) consciences work is explored.

*6*One might expect (subjects, subject's) such as hating evil and praising good to be heavy or boring. *7*Instead, the (stories', storie's) plots are usually charming. *8*Often they are funny, but just as often they catch (readers, readers') off guard. *9*Some (characters', character's) "flaws" seem to make them more likable. *10*(Other's, Others') virtues, which ought to make us admire the characters, don't appeal to us at all. *11*The (truth's, truths) that come out of the stories may seem sad or unfair. *12*Sometimes, however, the (tales, tale's) are simple and truly heartwarming.

3.2 Pronoun Forms

A personal pronoun is a word that can take the place of a noun or another pronoun. A personal pronoun has three forms: the subject form, the object form, and the possessive form.

Subject Pronouns

Use the subject form of a pronoun when it is the subject of a sentence or the subject of a clause. *I, you, he, she, it, we,* and *they* are subject pronouns.

Using the correct pronoun form is not a problem when the sentence has just one pronoun. Problems can arise, however, when a noun and a pronoun—or two pronouns—are used in a compound subject or compound object. To see whether you are using the correct pronoun form, read the sentence with only one pronoun.

> "The Circuit" tells the story of a boy and his family of migrant workers. The story begins and ends as he and
> *they*
> ~~them~~ pack to move on to yet another "home."

Use the subject form of a pronoun when it is a predicate pronoun following a linking verb.

You often hear the object form of a predicate pronoun used in casual conversation (*It is me*). For this reason, the subject form may sound awkward to you, though it is preferred for more-formal writing.

> *he*
> The boy is the narrator. It is ~~him~~ who helps the readers feel his joy and pain.

Object Pronouns

Use the object form of a pronoun when it is the object of a sentence, the object of a clause, or the object of a preposition. *Me, you, him, her, it, us,* and *them* are object pronouns.

LINK TO LITERATURE

Notice how Francisco Jiménez uses pronouns to avoid repetition of the same nouns and to link ideas in different sentences throughout his short story "The Circuit," on page 545.

REVISING TIP

To check for a correct pronoun, see whether the sentence still makes sense when the subject and the pronoun are reversed. (*It was she. She was it.*)

> We share with his family and ~~he~~ *him* the frustration caused
> by not staying anywhere long. One of the teachers
> treats ~~he~~ *him* and the other students with kindness.

Possessive Pronouns

**Never use an apostrophe in a possessive pronoun. *My,
mine, your, yours, his, her, hers, its, our, ours, their,* and
theirs are possessive pronouns.**

Writers often confuse the possessive pronouns *its, your,* and
their with the contractions *it's, you're,* and *they're*. Remember
that the pairs are spelled differently and that they have different
meanings.

> *Their*
> ~~They're~~ disappointment at putting down roots only to
> pull them up again touches us. Its as if we, and not
> *they*
> ~~them~~, come home to find boxes packed. The sad circuit,
> or cycle, is our's.

APPLY WHAT YOU'VE LEARNED

**Write the correct pronoun form given
in parentheses.**

1The life of a migrant worker would be
hard for you and (I, me). **2**(Them, They) and
other workers must struggle at low-paying
jobs just to survive. **3**(They're, Their) working conditions are sometimes intolerable.
4Not only must workers settle for extremely
low wages, but (they're, their) often unable
to find any jobs for half the year. **5**When
(they, them) do, employers provide poor
housing for (they, them). **6**No sick days, holidays, or other benefits are offered their
families or (them, they). **7**You and (I, me)

might wonder why anyone would settle for
such work. **8**Many workers come from
other countries, however, where (its, it's)
even harder to make a living. **9**Black and
Hispanic men, women, and children make
up most of the migrant work force; poor
whites and (they, them) suffer equally.
10Some travel with (they're, their) families;
others send money home to places such as
Haiti and the West Indies. **11**Compare (your,
you're) life with that of a migrant worker.
12At (its, it's) worst it may be easier than
what (he, him) or (she, her) must face.

3.3   Pronoun Antecedents

An antecedent is the noun or pronoun to which a personal pronoun refers. The antecedent usually precedes the pronoun.

Pronoun and Antecedent Agreement

A pronoun must agree with its antecedent in
- number—singular or plural
- person—first, second, or third
- gender—masculine, feminine, or neuter

Use a singular pronoun to refer to a singular antecedent; use a plural pronoun to refer to a plural antecedent.

Do not allow interrupting words to determine the number of the personal pronoun.

> In "In the Land of Small Dragon" it is the younger half-sister, not the two other characters, who ~~are~~ *is* unkind to the sweet Cinderella figure, Tâm.

If the antecedent is a noun that could refer to either a male or a female, use *he or she* (*him or her, his or her*), or reword the sentence to avoid the need for a singular pronoun.

> Somebody may wonder who Tâm is. ~~They~~ *He or she* might think she is a princess.
>
> *or*
>
> ~~Somebody~~ *People* may wonder who Tâm is. They might think she is a princess.

Be sure that the antecedent of a pronoun is clear.

In most cases, do not use a pronoun to refer to an entire idea or clause. Writing is much clearer if the exact reference is given.

LINK TO LITERATURE

"In The Land of Small Dragon," on page 662, was told by Dang Manh Kha to Ann Nolan Clark. The author presents an Asian Cinderella tale in poetic form. Her effective use of pronoun antecedents helps us to keep the characters separate in our minds.

Both this story and the Cinderella tale end happily, and
~~it is~~ *happy endings are* what we hope for.

"Goodness is always rewarded," "Beauty is as beauty
does," and "Actions speak louder than words"—all apply *these sayings*
in the tale "In the Land of Small Dragon."

Indefinite Pronouns as Antecedents

When a singular indefinite pronoun is the antecedent, use
***he or she** (**him or her, his or her**), **or rewrite the sentence**
to avoid the need for a singular pronoun.

Each person at the festival rejoiced. ~~They~~ *He or she* shared in the
joy of the prince and princess.

or

~~Everyone~~ *All who were* at the festival rejoiced. They shared in the joy
of the prince and princess.

REVISING TIP

Avoid the indefinite use of
you and *they*.

~~They say in~~ the story *tells us to*
~~that you should~~ be kind
and good to everybody.

Indefinite Pronouns					
Singular	another anybody anyone anything	each either	everybody everyone everything	neither nobody no one nothing one	somebody someone something
Plural	both	few	many	several	
Singular or Plural	all	any	most	none	some

Rewrite this paragraph to make the pronoun references clear.

1A tale like "In the Land of Small Dragon" is found in many countries; they remind you of Cinderella. **2**_Mufaro's Beautiful Daughters_ is one of these stories. The author drew upon traditional tales from Africa to write them. **3**In this story Nyasha was loved by everyone, but they usually did not like her sister. **4**She encouraged the snake to live in her garden, where it was very comfortable.

5Manyara was unkind and rude, and people could not help but see it. **6**One day a messenger arrived, and they said that the king was looking for a bride. **7**Manyara left on her journey to the king's city before Nyasha, and she was afraid she would be late. **8**On the way Manyara met an old woman; she reminded her to be helpful to anyone she met. **9**Instead, she was often rude to them. **10**Nyasha was kind and courteous, and it was rewarded in the end.

3.4   Pronoun Usage

The form that a pronoun takes is always determined by its function within its own clause or sentence.

Who and Whom

Use _who_ or _whoever_ as the subject of a clause or sentence.

> In "Three Strong Women" a wrestler meets three women whom are much stronger than he.

Use _whom_ as the direct or indirect object of a verb or verbal and as the object of a preposition.

People often use _who_ for _whom_ when speaking informally. However, in written English the pronouns should be used correctly.

> First he meets a young girl by who he is carried up a mountain. Then he learns that her mother and grandmother, who the girl introduces, are just as strong as she is.

REVISING TIP

Whom should replace _who_ in both sentences in the second example:
By whom—object of a preposition
Introduces whom—object of the verb in a clause

In trying to determine the correct pronoun form, ignore interrupters that come between the subject and the verb.

Whom, do you think, needs the most exercise to get into shape? Who would you choose to help move your furniture?

Pronouns in Contractions

Do not confuse the contractions *it's, they're, who's,* and *you're* with possessive pronouns that sound the same—*its, their, whose,* and *your*.

The story is amusing because its not about traditional Japanese women and strong sumo wrestlers. The characters roles seem switched, so their funnier.

APPLY WHAT YOU'VE LEARNED

Write the correct pronoun given in parentheses.

1. In recent years women's bodybuilding has come into (its, it's) own.
2. One reason may be that (its, it's) a challenge.
3. Some women (who, whom) take on this sport start by being concerned about (their, they're) safety.
4. Others, for (who, whom) health is a concern, also find bodybuilding very appealing.
5. (Who, Whom) is more interested in fitness today than the young?
6. People are more aware of (its, it's) importance now than ever before.
7. (Their, They're) finding bodybuilding more enjoyable than aerobics, jogging, or running.
8. Once people thought reducing diets were the only way to lose weight, but now we know (its, it's) more important to exercise.
9. Of all the people you know, (who, whom) do you most look up to?
10. (Who, Whom) do you think is the most fit?

4 Using Modifiers Effectively

4.1 Adjective or Adverb?

Use an adjective to modify a noun or a pronoun. Use an adverb to modify a verb, an adjective, or another adverb.

> In "Oh Broom, Get to Work" the author tells interest-
> ing about some especially boring visitors to her home. [*ly* inserted]
> These men usual were ministers, and they had some [*ly* inserted]
> peculiarly ways of acting.

REVISING TIP

Always determine first which word is being modified. For example, in the first sentence of the first example, *tells* is the verb being modified, so it takes an adverb, *interestingly.* In the second sentence, *ways* is a noun, so its modifier needs to be an adjective, *peculiar.*

Use an adjective after a linking verb to describe the subject.

Remember that in addition to forms of the verb *be,* the following are linking verbs: *become, seem, appear, look, sound, feel, taste, grow,* and *smell*.

> Yo Chan and her sister felt ~~unhappily~~ about the many [*unhappy* inserted]
> dull visitors. Only one minister seemed entertainingly.

APPLY WHAT YOU'VE LEARNED

Correct the modifiers throughout.

1In "Oh Broom, Get to Work" Yo Chan's parents are (proud, proudly) graduates of a Christian university in Japan. **2**Christianity was brought there by (fearlessly, fearless) missionaries. **3**The religion spread (quick, quickly) throughout Japan, beginning, in 1549. **4**The (stern, sternly) rulers of the nation thought that a Western religion would undermine their power. **5**In the early 1600s the (nervously, nervous) rulers began to limit the religion. **6**The number of people practicing Christianity dropped (great, greatly) by 1640. **7**Missionaries were (reluctant, reluctantly) allowed back into the country in 1873. **8**After two centuries they found some evidence of Christianity that had survived the (extensive, extensively) persecution.

Comparative and Superlative Adjectives

Use the comparative form of an adjective when comparing two things.

Comparative adjectives are formed by adding *-er* to short adjectives (*small—smaller*) or by using the word *more* with longer adjectives (*horrible—more horrible*).

> *a more impressive*
> "The Adoption of Albert" is an ~~impressiver~~ story than
>   ∧
> many I have read. The characters in the story are
>   *funnier*
> ~~more funny~~ than most.
>   ∧

Use the superlative form when comparing three or more things.

The superlative is formed by adding *-est* to short adjectives (*tall—tallest*) or by using the word *most* with longer adjectives (*interesting—most interesting*).

> *most*
> Of the characters, who is the ~~daringest~~? Who is the
>   ∧
> ~~most~~ quietest?

The comparative and superlative forms of some adjectives are irregular.

Adjective	Comparative	Superlative
good	better	best
well	better	best
bad	worse	worst
ill	worse	worst
little	less *or* lesser	least
much	more	most
many	more	most
far	farther *or* further	farthest *or* furthest

REVISING TIP

When comparing something with everything else of its kind, do not leave out the word *other*. (*Andy is quicker than any other player on the team.*)

Do not use both *-er* and *more* or *-est* and *most*.

Harry's piranha moves ~~more~~ faster than Jim's. It is the ~~most~~ boldest fish I've ever seen.

Comparative and Superlative Adverbs

When comparing two actions, use the comparative form of an adverb, adding *-er* or the word *more*.

More ~~oftener~~ than not, Aunt Rhoda behaved ~~oddlier~~ *more oddly* than anyone else in her family.

When comparing more than two actions, use the superlative form of an adverb, adding *-est* or the word *most*.

Of all the mistakes in the story, the one made by Louis's mother ended ~~humorousliest~~ *most humorously*.

Double Negatives

To avoid double negatives, use only one negative word in a clause.

Besides the compounds formed with *no,* the words *barely, hardly,* and *scarcely* also function as negative words.

No one ~~hardly~~ suspected that Albert's parents were searching for him. They couldn't find him ~~nowhere~~ *anywhere*.

APPLY WHAT YOU'VE LEARNED

Correct the mistakes in modifiers used in comparisons.

[1]Surely the importantest characters in "The Adoption of Albert" are the earthworms. [2]The very tinier earthworms grow only 0.04 inch long. [3]The most longest earthworms are 11 feet long. [4]Earthworms can tell the difference between more easier and more hard work. [5]After trying to move a leaf that was held down, they switched to a leaf that could be moved more faster. [6]The earthworm that lasted most longest in captivity lived ten years. [7]Some earthworms in Great Britain are the beautifullest green. [8]The more ordinarier red-brown color of common earthworms comes from iron pigment in their blood. [9]They burrow more deeper in winter or when the soil is dry.

Special Problems with Modifiers

The following terms are frequently misused in spoken English, but they should be used correctly in written English.

Them and Those

Them is always a pronoun and never a modifier of a noun. Those is a pronoun when it stands alone. It is an adjective when followed by a noun.

> In "Flowers and Freckle Cream" Elizabeth learns that
> ~~them~~ *those* freckles of hers aren't so bad after all.

Bad and Badly

Always use bad as an adjective, whether before a noun or after a linking verb. Badly should generally be used to modify an action verb.

> Grandpa saved the day when Elizabeth felt so bad~~ly~~.
> She acted bad *ly* when she refused to tell anyone what was
> wrong.

This, That, These, and Those

Whether used as adjectives or as pronouns, this and these refer to people and things that are nearby, and that and those refer to people and things that are farther away.

> All day long, Elizabeth worked outdoors in ~~this~~ *that* faraway
> field. When she came home, she had ~~these~~ *those* hateful freck-
> les on her face.

REVISING TIP

Avoid the use of *here* with *this* and *these*; also, do not use *there* with *that* and *those*.

Why did Elizabeth buy that ~~there~~ freckle cream? Those ~~there~~ products are expensive!

Good and Well

Good is always an adjective, never an adverb. Use *well* as either an adjective or an adverb, depending on the sentence.

When used as an adjective, *well* usually refers to a person's health. As an adverb, *well* modifies an action verb. In the expression "feeling good," *good* refers to being happy or pleased.

> Hoeing tobacco under the hot sun, Elizabeth did her
> work ~~good~~ well. She felt ~~well~~ good when she saw all her fine
> work.

Few and Little, Fewer and Less

Few refers to a number of things that can be counted; *little* refers to an amount or quantity. *Fewer* is used when comparing numbers of things; *less* is used when comparing amounts or quantities.

> Because Elizabeth felt appreciated by Grandpa, having
> ~~less~~ fewer freckles didn't matter. She decided that the ~~fewer~~ less
> she spent on freckle cream, the better.

Using Verbs Correctly

5

5.1   Verb Tenses and Forms

Verb tense shows the time of an action or condition. Writers sometimes cause confusion when they use different verb tenses in describing actions that occur at the same time.

Consistent Use of Tenses

When two or more actions occur at the same time or in sequence, use the same verb tense to describe the actions.

> "The Mushroom" tells about a fungus that starts small and then lived almost forever. It just got stronger and stronger all the time.

A shift in tense is necessary when two events occur at different times or out of sequence. The tenses of the verbs should clearly indicate that one action precedes the other.

> Now that the mushroom was a thousand years old, it weighed 38 tons. But at its birth, a slow, gentle rain helps the tiny mushroom spores grow.

Tense	Verb Form
Present	close/closes
Past	closed
Future	will/shall close
Present perfect	have/has closed
Past perfect	had closed
Future perfect	will/shall have closed

LINK TO LITERATURE

Throughout "The Mushroom," page 228, H. M. Hoover uses the past tense and past participles to describe a huge mushroom that lives a very long time. She shifts tense only twice. On page 230 she says, "A sheath of a thousand hyphae is no thicker than a human hair." She says it again on page 233. The shift in tense stands out, emphasizing the fact the author is presenting general information.

REVISING TIP

In telling a story, be careful not to shift tenses so often that the reader has difficulty keeping the sequence of events straight.

Past Tense and the Past Participle

The simple past form of a verb can always stand alone. Always use the past participles of the following irregular verbs when the verbs follow helping verbs.

Present Tense	Past Tense	Past Participle
know	knew	(have, had) known
lay	laid	(have, had) laid
lie	lay	(have, had) lain
ride	rode	(have, had) ridden
rise	rose	(have, had) risen
run	ran	(have, had) run
say	said	(have, had) said
see	saw	(have, had) seen
sing	sang	(have, had) sung
speak	spoke	(have, had) spoken
steal	stole	(have, had) stolen
swim	swam	(have, had) swum
take	took	(have, had) taken
teach	taught	(have, had) taught

Much history have went past while the mushroom had
            had gone
been growing. Even though humans paved it over when
they built a mall, the fungus have grown too big to die.
                              had

APPLY WHAT YOU'VE LEARNED

Write the correct verb for each sentence.

1. In "The Mushroom" we (seen, have seen) an interesting member of the fungus kingdom.
2. Naturalists have (saw, seen) as many as 3,300 kinds of mushrooms.
3. Of those, 2,000 (are, were) nonpoisonous.
4. The mushroom's gills turn black when it (matures, matured).
5. The indigo lactaria mushroom (is, was) totally blue.
6. Sharp, spiny structures (stick, stuck) out from hedgehog mushroom caps.
7. People have (spoke, spoken) of mushrooms growing 15 inches tall.
8. Humans aren't the only ones to have (took, taken) mushrooms into their diet.
9. People have (saw, seen) red squirrels putting mushrooms on branches to dry.
10. Then, as the people watched, the squirrels (ran, run) off to store the mushrooms.

5.2 Commonly Confused Verbs

The following verb pairs are easily confused.

Let and Leave

Let means "to allow or permit." Leave means "to depart" or "to allow something to remain where it is."

> "Aaron's Gift" ~~leaves~~ ^lets^ the reader imagine what to do about a wounded animal. Should you ~~let~~ ^leave^ it to die?

Lie and Lay

Lie means "to rest in a flat position." Lay means "to put or place."

> The pigeon ~~laid~~ ^lay^ down, almost dead. He ~~lied~~ ^laid^ his ruffled feathers as close as he could to his body.

Sit and Set

Sit means "to be in a seated position." Set means "to put or place."

> Pidge would often ~~set~~ ^sit^ quietly and look at Aaron. Aaron was glad he'd ~~sat~~ ^set^ out food to help the bird get well.

Rise and Raise

Rise means "to move upward." Raise means "to move something upward."

> Pidge escaped the gang by flying, ~~raising~~ ^rising^ up quickly. He ~~rose~~ ^raised^ his healed wing and flapped desperately.

REVISING TIP

If you're uncertain about which verb to use, check to see whether the verb has an object. The verbs *lie, sit,* and *rise* never have objects.

Learn and *Teach*

Learn means "to gain knowledge or skill." **Teach** means "to help someone learn."

> Pidge ~~learned~~ taught Aaron much about healing and about
> standing up for a friend.

Here are the principal parts of these troublesome verb pairs.

Present Tense	Past Tense	Past Participle
let leave	let left	(have, had) let (have, had) left
lie lay	lay laid	(have, had) lain (have, had) laid
sit set	sat set	(have, had) sat (have, had) set
rise raise	rose raised	(have, had) risen (have, had) raised
learn teach	learned taught	(have, had) learned (have, had) taught

---

APPLY WHAT YOU'VE LEARNED

Choose the correct verb from each pair in parentheses.

1. Biologists have (left, let) us know that rock doves are the ancestors of pigeons like the one in "Aaron's Gift."
2. Rock doves like to (sit, set) their nests on cliff ledges, so their descendants thrive in modern cities.
3. People started (raising, rising) rock doves for food around 4500 B.C.
4. (Leave, Let) me tell you that today there are about 285 kinds of pigeons.
5. Pigeons usually are active during the day, but do they ever (lay, lie) down to sleep?

6. Some kinds of pigeons weigh as much as three pounds, so they must be strong fliers to (raise, rise) into the air.
7. When we raised pigeons, they usually (lay, laid) two eggs at a time.
8. Biologists (teach, learn) us that some pigeons use the sounds their feathers make during flight to signal each other.
9. A crowned pigeon has plumage that (raises, rises) up from its head and looks like a peacock's tail.
10. Rats (setting, sitting) in shadowy corners are among a pigeon's enemies.
11. The rats and humans have (learned, taught) pigeons to beware of them.

Correcting
Capitalization

6.1 Proper Nouns and Adjectives

A common noun names a whole class of persons, places, things, or ideas. A proper noun names a particular person, place, thing, or idea. A proper adjective is an adjective formed from a proper noun. All proper nouns and proper adjectives are capitalized.

Names and Personal Titles

Capitalize the name and title of a person.

Also capitalize initials and abbreviations that stand for names and titles. *Captain Greaves, Blackbeard, Sir Henry Morgan, S. Bonnet,* and *Anne Bonny* are capitalized correctly.

> *Gold and Silver, Silver and Gold* tells about captain
> william kidd, famous as a Pirate. Others besides the
> Captain included "calico jack" rackham, charles vane,
> and two women—mary read and jeanne de belleville.
> Even sir francis drake was a Pirate before the queen
> knighted him.

Capitalize a word referring to a family relationship when it is used as someone's name (*Uncle Joseph*) but not when it is used to identify a person (*Andrea's aunt*).

> Charlie smith, my Uncle, says he's glad he didn't live in
> a world with pirates. I disagree with uncle charlie, but
> my Mother agrees with him.

LINK TO LITERATURE

In the excerpt from *Gold and Silver, Silver and Gold*, on page 430, notice how Alvin Schwartz refers to specific places, people, and things. These precise names help you visualize scenes. More-general words probably would not help you see the story or believe it as easily.

REVISING TIP

Do not capitalize personal titles used as common nouns. (*We met the emperor.*)

Languages, Nationalities, Religious Terms

Capitalize the names of languages and nationalities, as well as religious names and terms.

Capitalize words referring to languages and nationalities, such as *Spanish, Norwegian, Turkish, Yiddish,* and *Greek.* Capitalize religious names and terms, such as *Allah, Jehovah, Bible,* and *Koran.*

> Captain kidd took gold from a wrecked french ship,
> and he stole armenian trading ships owned by the
> emperor of India. He refused to raid a dutch ship,
> though.

School Subjects

Capitalize the name of a specific school course (*Choral Music, Physics I, Chemistry 2*). Do not capitalize a general reference to a school subject (*biology, geometry, health*).

> My Social Studies teacher said that next year in history 2
> we will learn about the New Orleans pirate Jean Laffite.

Organizations, Institutions

Capitalize the important words in the official names of organizations and institutions (*Parliament, Dutch West India Company*).

Do not capitalize words that refer to kinds of organizations or institutions (*college, hospital, museums*) or a word that refers to specific organization but is not its official name (*to the museum*).

> The smithsonian institution has materials on Captain
> Kidd. Maybe the new york historical society or another
> Library does too, since Kidd lived in New York.

REVISING TIP

Do not capitalize minor words in a proper noun that is made up of several words. (*Museum of Modern Art*)

Geographical Names, Events, Time Periods

Capitalize geographical names, as well as the names of events, historical periods and documents, holidays, and months and days, but not the names of seasons or directions.

Names	Examples
Continents	North America, Europe, Asia
Bodies of water	Caribbean Sea, Delaware Bay, Hudson River, Indian Ocean
Political units	France, the Netherlands, India, New Jersey
Sections of a country	the Midwest, New England
Public areas	Central Park, Yosemite National Park
Roads and structures	Wall Street, Taj Mahal
Historical events	French and Indian War, Russian Revolution
Documents	Treaty of Westminster, the Constitution
Periods of history	Dark Ages, Enlightenment
Holidays	Fourth of July, Veterans Day
Months and days	November, Monday
Seasons	spring, winter
Directions	east, northwest

REVISING TIP

Do not capitalize a reference that does not use the full name of a place, event, or period. (*Buckingham Palace is the most beautiful palace in the world.*)

Captain Kidd was born in scotland around 1645 and died on may 23, 1701, in london. When he was executed on that late Spring day, he left behind a wife and children on liberty street in new york city.

APPLY WHAT YOU'VE LEARNED

Correct any capitalization errors.

1. *Gold and Silver, Silver and Gold* made me curious about Pirates.
2. Therefore, I found out about buccaneers like barbarossa and henry jennings.
3. Kidd's treasure probably included persian gulf pearls, diamonds from india, and emeralds from south america.
4. My aunt theresa reminded me to check our Village Library for information.
5. I'm glad she's such a helpful Aunt.
6. Maybe the vatican library or the conde museum knows about kidd's life.
7. I could ask the Librarian just how to do this research for my History project.
8. My math II teacher, miss flanders, told me to read about less famous Pirates, like edward low.
9. Finally, uncle charlie said to look into the treaty of paris.
10. He said it outlawed privateering, which was a kind of legal Piracy.

6.2　Titles of Created Works

Titles follow certain capitalization rules.

Poems, Stories, Articles

Capitalize the first word, the last word, and all other important words in the title of a poem, a story, or an article. Enclose the title in quotation marks.

> Carl Sandburg's poem ˅"primer lesson˅" talks about risks you take when you say harsh things. Harsh words hurt people.

Books, Plays, Magazines, Newspapers, Films

Capitalize the first word, the last word, and all other important words in the title of a book, a play or musical, a magazine, a newspaper, or a film. Underline or italicize the title to set it off.

Within a title, don't capitalize articles, conjunctions, and prepositions of fewer than five letters.

> ˅"Primer lesson˅" appeared in Sandburg's book complete poems, published in 1950.

REVISING TIP

Underline the titles of books, plays, magazines and newspapers, and movies when they are typed or handwritten. Enclose the titles of poems, short stories, and articles in quotation marks.

APPLY WHAT YOU'VE LEARNED

Rewrite these sentences, correcting the punctuation and capitalization of titles.

1. Sandburg's poem primer lesson is just a tiny part of all the work he did.
2. Most people probably think of him as a poet, especially for his 1914 poem chicago.
3. He also wrote many volumes of historical biography about Lincoln. One set of these was abraham lincoln: the prairie years.
4. I wonder whether the song buffalo gals won't you come out tonight is in his collection called the american songbag.
5. In his early years he worked for the chicago daily news.
6. Critics think Sandburg's poetry was strongly influenced by Walt Whitman's poetry collection leaves of grass.

Correcting Punctuation

7.1   Compound Sentences

Punctuation helps organize longer sentences that have several clauses.

Commas in Compound Sentences

Use a comma before the conjunction that joins the clauses of a compound sentence.

> In "Matthew Henson at the Top of the World" Henson got to the North Pole‚ and he worked really hard to make the most of his opportunity.

Semicolons in Compound Sentences

Use a semicolon between the clauses of a compound sentence when no conjunction is used. Use a semicolon before, and a comma after, a conjunctive adverb that joins the clauses of a compound sentence.

Conjunctive adverbs include *therefore, however, nevertheless, consequently,* and *besides.*

> He made the dream of his boyhood come true‚ however‚ racism interfered with his ambition. The limits placed on African Americans closed doors for him‚ his abilities usually were ignored.

LINK TO LITERATURE

Notice on pages 56 and 57 of "Matthew Henson at the Top of the World" how Jim Haskins uses compound and complex sentences. He combines ideas and merges pieces of information in a way that shows their relation to one another.

REVISING TIP

Even when clauses are connected by a coordinating conjunction, you may use a semicolon between them if one or both clauses contain a comma.

Rewrite these sentences, adding commas and semicolons where necessary.

1 "Matthew Henson at the Top of the World" describes the discovery of the North Pole but the Peary expedition wasn't the first to seek it. **2** The earliest Arctic expedition probably took place in the late 300s B.C. a Greek explorer, Pytheas, said he found an island six days north of Scotland. **3** People didn't believe him they thought there was nothing but ice that far north. **4** In the late 1500s people wanted a quick way to the riches of the Orient therefore the Englishman Martin Frobisher tried to find a northwest passage through the Arctic. **5** In the 1770s Samuel Hearne was the first European to travel by land to the Arctic Ocean from Hudson Bay and much exploration followed his journey. **6** In 1926 Richard Byrd and Floyd Bennett made the first flight over the North Pole the next step was to complete an undersea passage over the pole. **7** A submarine, the *Nautilus,* crossed the North Pole under the icecap in 1958.

7.2 Elements Set Off in a Sentence

Most elements that are not essential to a sentence are set off by commas to highlight the main idea of the sentence.

Introductory Words

Use a comma to separate an introductory word from the rest of the sentence.

> Definitely␣ "The First Emperor" gets me thinking about
>
> what China was like in the 200s B.C.

Use a comma to separate an introductory phrase from the rest of the sentence.

Use a comma to set off more than one introductory prepositional phrase but not a single prepositional phrase in most cases.

> With its clear images of cruel behavior␣ this article
>
> makes me doubt I could have survived in that world.

Interrupters

Use commas to set off a word that interrupts the flow of a sentence.

What, perchance, would make a king of the smallest, weakest state want to unite all the neighboring states? Was it like, maybe, a kid who is picked on and finally stands up to a bully, except on a larger scale?

Use commas to set off a group of words that interrupts the flow of a sentence.

The discovery of Ch'in's tomb, including all the soldiers and horses guarding it, has astonished archaeologists.

Nouns of Address

Use a comma to set off a name or noun in direct address at the beginning or end of a sentence.

If I could talk with Emperor Ch'in, I'd say, "Emperor, why put people in danger for no reason? When you built the Great Wall, all those deaths weren't necessary."

Use commas to set off a noun in direct address in the middle of a sentence.

Then I'd say, "Maybe you saved lives when you stopped the wars between all those countries. But how many people, Emperor, did you kill because you were scared?"

Appositives

Set off with commas an appositive phrase that is not necessary to the meaning of the sentence.

The following sentence could be understood without the words set off by commas.

> The emperor˄a silly person about some things˄dug his
>
> own grave in more ways than one.

Do not set off with commas an appositive phrase that is necessary to the meaning of the sentence.

The following sentence could not be understood without the words set off by commas.

> Ch'in,⟋the warrior and unifier,⟋seems very different from
>
> Ch'in,⟋the shaking-in-his-shoes mouse.

For Clarity

Use commas to prevent misreading or misunderstanding.

> Excavators finally found the tomb of Ch'in that profes-
>
> sors had searched for˄for a long time.

REVISING TIP

Sometimes if a comma is missing, parts of a sentence can be grouped in more than one way by a reader. A comma separates the parts so that they can be read in only one way.

APPLY WHAT YOU'VE LEARNED

Rewrite these sentences. Add or delete commas where necessary.

1Ch'in Shih Huang Ti "The First Emperor" sounds like a typical emperor. **2**An emperor rules not just one but several countries always staying alert to outside threats. **3**Clearly his country is the strongest one. **4**Usually an emperor holds the empire together by military force. **5**Empires those vast political machines are formed by war. **6**Once an empire is established however it reduces the number of wars for a while. **7**In an empire with strong central control everyone knows who's boss. **8**Empires can have good effects when for example they force people to exchange languages, art, and technology. **9**If I could, I'd say to Ch'in, "Tell me Emperor what you accomplished."

7.3   Elements in a Series

Commas should be used to separate three or more items in a series and to separate adjectives preceding a noun.

Subjects, Verbs, Objects, and Other Elements

Use a comma after every item except the last in a series of three or more items.

Subjects, verbs, objects, and other elements often appear in series.

> In *The Hobbit* Bilbo Baggins is rudely dragged from his familiar routine, asked to do more than he thinks he can, and congratulated by his comrades when he does it.

Predicate adjectives also occur in series.

> As the play begins, Bilbo Baggins is fearful, silly, and confused. His dwarf comrades, however, are jolly, boisterous, and rowdy.

Adverbs and prepositional phrases may also occur in series.

> When there's time, Bilbo handles his problems slowly, thoughtfully, and carefully. When he has to, though, he decides on a new course of action with speed, with wit, and with great accuracy.

REVISING TIP

Note in the example that a comma followed by a conjunction precedes the last element in the series. That comma is always used.

Two or More Adjectives

In many cases when two or more adjectives precede a noun, use a comma after each adjective except the last.

If you can reverse the order of adjectives without changing the meaning or if you can use *and* between them, separate them with commas.

> Bilbo's comrade Dwalin has a long bushy beard and wears a dark, green hood.

APPLY WHAT YOU'VE LEARNED

Rewrite each sentence, correcting the comma errors.

1. *The Hobbit* was written in 1937 by J.R.R. Tolkien, a novelist scholar and professor.
2. His major fantasy saga, *The Lord of the Rings,* is made up of three parts: *The Fellowship of the Ring The Two Towers* and *The Return of the King.*
3. Tolkien was born in South Africa was raised in England and became a teacher of medieval languages at Oxford in 1925.
4. His fantasy world is dramatic detailed and entertaining.
5. Gollum, a sleazy character in *The Hobbit,* hisses nervously slimily and nastily when he talks to Bilbo, the hero.
6. In *The Lord of the Rings* Frodo, Bilbo's cousin, learns that Bilbo's ring has powers of invisibility of evil and of danger.
7. Industrious and good-natured Bilbo meets the Elven-Queen, who wears elegant, forest green clothing and a simple, oak-leaf crown.

7.4 Dates, Addresses, and Letters

Punctuation in dates, addresses, and letters makes information easy to understand.

Dates

Use a comma between the day of the month and the year. If the date falls in the middle of a sentence, use another comma after the year.

> In "User Friendly" Kevin's computer might greet him with "Today is Monday, April 24, 1996, a nice spring day."

Addresses

Use a comma to separate the city and the state in an address or other location. If the city and state fall in the middle of a sentence, use a comma after the state too.

> Kevin's dad has gone to Chicago‸Illinois‸on business for three days. Meanwhile, the computer Kevin calls Louis has developed an outlaw personality.

Parts of a Letter

Use a comma after the greeting and after the closing in a letter.

> If the machine had been a person, its last message might have read as follows:
>
> Dear Kevin‸
> I will always love you.
>
> Sadly‸
> Louise

APPLY WHAT YOU'VE LEARNED

Rewrite the following sentences, correcting the comma errors.

1. After reading "User Friendly," I had to write to my friend Darlene in Lima Ohio my old home.
2. Dear Darlene
   The computer named Louis in a story I just read has an "inbuilt logic/growth program" that lets it think and learn like a person. Can computers really do that?
   Yours truly
   Markie Malone
3. Darlene told me that computer designers near San Francisco California are working on something called artificial intelligence.
4. On May 8 1996 I decided to write my friend Ernesto about artificial intelligence.
5. Dear Ernesto
   You said your mom designs computers. Could she send me stuff on artificial intelligence?
   Your friend
   Markie Malone
6. On May 15 1996 Ernesto and his mom replied that artificial intelligence programs can duplicate some human thinking skills, but not human common sense.

Quotation marks let readers know exactly who said what. Incorrectly placed or missing quotation marks cause confusion.

Quotation Marks

Use quotation marks at the beginning and the end of direct quotations and to set off titles of short works.

> In "The Red Lion" Azgid, prince of Persia, travels in secret, running away from what he's scared of. He keeps saying to people, "Forgive me if I do not reveal my name."

REVISING TIP

If quoted words form part of a sentence you are writing, you can begin them with a lowercase letter. (*Will Rogers said that everybody "is ignorant, only on different subjects."*)

Capitalize the first word in a direct quotation, especially in a piece of dialogue.

> One person he talks to replies, "You are welcome to stay with me."

End Punctuation

Place periods inside quotation marks. Place question marks and exclamation points inside quotation marks if they belong to the quotation; place them outside if they do not belong to the quotation. Place semicolons outside quotation marks.

> When I read this story, I said to my sister, "I would have been afraid of a lion too"!
>
> "Are you admitting that you're not brave"? she said.
>
> I responded, "Not really"; I added that I had really enjoyed "The Red Lion".

Use a comma to end a quotation that is a complete sentence but is followed by explanatory words.

> "God be with you," said the shepherd to the stranger.

Divided Quotations

Capitalize the first word of the second part of a direct quotation if it begins a new sentence.

> "Well, then, come up when you wish," said the emir. "yours is the first bedroom on the right."

Do not capitalize the first word of the second part of a divided quotation if it does not begin a new sentence.

> "My men are pleased with your spirit," the prince's host said to him, "And with your skill at hunting."

 REVISING TIP

Should the first word of the second part of a divided quotation be capitalized? Imagine the quotation without the explanatory words. If a capital letter would not be used, then do not use one in the divided quotation. Note that commas always go inside quotation marks.

APPLY WHAT YOU'VE LEARNED

Rewrite these sentences, inserting quotation marks and other appropriate punctuation and correcting capitalization.

1. Gail and Eric were discussing a fable, The Red Lion.
2. Gail said, "to get background, I checked out the new words in the story."
3. "That's just what I did," said Eric. "Because words like *emir, sheik,* and *vizier* looked different. They entered English around 1577."
4. Gail then noted that the dictionary "Comes in handy sometimes."
5. She continued, "The story takes place in Persia, so I checked the encyclopedia. Persia is the old name of Iran"!
6. "The fable," Eric said, "Probably comes from a peaceful time in Persia, the late 1500s to the early 1700s, right"?
7. Gail said, "Well, maybe;" then Eric continued, "Invasions from the west were stopped by some wise treaties."
8. "Except you're forgetting the Arab sheik" muttered Gail.
9. Remember that he and his people were preparing for a battle, she said.

Grammar Glossary

This glossary contains various terms you need to understand when you use the Grammar Handbook. Used as a reference source, this glossary will help you explore grammar concepts and the ways they relate to one another.

Adjective An adjective modifies, or describes, a noun or pronoun. (*sunny* morning, *lucky* me)

A *predicate adjective* follows a linking verb and describes the subject. (The puppy is *lively*.)

A *proper adjective* is formed from a proper noun. (*Canadian* bacon)

The *comparative* form of an adjective compares two things. (*more industrious, larger*)

The *superlative* form of an adjective compares three or more things. (*most serious, greatest*)

What Adjectives Tell	Examples
How many	*few* songs *many* chances
What kind	*bright* colors *colder* winters
Which one(s)	*this* meeting *those* athletes

Adverb An adverb modifies a verb, an adjective, or another adverb. (Yi-Ming spoke *softly*.)

The *comparative* form of an adverb compares two actions. (*more slyly, later*)

The *superlative* form of an adverb compares three or more actions. (*most rapidly, soonest*)

What Adverbs Tell	Examples
How	write *carelessly* eat *quickly*
When	*Soon* I'll be home. I'll see you *later.*
Where	They traveled *far.* Put it *someplace.*
To what extent	I am *rather* tired. This is *quite* odd.

Agreement Sentence parts that correspond with one another are said to be in agreement.

In *pronoun-antecedent agreement,* a pronoun and the word it refers to are the same in number, gender, and person. (*Ann* played *her* flute. *We* played *our* drums.)

In *subject-verb agreement,* the subject and the verb in a sentence are the same in number. (*They act* well. *She acts* well.)

Antecedent An antecedent is the noun or pronoun to which a pronoun refers. (If *Leo* hurts *his* leg, *he'll* miss the game. *I* lost *my* pen.)

Appositive An appositive is a noun or phrase that explains one or more words in a sentence. (Lee, *a good artist,* won the prize.)

Article An article is an adjective that makes specific or general references to things. (*the* lamp, *a* bee, *an* onion)

A *definite article* (the word *the*) is used when a noun refers to a specific thing. (*the* anteater)

An *indefinite article* is used with a noun that does not refer to a particular example of a thing. (*a* ribbon, *an* accordion)

Clause A clause is a group of words that contains a verb and its subject. (*we believe*)

A *main (independent) clause* can stand by itself as a sentence.

A *subordinate (dependent) clause* does not express a complete thought and cannot stand by itself as a sentence.

Clause	Example
Main (independent)	The fox hid her young
Subordinate (dependent)	until the hunters were gone.

Collective noun. *See* **Noun.**

Common noun. *See* **Noun.**

Complete predicate The complete predicate of a sentence consists of the main verb plus any words that modify or complete the verb's meaning. (The lantern *showed us the path to the lake.*)

Complete subject The complete subject of a sentence consists of a subject noun or pronoun plus any words that modify or describe it. (*The new red sweater* fits me.)

Complex sentence A complex sentence contains one main clause and one or more subordinate clauses. (*The box came before we left.*)

Compound sentence A compound sentence consists of two or more independent clauses. (*Jo tried calling home, but the line was busy.*)

Compound sentence part A sentence element that consists of two or more subjects, predicates, objects, or other parts is compound. (*Jay* and *Al* agreed. Lou *sang* and *played*. Ann saw *plays* and *movies*.)

Conjunction A conjunction is a word that links other words or groups of words.

A *coordinating conjunction* connects related words, groups of words, or sentences. (*and, but, or*)

A *correlative conjunction* is one of a pair of conjunctions that work together to connect sentence parts. (*either . . . or, neither . . . nor*)

A *subordinating conjunction* introduces a subordinate clause. (*unless, while, if*)

Conjunctive adverb A conjunctive adverb joins the clauses of a compound sentence. (*however, therefore, besides*)

Contraction A contraction is formed by joining two words and substituting an apostrophe for letters left out of one of the words. (*he'll*)

Coordinating conjunction. *See* **Conjunction.**

Correlative conjunction. *See* **Conjunction.**

Demonstrative pronoun. *See* **Pronoun.**

Dependent clause. *See* **Clause.**

Direct object A direct object receives the action of a verb. (Kim knew the *answer.*)

Double negative A double negative is the incorrect use of two negative words when only one is needed. (We *don't never* come late.)

End mark An end mark is any of the several punctuation marks that can end a sentence. See the chart at the bottom of page 855.

Fragment. *See* **Sentence fragment.**

Future tense. *See* **Verb tense.**

Gerund A gerund is a verbal that ends in -*ing* and functions as a noun. (*Swimming* is good exercise.)

Helping verb. *See* **Verb.**

Indefinite pronoun. *See* **Pronoun.**

Independent clause. *See* **Clause.**

Indirect object An indirect object tells to or for whom (sometimes to or for what) something is done. (Ann gave *Barb* a pencil.)

Infinitive An infinitive is a verbal that begins with the word *to* and functions as a noun, an adjective, or an adverb. (I like *to swim.*)

Intensive pronoun. *See* **Pronoun.**

Interjection An interjection is a word or phrase used to express strong feeling. (*Ugh!*)

Interrogative pronoun. *See* **Pronoun.**

Inverted sentence An inverted sentence is one in which the subject comes after the verb. (*How is your brother? Here come the clowns.*)

Irregular verb. *See* **Verb.**

Linking verb. *See* **Verb.**

Main clause. *See* **Clause.**

Modifier A modifier makes another word more precise; modifiers most often are adjectives or adverbs. (*tasty* sandwich, smiled *happily*)

Noun A noun names a person, a place, a thing, or an idea. (*Joe, school, flower, freedom*)

An *abstract noun* names an idea, a quality, or a feeling. (*happiness*)

A *collective noun* names a group of things. (*band*)

A *common noun* is the general name of a person, a place, a thing, or an idea. (*friend, office, coat, justice*)

A *compound noun* contains two or more words. (*steel wool, rainbow, T-square*)

A *noun of direct address* is the name of a person being directly spoken to. (*Sid,* tell us a story.)

A *possessive noun* shows who or what owns something. (*Fred's* socks, the *light's* glare)

A *predicate noun* follows a linking verb and renames the subject. (Marie was the *leader.*)

A **proper noun** names a particular person, place, or thing. (*Bill Clinton, Missouri, Grant's Tomb*)

Number A noun, pronoun, or verb is **singular** in number if it refers to just one person, place, thing, or idea; it is **plural** in number if it refers to more than one.

Object of a preposition The object of a preposition is the noun or pronoun after the preposition. (They moved from the old *house.*)

Object of a verb The object of a verb receives the action of the verb. (Gay finished her *work.*)

Participle A participle is often used as part of a verb phrase. (had *seen*) It can also be used as a verbal that functions as an adjective. (the *falling* rocks)

The **present participle** is formed by adding *-ing* to the present tense of a verb. (*Singing* merrily, the carolers greeted us.)

The **past participle** of a regular verb is formed by adding *-d* or *-ed* to the present tense. The past participles of irregular verbs do not follow this pattern. (*Discouraged,* they looked for the stolen bicycle.)

Past tense. *See* **Verb tense.**

Perfect tenses. *See* **Verb tense.**

Person The person of a pronoun depends on the person to whom it refers.

A **first-person** pronoun refers to the person speaking. (*We* sang.)

A **second-person** pronoun refers to the person spoken to. (*You* ate.)

A **third-person** pronoun refers to some other person(s) or thing(s) being spoken of. (*It* fell.)

Personal pronoun. *See* **Pronoun.**

Phrase A phrase is a group of related words that does not contain a verb and its subject. (*seeing to it*)

Possessive A noun or pronoun that is possessive shows ownership. (*Clare's* pen, *his* plan)

Possessive noun. *See* **Noun.**

Possessive pronoun. *See* **Pronoun.**

Predicate The predicate of a sentence tells what the subject is or does. (Ann *told about her vacation.*)

Predicate adjective. *See* **Adjective.**

Predicate noun. *See* **Noun.**

Predicate pronoun. *See* **Pronoun.**

Preposition A preposition relates a word to another part of the sentence or to the sentence as a whole. (stood *within* the circle)

Prepositional phrase A prepositional phrase consists of a preposition, its object, and the object's modifiers. (leader *of the big band*)

Present tense. *See* **Verb tense.**

Pronoun A pronoun replaces a noun or another pronoun. Some pronouns allow a writer or speaker to avoid repeating a particular noun. Other pronouns let a writer refer to an unknown or unidentified person or thing.

A **demonstrative pronoun** singles out one or more persons or things. (*That* is a nice sweater.)

An **indefinite pronoun** refers to an unknown or unidentified person or thing. (*Somebody* will help.)

An **intensive pronoun** emphasizes a noun or pronoun. (May *herself* set the table.)

An **interrogative pronoun** asks a question. (*What* should I do?)

A **personal pronoun** refers to the first, second, or third person. (*I* go. *You* see. *He* sings.)

A **possessive pronoun** shows ownership. (*Your* answer is right.)

A **predicate pronoun** follows a linking verb and renames the subject. (The winner is *she.*)

A **reflexive pronoun** reflects an action back on the subject of the sentence. (Rita asked *herself* why.)

A **relative pronoun** relates a subordinate clause to the word it modifies in the main clause. (We met the man *who* builds houses.)

Pronoun-antecedent agreement. *See* **Agreement.**

Pronoun forms

The **subject form of a pronoun** is used when the pronoun is the subject of a sentence or follows a linking verb as a predicate pronoun. (*We* arrived. The winner was *she.*)

The **object form of a pronoun** is used when the pronoun is the direct or indirect object of a verb or verbal or the object of a preposition. (Seeing *him* and his friend, we sent *them* to *her.*)

Proper adjective. *See* **Adjective.**

Proper noun. *See* **Noun.**

Punctuation Punctuation clarifies the structure of sentences. See the chart on the facing page.

Reflexive pronoun. *See* **Pronoun.**

Regular verb. *See* **Verb.**

Relative pronoun. *See* **Pronoun.**

Run-on sentence A run-on sentence consists of two or more sentences written incorrectly as one. (*I ran to the door no one was there.*)

Sentence A sentence expresses a complete thought. The chart on the facing page shows the four kinds of sentences.

Kind of Sentence	Example
Declarative (statement)	He helped me.
Exclamatory (strong feeling)	You're home!
Imperative (request, command)	Open the door.
Interrogative (question)	What's wrong?

Sentence fragment A sentence fragment is a group of words that is only part of a sentence. (*When the wind blew, looking at the photo*)

Subject The subject is the part of a sentence that tells whom or what the sentence is about. (*Lee* knitted.)

Subject-verb agreement. *See* **Agreement.**

Subordinate clause. *See* **Clause.**

 V

Verb A verb expresses an action, a condition, or a state of being.

When the subject of a sentence performs the action, the verb is **active.** (Ken *threw* the ball.)

When the subject receives the action or expresses the result of the action, the verb is **passive.** (The box *was opened.*)

A **helping verb** is used with a main verb; together they make up a verb phrase. (*will* ask)

A **linking verb** expresses a state of being or connects the subject with a word or words that describe the subject. (The cocoa *smells* delicious.)

A **main verb** describes action or state of being; it may have one or more helping verbs. (will *do*)

The past tense and past participle of a **regular verb** are formed by adding -*d* or -*ed.* (*jump, jumped*)

An **irregular verb** does not follow this pattern. (*speak, spoke, spoken*)

Verbal A verbal is formed from a verb and acts as a noun, an adjective, or an adverb. *See* **Gerund; Infinitive; Participle.**

Verb phrase A verb phrase consists of a main verb and one or more helping verbs. (*might have entertained*)

Verb tense Verb tense shows the time of an action or the time of a state of being.

The **present tense** places an action or condition in the present. (A maid *comes* to the door.)

The **past tense** places an action or condition in the past. (Sid *agreed.*)

The **future tense** places an action or condition in the future. (Rose *will forget.*)

The **present perfect tense** describes an action completed in an indefinite past time or begun in the past and continued in the present. (*has come, have ordered*)

The **past perfect tense** describes one action that happened before another action in the past. (*had announced, had seen*)

The **future perfect tense** describes a future event that will be finished before another future action begins. (*will have baked*)

Punctuation	Uses	Examples
Apostrophe (')	Shows possession	Heather's book the girls' shoes
	Forms a contraction	He'll help. Dad's here.
Colon (:)	Introduces a list or long quotation	these boys: Joseph, Raul, and Sherman
Comma (,)	Separates ideas Separates modifiers Separates items in series	I invited him, but he could not come. the noisy, happy crowd They ate bread, cheese, and fish.
Exclamation point (!)	Ends an exclamatory sentence	What a great time we had!
Hyphen (-)	Joins words in some compound nouns	daughter-in-law, great-grandmother
Period (.)	Ends a declarative sentence Indicates most abbreviations	The fish in the lake were biting. hr. sec. Rd. Mrs. Dec.
Question mark (?)	Ends an interrogative sentence	Where is the library?
Semicolon (;)	Divides some compound sentences Separates items in series that contain commas	The whistle shrieked; the train roared by. Bruce wore a dark, floppy hat; a warm, waterproof jacket; and tough, high boots.

Index of Fine Art

Index of Skills

Literary Concepts

Alliteration. *See* Poetry.
Anecdote, 221, 762
Audience, 762
Author's purpose, 534, 762
Autobiography, 52, 122, 762
Biography, 52, 63, 269, 762
Caricature, 327
Character, 19, 37, 195, 403, 514, 763
Characterization, 763
Cinderella tales, 681
Climax, 20, 763
Complication, 20
Conflict, 19, 48, 135, 242, 252, 289, 763
    external, 135, 242, 763
    internal, 242, 763
Couplet. *See* Poetry.
Description, 269, 764
Dialogue, 237, 310–11, 327, 357, 620, 764
Drama, 357–58, 764. *See also* Dialogue.
    acts, 358, 762
    cast of characters, 357, 762
    scenes, 358, 769
    script, 764
    stage directions, 357–58, 770
Essay, 52, 235, 764
Exaggeration, 327
Exposition, 19
Fables, 636, 764
Fantasy, 355, 765
Fiction, 19–20, 765
Figurative language, 103, 543, 765
Folklore, 636
Folk tales, 636, 748, 765
Foreshadowing, 765
Form, 223, 543, 765
Free verse. *See* Poetry.
Haiku. *See* Poetry
Historical fiction, 124, 136
Humor, 327, 766
Imagery, 102, 108, 182, 222, 468, 766
Interview, 412, 766. *See also* Speaking, Listening, and
    Viewing *index*.
Legends, 636, 766
Main idea, 766
Memoir, 178, 179

Metaphor, 103, 543, 766
Mood, 161, 767
Myth, 636, 767
Narration, 275
Narrative, 767
Narrator, 767
Nonfiction, 51–52, 767
    informative, 51
    literary, 51
Novel, 19, 767
Onomatopoeia, 484, 767
Oral tradition, 634–637
Personification, 103, 767
Play. *See* Drama.
Plot, 19–20, 48, 504
Poetry, 102–3, 768
    alliteration, 344
    concrete, 424, 429
    couplet, 344, 764
    form, 102, 765
    free verse, 115, 226, 227, 765
    haiku, 180, 182, 766
    narrative poem, 104, 767
    repetition, 102
    rhyme, 102, 108, 115, 168, 341
    rhyme, end, 168, 768
    rhyme, external, 168, 768
    rhyme, internal, 168, 768
    rhyme scheme, 428, 768
    rhythm, 102, 108, 168, 341, 344, 769
    sound in, 102
    speaker, 110, 770
    tone, 110
    word order in, 109, 341
Poetic language, 341
Point of view, 28, 275, 384, 768
Primary source, 768
Purpose, 73
Quests, 571, 619–20
Radio play, 768
Repetition, 428, 768
Resolution, 20
Rhyme. *See* Poetry.
Scene. *See* Drama.
Sarcasm, 327
Science fiction, 289, 769
Script, 357

Secondary source, 769
Sensory detail, 300, 553, 562, 769. *See also* Imagery,
    Figurative language.
Setting, 19, 22, 135, 146, 178, 241, 769
Short story, 19, 770
Simile, 103, 226, 543, 770
Sources
    primary, 339
    secondary, 339
Speaker. *See* Poetry.
Stage directions, 770
Story, structure of, 19–20, 328. *See also* Plot.
Suspense, 374, 385, 403, 504, 770
Style, 109, 116, 222, 227, 276, 524, 770
Symbols, 422, 515, 770
Theme, 100, 103, 195, 771
Tone, 159, 439, 771

Reading and Critical Thinking Skills

Advertising, 90–1, 207, 519
Analysis, 762
Appearance. *See* Interpreting appearances.
Audience, 91, 379, 509, 625.
    See also Peer response.
Author's purpose, 344, 534
Brainstorming, 18, 93, 146, 213, 455
Cartoons, 506
Cause and effect, 271, 384, 763, 782, 793
Character
    revelation of, 214
    tests of, 214, 456
Choices and consequences, 318
Choral reading, 537
Chronological order. *See* Organization.
Clarifying. *See* Reading strategies.
Classifying and diagramming. *See also* Classifying and
    diagramming *in the* Writing Skills *index.*
    cluster diagram, 727
    concept map, 440, 564
    graphs, 385, 480, 486
    problem solving chart, 252, 379
    pyramid graph, 470
    scale of difficulty, 18
    setting dial, 146
    story map, 141, 194, 312, 356, 504
    webs, 21, 117, 147
Comparing and contrasting, 73, 93, 136, 146, 150, 159,
    196, 252, 300, 339, 384, 403, 424, 484, 506–11,
    514, 535, 681, 698, 699, 763, 764, 727, 782, 791
Conclusions, 213, 511. *See also* Organization.

Conflict resolution. *See* Problem solving.
Connecting, 5, 20, 103, 333, 486, 563, 701, 763
    biographical, 104, 271
    cultural, 151, 215, 291, 319, 359, 405, 414, 480, 486,
        519, 545, 727, 747
    geographical, 21, 39, 53, 117, 161, 184, 237, 269
    historical, 30, 93, 124, 170, 257, 268, 329, 341, 389,
        430, 457, 470, 526
    literary, 110, 180, 223, 436, 571, 680, 698, 726, 746
    personal, 21, 30, 39, 53, 65, 93, 104, 110, 117, 124,
        146, 151, 161, 170, 180, 184, 215, 223, 224, 228,
        237, 257, 271, 275, 277, 289, 291, 319, 329, 341,
        346, 359, 389, 405, 414, 424, 430, 457, 470, 480,
        486, 519, 526, 537, 545, 571, 622
    scientific, 228, 277, 424, 525, 537, 681, 726
    through art, 49, 74, 136, 182, 328, 413, 429, 469,
        535, 620, 698
    through reading, 39, 53, 65, 117, 124, 151, 161, 180,
        184, 223, 229, 237, 257, 271, 278, 319, 329, 341,
        359, 389, 414, 424, 431, 457, 470, 486, 537, 545,
        571
    through social studies, 554, 680, 699, 727, 746, 747
    through writing, 21, 30, 93, 110, 170, 194, 215, 291,
        346, 405, 480, 519
Context clues, 389, 764
Critical analysis, 28, 37, 63, 73, 100, 108, 113, 115, 122,
    135, 159, 168, 178, 182, 194, 221, 223, 235, 241,
    268, 275, 289, 300, 327, 339, 344, 355, 373, 402,
    412, 422, 425, 428, 439, 468, 481, 484, 503, 524,
    534, 543, 553, 619, 794–95
Decision making, 18, 506, 524
Detail. *See* Supporting detail; Sensory detail.
Dialogue, as part of a story, 310–11
Difference, 511
Difficulty, scale of, 18
Domino effect, 318
Drama, strategies for reading, 358, 571
Emotional response, 91
Evaluating. *See* Reading strategies.
Fact, in fiction, 339
Fact vs. opinion, 52, 625, 765. *See also* Opinion.
Fiction, strategies for reading, 20
Folk tales, strategies for reading, 748, 795
Foreign language, use of, 554, 822
Goals
    obstacles to reaching, 518
    setting of, 147, 253, 385, 515, 570
Grammatical links to literature, 813, 815, 817, 820, 822,
    824, 826, 835, 839, 843
Graphic organizers, 509. *See also* Classifying and
    diagramming
Heroism, 570

Grammar, Usage, and Mechanics

Writing Skills, Modes, and Formats

Vocabulary Skills

Research and Study Skills

Speaking, Listening, and Viewing

Index of Titles and Authors

Acknowledgments *(continued)*

Little, Brown and Company: "My First Dive with the Dolphins," from *The Dolphins and Me* by Don C. Reed; Text Copyright © 1989 by Don C. Reed. By permission of Little, Brown and Company.

Elaine Markson Literary Agency, Inc.: "Tuesday of the Other June" by Norma Fox Mazer; Copyright © 1986 by Norma Fox Mazer. By permission of Norma Fox Mazer. All rights reserved.

Marian Reiner: "Mean Song," from *There Is No Rhyme for Silver* by Eve Merriam; Copyright © 1962 by Eve Merriam, renewed 1990 by Eve Merriam. Reprinted by permission of Marian Reiner.

McIntosh and Otis, Inc.: "Too Soon a Woman" by Dorothy Johnson; Copyright 1953 by Dorothy M. Johnson, renewed © 1981 by Dorothy M. Johnson. Reprinted by permission of McIntosh and Otis, Inc.

Brandt & Brandt Literary Agents, Inc.: "Western Wagons" by Rosemary and Stephen Vincent Benét; Copyright 1937 by Stephen Vincent Benét, renewed © 1965 by Thomas C. Benét, Stephanie B. Mahin, Rachel Benét Lewis. Reprinted by permission of Brandt & Brandt Literary Agents, Inc.

Random House, Inc.: "Life Doesn't Frighten Me," from *And Still I Rise* by Maya Angelou; Copyright © 1978 by Maya Angelou. Reprinted by permission of Random House, Inc.

Abiodun Oyewole: "Another Mountain," from *Rooted in the Soil,* first edition. Reprinted by permission of the author.

Macmillan Books for Young Readers: Excerpt from *Woodsong* by Gary Paulsen; Text Copyright © 1990 by Gary Paulsen. Reprinted by permission of Macmillan Books for Younger Readers, an imprint of Simon & Schuster Children's Publishing Division.

Estate of Louis Untermeyer: "The Dog of Pompeii," from *The Donkey of God* by Louis Untermeyer has been published with expressed permission by the Estate of Louis Untermeyer, Norma Anchin Untermeyer, c/o Professional Publishing Services.

Unit Two

HarperCollins Publishers, Inc.: "The Adoption of Albert," from *My Brother Louis Measures Worms* by Barbara Robinson; Copyright © 1988 by Barbara Robinson. "The Quarrel" from *Eleanor Farjeon's Poems for Children;* originally appeared in *Over the Garden Wall* by Eleanor Farjeon; Copyright 1933, renewed © 1961 by Eleanor Farjeon. "Aaron's Gift," from *The Witch of Fourth Street and Other Stories* by Myron Levoy; Text Copyright © 1972 by Myron Levoy. "Where The Sidewalk Ends," from *Where The Sidewalk Ends* by Shel Silverstein; Copyright © 1974 by Evil Eye Music, Inc. Reprinted by permission of HarperCollins Publishers.

Feinman & Krasilovsky: "The Cremation of Sam McGee," from *The Collected Poems of Robert Service* by Robert Service; Copyright 1910 by Dodd Mead & Company. Used by permission of the Estate of Robert Service.

Silver Burdett Press: "Chinatown," from *The Lost Garden* by Laurence Yep; Copyright © 1991 Laurence Yep. Used by permission of Julian Messner, a division of Silver Burdett Press. All rights reserved.

Penguin Books Ltd.: Haiku, "Beautiful, see through holes . . . ," by Kobayashi Issa (p. 123) from *The Penguin Book of Japanese Verse,* translated by Geoffrey Bownas and Anthony Thwaite (Penguin Books, 1964); Copyright © 1964 by Geoffrey Bownas and Anthony Thwaite. By permission of Penguin Books, Ltd.

Raymond R. Patterson: "Glory, Glory," from *26 Ways of Looking at a Black Man and Other Poems* by Raymond R. Patterson; Copyright © 1969 by Raymond R. Patterson. Reprinted by permission of the author.

F. E. Albi: "Street Corner Flight" by Norma Landa Flores, from *Sighs and Songs of Aztlan*; Copyright © 1975 by F. E. Albi and J. G. Nieto. Reprinted by permission of F. E. Albi, editor.

Piccadilly Press, Ltd.: *The Spider and the Fly* by Mary Howitt. First published by Piccadilly Press, Ltd, London 1987. Reprinted by permission of Piccadilly Press, Ltd.

New Directions Publishing Corporation: "Two girls of twelve or so at a table," from *By the Waters of Manhattan* by Charles Reznikoff; Copyright © 1959 by Charles Reznikoff. Reprinted by permission of New Directions Publishing Corporation.

N. Scott Momaday: "New World" by N. Scott Momaday. Reprinted by permission of the author.

Atheneum Books for Young Readers: "Something Told the Wild Geese," from *Poems* by Rachel Field; Copyright 1934 by Macmillan Publishing Company, renewed © 1962 by Arthur S. Pederson. Reprinted with the permission of Atheneum Books for Young Readers, an imprint of Simon & Schuster Children's Publishing Division.

Simon & Schuster: "Oh Broom, Get to Work," from *The Invisible Thread* by Yoshiko Uchida; Copyright © 1991. By permission of the publisher, Julian Messner, a Division of Simon & Schuster.

Harcourt Brace & Company and Penguin Books, Ltd.: "It Seems I Test People," from *When I Dance* by James Berry; Copyright © 1988, renewed 1991 by James Berry. Reprinted by permission of Harcourt Brace & Company and Penguin Books, Ltd.

HarperCollins Publishers, Inc., and Kids Can Press: "Growing Pains," from *Hey World, Here I Am!* by Jean Little; Text Copyright © 1968 by Jean Little. By permission of HarperCollins Publishers and Kids Can Press.

Helen M. Hoover: "The Mushroom," from *The Big Book for Our Planet* by Helen M. Hoover. By permission of Helen M. Hoover.

Andre Deutsch, Ltd.: "Cricket in the Road," from *Cricket in the Road* by Michael Anthony; Copyright © 1973 by Michael Anthony. Reprinted by permission of Andre Deutsch, Ltd., London.

Unit Three

HarperCollins Publishers, Inc.: "Abd al-Rahman Ibrahima," from *Now Is Your Time: The African–American Struggle for Freedom* by Walter Dean Myers; Copyright © 1991 by Walter Dean Myers. Reprinted by permission of HarperCollins Publishers.

Dudley Randall: "Ancestors," from *After the Killing* by Dudley Randall; Copyright © 1973 by Dudley Randall. Reprinted by permission of the author.

Susan Bergholz Literary Services: "Eleven," from *Woman Hollering Creek* by Sandra Cisneros; Copyright © 1991 by Sandra Cisneros. Published by Vintage Books, a division of Random House, Inc., New York and in hardcover by Random House, Inc., New York. Reprinted by permission of Susan Bergholz Literary Services.

Delacorte Press: "User Friendly" by T. Ernesto Bethancourt, from *Connections: Short Stories* edited by Donald R. Gallo; Copyright © 1989 by T. Ernesto Bethancourt. Used by permission of Delacorte Press, a division of Bantam

Farrar, Straus & Giroux, Inc.: Excerpt from *Gold and Silver, Silver and Gold* by Alvin Schwartz; Copyright © 1988 by Alvin Schwartz. By permissions of Farrar, Straus & Giroux, Inc.

Little, Brown and Company: "Diana Golden," from *Champions* by Bill Littlefield. Text Copyright © 1993 by Bill Littlefield. By permission of Little, Brown and Company.

Houghton Mifflin Company: "At Last I Kill a Buffalo," from *My Indian Boyhood* by Chief Luther Standing Bear; Copyright 1931 by Chief Luther Standing Bear, renewed © 1959 by May Jones. Reprinted by permission of Houghton Mifflin Company. All rights reserved.

Dutton Children's Books: "The Flower-Fed Buffaloes," from *Going to the Stars* by Vachel Lindsay; Copyright 1926 by D. Appleton & Co., renewed 1954 by Elizabeth C. Lindsay. Used by permission of Dutton Children's Books, a division of Penguin Books, USA.

Random House, Inc.: "Tomb of Tutankh-Amen," from *Lost Worlds* by Anne Terry White; Copyright 1941 by Random House, Inc., renewed © 1969 by Anne Terry White. Reprinted by permission of Random House, Inc.

Poetry Magazine and Constance Urdang: "Pole Vault" by Shiro Murano, translated by Constance Urdang and Satoru Sato; first appeared in *Poetry*, Copyright 1956 by The Modern Poetry Association. Reprinted by permission of the Editor of *Poetry*.

Simon & Schuster Books for Young Readers: "Analysis of Baseball," from *The Complete Poems to Solve* by May Swenson; Copyright © 1993 by The Literary Estate of May Swenson. Reprinted by permission of Simon & Schuster Books for Young Readers, an imprint of Simon & Schuster Children's Publishing Division.

John Hawkins & Associates, Inc.: "My Friend Flicka," by Mary O'Hara, published by *Story Magazine,* 1941; Copyright 1941 by Mary O'Hara. Reprinted by permission of John Hawkins & Associates, Inc.

Unit Five

Elizabeth Ellis: "Flowers and Freckle Cream," by Elizabeth Ellis from *Best-Loved Stories Told at the National Storytelling Festival.* Copyright © by Elizabeth Ellis. Reprinted by permission of Elizabeth Ellis.

Arte Publico Press: "Same Song," from *Borders* (Houston: Arte Publico Press—University of Houston, 1985) by Pat Mora is reprinted with the permission of Arte Publico Press.

Henry Morrison, Inc.: Excerpt from "The First Emperor," from *The Tomb Robbers* by Daniel Cohen, copyright © 1980 by Daniel Cohen. This selection is used by permission of the author and Henry Morrison, Inc., his agents.

Marian Reiner, Literary Agent: "Message from a Caterpillar," from *Little Raccoon and Poems from the Woods* by Lilian Moore; Copyright © 1975 by Lilian Moore. Reprinted by permission of Marian Reiner for the author.

HarperCollins Publishers, Inc.: "Chrysalis Diary," from *Joyful Noise* by Paul Fleischman; Text Copyright © 1988 by Paul Fleischman. Reprinted by permission of HarperCollins Publishers.

Francisco Jiménez: "The Circuit," from *Arizona Quarterly,* Autumn 1973. Reprinted by permission of the author.

BOA Editions Limited: "the 1st," from *Good Woman: Poems and a Memoir 1969–1980* by Lucille Clifton; Copyright © 1987 by Lucille Clifton. Reprinted with the permission of BOA Editions, Ltd., 92 Park Ave., Brockport, NY 14420.

Jane Dystel Literary Management: "The Scribe," from *Guests in the Promised*

Land by Kristin Hunter. Copyright © 1968, 1972, 1973 by Kristin Hunter. Reprinted by permission of the author.

The Dramatic Publishing Company: *The Hobbit,* a dramatization by Patricia Gray; Copyright © 1987 by Patricia Gray, based upon the book by J.R.R. Tolkien. Printed in the United States of America. All Rights Reserved. All inquiries regarding performance rights should be addressed to the Dramatic Publishing Company, 311 Washington St., Woodstock, IL 60098.

Unit Six

Harcourt Brace & Company: Entire text of *Wings* by Jane Yolen; Copyright © 1991 by Jane Yolen. Reprinted by permission of Harcourt Brace & Company.

Rosenstone/Wender: *The Red Lion* by Diane Wolkstein; Copyright © 1977 by Diane Wolkstein. By permission of Rosenstone/Wender.

Scholastic Inc.: "Why Monkeys Live in Trees," from *How Many Spots Does a Leopard Have?* by Julius Lester; Copyright © 1989 by Julius Lester. Reprinted by permission of Scholastic Inc.

Viking Penguin: Excerpt from *In the Land of Small Dragon* as told by Dang Manh Kha to Ann Nolan Clark; Copyright © 1979 by Ann Nolan Clark. Used by permission of Viking Penguin, a division of Penguin Books USA Inc.

Houghton Mifflin Company: "The Bamboo Beads," from *A Wave in Her Pocket* by Lynn Joseph; Copyright ©1991 by Lynn Joseph. "The Legend of Damon and Pythias," from *The Bag of Fire and Other Plays* by Fan Kissen; Copyright © 1964 by Houghton Mifflin Company, renewed © 1993 by John Kissen Heaslip. "Arachne," from *Greek Myths* retold by Olivia E. Coolidge; Copyright 1949, renewed © 1977 by Olivia E. Coolidge. Reprinted by permission of Houghton Mifflin Company. All rights reserved.

Penguin Books USA Inc.: "The Legend of the Hummingbird," from *Once in Puerto Rico* by Pura Belpré; Copyright © 1973 by Pura Belpré. Used by permission of Frederick Warne Books, a division of Penguin Books USA Inc.

Ricardo E. Alegría: "The Three Wishes," from *The Three Wishes: A Collection of Puerto Rican Folktales,* selected and adapted by Ricardo E. Alegría, translated by Elizabeth Culbert; Copyright © 1969 by Ricardo E. Alegría. Reprinted by permission of author.

Curbstone Press: Excerpt from "The Disobedient Child," from *The Bird Who Cleans the World and Other Mayan Fables* by Victor Montejo. Translated by Wallace Kaufman (Curbstone Press, 1991). Reprinted with permission of Curbstone Press.

Dial Books for Young Readers: "Three Strong Women," from *The Woman in the Moon and Other Tales of Forgotten Heroines* by James Riordan; Copyright © 1984 by James Riordan. Used by permission of Dial Books for Young Readers, a division of Penguin Books USA Inc.

Fulcrum Publishing: "The White Buffalo Calf Woman and the Sacred Pipe" by Joseph Bruchac, from *Native American Stories* told by Joseph Bruchac, from *Keepers of the Animals* by Michael J. Caduto and Joseph Bruchac, Fulcrum Publishing, Inc., 350 Indiana St., #350, Golden, CO 80401.

Houghton Mifflin Company and Carol Kendall: "The Living Kuan-yin," from *Sweet and Sour: Tales from China* by Carol Kendall and Yao-Wen Li; Copyright © 1980 by Carol Kendall and Yao-Wen Li. Reprinted by permission of Clarion Books/Houghton Mifflin Company and Carol Kendall. All rights reserved.

Philomel Books: "Sister Fox and Brother Coyote," from *Cut from the Same Cloth* by Robert San Souci; Text Copyright © 1993 by Robert D. San Souci. Reprinted by permission of Philomel Books, a division of the Putnam Publishing Group.

Doubleday: "King Thrushbeard," from *Grimms' Tales for Young and Old* by Jakob and Wilhelm Grimm; Copyright © 1977 by Ralph Manheim. Used by permission of Doubleday, a division of Bantam Doubleday Dell Publishing Group.

The following sections were prepared by **Ligature, Inc., of Chicago, Illinois:** Learning the Language of Literature, Writing About Literature, Writing from Experience, Writing Handbook, Multimedia Handbook, and Grammar Handbook.

Art Credits

Commissioned Art and Photography
2 *top*, 84 , 85, 88, 138, 139, 140 *bottom*, 144, 145, 206–210, top 245, 247, 310–315, 378 *top*, 379–381, 509–511, 513, 622, 623, 748, 749 *top right*, 751 *bottom*, 754, 755 Allan Landau. 4–5, 17, 29, 75, 86, 90–91, 109, 111–113, 118–119, 140 *top*, 142, 171, 173, 176, 180, 186, 188, 191, 216, 218, 222, 234, 238, 244 *bottom*, 246, 248–251, 256, 269, 279, 330, 332–336, 347, 351, 354, 356, 373–374, 376–377, 378 *bottom*, 382–383, 386, 388, 403, 406, 412, 415, 422, 433–438, 448–453, 471–472, 506–508, 512, 519–520, 523, 555, 557, 559–560, 562–569, 624–626, 629, 658, 662–663, 670–672, 676–678, 680, 698–705, 710–722, 726, 731, 741, 746, 747, 750, 751 *top*, 752 Sharon Hoogstraten. 29 Paul Dennis. 31 Karen Berntsen. 198–200 Russ Willms. 230-233 Mike Reed. 261–262, 264 Jennifer Carney. 302, 304, 307–308 Clare Hirn. 320–325 Laura Montenegro. 426–427 Barb Rohm. 487, 489, 492, 495, 496, 499 Fran Lee. 506 Josh Neufeld. 577, 580, 588, 594, 599, 600-601, 607, 613, 617 Anne Gavitt. 635 Richard Waldrep.

Maps: **632–633, 636–639, 660–661, 682, 708–709, 728–729** John Sandford. Maps on all Previewing and Responding pages: Robert Voights.

Author Photographs and Portraits
29 Willy Leon. 50 Courtesy of Mrs. Sperry. 74 Marine World Africa USA. 83 George Janoff. 101 Mansfield Library, University of Montana. 109, 345 Stock Montage. 116 UPI/Bettmann. 137 The Library of Congress. 169 Culver Pictures. 179 Photo by K. Yep. 183 *top* Courtesy of New Orleans (Louisiana) Museum of Art; *bottom* Heibonsha, Ltd., Japan. 197, 204, 205, 328, 429, 485, 621 AP/Wide World Photos, Inc. 201, 725 Copyright © Layle Silbert. 222 Copyright © June Finfer, Filmedia, Ltd. 227 Guelph (Ontario) *Daily Mercury*. 276 Rubén Guzmán. 301 National Archives. 375 CBS Photography. 423 Copyright © Jerry Bauer. 554 Courtesy of the University of Santa Clara (California). 561 John I. Lattony. 653 Rachel C. Zucker. 675 Ed Scott. 697 Mel Rosenthal. 745 The Granger Collection, New York.

Miscellaneous Art Credits
xiv *Mecklenberg County: High Cotton Mother and Child* (1978), Romare Bearden. Courtesy of the Estate of Romare Bearden. xix *The Hill: Hobbiton-*

Across-the-Water (1966), J.R.R. Tolkien. Illustration from *The Hobbit* by J.R.R. Tolkien. Copyright © 1966 J.R.R. Tolkien. Reprinted by permission of Houghton Mifflin Co. All rights reserved. **xxi** *Exotic Landscape* (1910), Henri Rousseau. Oil on canvas, $51\frac{1}{4}'' \times 64''$. The Norton Simon Foundation, Pasadena, California. **2** *bottom left* Copyright © Owen Franken/Stock, Boston; *bottom right* Copyright © Richard Hutchings/PhotoEdit. **2–3** *top* Copyright © Lorentz Gullachsen/Tony Stone Images. **3** *top* Copyright © 1990 Arnold Adler/Black Star; **22–23** Copyright © Hugh Sitton/Tony Stone Images. **40–41** Copyright © 1995 Cheryl Cooper. **49** Copyright © Marc Chamberlain/Tony Stone Images. **65** Copyright © François Gohier/Photo Researchers, Inc. **66** Copyright © Bill Wood/Westlight. **66** Copyright © Leland Bobbe/Tony Stone Images. **90** *bottom left* From *The Complete Book of Dog Care: How to Raise a Happy and Healthy Dog* by Ulrich Klever, Copyright © 1989 by Barron's Educational Series, Inc. Reprinted by arrangement with Barron's Educational Series, Inc., Hauppauge, New York. **92** Copyright © R. Walker/H. Armstrong Roberts. **93** The Granger Collection, New York. **124** Copyright © 1995 Everett Johnson/Frozen Images. **125** Doric pillars on Temple of Zeus, Nemea, Peloponnesus, Greece. Copyright © M. Thonig/H. Armstrong Roberts. **136** Detail of *Cave Canem* [Beware of dog], unknown artist. Roman mosaic, Museo Archeologico Nazionale, Naples, Italy, Scala/Art Resource, New York. **138** *right, Calvin and Hobbes* Copyright © 1986 Watterson. Distributed by Universal Press Syndicate. Reprinted with permission. All rights reserved. **151** Copyright © Robert E. Daemmrich/Tony Stone Images. **169** Copyright © Tom Walker/Tony Stone Images. **182** Detail of incense wrapper (Edo period, Japan; 17th–18th centuries) attributed to Ogata Korin. Wrapper mounted on hanging scroll, ink and color on gold-ground paper, 33 cm × 24.1 cm, The Art Institute of Chicago, Russell Tyson Purchase Fund (1966.470). Photo Copyright © 1994 The Art Institute of Chicago. All rights reserved. **193** Copyright © Leland Bobbe/Tony Stone Images. **195** The Bettmann Archive, New York. **212–213** From a production of *Bold Girls* by Rona Munro, produced by Eclipse Theatre Company, Chicago. Scenic design by Ken Puttbach. **228** NASA. **229** The Granger Collection, New York. **242** *left* Copyright © 1982 Tom Hollyman/Photo Researchers; *right* Copyright © Katrina Thomas/Photo Researchers. **244** *bottom left* Courtesy of Hayun Cho; *bottom right* Copyright © Philip Saltonstall. **245** *right* UPI/Bettmann. **247** *center* Courtesy of Lake Bluff Middle School, Lake Bluff, Illinois. **257** *Abd al-Rahman Ibrahima* (1828), Henry Inman. Reproduced from the collections of the Library of Congress. **272** Detail of *Cake Window (Seven Cakes)* (1970–1976), Wayne Thiebaud. Courtesy of Allan Stone Gallery, New York. **277** Archive Photos. **316–317** Copyright © Paul John Miller, all rights reserved. **319** The Bettmann Archive, New York. **328** Detail of *La cuillerée* [The spoonful of milk] (1912), Marc Chagall. Copyright © 1995 Artists Rights Society (ARS), New York/ADAGP, Paris. **329** Copyright © Frank Cezus/Tony Stone Images. **338** Smithsonian Institution, Washington, D.C. Pullman Negative Collection (Neg. # 4586). **342–343** Copyright © Ken Biggs/Tony Stone Images. **359** Copyright © 1995 Classic PIO Partners. **389** Copyright © 1995 Larry Stevens/Nawrocki Stock Photo Inc. All rights reserved. **390** Copyright © Camille Przewodek. **390** Copyright © Les Jorgensen/Photonica. **399** Detail of *Long Day's Shadow* (1994), Marilyn Sunderman. Courtesy of the artist, Sedona, Arizona. **405** Courtesy of Jerry Pinkney. **413** Detail of illustration by Jerry Pinkney. Illustration Copyright © 1994 Jerry Pinkney. From *John Henry* by Julius Lester, used with permission of Dial Books for Young Readers, a division of Penguin

707 *bottom* Copyright © 1982 Warner Bros., Inc. Photo courtesy of the Kobal Collection; *background,* Copyright © Cowgirl Stock Photography; 708 *Buffalo Calf Woman,* Oscar Howe. U.S. Department of the Interior, Indian Arts and Crafts Board, Sioux Indian Museum and Crafts Center, Rapid City, South Dakota. 709 Detail of illustration by Arvis Stewart, from *The Macmillan Book of Greek Gods and Heroes* by Alice Low. Copyright © 1985 Macmillan Publishing Company, reprinted with the permission of Simon & Schuster Books for Young Readers, an imprint of Simon & Schuster Children's Publishing Division. 709 Figure of a woman (late 1600s), unknown Japanese artist. Arita ware, Kakiemon porcelain with over-glaze polychrome enamel, $14\frac{1}{4}'' \times 5\frac{1}{2}''$, Asian Art Museum of San Francisco, The Avery Brundage Collection (B62 P5+). 728 Details Copyright © John Nieto. Courtesy of Bailey Nelson Gallery, Seattle, Washington. 729 Copyright © Joyce Patti. 735 Copyright © Jim Stamates/Tony Stone Images. 739 Details Copyright © John Nieto. Courtesy of Bailey Nelson Gallery, Seattle, Washington. 748 *center* Copyright © Felicia Martinez/PhotoEdit. 749 *top left* Copyright © George Mars Cassidy/Tony Stone Images; *center* Copyright © Dallas and John Heaton/Westlight; *bottom left* Copyright © Chris Cole/Tony Stone Images; *bottom right* Copyright © Tony Stone Images. 754 *center* Copyright © Hiroyuki Matsumoto/Black Star. 788 Copyright © Janet Gill/Tony Stone Images. 790 Copyright © Victoria Ross/Southern Stock Photo Agency. 796 Copyright © John Kelly/The Image Bank. 798 Copyright © Christina Rose Mufson/Comstock. 802 Netscape, Netscape Navigator and the Netscape Communications Corporation Logo are trademarks of Netscape Communications Corporation; *center* OpenNet Technologies, Inc. 805–807 Screen shots reprinted with permission from Microsoft Corporation. 808 Used with express permission. Adobe and Adobe Illustrator are trademarks of Adobe Systems Incorporated. 809 Copyright © Lori Adamski Peek/Tony Stone Images. 811 Copyright © Dennis O'Clair/Tony Stone Images.

Teacher Review Panels *(continued)*

Bonnie Garrett, Davis Middle School, Compton School District

Sally Jackson, Madrona Middle School, Torrance Unified School District

Sharon Kerson, Los Angeles Center for Enriched Studies, Los Angeles Unified School District

Gail Kidd, Center Middle School, Azusa School District

Corey Lay, ESL Department Chairperson, Chester Nimitz Middle School, Los Angeles Unified School District

Myra LeBendig, Forshay Learning Center, Los Angeles Unified School District

Dan Manske, Elmhurst Middle School, Oakland Unified School District

Joe Olague, Language Arts Department Chairperson, Alder Middle School, Fontana School District

Pat Salo, 6th Grade Village Leader, Hidden Valley Middle School, Escondido Elementary School District

FLORIDA

Judi Briant, English Department Chairperson, Armwood High School, Hillsborough County School District

Beth Johnson, Polk County English Supervisor, Polk County School District

Sharon Johnston, Learning Resource Specialist, Evans High School, Orange County School District

Eileen Jones, English Department Chairperson, Spanish River High School, Palm Beach County School District

Jan McClure, Winter Park High School Orange County School District

Wanza Murray, English Department Chairperson (retired), Vero Beach Senior High School, Indian River City School District

Shirley Nichols, Language Arts Curriculum Specialist Supervisor, Marion County School District

Debbie Nostro, Ocoee Middle School, Orange County School District

Barbara Quinaz, Assistant Principal, Horace Mann Middle School, Dade County School District

OHIO

Joseph Bako, English Department Chairperson, Carl Shuler Middle School, Cleveland City School District

Deb Delisle, Language Arts Department Chairperson, Ballard Brady Middle School, Orange School District

Ellen Geisler, English/Language Arts Department Chairperson, Mentor Senior High School, Mentor School District

Dr. Mary Gove, English Department Chairperson, Shaw High School, East Cleveland School District

Loraine Hammack, Executive Teacher of the English Department, Beachwood High School, Beachwood City School District

Sue Nelson, Shaw High School, East Cleveland School District

Mary Jane Reed, English Department Chairperson, Solon High School, Solon City School District

Nancy Strauch, English Department Chairperson, Nordonia High School, Nordonia Hills City School District

Ruth Vukovich, Hubbard High School, Hubbard Exempted Village School District

TEXAS

Anita Arnold, English Department Chairperson, Thomas Jefferson High School, San Antonio Independent School District

Gilbert Barraza, J.M. Hanks High School, Ysleta School District

Sandi Capps, Dwight D. Eisenhower High School, Alding Independent School District

Judy Chapman, English Department Chairperson, Lawrence D. Bell High School, Hurst-Euless-Bedford School District

Pat Fox, Grapevine High School, Grapevine-Colley School District

LaVerne Johnson, McAllen Memorial High School, McAllen Independent School District

Donna Matsumura, W.H. Adamson High School, Dallas Independent School District

Ruby Mayes, Waltrip High School, Houston Independent School District

Mary McFarland, Amarillo High School, Amarillo Independent School District

Adrienne Thrasher, A.N. McCallum High School, Austin Independent School District

Manuscript Reviewers *(continued)*

Maryann Lyons, Literacy Specialist, Mentor teacher, San Francisco Unified School District, San Francisco, California

Karis MacDonnell, Ed.D., Dario Middle School, Miami, Florida

Bonnie J. Mansell, Downey Adult School, Downey, California

Martha Mitchell, Memorial Middle School, Orlando, Florida

Nancy Nachman, Landmark High School, Jacksonville, Florida

Karen Williams Perry, English Department Chairperson, Kennedy Jr. High School, Lisle, Illinois

Julia Pferdehirt, free-lance writer, former Special Education teacher, Middleton, Wisconsin

Phyllis Stewart Rude, English Department Head, Mears Jr./Sr. High School, Anchorage, Alaska

Leo Schubert, Bettendorf Middle School, Bettendorf, Iowa

Gertrude H. Vannoy, Curriculum Liaison Specialist, Gifted and Horizon teacher, Meany Middle School, Seattle, Washington

Richard Wagner, Language Arts Curriculum Coordinator, Paradise Valley School District, Phoenix, Arizona

Stephen J. Zadravec, Newmarket Jr./Sr. High School, Newmarket, New Hampshire